Random House Reference

Timetables

of History

RANDOM HOUSE REFERENCE

New York   Toronto   London   Sydney   Auckland

First published in the United Kingdom in 1999
by Philip's, a division of Octopus Group
Publishing Ltd., as *Philip's World History:
People, Dates & Events*.

Published in the United States by Random
House Reference, an imprint of The Random
House Information Group, a division of
Random House, Inc., New York, and simulta-
neously in Canada by Random House of
Canada Limited, Toronto.

RANDOM HOUSE is a registered trademark
of Random House, Inc.

Please address inquiries about electronic
licensing of any products for use on a network, in software, or on CD-ROM to the
Subsidiary Rights Department, Random
House Information Group, fax 212-572-6003.
This book is available at special discounts for
bulk purchases for sales promotions or pre-
miums. Special editions, including personal-
ized covers, excerpts of existing books, and
corporate imprints, can be created in large
quantities for special needs. For more information, write to Random House, Inc., Special
Markets/Premium Sales, 1745 Broadway, MD
6-2, New York, NY, 10019 or e-mail special-
markets@randomhouse.com.

Visit the Random House Reference Web site:
www.randomwords.com

Printed in the United States of America

10 9 8 7 6 5 4 3 2 1

Library of Congress Cataloging in Publication
Data is available.

ISBN 978–0–375–72226–4

TEXT Clint Twist

EDITORS Lester Hawksby
        Christian Humphries
        Frances Adlington

ART EDITOR Mike Brown

PRODUCTION Lester Hawksby

PICTURE RESEARCH Sarah Moule

INDEX Ann Barret

PHOTOGRAPHIC CREDITS

INTRODUCTION

Dates are much more than isolated markers of events. Organized into a chronology, dates establish sequence and synchronicity. In creating this particular chronology of World History, every care has been taken to use accurate and informative dates. However, it is impossible to achieve 'definitive' dates when referring to events that occurred many thousands of years ago. Virtually all dates before CE 1 are based on archeology -- the dating of objects dug from the ground. The most useful and widespread method of dating such material is by measuring the decay of the isotope carbon-14 (radiocarbon dating). This method is reliable, but is not strictly precise. Even when correlated with dendrochronology (tree-ring dating) radio-carbon dates are at best accurate to within 50–100 years, and the further back the method is applied, the wider the margin for error. To spare the reader any confusion between correlated and uncorrelated dates, we have often selected a single date, pre-fixed by the abbreviation c. (circa) to indicate a date-range. Broadly speaking, the size of the date-range indicated by c. depends on the nature of the date: c.5500 BCE means 6000 BCE–5000 BCE; c.2500 BCE means 2750 BCE–2250 BCE. In more recent times, c. indi-cates a degree of uncertainty owing to the fact that definitive written records are rare, hence c.1500 BCE means 1600 BCE–1400 BCE; c.1000 BCE means 1050 BCE–950 BCE; c.500 BCE means 525 BCE–485 BCE. Other complications arise from the use of different dating systems by various peoples at different times in the past. Even the twentieth century is beset by chronological problems. The Russian Revolution of 1917, often called the "October Revolution", occurred in November in the Gregorian (New Style) Calendar.

The **chronology** section of this book is organized into six categories – Asia and Australasia, Africa, Europe, the Americas, sci-ence and technology, arts and humanities. The categories are distinguished by color, with darker bands of color across the spreads allowing for easy comparison between them. From 15000 BCE to 5000 BCE science and tech-nology, arts and humanities are treated as one category: technology and art. Following the chronology is an A–Z section of **people and peoples**, in which can be found articles on historical figures, tribes, dynasties, and

kingdoms. The existence of such an article is indicated by SMALL CAPITAL LETTERS in the chronology text. The book concludes with a comprehensive **index**, referenced by date. Instead of BC and AD we have used BCE and CE, which are abbreviations of before Christian era (or before common era) and Christian era (or common era).

PREHISTORY

15,000 mya (million years ago)
According to the Big Bang theory, the universe is formed.
4600 mya
The Earth is formed.
3800 mya
Simple single-celled life (bacteria) appears.
1200 mya
Complex single-celled plants and animals appear.
600 mya
Multicellular plants and animals appear.
560 mya
Beginning of Cambrian period of geological timescale, during which animals evolve eyes and jointed legs.
400 mya
The first land plants and animals appear.
220 mya
A massive extinction event wipes out 90% of species.
65 mya
An extinction event, probably caused by an asteroid impact, kills the land-living dinosaurs.
*c.*5 mya
Australopithicenes appear in s Africa.
*c.*2 mya
The most recent ice age starts; *Homo habilis* appears in SE Africa.
*c.*1.7 mya
Homo erectus appears in E Africa.
*c.*250,000 BCE
Archaic *Homo sapiens* appears in E Africa.
*c.*200,000 BCE
Homo neanderthalensis appears in Europe and Asia.
*c.*150,000 BCE
Modern *Homo sapiens* appears in E Africa.
*c.*55,000 BCE
Modern *Homo sapiens* moves into Europe and Australia.
*c.*35,000 BCE
Neanderthals become extinct in Europe.

ASIA AND AUSTRALASIA	AFRICA	EUROPE

15,000 BCE

10,000 BCE

8000 BCE

7000 BCE

6000 BCE

5001 BCE

ASIA AND AUSTRALASIA

*c.***15,000 BCE** End of the coldest period of the most recent ice age.

*c.***10,000 BCE** Emergence of Natufian culture in the Middle East to the W of the River Euphrates, based on the intensive gathering of wild cereals.

*c.***10,000 BCE** Earliest firm evidence of domesticated dogs (from a grave in Palestine).

*c.***9000 BCE** Earliest-known permanent human settlements established by Natufian peoples; they build villages with circular houses in parts of the Middle East and Asia Minor.

*c.***9000 BCE** Sheep and goats are domesticated in the Middle East.

*c.***8500 BCE** Earliest-known rectangular houses are built in Mesopotamia.

*c.***8500 BCE** Wheat (einkorn and emmer) and barley are domesticated in the Middle East.

*c.***8500 BCE** End of the Paleolithic period (Old Stone Age) in the Middle East.

*c.***8000 BCE** First pottery is made in China.

*c.***8000 BCE** Village of Jericho (on the West Bank of the River Jordan) has a population of *c.*1000, and is surrounded by a stone wall with a fortified tower.

*c.***7000 BCE** Cattle and pigs are domesticated in the Middle East.

*c.***7000 BCE** Pigs are domesticated in China.

*c.***7000 BCE** Tropical horticulture begins in the highlands of New Guinea.

c. **6500 BCE** Farming starts in the NE of the Indian subcontinent.

*c.***6000 BCE** Domestication of millet and broomcorn in N China and rice in S China; start of Yangshao culture.

*c.***5400** Start of the Early Ubaid period in Mesopotamia; beginnings of urbanization.

AFRICA

*c.***15,000 BCE** End of the coldest period of the most recent ice age.

wheat *A cereal grass originating in the Middle East, wheat is now grown worldwide and is one of the world's most important food crops.*

*c.***7500 BCE** Earliest-known African pottery is produced in S Sahara region.

mammoth *A hairy, elephantlike mammal, the mammoth inhabited the steppes and tundra of North America, Europe and Asia during the ice ages of the Pleistocene period.*

*c.***6000 BCE** Wheat, barley, sheep and goats are introduced to Egypt from the N.

*c.***6000 BCE** Onset of dryer climatic conditions begins the desertification of the Sahara.

*c.***5500 BCE** Bullrush millet is domesticated in the Sahara.

EUROPE

*c.***15,000 BCE** End of the coldest period of the most recent ice age.

*c.***9500 BCE** Ice sheets start to melt in Europe and North America.

*c.***8500 BCE** End of Paleolithic period in Europe; start of Mesolithic period (Middle Stone Age); bows and arrows come into widespread use.

*c.***6500 BCE** Farming (wheat, barley, goats and sheep) starts in Greece and the Balkans.

*c.***6400 BCE** Emergence of Karanovo culture in present-day S Bulgaria.

*c.***5400 BCE** Start of Vinca culture in present-day Bosnia.

*c.***5400 BCE** Farming spreads across the Hungarian Plain to central Europe.

*c.***5200 BCE** Farming starts in Spain.

THE AMERICAS

c.15,000 BCE End of the coldest period of the most recent ice age.

c.9500 BCE Ice sheets start to melt in Europe and North America.

c.9200–c.8900 BCE Clovis period hunters are active in North America.

c.8500 BCE Disappearance of the ice-bridge across the Bering Strait ends first period of human migration into the Americas.

c.8900–8400 BCE Fulsom period hunters are active in North America.

c.8000 BCE Large mammals (including the mammoth and the horse) become extinct in North America.

▶ **Lascaux** *This cave complex in the Pyrenees contains many different styles of Paleolithic wall paintings, depicting horses, ibex and stags.*

c.7000 BCE Beans and squash are first cultivated in Peru.

7000 BCE Start of the Archaic Period in Mesoamerican history.

c.5200 BCE Onset of drier climatic conditions on the Great Plains of North America forces people and animals to migrate E.

TECHNOLOGY AND ART

c.15,000 BCE Bow and arrow (the bow consisting of a single piece of wood) is invented toward the end of the Paleolithic period (Old Stone Age).

c.15,000–12,000 BCE Main period of European cave painting, including the sites of Lascaux in France and Altamira in Spain, although the earliest sites date from c.30–25,000 BCE.

c.11,000 BCE World's earliest-known fired-clay vessels (bag-shaped pots) are made by hunter-gatherers in Japan.

c.10,000 BCE Jomon cord-marked pottery is first produced in Japan.

c.8500 BCE Earliest-known mudbricks are used to build houses in Mesopotamia.

c.7500 BCE Peoples living in Mesopotamia use fermentation to produce the earliest-known beer.

c.7000 BCE Shrine at Çatal Hüyük in central Asia Minor is decorated with sculpted bull's heads and goddess figures.

c. 7000 BCE Copper (lumps of naturally occurring native copper hammered and cut into shape with stone tools) is first used for jewelry in parts of the Middle East.

c.7000 BCE Pottery comes into general use in many parts of the Middle East.

c.6500 BCE Earliest-known textile (linen) is woven at Çatal Hüyük.

c.5400 BCE Farmers in N central Europe produce distinctive pottery vessels.

c.5500 BCE Copper smelting (the extraction of metal from ore) starts in Asia Minor and present-day W Iran. Start of the Chalcolithic (or Copper) Age in the Middle East.

c.5300 BCE Earliest-known complex buildings are constructed in Mesopotamia, with upper stories and numerous internal rooms.

15,000 BCE

10,000 BCE

8000 BCE

7000 BCE

6000 BCE

5001 BCE

ASIA AND AUSTRALASIA	AFRICA	EUROPE
5000 BCE		
*c.*5000 BCE First permanent settlement is established at Eridu (by tradition the first city) in Mesopotamia.	*c.*5000 BCE Badarian culture emerges in central Egypt.	
*c.*5000 BCE Longshan culture emerges around the Shandong peninsula in N China.		

4800 BCE

cotton *Most cotton is grown for the fibers that can be made into fabric. Cotton seeds develop within seedpods (bolls). When mature, the bolls rupture and a soft cloud of cotton erupts.*

4600 BCE		
*c.*4500 BCE Zebu cattle are domesticated in Pakistan.	*c.*4500 BCE Start of cattle herding in the Sahara; either with locally domesticated stock or with animals introduced via Egypt.	*c.*4500 BCE Earliest megaliths are built in NW Europe to accommodate collective burials.
c. 4500 BCE Permanent settlement is established at Ur in S Mesopotamia.		*c.*4500 BCE Spread of farming reaches the Netherlands.

4400 BCE		
*c.*4300 BCE Start of the Late Ubaid period in Mesopotamia; many cities are established and temples and ziggurats are built.	*c.*4250 BCE Local sorghum and rice are domesticated in Sudan.	*c.*4400–4100 BCE Extensive forest clearance takes place in Britain.
		*c.*4400 BCE Start of Gumelnita culture in present-day N Bulgaria and S Romania.
		*c.*4250 BCE Plow is first used in the Balkans.

4200 BCE		
*c.*4200 BCE Copper mining starts in Oman in SE Arabia.		*c.*4200 BCE Horses are domesticated (for food) in Ukraine.
*c.*4200 BCE Elamites establish the city of Susa in present-day W Iran.	**sorghum** *A tropical cereal grass, sorghum is thought to have originated in Africa and is now its most widely cultivated grain.*	

4001 BCE

THE AMERICAS	TECHNOLOGY AND ART	
*c.*5000 BCE Guinea pigs are domesticated in Colombia.	*c.*5000 BCE Earliest-known canals are dug in Mesopotamia. They are used to irrigate crops and to drain marshy ground for settlement and cultivation.	5000 BCE
	*c.*5000 BCE *Thinker* (also known as the *Sorrowing God*) statue is carved at Cernavoda in present-day E Romania.	
*c.*4800 BCE Peoples from the Central American mainland become the first inhabitants of the Caribbean islands.	*c.*4800 BCE Stamp seals are first used to identify property and goods in Mesopotamia and SE Europe.	4800 BCE
	*c.*4500 BCE Ox-drawn plow is invented in Mesopotamia; crop farming is extended to soils too difficult to be worked with hand-held sticks.	4600 BCE
	*c.*4500 BCE Small clay tokens in different shapes are first used for accounting purposes in Mesopotamia	
c. 4300 BCE A variety of cotton is domesticated in Mexico.	*c.*4300 BCE Turntable (tournette or slow wheel) for pottery making is invented in N Mesopotamia.	4400 BCE

ox-drawn plow *The application of animal power to farming implements was a great advance in agricultural history. Primitive plows were drawn by a pair of oxen. The plow bar was tied to the center of a bar of wood which was lashed to the horns of the animals.*

	*c.*4200 BCE First deliberate production of bronze (copper alloyed with arsenic or tin) occurs in present-day W Iran.	4200 BCE
		4001 BCE

ASIA AND AUSTRALASIA	AFRICA	EUROPE
	c.4000 BCE Nagada culture emerges along the River Nile in Egypt.	**c.4000 BCE** Olives, figs, almonds and pomegranates are domesticated in the E Mediterranean region.
	c.4000 BCE Donkeys are domesticated in Egypt.	

4000 BCE

donkey *A member of the horse family, the donkey is a domesticated ass, descended from the African wild ass, which was tamed by humans thousands of years ago.*

3800 BCE

c.3800 BCE Rise of TRB (*Trichterbecher*) farming culture in Denmark and N Germany and Poland.

3600 BCE

| **c.3500 BCE** Floodplain of the River Indus in present-day Pakistan is settled by farmers who use some copper tools; start of the Early Indus period (*c.*3500–*c.*2800 BCE). | **c.3500 BCE** First fortified towns are built in Egypt; two distinct centers of urbanization emerge in Upper (S) and Lower (N) Egypt. | **c.3500 BCE** Copper mining starts near present-day Granada in S Spain. |
| **c.3500 BCE** Start of the Uruk period in S Mesopotamia; development of urban civilization. | | |

3400 BCE

| **c.3300 BCE** SUMERIANS (who probably originated in central Asia) settle in S Mesopotamia. | | **c.3400 BCE** Earliest evidence of wheeled vehicles in Europe (from a grave in Poland). |
| **c.3300 BCE** City-states develop in Syria and Palestine. | | **c.3300 BCE** Megalithic temple is built at Tarxien, Malta. |

Sumeria *This Sumerian vessel dates from c.3,500 BCE. It was made of clay, one of the few materials available. The quality of their glazes and decorations was very advanced.*

3200 BCE

c.3200 BCE Bronze comes into widespread use for tools in Mesopotamia; start of the Bronze Age in the Middle East.	**c.3100 BCE** Egypt is unified by King MENES (also known as Narmer) of Upper Egypt, who establishes a capital city at Memphis; start of the Early Dynastic period.	**c.3200 BCE** Farming spreads to S Sweden.
c.3100 BCE End of the Uruk period in S Mesopotamia; start of the Jamdat Nasr period.		**c.3200 BCE** The "Man in the Ice", equipped with a cast copper ax, dies in a blizzard while crossing the Alps near the present-day Italian–Austrian border.
		c.3100 BCE First ritual earthworks are constructed at Stonehenge, England.

3001 BCE

THE AMERICAS	TECHNOLOGY AND ART	
*c.***4000** BCE Llamas and alpacas are domesticated in Peru.	*c.***4000** BCE A burial at Varna in Bulgaria contains the earliest-known large deposit of gold objects (weighing more than 1.5kg/3.3lb).	**4000** BCE
*c.***4000** BCE Corn is domesticated in Mexico.	*c.***4000** BCE By using the Nilometer (which measures the height of the River Nile's annual flood), the Egyptians calculate that the year is 365 days long.	
	*c.***4000** BCE First copper axes are produced in present-day W Iran and SE Europe.	
	*c.***3800** BCE Earliest-known metal tools with an integrally cast shaft-hole are made at Sialk, present-day NW Iran.	**3800** BCE
	*c.***3800** BCE Wheel is invented in Mesopotamia; the first ox-drawn carts are used to transport agricultural produce.	
*c.***3600** BCE First American pottery is produced in Guyana on N coast of South America.	*c.***3500** BCE Start of the Secondary Products Revolution in agriculture; widespread use of animal power, use of wool for textiles, and introduction of dairying.	**3600** BCE
c. **3500** BCE A variety of cotton is domesticated in lowland Peru.	*c.***3500** BCE First systematic use of pictographs for writing occurs in Sumeria (S Mesopotamia).	
	*c.***3400** BCE Potter's wheel (fast wheel) is invented in Mesopotamia.	**3400** BCE
	c. **3400** BCE Cylinder seal is developed in Mesopotamia.	

Sumeria These Sumerian pictographs show a sled and a wheeled sled. Pictographic writing and wheeled vehicles were two of the many major advances of the Sumerians.

corn Also known as corn or sweetcorn, corn is a cereal plant of the grass family. Edible seeds grow in rows upon a cob, protected by a leafy sheath.

	*c.***3200** BCE Walls of the so-called Stone Mosaic temple at Uruk are decorated with thousands of small, multicolored, baked clay cones.	**3200** BCE
	*c.***3200** BCE Food rations for workers in the city of Uruk are distributed in pottery bowls mass-produced in molds.	
	*c.***3200** BCE Lost-wax technique (*cire perdue*) for casting metals is developed in Mesopotamia.	
		3001 BCE

ASIA AND AUSTRALASIA	AFRICA	EUROPE

3000 BCE

*c.*3000 BCE Agriculture starts at oases in SE Arabia.

▼ *pyramid* The three pyramids at Giza have survived virtually intact into the modern age. The largest was built for the pharaoh Khufu, the other two for Khafre and Menkaure.

*c.*3000 BCE First copper working in Italy.

c. 3000 BCE Lake villages are built at Clairvaux and Charavines in France.

2900 BCE

*c.*2900 BCE First sizable town is established on the site of Troy, NW Asia Minor.

*c.*2900 BCE Start of the Early Dynastic period in Sumerian Mesopotamia; the first conflicts between rival city-states occur.

2800 BCE

*c.*2800 BCE AKKADIANS establish a kingdom to the N of Sumeria.

*c.*2800 BCE Indus valley civilization emerges in present-day Pakistan.

*c.*2800 BCE EGYPTIAN expeditions make first contact with Nubian cultures to the S.

*c.*2800 BCE Stone-walled fortresses are built in Portugal and S Spain.

*c.*2750 BCE Start of Bronze Age in SE Europe.

2700 BCE

*c.*2700 BCE Reign of GILGAMESH, the legendary Sumerian king of Uruk.

breadfruit *Cultivated in the Malay archipelago since the third millennium BCE, the breadfruit spread from there to the whole of SE Asia and the S Pacific region.*

2686 BCE Early Dynastic period ends in Egypt; start of the Old Kingdom period (2686–2181 BCE).

*c.*2700 BCE Start of notable decline of central and E European farming cultures, possibly due to soil exhaustion or population movements.

2600 BCE

*c.*2600 BCE Domestication of breadfruit in SE Asia.

*c.*2600 BCE Walled towns are built in N China.

*c.*2550–*c.*2525 BCE Great Pyramid is built for the Egyptian pharaoh CHEOPS (Khufu) at Giza.

*c.*2600 BCE Emergence of Early MINOAN CIVILIZATION in Crete.

2501 BCE

THE AMERICAS	TECHNOLOGY AND ART	
*c.***3000** BCE Start of Old Copper Culture on s shore of Lake Superior; jewelry and other artifacts are produced from hammered native copper.	*c.***3000** BCE Hieroglyphic writing is first used in Egypt.	3000 BCE
*c.***3000** BCE Chilis, avocados, peanuts and sweet potatoes are domesticated in the coastal region of Peru.		
	*c.***2850** BCE First Cycladic statues are produced on Mediterranean islands to the E of Greece.	2900 BCE
*c.***2800** BCE Several varieties of potato are domesticated in highland Peru.	*c.***2800** BCE Silkworms and mulberry trees are domesticated in China.	2800 BCE

peanut Native to South America, peanuts are now grown in many temperate parts of the world. The nuts are a valuable source of protein.

	*c.***2700** BCE Earliest examples of Egyptian literature, the Pyramid Texts, containing prophesies and moralistic tales, are written down on papyrus using a brush and ink.	2700 BCE
	*c.***2700** BCE Cuneiform writing (wedge-shaped marks made by pressing the end of a reed into clay tablets) is developed in Mesopotamia.	
	*c.***2650** BCE Egyptian architect IMHOTEP designs the world's earliest-known pyramid (the so-called stepped pyramid) for the pharaoh Zoser	
*c.***2600** BCE First temple mounds are constructed in Peru.	*c.***2600** BCE Earliest-known glass is made for jewelry beads in Mesopotamia.	2600 BCE
	*c.***2600** BCE Earliest-known large-scale use of fired bricks occurs with the construction of the Indus valley cities of Harappa and Mohenjo Daro.	

ASIA AND AUSTRALASIA	AFRICA	EUROPE

2500 BCE

*c.*2500 BCE Potters wheel is first used in China.

*c.*2500 BCE One-humped dromedary camel in Arabia and two-humped Bactrian camel in central Asia are domesticated.

*c.*2500 BCE EGYPTIANS establish a trading post in Nubia, at Buhen near the second cataract of the River Nile

*c.*2500 BCE Horses are introduced to Ireland.

camel There are two species of camel – the dromedary (above) and the Bactrian (below). Camels are well adapted to their desert environment: they are able to walk for eight days without drinking or eating by using up fat stored in their humps.

2400 BCE

*c.*2400 BCE City of Ebla in N Syria becomes a major trading and commercial center.

2334 BCE AKKADIANS under SARGON establish an empire in Mesopotamia.

*c.*2400 BCE So-called BEAKER PEOPLE begin migration from Spain to France, Germany and Britain.

2300 BCE

*c.*2300 BCE Indus valley civilization starts trade with Mesopotamia and the Arabian Gulf region via the port of Lothal.

*c.*2300 BCE Start of Bronze Age in central Europe.

2200 BCE

2190 BCE Akkadian empire collapses under attack from the nomadic Guti people.

2119 BCE Utuhegal, king of Uruk, defeats the Gutians in battle and re-establishes Sumerian control.

2112 BCE King Urnammu takes control of Mesopotamia and founds the Third Dynasty of Ur.

2181 BCE End of Old Kingdom in Egypt; collapse of central control; start of the First Intermediate period.

sunflower Originating in North America, sunflowers were not introduced to Europe until the 16th century. Their nutritious seeds yield a high-quality oil.

2100 BCE

*c.*2100 BCE AMORITE nomads move into Mesopotamia from the E.

2004 BCE Ur is destroyed by ELAMITES from present-day SW Iran.

2040 BCE Pharaoh MENUHOTEP re-establishes central control in Egypt; end of the First Intermediate period; start of Middle Kingdom period (2040–1640 BCE).

*c.*2100 BCE Circle of bluestones at Stonehenge, England, is erected.

2001 BCE

THE AMERICAS	TECHNOLOGY AND ART	
	c.2500 BCE Earliest-known examples of Sumerian literature are written down at Abu Salabikh in Mesopotamia.	2500 BCE
	c.2500 BCE Reflex bow made from a composite of wood and horn is invented in N Mesopotamia.	
	c.2500 BCE Royal burials at Ur contain lavishly decorated musical instruments.	
	c.2450 BCE Vultures Steele is carved to commemorate the victories of the Sumerian king Eannatum of Lagash in Mesopotamia.	
c.2400 BCE First Mesoamerican pottery is made.	**2350** BCE Earliest-known law code is compiled for Urukagina, the Sumerian king of Lagash in S Mesopotamia.	2400 BCE
c.2300 BCE Stone temple and ritual center is built at La Galada in lowland Peru.	***c.2300*** BCE First houses with mains drainage are built in Indus valley cities.	2300 BCE
	c.2300 BCE An as-yet-undeciphered script is developed in the Indus valley.	
	c.2225 BCE Stone victory steele is carved to commemorate the military success of of the Akkadian king Naramsin.	
c.2200 BCE People in present-day SW USA first make pottery.	***c.2130*** BCE Stone statues of King Gudea of Lagash mark a brief revival of Sumerian art.	2200 BCE
c.2200 BCE Domestication in present-day E USA of sunflowers, sumpweed, goosegrass and a variety of squash.		
▶ *Beaker culture The people of this culture were accomplished metalworkers, as can be seen from the copper and flint dagger shown here. Such weapons often accompanied burials, along with the distinctive drinking vessel from which the culture gets its name.*		
	c.2100 BCE Mathematicians in Mesopotamia divide a circle into 360 degrees in accordance with their 60-based number system.	2100 BCE
		2001 BCE

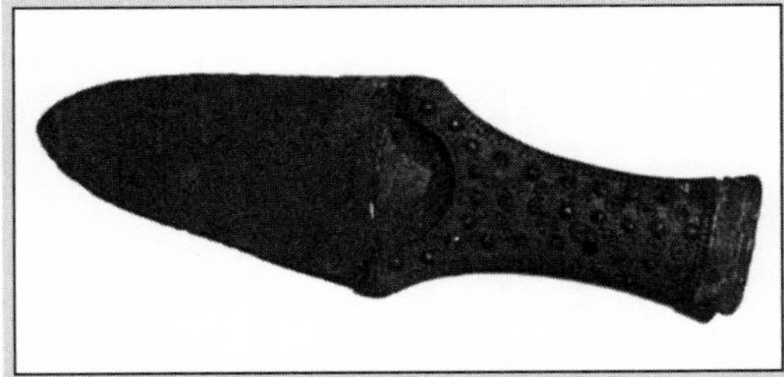

ASIA AND AUSTRALASIA	AFRICA	EUROPE

2000 BCE

*c.***2000 BCE** Start of the Bronze Age in China and SE Asia.

*c.***1994–1523 BCE** Xia dynasty establishes central control over city-states in N China.

*c.***2000 BCE** EGYPTIANS conquer N Nubia.

*c.***2000 BCE** Farming cultures of SE Europe collapse, perhaps because of population movements.

*c.***2000 BCE** Rise of Urnfield culture in E central Europe.

*c.***2000 BCE** Greek-speakers migrate into Greece from the N.

*c.***2000 BCE** Start of Old Palace period of MINOAN CIVILIZATION in Crete.

1900 BCE

*c.***1900 BCE** Start of the decline of the Indus valley civilization; collapse of international trade; port of Lothal is abandoned.

1830 BCE Having taken over several Mesopotamian cities, AMORITE king Sumuabum founds a new dynasty in BABYLONIA.

*c.***1900 BCE** Egyptians establish a series of fortresses around the second cataract of the Nile to protect against raids by Nubians from Kush (present-day Sudan).

*c.***1900 BCE** Large sarsen stones are added to Stonehenge in England.

1800 BCE

1792–1750 BCE King HAMMURABI of Babylonia extends Amorite control over all Mesopotamia.

▶ *Stonehenge The largest megalith in Europe, Stonehenge dates from the early 3rd millennium BCE, although the main stones were erected c.2000–1500 BCE.*

1700 BCE

*c.***1650 BCE** HITTITES settle in Asia Minor and establish a capital at Hattusas.

*c.***1700 BCE** HYKSOS peoples from Palestine introduce horses into Egypt.

*c.***1650 BCE** MYCENAEAN warlords establish control of Greek mainland and engage in long-distance trade with central and N Europe.

1600 BCE

*c.***1600 BCE** Chariots are introduced to China from central Asia.

*c.***1600 BCE** Start of Polynesian expansion by boat E from NE New Guinea.

*c.***1600 BCE** Aryan peoples begin migrating into the Indus valley region.

1595 BCE Hittites sack Babylonia and establish temporary control in Mesopotamia.

1640 BCE Hyksos peoples establish control of the Nile delta region; end of the Middle Kingdom period; start of Second Intermediate period.

*c.***1620 BCE** Massive eruption of the Thíra volcano buries the city of Acrotiri on the island of Thíra.

*c.***1550 BCE** HURRIANS in N Syria unite to create the kingdom of Mitanni.

1530 BCE KASSITES from present-day NW Iran invade Mesopotamia and take over Hammurabi's empire.

1523 BCE Beginning of the SHANG DYNASTY in China.

*c.***1550 BCE** Pharaoh AHMOSE unites Egyptians and expels the Hyksos; end of the Second Intermediate period; start of the New Kingdom period.

*c.***1600 BCE** Cretan palaces are destroyed then rebuilt; start of the New Palace period of Minoan civilization.

1501 BCE

THE AMERICAS

*c.*2000 BCE Establishment of irrigated farming villages in coastal Peru, with terracing on mountainsides; start of Initial Period of South American history.

*c.*2000 BCE People in present-day E USA first make pottery.

*c.*1800 BCE People in Peru first make pottery.

*c.*1700 BCE Ritual center is established at Poverty Point, Louisiana (in present-day USA).

TECHNOLOGY AND ART

*c.*2000 BCE Egyptian scribes develop their cursive hieratic script.

*c.*2000 BCE Minoans in Crete develop a pictographic writing system.

*c.*2000 BCE Carved statue menhirs are erected in S France and N Italy.

*c.*1900 BCE Earliest-known copy of the Epic of Gilgamesh is written down in Babylon, Mesopotamia.

*c.*1800 BCE Horse-drawn, two-wheeled war chariot is invented on the SW fringes of the Eurasian steppes.

*c.*1780 BCE Law code of King Hammurabi of Babylon is written down and publicized throughout his empire.

*c.*1700 BCE Earliest-known Chinese script is used to pose questions on oracle bones thrown into a fire.

Minoan civilization *This period was noted for decorative pottery, frescos and costumes. The woman's costume shown here comprises a sleeved bodice, joined under bare breasts; the hip corselet and bell-shaped flounced skirt are tightly belted. The narrow-waisted effect is echoed in the man's costume – a simple loin cloth worn tightly belted. Bright materials, bracelets and fillets are worn by both.*

*c.*1600 BCE Minoans in Crete begin to use the as-yet-undeciphered Linear A script.

*c.*1600 BCE Hittites in Asia Minor develop the first iron-making techniques; the invention remains a Hittite "secret weapon" for several centuries.

2000 BCE

1900 BCE

1800 BCE

1700 BCE

1600 BCE

1501 BCE

ASIA AND AUSTRALASIA	AFRICA	EUROPE

1500 BCE

*c.*1500 BCE Sabaeans establish a state in present-day Yemen, SW Arabia.

*c.*1500 BCE Egypt regains control of N Nubia.

*c.*1490 BCE Queen HATSHEPSUT of Egypt (r.1494–1482 BCE) sends expeditions to Punt (present-day Somalia).

*c.*1480 BCE Following victory at the battle of Megiddo, Egypt conquers the city-states of present-day Lebanon and Israel; beginning of the Egyptian empire.

*c.*1500–*c.*1200 BCE Spread of Urnfield culture to Germany and Italy.

*c.*1450–1375 BCE MYCENAEANS conquer Crete; MINOAN palaces are sacked.

1400 BCE

c. 1400 BCE KASSITES from present-day NW Iran overthrow the AMORITES and establish control in Mesopotamia.

*c.*1350 BCE HITTITES conquer the kingdom of Mitanni; the Hittite empire reaches its greatest extent under King Suppiluliumas (*c.*1380–*c.*1346 BCE).

*c.*1450 BCE EGYPTIANS establish the fortified town of Napata in central Nubia, near the fourth cataract of the River Nile.

*c.*1360 BCE Pharaoh AKHNATEN (r.*c.*1379–1362 BCE) unsuccessfully tries to replace traditional Egyptian religion with sun-worship.

1300 BCE

*c.*1300 BCE Emergence of the first ASSYRIAN EMPIRE in present-day S Syria.

1275 BCE Battle of Kadesh in present-day Syria between the Egyptians and Hittites establishes the frontier between their empires.

*c.*1225 BCE Legendary Trojan War ends with the capture of Troy by Greeks.

1200 BCE

*c.*1220–1190 BCE East Mediterranean is raided by Sea Peoples, who weaken the Hittite empire.

*c.*1200 BCE Hittite empire collapses under attacks from the Sea Peoples and the Assyrians.

1154 BCE Kassites are conquered by the Assyrians, who extend their empire into S Mesopotamia.

*c.*1190 BCE Sea Peoples attack Egypt, but are defeated by pharaoh RAMSES III (r.*c.*1194–1163 BCE).

*c.*1200 BCE Citadel at Mycenae is sacked; end of the Mycenaean civilization.

1100 BCE

*c.*1100 BCE Rise of PHOENICIAN city-states in present-day Lebanon, Palestine and Israel.

*c.*1100 BCE Jews establish the kingdom of Israel in Palestine.

1076 BCE First Assyrian empire reaches its greatest extent under King Tiglath-Pileser I (r.1114–1076 BCE).

1030 BCE End of the SHANG DYNASTY in China; start of the ZHOU DYNASTY.

1085 BCE End of the New Kingdom period in Egypt; end of the Egyptian empire; start of the Late Period.

*c.*1100 BCE Iron is first used in SE Europe and Italy.

*c.*1100 BCE ETRUSCAN peoples migrate into N Italy.

*c.*1050 BCE Start of first period of Greek migration to Aegean islands and W coast of Asia Minor.

1001 BCE

14

THE AMERICAS

1500 BCE Start of the Formative period in Mesoamerican history; beginnings of OLMEC civilization on Mexico's Gulf coast.

c.1200 BCE End of the Initial period in South American history; start of Early Horizon period; beginnings of CHAVÍN CULTURE in Andes region.

c.1150 BCE Town of San Lorenzo becomes the Olmec political and ritual center.

TECHNOLOGY AND ART

c.1500 BCE Earliest-known alphabet is devised in the city of Ugarit in present-day Syria.

c.1500 BCE Mycenaeans build beehive tombs in Greece.

c.1500 BCE Earliest-known glass vessels are buried in an Egyptian pharaoh's tomb.

1500 BCE

c.1400 BCE Mycenaeans in Crete begin to use Linear B script to write the Greek language.

1323 BCE Pharaoh TUTANKHAMON (b.1341 BCE) is buried in the Valley of the Kings near Luxor in Egypt.

1400 BCE

c.1250 BCE Rock-cut temple at Abu Simbel is constructed on the orders of pharaoh RAMSES II (r.1290–1224 BCE).

1300 BCE

◄ *Mycenaean soldier* This soldier dates from between 1400 and 1200 BCE. Excavations in Mycenae have revealed fortifications, weapons and armor, indicating that warfare was an important factor of life at this time.

c.1200 BCE Egyptian capital Memphis is the world's largest city with a population of up to one million.

1200 BCE

c.1200 BCE The *Vedas*, ancient and most sacred writings of Hinduism, are composed by the Aryan invaders of India.

c.1200 BCE Start of the Iron Age in the Middle East – the breakup of the Hittite empire ends their monopoly on iron production.

c.1100 BCE An alphabet is developed by Phoenicians in present-day Lebanon.

1100 BCE

◄ *Abu Simbel* is the location of two rock-cut sandstone temples built by Ramses II. In front of the façade of the Great Temple are four seated colossi of Ramses, two of which are shown here, each over 19m (62ft) high. Between 1963 and 1966, the temples and statuary were cut into some 1,000 blocks and reassembled on higher ground in order to prevent their disappearance under the waters of Lake Nasser, created by the construction of the Aswan High Dam.

1001 BCE

ASIA AND AUSTRALASIA	AFRICA	EUROPE
1000 BCE *c.*1000 BCE Polynesian expansion across the Pacific Ocean reaches Samoa and Tonga.	*c.*1000 BCE Horses are introduced into sub-Saharan Africa via Egypt.	*c.*1000 BCE Start of the Iron Age in S and central Europe.
962 BCE SOLOMON (r.962–922 BCE) succeeds DAVID (r.1000–962 BCE) as king of Israel.	*c.*920 BCE Nubian peoples establish KUSH (capital Napata) as an independent state in present-day Sudan.	*c.*900 BCE ETRUSCAN civilization emerges in N Italy.
935 BCE Second ASSYRIAN EMPIRE is established by King ASSURDAN II.		*c.*800 BCE Establishment of a town near salt and iron ore mines at Hallstatt, Austria.
900 BCE *c.*900 BCE Kingdom of Urartu is founded in present-day Armenia.	814 BCE Traditional date for the founding of the city of Carthage, near present-day Tunis, by PHOENICIANS from the city of Tyre.	776 BCE Traditional date for the founding of the Olympic Games.
800 BCE 771 BCE Western capital of the Chinese ZHOU emperors is sacked by warrior nomads.	727 BCE King Piankhi of Kush completes his conquest of Egypt and establishes the Kushite dynasty.	753 BCE Traditional date for the founding of Rome by ROMULUS AND REMUS.
*c.*750 BCE Start of the Iron Age in China and SE Asia.		*c.*750 BCE Rise of city-states in mainland Greece.
722 BCE Collapse of central control in China; Zhou emperors rule in name only; start of the Spring and Autumn period; rival states emerge.		733 BCE GREEK settlers found the city of Syracuse in Sicily.
		730–710 BCE City-state of Sparta in Greece conquers neighboring Messenia.
700 BCE *c.* 650 BCE SCYTHIAN peoples from the steppes begin raiding the Middle East.	671 BCE Kushite dynasty overthrown by ASSYRIAN conquest of Egypt.	669 BCE Defeat by rival city-state Argos and revolt of subjugated Messenians (helots) causes militarization of Spartan society.
627 BCE Under Chaldean rulers, the Neo-BABYLONIAN kingdom breaks away from the Assyrian empire.	664 BCE King Psamtek I establishes a Saite dynasty in N Egypt under Assyrian overlordship.	*c.*650 BCE Greek colonies are established by the Black Sea.
605 BCE MEDES and Neo-Babylonians under King NEBUCHADNEZZAR II (d.562 BCE) defeat the Assyrians at the battle of Carchemish; end of the Assyrian empire.	*c.*620 BCE Greek traders establish the port of Naucratis in the Nile delta.	621 BCE DRACO introduces a strict (hence draconian) law code in the Greek city-state of Athens.
		*c.*600 BCE Rome is conquered by the Etruscans.
600 BCE 586 BCE Neo-Babylonian empire conquers Jerusalem and destroys the Temple.	*c.*600 BCE Beginnings of Nok culture in the River Niger valley.	600 BCE Greek traders establish a colony at Massilia, S France.
550 BCE CYRUS THE GREAT (600–529 BCE) of Persia establishes the Persian ACHAEMENID DYNASTY.	*c.*600 BCE Phoenician seafarers circumnavigate Africa.	594 BCE SOLON (*c.*639–*c.*559 BCE) begins reforms in Athens.
550 BCE Zoroastrianism, based on the teachings of ZOROASTER (Zarathustra), becomes the state religion of the Persian empire.	591 BCE Saite dynasty sacks Napata; the capital of Kush moves to Meroë.	*c.*580 BCE Phoenicians establish colonies in W Sicily.
546 BCE Persians conquer the Greek cities in Asia Minor.	*c.*580 BCE First African production of iron takes place in Meroë.	540 BCE A Greek fleet is defeated by an alliance of Etruscans and Carthaginians near Corsica.
545 BCE King Bimbisara of MAGADHA in the Ganges valley of India initiates a policy of expansion.	*c.*550 BCE Kushite kingdom is extended S to present-day Khartoum.	512 BCE Persian armies invade Europe and occupy NE Greece.
	525 BCE Persians conquer Egypt.	509 BCE TARQUIN SUPERBUS, last of the Etruscan kings of Rome, is expelled; start of ROMAN Republic.
538 BCE Persians capture Babylonia.		507 BCE Reforms of Cleisthenes mark beginnings of Athenian democracy.
501 BCE		

THE AMERICAS

c.1000 BCE Beginning of Adena culture in Ohio valley, present-day USA; it is also known as Early Woodland culture.

c.1000 BCE Cultivation of corn is introduced to present-day SW USA from Mexico.

c.900 BCE OLMEC capital San Lorenzo, on Gulf coast of Mexico, is destroyed by warfare; the town of La Venta becomes the new political center of the region.

c.850 BCE Emergence of ZAPOTEC civilization around the town of San Jose Mogote in the Oaxaca valley region of Mexico.

c.850 BCE Temple center at Chavín de Huántar is established in Peru.

c.700 BCE Abandonment of the ritual center at Poverty Point, Louisiana, marks the end of the Archaic period in North American history.

c.600 BCE MAYAN people start the construction of the city of Tikal in present-day Guatemala.

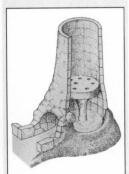

Etruscan kiln *The wealth of the Etruscan civilization was based on their iron-working skills. This Etruscan iron-smelting kiln dates from the 7th century BCE. It probably provided iron for the grave goods found in their elaborate tombs.*

TECHNOLOGY AND ART

c.1000 BCE Developments in EGYPTIAN writing produce demotic script. — 1000 BCE

c.900 BCE First Geometric-style pottery is produced in Athens. — 900 BCE

c.900 BCE Peoples of the Eurasian steppes invent the saddle and develop horse-archer cavalry.

c.900 BCE *Brahmanas* and *Aranyakas*, ancient writings of Hinduism, are composed in India.

c.800 BCE Latest date for the introduction of the Phoenician alphabet to Greece. — 800 BCE

c.750 BCE *Illiad* and *Odyssey* are written down in their final form, supposedly by the poet HOMER.

c.750 BCE City of Argos in Greece develops an army of hoplites — armored citizen soldiers.

c.750 BCE Start of the Halstatt period of Celtic art.

c.730–c.680 BCE Orientalizing period of Greek art.

c.720 BCE First black-figure pottery is produced in Athens.

c.700 BCE Greek author HESIOD writes his *Theogeny* and *Works and Days*. — 700 BCE

c.700 BCE Coinage is invented in Greek colonies in SW Asia Minor.

c.700 BCE Etruscans adopt the Greek alphabet.

c.690 BCE Sabaeans complete the Marib dam in present-day Yemen.

c.600 BCE Development in present-day Mexico of Zapotec pictograph writing. — 600 BCE

c.600 BCE *Upanishads*, texts of Hinduism, are compiled in India.

585 BCE THALES OF MILETUS (636–546 BCE) predicts an eclipse of the Sun; this traditionally marks the beginning of Greek philosophy.

c.575 BCE Etruscan engineers dig the Cloaca Maxima sewer in Rome.

c.570 BCE Death of the Greek poet SAPPHO.

c.563 BCE Birth of Siddhartha Gautama (d.483 BCE) – the BUDDHA.

c.560 BCE Death of AESOP (b.c.620 BCE), reputed author of animal fables.

c.557 BCE Indian teacher Mahavira (c.599–527 BCE) develops the philosophy of Jainism.

551 BCE Birth of the philosopher CONFUCIUS (d.479 BCE) in China

c.550 BCE Method for mass-producing cast iron is invented in China.

c.534 BCE First Greek tragedy is written by Thespis.

531 BCE Death of the Chinese philosopher LAO TZU (b.604 BCE), the founder of Taoism.

c.530 BCE Red-figure pottery replaces black-figure pottery at Athens.

c.530 BCE Greek philosopher PYTHAGORAS (c.580–500 BCE) moves from the island of Samos to Croton in Italy.

501 BCE

ASIA AND AUSTRALASIA	AFRICA	EUROPE

500 BCE

499–494 BCE Greek-speaking cities in w Asia Minor revolt against Persian overlordship; Athens and Sparta lend assistance but the revolt is crushed.

*c.***500 BCE** Peoples from sw Arabia settle in Ethiopia.

*c.***500 BCE** Iron-working techniques reach w Africa.

499 BCE Rome defeats neighboring Latin cities at battle of Lake Regillus.

490 BCE Persians under DARIUS I (r.521–486 BCE) invade Greece, but are defeated by Athens and Sparta at the battle of Marathon.

480 BCE

480 BCE Carthaginians under Hamilcar invade Sicily in support of PHOENICIAN colonies on the island; they are defeated by Greek forces led by Gelon of Syracuse.

*c.***470 BCE** Carthaginians under Hanno explore w African coast.

480 BCE Persians under XERXES (r.486–465 BCE) invade Greece and sack Athens after the battle of Thermopylae; they are defeated by a GREEK fleet at the battle of Salamis.

479 BCE Persians are defeated at the battle of Plataea and driven from Greece.

477 BCE Foundation of Delian League; start of Athenian empire under CIMON's leadership.

460 BCE

*c.***460 BCE** State of Qin in w China is partitioned; end of the Spring and Autumn period.

449 BCE Peace treaty signed between Athens and Persia.

460–454 BCE Athens sends an expedition to support an EGYPTIAN revolt against the Persians; the Greek troops are defeated in battle and wiped out.

464 BCE Earthquake in Sparta followed by a helot revolt.

461 BCE PERICLES (490-429 BCE) leads democratic revolution in Athens.

461–451 BCE First Peloponnesian War between Athens and Sparta.

445 BCE Athens and Sparta sign the Thirty Year Peace agreement.

440 BCE

431 BCE Start of the Second Peloponnesian War between Athens and Sparta.

425–424 BCE Sparta and its ally Thebes win a series of victories against Athens.

421 BCE Peace of Nicias between Athens and Sparta fails to end hostilities.

420 BCE

*c.***420 BCE** Nabataeans establish a kingdom with its capital at Petra in present-day Jordan.

*c.***403 BCE** Start of Warring States period in China as rival states battle for overall control.

▲ *Parthenon* Dominating the Acropolis, the Parthenon was erected by the Athenian ruler Pericles to replace the temple destroyed by the Persians in 480 BCE. Under the overall direction of the sculptor Phidias, with Ictinus and Callicrates as architects, it took shape in the years after 445 and was completed by 438 BCE, except for the sculptures, which took a further six years. Designed as an expression of Athens' supremacy and civic pride, it was Greece's largest and most costly building.

415–413 BCE Athenian naval expedition to capture Sicily ends in defeat and disaster.

411 BCE Sparta makes an alliance with Persia against Athens.

411 BCE Council of Four Hundred takes control in Athens.

405 BCE Persia destroys the Athenian fleet at battle of Aegospotami.

404 BCE Athens surrenders to Sparta; end of Second Peloponnesian War.

401 BCE

THE AMERICAS

***c.*500 BCE** Emergence of PARACAS culture in s Peru.

***c.*500 BCE** ZAPOTECS build a new ritual and political center at Monte Albán.

▲ **Petra** *The capital of the Nabataean kingdom, Petra was carved from the high, pinkish sandstone cliffs that protected it. The monastery, shown here, is situated on a high plateau above the rest of the city.*

SCIENCE AND TECHNOLOGY

***c.*500 BCE** First Chinese coins are manufactured, in the shapes of miniature tools.

***c.*430 BCE** Earliest-known woven wool carpet is buried with a Scythian chief in s Siberia.

***c.*425 BCE** Greek philosopher DEMOCRITUS (460–370 BCE) theorizes that all matter is made of very small atoms.

423 BCE Greek astronomer Meton proposes inserting extra months into a 19-year cycle to align the calendar.

◄ **Sophocles** *was a popular and prominent figure in his day. With Aeschylus and Euripides, he was considered one of the three great tragedians of ancient Greece.*

ARTS AND HUMANITIES

***c.*490 BCE** Multicolored enameled bricks are used to decorate the palace of Darius I at Susa.

***c.*490 BCE** Start of the Classical period of Greek art.

487 BCE Comedies are entered for the first time in literary competition in Athens.

476 BCE Greek poet PINDAR (522–438 BCE) visits Sicily at the invitation of the tyrant Hiero I of Syracuse.

***c.*475 BCE** Bronze statue of a *Charioteer* (from Delphi) is cast in Greece.

***c.*458 BCE** Greek dramatist AESCHYLUS (525–456 BCE) completes the *Oresteia*.

450 BCE Greek philosopher Xeno publishes his logical paradoxes.

***c.*445–438 BCE** Parthenon in Athens is rebuilt under the direction of the sculptor PHIDIAS (490–430 BCE).

430 BCE Greek dramatist SOPHOCLES (496–406 BCE) writes *Oedipus Rex*.

425 BCE Greek historian HERODOTUS (b. *c.*485 BCE) dies at Thurii in s Italy.

415 BCE Greek dramatist EURIPIDES (480–406 BCE) writes his *Trojan Women*.

405 BCE Greek dramatist ARISTOPHANES (448–380 BCE) writes his comedy *Frogs*.

500 BCE

480 BCE

460 BCE

440 BCE

420 BCE

401 BCE

ASIA AND AUSTRALASIA	AFRICA	EUROPE

400 BCE

c.400 BCE The s Indian kingdoms of the CHOLAS and the PANDYAS are established.

340 BCE

334 BCE ALEXANDER THE GREAT (Alexander of Macedon, 356–323 BCE) invades Persian empire, defeats king DARIUS III (380–330 BCE) at the River Granicus, and gains control of Asia Minor.

333 BCE Alexander cuts the legendary Gordian knot, and defeats the Persians at the battle of Issus on the N border of Syria.

331 BCE Victory over the Persians at the battle of Gaugamela gives Alexander control of Mesopotamia.

330 BCE Alexander's troops burn the Persian royal palace at Persepolis; Darius is murdered by his bodyguard; end of the Persian empire.

c. 330 BCE Chinese philosopher MENCIUS (Mengzi) (c.372–289 BCE) expands and develops the ideas of CONFUCIUS.

329 BCE Alexander invades Bactria and Sogdiana (present-day Afghanistan and Turkistan); he founds cities and attempts to establish control over local rulers.

326 BCE Alexander crosses Hindu Kush mountains, invades NW India and defeats King Poros at battle of Hydaspes.

325 BCE Alexander leads his army back to Persia.

323 BCE Alexander dies in Babylon.

321 BCE CHANDRAGUPTA (d.297 BCE) takes over kingdom of MAGADHA in N India; start of MAURYAN EMPIRE.

320 BCE

312 BCE SELEUCUS I (d.281 BCE) establishes control of Asia Minor, Persia and Alexander's E conquests; start of SELEUCID EMPIRE.

303 BCE Seleucus loses control of Indus valley region and present-day s Afghanistan to Mauryan empire.

301 BCE

---

c.400 BCE Start of migration E and s by iron-working Bantu farmers from w Africa.

> "Socrates is guilty of corrupting the minds of the young, and of believing in deities of his own invention instead of the gods recognized by the State."
>
> Socrates, as reported by Plato (*Apology*)

331 BCE Alexander the Great (Alexander of Macedon) invades Egypt, visits the oracle of Ammon at Siwa. and founds the city of Alexandria.

304 BCE PTOLEMY I (d.283 BCE) establishes control over Egypt; start of Ptolemaic period.

---

396 BCE Start of the Corinthian War, in which Sparta fights against Athens and Corinth allied with Persia.

396 BCE ROMANS capture the Etruscan city of Veii.

390 BCE Rome is sacked during a Celtic raid into central Italy.

386 BCE King's Peace ends the Corinthian War; Persia regains control of the GREEK cities in Asia Minor.

371 BCE Thebes allied with Athens defeats Sparta at battle of Leuctra; end of Spartan power; Thebes becomes the dominant city-state in Greece.

359 BCE PHILIP II (382–336 BCE) becomes king of Macedon.

355 BCE Athenian orator DEMOSTHENES (383–322 BCE) denounces the growing power of Philip of Macedon.

343 BCE Rome fights the First SAMNITE War.

340 BCE Athenians declare war on Philip.

338 BCE Victory against Athens at the battle of Chaeronea establishes Philip of Macedon as sole ruler of Greece; end of independent Greek city-states.

336 BCE Philip dies during an attempted invasion of Persia; he is succeeded by his son Alexander III (also known as Alexander the Great or Alexander of Macedon).

327–304 BCE During the Second Samnite War, Roman control expands into central Italy.

323 BCE Start of power struggle between various contending successors (the Diadochi) to Alexander the Great.

THE AMERICAS

*c.***400 BCE** Start of NAZCA culture in coastal S Peru.

*c.***400 BCE** Sack of the OLMEC capital La Venta and collapse of Olmec power; start of Late Formative period in Mesoamerican history.

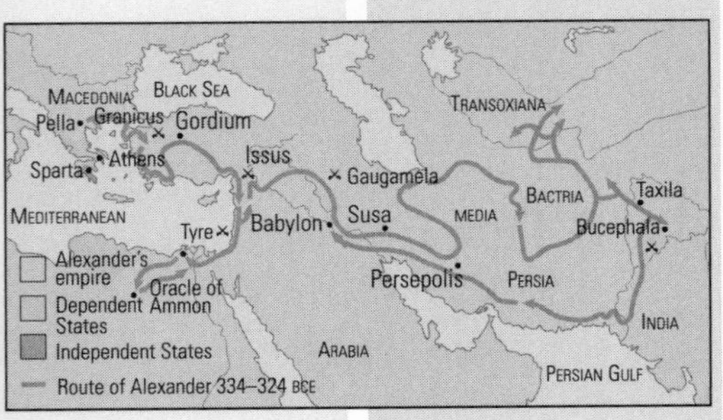

◄ Celtic soldier Warfare was an essential part of Celtic life. Celtic soldiers, such as the one shown here, were armed with highly efficient iron weapons. They swept through central Europe in the fourth and third centuries BCE.

SCIENCE AND TECHNOLOGY

*c.***400 BCE** Horse-collar is invented in China.

*c.***400 BCE** Crossbow is invented in China.

▼ Alexander the Great The map, shown below, illustrates how, between 334 and 332 BCE, Alexander expanded his territory eastward. His journey began in Macedonia and ended with his death in Babylon.

MACEDONIA BLACK SEA
Pella Granicus Gordium
Sparta Athens Issus TRANSOXIANA
MEDITERRANEAN Gaugamela BACTRIA Taxila
Tyre Babylon Susa MEDIA Bucephala
Alexander's empire Oracle of Persepolis PERSIA
Dependent States Ammon INDIA
Independent States ARABIA
— Route of Alexander 334–324 BCE PERSIAN GULF

337 BCE Greek scientist and philosopher ARISTOTLE (384–322 BCE) founds the Lyceum in Athens.

*c.***325 BCE** Indian mathematicians add a symbol for zero to their numerals 1–9 to create a decimal positional number system.

*c.***325–300 BCE** Influenced by Alexandria, many Greek cities are built (or existing ones rebuilt) on a grid pattern.

*c.***310 BCE** First Roman aqueduct, the Aqua Appia, is completed.

ARTS AND HUMANITIES

399 BCE Greek philosopher SOCRATES (b.469 BCE) is condemned to commit suicide by drinking hemlock having been found guilty of corrupting Athenian youth.

400 BCE

395 BCE Greek historian THUCYDIDES (460–400 BCE) publishes his *History of the Peloponnesian War*.

387 BCE Greek philosopher PLATO (427–347 BCE) founds his Academy at Athens.

377 BCE Death of HIPPOCRATES of Cos (b.460 BCE), who is considered to be the father of western medicine.

380 BCE

*c.***350 BCE** Greek theater at Epidaurus is built.

360 BCE

*c.***330 BCE** Start of the Hellenistic period in European and W Asian art.

340 BCE

*c.***320 BCE** Nabataeans construct the first of the monumental rock-cut tombs at Petra.

320 BCE

*c.***315–c.305 BCE** MENANDER (342–292 BCE) writes plays in the New Comedy style in Athens.

307 BCE EPICURUS (341–270 BCE) founds a school of philosophy in Athens.

301 BCE

21

	ASIA AND AUSTRALASIA	AFRICA	EUROPE
300 BCE	**c.300 BCE** Settlers from Korea introduce agriculture into Japan.	**295 BCE** Independent kingdom of Meroë is established in present-day Sudan.	**295 BCE** ROMANS defeat an ETRUSCAN/SAMNITE confederation at the battle of Sentinum.
280 BCE	**c.280 BCE** King Bindusara (r.298–c.270 BCE) extends the MAURYAN EMPIRE into central India.	**274–217 BCE** Four wars are fought between Ptolemaic Egypt and SELEUCID Persia for control of Palestine.	**280 BCE** King PYRRHUS of Epirus (c.319–272 BCE) sends troops to Italy to help the Greek-speaking cities resist Roman expansion.
260 BCE	**c.260 BCE** King Eumenes (r.263–241 BCE) establishes Pergamum in S Asia Minor as an independent kingdom.		**279 BCE** CELTS pillage the sacred Greek shrine at Delphi.
	256 BCE Sickened by the excesses of warfare, King ASHOKA (r.264–238 BCE) declares Buddhism to be the state religion of the Mauryan empire.		**275 BCE** Pyrrhus withdraws his support, and S Italy falls under Roman control.
	256 BCE ZHOU DYNASTY in China is overthrown by QIN DYNASTY.	**256 BCE** Romans invade North Africa and march on Carthage.	**264 BCE** First Punic War (between Rome and Carthage) breaks out over Roman intervention in Sicily.
	c.250 BCE Diodotus, ruler of Bactria, breaks away from the Seleucid empire.	**255 BCE** Spartan-trained Carthaginian troops crush the Roman invaders.	**260 BCE** First Roman naval battle (against the Carthaginians at Mylae) results in victory.
	c.250 BCE Emergence of Theravada (Hinayana) Buddhism in S India.	**c.250 BCE** Dromedaries (one-humped camels) are introduced into Egypt.	**241 BCE** Roman naval victory off the Aegates Islands ends the First Punic War; Rome gains Sicily.
	248 BCE Parthian leader Arsaces I revolts against Seleucid rule in NE Persia; beginnings of the PARTHIAN empire.		**237 BCE** Rome conquers Sardinia and Corsica from the Carthaginians.
			c.235 BCE HAMILAUTOMOBILE BARCA (d.228 BCE) revives Carthaginian power in E Spain.
240 BCE	**238 BCE** King Attalus I of Pergamum defeats the Galatian Celts in Asia Minor.		**225 BCE** Romans defeat the Celts at battle of Telamon in N Italy.
	221 BCE Qin king completes the conquest of other Chinese states and declares himself emperor of China.		**219 BCE** Romans gain control of E coastline of the Adriatic Sea.
220 BCE	**210 BCE** Death of Chinese emperor leads to collapse of central power and civil wars.	**204 BCE** Roman general SCIPIO AFRICANUS MAJOR (236–183 BCE) invades Africa.	**218 BCE** Carthaginians from Spain under HANNIBAL (247–183 BCE) invade Italy by crossing the Alps; start of the Second Punic War.
	c.210 BCE Seleucids make unsuccessful attempt to regain control of Bactria and N India.	**202 BCE** Scipio defeats the Carthaginians at the battle of Zama S of Carthage; end of the Second Punic War.	**217 BCE** Hannibal defeats the Romans at battle of Lake Trasimene.
	c.210 BCE Emergence of Mahayana Buddhism in N India.		**216 BCE** Massive victory over the Romans at the battle of Cannae gives Hannibal control of S Italy.
	c.209 BCE Nomadic HUN tribes (known to the Chinese as Xiongnu) form a confederation to the N and W of China.		**211 BCE** Hannibal makes unsuccessful attempt to capture the city of Rome.
	202 BCE Liu Bang declares himself emperor of China; start of the HAN DYNASTY.		**211–206 BCE** Roman victories bring much of Spain under Roman control.
201 BCE			**202 BCE** Rome gains Spain at the end of the Second Punic War.

THE AMERICAS

c.300 BCE Domestication in present-day E USA of knotweed, maygrass and little barley.

c.300 BCE MAYA build cities in the lowland region of Peten in Guatemala.

▲ **terracotta warrior** The elaborate tomb of Qin Shihuangdi, the founder of the Qin dynasty, was constructed at Xianyang (near present-day Xian), the capital of the dynasty. Many thousands of life-sized warriors and horses were built to guard the emperor.

SCIENCE AND TECHNOLOGY

c.300 BCE Museum and Great Library are founded at Alexandria, Egypt.

c.290 BCE Greek mathematician EUCLID (c.330–260 BCE) publishes his *The Elements*, which codifies the mathematical knowledge that the GREEKS had inherited from the BABYLONIANS and EGYPTIANS.

c.280 BCE King PTOLEMY II (r.284–246 BCE) of Egypt completes a canal between the Mediterranean Sea and the Red Sea and builds a lighthouse at Alexandria.

c.275 BCE Greek astronomer ARISTARCHUS (c.310–230 BCE) of Samos proposes that the Earth orbits the Sun.

c.260 BCE Roman naval architects invent the *corvus* – a weighted gangplank for boarding enemy ships in battle.

c.240 BCE Greek astronomer ERATOSTHENES (c.276–194 BCE) of Cyrene calculates the tilt of the Earth's axis.

238 BCE Ptolemy II orders the length of the year in the Egyptian calendar revised from 365 days to 365.25 days.

c.214 BCE Chinese emperor QIN SHIHUANGDI orders existing scattered fortifications to be joined together to make the Great Wall.

212 BCE Greek mathematician and engineer ARCHIMEDES (b. 287 BCE) is killed during the Roman attack on Syracuse in Sicily.

ARTS AND HUMANITIES

300 BCE ZENO OF CITIUM (c.334–c.262 BCE) founds the Stoic school of philosophy, which meets under a stoa (portico) in Athens.

c.250 BCE Development in present-day Mexico of Mayan hieroglyphs.

241 BCE First play in Latin (translated from a Greek original) is performed in Rome.

c.240 BCE Ashoka builds the Great Stupa at Sanchi, India.

c.220 BCE Roman dramatist PLAUTUS (c.254–184 BCE) completes his first comedy.

c.220 BCE Work starts on the construction of the 7,000-strong terracotta army that is to be buried alongside the Qin emperor of China, Qin Shihuangdi.

204 BCE Poet ENNIUS (239–169 BCE), author of the *Annals*, is brought to Rome by CATO THE ELDER (234–149 BCE).

202 BCE Fabius Pictor publishes the first history of Rome (in Greek).

300 BCE

280 BCE

260 BCE

240 BCE

220 BCE

201 BCE

ASIA AND AUSTRALASIA	AFRICA	EUROPE
200 BCE **190 BCE** Artaxiad I establishes the independent Kingdom of Armenia.		**197 BCE** ROMAN victory at the battle of Cynoscephalae ends the Second Macedonian War (200–197 BCE).
187 BCE Collapse of the MAURYAN EMPIRE in India; in the River Ganges valley region the Sunga dynasty seizes control.		**196 BCE** SELEUCID king ANTIOCHUS III (r.223–187 BCE) occupies NW Greece.
180 BCE **171 BCE** Revolt by Eucratides in Bactria establishes rival Indo-Greek kingdoms in NW India.		**191 BCE** Roman victory at the battle of Thermopylae drives the Seleucids from Europe.
171 BCE PARTHIAN king Mithridates I (r.171–138 BCE) establishes complete independence from the Seleucid empire.		**190 BCE** Roman victory at Magnesia reduces Seleucid power in Asia Minor.
170 BCE Nomadic warriors Xiongnu (HUNS) drive the Yuehchi confederation from the steppe N of China.		**190–180 BCE** Roman troops force the CELTS out of N Italy.
167 BCE Led by Judas MACCABAEUS (d.161 BCE), the Jews revolt against Seleucid rule.	**168 BCE** Seleucid king ANTIOCHUS IV (r.175–164 BCE) invades Egypt, but retreats after being intimidated by a Roman envoy.	**168 BCE** Roman victory at the battle of Pydna ends the Third Macedonian War (171–168 BCE).
160 BCE **160 BCE** Wu Ti (d.86 BCE) becomes emperor of China and begins a series of campaigns against the Huns.	**150 BCE** A Carthaginian army is wiped out in battle against the forces of King MASINISSA (238–149 BCE) of neighboring Numidia.	**151 BCE** While suppressing a revolt in Spain, the Romans massacre 20,000 men in the city of Cauca.
c.150 BCE Nomadic Sakas (related to the SCYTHIANS) begin settling in parts of present-day Afghanistan.	**149 BCE** Romans lay siege to Carthage; start of the Third Punic War.	**148 BCE** Macedonia becomes a Roman province.
141 BCE Parthians capture the Seleucid capital; end of Seleucid control of Persia and Mesopotamia.	**146 BCE** Carthage falls to the Romans; the city is razed to the ground; end of the Third Punic war.	**146 BCE** Cities in Greece rise against Roman rule; after they are defeated, the city of Corinth is sacked and razed to the ground as punishment.
140 BCE **136 BCE** Confucianism is adopted as the state ideology in China, largely as a result of the work of the philosopher and scholar Dong Zongshu (179–104 BCE).		**133 BCE** Tiberius GRACCHUS (c.163–133 BCE) attempts land reforms in Rome.
133 BCE Kingdom of Pergamum is bequeathed to the Romans by its last king, ATTALUS III (r.138–133 BCE).		**122 BCE** Gaius GRACCHUS (c.153–121 BCE, brother of Tiberius) makes further attempts at land reform.
120 BCE **115 BCE** Chinese envoy Zhang Qian travels to Parthia to trade silk for horses.	**112 BCE** War breaks out between Rome and Numidia.	**121 BCE** Southern Gaul (France) is incorporated into the Roman Empire.
111 BCE Chinese emperor establishes control over SW China and Annam (present-day N Vietnam).	**106 BCE** Roman troops commanded by General Gaius Marius defeat the Numidians led by King JUGURTHA (156–104 BCE).	**102–101 BCE** General Gaius MARIUS (157–86 BCE) defeats the Cimbri and Teutones – Germanic tribes that had invaded S Gaul.
102 BCE China achieves temporary control of the oases of the Tarim Basin in central Asia.		
101 BCE		

THE AMERICAS

*c.*200 BCE Start of HOPEWELL CULTURE in the Ohio valley region of present-day USA; it is also known as Middle Woodland culture.

*c.*200 BCE Emergence of the ZAPOTEC state in present-day Mexico.

*c.*200 BCE Decline of the ritual center at Chavín de Huántar.

▶ *Tiberius Gracchus, a Roman tribune, attempted to redistribute land in order to benefit the poor. He is shown here in a painting by the Italian artist Luca Signorelli (1441–1523).*

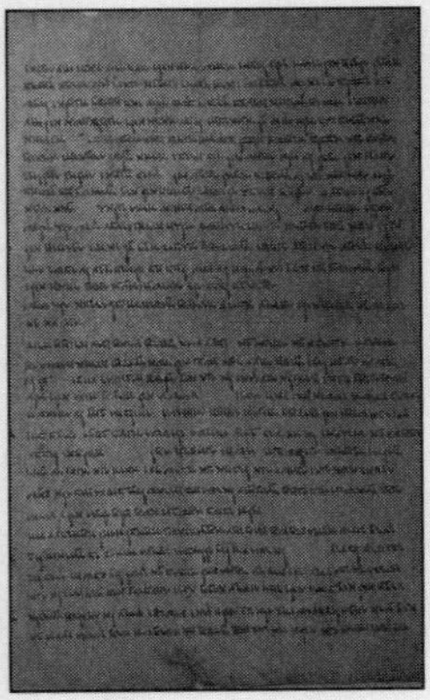

SCIENCE AND TECHNOLOGY

193 BCE Newly invented concrete is used to build the Porticus Aemilia in Rome.

*c.*130 BCE Greek astronomer HIPPARCHUS (d.127 BCE) discovers the precession of the equinoxes.

119 BCE Iron-making and salt production become state monopolies in China.

◀ *Dead Sea Scrolls Written in Hebrew or Aramaic, the Dead Sea Scrolls include versions of much of the Old Testament, some of which are a thousand years older than any other biblical manuscript. Shown here is a detail of the Isaiah Manuscript, c.100 BCE.*

ARTS AND HUMANITIES

*c.*200 BCE Greek influence produces the Gandaharan art style in NW India.

*c.*200 BCE Earliest of the Dead Sea Scrolls is written.

196 BCE Tri-lingual Rosetta Stone is inscribed in Egypt to record the gratitude of the priests of Memphis to King Ptolemy V.

*c.*190 BCE *Victory of Samothrace* statue is carved in Greece.

*c.*165 BCE Plays of TERENCE (190–159 BCE) become popular in Rome.

124 BCE Confucian university is established in China to prepare students for work in the civil service.

*c.*120 BCE *Venus de Milo* statue is carved in Greece.

200 BCE

180 BCE

160 BCE

140 BCE

120 BCE

101 BCE

ASIA AND AUSTRALASIA

100 BCE **92 BCE** First official contact between the PARTHIAN and Roman Empires takes place in Mesopotamia.

91 BCE HUNS inflict a crushing defeat on a Chinese army in central Asia.

90 BCE Sakas under Maues capture Taxila in present-day Pakistan and occupy parts of the Indus valley.

89 BCE King MITHRIDATES VI (r.120–63 BCE) of Pontus in Asia Minor forms an anti-Roman coalition.

80 BCE **73 BCE** Fall of Sunga dynasty in India. Kanva dynasty takes control of MAGADHA, the last remnant of the MAURYAN EMPIRE.

66–63 BCE Roman general POMPEY (106–48 BCE) conquers the remnants of the SELEUCID EMPIRE in Asia Minor and Syria.

60 BCE **58 BCE** Azes I becomes Saka ruler in N India; start of the Vikram era.

57 BCE Kingdom of Silla is established in S Korea during a period of decreased Chinese influence.

c.50 BCE Romans begin trade with India for spices and Chinese silk.

c.50 BCE Kushans under Kujula Kadphises emerge as the leaders of the Yueh-chi confederation and begin the takeover of Saka India; start of the KUSHAN EMPIRE.

43 BCE Huns make peace with the Chinese empire.

37 BCE HEROD THE GREAT is made King of Judaea by the Romans.

40 BCE **c.10 BCE** Last of the Indo-Greek kingdoms is overthrown by the **20 BCE** Sakas.

c.10 BCE Satavahana dynasty replaces the Kanvas in India's Magadha kingdom.

c.4 BCE Birth of JESUS CHRIST in Bethlehem.

1 BCE

AFRICA

c.100 BCE AKSUMITE state is established in present-day Ethiopia and Eritrea.

c.100 BCE Camels are introduced into the Sahara desert.

46 BCE Romans found a new city of Carthage on the site of the PHOENICIAN city.

> "I sing of arms and of the hero who first came from the shore of Troy, exiled by Fate, to Italy and its Lavinian shore."
>
> Virgil (*Aeneid*)

30 BCE Following the suicides of Antony and Cleopatra, Egypt becomes a province under Roman control.

c.25 BCE KUSHITES from Meroë invade S Egypt; a Roman reprisal raid sacks Napata.

EUROPE

88 BCE Mithridates VI of Pontus invades N Greece and liberates Athens from ROMAN control.

87 BCE Gaius MARIUS (157–86 BCE) declares himself dictator in Rome; he dies the following year.

85 BCE Roman general Lucius Cornelius SULLA (138–78 BCE) makes peace with Mithridates.

82 BCE Sulla declares himself dictator.

79 BCE Sulla retires from Roman politics.

73–71 BCE Slave uprising in Italy led by SPARTACUS (d.71 BCE).

60 BCE Establishment of First Triumvirate – POMPEY (106–48 BCE), Julius CAESAR (100–44 BCE) and CRASSUS (115–53 BCE) – to rule Rome.

58–52 BCE Roman legions under Julius Caesar conquer Gaul (present-day France).

55 BCE Romans invade Britain, but leave the following year.

53 BCE Crassus killed at battle of Carrhae against the Parthians.

49–47 BCE Civil war between Pompey and Caesar results in Pompey's death; Caesar becomes dictator of Rome.

44 BCE Caesar is assasinated in Rome.

43 BCE Second Triumvirate – Mark ANTONY (82–30 BCE), LEPIDUS (d. c.13 BCE) and Octavian (63 BCE–14 CE) – established to rule Rome and avenge Caesar's death.

42 BCE Caesar's assassins are defeated at battle of Philippi in Greece.

31 BCE ANTONY and CLEOPATRA are defeated by Octavian at the sea-battle of Actium; Octavian becomes sole ruler of Rome.

27 BCE Octavian takes the name AUGUSTUS. This date marks the end of the Roman republic and the beginning of the Principiate (ROMAN EMPIRE).

86 BCE Crop rotation is introduced in China.

100 BCE

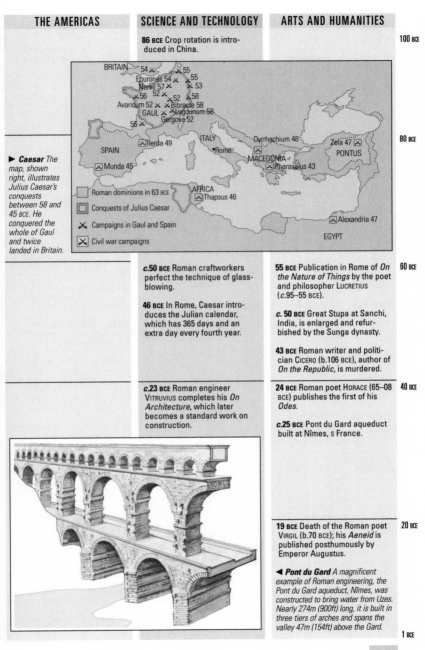

BRITAIN 54 × × 55
Eburones 54 × × 55
Nervii 57 × × 53
× 56 × 52 × 58
Avaricum 52 × × Bibracte 58
GAUL × × Lugdunum 58
Gergova 52
56 ×

ITALY
SPAIN •Rome
⊠ Ilerda 49

Dyrrhachium 48 ⊠
MACEDONIA
⊠ Pharsalus 43

Zela 47 ⊠
PONTUS

80 BCE

⊠ Munda 45

AFRICA
⊠ Thapsus 46

☐ Roman dominions in 63 BCE
☐ Conquests of Julius Caesar
✕ Campaigns in Gaul and Spain
⊠ Civil war campaigns

⊠ Alexandria 47

EGYPT

► **Caesar** The map, shown right, illustrates Julius Caesar's conquests between 58 and 45 BCE. He conquered the whole of Gaul and twice landed in Britain.

c.50 BCE Roman craftworkers perfect the technique of glass-blowing.

46 BCE In Rome, Caesar introduces the Julian calendar, which has 365 days and an extra day every fourth year.

55 BCE Publication in Rome of *On the Nature of Things* by the poet and philosopher LUCRETIUS (*c.*95–55 BCE).

60 BCE

c. 50 BCE Great Stupa at Sanchi, India, is enlarged and refurbished by the Sunga dynasty.

43 BCE Roman writer and politician CICERO (b.106 BCE), author of *On the Republic,* is murdered.

c.23 BCE Roman engineer VITRUVIUS completes his *On Architecture*, which later becomes a standard work on construction.

24 BCE Roman poet HORACE (65–08 BCE) publishes the first of his *Odes*.

40 BCE

c.25 BCE Pont du Gard aqueduct built at Nîmes, s France.

19 BCE Death of the Roman poet VIRGIL (b.70 BCE); his *Aeneid* is published posthumously by Emperor Augustus.

20 BCE

◄ **Pont du Gard** A magnificent example of Roman engineering, the Pont du Gard aqueduct, Nîmes, was constructed to bring water from Uzes. Nearly 274m (900ft) long, it is built in three tiers of arches and spans the valley 47m (154ft) above the Gard.

1 BCE

ASIA AND AUSTRALASIA	AFRICA	EUROPE

CE 1

CE 8 Regent WANG MANG (33 BCE–CE 23) appoints himself emperor of China and begins radical reforms; end of the Former HAN DYNASTY.

CE c.15 Death of King Natakamani of Meroë (ruled from c.15 BCE), who built the Lion Temple at Naqa.

CE 9 Germanic tribes led by Arminius (d.19) ambush and destroy three ROMAN legions in the Tutoberg Forest, present-day NW Germany.

14 Roman emperor AUGUSTUS dies. His will names his son-in-law TIBERIUS (42 BCE–CE 37) as the next emperor; this establishes the principle of succession for Roman emperors.

20

23 Rebels kill Wang Mang; a Han emperor is restored in China; start of Later Han dynasty.

30 JESUS CHRIST (b.c.4 BCE) is crucified outside Jerusalem, under the orders of PONTIUS PILATE.

37–41 Short reign of Roman emperor Gaius (better known as CALIGULA, b.12) is marked by extravagance and decadence.

41 CLAUDIUS (10–54) becomes Roman emperor.

43 Romans occupy S Britain.

59 Emperor NERO (r.54–68) murders his mother AGRIPPINA (b.15).

40

53 Tiridates I (d.75) becomes king of Armenia and founds the Arsacid dynasty.

53–63 Roman general Corbulo (d.67) campaigns unsuccessfully against the PARTHIANS over control of Armenia.

40 Roman emperor Gaius (Caligula) annexes Mauretania (present day Algeria and Morocco).

60 BOADICEA (Boudicca, d.62), queen of the Iceni, leads a short-lived revolt against the Romans in Britain.

64 Great Fire of Rome is blamed on Christians and leads to their first persecution.

68–69 Death of Nero leads to civil war in the Roman Empire. There are four self-proclaimed emperors; VESPASIAN (9–79) emerges as the victor and founds the Flavian dynasty.

60

70 Roman legions under General TITUS (39–81) sack Jerusalem and destroy the temple while crushing a Jewish revolt.

78 Accession of King Kaniska (d.103) marks the highpoint of the KUSHAN EMPIRE in N India and S central Asia.

79 Eruption of Mount Vesuvius in S Italy buries the towns of Pompeii and Herculaneum.

79 Titus succeeds his father Vespasian as Roman emperor.

81 DOMITIAN (51–96) succeeds his brother Titus as emperor.

80

90 Chinese troops under General Ban Chao curtail Kushan expansion in central Asia.

c.95 Nahapana, the Kushan-appointed Saka satrap (governor) of W India forms an independent state.

97 Chinese military expedition attempts to establish control over the Silk Road to the Middle East; an advance party reaches the Black Sea.

82–86 Eastern border of the Roman Empire is established along the rivers Rhine and Danube.

83 Roman control in Britain is extended to S Scotland.

96 Domitian is assassinated and NERVA (30–98) is appointed.

98 TRAJAN (53–117) becomes emperor when Nerva dies.

99

▲ **Boadicea**, the queen of the Iceni, led a revolt against the Romans when they brutally seized her territory. Her army is thought to have killed 70,000 Roman soldiers before her capture and suicide.

THE AMERICAS

CE *c*.1 Basketmaker culture emerges in present-day SW USA; villages of circular houses are built.

***c*.25** Mochica (Moche) state is established in river valleys along the N coast of Peru.

***c*.50** City of Teotihuacán establishes control of the valley of Mexico; work starts on the construction of the Pyramid of the Sun.

SCIENCE AND TECHNOLOGY

CE *c*.10 Greek geographer STRABO (*c*.63 BCE–CE *c*.24) produces a reasonably accurate map of the Roman world.

***c*.39** A wooden ship 71m (233ft) long and 24m (80ft) wide is built on Lake Nemi near Rome for the entertainment of the emperor Gaius (Caligula).

► ***Teotihuacán*** *This city was the center of a considerable empire and, at its greatest, housed* c.*100,000 people. It was built on a cruciform shape, with the Pyramid of the Moon, shown here, in the* N, *and the great Pyramid of the Sun in the* E.

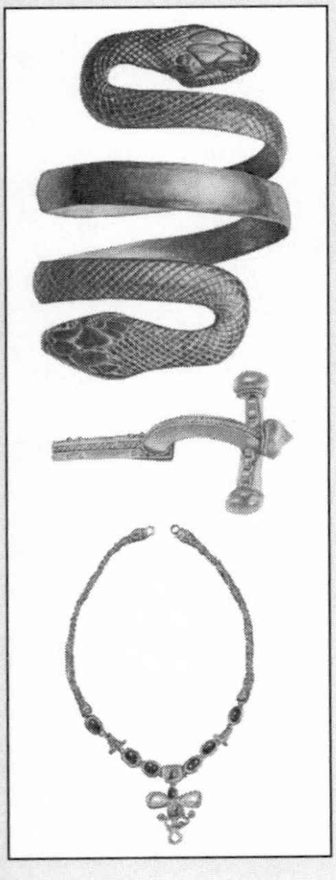

***c*.50** Rome is the world's largest city, with a population of about one million.

***c*.60** Greek engineer HERO OF ALEXANDRIA (b. *c*.20) experiments with hydraulic machinery and invents a simple steam engine.

***c*.67** Emperor Nero completes the construction of his palace in Rome – the Golden House – on the ruins of the Great Fire.

79 Roman encyclopedist PLINY THE ELDER (b.23), author of *The Natural History,* dies in the eruption of Mount Vesuvius.

80 Construction of the Colosseum begins in Rome.

◄ ***Roman jewelry*** *During the Roman Empire jewelry-making flourished. Early on, the snake motif was popular, along with other styles borrowed from Greek and Etruscan culture. Soon, however, Roman jewelry began to make greater use of gemstones and intricate, pierced decoration.*

ARTS AND HUMANITIES

CE *c*.3 Roman poet OVID (43 BCE–CE 18) publishes his *Metamorphoses*. CE 1

17 Death of the Roman historian LIVY (b.59 BCE), author of a 142-volume history of Rome entitled *From the Beginning of the City*.

20

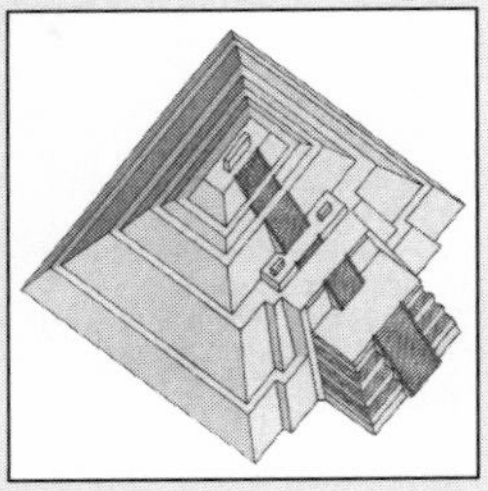

***c*.50** Under KUSHAN patronage, the Mathura art style develops in N India. 40

65 SENECA (b.4), the orator, philosopher and tutor of Nero, commits suicide in Rome after being condemned for undue political influence. 60

66–70 Dead Sea Scrolls are concealed in a cave during the Jewish revolt.

80

99

ASIA AND AUSTRALASIA	AFRICA	EUROPE

100 *c.*100 Buddhism spreads to China via central Asia.

106 Romans annexe the Nabataean kingdom – the Roman province of Arabia is created.

114–16 Roman emperor Trajan invades Parthia and occupies Armenia and Mesopotamia – the Roman Empire reaches its greatest extent.

117 Hadrian abandons Armenia and Mesopotamia.

120 *c.*130 Saka state in W India establishes control over the city of Ujain in central India.

132–35 Second Jewish revolt against the Romans.

138 Independent kingdoms of Palmyra in Syria and Elymais in SW Persia attempt a trade alliance to circumvent the PARTHIAN empire.

140 *c.*150 HUNS drive the Chinese out of Central Asia.

▲ *Ptolemy* was highly influential as an astronomer and as a geographer. His description of a geocentric universe, known as the Ptolemaic system, remained the accepted view for 1300 years.

*c.*150 Kingdom of Meroë goes into decline because of trade competition from AKSUM.

101 Emperor TRAJAN (53–117) invades Dacia.

106 Trajan defeats the Dacian king Decebalus; Dacia becomes part of the ROMAN EMPIRE.

117 Trajan dies and is succeeded as Roman emperor by HADRIAN (76–138).

121 Hadrian's Wall is built across Britain as the N border of the Roman Empire.

138 Hadrian is succeeded as emperor by ANTONINUS PIUS (86–161), whose reign is regarded as the Golden age of the Roman Empire.

160 **166** Roman merchants visit China for the first time.

162 Lucius Septimius SEVERUS (146–211) leads a Roman campaign against the Parthians.

168 Romans capture from the Parthians the trade center of Dura Europos near the end of the Silk Road in Mesopotamia.

161 MARCUS AURELIUS (121–80) succeeds Antoninus Pius as Roman emperor.

161 Outbreak of plague devastates the city of Rome.

168 Germanic tribes invade the Roman Empire across the River Danube.

175 Germanic tribes are defeated and expelled from the empire.

180 **184** Yellow Turbans rebellion breaks out in China.

190 Chinese HAN emperor is murdered and civil wars ensue.

197–99 Severus invades Parthia and temporarily adds Mesopotamia to the Roman Empire.

180 COMMODUS (161–92) becomes emperor on the death of his father Marcus Aurelius.

192 Assassination of Commodus precipitates civil wars between rival emperors for control of the empire.

197 Severus emerges as sole emperor and founds the Severan dynasty.

199

c.100 Adena culture in the Ohio valley becomes absorbed into the geographically more extensive HOPEWELL CULTURE.

c.100 Single-wheeled cart or wheelbarrow is invented in China.

c.100 Knowledge of the monsoon wind systems of the Indian Ocean becomes widespread, leading to an increase in trade between India and the Arabian Gulf.

105 Invention of paper is announced to the Chinese court.

c.110 Greek mathematician Menelaus writes *Sphaerica*, a treatise on trigonometry.

c.118 Pantheon is built in Rome with a 43-m (140-ft) concrete dome.

c.105 Roman historian SUETONIUS (c.69–140) writes his *The Lives of the Caesars*.

c.110 Roman historian TACITUS (55–120) writes his *Annals* and *Histories*.

110 Roman writer JUVENAL (55–140) publishes the first of his *Satires*.

112 Trajan's Column is erected in Rome.

114 Death of the historian Ban Zhou (b.45), the leading woman intellectual in China.

100

120 Death of the Greek writer PLUTARCH (b.46), author of *The Parallel Lives*.

120

c.150 End of the Formative period in Mesoamerican history; start of the Classic period.

c.150 Roman doctor GALEN (129–99) uses dissection and experimentation to establish the function of bodily organs.

c.150 Earliest-known inscription in Sanskrit is carved in w India.

140

c. 160 Greek astronomer PTOLEMY (90–168) publishes his *The Mathematical Collection* (later known as *The Almagest*).

c.165 Roman novelist APULEIUS (c.125–c.170) writes the *The Golden Ass*.

172–80 Emperor Marcus Aurelius composes his *Meditations*.

160

180

◄ **Pantheon** *One of the most influential buildings in the history of architecture, the Pantheon was the largest domed structure until modern times. The dome, a perfect hemisphere, is remarkable not only for its size but also for its apparent lightness, an illusion skillfully created by the use of coffering, once stuccoed and gilded, and a single central light source.*

199

ASIA AND AUSTRALASIA	AFRICA	EUROPE
	*c.*200 Bantu peoples reach the E coast of Africa.	211 Lucius Septimius SEVERUS dies and his sons, Caracalla and Geta, succeed as joint emperors. Caracalla has Geta murdered.
220 Civil wars bring the HAN DYNASTY in China to an end; start of the Three Kingdoms (Wei, Wu and Shu) period.		212 CARACALLA (118–217) extends ROMAN citizenship to all free subjects of the empire.
224 King ARDASHIR of Persis, S Persia, takes over the PARTHIAN empire; start of the SASSANIAN empire.		218–22 Emperor Elagabalus (204–22) introduces sun-worship to Rome, which leads to his assassination.
*c.*235 Sassanians defeat the Kushans near the River Oxus, central Asia.		
*c.*240 KUSHAN EMPIRE in India breaks up, with local rulers coming to power.		235 Death of emperor SEVERUS ALEXANDER (b.208) marks the end of the Severan dynasty. During the next fifty years there are 36 Roman emperors.
244 Sassanians under Shapur I (r.244–72)conquer Armenia.		
238 Sassanians conquer Mesopotamia from the Romans.		
*c.*250 Chief of the Yamato clan establishes control over central Japan.	249 Bishop Cyprian of Carthage (d.258) leads the Christians during the persecution initiated by the Roman emperor DECIUS (200–51).	248 Emperor Philip I (r.244–49) holds games to celebrate Rome's 1000th anniversary.
253 Sassanians sack the Roman city of Antioch, present-day Syria.		
260 Roman emperor VALERIAN (r.253–60) is captured while campaigning against the Sassanians under Shapur I.		260 Roman emperor GALLIENUS (r.253–68) defeats the invading Germanic tribe, the ALEMANNI, near present-day Milan, N Italy.
260 King Odaenath (d.267) of Palmyra declares his independence from Rome.		260–74 Gallic empire (parts of present-day France and Germany) under Postumus and his successors breaks away from Rome.
267 Zenobia makes herself queen of Palmyra and establishes control over Egypt and much of Asia Minor.		*c.*260 GOTHS migrate from Scandinavia to the shores of the Black Sea.
271 Zenobia declares her son to be Roman emperor.		267 Five hundred-ship fleet of Goths and other Germanic tribes raids the coast of Greece and sacks the city of Athens.
273 Roman legions under AURELIAN (*c.*215–75) crush the Palmyrans; Zenobia is taken to Rome in chains.		274 Emperor Aurelian re-establishes Roman control over the Gallic empire.
280 China is reunified under the Western Jin dynasty.	*c.*285 King Aphilas of AKSUM invades SW Arabia.	284 Roman general DIOCLETIAN (245–313) makes himself emperor.
297 Roman legions under GALERIUS (d.311) defeat the Sassanians. A peace treaty gives the Sassanians a monopoly over the silk trade with Rome.		293 Diocletian introduces the Tetrarchy, under which the Roman Empire is ruler by two joint emperors (*Augustii*) each assisted by a deputy (*Caesar*).

200
220
240
260
280
299

THE AMERICAS	SCIENCE AND TECHNOLOGY	ARTS AND HUMANITIES	

THE AMERICAS

c.200 Warfare breaks out between rival MAYAN city-states in the Yucatán region of Mexico.

c.200 City of Teotihuacán establishes an empire than controls most of highland Mexico.

SCIENCE AND TECHNOLOGY

c.216 Baths of Caracalla in Rome are completed.

Diocletian *This gold coin (aureus) depicts the head of Emperor Diocletian. The restoration of order to the Roman Empire under Diocletian and Constantine prompted the standardization of Roman coinage. Representations of rulers became stylized with religious overtones – a typical aspect of late Roman art, which foreshadowed that of Byzantium.*

c.250 DIOPHANTUS of Alexandria establishes algebra as a branch of mathematics and introduces the use of symbols in equations.

c.260 Sassanian royal palace Taq-i-Kisra, containing a 22-m (75-ft) wide arch, is built at Ctesiphon near present-day Baghdad, Iraq.

c.265 Rock-cut reliefs at Bishapur, Persia, celebrate the Sassanian's humiliation of the Roman emperor Valerian.

▶ ***Caracalla*** *succeeded his father, Lucius Septimius Severus, in 211, and, in order to be sole ruler, he had his brother Geta murdered. He also ordered the deaths of many of Geta's friends, fueling his reputation as a bloodthirsty tyrant.*

ARTS AND HUMANITIES

c.244 Philosopher PLOTINUS (205–70) opens a school in Rome where he teaches the ideas of Neoplatonism.

c.250 Prophet MANI (216–76) preaches his new philosophy of Manichaeism in Persia.

200

220

240

260

280

299

ASIA AND AUSTRALASIA	AFRICA	EUROPE

300

311 HUNS and other nomad peoples sack the Chinese city of Luoyang.

316 Western Jin emperor is captured by the Huns who occupy N China.

*c.*305 ANTHONY the Hermit (*c.*250–*c.*355) establishes the tradition of Christian monasticism in Egypt.

305 DIOCLETIAN's retirement begins a 20-year period of rivalry for control of the ROMAN EMPIRE.

312 CONSTANTINE I (285–337) converts to Christianity and becomes Roman emperor in the W after the battle of the Milvian Bridge near Rome.

320

320 Accession of King CHANDRAGUPTA I at Palipatura (present-day Patna) in India marks the beginning of the GUPTA DYNASTY.

325 Council of Nicaea (in present-day NW Turkey) establishes the basis of Christian belief and denounces the heresy of ARIUS (*c.*250–336).

313 Edict of Mediolanum (present-day Milan) declares that Christianity is to be tolerated throughout the Roman Empire.

324 Constantine defeats LICINIUS (*c.*270–325) and becomes sole Roman emperor.

330 Constantine founds Constantinople, on the site of the Greek city of Byzantium, as the E capital of the Roman Empire.

340

343 King Ezana of AKSUM is converted to Christianity by missionaries from Egypt.

*c.*350 King Ezana conquers the kingdom of Meroë and sacks the capital city.

*c.*330 Christianity is proclaimed as the only official religion of the Roman Empire.

337 After the death of Constantine, the empire is divided between his sons Constans (emperor in the W) and Constantius II (emperor in the E).

350 CONSTANS (b.*c.*323) is killed in battle against the usurper Magnentius in Gaul (present-day France).

360

*c.*360 King Samudragupta (r.335–76) conquers N and NE India and expands the Gupta empire.

363 Roman emperor Julian is killed in battle against the SASSANIANS.

369 Japanese empress Jing orders the invasion of Korea.

374 Huns attack the Alans (nomads living on the W bank of the River Volga), who are driven W and in turn attack and defeat the VISIGOTHS.

353 CONSTANTIUS II (317–61) re-establishes sole control of the Roman Empire.

361 JULIAN (331–63) becomes Roman emperor and briefly reintroduces pagan worship.

364 VALENTINIAN I (321–75) and VALENS (328–78) become Roman emperors in W and E respectively.

378 Visigoths invade SE Europe and defeat the Romans, led by the emperor Valens, at the battle of Adrianople.

380

383 Chinese victory at the battle of River Fei repulses a Hun invasion of S China.

*c.*395 King CHANDRAGUPTA II (r. *c.*380–414).conquers W India; the Gupta empire reaches its greatest extent.

392 THEODOSIUS (347–95) becomes sole Roman emperor.

395 On the death of Theodosius the Roman Empire is formally split into W and E parts ruled respectively by his sons Honorius and ARCADIUS (*c.*377–408).

399

THE AMERICAS	SCIENCE AND TECHNOLOGY	ARTS AND HUMANITIES	
c. **300** City of Teotihuacán establishes control over the highland MAYAN cities in present-day Gautemala. *c.***300** Lowland Mayan city-state of Tikal conquers neighboring El Mirador.			300
	321 Constantine I introduces the seven-day week into the calendar used throughout the Roman Empire.		320
*c.***350** City of Teotihuacán extends its influence over the lowland Mayan cities in the Yucatán region of Mexico.	*c.***340** Greek mathematician PAPPUS OF ALEXANDRIA explores the geometry of curved surfaces.	**341** Ulfilas devises the Gothic alphabet for his translation of the Bible into Gothic.	340
	*c.***375** Stirrups are invented in w China, from where they spread to Europe with the AVARS.	**365** Birth of the Chinese writer and landscape poet TAO CH'IEN (d.427), author of the short story *Peach Tree Spring*. **375** Wall painting in caves at Ajanta, India, mark the flowering of Gupta-period art.	360
		*c.***380** AMBROSE (339–97), bishop of Milan, introduces plainsong into Christian services. *c.***385** JEROME (347–420) starts translating the Bible from Greek into Latin (the Vulgate Bible). *c.***397** Christian philosopher AUGUSTINE of Hippo (354–430) writes his *Confessions*.	380
			399

Constantine I This gold coin (aureus) depicts the head of Constantine I. Born and educated a pagan, Constantine had nevertheless appealed to the God of the Christians before the battle of Milvian Bridge (312) for help against the pagan forces of his rival Maxentius. Constantine regarded his victory as the answer to his appeal and converted to Christianity.

ASIA AND AUSTRALASIA	AFRICA	EUROPE
400	**c.400** Seafaring peoples from Indonesia begin settling on the island of Madagascar off the E coast of Africa.	**407** Burgundians establish a kingdom in present-day central and SE France. **409** VANDALS and SUEVI move into Spain. **410** GOTHS under ALARIC (370–410) sack Rome. **418** VISIGOTHS establish a kingdom in S France.
420 **420** Fall of the Eastern Jin dynasty in central China; it is replaced by the Former Song dynasty.	**429** Vandals under Gaeseric cross from Spain to N Africa. **439** Vandals capture the city of Carthage and establish a kingdom.	**c.420** ANGLES, SAXONS and JUTES begin settling in Britain. **c.430** FRANKS begin settling in N France. **c.430** Visigoths take over most of Spain. **434** ATTILA (406–53) is declared leader of the HUNS.
440 **c.450** Ruan-ruan nomads replace the Huns as the dominant force on the steppes of central Asia. **c.450** Steppe nomads the Hepthalites (White Huns) invade N India and occupy the Punjab; they are fought to a standstill by GUPTA king Skandagupta.	**451** Council of Chalcedon results in the Coptic Christians in Egypt splitting away from the influence of Rome and Constantinople.	**441–48** Huns plunder the Balkans until bribed by E Roman emperor to turn W. **451** Huns under Attila are defeated at the battle of Chalons in France. **452** Huns plunder N Italy. **453** Death of Attila. **455** Vandals sack Rome. **458** Sicily is captured by the Vandals.
460 **479** Former Song dynasty in China is replaced by the Southern Ch'i dynasty.	**468** Combined forces of the E and W Roman Empire make disastrous attempt to invade Vandal kingdom.	**476** Overthrow of Emperor Romulus AUGUSTULUS (r.475–76) by ODOACER (433–93) marks end of W Roman Empire.
480 **484** Hepthalites attack the SASSANIAN EMPIRE, kill King Peroz and occupy parts of E Persia. **c.495** Hepthalites invade central India and conquer some Gupta territory. **495** Northern Wei dynasty in N China moves its capital from Tatung to Luoyang. **499**	"For in all adversity of fortune the worst sort of misery is to have been happy." Boethius (*Consolation of Philosophy*)	**481** CLOVIS I (465–511) establishes a Frankish kingdom in France; start of MEROVINGIAN DYNASTY. **491–99** Fiscal and administrative reforms of the emperor ANASTASIUS I (d.518) revive the E Roman Empire. **493** THEODORIC (454–526) assassinates Odoacer and establishes an OSTROGOTH kingdom in Italy. **498** Clovis I is converted to Christianity.

THE AMERICAS

401–50 HOPEWELL CULTURE declines and collapses.

*c.***425** Teotihuacán completes its subjugation of the lowland MAYAN cities of Tikal, Uaxactun and Becan

SCIENCE AND TECHNOLOGY

*c.***400** Supposedly rustproof pillar of pure iron is erected in Delhi, India.

415 Philosopher and mathematician HYPATIA (b.370) is killed in Alexandria by a Christian mob, who equate her learning with paganism.

ARTS AND HUMANITIES

*c.***405** Indian poet and dramatist KALIDASA writes *Sakuntala Recognized* at the Gupta court.

413 Traveler monk Faxian returns to China with large numbers of Buddhist texts.

*c.***425** Galla PLACIDIA (388–450) adorns her mausoleum in Ravenna, Italy, with mosaics.

438 Law code of THEODOSIUS II (r.408–50) published throughout the ROMAN EMPIRE; the code is later adopted by many Germanic rulers.

Frankish soldier
At the time of their invasion of Gaul in the 5th century, all freemen within the Frankish tribe were warriors. Their most formidable weapon was the battleax (the francisca), as shown in this illustration. Because metal was scarce, the round shield was made of wood covered with stretched hide.

Saxon soldier
During the 5th century, Angles, Saxons and Jutes began settling in England. Saxons, such as the soldier shown here, came to England as a result of Frankish expansion in Europe, which had put pressure on their homelands. The word Saxon survives in the names Sussex (South Saxon) and Essex (East Saxon).

*c.***485** Chinese mathematician Tsu Ch'ung Chi calculates the value of *pi* to an accuracy that is not bettered for a thousand years.

*c.***499** Indian mathematician Aryabhata (476–550) publishes his *Aryabhatiya*, a compendium of scientific knowledge.

480 Birth of the Italian scholar BOETHIUS (d.524), who translates the works of Aristotle into Latin.

400

420

440

460

480

499

ASIA AND AUSTRALASIA	AFRICA	EUROPE
500 *c.***500** Polynesians settle on Easter Island.	*c.***500** Bantu farmers reach Orange River in present-day South Africa.	**502** FRANKS defeat the ALEMANNI and conquer present-day S Germany. **511** OSTROGOTHS under THEODORIC (454–526) annexe Spain.
520 **527** Accession of JUSTINIAN (482–565) marks the end of the ROMAN EMPIRE in the E, and the start of the BYZANTINE EMPIRE. **535** Hepthalites invade the remaining GUPTA territories in India; end of the Gupta dynasty.	**533** Byzantine armies under General BELISARIUS (505–65) recapture N Africa from the VANDALS. **536** Byzantine authorities close the temple at Philae in Egypt; this marks the end of traditional Egyptian religion.	**527** Justinian becomes Roman emperor in Constantinople; start of the Byzantine empire. **532** Nika riots in Constantinople cause extensive damage to buildings. **534** Franks under Theudebert I conquer the Burgundian kingdom.
540 **540** SASSANIANS under King KHOSHRU I (r.531–79) sack the city of Antioch on the Mediterranean coast in Syria. *c.***550** Buddhism spreads to Japan. **552** Nomadic Turks under Bumin (r.546–53) win a decisive victory over the Ruan-ruan, and establish control across central Asia.	*c.***543** Ruling warlords of the Ethiopian highlands are converted to Christianity through the efforts of Bishop Frumentius. *c.***550** Kingdom of Ghana is established in W Africa.	**541** Europe's first encounter with smallpox devastates the Mediterranean region. *c.***540–50** Slav peoples migrate into the Balkans and Greece. **548** Frankish kingdom disintegrates on the death of Theudebert I. **552** Byzantine armies conquer S Spain from the Ostrogoths.
560 **561** Silkworms are smuggled to the Byzantine court from China. **562** Sassanians and Turks in alliance crush the Hepthalites, who cease to be an effective force. *c.***575** Sassanians expel the Aksumites and occupy present-day Yemen.	**570** AKSUMITE armies make an unsuccessful attempt to conquer the city of Mecca in W Arabia.	**557** AVAR nomads invade and settle in Hungary. **558** CLOTAIRE I (497–561) reunites the Frankish kingdom. **568** LOMBARDS invade N Italy and establish a kingdom in the Po valley.
580 **580** Marib dam in Yemen collapses, causing economic decline. **581** Sui Yang Jian (d.604) becomes emperor in China; start of the SUI DYNASTY. **589** Through military conquest, the Sui dynasty achieves the reunification of China under a single ruler. **591** KHOSHRU II (d.628) becomes Sassanian king with Byzantine military assistance. **599**		**582** Combined force of Avars and Slavs attacks Athens, Sparta and Corinth. **583** King Leovigild (r.569–86) defeats the SUEVI in NW Spain and reunites N and central Spain under VISIGOTH control. **599** Visigoth king Reccared (r.586–601) converts to Christianity.

THE AMERICAS

c.500 Settlement is established at Mesa Verde in SE Colorado, present-day USA.

c.500 MOCHICA state reaches its greatest extent along the lowland coast of Peru.

c.500 Cities of Tiahuanaco and Huari rise to prominence in the Andes highlands of central Peru.

▼ *Justinian The Byzantine emperor Justinian is the central figure in this 6th-century mosaic in the church of San Vitale, Ravenna, Italy. Justinian made a determined effort to reunite the old Roman Empire under Christianity. Byzantine churches, such as those at Ravenna, were built after Justinian's general, Belisarius, overran Italy as far N as Milan in the years following 535.*

SCIENCE AND TECHNOLOGY

▶ *Hagia Sophia Built for Emperor Justinian, Hagia Sophia is a masterpiece of Byzantine architecture. This illustration shows acanthus leaf decoration from an arch within it. The elaborate internal ornamentation of much Byzantine architecture contrasts with the simple exteriors.*

525 Mathematician Dionysius EXIGUUS (500–50) begins the practice of dating years using the birth of Jesus Christ as a starting point; beginning of the Christian, Common, or Current Era.

531–37 Church of Hagia Sophia is constructed in Constantinople.

ARTS AND HUMANITIES

500

520

540

560

580

599

ASIA AND AUSTRALASIA	AFRICA	EUROPE

600

*c.*600 Polynesians settle in Hawaii.

604 Prince Shotoku Taishi (573–621) establishes formal principles of government in Japan.

612–15 Sassanians under King KHOSHRU II (d.628) conquer Asia Minor, Syria and Palestine.

618 TANG DYNASTY is founded by the Sui official Li Yuan.

620

*c.*620 Ganges valley king Harsha (r.606–47) conquers and temporarily unites N India.

622 MUHAMMAD (*c.*570–632) and his followers flee from Mecca to Medina (the Hejira); start of the Islamic calendar.

*c.*625 Srong-brtsan (r.608–50) unifies the Tibetan peoples.

627 BYZANTINE army sacks the Sassanian capital of Ctesiphon.

630 Chinese establish control over much of central Asia.

630 Muhammad's army marches on Mecca, which surrenders.

632 Death of the prophet Muhammad marks the beginning of the Arab empire.

636–37 Arab armies under the caliph OMAR (r.634–44) conquer Syria and Palestine.

640

642 Arabs defeat the Sassanians at the battle of Nihawand and overrun Persia; end of the Sassanian empire.

645 Taika reforms establish central government over all Japan.

656–61 Civil wars are waged for control of the Arab empire during the caliphate of ALI (*c.*600–61); the UMAYYAD family emerges as the ruling dynasty.

660

668 Kingdom of Silla unifies most of Korea under its rule.

680

690 Wu (d.705), the only woman emperor of China, becomes sole ruler.

699

---

616 SASSANIANS conquer Egypt.

628 Byzantine emperor HERACLIUS (575–641) restores Byzantine control over Egypt.

639–42 Arab armies conquer Egypt.

648 Byzantine forces temporarily halt Arab expansion in N Africa.

c.650 Traders from Arabia establish the first Islamic settlements on the E coast of Africa.

652 Arab rulers of Egypt agree to respect the existing borders of the Nubian kingdoms.

670 Arab forces move into present-day Tunisia.

697 Arab forces destroy the Byzantine city of Carthage.

---

626 Combined force of AVARS and Sassanians besiege Constantinople.

629 VISIGOTHS drive the Byzantines from S spain.

663 Byzantine emperor Constans II (630–68) leads an army against the LOMBARDS, but retreats to Sicily.

673–78 Arab armies besiege Constantinople by land and sea.

673 Visigoth king Wamba (r.672–81) defeats an Arab fleet near the Straits of Gibraltar.

681 Onogur HUNS establish the kingdom of Bulgaria.

687 Victory over dynastic rivals at the battle of Tertry in N France extends the power of the Frankish king PEPIN II (d.714).

THE AMERICAS	SCIENCE AND TECHNOLOGY	ARTS AND HUMANITIES	
***c.*600** MOCHICA state in Peru is absorbed by the city-state of Huari.	***c.*600** Earliest-known windmills are used to grind flour in Persia.	***c.*600** Pope GREGORY (540–604) reforms the use of plainsong in Christian services and is thought to have introduced Gregorian chant.	600
	***c.*628** Indian mathematician Brahmagupta (598–665) publishes his *The Opening of the Universe.*	***c.*635** Sutras of the Koran are collected and distributed.	620
***c.*650** City of Teotihuacán is destroyed by warfare: collapse of the Teotihuacán empire.	***c.*650** Chinese scholars develop a technique for printing texts from engraved wooden blocks. ***c.*650** Chinese capital Changan (Xian) is the world's largest city, with a population of about one million.	**641** Great Library at Alexandria is destroyed by fire during an Arab attack.	640
	***c.*675** Byzantine defenders of Constantinople deploy a new weapon, Greek fire – a type of flamethrower.		660
682 King Ah-Cacaw becomes ruler of the MAYAN city of Tikal.	**685–92** Dome of the Rock mosque (Qubbat al-Sakhrah) is built in Jerusalem. ▶ ***Gregory the Great*** *is shown here in a painting by Carlo Saraceni (c.1580–1620). Gregory's dedication enabled him to give the Roman Church a status it had never previously enjoyed. The Papacy henceforth existed as a temporal as well as a spiritual power in the West.*		680
			699

ASIA AND AUSTRALASIA	AFRICA	EUROPE
700 **705** Arab armies carry Islam into Turkistan, central Asia.	**702** AKSUMITES attack the port of Jiddah in present-day Saudi Arabia.	**711–18** Arab and Berber armies invade and conquer VISIGOTH Spain.
710 City of Nara is established as the capital of Japan.	**702–11** Arab conquests are extended W along the N African coastline to the Atlantic ocean.	**717–18** Arab armies besiege Constantinople.
713 Arab expansion to the E reaches the upper Indus valley.		
c.710 Rise of the city of Srivijaya in Sumatra as an important trade center.		
720	**739** Port of Zanzibar on the E coast of Africa is founded by Islamic traders from S Arabia.	**732** Frankish armies led by CHARLES MARTEL (688–741) defeat the Arabs at the battle of Tours and confine them S of the Pyrenees mountains.
740 **744** Revolt by the ABBASID family in present-day Iran leads to civil war in the Arab empire.		
745 Uighurs establish themselves as the ruling dynasty of the Turks.		
747 RAJPUTS (the descendants of Hepthalites and other central Asian invaders in NW India) formally join the Hindu warrior caste.	**c.740** Berber peoples in the N Sahara region revolt against UMAYYAD rule and form independent Islamic kingdoms.	**750** Palace coup makes PEPIN III (714–68) king of the FRANKS; end of the MEROVINGIAN DYNASTY.
	753 Arab expedition crosses the Sahara desert and makes contact with the kingdom of Ghana.	**756** Pepin gives territories in central Italy to the pope; these become the Papal States.
750 Abbasids defeat the Umayyads at the battle of Zab and take over as the ruling Islamic dynasty in the Middle East.		**756** Umayyads retain power in Islamic Spain and establish the independent Emirate of Córdoba.
c.750 Palla dynasty establishes control over present-day Bangladesh.		
751 Combined armies of the Arabs and Turks defeat the Chinese at the battle of Talas; TANG DYNASTY control of central Asia is lost.		**772** New Frankish king CHARLEMAGNE (742–814) campaigns against the SAXONS in present-day N Germany.
753 Rashtrakuta dynasty establishes control over W central India.		**774** Charlemagne defeats the LOMBARDS and annexes N and central Italy.
755–63 Revolt of General An Lushan (703–57) seriously weakens Tang dynasty control of China for the next half century.	**789** Idrisid dynasty establishes Morocco as an independent Islamic kingdom.	**781** Charlemagne establishes his capital at Aachen.
760 **762** Abbasids found the city of Baghdad as their new capital.		**793** Danish raiders (VIKINGS) pillage the island monastery of Lindisfarne off NE England.
763 Tibetan power in central Asia reaches its height with the sacking of the Chinese capital of Changan.		**795** Charlemagne extends Frankish territory to S of the Pyrenees.
780 **794** Capital of Japan moves to Kyōto, start of the HEIAN period.		**796** Frankish armies defeat and conquer the AVARS in present-day Hungary.
799		

THE AMERICAS	SCIENCE AND TECHNOLOGY	ARTS AND HUMANITIES

715 Great Mosque at Damascus is built.

700 Greek language is banned from public documents throughout the Arab empire.

700

726 Iconoclasm movement starts in the BYZANTINE EMPIRE when emperor LEO III (*c*.750–816) bans the use of figurative images in Christian art.

720

731 English monk and scholar BEDE (673–735) publishes his *Ecclesiastical History of the English People.*

c.**750** Start of the decline of classic MAYAN civilization.

c.**750** Decline of Huari control in highland Peru.

▲ *Charlemagne* is shown here, in a ceiling by Victor Schnetz, receiving the theologian and scholar Alcuin. Charlemagne was the most powerful ruler in early medieval Europe. He unified W Europe, recreating an equivalent of the old Roman Empire.

c.**750** Anglo-Saxon poem *Beowulf* is written down.

740

c.**750** *Book of Kells* illuminated manuscript is produced in Ireland.

c.**750** Poets LI PO (701–62) and TU FU (712–70) become popular in China.

Viking longship These fast, graceful ships brought the greatly feared Viking raiders to the coasts of NW Europe. The hull was built from overlapping oak planks and the keel from a single piece of timber. The high stem was elaborately carved. The ship was primarily wind-driven but could also be rowed. It was steered by an oar-shaped rudder at starboard. The shields at each side were probably only displayed when in harbor or on show.

760

780 Birth in central Asia of the Islamic mathematician AL-KHWARIZMI, who wrote *Calculation with Hindu Numerals* (825), which adopted the Indian 10-digit number system and positional notation.

780 Birth of SANKARA (d.820), the Indian philosopher who founded the Advaita Vedanta branch of Hinduism.

780

c.**784** First Arab paper factory opens in Baghdad using skills learned from Chinese prisoners taken at the battle of Talas.

799

800

*c.*800 Polynesians reach New Zealand.

802 Jayavarman II (*c.*770–850) establishes the kingdom of Angkor in present-day Cambodia.

818 TANG DYNASTY re-establishes strong central control in China.

820

823 Arabs conquer Sicily from the Byzantine empire.

▶ *Toltec* A warrior people from highland Mexico, the Toltecs were powerful from the 9th until the 13th centuries. The columns carved in human form, shown right, are part of a 12th-century Toltec temple.

840

845 Buddhism is banned in China and Confucianism is restored as the state ideology.

849 City-state of Pagan is founded in Burma.

857 Yoshifusa (804–72) establishes the FUJIWARA family as the power behind the emperor in Japan.

860

880

*c.*880 Tibetan unity dissolves into local rivalries

899

800 Aghlabids establish an independent Islamic dynasty in present-day Tunisia.

*c.*800 Kingdom of Kanem is established around the w shore of Lake Chad.

808 City of Fez becomes the capital of the kingdom of Morocco.

868 Independent Tulunid dynasty is established in Egypt.

"If many people follow your enthusiastic endeavors, perhaps a new Athens might be created in the land of the Franks, or rather a much better one."

Alcuin (letter to Charlemagne)

800 CHARLEMAGNE (742–814) is crowned Holy Roman emperor in Aachen by Pope LEO III (*c.*750–816); start of the HOLY ROMAN EMPIRE.

804 Charlemagne completes the conquest of present-day N Germany.

812 BYZANTINES recognize Charlemagne as emperor in the w in return for Venice and present-day N Yugoslavia.

825 Islamic fleet captures the island of Crete.

*c.*830 King Egbert of Wessex (d.839) establishes control over the Anglo-Saxon states in England

843 Treaty of Verdun divides the CAROLINGIAN empire into three kingdoms.

846 Arab army raids Italy and sacks Rome.

*c.*850 MAGYARS migrate into Hungary, replacing the AVARS, and begin raiding w Europe.

858 Swedes establish the state of Kiev in Ukraine.

859–62 Danes raid along the coast of present-day s France.

*c.*865 Bulgarians are converted to Christianity.

866 Danes invade SE England

867 BASIL I (*c.*813–86) becomes Byzantine emperor and founds the Macedonian dynasty.

869 Swedish warrior RURIK (d.879) founds the town of Novgorod, NW Russia.

874 Norwegians begin to settle in Iceland.

878–85 King Alfred of Wessex (ALFRED THE GREAT, 849–99) defeats the Danes and confines them to E England (Danelaw).

882 Unification of Novgorod and Kiev under King Oleg creates the first Russian state.

c.800 Metalworking is introduced into Mesoamerica from the s.

c.800 Cultivation of beans and corn is introduced to present-day E USA.

c.800 Huari abandon their capital city in highland Peru.

804 Death of the Anglo-Saxon monk Alcuin (b.c.732), who instigated civil service training and a revival of classical learning at Charlemagne's court. — 800

c.825 Abbasid caliph Al-Mamun (786–833) establishes the House of Wisdom, a library and translation academy at Baghdad.

839 Birth of the Islamic historian Al-Tabri (d.923), who wrote a world history detailing the conquests of the Arabs.

c.820 Reign of the ABBASID caliph HARUN AL-RASHID (r.786–809) inspires the writing of the *Thousand and One Nights*. — 820

824 Death in China of Han Yu (b.768), the leading exponent of Neo-Confucianism.

c.850 TOLTECS establish military supremacy in central Mexico.

c.850 Gunpowder is invented in China.

c.850 First European windmills are built in Islamic Spain.

843 End of iconoclasm in the Byzantine empire; images (icons) are once again permitted in Christian art. — 840

870 Birth of the Islamic philosopher Al-Farab (d.950), who studied the works of Plato and Aristotle, and wrote *Views of the Perfect Citizen of the Perfect State*.

c.860 Cyril (*c.*827–69) and Methodius (*c.*825–84) devise the Cyrillic alphabet to assist their conversion of the Slavs. — 860

868 Earliest-known printed book, the *Diamond Sutra*, is produced in China.

869 Death of the Islamic philosopher and essayist Al-Jahiz (b.776).

◄ *Carolingian architecture* The — 880
monastery church of St. Riquier at Centula near Abbeville, France, was a celebrated example of a Carolingian double-ended church. Built in the decade after 790, it was largely financed by Charlemagne. The church no longer exists; this reconstruction uses details of its exterior and layout found in the present church and in contemporary illustrations.

899

ASIA AND AUSTRALASIA	AFRICA	EUROPE

900

907 Rebellion in China leads to the end of the TANG DYNASTY; disunity and civil wars ensue – the period of the Five Dynasties.

905 Ikhshidids replace the Tulunids as the ruling dynasty in Egypt.

909 FATIMID DYNASTY seizes power in W Tunisia.

911 Danish warleader ROLLO (c.860–931) establishes an independent dukedom of Normandy in NW France.

919 HENRY I (THE FOWLER) (c.876–936) is elected the first king of Germany.

920

c.925 CHOLA kingdom in S India annexes the neighboring PALLAVA kingdom.

927 Anglo-Saxon king Ethelstan (d.939) expels the Danes from England.

940

945 Buyid dynasty from present-day N Iran captures Baghdad from the ABBASID DYNASTY.

944 Russians from Kiev attack Constantinople.

952 King OTTO I of Germany (912–73) declares himself king of Lombardy.

955 MAGYARS are decisively defeated by Otto I at the battle of Lechfield (near present-day Augsburg) in Germany.

960

960 General Zhao Kuang-yin reunifies N China and establishes the SONG DYNASTY.

971 Fatimids conquer Syria and Palestine from the Abbasids.

974 Byzantines establish control over N Syria and N Palestine.

960 Falasha warriors under Queen Gudit sack the city of Aksum.

969 Fatimids invade Egypt and establish Cairo as their capital.

961 BYZANTINES recapture Crete from the Arabs.

962 Otto I is crowned Holy Roman emperor in Rome.

c.969 Miezko I (d.992) establishes the Christian kingdom of Poland.

973 Christian kingdom of Bohemia is established in present-day Czech Republic.

980

985 Cholas invade the island of Sri Lanka.

998 Warlord Mahmud (971–1030) seizes control in Afghanistan and E Persia and expands the GHAZNAVID DYNASTY.

▼ **Anasazi** Various examples of Anasazi pottery have been found in present-day SW USA. The pottery was generally painted with black-on-white designs, though other colors were sometimes used.

986 Emirate of Córdoba conquers the remaining Christian kingdoms in N Spain.

987 Hugh CAPET (938–96) becomes king of France; start of the CAPETIAN DYNASTY.

988 Russian king VLADIMIR I (956–1015) converts to Christianity.

996 Byzantines recapture Greece from the Bulgarians.

997 Following their conversion to Christianity, the Magyars establish a kingdom in Hungary under STEPHEN I (977–1038).

999

THE AMERICAS

900 End of the Classic period of Mesoamerican history; start of the Early Postclassic period.

***c*.900** CHIMÚ people establish the city-state of Chan Chan in N Peru.

***c*.900** MAYA abandon their cities in Guatemala and retreat to the Yucatán region of Mexico.

***c*.900** Anasazi peoples establish towns around Chaco Canyon in New Mexico, with a ritual center at Pueblo Bonito.

***c*.900** HOHOKAM people establish a town and ritual center at Snaketown in S Arizona.

***c*.950** TOLTECS build a capital city at Tula in central Mexico.

982–86 Norwegian explorers discover Greenland and establish a colony.

***c*.987** Toltecs seize control of the Mayan city of Chichén Itzá.

▶ ***Chichén Itzá*** *Shown right is a conjectural reconstruction of the astronomical observatory at Chichén Itzá, the chief city and shrine of the Mayan and Toltec peoples. There were two distinct cities; the earlier Mayan city was abandoned* c.*900 and the new Toltec city was built* c.*1.5km (1mi) away. The style of the vaulting and lintels on the observatory is Mayan and the general design of the tower is Toltec.*

SCIENCE AND TECHNOLOGY

925 Death of the Islamic doctor Al-Razi (b.865), author of *Al-Hawi* – a comprehensive survey of Greek, Arab and Indian medical knowledge.

929 Death of the Islamic mathematician Al-Battani (Albategnius) (b.850), author of *On the Motion of Stars.*

953 Arab mathematician Al-Uqlidsi produces the first decimal fractions.

973 Birth of the Islamic scientist Al-Biruni (d.1048), who compiled an analysis of Indian mathematics.

976 Arabic (Indian) numerals are first used in Europe (in N Spain).

ARTS AND HUMANITIES

965 Death of the Arab poet Al-Mutanabbi (b.915), who worked at the Ikhshidid court in Egypt.

978 Birth of the Japanese woman novelist MURASAKI SHIKIBU (d.1014), author of *The Tale of Genji.*

	900
	920
	940
	960
	980
	999

ASIA AND AUSTRALASIA

1000 GHAZNAVID armies begin raiding and pillaging cities in N India.

1022 CHOLA king Rajendra I (r.1016–44) conquers the E coast of India.

1026 Cholas invade Sumatra and Malaya.

1040 SELJUK Turks defeat the Ghaznavids and invade Persia.

1055 Seljuk Turks under Tughril Bey (c.990–1063) capture Baghdad.

1064 Armenia is incorporated into the Byzantine empire.

1060–67 King Anawrahta (r.1044–77) of Pagan unifies Burma under his rule.

1071 Seljuks led by ALP ARSLAN (1029–72) defeat the Byzantines at the battle of Manzikert and occupy most of Asia Minor.

1075–78 Turks occupy Syria and Palestine.

1096 People's Crusade is massacred by Turks in NW Asia Minor.

1099 First Crusade, under GODFREY OF BOUILLON (1060–1100), captures Jerusalem; independent Christian kingdoms are established along the E coast of the Mediterranean.

AFRICA

▲ *Canute* built a unified Danish empire comprising England, Norway and Denmark. He is depicted, above, in the manuscript Liber Legum Antiquorum Regum *(1321)*.

1054 Berber chieftain Abu Bakr (d.1087) launches an empire-building campaign in N Africa and establishes the ALMORAVID dynasty.

1070 Abu Bakr founds the city of Marrakesh in s Morocco.

1075–77 Almoravids conquer N Morocco and W Algeria.

1076 City of Kumbi, capital of Ghana, is sacked by an Almoravid army.

EUROPE

1003 War between Pisa and Florence is the first recorded war between Italian city-states.

1008–28 Civil wars fragment the Emirate of Córdoba; Christian kingdoms re-emerge in N Spain; end of the UMAYYAD DYNASTY.

1013 Danes conquer England.

1014 Emperor BASIL II (c.958–1025) completes the BYZANTINE reconquest of Bulgaria and the Balkan region.

1016 Danish prince CANUTE (c.994–1035) is elected king of England.

1028 Danes under King Canute conquer Norway.

1033 German emperor CONRAD II (990–1039) adds Burgundy to the HOLY ROMAN EMPIRE.

1037 Christian kingdoms of León and Navarre in N Spain form an alliance and attack the Islamic s.

1040–52 Normans establish control over Byzantine s Italy.

1054 Great Schism divides the Catholic and Orthodox churches.

1054 Following the death of King YAROSLAV (b.980), the Russian state breaks up.

1061–72 Normans under Roger I conquer Sicily from the Arabs.

1066 William of Normandy (1027–87) invades England, wins the battle of Hastings, and becomes King WILLIAM I (THE CONQUEROR).

1085 Christian forces capture the city of Toledo in central Spain.

1086 Berber Almoravids under Yusuf (d.1106) are invited to intervene against the Christians in Spain.

1095 Following the Council of Clermont in France, pope URBAN II (c.1035–99) proclaims a Crusade to free Palestine from Islamic rule.

1096 First Crusade departs.

THE AMERICAS	SCIENCE AND TECHNOLOGY	ARTS AND HUMANITIES	
			1000

THE AMERICAS

*c.*1000 Norwegian explorers discover North America and establish temporary settlements on the E coast of Canada.

SCIENCE AND TECHNOLOGY

1003 Death of the scholar Gerbert of Aurillac (b.946), who translated Arabic texts on the abacus and astrolabe into Latin.

1010 Arab mathematician Ibn al-Haytham (*c.*965–1039), known in Europe as Alhazen, describes the properties of glass lenses.

1037 Death of the Islamic doctor and philosopher Ibn Sina (b.979), known in Europe as AVICENNA, who wrote *Canon of Medicine*.

1050 Technique for printing using movable ceramic type is invented in China.

1054 Chinese astronomers observe the supernova explosion that creates the Crab nebula.

1055–65 Westminster Abbey is built in London, England.

ARTS AND HUMANITIES

1020 Death of the Persian Islamic poet FIRDAUSI (b.935) author of the historical epic *Shah-nameh*.

1033 Birth of the philosopher ANSELM OF CANTERBURY (d.1109), who proposed a logical proof for the existence of God.

1048 Birth of the Islamic scientist and poet OMAR KHAYYÁM (d.1131).

1000

1020

1040

*c.*1070–80 Bayeux tapestry is woven to commemorate William of Normandy's invasion of Britain.

1078 Death of the historian Michael Psellus (b.1018), author of *Chronographia*, a history of the reigns of 14 Byzantine emperors.

1088 First officially sanctioned university in Europe is established in Bologna, Italy.

◀ *Romanesque architecture* The west façade of the Cathedral of San Maggiori, Pisa, Italy, is a fine example of Romanesque architecture. Construction of the cathedral, designed by Buscheto, started in 1063, was interrupted in 1095 and resumed in 1099.

1060

1080

1099

ASIA AND AUSTRALASIA	AFRICA	EUROPE

1100

1100 BALDWIN (1058–1118) becomes king of Jerusalem.

1118 Order of the Knights Templar is established in Jerusalem.

1117 City of Lalibela becomes the capital of Christian Ethiopia.

1108 LOUIS VI (1081–1137) becomes king of France and extends the power of the CAPETIAN DYNASTY.

1138 CONRAD III (1093–1152) becomes Holy Roman emperor and establishes the HOHENSTAUFEN DYNASTY.

1120

1127 Jurchen nomads overrun N China; the SONG DYNASTY retreats to S China; start of the Southern Song dynasty.

1147 Second Crusade departs under the leadership of German emperor Conrad III and King LOUIS VII (c.1120–80) of France.

*c.*1150 Almohad dynasty establishes control over Islamic Spain.

1151 Independent Serbian kingdom is established.

1153 FREDERICK I (1123–90) becomes Holy Roman emperor.

Knights Templar *The military religious order of the Knights Templar had its headquarters in the Temple of Solomon, Jerusalem. The Templars protected routes to Jerusalem for Christians during the Crusades.*

1140

1149 Second Crusade ends after unsuccessful campaigns against the Turks in Palestine.

1156 Civil war between rival clans breaks out in Japan; end of the HEIAN period.

1143–47 Berber ALMOHAD dynasty overthrows the ALMORAVIDS in NW Africa.

1154 Dynastic disputes in the HOLY ROMAN EMPIRE erupt into open warfare in Italy.

1154 HENRY II (1133–89) becomes king of England and establishes the PLANTAGENET DYNASTY.

1158 German merchants found the Baltic port of Lübeck.

1159 Contested papal elections result in both a pope and an antipope being recognized by the warring factions in Italy.

1160

1173 Muhammad of Ghur overthrows the GHAZNAVID DYNASTY in Afghanistan.

1171 Turkish general SALADIN (1138–93) overthrows the FATIMID DYNASTY in Egypt and establishes the AYYUBID dynasty.

1167 Lombard League is formed against Frederick I in N Italy.

1171–73 Henry II of England establishes formal control over Ireland, Wales and Scotland.

1177 Peace treaty of Venice reestablishes a single papacy.

1186 Independent Bulgarian kingdom is re-established.

1180

1187 Victory over Christian forces at the battle of Hattin allows the Islamic general Saladin to recapture Jerusalem.

1191 Third Crusade captures the island of Cyprus and the town of Acre but fails to recapture Jerusalem.

1192 Yoritomo Minamoto (d.1199) institutes the shōgunate in Japan.

1192 Muhammad of Ghur's victory over the RAJPUTS at the battle of Thanesar leads to the Islamic conquest of N India.

1197 Fourth Crusade ends in failure.

1189 Third Crusade departs under the leadership of Frederick I.

1198 OTTO IV (1174–1218), a GUELPH, becomes Holy Roman emperor after the death of HOHENSTAUFEN king HENRY VI (1165–97); civil war breaks out in Germany.

1199 JOHN (1167–1216) becomes king of England on the death of his brother RICHARD I (b.1157).

1199

THE AMERICAS	SCIENCE AND TECHNOLOGY	ARTS AND HUMANITIES	
	1104 Construction of the Arsenal begins in Venice, Italy.	**1111** Death of the Islamic philosopher Al-Ghazali (b.1058), who wrote *The Revival of the Religious Sciences* to counter the Greek-influenced philosophies of AVICENNA and AVERRÖES.	1100
	1120 Robert of Chester visits Spain and translates AL-KHWARIZMI's *Calculation with Hindu Numerals* into Latin.	*c.***1120** Scholar Pierre ABÉLARD (1079–1142) revives the teaching of ARISTOTLE in Paris, France.	1120
		*c.***1130** Construction of the temples at Angkor Wat in Cambodia begins.	
		1139 GEOFFREY OF MONMOUTH (1100–54) composes his *History of the Kings of Britain*.	
1156 Last TOLTEC king, Heumac, flees the destruction of Tula.	*c.***1140** Adelard of Bath (*c.*1075–1160) translates Euclid into Latin using both Greek and Arabic texts.	**1140** Birth of the Japanese philosopher Eisa (d.1215) whose teachings founded Zen Buddhism.	1140
	1150 A university is established in Paris, France.	**1153** Death of the Byzantine scholar Anna Comnena (b.1083), author of *The Alexiad*, a biography of her father the emperor ALEXIUS (1048–1118).	
	1163 External flying buttresses are used for the first time, in the construction of Notre Dame in Paris.		1160
	1167 A university is established in Oxford, England.		
	1170 Roger of Salerno writes the first European surgery textbook, *Practica chirurgiae*.		
	1174 Construction work begins on the unintentionally leaning tower in Pisa, Italy.		
1187 Mayan leader Hunac Ceel leads a rebellion that evicts the Toltecs from Chichén Itzá and establishes a new Mayan capital at Mayapan.	**1187** Death of the Italian scholar Gerard of Cremona (*c.*1114–87) who translated the works of GALEN (129–99) from Arabic texts captured at Toledo.	*c.***1180** Chinese philosopher Zhu Xi (1130–1200) compiles the Confucian Canon.	1180
*c.***1190** AZTECS establish a small state on the shore of Lake Texcoco in Mexico.		**1198** Death of the Islamic philosopher Ibn Rushd (b.1126), known in Europe as Averroës, who wrote an extended commentary on Aristotelian thought.	
			1199

Angkor Wat Created by Suryavarman II, Angkor Wat was the ritual center of his kingdom. The outer cloister enclosed a complex of buildings, the main group arranged as a square of four at the corners and one in the center. All were covered in exquisite low relief with divine dancers, plants, birds and animals.

ASIA AND AUSTRALASIA	AFRICA	EUROPE

1200

AFRICA

*c.***1200** Kingdom of Mwenemutapa is established in Zimbabwe.

1203 Samanguru establishes himself as ruler of the remnants of the kingdom of Ghana.

EUROPE

1201 German Crusaders establish the town of Riga in present-day Latvia.

1203 Fourth Crusade captures the Byzantine port of Zara (in present-day Yugoslavia) for Venice.

1204

1204 Empires of Nicaea (NW Asia Minor) and Trebizond (NE Asia Minor) are created out of the remnants of the BYZANTINE EMPIRE.

1206 Islamic DELHI SULTANATE is established in N India.

1206 MONGOL warrior Temujin (1167–1227) establishes control over the nomads of the Eurasian steppes and adopts the title GENGHIS KHAN (Emperor of the World).

1204 Danes under King Waldemar II (d.1241) conquer Norway.

1204 At the behest of Venice, the Fourth Crusade captures and sacks Constantinople; the Latin empire is created on former Byzantine territory in Greece and the Balkans; Venice gains key ports and Crete.

1208

1211 Mongol warriors invade Jurchen-controlled N China.

Pope Innocent III *The medieval Papacy was brought to the height of its powers by Innocent III. Through the legislative power of the papal Curia, his tight control of ecclesiastical affairs and his influence in imperial elections, Innocent directed the affairs of the entire secular European world.*

1209 At the request of Pope INNOCENT III (1161–1216), an English-led Crusader army invades S France to suppress the Albigensian heretics (Cathars); the town of Beziers is burned.

1212

1215 Mongol advance in China reaches the Yellow River.

1212 Thousands of children who joined the Children's Crusade are sold into slavery in Alexandria, Egypt.

1212 Civil wars in Germany end with FREDERICK II (1194–1250) becoming the German king.

1212 Christian victory at the battle of Las Navas de Toloso leads to the downfall of the Islamic ALMOHAD dynasty in Spain.

1214 French king PHILIP II (1165–1223), supported by Frederick II, defeats the English, supported by Otto IV (1174–1218), at the battle of Bouvines; he conquers the English-controlled territory N of the River Loire.

1215 King JOHN (1167–1216) signs the Magna Carta at Runnymede, England.

1216

1218–25 Mongols conquer E Persia.

1219 Last shōgun of the Minamoto family is killed in Japan; after the brief Shokyu war, the Hojo family takes control.

1219 Fifth Crusade captures the Egyptian port of Damietta, but fails to take Cairo.

*c.***1218** Rivalry between GUELPHS (supporters of papal authority) and GHIBELLINES (supporters of the German emperor) becomes a major factor in Italian politics.

1219

THE AMERICAS	SCIENCE AND TECHNOLOGY	ARTS AND HUMANITIES	

THE AMERICAS

c.1200 Manco Capac establishes the INCA ruling dynasty with its capital at Cuzco, Peru.

c.1200 Monks Mound is constructed at Cahokia, Illinois, present-day USA.

> "To no one will we sell, or deny, or delay, right or justice."
>
> Magna Carta (clause 40)

SCIENCE AND TECHNOLOGY

c.1200 Stern post rudders (invented in China) are first used on European ships.

1202 Italian mathematician Leonardo FIBONACCI of Pisa (*c.*1170–*c.*1240) publishes his *Book of the Abacus* – the first European book to explain Indian numerals.

Franciscan *The friars belonging to the religious order of the Franciscans traveled Europe preaching, possessing neither property nor money and relying on begging for a livelihood. Originally called Grayfriars, Franciscans now wear brown robes.*

1215 Syllabus of the university of Paris is revised, with logic replacing Latin literature.

ARTS AND HUMANITIES

c.1200 Churches, such as that of St. George, are carved out of solid rock at Lalibela in Ethiopia.

1200 Birth of the Japanese Zen master Dogen (d.1253).

1209 Franciscans, the first order of mendicant friars, are founded by FRANCIS OF ASSISI (1182–1226).

c.1210 German minnesinger WOLFRAM VON ESCHENBACH (1170–1220) writes the romance *Parzival*.

1210 German poet Gottfried von Strassburg writes his version of *Tristan and Isolde*.

1212 Order of the Poor Clares is founded.

1213 French historian Geoffrey de Villehardouin (1150–1213) writes an account of the Fourth Crusade, *Conquest of Constantinople*.

◄ ***Crusades*** *The Fourth Crusade aimed to recover Jerusalem but was diverted by the Venetians and ended in the sacking of Constantinople. The fifth Crusade targeted the Islamic stronghold of Egypt. Under the leadership of John of Brienne, the crusaders captured Damietta. Frederick II led the sixth Crusade. He negotiated a truce with the sultan of Egypt that recovered Jerusalem and other holy cities. Jerusalem was retaken for Islam in 1244. The seventh Crusade, led by Louis IX, responded by attacking Egypt. A march on Cairo resulted in a rout and Louis was captured.*

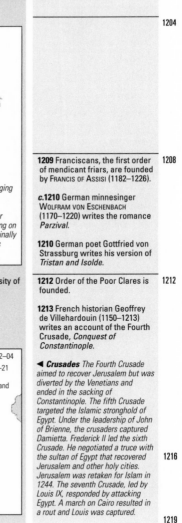

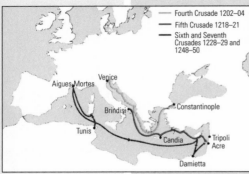

Fourth Crusade 1202–04
Fifth Crusade 1218–21
Sixth and Seventh Crusades 1228–29 and 1248–50

Venice
Aigues-Mortes
Brindisi
Constantinople
Tunis
Candia
Tripoli
Acre
Damietta

(timeline markers, right margin) 1200 · 1204 · 1208 · 1212 · 1216 · 1219

ASIA AND AUSTRALASIA	AFRICA	EUROPE
1220		
1222 MONGOLS conquer Afghanistan and invade N India.		**1220** FREDERICK II (1194–1250) becomes Holy Roman emperor. and king of S Italy.
1224		
1227 Mongols conquer the Xi-Xia kingdom in NW China. GENGHIS KHAN (b.1167) dies and the Mongol empire is divided between his three sons and a grandson.		**1226** Teutonic Knights settle in Riga and NE Poland. **1226** LOUIS IX (1214–70) becomes king of France, with his mother, Blanche of Castile, as regent. **1227** Della Torre family (GUELPHS) gains control of the city-state of Milan in Italy.
1228		
1228–29 Sixth Crusade, led by Frederick II of Germany, obtains Jerusalem, Bethlehem and Nazareth by treaty. **1229** Shan people establish the kingdom of Assam in E India. **1229** Genghis Khan's son Ogedei (1186–1241) is elected chief khan of the Mongol empire. **1231** Mongols invade Korea.	**1228** Hafsid dynasty takes over from the ALMOHADS in Tunisia. **1230** Sundiata I (d.1255) becomes king of the city-state of Mali.	**1228** Italian city-state of Florence adopts a democratic constitution. **1228** Mercenaries are used for the first time in Europe in wars between Italian city-states. **1229** At the end of the wars against the Albigensians, the French crown acquires territory in S France. **1231** Constitutions of Melfi establish a modern administrative state in Sicily. **1231** Teutonic Knights begin the conquest of Prussia.
1232		
1234 Islamic DELHI SULTANATE sacks the Hindu city of Ujjain in central India. **1234** Mongols complete their conquest of N China.	▲ **Genghis Khan** united the Mongol tribes. Demonstrating military genius and ruthlessness, he created a huge empire, stretching across Asia from the Caspian Sea to the Sea of Japan.	**1232** Frederick II's son, Henry, leads the N Italian cities in a revolt against German control. **1232** Emirate of Granada is established by the Islamic Nasrid dynasty in S Spain. **1235** Kingdom of Aragón, N Spain, captures the Balearic Islands from Islamic rule.
1236		
	1239 Ziyanid dynasty overthrows the Almohads in Algeria.	**1236** FERDINAND III (1199–1252) of Castile captures Córdoba and conquers most of S Spain. **1236** Mongols invade Europe. **1237** Armies of Frederick II defeat the N Italian cities at the battle of Cortenuova. **1237** Mongol khanate of the Golden Horde is established in S Russia.
1239		

SCIENCE AND TECHNOLOGY

c.1220 Explosive bombs and rockets are first used by the defenders of Chinese cities against the Mongols.

Teutonic Knight The military religious order of the Teutonic Knights was founded (1190–91) during the Third Crusade. Its members, of aristocratic class, took monastic vows of poverty and chastity. They waged war on non-Christian peoples.

ARTS AND HUMANITIES

c.1220 In S China the landscape artists Ma Yuan (1190–1224) and Xia Gui (1180–1230) emphasize mist and clouds.

1220 Building of Amiens cathedral marks the beginning of the Rayonnant Gothic style of architecture, characterized by large circular windows.

1222 Icelandic poet SNORRI STURLUSON (1179–1241) writes the epic *Prose Edda*.

1225 Qutb Minar tower is built in Delhi, India.

1225 FRANCIS OF ASSISI (1182–1226) writes his *Canticle of Brother Sun*.

c.1230 French poet GUILLAUME DE LORRIS (1210–37) writes the first part of *Roman de la Rose*.

▼ **Mongol conquest** Corruption at court and discontent among the Chinese people permitted the ascendancy of the Mongol empire in the early 13th century. Genghis Khan invaded N China and by 1234 had conquered most of the country north of the Huang He (Yellow River). In 1267 his grandson Kublai Khan moved the capital from Karakorum in Mongolia to Beijing, and in 1279 he overthrew his former allies the southern Song. Mongol rule, officially known as the Yuan dynasty, reached its peak under Kublai Khan.

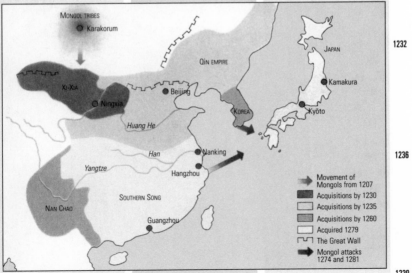

1220
1224
1228
1232
1236
1239

ASIA AND AUSTRALASIA	AFRICA	EUROPE
1240		
1242 Mongols capture the city of Lahore in present-day Pakistan.	**1240** Sundiata, king of Mali, defeats Samanguru, king of Ghana, and establishes the empire of Mali.	**1240** MONGOLS destroy Kiev.
		1240 Prince of Novgorod, ALEXANDER NEVSKI (1220–63), defeats a Swedish invasion on the River Neva.
1244		**1241** Mongols defeat an army of Polish and German knights at the battle of Liegnitz.
1244 Jerusalem is captured by Islamic armies.		
		1241 Mongols defeat the Hungarians at the battle of Sajo.
1248	**1249** Seventh Crusade, led by LOUIS IX (1214–70) of France, invades Egypt and captures the port of Damietta.	**1241** Conflicts between FREDERICK II (1194–1250) and the pope lead to German troops pillaging central Italy.
c.1250 Turks begin settling in Asia Minor.		
	1250 Louis IX is defeated by the Egyptians and is taken prisoner.	**1242** Teutonic Knights attack Novgorod, but are defeated by Alexander Nevski at the battle of Lake Peipus.
	1250 MAMELUKES (Turkish slave bodyguards), led by Baybars, seize power in Egypt; end of the FATIMID DYNASTY; start of the Bahri Mameluke dynasty.	**1242** Mongols withdraw from Europe after the death of Khan Ogedei (1186–1241).
		1242 English under King HENRY III (1207–72) invade France.
1252		**1250** Frederick II dies and is succeeded by his son CONRAD IV (1228–54).
1253 Mongols under HULEGU (1217–65) invade w Persia and establish the Ilkhanid dynasty.		
1253 Mongols capture the N Burma region; Thai peoples migrate s.		**1253** Kingdom of Portugal conquers the Algarve region from Islamic rule.
1253 Rivalry between Venetian and Genoese merchants at Acre, Palestine, leads to war between the two Italian city-states.		**1254** Death of Conrad IV marks the end of the HOHENSTAUFEN DYNASTY in Germany and the beginning of an interregnum.
1255 Mongol khan Mongke (1208–59) bans Taoist books in China.		
1256		**1258** English barons rebel against King Henry III.
1256 Mongols exterminate the ASSASSINS in Syria.		
1257 Mongol armies conquer present-day N Vietnam.		**1259** English are forced to cede territory to the French king, Louis IX, at the Peace of Paris.
1258 Mongols launch attacks against the Southern SONG DYNASTY in s China.		**1259** German port cities of Lübeck, Hamburg and Rostock form a Hansa (union).
1258 Baghdad is destroyed by Mongol armies.		
1259 Following the death of Mongke, the division of the Mongol empire into four khanates becomes permanent.		
1259		

THE AMERICAS	SCIENCE AND TECHNOLOGY	ARTS AND HUMANITIES

1240

▶ *Alhambra* The Spanish citadel of the sultans of Granada, the Alhambra is one of the most beautiful examples of medieval Islamic architecture. Parts of the complex date from the period of the Nasrid dynasty (1238–1358), but much was added later, including a palace begun by Holy Roman Emperor Charles V in 1526.

1244

*c.*1250 Gunpowder is first mentioned in European manuscripts; the secret of its manufacture was learned either from Arabs in Spain or from Mongol prisoners.

1248 Construction starts on the Alhambra fortress and palace in Granada, s Spain.

1248 Building of Cologne cathedral marks the spread of Gothic architecture across N Europe.

*c.*1250 "Black Pagoda" Temple of the Sun at Konarak in India is built by King Narasimhadeva (r.1238–64).

1248

1252

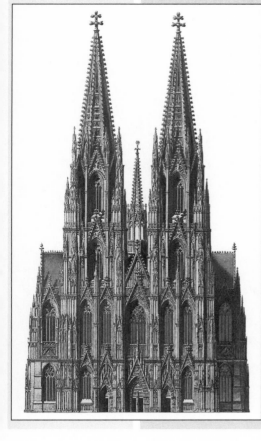

1259 Death of the English historian and biographer Matthew PARIS, author of *Great Chronicle*.

1256

◀ *Cologne Cathedral* Begun in 1248, Cologne cathedral is the largest Gothic church in N Europe. The present building was completed between 1842 and 1880. The illustration shows the w façade. The cathedral's grandeur lies predominantly in its highly decorated twin towers, which rise to 152m (502ft).

1259

1260

1260 MONGOLS are defeated by the MAMELUKES at the battle of Ain Jalut in Palestine.

1260 Mongol khan KUBLAI (1215–94) becomes emperor of N China.

1264

1267 Kublai establishes as his capital the city of Khanbalik, which later becomes Beijing.

1268

1268 Mamelukes sack the city of Antioch in Syria.

1268 Mongols invade S China.

1271 Mamelukes capture the Christian fortress of Krak des Chevaliers in Syria.

1272

1274 Mongols make an unsuccessful attempt to invade Japan.

1276

1277 Mongol forces capture the city of Guangzhou (Canton) in S China.

1277 Mamelukes invade Asia Minor and defeat the Mongols, but later withdraw.

1279 PANDYA DYNASTY completes its conquest of S India; end of the CHOLA DYNASTY.

1279 Mongols complete their conquest of S China; end of the Southern SONG DYNASTY, start of the YUAN DYNASTY.

1279

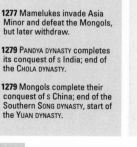

Church at Lalibela, Ethiopia
The 13th-century church at Lalibela was one of several hewn out of solid rock. The Middle Ages was a time of great church building and of revival and expansion in the ancient Christian empire of Ethiopia.

1269 Marinid dynasty takes over from the ALMOHADS in Morocco.

1270 Warlord Yekuno Amlak (r.1270–85) seizes control of Ethiopia and establishes the Solomonid dynasty.

1270 Louis IX of France leads the Eighth Crusade to Tunis, where he dies of fever.

1260 City of Siena defeats the ruling GUELPH faction of Florence at the battle of Montaperti.

1261 King Ottokar II (d.1278) of Bohemia captures Austria from Hungary; this marks the high-point of Bohemian power.

1261 Greeks, with Genoese assistance, seize Constantinople and re-establish the BYZANTINE EMPIRE; end of the Latin empire.

1264 Venice regains control of Constantinople after defeating Genoa at the battle of Trepani.

1266 French invade S Italy. CHARLES (1226–85), brother of French king LOUIS IX (1214–70), becomes king of Sicily.

1265 Rebellious English barons are defeated by Prince Edward (later EDWARD I) at the battle of Evesham.

1271 Marco POLO (1254–1324) departs for China.

1277 Visconti family (GHIBELLINES) gains control of Milan.

1277 Genoese merchants establish the first regular Atlantic sea-route between the Mediterranean Sea and N Europe.

1278 After victory over Ottokar II of Bohemia at the battle of Marchfeld, RUDOLF I (1218–91) of HAPSBURG gains control of Austria.

1278–84 Edward I (1239–1307) of England invades and conquers Wales.

THE AMERICAS

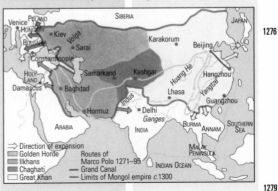

▲ **Kublai Khan** expanded the empire of his grandfather, Genghis Khan, completing the conquest of China. He brought economic prosperity through his encouragement of trade.

▶ **Marco Polo** Despite the terror that the Mongols inspired, their domination of large areas of Asia and parts of Europe led to the development of trade routes used by traders of many nations in the 13th century. Marco Polo set out for Beijing in 1271. It was more than 20 years before he returned to Europe to describe the wealth and splendor of the Khan's court.

SCIENCE AND TECHNOLOGY

1262 Death of the Islamic astronomer Ibn Omar al-Marrakashi, who wrote *Of Beginnings and Ends.*

1264 French scholar Vincent of Beauvais (1190–1264) publishes his *Great Mirror*, a combination of encyclopedia and universal history.

1266 English scholar and mathematician Roger Bacon (1220–92) completes his *Longer Work*, which advocates the use of scientific experiment.

c.1270 Firearms and cannon (made of reinforced bamboo) are first used in battles between the Mongols and the Chinese.

c.1270 Double-entry book-keeping is developed in the Italian city of Florence.

1275 German scholar and scientist Theodoric of Freiburg describes how a rainbow is formed by reflections within raindrops.

ARTS AND HUMANITIES

1260 Italian artist Nicola Pisano (1225–84) sculpts a pulpit for the Baptistry in Pisa.

1262 Death of the philosopher and reformer Shinran (b.1173), who established True Pure Land Buddhism in Japan.

> "The whole city is arrayed in squares just like a chessboard, and disposed in a manner so perfect and masterly that it is impossible to give a description that should do it justice."
>
> Marco Polo, referring to Kublai Khan's capital Khanbalik
> (*The Book of Marco Polo*)

1273 Italian scholar and philosopher Thomas Aquinas (1225–74) completes his *Theological Digest.*

1260

1264

1268

1272

1276

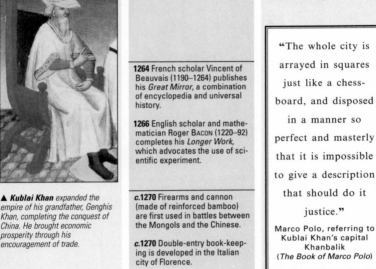

⇒ Direction of expansion
▨ Golden Horde
▨ Ilkhans
▨ Chaghati
☐ Great Khan

Routes of Marco Polo 1271–95
— Grand Canal
— Limits of Mongol empire c.1300

1279

ASIA AND AUSTRALASIA	AFRICA	EUROPE
1280		
1281 MONGOLS attempt to invade Japan but are repulsed by samurai; the Mongol fleet is destroyed by a storm – the *kamikaze* (divine wind).		**1282** French soldiers in Palermo are massacred during the "Sicilian Vespers"; the Sicilians invite Pedro of Aragón to be their king.
1282–88 Mongols make repeated attempts to subdue the kingdom of Champa in present-day S Vietnam.		**1283** Teutonic Knights complete the conquest of Prussia.
1284		
1287 Mongols conquer and destroy the kingdom of Pagan in Burma.		**1284** Italian city-state of Genoa defeats Pisa at the battle of Meliora.
		1285 Bulgarian kingdom disintegrates under Mongol overlordship.
1288		
1291 MAMELUKES capture the city of Acre, Palestine, the last remnant of the Crusader kingdoms.		**1291** Three Swiss cantons revolt against HAPSBURG rule and form a confederation.
		1291 Knights of St. John move to Cyprus.
1292		
1292–93 Mongols attempt a seaborne invasion of Java.		
1294 Death of the Mongol Chinese emperor KUBLAI (b.1215).		
1296		
1297 DELHI SULTANATE conquers the Hindu kingdom of Gujarat in W India.		**1296** English king EDWARD I (1239–1307) invades Scotland to suppress a rebellion.
1299 Mongol Chaghati khanate of central Asia invades N India.		**1297** William WALLACE (1270–1305) leads a rising against English rule in Scotland.
		1297 Edward I invades France in support of Flanders.
		1297 French king PHILIP IV (1268–1314) occupies Flanders (NE France and Belgium).
		1299 Genoa defeats Venice at a naval battle near the island of Curzola in the Adriatic Sea.
1299		

Knights of St. John The Order of the Hospital of St. John of Jerusalem dates from the early 11th century, when a hospital was founded in Jerusalem for Christian pilgrims. The knights adopted a military role in the 12th century to defend Jerusalem and, later, Acre, Cyprus and Rhodes.

THE AMERICAS	SCIENCE AND TECHNOLOGY	ARTS AND HUMANITIES	

THE AMERICAS

SCIENCE AND TECHNOLOGY

*c.*1280 Belt-driven spinning wheel is introduced to Europe from India.

1280s Establishment of the Mongol empire across Asia re-opens overland trade routes, such as the Silk Road, between Europe and the Far East.

ARTS AND HUMANITIES

*c.*1280 Tibetan scholar Phags-pa devises a script for writing Mongolian.

1282 Death of the philosopher Nichiren (b.1222), who established Lotus Sutra Buddhism in Japan.

1283 Italian artist Giovanni CIMABUE (*c.*1240–*c.*1302) paints his *Sta Croce* crucifix.

1283 Catalan scholar and author Raimon LULL (1235–1315) writes his utopian novel *Blanquerna*.

1285 Italian artist DUCCIO DI BUONINSEGNA (*c.*1265–1319) paints the *Rucellai Madonna*, which revolutionizes the Byzantine style of Sienese painting.

1291 Venetians move their glass factories to the island of Murano for fire safety.

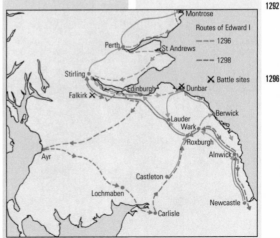

▶ **Edward I** *The Scottish royal line ended with the deaths of Alexander III in 1286 and his granddaughter, who was married to Edward I of England's son, in 1290. The decision about the succession was left to Edward, who chose John Balliol. Edward's attempts to dictate to Balliol led to an unsuccessful rebellion in 1296. Edward invaded, and his route is illustrated on the map. Balliol resigned and the Stone of Scone, on which Scottish kings were enthroned, was removed to Westminster. In 1297 William Wallace launched a more serious rebellion, which was not suppressed for several years.*

1280

1284

1288

1292

1296

1299

ASIA AND AUSTRALASIA	AFRICA	EUROPE

1300		
1300 Turkish general OSMAN I (1258–1326) proclaims himself sultan of the Turks in Asia Minor; start of the OTTOMAN EMPIRE.	*c.*1300 Kingdom of Benin is established on the w coast of Africa.	**1302** Citizens of Flanders defeat the French at the battle of the Spurs at Courtrai.
1300 Thai peoples under king Rama Kamheng establish a kingdom around the city of Sukhothai in present-day Thailand.		
1303 DELHI SULTANATE conquers the RAJPUT fortress of Chitor, the last Hindu stronghold in N India.		
1304		
1306 Chaghati MONGOLS are expelled from India by the Delhi Sultanate.		**1305** Flanders submits to French rule.
		1305 English execute the Scottish rebel William WALLACE (b.1270).
		1307 Knights Templar are disbanded in Paris.
1308		
1311 Delhi Sultanate annexes the PANDYA kingdom in s India.		**1309** French king PHILIP IV (1268–1314) compels the pope, Clement V, to move to Avignon in s France; start of the "Babylonian Captivity".
		1309 Teutonic Knights make Marienburg their capital.
		1309 A Bourse (stock exchange) is founded at Bruges, present-day Belgium.
		1309 Knights of St. John move to the island of Rhodes.
		1310 City-state of Venice establishes its Council of Ten.
1312		
1313 Delhi Sultanate conquers central India.		**1314** Scots, led by ROBERT THE BRUCE (1274–1329), defeat the English, under EDWARD II (1284–1327), at the battle of Bannockburn and establish Scottish independence.
		1314 First Venetian merchant ships visit N Europe.
		1315 Swiss defeat the Austrian army at the battle of Morgarten.
1316		
	1316 Military expedition from Egypt establishes an Islamic ruler in Nubia.	**1319** Sweden and Norway are united under the rule of MAGNUS VII (1316–74).
1319		

▲ *Osman I was the founder of the Ottoman Empire. The Ottoman Turks were originally Muslim warriors who patrolled the E borders of the Byzantine world. Osman's military genius raised them from nomadic tribesmen lacking any political institution or national consciousness to become the formidable potential masters of a great empire.*

THE AMERICAS	SCIENCE AND TECHNOLOGY	ARTS AND HUMANITIES	
c.1300 CHIMÚ state in Peru expands to rival that of the INCAS.	**c.1300** Earliest-known European spectacles are manufactured in Italy.	**c.1300** Polynesian settlers on Easter Island begin a period of intensive statue carving.	1300

c.1300 Mesa Verde and other Anasazi centers in present-day sw USA are abandoned.

> "All abandon hope,
> ye who enter here."
>
> Dante (*Divine Comedy*,
> "Inferno")

1304–09 Italian artist GIOTTO DI BONDONE (1266–1337) begins painting his frescos in the Arena chapel, Padua. — 1304

1311 Pietro Vesaconte makes the earliest-known portolan sea-chart (navigational chart) of the Mediterranean.

1309 French knight Jean, Sire de Joinville (1224–1319) publishes his *Life of St. Louis* (the French king LOUIS IX). — 1308

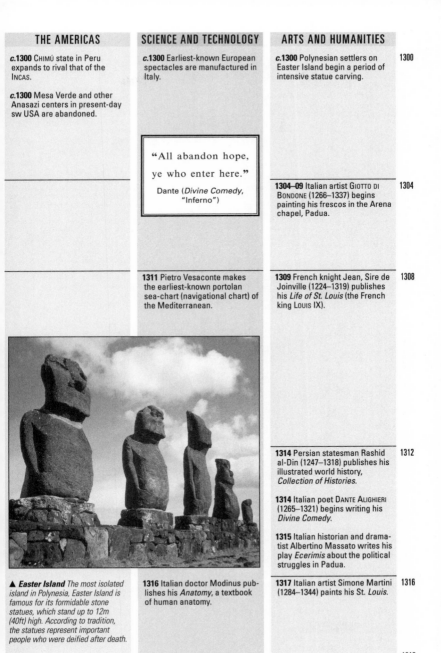

1314 Persian statesman Rashid al-Din (1247–1318) publishes his illustrated world history, *Collection of Histories*. — 1312

1314 Italian poet DANTE ALIGHIERI (1265–1321) begins writing his *Divine Comedy*.

1315 Italian historian and dramatist Albertino Massato writes his play *Ecerimis* about the political struggles in Padua.

▲ *Easter Island* The most isolated island in Polynesia, Easter Island is famous for its formidable stone statues, which stand up to 12m (40ft) high. According to tradition, the statues represent important people who were deified after death.

1316 Italian doctor Modinus publishes his *Anatomy*, a textbook of human anatomy.

1317 Italian artist Simone Martini (1284–1344) paints his St. *Louis*. — 1316

1319

ASIA AND AUSTRALASIA	AFRICA	EUROPE

1320

1320 Turkish Tughluk dynasty takes over control of the DELHI SULTANATE.

1323 Delhi Sultanate conquers the Hindu kingdom of Telingana in India.

1320 King Amda Seyon (r.1314–44) extends Christian control to s Ethiopia.

1324

1324 Pilgrimage of MANSA MUSA (r.1312–37) to Mecca marks the highpoint of the empire of Mali.

▼ *Mosque, Timbuktu* *The great mosque at Timbuktu was designed in the 14th century by As Saheli, one of the Egyptians brought back to Mali by Mansa Musa after his pilgrimage to Mecca. Timbuktu grew to be an important center of commerce, religion and learning.*

1325 Ivan I becomes ruler of the Grand Duchy of Moscow under the overlordship of the khanate of the Golden Horde.

1328

1330 Hindu kingdom of Madjapahit in Java begins extending its control over nearby islands.

1328 Seat of the Russian Church is moved from Vladimir to Moscow.

1328 Death of the French king CHARLES IV (b.1294) ends the CAPETIAN DYNASTY; start of the VALOIS DYNASTY, under PHILIP VI (1293–1350).

1329 BYZANTINES capture the island of Chios from Genoa.

1330 After defeating the Greeks and Bulgarians at the battle of Velbuzdhe, Serbia becomes the dominant power in the Balkans.

1331 Cities in s Germany, including Ulm and Augsburg, establish the Swabian League.

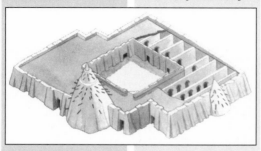

1332

1333 Emperor Go-daigo tries to re-establish imperial power in Japan.

1335 MONGOL Ilkhanid dynasty in Persia is overthrown.

*c.*1335 Epidemic of plague, which later becomes known as the Black Death, breaks out in China.

1332 War breaks out between Christian Ethiopia and neighboring Islamic kingdoms.

1332 Gerhard of Holstein, supported by the Hanseatic League, seizes the Danish crown.

1332 Lucerne is the first city to join the Swiss Confederation.

1336

1336 Revolt establishes the Hindu kingdom of Vijayanagar in s India; start of the Sangama dynasty.

1336 Civil wars break out in Japan, which is split between rival imperial courts.

1337 OTTOMAN Turks capture Nicaea, the last remaining Byzantine territory in Asia Minor.

1338 Bengal breaks away from the Delhi Sultanate to become an independent Islamic state.

1337 EDWARD III (1312–77) of England lays claim to the French throne; beginning of the Hundred Years War (to 1453).

1339 City of Genoa in Italy adopts a republican constitution.

1339 Island city of Venice conquers the town of Treviso on the Italian mainland.

1339

THE AMERICAS

c.1325 AZTECS establish the city of Tenochtitlán on an island in Lake Texcoco, Mexico.

SCIENCE AND TECHNOLOGY

c.1320 Cannon are first used on a European battlefield.

1324 Earliest-known European cannon are manufactured in France.

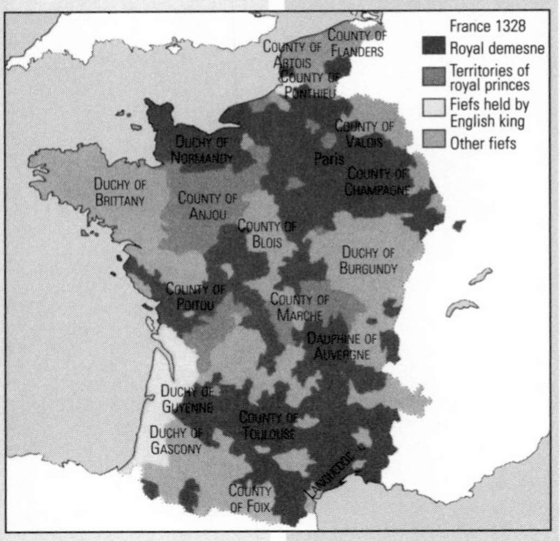

ARTS AND HUMANITIES

1324 Italian politician Marciglio of Padua (c.1275–1342) writes his *Defensor Pacis*, an essay on relations between church and state.

c.1325 Beginning of the Renaissance in Italian art is accompanied by a revival of interest in ancient Greece and Rome, and the development of secular thought – humanism.

1332 Birth of the Islamic philosopher IBN KHALDUN (d.1406), author of an *Introduction to History*.

1334 GIOTTO DI BONDONE (1266–1337) designs the bell tower of Florence cathedral.

1335 Italian artist Andrea Pisano (d.1348) casts the bronze s doors of the baptistry in Florence.

1335 Mosque of Al-Nasir in Cairo is completed.

1337 Italian artist Ambrogio Lorenzetti paints frescos of *Good and Bad Government* in the town hall in Siena.

1337 Death of the Chinese dramatist Wang Shifu (b.1250), author of *The Romance of the Western Chamber*.

1338 Italian artist Taddeo Gaddi (c.1300–c.1366) paints frescos in the church of Santa Croce, Florence.

▼ *France* The map shows the distribution of French lands in 1328. The Capetian dynasty had established its hold on the former Plantagenet lands, and all the feudatories in Burgundy, Brittany and Languedoc acknowledged it, as did the English king in Guyenne. But the many enclaves and noble houses indicate how shallow were the roots of royal authority.

France 1328
- Royal demesne
- Territories of royal princes
- Fiefs held by English king
- Other fiefs

COUNTY OF FLANDERS
COUNTY OF ARTOIS
COUNTY OF PONTHIEU
DUCHY OF NORMANDY
COUNTY OF VALOIS
Paris
COUNTY OF CHAMPAGNE
DUCHY OF BRITTANY
COUNTY OF ANJOU
COUNTY OF BLOIS
DUCHY OF BURGUNDY
COUNTY OF POITOU
COUNTY OF MARCHE
DAUPHINE OF AUVERGNE
DUCHY OF GUYENNE
DUCHY OF GASCONY
COUNTY OF TOULOUSE
LANGUEDOC
COUNTY OF FOIX

1320
1324
1328
1332
1336
1339

ASIA AND AUSTRALASIA	AFRICA	EUROPE

1340

1341–43 Epidemic of plague – the Black Death – sweeps across China.

1340 Portuguese sailors discover the Canary Islands.

1340 English defeat the French at a naval battle near the port of Sluys (in present-day Belgium).

1340 Spanish king of Castile, Alfonso XI (1311–50), decisively repels an Islamic attack at the battle of Rio Salado.

1341–47 Civil war further disrupts the Byzantine empire.

1344

1344 Flooding of the Yellow River devastates e China.

1346 Independent Islamic dynasty is founded in Kashmir, n India.

1347 Thai capital is moved to the city of Ayutthaya.

1344 Canary Islands are allocated to Castile by the pope.

1348 Black Death devastates Egypt.

1349 Moroccan traveler Ibn Battutah (1304–68) returns home after a 25-year journey to India and China.

1344 Hungarian king Louis I (1326–82) expels the Mongols from Transylvania.

1346 Black Death sweeps through s Russia.

1346 Teutonic Knights gain control of Estonia.

1346 English defeat the French at the battle of Crécy, the first major battle of the Hundred Years War.

1347 English capture the French port of Calais.

1347 Black Death reaches Constantinople, Italy and s France; in 1348 it reaches Spain. n France and Britain; in 1349 Germany and Scandinavia. This initial outbreak kills c.25% of Europe's population.

Crimea 1347

China 1335

1348

1350 Unrest begins in China among workers repairing the Grand Canal. They are followers of the Buddhist White Lotus cult and wear red turbans.

1352

1353 Kingdom of Laos is established in se Asia.

1355 Red Turbans, led by former monk Hong-wu (1328–98), foment a popular revolt against Mongol rule in China.

1356

June 1350

December 1347

▲ **Black Death** Originating in China c.1335, the Black Death spread w across Asia and Europe, via trade and pilgrimage routes, reaching the Crimea in 1347, as illustrated in the larger map. From the Crimea, the plague spread throughout Europe. The red lines on the smaller map indicate the approximate extent of plague in Europe at six monthly intervals from 31 December 1347 to 30 June 1350. The region spared partly or wholly from the plague is in white.

1348 Danish king Waldemar IV (1320–75) recaptures Jutland from German control.

1351 War breaks out in Italy between Florence and Milan.

1352 Ottoman Turks establish a foothold in Europe at Gallipoli.

1354 Genoese destroy the Venetian fleet at the sea battle of Sapieanza.

1356 English, led by Edward the Black Prince (1330–76), defeat the French at Maupertuis and capture the French king.

1356 Hanseatic League (a commercial union of c.160 German, Dutch and Flemish towns) is formally established.

1358 Rising in Paris, led by Étienne Marcel (c.1316–58), and peasant revolts in the countryside weaken France.

1359

THE AMERICAS

c.1340 King Mayta Capa begins expanding INCA control in Peru.

▼ **Hundred Years War** The conflict between the Plantagenet and the Valois dynasties was marked by short campaigns, longer truces and periods of stalemate. English campaigns consisted of plundering raids on w and n France. Except for a few captured strongholds, from which expeditions could be launched, there was little attempt to conquer French territory until Henry V invaded Normandy in 1417. Various campaigns and possessions are illustrated on the map below.

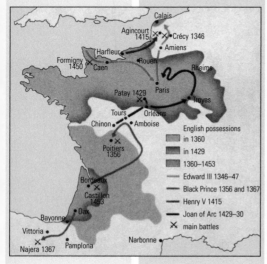

English possessions
- ▨ in 1360
- ▨ in 1429
- ▨ 1360–1453
- — Edward III 1346–47
- — Black Prince 1356 and 1367
- — Henry V 1415
- — Joan of Arc 1429–30
- ✕ main battles

SCIENCE AND TECHNOLOGY

1340 First European factory for making paper opens in Fabriano, Italy.

1340s Wind-driven pumps are used to drain marshes in Holland.

1343 English philosopher and scholar WILLIAM OF OCCAM (1285–1349) publishes his *Dialogus*, which contains his "razor" of logic.

ARTS AND HUMANITIES

1341 Italian poet Francesco PETRARCH (1304–74) publishes *Poems*, a collection of love poems

> "Entities should not be multiplied unnecessarily. No more things should be presumed to exist than are absolutely necessary."
>
> William of Occam's statement of the rule of economy that has come to be known as Occam's razor

1348 Death from plague of Italian historian Giovanni Villani (b.1276) brings to an end his chronicle of Florentine history.

1352 Palace of the popes at Avignon is completed.

1357 Italian artist Andrea Orcagna (1308–68) creates the altarpiece for the Strozzi family chapel in Florence.

1357 Death of the Italian lawyer Bartolus of Sassoferrato (b.1314), who advocated republican government in his *On the government of cities*.

1357 Italian scholar Zanobi da Strada discovers a forgotten manuscript copy of TACITUS' *Annals* in a monastery library.

1358 Italian poet and author Giovanni BOCCACCIO (1313–75) completes his *Decameron* of tales told during the Black Death.

1340

1344

1348

1352

1356

1359

ASIA AND AUSTRALASIA	AFRICA	EUROPE

1360

EUROPE

1360 By the Peace of Bretigny, EDWARD III (1312–77) of England gives up his claim to the French throne in return for sovereignty over SW France.

1361 OTTOMAN Turks capture the city of Adrianople; the BYZANTINE EMPIRE is reduced to the city of Constantinople..

1361–63 Second outbreak of the Black Death devastates parts of Europe.

1364

ASIA AND AUSTRALASIA

1367 Victory in battle by the DELHI SULTANATE over the Hindu kingdom of Vijayanagar leads to the massacre of 400,000 civilians.

AFRICA

1365 Crusade led by the king of Cyprus sacks the city of Alexandria in Egypt.

EUROPE

1361–70 Wars between the Hanseatic League and Denmark leave the League dominant in the Baltic region.

1368

1368 Red Turbans expel the MONGOLS from China and Hongwu (1328–98) becomes emperor; start of the MING DYNASTY.

1369 Thais sack the Khmer capital of Angkor.

1369 TAMERLANE (1336–1405), or Timur, a Turkish soldier, rebels against the Chaghati Mongols and captures their capital, Samarkand.

1367 Civil war breaks out between the Swabian League and the German emperor.

1369 French king CHARLES V (1337–80) attacks English possessions in France.

1370 Teutonic Knights defeat the Lithuanians at the battle of Rudau.

1370 Bastille fortress is built in Paris.

1371 Robert II (1316–90) becomes king of Scotland; start of the Stuart dynasty.

1372

AFRICA

1375 Kingdom of SONGHAI breaks away from the empire of Mali.

EUROPE

1372 Swabian League is defeated.

1372 Spanish, allied with the French, defeat the English at the sea battle of La Rochelle.

1375–78 War of the Eight Saints is fought between Florence and the papacy.

1376

1377 Islamic empire of Java conquers Hindu Sumatra.

1376 Swabian League is revived by the city of Ulm.

1377 Pope returns to Rome; end of the "Babylonian Captivity".

1378–1417 Schism occurs in the Catholic Church with rival popes at Rome and Avignon.

1378 Genoa captures the town of Chioggia, S of Venice.

▶ **Kraków University** Founded by Casimir III, the Jagiellonian University at Kraków is one of the oldest universities in Europe. One of its most famous alumni is Nicolas Copernicus.

1378 Flanders revolts against French rule.

1379

1363 French doctor Guy de Chauliac (d.1368) completes his textbook of surgery, *Great surgery*.

1360 Italian lawyer Giovanni di Legnano writes his *Treatise on War*.

1360

1360 Construction of the Alcázar palace in Seville begins.

*c.*1362 English priest William LANGLAND (1331–99) writes the poem *Piers Plowman*.

1364 A university is established in Kraków, Poland.

*c.*1365 Flemish painters establish the Bruges school of painting.

1364

*c.*1370 Acamapitchtli becomes king of the AZTECS.

*c.*1370 CHIMÚ complete their conquest of coastal N Peru.

1370 French king Charles V establishes standard time according to a weight-driven mechanical clock in the royal palace in Paris.

*c.*1370 Japanese dramatist Kanami Motokiyo (1333–84) establishes the classic form of No drama.

1368

1372 Egyptian scholar and zoologist Al-Damiri (1344–1405) writes his *Lives of animals*.

1372

▲ *Tamerlane controlled a vast empire that extended from the Black Sea to the Indus River and from the Persian Gulf to the Syr Darya River. The atrocities committed in the course of his conquests have become legendary. He is the subject of Christopher Marlowe's play* Tamburlaine the Great *(1590).*

*c.*1377 French scholar William of Oresme (1320–82) writes his essay on monetary policy, *On money*.

1377 Single arch bridge with a span of 72m (236ft) is completed at Trezzo, N Italy.

1379 Rockets are first used on a European battlefield by the army of Padua in Italy.

1378 Nun and philosopher CATHERINE OF SIENA (1347–80) writes her *Dialogo*.

1376

1379

1380

1381–87 TAMERLANE (Timur, 1336–1405) invades and conquers Persia.

1382 All districts of China are reunited under MING control.

1382 Burji MAMELUKES seize control from the Bahris in Egypt.

1380 Venice recaptures Chioggia and destroys the Genoese fleet.

1381 *Ciompi* (low-paid workers) revolt against the rule of the GUELPHS in Florence.

1381 Peasants' Revolt in England ends with the death of its leader, Wat TYLER.

1382 Flanders revolt is crushed at the battle of Roosebeke by PHILIP THE BOLD (1342–1404), who becomes overlord of the region.

1383 Venice captures Corfu.

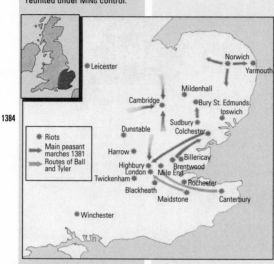

1384

* Riots
→ Main peasant marches 1381
→ Routes of Ball and Tyler

Leicester
Norwich
Yarmouth
Mildenhall
Cambridge
Bury St. Edmunds
Ipswich
Sudbury
Dunstable
Colchester
Harrow
Billericay
Highbury
Brentwood
London
Mile End
Twickenham
Rochester
Blackheath
Maidstone
Canterbury
Winchester

1385 Victory at the battle of Aljubarrota establishes Portuguese independence from Spain.

1386–88 Milan conquers the Italian cities of Verona, Vicenza and Padua.

1386 King Jagiello (1351–1434) of Poland forms a union with the Grand Duchy of Lithuania.

1387 Danish regent Margaret (1363–1412) becomes queen of Sweden and Norway.

1388

1389 Islamic empire of Java collapses after the death of king Rajasanagara (b.1334).

▲ **Peasants' Revolt** The rebellion in England, mainly a movement of farmers and tradesmen, with a following of farm laborers, was caused by the introduction of a poll tax, as well as resentment at feudal restrictions and statutory control of wages. Led by Wat Tyler and roused by the rebel priest John Ball, it occurred mainly in the southeast, as shown above. Rebels in Essex were in touch with those in Kent, from where the main march on London began. Townsmen as well as countrymen were involved. St. Albans, Bury St. Edmunds and towns in Norfolk all suffered violent movements. In general, risings took place in the prosperous areas, where legal restraints restricted virtually independent farmers from pursuing their own fortunes.

1389 OTTOMAN Turks defeat the Serbs at the battle of Kosovo.

1388–95 Tamerlane invades and conquers the territory of the Golden Horde but fails to take Moscow.

1392

1392 Yoshimitsu (1358–1408) becomes ruler of Japan and establishes the Muromachi shōgunate.

1392 General Yi Song-gye establishes the Yi (Choson) dynasty in Korea.

1393–94 Tamerlane invades and conquers Mesopotamia.

1394 Islamic kingdom of Jaunpur in N India is established.

1396 SIGISMUND (1368–1437) of Hungary attempts to break the Turkish encirclement of Constantinople but is defeated at the battle of Nicopolis

1396 Bulgaria becomes part of the Ottoman Empire.

1397 Treaty of Kalmar unites Denmark, Sweden and Norway under Danish control.

1397 Bank of Medici is established in Florence.

1396

1398–99 Tamerlane invades N India and sacks Delhi.

1399 RICHARD II (1367–1400) of England is overthrown by HENRY IV (1367–1413); end of the PLANTAGENET DYNASTY, start of the LANCASTER DYNASTY.

1399

THE AMERICAS	SCIENCE AND TECHNOLOGY	ARTS AND HUMANITIES	
		1380 English religious reformer John WYCLIFFE (1330–84) translates the Bible into English	1380
		c.1380 English poet Geoffrey CHAUCER (1346–1400) begins writing the first of his *Canterbury Tales.*	
	1385 Heidelberg university is established.	**1386** Construction of Milan cathedral begins.	1384

▶ **Ming dynasty** *During the early years of the Ming dynasty, China experienced a period of great artistic distinction. The street scene, shown right, dates from this period and provides an insight into the way of life in China at the time.*

		1391 Byzantine scholar Manuel Chrysolarus arrives in Italy and begins popularizing the Classical Greek philosophers.	1388
	1392 Movable metal type is first used for printing in Korea.		1392

"This world nis but a thurghfare ful of wo, / And we ben pilgrimes, passinge to and fro; / Dethe is an ende of every worldly sore."

Chaucer (*Canterbury Tales*)

		1396 Italian humanist philosopher Coluccio Salutati (1331–1406) publishes his *On destiny and fortune.*	1396
		1397 Chinese law code *Laws of the Great Ming* is published.	
		c.1399 Greek artist Theophanes (c.1330–1405) paints the icon *The Deeds of the Archangel Michael* for the Kremlin cathedral in Moscow.	
			1399

ASIA AND AUSTRALASIA

1400 TAMERLANE (Timur, 1336–1405) invades and conquers Syria.

1402 Tamerlane defeats the OTTOMAN Turks at the battle of Ankara; collapse of the Ottoman Empire in Asia.

1403 Islamic warlord establishes the city of Malacca in Malaya.

1404–07 Chinese admiral CHENG HO (1371–1433) subdues Sumatra.

1405 Tamerlane dies and his empire collapses; a Timurid dynasty continues to rule in Persia and Turkistan.

1408–11 Cheng Ho defeats the Ceylonese.

1409 Chinese invade Vietnam.

1413 Sultan Muhammad I (1389–1421) re-establishes Ottoman control over Asia Minor.

1416–19 Chinese fleet sails to Yemen.

1418 Vietnamese leader Le Loi organizes resistance against the Chinese.

1419 Sejong (1397–1450) becomes king of Korea.

AFRICA

▲ **Wycliffe** rejected the doctrine of transubstantiation and attacked the formation and hierarchical system of the Roman Catholic Church. His followers, the Lollards, helped to pave the way for the Reformation.

1415 Portuguese under king JOHN I (1357–1433) capture the town of Ceuta on the Mediterranean coast of Morocco.

1416 Portuguese explorers reach Cape Bojador on the w coast of Africa.

EUROPE

1400 Welsh led by Owain GLYN DWR (Owen Glendower, c.1359–1416) rebel against English rule.

1404 Territory of the Teutonic Knights reaches its greatest extent after acquisition of Brandenburg.

1405 Venetians attack and occupy the city of Padua in NE Italy, initiating their conquest of the *Terrafirma*.

1406 Italian city of Florence gains access to the sea through control of neighboring Pisa.

1408 Khanate of the Golden Horde unsuccessfully besieges Moscow, but re-establishes its overlordship

1410 Polish-Lithuanian armies defeat the Teutonic Knights at the battle of Tannenberg.

1413 HENRY V (1387–1422) becomes king of England and renews claims against France.

1414 Attempted rising by Lollards (followers of the religious reformer John WYCLIFFE) in England is suppressed.

1415 Czech religious reformer Jan Hus (b.1369) is executed.

1415 Henry V of England invades France, wins the battle of Agincourt, and occupies Paris.

1416 Venetians defeat the Ottoman Turks in a sea battle.

1417 Council of Constance restores a single papacy, ending the Great Schism.

1419 Predominantly Czech supporters of Hus rise against German rule in Bohemia (the defenestration of Prague); start of the Hussite Wars.

1400
1404
1408
1412
1416
1419

THE AMERICAS	SCIENCE AND TECHNOLOGY	ARTS AND HUMANITIES	
***c.*1400** Start of the Middle Period of Mississippi mound-building.		**1400** French scholar Jean Froissart (*c.*1337–1410) completes his *Chronicles*, describing events in the Hundred Years War. **1402** Italian humanist Pietro Paulo Vergerio (1370–1444) writes his *Conduct worthy of free men*.	1400
		1406 Construction work starts on the Forbidden Palace in Beijing.	1404
	1410 Flagship of the Chinese admiral Cheng Ho is 130m (426ft) long and has five masts and 12 decks; it is the biggest wooden sailing ship ever built.	**1410** French artists the LIMBOURG brothers produce the illustrated *Les tres riches heures du Duc de Berry*.	1408
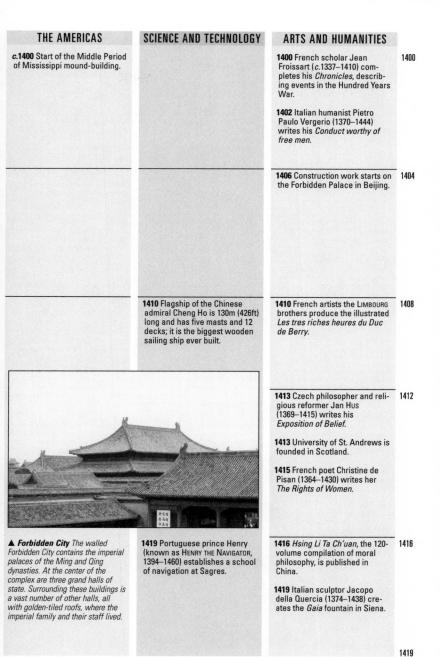		**1413** Czech philosopher and religious reformer Jan HUS (1369–1415) writes his *Exposition of Belief*. **1413** University of St. Andrews is founded in Scotland. **1415** French poet Christine de Pisan (1364–1430) writes her *The Rights of Women*.	1412
▲ *Forbidden City* The walled Forbidden City contains the imperial palaces of the Ming and Qing dynasties. At the center of the complex are three grand halls of state. Surrounding these buildings is a vast number of other halls, all with golden-tiled roofs, where the imperial family and their staff lived.	**1419** Portuguese prince Henry (known as HENRY THE NAVIGATOR, 1394–1460) establishes a school of navigation at Sagres.	**1416** *Hsing Li Ta Ch'uan*, the 120-volume compilation of moral philosophy, is published in China. **1419** Italian sculptor Jacopo della Quercia (1374–1438) creates the *Gaia* fountain in Siena.	1416
			1419

ASIA AND AUSTRALASIA	AFRICA	EUROPE

1420

1420 Beijing replaces Nanking as the the capital of China.

*c.***1420** Coffee, introduced from Ethiopia via Yemen, is domesticated near Mecca, Arabia.

1420 Portuguese occupy the island of Madeira.

1421 Ships from MING China establish direct contact with the Islamic towns of E Africa.

1420–22 Supporters of Jan Hus (1369–1415) in Bohemia defeat a Crusade against them led by SIGISMUND (1368–1437) of Hungary.

1424

1424 Chinese ships again visit E Africa.

1425 Portuguese fail to conquer the Canary Islands from Castile.

1425 Cities of Florence and Venice ally against Milan.

1427 War breaks out between Denmark and the Hanseatic League.

1427 Venetians conquer the city of Bergamo in NE Italy, and complete their *Terrafirma*.

1428

1429 City of Bidur becomes the capital of the much-reduced DELHI SULTANATE.

1428 Le Loi declares himself ruler of Annam (N Vietnam).

1431 Annam wins independence from China.

1430 Portuguese discover the Azores.

1429 JOAN OF ARC (1412–31) leads French forces to relieve the English siege of Orléans, and escorts CHARLES VII (1403–61) of France to his coronation at Reims.

1429 Florence attacks the nearby city of Lucca.

1430 OTTOMAN Turks capture the city of Thessaloníki from the Venetians.

1431 Joan of Arc is executed by the English.

1432

1433 Chinese emperor Xuan-zong prohibits any further long-distance sea voyages.

▼ *Joan of Arc, dressed as a man. led the French troops to break the long English siege of Orléans. She drove the English from the town and defeated them at Patay. In early 1430 she was captured by the*

1436

Burgundians and handed over to the English. She was burned at the stake for witchcraft and heresy.

1433 Chinese ships make a final visit to E Africa.

1433 Desert nomads capture the city of Timbuktu in the SW Sahara desert.

1434 Zara Yaqob (d.1468) becomes king of Ethiopia.

1437 Portuguese make a disastrous attempt to capture Tangier, Morocco.

1433 Hungarian king Sigismund, also king of Germany and Bohemia, becomes Holy Roman emperor.

1434 Defeat by the Holy Roman emperor at the battle of Lipany leads to civil war between moderate and radical Hussites; it ends in the defeat of the radicals.

1434 Cosimo de' MEDICI (1389–1464) becomes the effective ruler of Florence.

1435 Spanish ruler of Sicily, Alfonso V, unites his kingdom with that of Naples.

1436 French recapture Paris from the English.

1438 Albert of HAPSBURG (1397–1439) becomes German emperor and king of Hungary and Bohemia as ALBERT II.

1439

THE AMERICAS

SCIENCE AND TECHNOLOGY

ARTS AND HUMANITIES

1420 Italian architect Filippo BRUNELLESCHI (1377–1446) begins designing the dome of Florence cathedral.

1423 Italian artist GENTILE DA FABRIANO (c.1370–1427) paints his *Adoration of the Magi*.

1426 Itzcoatl (d.1440) becomes AZTEC king and begins a policy of military expansion.

1424 Persian mathematician al-Kashi (d.1429) publishes a value for pi (π) that is correct to 16 decimal places.

1424 French poet Alain Chartier (1385–1440) writes his *La Belle Dame Sans Merci*, an attack on courtly love.

1425 Italian sculptor Lorenzo GHIBERTI (1378–1455) begins work on the bronze N doors of the Baptistry in Florence.

1426 Italian artist MASACCIO (1401–28) paints his polyptych panels for the Carmelite Church, Pisa.

▲ **coffee** *It is thought that coffee originated in Ethiopia and reached Arabia soon after. Before its use as a beverage, it was a medicine. The Arabian coffee plant* (Coffea arabia) *shown here is the most common kind. The white blossoms are followed by berries, which ripen to a deep red and are then ready for picking.*

c.1430 Hussite leader Jan Zizka (c.1376–1424) invents the cannon-equipped armored fighting vehicle.

1429 Italian humanist Guarino da Verona (1374–1460) becomes professor of Classics at Ferrara University.

1435 Italian architect Leon ALBERTI (1404–72) outlines the mathematical laws of perspective in painting in his *On painting*.

1434 Flemish artist Jan van EYCK (c.1390–1441) paints the *Arnolfini Wedding*.

1434 Italian sculptor DONATELLO (1386–1466) casts his bronze statue of *David* in Florence.

1437 While the Lord INCA is campaigning elsewhere, Cuzco is besieged by the neighboring Chanca people.

1438 Incas led by Pachacuti conquer the Chancas.

1437 Islamic astronomers in Samarkand publish the *Tables of Ulugh Beg*, named for the Mongol ruler who established their observatory.

1436 Italian artist Paolo Uccello (1397–1475) paints a frescoed portrait for the tomb of the English condottieri (mercenary) John Hawkwood (d.1394).

1439 Cosimo de' Medici founds the Florentine Academy.

1439 Byzantine scholar Gemistus Pletho (1355–1452) publishes his treatise on the differences between the Platonic and Aristotelian philosophies.

ASIA AND AUSTRALASIA	AFRICA	EUROPE

1440

> "Of the two lights of Christendom, one has been extinguished."
>
> Aeneas Silvius, Bishop of Trieste, on hearing of the fall of Constantinople to the Turks

1444

1448

1452

1456

1459

AFRICA

*c.***1440** Walled enclosure and tower are built at Great Zimbabwe, capital of the Mwenemutapa kingdom.

1445 Portuguese explorers reach Cape Verde on the w coast of Africa.

1448 Portuguese establish a settlement on Arguim Island off the coast of Mauritania.

1455 Portuguese explorers discover the Cape Verde islands.

EUROPE

1440 Alliance between Florence and Venice defeats Milan at the battle of Anghiari.

1444 OTTOMAN sultan Murad II (1403–51) defeats a Christian army at the battle of Varna in Bulgaria.

1445 African slaves are auctioned for the first time in Portugal.

1449 Milan defeats Venice and conquers the Lombardy region of N Italy.

1449 French invade the English territory in w France.

1450 Denmark and Norway are united under Danish king CHRISTIAN I (1426–81).

1450 Sforza family gains control of Milan

1452 FREDERICK III (1415–93) becomes the first HAPSBURG Holy Roman emperor.

1453 Ottoman Turks besiege and capture Constantinople, which is henceforth known as Istanbul.

1453 French victory over the English at the battle of Castillon near Bordeaux marks the end of the Hundred Years War.

1454 Peace of Lodi brings to an end the wars in Italy between Milan, Venice and Florence.

1455 Wars of the Roses break out in England between the rival dynasties of LANCASTER and YORK.

1456 Turks capture Athens.

1457 Poland captures Marienberg from the Teutonic Knights who move their capital to Königsberg.

1459 Turks conquer Serbia.

ASIA AND AUSTRALASIA

1448 Trailok (r.1448–88) becomes king of Thailand.

1449 Chinese emperor is captured by a MONGOL raiding party.

▼ *Great Zimbabwe* *The walled enclosure was built mainly in the 14th and 15th centuries on a site used for ritual purposes since* c.*1000. The Mwenemutapa kingdom, of which Great Zimbabwe was the capital, traded gold with Arabs on the E African coast.*

THE AMERICAS

1440 Montezuma I (r.1440–69) becomes the Aztec king.

1441 Aztecs conquer Mayapan.

1450 Incas under Pachacuti conquer the Lake Titicaca region.

SCIENCE AND TECHNOLOGY

1443 Phonetic alphabet is developed in Korea.

*c.***1445** German goldsmith Johann Gutenberg (1400–68) develops movable metal type for printing.

1449 Italian artist and inventor Mariano di Jacopo Taccola (1381–1453) completes his 10 books of civil and military machines.

1453 Hungarian armorers cast a 7.3m (26ft), 50-ton cannon to be used by the Ottoman Turks in the siege of Constantinople.

1455 Construction of the Grand Bazaar begins in Istanbul.

ARTS AND HUMANITIES

c.1440 Italian artist Pisanello (c.1395–1455) turns the making of bronze portrait medals into an art form.

1444 Italian architect Michelozzi di Bartolommeo (1396–1472) designs the Medici Palace in Florence.

1445 Italian sculptor Bernado Rossellino (1409–64) carves a marble tomb in Florence for the humanist Leonardo Bruni.

1446 Flemish artist Rogier van der Weyden (1400–64) paints his *The Last Judgment.*

1449–52 *Gideon Tapestries* are woven in Tournais, present-day Belgium, for Philip the Good (1396–1467), Duke of Burgundy.

1452 Italian artist Fra Filippo Lippi (1406–69) paints his frescos for Prato cathedral.

1455 *Gutenberg Bible* is printed.

1440

1444

1448

1452

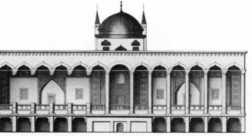

Istanbul *The Topkapi Sarayi (Old Palace) was built by Muhammad II, the conqueror (1453) of Constantinople, on the site of the old Acropolis. One of the earliest Ottoman buildings in the new capital, it was the sultan's official residence and also housed the harem. It was conceived on a grand scale.*

1456 German astronomer Johannes Regiomontanus (1436–76) introduces the mathematical symbols for plus and minus in an unpublished manuscript.

1456 French poet François Villon (1430–63) completes his *Le petit testament.*

1457 Italian artist Antonio Pollaiuolo (1432–98) completes a silver reliquary of St. Giovanni in Florence.

1456

1459

ASIA AND AUSTRALASIA	AFRICA	EUROPE
1460		
1461 Trebizond, the last remnant of the BYZANTINE EMPIRE, is conquered by the OTTOMANS.	**1463** Portuguese capture Casablanca in Morocco.	**1462** IVAN III (1440–1505) becomes the first ruler of Moscow not to pay tribute to the Golden Horde; end of the "Tartar Yoke".
1464		
1467 Onin War starts in Japan between rival feudal warlords.	**1464** King of SONGHAI, Sunni Ali (d.1492), begins campaigns to overthrow Mali; start of Songhai empire.	**1466** Teutonic Knights accept Polish overlordship.
1468		
1469 Last Timurid ruler of Persia is overthrown by Uzun Huzan (c.1420–78), leader of the White Sheep Turkmens.

1471 Annam (N Vietnam) conquers Champa (S Vietnam). | **1468** Songhai empire conquers Timbuktu.

1469 Portuguese explorers cross the equator.

1471 Portuguese establish a trading post at El Mina on the coast of present-day Ghana.

1471 Portuguese capture the city of Tangier on the N coast of Morocco. | **1468** CHARLES THE BOLD (1433–77), duke of Burgundy (NE France, Belgium and Holland), allies with England against the French.

1469 Lorenzo "il Magnifico" MEDICI (1449–92) becomes ruler of Florence.

1470 LOUIS XI (1423–83) of France allies with the Swiss against Burgundy.

1471 Right to feud is formally abolished in Germany in an attempt to stem rising lawlessness. |
1472		
		1475 Ottoman Turks conquer the Crimean peninsula on the N coast of the Black Sea
1476		
1477 At the end of the Onin War in Japan, power lies in the hands of new *daimyo* (territorial rulers).

1479 Vietnam conquers the kingdom of Laos. | **1478** Portuguese ships defeat a fleet sent from Spain and establish supremacy along the W African coast. | **1477** Inquisition is revived in Spain.

1477 Charles the Bold is killed at the battle of Nancy. France occupies parts of Burgundy; the Low Countries come under HAPSBURG control by marriage.

1478 Albania is conquered by the Ottomans.

1479 Hapsburg heir, MAXIMILIAN (1459–1519), defeats French attempts to gain control of the Low Countries.

1479 FERDINAND V (1452–1516) becomes Spanish king, uniting Castile and Aragón. |
| **1479** | | |

THE AMERICAS	SCIENCE AND TECHNOLOGY	ARTS AND HUMANITIES	
*c.*1460 Manchancaman becomes CHIMÚ king and attacks the INCAS.	*c.*1460 Italian glassmaker Anzolo Barovier perfects the technique of making completely colorless glass by adding manganese.		1460
1463 Pachacutec becomes the Inca king.	1462 Pope declares his monopoly over the supply of alum (used in the dyeing industry) to Europe.		
		1465 Italian artist Andrea del Verrocchio (1435–88) starts work on his bronze statues of *Christ and St. Thomas* in Florence.	1464
1470 Incas defeat and annex the Chimú kingdom.	1469 PLINY THE ELDER's *Natural History* is printed for the first time.	1469 Birth of NANAK (d.1539) the Indian philosopher and founder of Sikhism.	1468
1471 Tupac Yupanqui becomes the Inca king.		1470 Italian artist PIERO DELLA FRANCESCA (1415–92) paints portraits of the Duke and Duchess of Urbino.	
	1474 Government of Venice issues the world's first patents to protect inventors' rights.	*c.*1472 Italian artist Giovanni BELLINI (*c.*1430–1516) paints his Pesaro altarpiece in Venice.	1472
	*c.*1475 Italian astronomer and mathematician Paolo Toscanelli (1397–1482) proposes voyaging to China by sailing w across the Atlantic ocean.		
		*c.*1478 Italian artist Sandro BOTTICELLI (1444–1510) paints his *Primavera*.	1476

◄ *Renaissance* Prominent figures in the Florentine Renaissance often worked in a variety of cultural and political fields. Illustrated here are, from left to right: Macchiavelli, statesman and political theorist; Leonardo da Vinci, painter, sculptor, architect, engineer and scientist; Verrocchio, sculptor and painter; and Michelangelo, sculptor, painter, architect and poet.

1479

ASIA AND AUSTRALASIA	AFRICA	EUROPE

1480

1480 Under the treaty of Toledo, Portugal gets exclusive trading rights in Africa in return for agreeing to Spanish control of the Canary Islands.

1482 Portuguese build the fort of São Jorge to protect El Mina in Ghana.

1483 Tomás TORQUEMADA (1420–98) becomes head of the Spanish Inquisition.

1484 **1487** Portuguese explorers sailing from the Red Sea visit India.

1483 Portuguese explorers make contact with the w African kingdom of KONGO.

1487 Portuguese explorer Bartholomeu DIAZ (c.1450–1500) sails around the s tip of Africa into the Indian Ocean.

1485 Battle of Bosworth ends the Wars of the Roses in England. HENRY VII (1547–1509) becomes king; start of the TUDOR DYNASTY.

1486 HAPSBURG MAXIMILIAN I (1459–1519) is elected king of Germany.

1488

1489 Portuguese explorers sailing from the Red Sea visit E Africa.

1490 Nzinga Nkuwu (d.c.1506), king of Kongo, converts to Christianity.

1488 Great Swabian League of princes, knights and cities is formed in s Germany.

1492

1493 Muhammad Askia becomes emperor of SONGHAI, with the city of Gao as his capital.

1492 Spanish, under FERDINAND V (1452–1516) and ISABELLA I (1451–1504), conquer the Islamic emirate of Granada; the whole of Spain is united under Christian rule

1493 Maximilian I becomes Holy Roman emperor.

1493 OTTOMAN Turks invade Croatia.

◄ *Columbus' voyages marked the start of intensive European exploration of the Americas. On his final voyage (1502) he sailed past Hispaniola and south along the coast of Honduras. Attempting to return to Hispaniola, he was shipwrecked on Jamaica and forced to return to Spain, abandoning his travels.*

1493 By the treaty of Senlis, France cedes the rest of Burgundy to Hapsburg control.

1494–95 French under CHARLES VIII (1470–98) invade Italy, capture Florence and Naples, but are then forced to retreat.

1496 **1498** Portuguese explorer Vasco da GAMA (1469–1524) reaches the port of Calicut in India.

1496 Spanish capture the town of Melilla on the N coast of Morocco.

1498 Sailing from Portugal, Vasco da Gama calls at the E African port of Mombasa en route to India.

1497 Denmark enforces union on Sweden.

1499 French under LOUIS XII (1462–1515), allied with Venice, invade Italy, capture Milan and dispossess Ludovico SFORZA (c.1451–1508).

1499 Switzerland wins political independence from the Hapsburg empire in the Swabian War.

1499 Cesare BORGIA (1475–1507), son of Pope Alexander IV, begins the conquest of central Italy.

1499

THE AMERICAS

*c.*1490 INCAS expand their empire into parts of Bolivia and Colombia.

1492 Christopher COLUMBUS (1451–1506), a Genoese in the service of Spain, reaches an island he names San Salvador in the Bahamas. He founds the first European settlement, Navidad, on the island of Hispaniola.

1493 On his second voyage, Columbus plants the first sugar-cane cuttings in the Caribbean.

1494 Treaty of Tordesillas between Spain and Portugal grants most of the New World to Spain.

1496 Town of Santo Domingo is established on Hispaniola as the Spanish center of government in the Americas.

1497 John CABOT (*c.*1450–*c.*1498), a Genoese sailing from England, discovers the coast of Newfoundland.

1498 Columbus reaches the American mainland at the mouth of the River Orinoco.

1499 Italian explorer Amerigo VESPUCCI (1454–1512) discovers the mouth of the River Amazon.

SCIENCE AND TECHNOLOGY

1480 Italian artist and inventor LEONARDO DA VINCI (1452–1519) designs a parachute.

▲ **Hapsburgs** *The Hapsburg dynasty was the leading ruling house in Europe from the 13th to the 19th century. Maximilian I (top left) and his family are shown in this picture by Bernard Strigel. Maximilian inherited the Low Countries through his marriage to Mary of Burgundy (top right).*

1494 Italian mathematician Luca Pacioli (*c.*1445–1517) introduces algebra to Europe in his *Survey of Arithmetic, Geometry, Proportions and Proportionality.*

ARTS AND HUMANITIES

1481 Death of the French artist Jean Fouquet (b.1420), who painted miniature portraits and illustrated manuscripts.

*c.*1482 Italian architect Giuliano da Sangallo (1445–1516) designs the villa Poggio a Caiano in Florence.

1485 William CAXTON (1422–91) prints *Le Morte D'Arthur* by Sir Thomas MALORY.

1486 Italian humanist Giovanni Pico della Mirandola (1463–94) writes his *Oration on the Dignity of Man.*

1486 Italian artist Andrea MANTEGNA (1431–1506) paints his *Triumphs of Caesar* in Mantua.

1489 German inquisitors publish the *Hammer of Witchcraft.*

1489 German sculptor Viet Stoss (1440–1533) completes his carved limewood altar for the church of St. Mary's in Kraków, Poland.

1494 German humanist poet Sebastian Brandt (1458–1521) writes his *Ship of Fools.*

1495 Flemish painter Hieronymus BOSCH (*c.*1450–1516) paints his *The Garden of Earthly Delights.*

1496 Japanese artist-priest Sesshū Toyo (1420–1506) paints his *Winter Landscape.*

1498 German artist Albrecht DÜRER (1471–1528) publishes his album of woodcuts *The Apocalypse.*

1498 Ottavanio Petrucci (1466–1539) obtains a license in Venice to become the first commercial music printer.

1480

1484

1488

1492

1496

1499

ASIA AND AUSTRALASIA	AFRICA	EUROPE

1500

1501 Persian leader ISMAIL (1486–1524) defeats Turkish tribes at the battle of Shurur and gains control of Persia.

1502 Portuguese ships commanded by Vasco da GAMA (1469–1524) destroy the Indian port of Calicut.

1502 Ismail is proclaimed shah of Persia; start of the SAFAVID DYNASTY in Persia.

1501 Portuguese attempt to close the Red Sea to Islamic shipping.

1501 French invade Italy and conquer Naples.

1501 Portuguese establish a direct sea-route to import pepper and spices from India into Europe.

1504 Spain regains control of Naples.

1504

1504 Warlord Babur (1483–1530) captures Kabul, Afghanistan.

1506 Portuguese build a fort at Cochin in India.

1507 Portuguese sack the port of Muscat near the mouth of the Arabian Gulf.

1504 Christian kingdom of Soba in Nubia is conquered by Islamic forces.

1505 Portuguese under Francisco de Almeida (1450–1510) sack the Islamic ports of Kilwa and Mombasa in E Africa.

1506 Portuguese build a fort at Sofala on the E coast of Africa.

1509 French-led coalition attacks and captures Venetian-controlled towns in N Italy.

1511 HENRY VIII (1491–1547) of England joins the Holy League against France in Italy.

1512 Hanseatic League permits Dutch ships to trade in the Baltic Sea.

1508

1508 Turkish fleet destroys some Portuguese ships at the Indian port of Chaul.

1509 Portuguese destroy a combined Turkish-Indian fleet near the island of Diu.

1510 Portuguese conquer Goa and make it their capital in India.

1511 Portuguese, led by Afonso d'ALBUQUERQUE (1453–1515), capture Malacca in Malaya.

1509 Spanish capture the town of Oran on the coast of Algeria.

1510 Spanish capture the town of Tripoli in Libya.

1513 French are defeated at the battle of Novara in Italy.

1513 English destroy the Scottish army at the battle of Flodden.

1515 A marriage alliance gives the HAPSBURGS control over Spain.

1515 German emperor obtains Bohemia and Hungary from Poland in exchange for Prussia.

1515 After defeat by the French at the battle of Marignano, Switzerland adopts a policy of neutrality.

1512

1512 Portuguese reach the Spice Islands (the Moluccas).

1514 OTTOMAN Turks invade Persia and defeat the Safavids at the battle of Chaldiran.

1515 Ottoman Turks conquer Kurdistan.

1515 Portuguese capture and fortify Hormuz in Yemen.

helicopter *Leonardo da Vinci sketched this design for a rotating-wing aircraft in c.1500. The spiral wing would have lifted the machine in much the same way as the rotor of a helicopter. It is certain, however, that this machine never flew because there was no engine in existence that was capable of powering the device.*

1517 Pope LEO X (1475–1521) revives the sale of indulgences to pay for the rebuilding of St. Peter's cathedral in Rome.

1517 German priest and reformer Martin LUTHER (1483–1546) writes his 95 theses against Church corruption; start of the Reformation in Europe.

1516

1516 Ottoman Turks defeat the Egyptian MAMELUKES and the Persian Safavids at the battle of Marj Dabik in Syria.

1516 Portuguese establish a trading post at Guangzhou (Canton) in S China.

1517 Portuguese establish a trading post at Columbo in Ceylon.

1517 Ottomans under sultan SELIM I (1467–1520) conquer Egypt; end of the Mameluke dynasty.

1517 HAUSA states defeat the SONGHAI empire in W Africa.

1518 Swiss religious reformer Ulrich ZWINGLI (1484–1531) begins preaching in Zurich.

1519 CHARLES V (1500–58), Hapsburg king of Spain and Burgundy, wins election as German emperor over FRANCIS I (1494–1547) of France.

1519

THE AMERICAS

1500 Portuguese explorer Pedro CABRAL (1467–1520) lands in Brazil and establishes Vera Cruz.

1501 First African slaves are landed in the West Indies.

1502 MONTEZUMA II (r.1502–20) becomes the AZTEC king.

1507 German mapmaker Martin Waldseemüller (c.1470–c.1518) proposes that the New World be named America.

wheel lock A device for igniting the powder in a firearm, the wheel lock was invented c.1515. Sparks, produced by holding a piece of pyrite against a revolving steel wheel, are directed into the priming powder. The wheel lock is shown externally (above) and internally.

1508–15 Spanish conquer Puerto Rico and Cuba.

1509 Spanish establish a colony on the isthmus of Panama.

1512 Spanish governor of Puerto Rico, Juan PONCE DE LEÓN (1460–1521), discovers Florida.

1513 Spanish explorer Vasco Núñez de BALBOA (1475–1519) crosses the Ithsmus of Panama and discovers and names the Pacific Ocean.

1516 Bananas are introduced into the Caribbean from the Canary Islands.

1517 Spanish explorer Francisco de Córdoba discovers the Yucatán peninsula in Mexico.

1517 First asiento (agreement) for the supply of African slaves to the American colonies is issued to a Flemish merchant by the Spanish government.

1518 Spanish conquistador Hernán CORTÉS (1485–1547) lands in Mexico and conquers the Tlaxcalans.

1519 Cortés enters the Aztec capital Tenochtitlan, captures Montezuma II and establishes Spanish control.

SCIENCE AND TECHNOLOGY

1500 LEONARDO DA VINCI (1452–1519) designs an impractical, but correctly principled, helicopter.

1502 Italian mineralogist Leonardus Camillus publishes his *Speculum Lapidum*, which catalogs over 250 minerals.

c.1505 Pocket watch is invented by German clockmaker Peter Henlein (1480–1542).

c.1510 Polish astronomer and mathematician Nicolas COPERNICUS (1473–1543) formulates his theory that the Earth orbits the Sun.

c.1515 Wheel lock for igniting firearms is invented in Italy.

▲ **Copernicus**' study of planetary motions led him to develop a Suncentered theory of the Universe known as the Copernican system.

ARTS AND HUMANITIES

1502 Italian architect Donato BRAMANTE (1444–1514) reintroduces the Doric order in his tempietto at San Pietro in Montorio, Rome.

1503 Leonardo da Vinci paints the *Mona Lisa*.

1504 Italian artist MICHELANGELO BUONAROTTI (1475–1564) carves his marble sculpture of *David* in Florence.

c.1504 Flemish composer JOSQUIN DESPREZ (1445–1521) writes the mass *Hercules Dux Ferrariae*.

c.1505 Italian artist GIORGIONE (c.1478–1510) paints his *Tempest*.

1506 Ancient Roman sculpture known as the *Laocoön* is rediscovered in Rome.

1511 Dutch humanist Desiderius ERASMUS (1466–1536) publishes his *In Praise of Folly*.

1512 Michelangelo finishes painting the ceiling of the Sistine Chapel in Rome.

1512 Italian artist Raphael Santi (1483–1520) paints a portrait of Pope Julius II.

1513 Italian politician Niccolò MACHIAVELLI (1469–1527) writes his *The Prince*.

1515 German artist Mathias Grünewald (1470–1528) paints his *The Crucifixion* for the Isenheim altarpiece, Alsace.

1516 English scholar Thomas MORE (1478–1535) publishes his *Utopia*.

1516 Italian poet Lodovico ARIOSTO (1474–1533) publishes his epic *Orlando Furioso*.

1520

1521 Ferdinand MAGELLAN (1480–1521) discovers and claims the Philippine Islands for Spain.

1521 Portuguese establish a settlement on Amboina, one of the Spice Islands.

1522 Portuguese traders are expelled from China.

1523 Afghan warlord BABUR (1483–1530) invades India and captures the city of Lahore.

"Be a sinner and strong in your sins, but be stronger in your faith and rejoice in Christ."

Martin Luther (letter to Melanchthon)

1521 At the diet of Worms, Emperor CHARLES V (1500–58) condemns Martin Luther's ideas.

1521 OTTOMAN Turks capture Belgrade and raid s central Europe.

1521–26 First war for control of Italy is fought between France and Spain.

1522 Knights of St. John surrender the island of Rhodes to the Turks after a siege.

1523 GUSTAVUS I (1496–1560) establishes the Swedish state; start of the Vasa dynasty.

1524

1526 Babur conquers the w half of the DELHI SULTANATE after the battle of Panipat and establishes the MUGHAL EMPIRE.

1526 Portuguese explorers reach New Guinea.

1527 Islamic Somalis invade Ethiopia.

▼ *Château de Chambord* Built for French king Francis I, the château was probably designed by Italian architect Domenica da Cortona.

1524–25 Violent peasant uprisings sweep across Germany.

1525 Spain defeats France at the battle of Pavia in Italy and captures FRANCIS I (1494–1547).

1526 King LOUIS II (b.1506) of Hungary is killed in the battle of Mohács against the Ottoman Turks; the Hungarian crown passes to the HAPSBURGS.

1527 During his second Italian war (1526–29), Spanish king and Hapsburg emperor Charles V sacks Rome.

1528

1529 Victory at the battle of the River Gogra completes the Mughal conquest of n India.

1529 Ottoman Turks invade and conquer Algeria.

1528 Genoese admiral Andrea Doria (1466–1560) frees Genoa from French rule.

1532

1534 Ottomans conquer Mesopotamia.

1535 Charles V campaigns against the Turkish pirate Khayr ad-Din (BARBAROSSA, 1466–1546) and captures the city of Tunis.

1529 Ottoman Turks unsuccessfully besiege Vienna.

1529 German emperor Charles V ends toleration of Lutheran reforms. Some German princes protest, becoming Protestants.

1536

1537 Portuguese obtain trading concessions at Macao on the coast of s China.

1538 Alliance of Ottoman Turks and Gujaratis fails to evict the Portuguese from Diu in India.

1538 Turkish naval expedition conquers the w coast of Arabia.

1539 Mughal dynasty in India is overthrown by the Afghan warlord Sher Shah (d.1545).

1531 War breaks out between Protestant and Catholic cantons in Switzerland.

1531 Hungary is partitioned between the Hapsburgs and the Ottomans.

1531 Protestant rulers in Germany form the Schmalkaldic League.

1534 Act of Supremacy is passed in England, making HENRY VIII (1491–1547) head of the English Church.

1539

THE AMERICAS

1520 MONTEZUMA II dies and the AZTECS force the Spanish from Tenochtitlan.

***c*.1520** INCA king Huayna Capac conquers parts of Ecuador.

1521 Spanish attack and destroy Tenochtitlan.

1522 Viceroyalty of New Spain is created and Mexico City is founded on the ruins of Tenochtitlan.

1521 Sailing in the pay of Spain, the Portuguese navigator Ferdinand Magellan sails around Cape Horn at the S tip of South America.

1522 Spanish expedition from Panama reaches Peru.

1525 Death of Inca king Huayna Capac leads to dispute over throne between sons Huáscar(d.1532) and ATAHUALPA (1502–33).

1529 Welser family (German bankers) establish a colony in Venezuela.

1530 Portuguese begin the colonization of Brazil.

1531 Inca king Atahualpa invites Spanish soldiers, led by Francisco PIZARRO (1471–1541), to join his side in the Inca civil war.

1532 Pizarro captures Atahualpa and holds him to ransom.

1533 Atahualpa is killed by the Spanish, who occupy Cuzco and conquer the Inca empire.

1535 Pizarro founds the city of Lima in Peru.

1537 Spanish establish colonies at Buenos Aires, at the mouth of the River Plate, and Asunción, on the River Paraguay.

1538 Spanish conquistador Gonzalo de Quesada founds the city of Bogotá.

1539 Spanish begin the conquest of the MAYAN cities in the Yucatán region of Mexico.

SCIENCE AND TECHNOLOGY

***c*.1520** Rifling for firearms is invented in central Europe.

1522 Spanish ships returning from Ferdinand Magellan's voyage complete the first circumnavigation of the world.

1525 German mathematician Christoff Rudolff introduces the square root symbol in his *Die Coss.*

▲ *Pizarro* arrived in the New World in 1502. Of modest origins, he became a prosperous landowner in Panama City before receiving a commission from the Crown for the conquest of Peru.

1533 German surveyor Gemma Frisius (1508–55) discovers the principles of triangulation.

1537 Italian mathematician Niccoló TARTAGLIA (1449–1557) discusses the trajectory of projectiles in his *New Science.*

ARTS AND HUMANITIES

1520 German Christian reformer Martin LUTHER (1483–1546) writes his *The Freedom of a Christian Man,* which proclaims salvation through faith.

1524 German artist Lucas Cranach (1472–1553) paints his *Judgment of Paris.*

1525 Luther writes his *Against the Murderous Thieving Hordes of Peasants.*

1525 English religious reformer William TYNDALE (*c*.1494–1536) starts printing English versions of the New Testament in Cologne, Germany.

1528 Italian courtier Baldassare Castiglione (1478–1529) publishes his *Book of the Courtier.*

***c*.1528** German artist Albrecht Altdorfer (1480–1538) paints unpopulated landscapes.

1530 German religious reformer Philip MELANCHTHON (1497–1560) writes the *Confessions of Augsburg,* a statement of Protestant beliefs.

1530 Italian artist CORREGGIO (*c*.1490–1534) paints his *Adoration of the Shepherds.*

1533 German artist Hans HOLBEIN the Younger (1497–1543) paints his *The Ambassadors.*

1534 Luther completes his translation of the Bible into German.

1534 French humanist François RABELAIS (1494–1553) writes his satire *Gargantua.*

1534 Society of Jesus (Jesuits) is founded by IGNATIUS LOYOLA (1491–1556) and FRANCIS XAVIER (1506–52).

***c*.1535** Italian artist PARMIGIANO (1503–40) paints his *Madonna with the Long Neck.*

1538 Italian artist TITIAN (1485–1576) paints his *Venus of Urbino.*

1520

1524

1528

1532

1536

1539

ASIA AND AUSTRALASIA

1540

1543 Portuguese first make contact with Japan.

1544

1546 With Portuguese assistance, Tabin Shwehti (r.1531–50) makes himself king of Burma.

▶ *theodolite Dating from the 16th century, theodolites are surveying instruments used to measure horizontal and vertical angles. The 16th-century instrument shown here was designed by the German cartographer Martin Waldseemüller.*

1548

1552

1555 Burmese invade N Thailand.

1555 Peace treaty is signed between the Ottoman Turks and SAFAVID Persia.

1556

1556 Emperor AKBAR I (1542–1605) restores Mughal rule in India and defeats Hindu forces at the second battle of Panipat.

1557 Portuguese establish a colony at Macao in China.

AFRICA

1541 Expedition of CHARLES V (1500–58) against the OTTOMAN Turks at Algiers fails.

1543 Ethiopian forces, assisted by Portuguese troops, expel Islamic invaders.

▼ *Palladio The Villa Rotunda was begun c.1550 in Vicenza. Designed by Italian architect Palladio, it is exceptional among villas for its perfect symmetry, designed to take advantage of the view from the hilltop site.*

EUROPE

1541 French religious reformer John CALVIN (1509–64) establishes religious rule in Geneva.

1541 Ottoman Turks capture Budapest and conquer Hungary.

1545 Council of Trent meets to reform the Catholic Church.

1546–47 Charles V defeats the Protestants in the Schmalkaldic War in S and central Germany.

1547 Protestant reformer John KNOX (1514–72) is arrested by French soldiers in Scotland.

1547 IVAN IV (1530–84) of Moscow is crowned first czar of Russia.

1552 Emperor Charles V invades E France.

1553 Following the death of HENRY VIII in 1547, and his only son, EDWARD VI, in 1553, his daughter Mary (1516–58) becomes queen as MARY I. She marries the future PHILIP II (1527–98) of Spain and restores Catholic worship in England; Protestants are persecuted.

1555 Religious peace of Augsburg establishes freedom of worship in Germany.

1556 Charles V abdicates; his empire is split between FERDINAND I (Austria and Germany) and Philip II (Spain, Low Countries, parts of Italy, and America).

1557 Russia invades Livonia, the former territory of the Teutonic Knights.

1558 English, allied to Spain, lose the port of Calais to the French.

1558 Ivan IV orders the colonization of Siberia.

1558 ELIZABETH I (1533–1603) becomes queen of England

1559 Philip II of Spain defeats France; the Peace of Château-Cambrésis restores Naples and the Low Countries to Spanish control.

1559

THE AMERICAS

1540–42 Spanish expedition led by Francisco de CORONADO (1510–54) discovers the Grand Canyon.

1541 Spanish explorer Hernando DE SOTO (1500–42) discovers the River Mississippi.

1541 Spanish explorer Francisco de Orellana (*c*.1490–*c*.1546) completes his journey down the River Amazon from the Andes to the Atlantic Ocean.

1541 French explorer Jacques CARTIER (1491–1557) makes an unsuccessful attempt to establish a colony at Quebec in Canada.

1541 Spanish found the city of Santiago in Chile.

1542 Spanish create the Viceroyalty of Peru.

1545 Spanish begin mining silver at Potosi in Peru.

1546 Revolt by the MAYA against Spanish rule in Mexico is crushed.

1548 Spanish open silver mines at Zaatecar in Mexico.

1548 Spanish Viceroyalty of New Galicia is created in NW Mexico with Guadalajara as its capital.

1549 The Spanish Viceroyalty of New Granada is created, comprising South America E of the Andes and N of the River Amazon.

1549 Portuguese establish the port of Bahia in Brazil.

1554 Portuguese establish the city of São Paulo in Brazil.

1555 Dutch, English and French sailors form the Guild of Merchant Adventurers to raid Spanish shipping routes from America.

1555 French establish a colony at the bay of Rio de Janeiro on the coast of Brazil.

SCIENCE AND TECHNOLOGY

1540 Italian gunsmith Vannoccio Biringuccio's *Concerning Pyrotechnics*, a handbook of metal smelting and casting techniques, is published.

1542 French scholar Konrad Gesner (1516–65) publishes his *Historia Plantarum*, the first modern work of botany.

1543 Polish astronomer and mathematician Nicolas COPERNICUS' (1473–1543) heliocentric theory is published in his *On the Revolutions of the Celestial Spheres*.

1543 Belgian doctor Andreas VESALIUS (1514–64) publishes his *On the Structure of the Human Body*, an illustrated handbook of human anatomy based on dissection.

1545 Italian scientist Giramolo Cardano (1501–76) introduces negative numbers to European mathematics in his book *The Great Art*.

1551 English mathematician Leonard Digges (*c*.1520–59) invents the theodolite.

1551 German mathematician Georg Rhaeticus (1514–74) publishes the six basic trigonometrical functions in his *Canon doctrinae triangulorum*.

1556 German mineralogist Georg Bauer (1494–1555), also known as Agricola, publishes his *De re metallica*, a systematic study of mining and assaying techniques.

1557 English mathematician Robert Recorde (*c*.1510–58) introduces the symbol for equality in his algebra textbook *The Whetstone of Whit*.

ARTS AND HUMANITIES

1540 Holy Carpet of Ardebil, with an area of 61sq m (72sq yd), is woven in N Persia.

1541 Spanish priest and protector of Native Americans Bartolomé de LAS CASAS (1474–1566) writes his *Very Brief Account of the Destruction of the Indies*.

1541 Death of the Swiss doctor known as PARACELSUS (b.1493).

1545 Indian architect Aliwal Khan designs the octagonal tomb of the Afghan warlord Sher Shah at Sasaram, India.

1545 Italian goldsmith and sculptor Benvenuto CELLINI (1500–71) casts his bronze statue of *Perseus* in Florence.

1548 Italian artist TINTORETTO (1518–94) paints his *The Miracle of the Slave* in Venice.

1549 French poet Joachim du Bellay (1522–60) writes his *Defense and Illustration of the French Language*.

1549 English priest Thomas CRANMER (1489–1556) publishes his *Book of Common Prayer*.

1555 Italian architect Andrea PALLADIO (1508–80) publishes a guidebook to Roman antiquities.

1559 *Index of Forbidden Books* is published by the Roman Catholic Church.

ASIA AND AUSTRALASIA	AFRICA	EUROPE
1560		
1561 Mughals under AKBAR (1542–1605) conquer Malwa in central India.	**1561** Portuguese expedition up the River Zambezi makes contact with the kingdom of Mwenemutapa.	**1560** Scottish parliament establishes Presbyterianism as the state religion.
1563 Chinese destroy Japanese pirates who have been raiding coastal cities.		**1560** CHARLES IX (1550–74) becomes boy-king of France with his mother Catherine de MEDICI (1519–89) as regent.
		1562 Massacre of Huguenots (French Protestants) at Vassy in France starts a series of religious civil wars.
		1563 Start of the Catholic Counter Reformation in s Germany.
1564		
1565 Mughals conquer the Hindu kingdom of Vijayanagar in s India after the battle of Talikota.		**1564** Boyars (Russian aristocrats) revolt against IVAN IV (1530–84).
		1566 Dutch nobles form an anti-Spanish alliance.
		1567 Duke of Alba enforces Spanish control in the Low Countries.
1568		
1568 Oda Nobunaga (1534–82) seizes power in central Japan; start of the Azuchi-Momoyama period.	**1571** Idris III (d.1603) becomes king of Kanem and establishes control of the Lake Chad region.	**1569** Poland and Lithuania unite under Polish control.
1570 Port of Nagasaki in Japan is opened to foreign traders.	**1571–73** Portuguese make a disastrous attempt to conquer Mwenemutapa.	**1569–71** Revolt by former Muslims is crushed in Spain.
1571 Spanish found the city of Manila in the Philippines.		**1570** Novgorod is destroyed by armies from Moscow.
		1570 Turks attack Cyprus.
		1571 Stock Exchange is established in London, England.
		1571 Venetian and Spanish fleets defeat the Ottoman Turks at the Mediterranean sea battle of Lepanto.
1572		
1573 Mughals under Akbar conquer Gujarat in w India.	**1572** Spanish capture Tunis from the Ottoman Turks.	**1572** Thousands of Huguenots (French Protestants) are massacred on St. Bartholomew's Day.
	1574 Portuguese found the city of Luanda in Angola.	**1573** Venetians abandon Cyprus to the Turks.
	1574 Ottoman Turks recapture Tunis.	**1574** Dutch under WILLIAM I (THE SILENT), Prince of Orange, open dykes to relieve the Spanish siege of Leyden.
1576		
1576 Mughals conquer Bengal in E India.	**1578** Portuguese attempt to conquer the interior of Morocco is defeated at the battle of Alcázar-Kabir.	**1576** Following the Spanish sack of Antwerp, the Dutch provinces unite under William I (the Silent).
		1579 Dutch republic is formed; Belgium remains under Spanish control.
1579		

THE AMERICAS

1561 Following the failure of a settlement at Pensacola, South Carolina, present-day USA, the Spanish king abandons attempts to colonize the E coast of North America.

1561 Spanish treasure fleets are forced to adopt a convoy system as a defense against "pirate" attacks.

1564 French establish a colony at Fort Caroline in Florida, present-day USA.

1565 Spanish destroy Fort Caroline and found the town of St. Augustine in Florida.

1567 Portuguese destroy the French colony in Brazil and found the city of Rio de Janeiro.

1568 Spanish destroy the fleet of the English slave-trader John HAWKINS (1532–95) at Vera Cruz.

1578 English explorer Francis DRAKE (1540–96) sails along the W coast of present-day USA and lays claim to California.

SCIENCE AND TECHNOLOGY

▲ **Brahe** could not accept the Sun-centered world system put forward by Copernicus. In Brahe's planetary theory, the planets move around the Sun, and the Sun, like the Moon, moves round the stationary Earth.

1569 Flanders mapmaker Gerardus MERCATOR (1512–94) publishes a world navigation chart that has meridians and parallels at right-angles

1572 Italian mathematician Raffaele Bombelli (1526–72) introduces imaginary numbers in his *Algebra*.

1576 Danish astronomer Tycho BRAHE (1546–1601) builds a royal observatory for King Frederick II (1534–88).

ARTS AND HUMANITIES

1562 Italian artist Paolo VERONESE (1528–88) paints his *The marriage of Cana*.

1563 Dutch artist Pieter BRUEGEL the Elder (1525–69) paints his *The Tower of Babel*.

1563 English historian John FOXE (1516–87) publishes the book known as *Foxe's Book of Protestant Martyrs*.

1563 Building work starts on the monastery and palace of Escorial near Madrid, Spain, designed by Juan de Herrera (c.1530–97).

1568 Italian art critic Giorgio VASARI (1511–74) publishes a revised edition of his *Lives of the most excellent Painters, Sculptors and Architects*.

◀ **Golden Hind** In 1577–80 Francis Drake circumnavigated the world, the first Englishman to do so. Sailing in the Golden Hind, Drake looted Spanish ships and settlements in the Pacific, claimed California for England, and then

1572 Portuguese poet Luíz vaz de CAMÕES (1524–80) publishes his epic *The Lusiads*.

1575 Italian architect Giacomo della Porta (1537–1602) designs the church of Il Gesù in Rome; this marks the beginning of the baroque period of European art.

1576 French political philosopher Jean BODIN (1530–96) publishes his *Of the Republic*.

1580

1581 Cossack chieftain Yermak Timofeyevich (d.1584) begins the Russian conquest of Siberia.

1581 AKBAR I (1542–1605) conquers Afghanistan.

1581 Turkish ships sack the Portuguese fortress at Muscat.

1583 Mughal emperor Akbar I proclaims toleration of all religions in India.

1584

1584 General Toyotomi Hideoshi (1536–98) establishes himself as ruler of central Japan.

1586 ABBAS I (1571–1629) becomes shah of SAFAVID Persia.

1588

1590 Ottoman Turks wrest control of Georgia and Azerbaijan from Persia.

1590 Hideoshi conquers E and N Japan, reuniting the country under his rule.

1592

1592 Akbar conquers S Pakistan.

1592 Japanese invade Korea, but are forced out by the Chinese.

1596

1597 Japanese again invade Korea, then withdraw.

1597 Persians defeat the nomadic Uzbeks and expel them from W Afghanistan.

1598 TOKUGAWA IEYASU (1543–1616) seizes power in Japan on the death of Hideoshi.

1599

1581 Morocco begins expanding S into the W Sahara and captures the town of Tuat.

▲ *Pope Gregory XIII* promoted church reform and sought to carry out the decrees of the Council of Trent. He is best known for his reform of the Julian calendar, in which he refined the system of leap years to increase its accuracy.

1589 Portuguese defeat the Ottoman Turks at Mombasa, E Africa.

1591 Invading Moroccans crush SONGHAI forces at the battle of Tondibi and destroy the city of Gao; end of the Songhai empire.

1595 Dutch establish a trading post in Guinea on the W coast of Africa.

1598 Dutch establish a small colony on the island of Mauritius.

1580 King PHILIP II (1527–98) of Spain succeeds to the throne of Portugal and the two countries are united under HAPSBURG rule.

1581 Spain agrees a peace treaty with the OTTOMAN Turks.

1584 Dutch leader WILLIAM I of Orange (b.1533) is murdered and is succeeded by Maurice of Nassau (1567–1625).

1585 Queen ELIZABETH I (1533–1603) of England refuses the Dutch throne but takes the Netherlands under her protection by the treaty of Nonsuch.

1585–89 War of the Three Henrys is fought for the French throne.

1588 Spanish invasion fleet (the Armada) sent against England is defeated at the naval battle of Gravelines.

1589 Russian Church becomes independent of the Greek Orthodox Church.

1589 Victorious HENRY III (b.1551) of France is assassinated; HENRY IV (1553–1610) accedes to the throne; start of the BOURBON DYNASTY.

1593 War breaks out in Transylvania between Austria and the Ottoman Turks.

1595 After intervening in the Livonian wars, Sweden acquires Estonia by the treaty of Teusina.

1598 Boris GODUNOV (1551–1605) becomes czar of Russia.

1598 Edict of Nantes grants limited freedom of worship and legal equality for Huguenots (Protestants) in France.

THE AMERICAS	SCIENCE AND TECHNOLOGY	ARTS AND HUMANITIES

SCIENCE AND TECHNOLOGY

1582 Pope Gregory XIII (1502–85) introduces the New Style (Gregorian) calendar to Catholic countries.

1583 Danish mathematician Thomas Finke (1561–1656) publishes the law of tangents in his *Geometriae rotundi*.

ARTS AND HUMANITIES

1580 French scholar and author Michel Montaigne (1533–92) publishes the first of his *Essays*.

1580 Flemish sculptor Jean de Boulogne (1529–1608) cast his bronze statue of *Mercury*.

1582 Death of the Spanish religious philosopher TERESA OF AVILA (b.1515).

1580

THE AMERICAS

1585 Expedition organized by Walter RALEIGH (1552–1618) establishes a colony (which immediately fails) on Roanoke Island off the coast of Virginia, present-day USA.

1587 Second, unsuccessful attempt is made to found an English colony on Roanoke Island.

1586 Dutch mathematician Simon Stevin (1548–1620) demonstrates that objects fall at an equal rate in a vacuum, irrespective of their weights.

1586 Greek-born Spanish artist EL GRECO (1541–1614) paints his *Burial of Count Orgasz* in Toledo, Spain.

1584

1589 Stocking-frame knitting machine is invented by William Lee (*c*.1550–*c*.1610) in Cambridge, England.

1591 French mathematician François Viete (1540–1603) introduces literal notation to algebra, with the systematic use of letters to represent unknowns and coefficients.

1589 English poet and dramatist William SHAKESPEARE (1564–1616) writes his first play *Henry VI (part I)*.

1590 English dramatist Christopher MARLOWE (1564–93) writes his play *Tamburlaine the Great*.

1588

Globe Theater *Built in 1599 but destroyed by fire in 1613, the Globe Theater was rebuilt (1614) in the form shown above. It was a tiled and brick-built, three-story structure, surrounding an uncovered yard, where poorer patrons could stand. It was a small building, with a diameter of only 25m (83ft), but with its galleries it could hold 2000. It was closed down by the Puritans in 1642, demolished in 1644 and finally rebuilt and reopened in 1995.*

1593 German astronomer Christopher Clavius (1537–1612) invents and uses the decimal point in a table of mathematical sines.

1593 Death of doctor Li Shizen (b.1518) who compiled *The Comprehensive Pharmacopoeia* of traditional Chinese medicine.

1595 William Shakespeare writes his play *Romeo and Juliet.*

1592

1596 English poet (1552–99) Edmund SPENSER completes his *The Faerie Queen*.

1597 Italian composer Giovanni Gabrieli (c.1553–1612) writes his *Sonata Pian'e Forte*.

1598 Italian artist CARAVAGGIO (1571–1610) paints his *Supper at Emmaus*.

1599 Globe Theater is built in London.

1596

1599

1600

1600 Victory at the battle of Sekigahara leaves TOKUGAWA IEYASU (1543–1616) as sole ruler of Japan; start of the Tokugawa (or Edo) period.

1600 English East India Company is formed.

1602 Dutch East India Company is formed.

1603 Persians under Abbas I (1571–1629) capture Baghdad from the OTTOMANS.

1604

1605 Dutch seize the spice island of Amboina from the Portuguese.

1606 Turkey makes peace with Austria.

1606 Spanish explorer Luis de Torres sights the York peninsula on the N coast of Australia.

1608

1609 Dutch conquer Ceylon from the Portuguese.

1609 Dutch establish a trading mail at Hirado, W Japan.

1609 Persians defeat the Turks at the battle of Urmia and recapture Baghdad.

1610 Russian expansion E into Siberia reaches the River Yenisei.

▶ **tobacco** *Produced mainly from the plant* Nicotiana tabacum, *tobacco is cultivated worldwide. Native Americans smoked tobacco leaves for ceremonial and medicinal purposes long before the arrival of Europeans in the New World.*

1612

1612 England gains trading rights at Surat in India after defeating the Portuguese in a naval battle.

1615 Nomad tribes of Manchuria form a military coalition under their leader NURHACHI (1559–1626).

1615 Japanese ruler Ieyasu destroys Osaka castle after a siege.

1616

1619 Dutch establish the fortified port of Batavia (present-day Jakarta) on the island of Java.

1619

▲ **Galileo Galilei** *is well known for his discovery that a pendulum could be used for timekeeping. His support for the Copernican view of the Universe, with the Earth moving round the Sun, brought him into conflict with the Church.*

1612 City-state of Timbuktu becomes independent of Morocco.

1603 James VI (1566–1625) of Scotland, son of MARY, QUEEN OF SCOTS (1542–87), inherits the English throne as JAMES I on the death of ELIZABETH I (b.1533); end of the TUDOR DYNASTY, start of the STUART DYNASTY.

1604 Protestant CHARLES IX (1550–1611) becomes king of Sweden.

1605 Gunpowder Plot fails to blow up the English parliament; Guy FAWKES (b.1570) is executed the following year.

1608 Protestant Union of German rulers is formed.

1609 Catholic League of German rulers is formed.

1609 Truce ends the fighting in the Netherlands between PHILIP III (1578–1621) of Spain and the Dutch rebels.

1610 HENRY IV (b.1553) of France is assassinated; LOUIS XIII (1601–43) becomes king with his mother Marie de' MEDICI (1573–1642) as regent.

1610 Poland invades Russia and occupies Moscow in an attempt to gain control of the Russian throne.

1613 Following the expulsion of the Poles, Michael Romanov (d.1645) becomes Russian czar; start of ROMANOV DYNASTY.

1617 Under the peace of Stolbovo with Sweden, Russia loses access to the Baltic Sea.

1618 Protestant revolt in Prague (the second defenestration) begins the Bohemian War; it marks the start of the Thirty Years War.

THE AMERICAS	SCIENCE AND TECHNOLOGY	ARTS AND HUMANITIES

SCIENCE AND TECHNOLOGY

1600 English scientist William Gilbert (1544–1603) publishes his *Concerning Magnetism*, which discusses the Earth's magnetism.

1602 Italian astronomer and scientist GALILEO Galilei (1564–1642) discovers the constancy of a swinging pendulum.

1606 Belgian scholar Justus Lipsius (1547–1606) completes the final revisions and corrections to his edition of Tacitus' *Annals*.

ARTS AND HUMANITIES

1600 Italian artist Annibale Carracci (1560–1609) paints his *The Virgin mourning Christ*. `1600`

1600 William SHAKESPEARE (1564–1616) writes *Hamlet*.

1602 Italian philosopher Tommaso Campanella (1568–1639) publishes his *City of Sun*.

1604 Confucian Tung-lin Academy is founded in China. `1604`

1605 Spanish author Miguel de CERVANTES (1547–1616) publishes the first volume of *Don Quixote of the Mancha*.

1605 English dramatist Ben JONSON (1572–1637) writes his *Volpone*.

1605 English philosopher Francis BACON (1561–1626) publishes his *Advancement of Learning*.

THE AMERICAS

1606 London Company and Plymouth Company are established in England.

1607 London Company establishes a colony at Jamestown, Virginia, under the leadership of John SMITH (1580–1631).

1608 French explorer Samuel de CHAMPLAIN (1567–1635) founds Quebec as the capital of the colony of New France.

1609 English explorer Henry HUDSON (d.1611) discovers and sails up the Hudson River.

1610 Sailing in search of a Northwest Passage to the Far East, Hudson discovers Hudson Bay.

1612 English establish a settlement on the island of Bermuda.

1612 Tobacco is first cultivated by English settlers in Virginia.

1612 French establish a colony on the island of Maranhão at the mouth of the River Amazon.

1613 Dutch set up a trading post on Manhattan Island.

1608 Dutch optician Hans Lippershey (1570–1619) invents a refracting telescope.

1611 Flemish artist Peter Paul RUBENS (1577–1640) paints his *Raising of the Cross*. `1608`

1614 Expedition organized by the Plymouth Company makes an unsuccessful attempt to establish a colony in New England.

1614 Dutch New Netherland Company is established.

1616 Portuguese conquer the French colony at the mouth of the Amazon and found the city of Belém.

1614 Scottish mathematician John Napier (1550–1617) invents logarithms.

1615 Dutch mathematician Ludolp van Ceulen (1540–1610) publishes a value for pi (π) that is correct to 32 decimal places in his posthumous *Arithmetische en Geometishe fondamenten*.

1612 English poet John DONNE (1572–1631) writes his *Of the Progress of the Soul*. `1612`

c.1613 Spanish poet and dramatist Felix Lope de VEGA CARPIO (1562–1635) writes his *All Citizens are Soldiers*.

1615 *Bukeshohatto* book of warriors' wisdom is published in Japan.

1616 Dutch establish the colony of New Netherland on the site of present-day New York, USA.

1616 English explorer William BAFFIN (1584–1622) discovers Baffin Bay.

1619 First African slaves arrive in Virginia, and the first representative assembly is held.

1618 Dutch scientist Snellius (1591–1626) discovers his law of the diffraction of light.

1619 German astronomer Johannes KEPLER (1571–1630) outlines the third of his three laws of planetary motion in *Harmonies of the World*.

1619 English architect Inigo JONES (1573–1652) designs the Banqueting House in London. `1616`

`1619`

ASIA AND AUSTRALASIA	AFRICA	EUROPE

1620
1624
1628
1632
1636
1639

ASIA AND AUSTRALASIA

1620 English defeat the Portuguese at the sea battle of Jask off the w coast of India.

1622 English, allied with the Persians, capture Hormuz from the Portuguese.

1623 Dutch massacre English merchants on the island of Amboina.

1624 Spanish traders are expelled from Japan.

1624 Dutch establish a trading post on the island of Formosa.

1625 Janissaries (slave soldiers) revolt against OTTOMAN rule in Turkey.

1635–37 Manchurian confederation conquers s Mongolia and Korea.

1637 Christian-led Shimabara rebellion is suppressed in Japan.

1638 Japan is closed to foreigners.

1638 Ottoman Turks under Murad IV (1607–1640) recapture Baghdad.

1639 Treaty of Kasr-i-Shirim establishes a permanent border between Turkey and Persia.

1639 English acquire a site for a colony at Madras in India.

AFRICA

1621 Dutch capture the w African island slave ports of Arguin and Goree from the Portuguese.

1626 French establish the colony of St. Louis at the mouth of the River Senegal.

1626 French settlers and traders establish a colony on the island of Madagascar

▲ *Taj Mahal* Ranking among the world's most beautiful buildings, the Taj Mahal stands in a Persian water garden that represents Paradise. It was by far the largest Islamic tomb ever destined for a woman.

1637 Dutch capture the fortified port of El Mina from the Portuguese.

EUROPE

1620 Catholic victory at the battle of the White Mountain leads to the dissolution of the Protestant Union in Germany.

1621 Gustavus II (1594–1632) of Sweden creates the first modern army and conquers Livonia from Poland.

1621 Warfare between the Dutch and Spanish is renewed.

1625 Huguenots rebel in NW France.

1625 CHARLES I (1600–49) becomes king of England, Scotland and Ireland.

1625 CHRISTIAN IV (1577–1648) of Denmark intervenes as leader of the Protestants in Germany; start of the Danish phase of the Thirty Years War.

1628 French forces under chief minister cardinal Armand Richelieu capture the Huguenot stronghold of La Rochelle.

1629 After defeat by Catholic armies, Denmark withdraws from German politics under the peace of Lübeck.

1630 Gustavus II of Sweden lands in N Germany in support of the Protestants; start of the Swedish phase of the Thirty Years War.

1631 Swedes defeat the German Catholics at the battle of Breitenfeld and invade s Germany.

1632 Gustavus II dies following his victory at the battle of Lutzen.

1635 Catholic victory at the battle of Nordlingen forces the Swedes out of s Germany; France enters the Thirty Years War as Sweden's ally.

THE AMERICAS

1620 English Protestant settlers cross the Atlantic in the *Mayflower* and establish a colony in Massachusetts, present-day USA.

1623 English Council for New England establishes colonies at Dover and Plymouth in New Hampshire.

1624 English settlement in Virginia becomes a royal colony.

1624–25 Dutch capture and briefly hold the port of Bahía in Brazil.

1625 English settlers establish a colony on the island of Barbados.

1626 Dutch administrator Peter Minuit (1580–1638) purchases Manhattan Island and establishes the city of New Amsterdam.

1627 French minister Armand Richelieu (1585–1642) organizes the Company of 100 Associates to colonize New France.

1628 John Endicott (c.1588–1665) establishes an English colony at Salem.

1630 Dutch capture the port of Recife in Brazil from the Portuguese.

1630 Twelve-year period of intensive migration from England to Massachusetts begins.

1632 English colony of Maryland is established by George Calvert (1580–1632).

1635 French establish colonies of the islands of Martinique and Guadeloupe.

1636 Dutch capture the island of Curaçao from the Spanish.

1636 English colonist Roger Williams (1603–83) settles in Providence, Rhode Island.

1638 English colony is established at New Haven on Long Island.

1638 Swedes establish the colony of New Sweden in Delaware.

SCIENCE AND TECHNOLOGY

1628 English doctor William Harvey (1578–1657) explains the circulation of blood pumped around the body by the heart.

1631 French mathematician Pierre Vernier (1580–1637) invents an accurate measuring calliper.

1631 English scientist Thomas Harriot (c.1560–1621) introduces the symbols for "greater than" and "less than" in his posthumously published *The Analytical Arts*.

1631 English mathematician William Oughtred (1575–1660) introduces the symbol for multiplication in his *The Keys to Mathematics*.

1635 Italian mathematician Bonaventura Cavalieri (1598–1647) publishes the first textbook on integration, *Geometry of Continuous Indivisibles*

1637 French philosopher and mathematician René Descartes (1596–1650) introduces analytical geometry in his *Geometry*.

1639 French mathematician Girard Desargues (1591–1661) introduces the study of projective geometry in his *Brouillon project*.

RELIGION AND THE ARTS

1623 Death of the Indian poet Tulsi Das (b.1532), author of the Hindu classic *Tulsi-krit Ramayan*.

◄ *Harvey was one of England's most prestigious physicians, being successively physician to James I and Charles I.*

1624 Dutch artist Frans Hals (c.1580–1666) paints his *Laughing Cavalier.*

1625 Dutch lawyer Hugo Grotius (1583–1645) publishes his *On the laws of war and peace.*

1632 Dutch artist Rembrandt Harmenszoon van Rijn (1606–69) paints his *Anatomy Lesson of Dr. Tulp.*

1632 Flemish artist Anthony Van Dyck (1599–1641) becomes court painter to English king Charles I.

1633 Italian architect and sculptor Gianlorenzo Bernini (1598–1680) designs the canopy over the altar at St. Peter's in Rome.

1634 Taj Mahal is built in Agra, India, as a tomb for Mumtaz Mahal the wife of Mughal emperor Shah Jahan (1592–1666).

1634 Passion play is inaugurated at Oberammagau, s Germany

1635 Académie Française is established.

1637 French dramatist Pierre Corneille (1606–84) writes his play *Le Cid.*

1638 Italian architect Francesco Borromini (1599–1667) designs the church of San Carlo alle Quattro Fontane in Rome.

1638 Spanish dramatist Pedro Calderón de la Barca (1600-81) writes his play *Life is a Dream.*

c.1637 French artist Nicolas Poussin (1594–1665) paints his *The Rape of the Sabine Women.*

1620

1624

1628

1632

1636

1639

ASIA AND AUSTRALASIA	AFRICA	EUROPE

1640

1641 Dutch capture the Malaysian port of Malacca from the Portuguese.

1641 Dutch traders are permitted to operate from an island in Nagasaki harbor in Japan.

1643 Dutch explorer Abel TASMAN (1603–59) discovers New Zealand and Tasmania.

1644

1644 Manchurians enter Beijing at the invitation of the last Ming emperor; end of the MING DYNASTY in China; start of the QING DYNASTY.

1645 Russian explorers in Siberia reach the Sea of Okhotsk.

1648

1648 Janissaries revolt in Turkey and depose Sultan Ibrahim I (1615–48).

1652

1652 Russian colonists found the city of Irkutsk in Siberia.

1656

1656 OTTOMAN Turks are defeated by the Venetians at a sea battle near the Dardanelles.

1656 Muhammad Köprülü (c.1586–1661) becomes Ottoman vizier (chief minister) and stabilizes the Ottoman Empire.

Cromwell *An outstanding parliamentary commander, Cromwell rose to prominence in the English Civil War. Guided by his Calvinist faith, he attributed the victory of his New Model Army to God's providence.*

1650 Ali Bey establishes himself as hereditary ruler of Tunis.

1652 Dutch settlers found the colony of Capetown in South Africa.

1654 French occupy the island of Réunion.

▼ Dam Palace, Amsterdam
Begun in 1648, the year in which Dutch independence was recognized, the Dam Palace is covered with symbols in sculpture of Dutch maritime and commercial supremacy. The palace was designed by Jan van Campen in the style of Palladio.

1640 Portugal and Catalonia revolt against Spanish rule.

1640 FREDERICK WILLIAM (1620–88) becomes Great Elector of Prussia.

1642 Civil War breaks out in England between Royalists and Parliamentarians.

1646 French and Swedes invade Bavaria in s Germany.

1648 Spain recognizes Dutch independence.

1648–53 Fronde rebellions erupt in France.

1648 Treaty of Westphalia ends the Thirty Years War.

1649 CHARLES I (b.1600) of England is executed; the monarchy is abolished and a Commonwealth is established.

1652 Spain is reunited when Catalonia submits to Spanish rule.

1652–54 England wins a naval war against the Dutch over shipping rights.

1653 Oliver CROMWELL (1599–1658) becomes Lord Protector of England.

1654 Cossacks in the Ukraine defect from Poland to Russia, starting a war.

1656 War breaks out between Protestant and Catholic cantons in Switzerland.

1656 English ships capture a Spanish treasure fleet near the port of Cadiz.

1656 Swedes invade Poland and capture Warsaw.

1658 English, allied with the French, capture the Spanish-held port of Dunkirk after the battle of the Dunes.

1659 Peace of the Pyrenees ends recent warfare between France and Spain.

1659

THE AMERICAS	SCIENCE AND TECHNOLOGY	RELIGION AND THE ARTS	

1641 Body of Liberties law code is established in Massachusetts.

1643 French establish the city of Montreal in Canada.

1643 English colonies form the New England Confederation.

1641 French scientist Blaise PASCAL (1623–62) invents a mechanical adding machine.

1643 Italian scientist Evangelista TORRICELLI (1608–47) invents the mercury barometer.

1642 Italian composer Claudio MONTEVERDI (1567–1643) completes his opera *The Coronation of Poppea*.

1640

1645 Portuguese settlers revolt against Dutch rule in N Brazil.

1644 French mathematician Marin Mersenne (1558–1648) studies prime numbers.

1647 German astronomer Johannes Hevelius (1611–87) draws a map of the Moon's surface.

1646 Spanish artist Bartolomé Murillo (1617–82) completes his paintings of the lives of Franciscan saints.

1644

1649 HURONS are defeated by the IROQUOIS CONFEDERACY in wars to control the fur trade.

1650 German scientist Otto von Guericke (1602–86) invents a vacuum pump.

1650 German scientist Athanasius Kircher (1601–80) discovers that sound will not travel in a vacuum.

1651 English political philosopher Thomas HOBBES (1588–1679) publishes his *Leviathan*.

1648

1654 Portuguese expel the Dutch from Brazil.

1655 French capture the island of Haiti from Spain.

1656 English ships capture Jamaica from Spain, provoking a war.

1655 Under Dutch governor Peter STUYVESANT (1610–72), New Netherland occupies New Sweden.

1654 German engraver Ludwig von Siegen (*c*.1609–80) reveals his methods of producing mezzotints.

1655 English mathematician John Wallis (1616–1703) introduces the symbol for infinity in his *The Arithmetic of Infinitesimals*.

***c*.1652** English religious reformer George FOX (1624–91) founds the Society of Friends, whose adherents become known as Quakers.

1654 Dutch poet and dramatist Joost van den Vondel (1587–1679) writes his play *Lucifer*.

1652

---

mechanical adding machine
Blaise Pascal's adding machine was made up of rotating cylinders each with the numbers 0–9 painted on the surface. The cylinders are moved by trains of toothed wheels, and so connected that when a cog is rotated ten places, the cog on its left, that is the cog representing the next order of ten, is rotated one place.

1657 Academia del Cimento, the first scientific research institute, is established in Florence, Italy.

1657 Dutch scientist Christiaan HUYGENS (1629–95) constructs a pendulum clock.

1659 Swiss mathematician Johann Rahn (1622–76) introduces the symbol for division in his *Teutsche Algebra*.

1659 French mathematician Pierre de FERMAT (1601–65), in correspondence with Pascal, develops the theory of probability.

1656 Spanish artist Diego VELÁZQUEZ (1599–1660) paints his *The Maids of Honor*.

1656 Dutch artist REMBRANDT HARMENSZOON VAN RIJN (1606–69) paints his *Jacob Blessing the Sons of Joseph*.

1656

1659

ASIA AND AUSTRALASIA	AFRICA	EUROPE

ASIA AND AUSTRALASIA

1660

1661 English establish a colony at Bombay in s India.

1662 Chinese pirate warlord Jeng Cheng-gong (Koxinga, 1624–62) expels the Dutch from Formosa.

1662 Kang-Xi (1654–1722) becomes emperor of China.

1664

1664 Hindu raiders sack the Mughal port of Surat in India.

1664 Russian cossacks raid N Persia.

1668

1669 Hindu religion is prohibited throughout the Mughal empire in India and Hindu temples are destroyed.

1672

1674 French establish a colony at Pondicherry in E India.

1674 Hindu raider Sivaji (1630–80) becomes independent ruler of Maratha in India.

1674 Regional rulers rebel against central control in China.

1675–78 Sikhs rebel against their Mughal overlords in India.

1676

1679

AFRICA

1662 Portugal cedes the city of Tangier in Morocco to England.

1662 English build a fort at the mouth of the River Gambia, w Africa.

▲ **Newton** developed theories of mechanics and of gravitation that survived unchallenged until the 20th century.

"A thing well said will be wit in all languages."

Dryden (*Of Dramatick Poesie*)

1677 French expel the Dutch from Senegal in w Africa.

EUROPE

1660 Monarchy is re-established in England with the accession of CHARLES II (1630–85).

1660 By the peace of Olivia, Sweden gains territory from Poland.

1661 On the death of cardinal MAZARIN (b.1602), LOUIS XIV (1638–1715) becomes sole ruler of France.

1662–63 Spanish invade Portugal in an attempt to re-establish control, but are defeated.

1664 Austria defeats the OTTOMAN Turks at the battle of St. Gotthard.

1665 War breaks out between the Dutch, supported by France, and England.

1667 By the treaty of Andrussovo, Russia acquires E Ukraine from Poland.

1667 France occupies Spanish towns in Flanders.

1668 Spain recognizes Portuguese independence.

1669 Ottoman Turks capture Crete from Venice.

1670 Peasants and cossacks revolt in s Russia.

1672 France invades the Netherlands; WILLIAM III OF ORANGE (1650–1702) becomes Dutch head of state and opens the sluices to save Amsterdam.

1674 German emperor enters the wars against France.

1675 Prussian army defeats France's ally Sweden at the battle of Fehrbellin.

1678 French capture the towns of Ypres and Ghent in Belgium from Spain.

1678 Treaties of Nijmegen end the wars between France and the Dutch, Germans and Spanish; France gains territory from Spain.

THE AMERICAS

1663 English colony of Carolina is established.

1664 Colonies of New Haven and Connecticut unite.

1664 New Amsterdam surrenders to the English; the city becomes known as New York.

1667 Bahamas are added to the colony of Carolina

1667 Under the treaty of Breda, English occupation of New Netherland is exchanged for the Dutch occupation of Surinam.

1669 English philosopher John LOCKE (1632–1704) writes the Fundamental Constitutions for Carolina.

1673 French priests Jacques MARQUETTE (1637–75) and Louis JOLIET (1646–1700) explore the upper reaches of the River Mississippi.

1673 Dutch briefly recapture New York.

1674 English establish the Hudson's Bay trading post.

1675–76 English colonists fight King Philip's War against Massoit Native Americans.

1676 Nathaniel Bacon (1647–76) leads a rebellion in Virginia.

SCIENCE AND TECHNOLOGY

1662 Royal Society of London is established.

1662 Irish scientist Robert BOYLE (1627–91) formulates his law of gas expansion.

c.1665 English scientist Isaac NEWTON (1642–1727) formulates the law of gravity.

1666 Italian astronomer Giovanni Cassini (1625–1712) discovers polar icecaps on Mars.

1666 French minister Jean COLBERT (1619–83) orders the construction of the Canal du Midi.

1667 French king Louis XIV founds the Observatoire de Paris.

1668 English mathematician John Wallis (1616–1703) discovers the principle of conservation of momentum.

1669 Isaac Newton creates the first system of calculus.

1672 French astronomer N. Cassegrain invents an improved reflecting telescope.

1673 German scientist Gottfried von LEIBNIZ (1646–1716) invents a calculating machine.

1673 French military engineer Sebastien de Vauban (1633–1707) introduces his system for attacking fortresses at the siege of Maastricht.

1675 Isaac Newton proposes the particle theory of light.

1675 Royal Observatory at Greenwich, near London, is established.

1676 Danish astronomer Ole Romer (1644–1710) discovers that light travels at a finite speed.

1678 Dutch scientist Christiaan HUYGENS (1629–95) proposes the wave theory of light.

1679 French scientist Denis Papin (1647–c.1712) invents the pressure cooker.

RELIGION AND THE ARTS

1662 French landscape gardener André Le Nôtre (1613–1700) designs the grounds of the palace of Versailles in France.

c.1663 French artist CLAUDE LORRAIN (1600–82) paints his *Landscape with sacrifice to Apollo.*

1664 French dramatist Jean Baptiste RACINE (1639–99) writes his *La Thebaïde.*

1667 French dramatist MOLIÈRE (1622–73) writes his comedy *The Misanthrope.*

1667 English poet John MILTON (1608–74) publishes his epic *Paradise Lost.*

1668 Dutch artist Jan VERMEER (1632–75) paints his *Astronomer.*

1668 English poet and dramatist John DRYDEN (1631–1700) writes his essay *Of Dramatick Poesie.*

1669 German author Hans von Grimmelshausen (1621–76) writes his novel *Simplicissimus.*

1669 English government official Samuel PEPYS (1633–1703) completes his 10-year diary of life in London.

1670 English architect Christopher WREN (1632–1723) begins rebuilding 50 London churches destroyed by the Fire of London (1666).

1673 French composer Jean-Baptiste LULLY (1632–87) writes his opera *Cadmus and Hermione.*

1677 Dutch philosopher Baruch SPINOZA (1632–77) publishes his *Ethics.*

1678 English preacher John BUNYAN (1628–88) writes his *The Pilgrim's Progress.*

1678 French architect Jules HARDOUIN-MANSART (1646–1708) designs the Hall of Mirrors for the palace of Versailles.

1678 French poet Jean de La Fontaine (1621–95) publishes his second book of *Fables.*

1660

1664

1668

1672

1676

1679

ASIA AND AUSTRALASIA	AFRICA	EUROPE

1680

1681 Manchu QING DYNASTY re-establishes central control in China.

1683 Qing dynasty conquers the island of Formosa, which comes under direct rule from the Chinese mainland for the first time.

1683 Prussians build a fort on the coast of Guinea in w Africa.

1683 OTTOMAN Turks under Vizier Kara Mustafa (1634–83) besiege Vienna and are defeated by a German-Polish army at the battle of the Kahlenberg.

1683 French under LOUIS XIV (1638–1715) invade Belgium and occupy Luxembourg and Lorraine.

1684

1685 Mughal emperor AURANGZEB (1619–1707) attempts to expel English merchants from Surat.

1684 England gives Tangier back to Morocco.

1684 French mount naval expeditions to suppress the Islamic pirates at Algiers.

1686 French formally annex Madagascar

1684 Venice, Austria and Poland form a Holy Alliance against the Turks.

1685 Louis XIV revokes the Edict of Nantes in France (1598).

1686 German rulers form the League of Augsburg against France.

1688

1689 Russian settlers are forced to withdraw from NW China; the treaty of Nerchinsk establishes the Russian–Chinese border in the Amur region.

1690 English establish a colony at Calcutta, N India.

1691 Mughal empire in India reaches its greatest extent.

▶ **Leeuwenhoek's microscope**
With the powerful, single-lens microscopes that he designed, such as the one shown right, Leeuwenhoek was able to study blood and spermatozoa as well as microscopic life forms. It was with one of these microscopes that he discovered bacteria in 1680.

1688 Huguenot refugees from France arrive in S Africa.

1688 France invades the Rhineland region of Germany.

1688 Austrian armies liberate Belgrade from the Turks.

1688 Glorious Revolution in England deposes Catholic king JAMES II (1633–1701); the Dutch Protestant ruler WILLIAM OF ORANGE (1650–1702) becomes William III of England.

1689 PETER I (1672–1725) becomes sole ruler of Russia.

1689 England and the Netherlands join the League of Augsburg against France.

1690 William III of England defeats French troops under former king James II at the battle of the Boyne in Ireland.

1692

1692 English and Dutch ships defeat a French fleet at Cap La Hogue.

1696

1696 Chinese establish a protectorate in N Mongolia.

1697 French complete the conquest of Senegal.

1698 Portuguese are expelled from most E African ports by Omanis from SE Arabia.

1696 Russians capture Azov from the Turks.

1697 Austrians defeat the Turks at the battle of Zenta.

1697 Peace of Ryswick ends the War of the League of Augsburg against France.

1699 Turks lose territory to the Holy Alliance under the peace of Kalowitz.

1699

| THE AMERICAS | SCIENCE AND TECHNOLOGY | ARTS AND HUMANITIES | |

THE AMERICAS

1680 Colony of New Hampshire is separated from Massachusetts.

1680 Portuguese establish the colony of Sacramento in w Brazil.

1680 Revolt by Pueblo Native Americans drives the Spanish from New Mexico.

1682 French explorer Robert de LA SALLE (1643–87) reaches the mouth of the Mississippi and claims the Louisiana Territory for France.

1683 Portuguese establish the colony of Colonia on the River Plate in Argentina.

1682 English Quaker William PENN (1644–1718) establishes the colony of Pennsylvania.

1684 Charter of Massachusetts is annulled.

1686 English colonies are organized into the Dominion of New England.

1689–97 King William's War is fought between English and French colonists and their native allies.

1691 King William III issues a new charter for Massachusetts.

1692 Witchcraft trials are held in Salem, Massachusetts.

1693 College of William and Mary is established in Virginia.

1696 Spanish reconquer New Mexico.

1699 French establish a colony at Biloxi in Louisiana.

SCIENCE AND TECHNOLOGY

1680 Dutch scientist Anton van LEEUWENHOEK (1632–1723) discovers bacteria.

1681 Dodo becomes extinct on the island of Mauritius in the Indian Ocean.

1682 English astronomer Edmond HALLEY (1656–1742) establishes the periodicity of Halley's Comet.

1684 German scientist Gottfried von LEIBNIZ (1646–1716) publishes his differential calculus and introduces the integral symbol.

1687 English scientist Isaac NEWTON (1642–1727) publishes his *Mathematical Principles of Natural Philosophy*.

1694 Bank of England is established in London.

1696 French Mathematician Guillaume de L'Hôpital (1661–1704) publishes *Analysis of the Infinitesimals*, the first textbook of infinitesimal calculus.

1698 Swiss mathematician Jakob Bernoulli (1654–1705) studies the properties of the logarithmic spiral.

1698 English engineer Thomas Savery (*c.*1650–1715) invents a practical steam-driven water pump.

ARTS AND HUMANITIES

1681 Italian composer Arcangelo CORELLI (1653–1713) writes his 12 trio sonatas op.1, *sonate da chiesa*.

1689 English composer Henry PURCELL (1659–95) writes his opera *Dido and Aeneas*.

1689 English philosopher John LOCKE (1632–1704) publishes his *Two Treatise on Government*.

1690 Italian musical instrument maker Antonio STRADIVARI (1644–1737) introduces his "long" pattern with his "Tuscan" violin.

◄ *Peter I the Great* and Catherine II were the two rulers chiefly responsible for the transformation of Russia from a medieval czardom into a powerful, modern state. Peter's modernizations included the rebuilding of the army on a permanent basis and the creation of a navy.

1694 Death of the Japanese haiku poet Matsuo Bashō (b.1644).

1696 German architect Fischer von Erlach (1656–1723) introduces Italian baroque to central Europe with his collegiate church in Salzburg, Austria.

1697 French scholar Pierre BAYLE (1647–1706) sets the trend for the Enlightenment with his *Historical and Critical Dictionary*.

1680

1684

1688

1692

1696

1699

1700

1700 Charles Eyre reorganizes the administration of English Bengal.

1702

1703 The "Forty-seven *ronin*" avenge the execution of their lord in Japan, and are ordered to commit suicide.

▼ *Armies* In the 18th century armies consisted of long-service volunteers or conscripts. Harsh discipline, low pay and bad conditions attracted only the poor and criminals into the ranks. Officers, from the nobility, used influence to gain commissions. Distinctive uniforms were chosen because long-range weapons were inaccurate. Illustrated below are, from left to right, a British Grenadier, an Austrian infantryman and a soldier of the Spanish Imperial Army.

1700 Sweden is attacked by Poland, allied to Denmark and Russia; start of the Great Northern War. Swedes, under CHARLES XII (1682–1718), defeat the Russians, under PETER I (1672–1725), at the battle of Navara.

1700 Charles II (b.1661) of Spain dies childless; the French duke of Anjou is proclaimed King PHILIP V (1683–1746); end of the HAPSBURG DYNASTY in Spain; start of the BOURBON DYNASTY.

1701 Frederick III (1657–1713) of Brandenburg is crowned FREDERICK I king of Prussia at Königsburg.

1701 England, Holland and Austria form the Grand Alliance against France.

1702 JAMES II's daughter ANNE (1665–1714) becomes queen of England.

1702 Grand Alliance declares war on France and Spain; the War of the Spanish Succession begins.

1702 Swedes invade Poland and capture Warsaw and Kraków.

1703 Peter I establishes the city of St. Petersburg at the mouth of the River Neva.

1704

1705 Chinese attempt to impose their candidate for Dalai Lama provokes risings and unrest in Tibet.

1704 British capture Gibraltar from Spain.

1705 Husseinid dynasty takes control in Tunis and establishes independence from the Turks.

1704 English army led by John Churchill (1650–1722), 1st Duke of MARLBOROUGH, defeats the French at the battle of Blenheim.

1706

1707 Death of Emperor AURANGZEB (b.1619) leads to the rapid disintegration of the MUGHAL EMPIRE in India.

1706 Following their defeat at Turin, the French are expelled from Italy.

1706 English defeat the French at the battle of Ramilles and conquer Belgium.

1707 England and Scotland are united as Great Britain.

1708

1708 Sikhs establish independent control of the Punjab region of N India.

1709 Mir Vais, Afghan chieftain of Kandahar, rebels against Persian rule and proclaims independence.

1708 Spanish are expelled from Oran in Algeria.

1709 Dutch cattle farmers in South Africa trek E across the Hottentot Holland Mountains.

1709 British defeat the French at the battle of Malplaquet.

1709 Swedes in alliance with Ukrainian cossacks invade Russia but are defeated at the battle of Poltava.

1709

THE AMERICAS

1701 French explorer Antoine de CADILLAC (1658–1730) founds the town of Detroit between lakes Erie and Huron.

1701 Yale College is founded in Connecticut, present-day USA.

1702 French acquire the asiento to supply African slaves to the Spanish colonies in America.

1702 English attack and burn St. Augustine in Florida at the start of Queen Anne's War (the American phase of the War of the Spanish Succession).

1703 English colony of Delaware separates from Pennsylvania.

1704 Native Americans allied to the French massacre English settlers at Deerfield in Connecticut.

1706 Spanish establish the town of Albuquerque in New Mexico.

1707 British troops from New England march into Canada and besiege French settlers at Port Royal, Nova Scotia.

▶ **seed drill** *Illustrated right is Jethro Tull's famous horse-drawn seed drill. First used in 1701, it is regarded as having initiated the mechanization of agriculture. Before this invention, seed was laboriously broadcast by hand.*

1708–09 Portuguese destroy the power of the Paulistas (slave-raiders) in s Brazil in the War of the Emboabas.

1709 Large numbers of Germans from the Palatinate region begin migrating to the English colonies in North America, especially Pennsylvania.

SCIENCE AND TECHNOLOGY

1700 German Protestants adopt the Gregorian calendar.

1701 English farmer Jethro TULL (1674–1741) invents the seed drill.

1701 Academy of Sciences is established in Berlin.

1705 English engineer Thomas NEWCOMEN (1663–1729) invents the atmospheric steam engine, which uses a vacuum to drive a piston.

1706 English mathematician William Jones (1675–1749) introduces the symbol for pi (π) in his *Synopsis palmariorum matheseos*.

1709 British ironworker Abraham Darby (c.1677–1717) perfects a technique for producing iron in a coke-fired blast furnace.

ARTS AND HUMANITIES

1700 English dramatist William Congreve (1670–1729) writes his comedy *The Way of the World*.

1700 Samuel Sewall (1652–1730) publishes his antislavery tract, *The Selling of Joseph*, in Boston, Massachusetts, present-day USA.

1702 World's first daily newspaper, the *Daily Courant*, is published in London.

1705 French writer Bernard de Mandeville (1670–1733) argues that self-interest leads to the general good in his book *The Grumbling Hive*.

1705 German-born English composer George Frideric HANDEL (1685–1759) writes his opera *Almira*.

1708 Death of GOBIND SINGH (b.1666), the tenth and last guru of Sikhism, who promoted the warrior ethic.

1709 Italian instrument-maker Bartolomeo Cristofori (1655–1731) invents the piano by substituting hammer action for the plucking action of the harpsichord.

1700

1702

1704

1706

1708

1709

ASIA AND AUSTRALASIA

1710

1711 Mir Vais, Afghan chieftain of Kandahar, defeats an invading Persian army.

1712

1712 War of succession in India between the sons of the MUGHAL emperor Bahadur divides India.

1714

1716

1717 Abdali dynasty of Herat establishes another independent Afghan state.

1717 MONGOL army seizes control of Lhasa, the Tibetan capital.

1717 British East India Company obtains trading concessions from the Mughal emperor.

1718

1718 Chinese army sent to Tibet is destroyed by Mongol warriors.

1719

AFRICA

1710 French take the island of Mauritius from the Dutch.

▼ *East Indiaman ship* During the 18th century, Europe's trading empire expanded worldwide. Such expansion was made possible by the development of fast and reliable sailing ships such as the Dutch East Indiaman illustrated below. Heavily armed and extremely robust, these merchant ships could also be used as warships.

1714 Ahmed Bey establishes the Karamanlid dynasty as independent rulers in Tripoli, Libya.

1717 Dutch begin importing slaves to Cape Colony, South Africa.

EUROPE

1710 South Sea Company is set up in London.

1711 Turks regain Azov from Russia under the treaty of Pruth.

1711 Following an uprising, Austria grants Hungary self-administration under the peace of Sathmar.

1711 CHARLES XII (1682–1718) of Sweden persuades the Turks to attack Russia.

1713 Treaty of Utrecht between Britain and France ends the War of the Spanish Succession; Britain gains overseas colonies in the Mediterranean and America.

1713 FREDERICK WILLIAM I (1688–1740) becomes king of Prussia.

1713 Austrian emperor CHARLES VI (1685–1740) issues the Pragmatic Sanction, which allows a female to inherit the Hapsburg throne.

1714 Russia captures Finland from Sweden after victory at the battle of Storkyro.

1714 Austria makes a separate peace with France and gains territory in Italy and Belgium.

1714 George, Elector of Hanover, becomes King GEORGE I (1660–1727) of Britain on the death of Queen ANNE (b.1665).

1715 LOUIS XV (1710–74) becomes king of France with Philip of Orléans as regent.

1715 First Jacobite rebellion in Scotland is defeated by British troops.

1717 Spain conquers Sardinia.

1717 Austria liberates Belgrade from the Turks.

1718 Spain conquers Sicily; Britain, Austria, France and Holland form the Quadruple Alliance and defeat Spain at the sea battle of Cape Passaro.

1719 Russia invades Sweden.

THE AMERICAS

1710–11 Portuguese defeat Brazilian natives in the War of the Mascates.

1711–12 Tuscarora Native Americans massacre British colonists in North Carolina and are subsequently defeated.

1711 French capture and ransom Rio de Janeiro in Brazil.

1713 By the treaty of Utrecht, Britain gains Newfoundland and Nova Scotia from the French, and acquires a monopoly on the asiento slave trade with Spanish colonies.

1715 British colonists defeat the Yamasee Native Americans in South Carolina.

1715 Scots-Irish immigrants begin the settlement of the Appalachian foothills.

1716 Governor Alexander Spotswood (1676–1740) of Virginia leads an expedition into the Shenandoah valley.

1717 Mississippi Company, promoted by Scottish economist John LAW (1671–1729), is given a monopoly on trade with the French colony of Louisiana.

1717 Portuguese build a fort at Montevideo on the River Plate in Uruguay.

1718 French found the port of New Orleans in Louisiana.

1718 Spanish establish the settlement of Pensacola in Florida.

1718 Warfare breaks out between France and Spain in Florida and Texas.

SCIENCE AND TECHNOLOGY

1711 Italian naturalist Luigi Marsigli (1658–1730) shows that corals are animals not plants.

1712 British clockmaker John Rowley constructs the first clockwork orrery.

1714 German scientist Gabriel FAHRENHEIT (1686–1736) invents the mercury thermometer.

St Paul's Cathedral Illustrated above is the dome of St. Paul's Cathedral, London, designed by Christopher Wren. It has a triple construction: a brick inner dome (1), with its "eye" rising 65m (213ft) above the floor; an intermediate, brick cone (2), reinforced with iron chains (3); and, resting on the intermediate cone, an outer dome (4), which is built out with timber framing (5) and lead covering to obtain the desired silhouette.

ARTS AND HUMANITIES

1710 Irish bishop George BERKELEY (1685–1753) introduces empiricist philosophy in his *Treatise concerning the Principles of Human Knowledge.*

1710 Puritan minister Cotton MATHER (1663–1728) publishes his *Essays to do Good.*

1710 English architect Christopher WREN (1632–1723) completes his rebuilding of St. Paul's Cathedral, London.

1712 British poet Alexander POPE (1688–1744) publishes his *Rape of the Lock.*

1713 School of dance is established at the Paris Opéra.

1714 German philosopher Gottfried LEIBNIZ (1646–1716) outlines his philosophy in *Monadologie.*

1715 Italian composer Alessandro Scarlatti (1660–1725) writes his opera *Il Tigrane.*

1715 French novelist Alain le Sage (1688–1747) publishes his *Gil Blas.*

c.1715 Japanese dramatist Chikamatsu Mozaemon (1652–1725) writes his *Love Suicides.*

1716 French artist Jean Antoine Watteau (1684–1721) paints his *The Lesson of Love.*

1717 German-born English composer George Frideric HANDEL (1685–1759) composes his *Water Music.*

1719 British author Daniel DEFOE (1660–1731) publishes his novel *Robinson Crusoe.*

1710
1712
1714
1716
1718
1719

ASIA AND AUSTRALASIA	AFRICA	EUROPE

1720

1720 Japanese shōgun Yoshimune (d.1751) permits the importation of nonreligious European books.

1720 Defeat in the Great Northern War ends Swedish dominance in the Baltic region; Russia gains Livonia and Estonia under the treaty of Nystad.

1720 Savoy gains Sardinia in return for Austrian control of Sicily.

1722

1722 Dutch explorer Jacob Roggeveen (1659–1729) discovers Easter Island and Samoa.

1722 Afghan ruler of Kandahar, Mir Mahmud (d.1725), invades Persia and makes himself shah.

1723 Russians capture Baku on the Caspian Sea from Persia.

1723 British Africa Company claims the Gambia region of W Africa.

1720 Collapse of John Law's Mississippi Company leads to widespread bankruptcies in France.

1720 South Seas Company fails and creates financial panic in London.

1721 Robert WALPOLE (1676–1745) becomes Britain's first prime minister.

1724

1724 Chinese establish a protectorate over Tibet.

1724 Russia and Turkey agree to divide Persia between them.

1724 Persian shah Mahmud goes insane and orders the massacre of the Persian aristocracy.

> "I told him... that we ate when we were not hungry, and drank without the provocation of thirst."
>
> Jonathan Swift
> (*Gulliver's Travels*)

1722 PETER I (1672–1725) makes administrative reforms in Russia and limits the traditional privileges of the aristocracy.

1723 FREDERICK WILLIAM I (1688–1740) establishes the General Directory for the centralized administration of Prussia.

1726

1726 Ashraf (d.1730), the Afghan shah of Persia, defeats an invading Turkish army.

1727 Kiakhta treaty fixes the borders between Russia and China.

1725 French king LOUIS XV (1710–74) breaks his engagement to a Spanish princess and marries the daughter of the ex-king of Poland; as a result the Spanish make an alliance with Austria.

1725 Following the death of Peter I, his wife, CATHERINE I (1684–1727), becomes the first of a series of weak Russian rulers.

1726 Cardinal Andre Hercule de Fleury (1653–1743) becomes chief minister in France.

1728

1728 Dutch explorer Vitus BERING (1680–1741), sailing for Russia, discovers the Bering Strait, between Siberia and Alaska.

1728–29 Portuguese briefly re-occupy the E African port of Mombasa.

1727 GEORGE II (1683–1760) accedes to the British throne.

1727 War breaks out between Spain and Britain allied with France.

1729 Treaty of Seville ends the war between Britain and Spain.

1729 Corsica revolts against Genoese rule.

1729

THE AMERICAS

1720 Spain occupies Texas after hostilities with France.

1720 British establish the colony of Honduras in Central America.

1721 Jose de Antequerra leads the revolt of the communeros against the Spanish in Paraguay.

▶ **Africa** Although Africa was a major source of a variety of goods, as illustrated on the map right, it was primarily the slave trade that established its links with the outside world and encouraged trade routes to develop within it. There was a steady flow of slaves to Muslim lands but most were shipped from west and west-central Africa for labor in the New World. The first cargo of slaves was shipped across the Atlantic Ocean in the 16th century, and the trade lasted until the 1870s.

1726 Spanish capture Montevideo in Uruguay from the Portuguese.

1726 British colonists from New York make a treaty with the Native American IROQUOIS CONFEDERACY against the French

1729 NATCHEZ Native Americans massacre French settlers at Fort Rosalie in Louisiana.

1729 British colonies of North and South Carolina are brought under royal control.

SCIENCE AND TECHNOLOGY

1721 First smallpox inoculations are carried out in Boston.

1725 Academy of Sciences is established at St. Petersburg, Russia.

1725 Italian philosophical historian Giambattista VICO (1668–1744) emphasizes the importance of social and cultural history in his *New Science*.

1727 British biologist Stephen Hales (1677–1761) publishes his *Vegetable Staticks*, which establishes the science of plant physiology.

1728 British astronomer James Bradley (1693–1762) discovers the aberration of light.

ARTS AND HUMANITIES

1721 German composer Johann Sebastian BACH (1685–1750) completes his *Brandenburg Concertos*.

1721 French philosopher Charles de Montesquieu (1689–1755) publishes his *Persian Letters* – the first major work of the Enlightenment.

1725 Italian artist CANALETTO (1697–1768) paints his *Four Views of Venice*.

1725 Italian composer Antonio VIVALDI (1675–1741) publishes his *The Four Seasons*.

1726 British author Jonathan SWIFT (1667–1745) publishes his satirical *Gulliver's Travels*.

1726 Chinese Academy of Letters publishes its *c.*5000-volume *T'u Shu Chi Ch'eng* encyclopedia.

1728 British poet John Gay (1685–1732) writes his *The Beggar's Opera*.

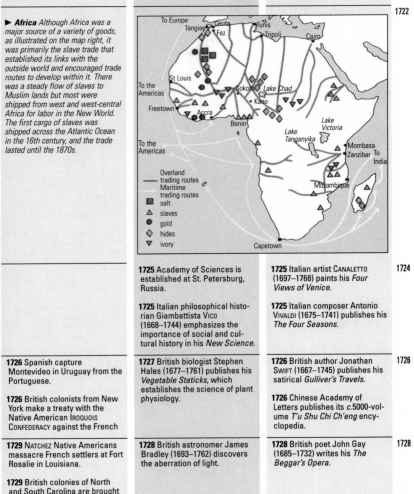

1730 **1730** Persian chieftain NADIR Kuli (1688–1747) drives the Afghans from Persia and restores the SAFAVID DYNASTY.

1731 Trade rivalries in India between Britain and Austria are settled in Britain's favor by the treaty of Vienna.

1730 Dutch northward expansion in South Africa reaches the River Olifants.

1732 **1733** Turks defeat the Persians at the battle of Kirkuk.

1732 Spanish recapture Oran in Algeria.

1732 Genoa suppresses the Corsican revolt.

1732 Military conscription is introduced in Prussia.

1733–35 Russia invades Poland after the death of King AUGUSTUS II (1670–1733); France allied to Spain fights the War of the Polish Succession against Austria allied to Russia.

rococo This style of art, architecture and decoration developed in early 18th-century France and soon spread to Germany, Austria, Italy and Britain. The style was particularly suited to interiors, as illustrated right. Doors and windows alternated with decorative panels. Square ceiling structures and corners were softened by curved and molded paneling, minimizing the transition from wall to ceiling. Ground plans followed the serpentine curves of the interiors.

1733 Treaty (the first Family Compact) between France and Spain declares the indivisibility of the two branches of the BOURBON DYNASTY.

1734 Russians capture Danzig in Poland.

1734 Spanish troops conquer Sicily and Naples from Austria.

1734 **1735** Russia allies with Persia against the Turks, who are defeated at the battle of Baghavand.

1735 CHARLES III (1716–88), son of PHILIP V (1683–1746) of Spain, becomes king of Sicily and Naples.

1735 French troops occupy Lorraine.

1736 **1736** Nadir becomes shah of Persia on the death of Abbas III; end of the Safavid dynasty.

1737 Persians invade Afghanistan.

1736–39 War between Austria allied to Russia and the Turks results in Russia regaining Azov and Austria losing Serbia.

1738 **1739** Persians invade India, defeat a MUGHAL army at the battle of Karnal, and capture Delhi.

1738 Treaty of Vienna settles the War of the Polish Succession; Spain gains Naples and Sicily on condition they are never united with Spain; France gains the promise of Lorraine.

▲ *Hume's* Treatise of Human Nature *was initially a literary failure. He achieved greater success with his* History of England *and various essays and philosophical "inquiries".*

1738 Corvée system of forced labor for road repairs is introduced in France.

1739 War of Jenkin's Ear breaks out between Britain and Spain.

1739

THE AMERICAS

1730 CHEROKEE Native Americans acknowledge British supremacy.

1731 Paraguayan revolutionary Jose de Antequerra is defeated and executed.

1733 British colony of Georgia is established by James OGLETHORPE (1696–1785).

1733 Molasses Act places prohibitive duties on non-British sugar products imported into British North America

1735 Spanish authorities finally suppress the revolt of the comuneros in Paraguay.

1735 Trial in New York of newspaperman John ZENGER (1697–1746) establishes the freedom of the press in the British colonies.

1737 William Byrd (1674–1744) founds Richmond, Virginia.

1739 British capture the Spanish settlement of Porto Bello in Panama.

1739 African slaves revolt and kill white settlers at Stono River, South Carolina.

SCIENCE AND TECHNOLOGY

1730 British navigator John Hadley (1682–1744) invents the reflecting quadrant.

1730 British politician and farmer Charles Townshend (1674–1738) introduces four-course crop rotation with turnips and clover.

1730 French scientist René RÉAUMUR (1683–1757) invents an alcohol thermometer.

1732 English farmer Jethro TULL (1674–1741) publishes his *Horse Hoeing Husbandry*.

1732 French engineer Henri de Pitot (1695–1771) invents a tube for measuring the speed of fluid flow.

1732 Dutch scientist Hermann Boerhaave (1668–1738) publishes his chemistry textbook *Chemical Elements*.

1733 French scientist Charles du Fray (1698–1739) identifies positive and negative static electricity.

1733 British clothworker John KAY (1704–64) invents the flying shuttle.

1735 Explorer Charles Condamine (1701–74) discovers rubber trees in South America.

1735 Swedish scientist Carolus LINNAEUS (1707–78) publishes his *Systema naturae*, which classifies all living organisms according to a binomial nomenclature.

1736 Swiss mathematician Leonhard EULER (1707–83) publishes his textbook of mechanics *Mechanica sive mortus analytice exposita*.

1738 Swiss mathematician Daniel Bernoulli (1700–82) demonstrates the relationship between pressure and velocity of fluid flow in his *Hydrodynamics*.

ARTS AND HUMANITIES

1731 French author Antoine Prévost (1697–1763) publishes his novel *Manon Lescaut*.

1732 Italian sculptor Niccolo Salvi (1697–1751) begins work on his Trevi fountain in Rome.

1732 American writer, scientist and politician Benjamin FRANKLIN (1706–90) publishes the first issue of *Poor Richard's Almanac*.

1734 Johann Sebastian BACH (1685–1750) composes his *Christmas Oratorio*.

1734 French philosopher and author VOLTAIRE (1694–1778) publishes his *English or Philosophical Letters*.

1735 French composer Jean Rameau (1683–1764) writes his ballet *Les Indes Galantes*.

1735 British artist William HOGARTH (1697–1764) publishes his engravings of *A Rake's Progress*.

1738 John WESLEY (1703–91) experiences a religious conversion and lays the foundations of Methodism.

1738 Archaeological excavation starts of the Roman town of Herculaneum in Italy.

1738 Russian Imperial Ballet School is founded in St. Petersburg.

1739 Scottish philosopher David HUME (1711–76) publishes his *Treatise on Human Nature*.

1739 Prince Frederick of Prussia, later FREDERICK II (THE GREAT), publishes his political theories in *Anti-Machiavelli*.

1739 French architect François de Cuvilliés (1695–1768) completes his rococo Hall of Mirrors in the Amalienburg, near Munich.

1730

1732

1734

1736

1738

1739

ASIA AND AUSTRALASIA	AFRICA	EUROPE

1740

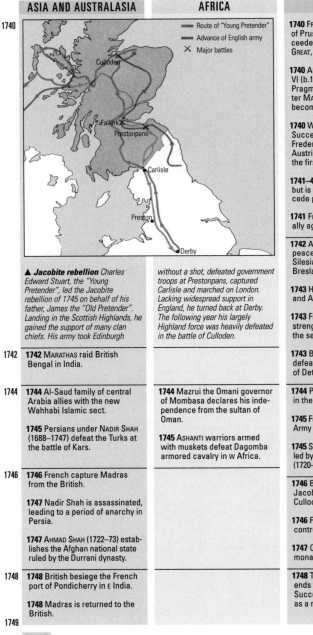

Route of "Young Pretender"
Advance of English army
✕ Major battles

Culloden

Falkirk ✕
Prestonpans

Carlisle

Preston

Derby

▲ **Jacobite rebellion** Charles Edward Stuart, the "Young Pretender", led the Jacobite rebellion of 1745 on behalf of his father, James the "Old Pretender". Landing in the Scottish Highlands, he gained the support of many clan chiefs. His army took Edinburgh

without a shot, defeated government troops at Prestonpans, captured Carlisle and marched on London. Lacking widespread support in England, he turned back at Derby. The following year his largely Highland force was heavily defeated in the battle of Culloden.

1740 FREDERICK WILLIAM I (b.1688) of Prussia dies and is succeeded by FREDERICK II (THE GREAT, 1712–86).

1740 Austrian emperor CHARLES VI (b.1685) dies; under the Pragmatic Sanction his daughter MARIA THERESA (1717–80) becomes empress.

1740 War of the Austrian Succession begins when Frederick II (the Great) invades Austrian-controlled Silesia in the first Silesian War.

1741–43 Sweden attacks Russia, but is defeated and forced to cede parts of Finland.

1741 France, Spain and Prussia ally against Austria.

1742 Austrians make a separate peace with Prussia, ceding Silesia under the treaty of Breslau and Berlin.

1743 Holland allies with Britain and Austria against France.

1743 France and Spain strengthen their alliance, with the second Family Compact.

1743 British-led Pragmatic Army defeats the French at the battle of Dettingen.

1742

1742 MARATHAS raid British Bengal in India.

1744

1744 Al-Saud family of central Arabia allies with the new Wahhabi Islamic sect.

1745 Persians under NADIR SHAH (1688–1747) defeat the Turks at the battle of Kars.

1744 Mazrui the Omani governor of Mombasa declares his independence from the sultan of Oman.

1745 ASHANTI warriors armed with muskets defeat Dagomba armored cavalry in W Africa.

1744 Prussians invade Bohemia in the second Silesian War.

1745 French defeat the Pragmatic Army at the battle of Fontenoy.

1745 Second Jacobite rebellion, led by Charles Edward STUART (1720–88), breaks out in Scotland.

1746

1746 French capture Madras from the British.

1747 Nadir Shah is assassinated, leading to a period of anarchy in Persia.

1747 AHMAD SHAH (1722–73) establishes the Afghan national state ruled by the Durrani dynasty.

1746 British troops defeat the Jacobite Scots at the battle of Culloden and the rebellion ends.

1746 French conquer Austrian-controlled Belgium.

1747 Orangists restore the monarchy in Holland.

1748

1748 British besiege the French port of Pondicherry in E India.

1748 Madras is returned to the British.

1748 Treaty of Aix-la-Chapelle ends the War of the Austrian Succession; Prussia emerges as a major European power.

1749

THE AMERICAS	SCIENCE AND TECHNOLOGY	ARTS AND HUMANITIES	
1740 British colonists from Georgia invade Spanish Florida but fail to take St. Augustine.	***c.*1740** British ironworker Benjamin Huntsman perfects the crucible process for casting steel.	**1740** British author Samuel RICHARDSON (1689–1761) publishes his novel *Pamela*.	1740
		1741 Italian architect Bartolomeo Rastrelli designs the Summer Palace in St. Petersburg.	
		1741 German-born English composer George Frideric HANDEL's oratorio *Messiah* is first performed in Dublin.	
1742 Spanish attack Georgia from Florida.	**1742** Swedish astronomer Anders CELSIUS (1701–44) invents the Celsius, or centigrade, temperature scale.	**1742** French artist François BOUCHER (1703–70) paints his *Bath of Diana*.	1742
1743 Hostilities between Britain and Spain become absorbed into King George's War, the American phase of the War of the Austrian Succession.	**1742** French scientist Paul Malouin invents a process for galvanizing steel.		
	1743 American Philosophical Society is founded in Philadelphia.		
1745 British colonists from New England besiege and capture the French fortress of Louisburg, Nova Scotia.	***c.*1745** Leyden jar electrical capacitor is invented in Holland.	**1745** Italian dramatist Carlo Goldoni (1707–93) publishes his comedy *The Servant of Two Masters*.	1744
	1745 French astronomer Pierre Maupertuis (1698–1759) publishes his *Venus physique*.		
1746 Princeton University is founded in New Jersey.	**1746** British chemist John Roebuck (1718–94) develops a process for manufacturing sulfuric acid.	**1746** French philosopher Denis DIDEROT (1713–84) publishes his *Philosophic Thoughts*.	1746
	1747 German scientist Andreas Marggraf (1709–82) invents a process for extracting sugar from sugar beet.	**1746** French philosopher Étienne Condillac (1715–1780) publishes his *Essay on the Origin of Human Knowledge*.	
		1747 French philosopher Julien La Mettrie (1709–51) publishes his atheist views in his book *Man, A Machine*.	
1748 British fleet captures Port Louis in Haiti from the French.	**1749** French naturalist Georges Buffon (1707–88) publishes the first volumes of his *Natural History*.	**1748** French philosopher Charles de Montesquieu (1689–1755) publishes his *The Spirit of Laws*.	1748
1748 Treaty of Aix-la-Chapelle ends King George's War.		**1749** British novelist Henry FIELDING (1707–54) publishes his *Tom Jones*.	
1749 British establish the town of Halifax in Nova Scotia.			
1749 British colonists form the Ohio Company to extend British territory w.			
1749 French build Fort Rouille on the site of present-day Toronto.			
			1749

ASIA AND AUSTRALASIA	AFRICA	EUROPE

1750

1750 Tibetans rebel against Chinese overlordship.

1750 French colonial administrator Joseph DUPLEIX (1697–1763) wins the battle of Tanjore and gains control of the Carnatic region of S India.

1750 KARIM KHAN (1705–79) establishes himself as shah of Persia and founds the Zand dynasty.

1751 China invades Tibet.

1751 British colonial administrator Robert CLIVE (1725–74) captures Arcot and ends French control of the Carnatic.

1752

1752 British troops under Robert Clive capture Trichinopoly in S India from the French.

1752 Afghans capture the city of Lahore in N India from the Mughals.

1753–55 King ALAUNGPAYA (1711–60) reunites Burma, with British assistance, and founds a new capital city at Rangoon.

1754

1755 Afghans conquer the Punjab region of N India and plunder Delhi.

1756

1756 Indian ruler of Bengal captures Calcutta from the British and imprisons British soldiers in the "Black Hole".

1757 Robert Clive recaptures Calcutta and defeats the native ruler of Bengal at the battle of Plassey.

1758

1758 MARATHAS occupy the Punjab region of N India.

1758 China occupies E Turkistan.

1759 British defeat a Dutch naval expedition and capture Chinsura.

1759

1750 French establish a settlement on the island of Sainte Marie off Madagascar

> "All is for the best in the best of all possible worlds."
>
> Voltaire (*Candide*)

1752 Portuguese settlements in SE Africa are placed under a separate government from that of Goa in India.

1755 Death of Emperor Jesus II marks the end of strong government in Ethiopia, which becomes divided between rival claimants to the throne.

1756 City of Tunis is captured by the Algerians.

1757 Muhammad XVI (d.1790) becomes ruler of Morocco and starts economic and military reforms.

1758 British capture Senegal from the French.

1750 Joseph I (1714–77) becomes king of Portugal, although the real ruler is the future marquês de POMBAL (1699–1782).

1753 Wenzel von KAUNITZ (1711–94) becomes chancellor of Austria. His negotiations, through the marquise de POMPADOUR (1721–64), the mistress of LOUIS XV, persuade France to ally with Austria.

1755 Portuguese capital, Lisbon, is destroyed by an earthquake.

1756 French capture the island of Minorca from the British.

1756 Russia and Sweden join the Franco-Austrian alliance against Prussia.

1756 Prussia allies with Britain, invades Saxony, and starts the Seven Years War.

1757 Prussia invades Bohemia and defeats the French and Austrians at the battle of Rossbach in Bohemia.

1757 William PITT the Elder (1707–78) becomes prime minister of Britain.

1758 Prussians fight the Russians to a standstill at the battle of Zorndorf in S Germany.

1759 Combined Austrian-Russian army defeats the Prussians at the battle of Kunersdorf.

1759 British defeat the French at the naval battle of Quiberon Bay.

1759 Prussians defeat the French at the battle of Minden.

1759 Jesuits are expelled from Portugal.

1759 CHARLES III (1716–88) becomes king of Spain and hands the throne of Sicily and Naples to his son FERDINAND (1751–1825).

THE AMERICAS

1750 By the treaty of Madrid, Spain recognizes Portuguese claims in s and w Brazil.

1752 French capture a British trading post in the Ohio valley.

1753 French build Fort Duquesne (present-day Pittsburgh) on the River Ohio.

1754 French troops attack the British Fort Necessity in the Ohio valley.

1754 At the Albany Congress, Benjamin Franklin proposes limited union of the British colonies to combat French aggression.

1755 Start of the French and Indian War between French and British settlers, which becomes the American phase of the Seven Years War.

1755 British expedition against Fort Duquesne is defeated at the battle of the Wilderness.

1756 Leading Quakers resign from the Pennsylvania Assembly in protest against participation in hostilities.

1756 French under the marquis de MONTCALM (1712–59) drive the British from the Great Lakes region.

1757 French capture Fort William Henry; the British garrison is massacred by Native Americans.

1758 British forces capture forts Frontenac and Duquesne.

1759 City of Quebec in Canada is captured after British general James WOLFE (1727–59) wins the battle of the Plains of Abraham.

1759 British capture the island of Guadeloupe from the French.

SCIENCE AND TECHNOLOGY

1750 British astronomer Thomas Wright (1711–1786) suggests that the Milky Way is a huge disk of stars.

1752 Gregorian calendar is adopted in Britain.

1752 American writer, scientist and politician Benjamin FRANKLIN (1706–90) publishes his *Experiments and Observations in Electricity*.

▲ *Franklin* was a gifted scientist as well as a highly respected statesman. He spent 16 years in England prior to the American Revolution attempting to reconcile the differences between Britain and the colonies. He was later a signatory of the peace treaty.

1757 British optician John Dollond (1706–61) produces the first achromatic lenses.

1758 French economist François Quesnay (1694–1774) sums up his physiocratic system of political economy in his *Tableau economique*.

1758 British optical instrument maker John Bird (1709–76) invents an improved sextant.

1758 British wheelwright Jebediah Strutt (1726–97) invents a ribbing machine for making hosiery.

1759 British clockmaker John HARRISON (1693–1776) constructs the first marine chronometer.

ARTS AND HUMANITIES

1751 First volume of the French *Encyclopedia, or Classified Dictionary of Sciences, Arts and Trades* is published.

1752 Death of the German preacher Johann Bengel (b.1687), who established the evangelical movement Pietism.

1753 Italian artist Giovanni Tiepolo (1696–1770) completes his frescos decorating the Kaisersaal in Wurzburg, Germany.

1754 British furniture-maker Thomas Chippendale (1718–79) publishes his *The Gentleman and Cabinetmaker's Directory*.

1755 Austrian composer Franz HAYDN (1732–1809) writes his first string quartet.

1755 British writer Samuel JOHNSON (1709–84) publishes his *Dictionary of the English Language*.

1755 French philosopher Jean Jacques ROUSSEAU (1712–78) writes his essay *A Discourse upon the Origin of Inequality*.

1755 German archaeologist Johann Winckelmann (1717–68) publishes his *Thoughts on the Imitation of Greek Painting and Sculpture*.

1756 Italian artist Giambattista Piranesi (1720–78) publishes his book of engravings *The Roman Antiquities*.

1757 Scottish philosopher David HUME (1711–86) publishes his *Natural History of Religion*.

1758 French philosopher Claude HELVETIUS (1715–71) publishes his atheistic book *On the Mind*, which is condemned and burned.

1758 Swedish scientist Emanuel SWEDENBORG (1688–1772) publishes his religious treatise *The New Jerusalem*.

1759 French philosopher and author VOLTAIRE (1694–1778) publishes his satirical novel *Candide*.

1750
1752
1754
1756
1758
1759

ASIA AND AUSTRALASIA

1760 British defeat the French at the battle of Wandiwash in s India.

1760 Chinese emperor declares that all foreign trade shall pass through the port of Canton (Guangzhou).

1761 British capture Pondicherry from the French.

1761 HYDER ALI (1722–82) makes himself ruler of Mysore in s India.

1761 Afghans invade N India and defeat the MARATHAS at the battle of Panipat.

1762 Afghans defeat the Sikhs at Lahore.

1762 British bombard Manila and capture the Philippines from Spain.

1763 British establish a trading post at Bushire in sw Persia.

1764 British return the Philippines to Spain.

1764 British defeat a native coalition at the battle of Baskar and gain control of the whole of Bengal.

1765–69 Chinese invade Burma and establish overlordship.

1767 Burma invades and conquers Thailand.

1767–69 War between British troops and the Indian state of Mysore ends in a truce.

1768 French explorer Louis de BOUGAINVILLE (1729–1811) claims Tahiti for France.

AFRICA

1760 Dutch farmers moving N cross the Orange River in South Africa.

1763 Kayambugu (d.1780) becomes king of Buganda in E Africa.

1763 Treaty of Paris confirms British control of Senegal.

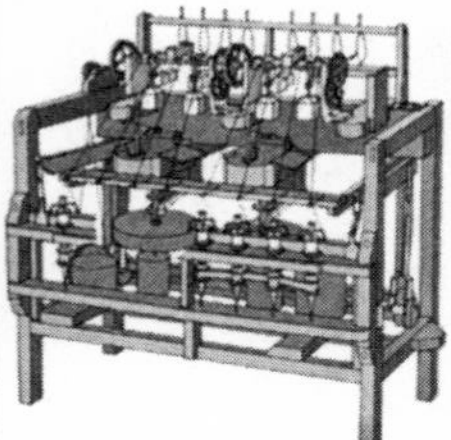

spinning frame *Shown here is Arkwright's spinning frame of 1769, which introduced powered machinery to the textile industry. The machine produced an unusually firm thread, which made it possible for the first time to produce a fabric consisting wholly of cotton. Arkwright called his invention a water frame, as it was powered by a water wheel. Spinning frames of this kind were made and used by Arkwright at Cromford, Derbyshire, from 1775.*

1768 ALI BEY (1728–73) establishes himself as ruler of Egypt and declares independence from the Turks.

EUROPE

1760 GEORGE III (1738–1820) becomes king of Britain.

1760 Russian army sacks Berlin.

1761 Third Family Compact strengthens the alliance between France and Spain.

1762 CATHERINE II (1729–96) seizes power in Russia by overthrowing her husband, PETER III (1728–62); she restores strong government.

1762 Spain invades Portugal but is repulsed.

1763 Austria makes the peace of Hubertsburg with Prussia, ending the European phase of the Seven Years War.

1763 "Whiteboys" revolt against British rule in Ireland.

1764 Russia and Prussia form an alliance to control Poland.

1764 Jesuits are expelled from France.

1765 JOSEPH II (1741–90) is elected Holy Roman emperor and becomes coruler, with his mother MARIA THERESA (1717–80), of the Austrian empire.

1766 Lorraine formally becomes a part of France.

1767 Jesuits are expelled from Spain.

1767 Catherine II of Russia appoints a commission for the modernization of the Russian state.

1768 Anti-Russian confederation is formed in Poland; its formation leads to a civil war in which Russia intervenes.

1768 Turkey declares war on Russia in defense of Poland.

1768 Genoa cedes Corsica to France.

1760

1762

1764

1766

1768

THE AMERICAS	SCIENCE AND TECHNOLOGY	ARTS AND HUMANITIES	

THE AMERICAS

1760 British capture Montreal from the French.

1761 British capture Cuba from the Spanish.

1761 James OTIS (1725–83) argues against British writs of assistance in a Massachusetts court.

1763 Peace of Paris ends the French and Indian War; Britain gains Canada, Tobago and Grenada from France and Florida from Spain; France cedes Louisiana to Spain.

1763 King George III of Britain issues a proclamation prohibiting N and W expansion from British colonies in North America.

1763 Surveyors Charles Mason and Jeremiah Dixon establish the boundary between Pennsylvania and Maryland.

1763–66 PONTIAC (1720–69), chief of the OTTAWA Native Americans, wages an unsuccessful war against the British.

1765 Stamp Act places a tax on books and documents in British North America; rioting breaks out in Boston and other cities.

1765 In New York, the Stamp Act Congress adopts a declaration of rights and liberties.

1765 British establish a colony on the Falkland Islands.

1766 Stamp Act is repealed.

1767 New York Assembly is suspended by the British.

1767 Townshend Acts place duties on many goods imported to British North America.

1768 Boston lawyer Samuel ADAMS (1722–1803) calls for united action against Britain.

1769 American explorer Daniel BOONE (1734–1820) opens a route into Kentucky.

1769 Spanish establish a settlement at San Diego in California.

SCIENCE AND TECHNOLOGY

1763 First exhibition of industrial arts is held in Paris.

1763 Scottish scientist Joseph BLACK (1728–99) discovers latent heat.

1764 British engineer James HARGREAVES (1722–78) invents the Spinning Jenny.

1765 Scottish engineer James WATT (1736–1819) improves the steam engine by adding a separate condenser.

1766 American writer, scientist and politician Benjamin FRANKLIN (1706–90) invents bifocal spectacles.

1766 British chemist Henry CAVENDISH (1731–1810) discovers hydrogen.

1769 British engineer Richard ARKWRIGHT (1732–92) invents a water-powered spinning frame.

ARTS AND HUMANITIES

1760 English novelist Laurence Sterne (1713–68) publishes the first volumes of his *Tristram Shandy*.

1760 British artist Joshua REYNOLDS (1723–92) paints his portrait of *Georgiana, Countess Spencer*.

1762 British artist George Stubbs (1724–1806) paints his *Mares and Foals*.

1762 French philosopher Jean Jacques ROUSSEAU (1712–78) publishes his *The Social Contract*.

1762 Scottish poet James Macpherson (1736–96) –"Ossian" – publishes his *Fingal*.

1762 German composer Christoph Gluck (1714–87) writes his opera *Orfeo and Euridice*.

1762 Building work starts on the Petit Trianon at Versailles in France.

1764 British author Horace Walpole (1717–97) publishes his Gothic horror novel *Castle of Otranto*.

1766 Irish novelist Oliver Goldsmith (1730–74) publishes his *The Vicar of Wakefield*.

1766 German philosopher and critic Gotthold Lessing (1729–81) publishes his *Laocoön*.

1766 First purpose-built American theater opens in Philadelphia.

1766 German poet Heinrich Gerstenberg (1737–1823) publishes the first of his *Letters on the Curiosities of Literature*; this work establishes the *Sturm und Drang* literary movement.

1760

1762

1764

1766

1768

1769

1770

1770 British establish a trading post at Basra, s Iraq.

1770 British explorer James Cook (1728–79) lands at Botany Bay and claims SE Australia for Britain.

1772

1773 British merchants obtain a monopoly over opium production in Bengal.

▼ *Continental Congress The first Congress met in Philadelphia on 5 September 1774. It was called to prepare a declaration condemning British actions in North America. The British government treated the actions of the Congress as rebellion. When the Second Congress met the following year, fighting had broken out. The Congress was accepted as the effective governing body of the rebels, although it had no statutory powers. It was the Congress that took the vital steps to issue the Declaration of Independence.*

1770 Louis (1754–93), later Louis XVI, marries MARIE ANTOINETTE (1755–93), daughter of MARIA THERESA.

1770 Russian fleet defeats the Turks at the battle of Chesme.

1770 John Struensee (1737–72) attempts radical reforms in Denmark.

1770 Lord NORTH (1732–92) becomes British prime minister.

1771 Russians conquer the Crimea from the Turks.

1771 Louis XV (1710–74) abolishes the French *parlements*.

1772 John Struensee is executed after an aristocratic coup.

1772 GUSTAVUS III (1746–92) restores the power of the monarchy in Sweden.

1772 Following Russian victories against the Turks, Austria and Prussia enforce the first partition of Poland. Russia, Austria and Prussia annex about 30% of Polish territory.

1773–75 Emelyan PUGACHEV (1726–75) leads a revolt of cossacks and peasants in SE Russia.

Jefferson · Samuel Adams · Franklin · Hancock · John Adams · Washington

1774

1774 British appoint Warren HASTINGS (1732–1818) as governor of India; he begins economic and administrative reforms.

1774 White Lotus Society foments a rebellion in NE China.

1775 War breaks out between the British and the MARATHAS in India.

1775 Persians attack and briefly capture Basra from the British.

▶ *North America The pattern of settlement in America between 1700 and 1774 is illustrated on the map. The first permanent settlement was founded by the Spanish in 1565. In the 17th century the English and the French went to the West Indies and North America. After 1700 free migration, as distinct from the importation of African slaves, was nearly all into the English colonies of the E seaboard.*

1774 Abiodun (d.1789) becomes king of Oyo in present-day s Nigeria.

1775 Maritius Benyowski establishes the town of Louisbourg on the coast of Madagascar for the French, who later refuse to support him.

1774 Louis XVI becomes king of France and restores the *parlements*.

1774 Treaty of Kuchuk Kainarji ends the war between Russia and Turkey; Russia gains Crimean ports.

Baltimore · RHODE ISLAND
NORTH CAROLINA · New Bern
English · SOUTH CAROLINA · Brunswick
African · GEORGIA · Georgetown · Savannah
German
Scottish/Irish · NEW ORLEANS

THE AMERICAS

1770 British troops shoot several Massachusetts citizens in what becomes known as the "Boston Massacre".

1772 American protesters burn the British customs ship *Gaspee* off Rhode Island.

1773 "Boston Tea Party" occurs when protesters dressed as Native Americans board British ships and dump tea into Boston harbor.

1773–74 Committees of Correspondence are set up throughout the British colonies.

1774 British pass the so-called Coercive Acts restricting American colonial rights.

1774 British fight and win Lord Dunmore's War against the SHAWNEE Native Americans.

1774 First Continental Congress meets at Philadelphia and draws up a Declaration of Rights and Grievances to be presented to Britain.

1774 Ann LEE (1736–84) establishes the first Shaker colony.

1775 American Revolution (American War of Independence) starts with the battles of Lexington and Concord, after which the British retreat to Boston.

1775 American general Ethan ALLEN (1738–89) captures Fort Ticonderoga from the British.

1775 Second Continental Congress meets at Philadelphia.

1775 Continental Army is formed outside Boston with George WASHINGTON (1732–99) as commander-in-chief.

SCIENCE AND TECHNOLOGY

1770 Grand Trunk Canal is completed in Britain.

1771 French astronomer Charles Messier (1730–1817) publishes the first volume of his star catalog.

1771 Italian scientist Luigi GALVANI (1737–98) conducts experiments that demonstrate a connection between muscular contractions and electricity.

1772 Imperial library in China begins compiling the *Complete Works of the Four Treasuries*, which contains more than 3000 works of literature.

1774 British chemist Joseph PRIESTLEY (1733–1804) discovers oxygen.

1774 British astronomer Nevil Maskelyne (1732–1811) discovers the value of the gravitational constant.

1774 British engineer John Wilkinson (1728–1808) invents a boring machine for making steam-engine cylinders and cannon.

1774 French chemist Antoine LAVOISIER (1743–94) demonstrates the conservation of mass in chemical reactions.

1775 Austrian physician Franz Mesmer (1734–1815) claims to be able to heal using "animal magnetism".

ARTS AND HUMANITIES

1770 British artist Thomas GAINSBOROUGH (1727–88) paints his *Blue Boy*.

1770 French philosopher Paul Holbach (1723–89) expounds materialism and determinism in his *System of Nature*.

1770 American artist Benjamin West (1738–1820) paints his *The Death of General Wolfe*.

1771 Encyclopedia Britannica is first published.

1772 French *L'Encyclopédie* is completed with the publication of the *Supplement to Bougainville's Voyage* by French philosopher and writer Denis DIDEROT (1713–84).

1773 Scottish architects Robert (1728–92) and James Adams publish their *Works of Architecture*.

1774 German poet and author Johann GOETHE (1749–1832) publishes his novel *The Sorrows of Young Werther*.

1775 German historian Johann HERDER (1744–1803) publishes his *Philosophy of History and Culture*.

> "Stand your ground. Don't fire unless fired upon, but if they mean to have a war, let it begin here!"
>
> US general John Parker (command given at the start of the battle of Lexington)

1770

1772

1774

1775

1775 cont.

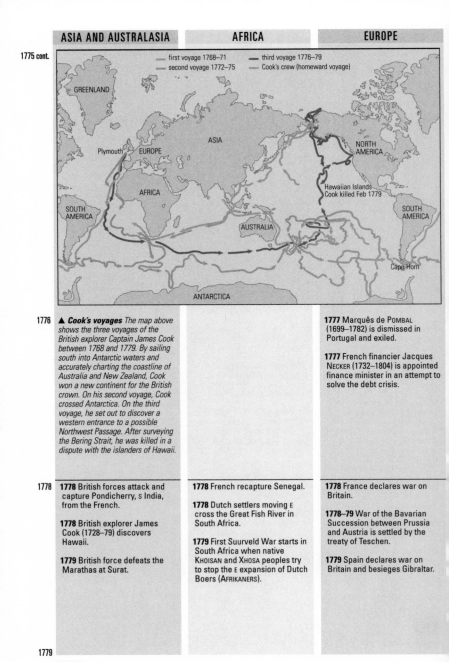

first voyage 1768–71 — third voyage 1776–79
second voyage 1772–75 — Cook's crew (homeward voyage)

GREENLAND

ASIA

Plymouth EUROPE

NORTH
AMERICA

AFRICA

Hawaiian Islands
Cook killed Feb 1779

SOUTH
AMERICA

SOUTH
AMERICA

AUSTRALIA

Cape Horn

ANTARCTICA

1776 ▲ **Cook's voyages** The map above shows the three voyages of the British explorer Captain James Cook between 1768 and 1779. By sailing south into Antarctic waters and accurately charting the coastline of Australia and New Zealand, Cook won a new continent for the British crown. On his second voyage, Cook crossed Antarctica. On the third voyage, he set out to discover a western entrance to a possible Northwest Passage. After surveying the Bering Strait, he was killed in a dispute with the islanders of Hawaii.

1777 Marquês de POMBAL (1699–1782) is dismissed in Portugal and exiled.

1777 French financier Jacques NECKER (1732–1804) is appointed finance minister in an attempt to solve the debt crisis.

1778 **1778** British forces attack and capture Pondicherry, s India, from the French.

1778 British explorer James Cook (1728–79) discovers Hawaii.

1779 British force defeats the Marathas at Surat.

1778 French recapture Senegal.

1778 Dutch settlers moving E cross the Great Fish River in South Africa.

1779 First Suurveld War starts in South Africa when native KHOISAN and XHOSA peoples try to stop the E expansion of Dutch Boers (AFRIKANERS).

1778 France declares war on Britain.

1778–79 War of the Bavarian Succession between Prussia and Austria is settled by the treaty of Teschen.

1779 Spain declares war on Britain and besieges Gibraltar.

1779

THE AMERICAS

1775 British win the battle of Bunker Hill; the Americans besiege Boston.

1775 American troops capture Montreal, but fail to take Quebec.

1776 British evacuate Boston.

1776 Congress adopts the Declaration of Independence written by American Statesman Thomas JEFFERSON (1743–1826).

1776 British win the battle of Long Island and occupy New York City.

1776 British defeat George WASHINGTON (1732–99) at the battle of White Plains and force an American retreat.

1776 Washington crosses the River Delaware and defeats the British at the battle of Trenton.

1777 Washington defeats the British at the battle of Princeton.

1777 Following defeat at the battle of Saratoga, British general John BURGOYNE (1722–92) surrenders to the Americans.

1777 British win the battle of Brandywine and occupy Philadelphia.

1777 British defeat Washington at the battle of Germanstown.

1777 Congress approves the Articles of Confederation that create the United States.

1778 France makes an alliance with the United States and sends a fleet.

1778 British evacuate Philadelphia.

1778 Washington wins the battle of Monmouth.

1778 British capture Savannah.

1779 American privateer John Paul JONES (1747–92) captures the British ship *Serapis*.

1779 Britain captures St. Lucia from the French.

SCIENCE AND TECHNOLOGY

▼ American Revolution
Illustrated below are an American soldier, left, and a British soldier, right. British "redcoats" were professional soldiers who were generally superior in conventional battles to the imperfectly trained American volunteers. Commander in chief George Washington kept the American army in existence despite repeated disappointments and used the American skill in guerrilla tactics to wear down the British until they could be outmaneuvered.

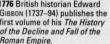

1779 British engineer Samuel CROMPTON (1753–1827) invents the spinning mule.

1779 Cast-iron bridge is completed at Coalbrookdale in Britain.

RELIGION AND THE ARTS

1775 cont.

1776 British historian Edward GIBBON (1737–94) publishes the first volume of his *The History of the Decline and Fall of the Roman Empire*.

1776 British economist Adam SMITH (1723–90) publishes his *An Inquiry into the Nature and Causes of the Wealth of Nations*.

1777 British dramatist Richard Sheridan (1751–1816) writes his *School for Scandal*.

1778 La Scala in Milan hosts its first opera.

1779 Italian sculptor Antonio Canova (1757–1822) carves his *Daedalus and Icarus*.

1776

1778

1779

1780	**1781** Assisted by the French, HYDER ALI (1722–82), sultan of Mysore, attacks the British and is defeated at the battle of Porto Novo. **1781** British conquer the Dutch settlements in Sumatra.	**1781** First Suurveld War in E South Africa ends with Boer (AFRIKANER) victory.	**1780** Russia forms the League of Armed Neutrality against British interference with shipping. **1780** Britain declares war on Holland. **1780** Anti-Catholic Gordon Riots occur in London. **1781** French financier Jacques NECKER (1732–1804) is dismissed as French finance minister. **1781** Russia and Austria form an anti-Turkish treaty for control of the Balkans. **1781** JOSEPH II (1741–90) of Austria abolishes serfdom and establishes freedom of worship.
1782	**1782** Sultan of Mysore, Hyder Ali, dies during a campaign against the British; his son TIPU SULTAN (1747–99) continues the war. **1782** New Thai king Rama I (1737–1809) expels the Burmese and establishes a new capital at Bangkok. **1782** Treaty of Salbai ends the war between the British and the MARATHAS in India.	**1783** Portuguese build a fort at Cabinda in Angola, SW Africa.	**1782** Spanish capture Minorca from the British. **1783** Treaty of Paris ends the war against Britain by France, Spain and the USA. **1783** Russia annexes the Crimea. **1783** William PITT the Younger (1759–1806) becomes British prime minister.
1784	**1784** India Act places the British colonies in India under government control. **1784** Tipu Sultan is defeated by the British when the French fail to send aid; he signs the treaty of Mangalore. **1784** US merchants start trading with China. **1784** Dutch cede the settlement of Negapatam in SE India to the British.	 ▲ ***Montgolfier's balloon*** *The first manned balloon flight took place on 21 November 1783. Jean François Pilâtre de Rozier and the Marquis d'Arlandes traveled about 8km (5mi) across Paris in a balloon made of paper-lined linen and coated with alum to reduce the fire risk.*	**1784** Treaty of Versailles ends the war between Holland and Britain. **1785** CATHERINE II (1729–96) issues charters recognizing the rights of the Russian aristocracy and towns. **1785** Prussia forms the League of German princes against Austria.
1786	**1786** British establish a settlement at Rangoon in Burma.	**1786** United States pays a bribe to Morocco to purchase immunity from pirate attacks. **1786** French expedition attacks Louisbourg in Madagascar and kills Maritius Benyowski.	**1786** FREDERICK WILLIAM II (1744–97) becomes king of Prussia.

THE AMERICAS

1780 British capture Charleston.

1780 British defeat the Americans at the battle of Camden.

1780 Treacherous American general Benedict ARNOLD (1741–1801) flees to the British.

1780 American troops drive the IROQUOIS Native Americans from the state of New York.

1780 British defeat the Americans at the battle of King's Mountain.

1780 TUPAC AMARU (c.1742–81), a descendant of the INCA rulers, leads a short-lived rebellion against the Spanish in Peru.

1780 French general the marquis de LAFAYETTE (1757–1834) persuades French king LOUIS XVI (1754–93) to send troops to reinforce the Americans.

1781 Americans win the battle of the Cowpens.

1781 Combined American and French force besieges the British at Yorktown.

1781 British under General Charles CORNWALLIS (1738–1805) surrender to the Americans at Yorktown.

1781 Communeros revolt against the Spanish breaks out in Colombia.

1782 British fleet under Admiral George RODNEY (1718–92) defeats the French at the battle of the Saints in the Caribbean.

1783 Britain recognizes US independence and cedes Tobago to France and Florida to Spain.

1784 Russia establishes a colony on Kodiak Island, Alaska.

1786 Shays' rebellion is suppressed in Massachusetts.

SCIENCE AND TECHNOLOGY

1781 German-born English astronomer William HERSCHEL (1738–1822) discovers Uranus.

1782 Scottish engineer James WATT (1736–1819) perfects the double-acting steam engine producing rotary motion.

1783 Hot-air balloon built by the French MONTGOLFIER brothers, Joseph (1740–1810) and Jacques (1745–99), makes the first crewed flight.

1783 French physicist Jacques CHARLES (1746–1823) makes the first hydrogen balloon flight.

1783 Swiss scientist Horace de Saussure (1740–99) invents an improved hair hygrometer.

1783 French engineer Claude de Jouffroy d'Abbans (1751–1832) builds a full-sized, paddle-wheel steamboat.

1784 British chemist Henry CAVENDISH (1731–1810) establishes the chemical composition of water.

1784 British ironworker Henry Cort (1740–1800) devises the puddling process to produce wrought iron.

1785 British clergyman Edmund CARTWRIGHT (1743–1823) invents the power loom.

1785 French physicist Charles COULOMB (1736–1806) publishes his law of electrical attraction in his *Memoirs on Electricity and Magnetism*.

1785 French chemist Claude Berthollet (1748–1822) invents chlorine bleach.

1785 Steam engine produced by James Watt and Matthew BOULTON (1728–1809) is installed in a British factory

ARTS AND HUMANITIES

1781 German philosopher Immanuel KANT (1724–1804) publishes his *Critique of Pure Reason*.

1782 British artist Henry Fuseli (1741–1825) paints his *The Nightmare*.

1783 Death of the French philosopher and mathematician Jean d'ALEMBERT (b.1717) who jointly edited *L'Encyclopédie* with French philosopher and writer Denis DIDEROT (1713–84).

1783 American publisher Noah Webster (1758–1843) produces *The American Spelling Book.*.

1785 French artist Jacques DAVID (1748–1825) paints his *Oath of the Horatii*.

1786 Austrian composer Wolfgang Amadeus MOZART (1756–91) writes his opera *Marriage of Figaro*.

1786 Scottish poet Robert BURNS (1759–96) publishes his *Poems, Chiefly in the Scottish Dialect*.

1787

1787 Chinese suppress a rebellion in Formosa (present-day Taiwan).

1787 Matsudaira Sadanobu (1759–1829) becomes chief minister to the infant Japanese shōgun Ienari (d.1838) and introduces a series of administrative reforms.

1787 British establish the colony of Sierra Leone in w Africa.

> "A bill of rights is what the people are entitled to against every government on earth... and what no just government should refuse to rest on inference."
>
> Thomas Jefferson (letter to James Madison)

1787 Dutch ruler William V (1748–1806) calls in Prussian troops to suppress the pro-French Patriot Party.

1787 CHARLES III (1716–88) of Spain establishes the *junta* (council of ministers).

1787 French king Louis XVI (1754–93) dismisses an assembly of notables and banishes, then recalls, the Paris *parlement*.

1787 Russia allied to Austria attacks the Turks.

1787 Britain, Holland and Prussia form an alliance against France.

1787 Austria incorporates Belgium as a royal province.

1788

1788 Britain transports the first shipment of convicts to Australia.

1789 Crew of the British ship *Bounty* mutiny and cast captain William BLIGH (1754–1817) adrift in an open boat.

1789 On the death of Abiodun, Awole becomes king of Oyo in present-day s Nigeria.

1789 Second Suurveld War breaks out when the Xhosa attempt to regain their traditional lands.

1788 Paris *parlement* presents a list of grievances to Louis XVI, who recalls Jacques Necker and summons the States General.

1788 Sweden invades Russian-controlled Finland.

1789 Austrians capture Belgrade from the Turks; Russian advance reaches the River Danube.

1789 States General meets at Versailles; the third estate declares themselves the National (Constituent) Assembly and takes the "tennis court oath" to establish a constitution.

1789 Louis XVI dismisses Jacques Necker again; the Paris mob storms the Bastille and establishes a Commune as a provisional government; the marquis de LAFAYETTE (1757–1834) becomes commander of the National Guard; peasant risings and urban rioting create the "Great Fear"; the National Assembly abolishes the feudal system and issues the Declaration of the Rights of Man.

1789 Mob of Parisian women march to Versailles and escort Louis XVI to Paris; the National Assembly moves to Paris and debates a constitution.

1789 Belgians rise against Austrian rule and defeat an Austrian army at Turnhout.

French Revolution *Shortly before the Revolution, Paris' city limits had been extended by the building of the "tax-farmers" wall (1785), authorized by the finance minister, Calonne, to facilitate the collection of tolls from those entering the city. The wall, 3m (7ft) high, ran concentrically with the* old city boundaries and took in several of the surrounding districts (faubourgs). Access was gained through 54 gates (barrières), which were largely destroyed by the crowds during the Revolution. The city's population in 1789 was approximately 600,000.

- ● Réveillon riots (April 1789)
- ● Bastille stormed (July 1789)
- ● March to Versailles (October 1789)
- ● Tuileries sacked (August 1792)
- ⌐ Tax-farmers wall built (1785)
- ■ Remains of old city wall
- ☐ Inner boulevards
- ■ Palace of Louis XV (site of guillotine)

THE AMERICAS

1787 Northwest Ordinance regulates the creation of new states in the USA.

1787 Constitutional Convention meets in Philadelphia and signs the US constitution.

1788 US constitution comes into effect when New Hampshire becomes the ninth state to ratify it.

1788 New York becomes the capital of the USA.

1789 George WASHINGTON (1732–99) is elected the first president of the United States.

1789 Attempted revolution in s Brazil is led by army officer Joaquim de Silva.

1789 US Congress adopts the Bill of Rights, 10 amendments to the constitution.

1789 Spanish challenge British claims to the Nootka Sound region of w Canada.

SCIENCE AND TECHNOLOGY

1787 French mathematician Joseph Lagrange (1736–1813) publishes his *Analytical Mechanics*.

1788 Scottish engineer Andrew Meikle (1719–1811) patents a threshing machine.

1789 French chemist Antoine LAVOISIER (1743–94) expounds his theory of combustion in his *Elementary Treatise on Chemistry*.

▲ *Marquis de Lafayette* became a popular hero when he led the French volunteers who helped the American colonists break free from Britain. He joined the French National Assembly in 1789, presenting a declaration of rights and organizing the National Guard. A moderate reformer, he became trapped between Jacobin extremists and the court and fled in 1792.

RELIGION AND THE ARTS

1787 Freed African slave Ottobah Cugoana publishes his book *Thoughts and Sentiments on Slavery*.

1788 German philosopher Immanuel KANT (1724–1804) publishes his *Critique of Practical Reason*.

1788 *Times* newspaper is founded in London.

1789 English social philosopher Jeremy BENTHAM (1748–1832) expounds his theory of utilitarianism in his *Introduction to the Principles of Morals and Legislation*.

1789 British poet William BLAKE (1757–1827) publishes his *Songs of Innocence*.

1789 French revolutionary Camille DESMOULINS (1760–94) publishes his republican manifesto *Free France*.

1789 French politician Emmanuel Joseph SIÈYES (1748–1836) publishes his pamphlet *What is the Third Estate?*

1790

1790 TIPU SULTAN (1747–99) attacks the pro-British s Indian state of Travancore.

1791 Fulani scholar and poet Usman dan Fodio (1754–1817) is appointed tutor to the rulers of Gobir in present-day N Nigeria.

1790 French revolutionary leader Maximilien ROBESPIERRE (1758–94) is elected leader of the Jacobin political club in Paris.

1792

1792 Tipu Sultan is defeated by the British.

1792 RANJIT SINGH (1780–1839) becomes king of the Sikhs.

1793 Burma under King Bodawpaya (d.1819) acquires coastal territory Thailand.

1793 French royalists surrender Pondicherry to the British.

1793 Shōgun Ienari (d.1838) takes personal control of the Japanese government.

1793 Chinese emperor refuses to lift restrictions on the import of British goods.

1793 First free settlers arrive in Australia.

1793 Second Suurveld War ends when Dutch magistrates compel the AFRIKANERS to concede territory to the XHOSA.

▼ **slave trade** The triangular route taken by slave ships from European ports such as Liverpool, Bristol and Bordeaux took them to Africa to collect slaves, across the Atlantic Ocean to sell them and back again with cargos bartered in exchange. By the end of the 18th century, the major share of the slave traffic was carried on by Great Britain, supplying slaves to plantations in the West Indies and the Americas.

1791 Wolfe TONE (1763–98) founds the society of United Irishmen.

1791 LOUIS XVI (1754–93) attempts to flee France but is escorted back to Paris; a constitution is proclaimed and elections held for the new Legislative Assembly.

1792 Paris mob storms the Tuileries palace and imprisons the royal family; Georges DANTON (1759–94) takes control of a provisional government; National Convention is elected; France is proclaimed a republic.

1792 Austria and Prussia form an alliance against France; France declares war on Austria.

1792 Austria and Prussia invade France; the French defeat the Prussians at the battle of Valmy and the Austrians at the battle of Jemappes; they conquer Belgium and annex Savoy.

1793 Poland loses 60% of its territory to Russia and Prussia in the second partition of Poland.

1793 Louis XVI is guillotined; Jacobins take control of the national convention; revolutionary Jean MARAT (b.1743) is murdered by Charlotte CORDAY (1768–93); revolutionary tribunal is set up to judge "enemies of the state"; start of the Reign of Terror; Lazare CARNOT (1753–1823) reorganizes the French army; Corsican officer NAPOLÉON Bonaparte (1769–1821) is promoted to general.

1793 Britain, Holland and Spain declare war on France; Austria recaptures Belgium; Britain attempts to invade s France.

slave trade
1790

SENEGAL
GOLD COAST

Palmares
Bahia
Rio de
Janeiro
JAMAICA
BAHAMAS
HAITI

ANGOLA

ANTIGUA
GUADELOUPE and
MARTINIQUE

British
38,000

French
20,000

BARBADOS

Portuguese
10,000

GRENADA
TRINIDAD
CURAÇAO

Dutch
4,000

British slave triangle

1794

1794 Last Persian shah of the Zand dynasty is killed; Aga Muhammad (d.1797) founds the Kajar dynasty.

1794 British capture the Seychelles from the French.

1795 British take Dutch Malacca to deny it to the French.

1795 British capture Cape Colony in South Africa from the Dutch.

1794 Robespierre and followers are condemned by the National Convention and executed; revolutionary tribunal is abolished; end of the Reign of Terror.

1794 French reconquer Belgium and invade Spain; British capture Corsica.

THE AMERICAS

1790 Spain withdraws its claims to Nootka Sound.

1790 Washington D.C. is designated the US capital.

1791 US Bill of Rights is ratified.

1791 Alexander HAMILTON (1755–1804) founds the Bank of the United States.

1791 Remaining British possessions in North America are organized into French-speaking Lower Canada and English-speaking Upper Canada.

1791 Slave revolt breaks out on the French island of Haiti in the Caribbean.

1791 Vermont becomes a state of the USA.

1792 New York Stock Exchange is established.

1792 George WASHINGTON (1732–99) is re-elected US president.

1792 Kentucky becomes a state of the USA.

1793 Slave rising causes extensive damage in Albany, New York.

1794 Slavery is abolished in French colonies.

1794 Whiskey Insurrection in Pennsylvania is suppressed.

1794 USA signs Jay's treaty regularizing trade with Britain and borders with Canada.
1794 US general Anthony WAYNE

SCIENCE AND TECHNOLOGY

1790 British engineer Matthew BOULTON (1728–1809) patents the steam-powered coining press.

1790 French adopt the decimal system of weights and measures.

1791 French military engineer Claude Chappe (1763–1805) invents the semaphore tower for long-distance communication.

1792 French revolutionaries adopt a new calendar starting at Year 1.

1792 Scottish engineer William Murdock (1754–1839) produces coal gas.

1793 US engineer Eli WHITNEY (1765–1825) invents the cotton gin.

1794 French revolutionary calendar is modified to have three 10-day weeks per month.

1795 Scottish geologist James Hutton (1726–97) publishes his *Theory of the Earth*.

ARTS AND HUMANITIES

1790 British author Edmund BURKE (1729–97) criticizes liberalism in his *Reflections on the Revolution in France*.

1791 British biographer James BOSWELL (1740–95) publishes his *Life of Samuel Johnson*.

1791 French revolutionary Louis de SAINT-JUST (1767–94) publishes his *The Spirit of the Revolution*.

1791 French author the marquis de Sade (1740–1814) publishes his *Justine*.

1791 Austrian composer Wolfgang Amadeus MOZART (1756–91) writes his opera *The Magic Flute*.

1792 US writer Thomas PAINE (1737–1809) publishes his *The Rights of Man*.

1792 British feminist Mary WOLLSTONECRAFT (1759–97) publishes her *Vindication of the Rights of Women*.

1792 French revolutionary soldier Claude de l'Isle composes the *Marseillaise*.

◀ *Paine* emigrated to Philadelphia from England in 1774 and soon became one of America's most influential revolutionaries. His pamphlet *Common Sense* and his *Crisis* papers profoundly stirred popular sentiment, with their impassioned pleas for liberty, condemnation of tyranny and powerful arguments favoring American independence.

1794 British poet William BLAKE (1757–1827) publishes his *Songs of Experience*.

1795 Spanish artist Francisco GOYA (1746–1828) paints his portrait of *The Duchess of Alba*.

1790

1792

1794

ASIA AND AUSTRALASIA	AFRICA	EUROPE

1794 cont.

▶ *Jenner was a pioneer of the science of immunology. He coined the word vaccination to describe his use of cowpox inoculation to obtain immunity to smallpox.*

1794 Thadeus KÓSCIUSZKO (1746–1817) leads a popular rising in Poland; it is suppressed by Russian and Prussian troops.

1795 Some French aristocrats return and begin a White Terror in s France; new constitution establishes the Directory in Paris.

1795 France invades Holland and establishes the Batavian Republic; Prussia makes the peace of Basle with France.

1795 Polish state is dissolved by the third partition, between Russia, Austria and Prussia.

1796

1796 Britain conquers Ceylon (present-day Sri Lanka) from the Dutch.

1796 Jia Qing (d.1820) becomes Chinese emperor and begins campaigns to suppress the White Lotus society.

1797 US government agrees to pay bribes to Algiers and Tripoli to further safeguard US shipping from pirate attacks.

1796 France invades s Germany but is repelled; Bonaparte defeats the Austrians and captures Milan; Spain makes treaty of San Ildefonso with France and declares war on Britain; Spanish fleet is destroyed by the British at Cape St. Vincent.

1797 French conquer Venice and N Italy; the peace of Campo Formio ends hostilities with Austria; end of first war of the Coalition against France.

1797 FREDERICK WILLIAM III (1770–1840) becomes king of Prussia.

1798

1798 Persians under Shah Fath Ali (1771–1834) attack Afghanistan.

1799 TIPU SULTAN (b.1747) is killed fighting against British forces led by Arthur WELLESLEY (1769–1852).

1799 French invade Syria and capture Jaffa but withdraw after an outbreak of plague.

1798 Napoléon Bonaparte lands an army at Alexandria, invades Egypt, and defeats the MAMELUKES at the battle of the Pyramids.

1798 British admiral Horatio NELSON (1758–1805) destroys the French fleet at the naval battle of Aboukir.

1798 French settlers on the island of Mauritius overthrow the colonial government.

1799 Bonaparte defeats a Turkish attempt to recapture Egypt at the land battle of Aboukir.

1798 French occupy Rome and establish a republic; French invade Switzerland; French capture Malta; a second Coalition against France is formed; French conquer s Italy; Russians capture Corfu and the Ionian Islands

1798 British troops defeat the United Irishmen at Vinegar Hill.

1799 Austrians and Russians defeat the French at the battles of Zurich, the Trebbia and Novi; they regain control of Italy and drive the French from Switzerland; Russia withdraws from the Coalition.

1799 Bonaparte returns to Paris and abolishes the Directory; he establishes the Consulate with himself as First Consul.

1799 Balkan state of Montenegro becomes independent of the Ottoman Empire.

1799

THE AMERICAS

(1745–96) defeats the Ohio Native Americans at the battle of the Fallen Timbers.

1795 USA signs Pinckney's treaty with Spain establishing the border with Florida.

▶ *Qing dynasty* This Manchurian dynasty of China reached its greatest extent at the end of the 18th century. Its authority spread to Mongolia, Tibet and Turkistan and to Burma, Nepal and Annam (present-day Vietnam). As the empire grew in size and wealth, European expansion in search of trade threatened its security and stability.

1796 Tennessee becomes a state of the USA.

1796 US settlers found Cleveland in Ohio.

1796 John ADAMS (1735–1826) is elected US president.

1797 XYZ Affair leads to a naval war between the USA and France.

1798 Slave leader Pierre TOUSSAINT L'OUVERTURE (1744–1803) drives the French from Haiti.

1799 Russian governor of Alaska founds the city of Sitka.

SCIENCE AND TECHNOLOGY

Map legend:
- ▨ Manchu China
- ▢ under Manchu suzerainty

Labels on map: RUSSIAN EMPIRE, AMUR, USSURI, MANCHURIA, JUNGGAR PENDI, OUTER MONGOLIA, INNER MONGOLIA, XINJIANG, Beijing, JAPAN, KOREA, Tianjin, QINGHAI, Huang He, Kaifeng, Grand Canal, TIBET, Hankou, Nanjing, Hangzhou, Shanghai, Yangtze, CHINA, Fuzhou, NEPAL, BHUTAN, INDIA, FORMOSA, Guangzhou, BURMA, ANNAM, SIAM

1797 French scientist André Garnerin (1769–1823) demonstrates his parachute by jumping from a hot-air balloon.

1798 US engineer Robert Fulton (1765–1815) demonstrates his submarine *Nautilus* to the French navy.

1798 British physician Edward JENNER (1749–1823) inoculates patients against smallpox using cowpox vaccine.

1798 US scientist Benjamin Rumford (1753–1814) publishes his *Inquiry Concerning the Heat which is Caused by Friction*, outlining the kinetic theory of heat.

1799 German mathematician Karl Gauss (1777–1855) establishes the fundamental algebraic proof.

1799 French historians in Egypt discover the tri-lingual Rosetta stone.

RELIGION AND THE ARTS

1794 cont.

1796 US artist Gilbert Stuart (1755–1828) paints his unfinished portrait of George Washington.

1797 German philosopher Friedrich von Schelling (1775–1854) publishes his *Philosophy of Nature*.

1796

1798 British poets William WORDSWORTH (1770–1850) and Samuel Taylor COLERIDGE (1772–1834) publish their *Lyrical Ballads*.

1798 British economist Thomas MALTHUS (1766–1834) publishes the first edition of his *Essay on the Principle of Population*.

1799 German author and dramatist Friedrich von SCHILLER (1759–1805) completes his *Wallenstein* trilogy.

1798

1799

ASIA AND AUSTRALASIA	AFRICA	EUROPE
1800		
1800 Chinese emperor bans the smoking of opium.	**1800** French defeat the Turks and Egyptians outside Cairo.	**1800** NAPOLÉON Bonaparte (1769–1821) defeats the Austrians at the battle of Marengo; a French army captures Munich and defeats the Austrians at the battle of Hohenlinden; French begin the invasion of Austria.
1801		
1801 Britain annexes the Carnatic region of s India.	**1801** Yusef Karamanli of Tripoli demands an increased pirate-protection bribe from the USA and declares war; the USA blockades Tripoli; start of the Tripolitanian War.	**1801** ALEXANDER I (1777–1825) becomes czar of Russia.
	1801 British defeat the French at Alexandria.	**1801** Act of Union joins Ireland to Britain.
		1801 Concordat joins church and state in France.
		1801 Austria makes the peace of Luneville with France.
		1801 Russia makes peace with France and joins the neutral Northern Coalition.
1802		
1802 Vietnamese emperor Nguyen Anh (1762–1820) reunites Annam under his control.	**1802** French withdraw from Egypt.	**1802** Britain makes the peace of Amiens with France; peace is established throughout Europe.
1802 British return Malacca to the Dutch.	**1802** British return Cape Colony to the Dutch.	**1802** Bonaparte becomes consul for life and president of the Italian republic; France annexes Piedmont.
1802 RANJIT SINGH (1780–1839) leads the Sikhs into Amristar.		
1802 British gain control of central India by the treaty of Bassein.		
1803		
1803 British navigator Matthew Flinders (1774–1814) circumnavigates Australia.	**1803** Tripolitanians capture the US ship *Philadelphia*.	**1803** Switzerland regains its independence.
1803 Second Maratha War begins; the British capture Delhi; Arthur WELLESLEY (1769–1852) wins the battle of Assaye in s India.		**1803** Russia annexes Georgia.
		1803 France occupies Hanover and prepares to invade Britain.
1804		
1804 Founding of Hobart marks the beginning of the colonization of Tasmania.	**1804** US forces capture the port of Derna near Tripoli.	**1804** Bonaparte is crowned Napoleon I emperor of France by the pope; the Code Napoléon law code is issued.
1804 British annex Calcutta.	**1804** Usman dan Fodio (1754–1817) leads the Fulani people against the Hausa states in Nigeria and establishes the Sokoto caliphate.	**1804** KARAGEORGE (1766–1817) leads a Serbian insurrection against the Turks.
1804 Chinese emperor finally suppresses the White Lotus society.		

THE AMERICAS	SCIENCE AND TECHNOLOGY	ARTS AND HUMANITIES	

THE AMERICAS

1800 France acquires Louisiana from Spain.

1800 Leaders of an intended slave revolt are hanged in Virginia.

1800 Thomas JEFFERSON (1743–1826) is elected US president.

▲ **Napoleon** was a military and organizational genius who won France a short-lived supremacy over most of Europe. Among his greatest achievements, however, were his reforms of French society, such as codifying the law and rationalizing education and administration.

1803 Ohio becomes a state of the USA.

1803 USA purchases New Orleans and Louisiana from France.

1803 Russians occupy E Alaska.

1804 Haiti declares independence from France under Emperor Jacques DESSALINES (1758–1806).

1804 US vice president Aaron BURR (1756–1836) kills Alexander HAMILTON (b.1755) in a duel.

1804 Meriwether LEWIS (1774–1809) and William Clark (1770–1838) lead a US expedition across Louisiana.

SCIENCE AND TECHNOLOGY

1800 Italian scientist Alessandro VOLTA (1745–1827) invents the galvanic cell electrical battery.

1800 Joseph Finlay builds an iron chain suspension bridge in Pennsylvania.

1800 German-born English astronomer William HERSCHEL (1738–1822) discovers infrared light.

1801 German mathematician Karl GAUSS (1777–1855) publishes his *Arithmetical Investigations*.

1801 Italian astronomer Giuseppe Piazzi (1746–1826) discovers the asteroid Ceres.

1801 French clothworker Joseph Jacquard (1752–1834) invents a loom to make figured fabric.

1801 German scientist Johann Ritter (1776–1810) discovers ultraviolet light.

1802 British engineer Richard TREVITHICK (1771–1833) invents a high-pressure steam engine.

1802 French physicist Jacques CHARLES (1746–1823) formulates his law of gas expansion.

1803 British chemist William Henry (1774–1836) discovers his law of the volume of dissolved gases.

1804 Swiss scientist Nicholas de Saussure (1767–1845) discovers that carbon dioxide and nitrogen are essential for plant growth.

ARTS AND HUMANITIES

1800 German philosopher Johann Fichte (1762–1814) publishes his *The Destiny of Man*.

1800 German poet Friedrich von Hardenberg (1772–1801) – Novalis – publishes his *Hymns of the Night*.

1800 Library of Congress is established in Washington D.C.

1802 German composer Ludwig van BEETHOVEN (1770–1827) writes his *Moonlight* sonata.

▼ **Australia** Explorers during the early 19th century sailed around uncharted coasts of Australia and probed the interior from settled areas in the southeast. They journeyed up the great rivers and across mountains and deserts in search of fertile land and an inland sea which they believed to exist. The map shows areas explored between 1800 and 1830.

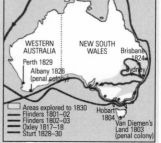

1800
1801
1802
1803
1804

ASIA AND AUSTRALASIA

1807 Ottoman Janisseries revolt and replace sultan SELIM III (1761–1808) with Mustafa IV (1779–1808).

1808 Colonial officers in Australia stage the Rum Rebellion against governor William BLIGH (1754–1817).

1808 Dutch conquer the independent state of Bantam in Indonesia.

1808 MAHMUD II (1785–1839) becomes Ottoman sultan.

1809 Treaty of Amritsar fixes the boundary between British territory in India and the Sikh kingdom.

1809 British make a defense treaty with the Afghans.

AFRICA

1805 Ottoman governor MUHAMMAD ALI (1769–1849) seizes power in Egypt.

1805 Tripolitanian War ends when the bey of Tunis renounces the right to levy pirate-protection bribes on the USA.

1806 British recapture Cape Colony in South Africa.

◀ **Nelson** broke the rigid tactical and strategic doctrines of his day in favor of imaginative decisions that seized the moment. His personal style of leadership won the loyalty of his crew. Nelson's "pell-mell" strategy at the Battle of Trafalgar (1805) destroyed Napoleon's invasion plans.

1807 Slave trade is abolished throughout the British Empire; a w African naval patrol is established to enforce the ban.

1807 British, allied to Russia, occupy Alexandria but withdraw after Turkish opposition.

> "Whither is fled the visionary gleam? / Where is it now, the glory and the dream? / Our birth is but a sleep and a forgetting. "
>
> William Wordsworth (*Ode on Intimations of Immortality*)

1809 British capture Senegal from the French.

EUROPE

1805 Britain forms a third Coalition with Russia, Sweden and Austria to make war on France; an Austrian army surrenders at Ulm; British under Horatio NELSON (1758–1805) win the naval battle of Trafalgar; French occupy Vienna; NAPOLEON defeats the Russians and Austrians at the battle of Austerlitz; Austrians sign the treaty of Pressburg; Napoleon becomes king of Italy.

1806 Turks, allied to France, attack the Russians.

1806 Napoleon organizes German states into a pro-French Confederation of the Rhine; his brother Joseph BONAPARTE (1768–1844) becomes king of Naples; the Holy Roman Empire is dissolved; Prussia attacks the French and is defeated at the battles of Jena and Auerstadt; Napoleon occupies Berlin and proclaims a blockade of Britain (the Continental System).

1807 French defeat the Prussians, capture Danzig and defeat the Russians at the battle of Friedland; peace of Tilsit ends fighting between France and Russia allied to Prussia; grand duchy of Warsaw is created in Poland; British destroy the Danish fleet; French marshal Andache Junot (1771–1813) conquers Portugal.

1808 Russia conquers Finland from Sweden.

1808 French troops invade Spain; CHARLES IV (1748–1819) abdicates and Joseph Bonaparte becomes king, marshal Joachim MURAT (1767–1815) takes the throne of Naples; British troops under Arthur WELLESLEY (1769–1852) land in Portugal and force a French evacuation; a Spanish revolt is suppressed by Napoleon.

1809 French win the battle of Coruña, force the British out of Spain, and invade Portugal; an Austrian uprising is defeated by Napoleon at the battle of Wagram; Austria signs the peace of Schönbrunn.

THE AMERICAS	SCIENCE AND TECHNOLOGY	ARTS AND HUMANITIES	
		1805 British artist Joseph TURNER (1775–1851) paints his *Shipwreck*.	1805
1806 British occupy Buenos Aires but are evicted by a colonial militia. **1806** Francisco de MIRANDA (1754–1816) leads an unsuccessful rebellion against the Spanish in Venezuela.	**1806** British admiral Francis Beaufort (1774–1857) devises a practical scale for measuring wind speed. **1806** British chemist Humphry DAVY (1778–1829) discovers sodium and potassium.	**1806** German bookseller Johann Palm publishes a pamphlet entitled *Germany in its Deepest Humiliation* and is executed by the French. **1806** French sculptor Claude Clodion (1738–1814) designs the Arc de Triomphe in Paris.	1806
1807 British fleet captures Montevideo but local opposition forces it to leave. **1807** Portuguese royal family flee to Brazil after the French invasion.	**1807** US engineer Robert Fulton (1765–1815) opens the first commercial steamboat service in New York. **1807** British physicist Thomas Young (1773–1829) discovers the modulus of elasticity.	**1807** British poet William WORDSWORTH (1770–1850) publishes his *Ode on Intimations of Immortality*.	1807
1808 Eastern part of Haiti returns to Spanish control. **1808** USA prohibits the importation of slaves. **1808** James MADISON (1751–1836) is elected US president.	**1808** British chemist John DALTON (1766–1844) outlines atomic theory in his *New System of Chemical Philosophy*. **1808** French physicist Étienne Malus (1775–1812) announces his discovery of the polarization of light. **1808** French chemist Joseph GAY-LUSSAC (1778–1850) announces his law of combining gas volumes.	**1808** French artist Jean INGRES (1780–1867) paints his *Bather of Valpinçon*. **1808** French reformer Charles FOURIER (1772–1837) proposes a system of cooperative farms in *Theory of the Four Movements*. **1808** German poet and author Johann GOETHE (1749–1832) publishes the first part of his drama *Faust*. **1808** German composer Ludwig van BEETHOVEN (1770–1827) writes his Symphony No.5 in C minor.	1808
1809 SHAWNEE Native American chief TECUMSEH (1768–1813) starts a campaign against US westward expansion.	**1809** Gas street lighting is installed in Pall Mall, London. **1809** French biologist Jean Baptiste LAMARCK (1744–1829) publishes his *Zoological Philosophy*.		1809

1810

1810 British capture Mauritius and Réunion from the French.

1810 Radama I (1791–1828) becomes king of the Hovas in Madagascar and encourages British influence.

1810 NAPOLEON (1769–1821) marries MARIE LOUISE (1791–1847), daughter of Austrian emperor FRANCIS I (1768–1835); France annexes Holland; in Spain Arthur WELLESLEY (1769–1852) captures Ciudad Rodrigo and Badajoz from the French and defeats them at the battle of Salamanca.

1811

1811 British recapture Malacca and invade Dutch Java and Sumatra.

1811 Ottoman governor MUHAMMAD ALI (1769–1849) secures his position in Egypt by massacring Mameluke generals in Cairo.

1811–12 Machine-breaking Luddite riots occur in Britain.

1812

1812 Russia defeats the Persians at the battle of Aslanduz.

1812 British build forts along the Fish River in South Africa.

1812 Turks cede Bessarabia (part of present-day Romania) to Russia.

1813

1813 Persia cedes Baku and Caucasus territories to Russia under the treaty of Gulistan.

1813 British government abolishes the East India Company's monopoly on trade with India.

1812 Napoleon invades Russia, wins the battles of Smolensk and Borodino, and occupies Moscow; the Russians burn Moscow and the French withdraw; most of the retreating French army dies.

1814

1814 Persia signs a defense treaty with Britain.

1814 Border dispute provokes a war between the British and the Gurkhas in Nepal.

▼ *Europe In 1812 almost all of Europe was ruled directly by Napoleon or by members of his family, or was allied with him, as illustrated in the map below. There was widespread support in Europe for Napoleon's revolutionary ideals of overthrowing the old order. Napoleon furthered his own power by using the desire of neighboring states for freedom, organizing many small states of Italy and Germany into dependent republics and setting up the Confederation of the Rhine, which effectively ended the Austrian-dominated Holy Roman Empire.*

1812 Liberal constitution is adopted by the Cortes of Spain.

1812 Russia gains control of Poland.

1813 Prussia declares war on France and is joined by Britain, Sweden and Austria; Napoleon is defeated at the battle of the Nations at Leipzig; Holland and Italy are freed from French rule; Wellesley wins the battle of Vittoria and drives the French from Spain; Swedes under French general Jean BERNADOTTE (1763–1844) invade pro-French Denmark.

KEY
- French Empire 1812
- Dependent states 1812
- French allies 1812

1814 Sweden and Norway are united under the Swedish king.

1814 FERDINAND VII (1784–1833) is restored as king of Spain; Prussians under Gebhard BLÜCHER (1742–1819) invade N France; British capture Bordeaux and Paris is occupied; a provisional government under Charles TALLEYRAND (1754–1838) exiles Napoleon to Elba; LOUIS XVIII (1755–1824) becomes king of France and issues a liberal constitution; peace of Paris restores the borders of Europe to the status quo of 1792; Austrian foreign minister Klemens METTERNICH (1773–1859) organizes the congress of Vienna; Wellesley becomes duke of WELLINGTON.

KINGDOM OF NORWAY AND DENMARK

PRUSSIA

GRAND DUCHY OF WARSAW

CONFEDERATION OF THE RHINE

FRENCH EMPIRE

SWITZERLAND

AUSTRIAN EMPIRE

KINGDOM OF ITALY

ILLYRIAN PROVINCES

LUCCA

SPAIN

KINGDOM OF NAPLES

BALEARIC ISLANDS

THE AMERICAS

1810 Provisional junta takes power in Buenos Aires.

1810 USA annexes w Florida.

1810 Mexican priest Miguel HIDALGO (1753–1811) leads a popular revolt against the Spanish.

1811 Paraguay declares independence from Spain.

1811 Venezuelan leader Francisco de MIRANDA (1750–1816) declares independence from Spain.

1811 US settlers defeat the SHAWNEE Native Americans at the battle of Tippecanoe.

1812 Louisiana becomes a state of the USA.

1812 USA declares war on Britain; British capture Detroit.

1813 Americans recapture Detroit but fail to take Montreal.

1813 Mexican revolutionary Jose Morelos (1765–1815) declares Mexican independence.

1813 Simón BOLÍVAR (1783–1830) takes command of Venezuelan independence forces.

1814 Americans defeat the British at a naval battle on Lake Champlain; British capture and burn Washington, D.C.; treaty of Ghent ends the war between Britain and the USA.

1814 Spanish regain control of Venezuela.

1814 José de Francia (c.1766–1840) is declared dictator of Paraguay.

SCIENCE AND TECHNOLOGY

1810 French chef Nicholas Appert (c.1750–1840) publishes his method for preserving food in tin cans.

1811 German printer Friedrich König (1774–1833) invents the power-driven, flat-bed, cylinder press.

1811 Italian physicist Amedeo AVOGADRO (1776–1856) discovers that equal volumes of gases have an equal number of molecules.

1812 French zoologist Georges CUVIER (1769–1832) publishes his *Researches into the Fossil Bones of Quadrupeds*.

1812 French mathematician Pierre LAPLACE (1749–1827) refines probability theory in his *Analytical Theory*.

1812 British scientist William Wollaston (1766–1828) invents the camera lucida.

1812 German mineralogist Friedrich Mohs (1773–1839) classifies the hardness of materials.

1814 British engineer George STEPHENSON (1781–1848) builds a steam locomotive, the *Blucher*.

1814 Swedish scientist Jöns Berzelius (1779–1848) introduces modern chemical symbols.

ARTS AND HUMANITIES

1810 Scottish poet Walter SCOTT (1771–1832) publishes *The Lady of the Lake*.   1810

1810 Spanish artist Francisco GOYA (1746–1828) begins his series of engravings *The Disasters of War*.

1810 British architect John NASH (1752–1835) begins designing the Royal Pavilion in Brighton, England.

1811 Swedish poet Esaias Tegner (1782–1846) publishes his *Svea*.   1811

1812 British poet George BYRON (1788–1824) publishes the first cantos of his *Childe Harold's Pilgrimage*.   1812

1812 German language scholars Jakob (1785–1863) and Wilhelm (1786–1859) GRIMM publish a collection of folktales and fairy stories.

1813 British novelist Jane AUSTEN (1775–1817) publishes her *Pride and Prejudice*.   1813

1813 French novelist Madame de STAËL (1766–1817) publishes her *On Germany*.

1813 British industrialist Robert OWEN (1771–1858) publishes his *A New View of Society*.

1814 Kurozumi Munetada (1780–1850) revives popular Shintoism in Japan.   1814

1815

1815 US navy threatens to bombard Algiers unless piracy against American shipping ends.

1815 France abolishes the slave trade.

1815 Revolt by AFRIKANERS is suppressed by British troops in South Africa.

1815 NAPOLEON (1769–1821) lands in s France, assembles an army, and marches to Paris; LOUIS XVIII (1755–1824) flees to Belgium; Austrians defeat Joachim MURAT (1767–1815) at the battle of Tolentino; FERDINAND I (1751–1825) is restored as the king of the Two Sicilies; Napoleon invades Belgium and defeats Gebhard BLÜCHER (1742–1819) at Ligny, but is defeated by the British and Prussians under the duke of WELLINGTON (1769–1852) at the battle of Waterloo; Napoleon is exiled to St. Helena; a second White Terror occurs.

> "Nothing except a battle lost can be half so melancholy as a battle won."
>
> Arthur Wellesley, Duke of Wellington (despatch from the battle of Waterloo)

1815 Congress of Vienna establishes the balance of power in Europe. Poland is united with Russia; Holland and Belgium are united as the Kingdom of the Netherlands; German Confederation is formed; neutrality of Switzerland is declared.

1815 Russia, Austria and Prussia form the antiliberal Holy Alliance.

1815 British parliament passes a protectionist Corn Law that restricts the importation of foreign grains.

1816

1816 Persians invade Afghanistan but are forced to withdraw.

1816 Nepal becomes an independent British protectorate.

1816 Britain returns Java and Sumatra to the Dutch.

1816–18 Egyptian army under General IBRAHIM PASHA (1789–1848) suppresses the Wahhabi state in w Arabia.

1817

1817–18 During the third Maratha War Britain gains control of the Rajput states of w central India.

1817 Senegal is returned to French control.

1817 Liberal German students protest in Wartburg.

1818

1818 Britain returns Malacca to the Dutch.

1818 Afghanistan disintegrates into small states after a tribal revolt.

1818 Miloš OBRENOVIĆ (1780–1860) leads a Serbian uprising against the Turks and establishes a degree of self-government.

1818 France joins the Holy Alliance by the treaty of Aix-la-Chapelle.

1818 Jean Bernadotte (1763–1844) becomes CHARLES XIV of Sweden.

1819

1819 Bagyidaw (d.1837) becomes king of Burma and continues the policy of expansion.

1819 Sikhs under RANJIT SINGH (1780–1839) conquer Kashmir.

1819 British colonial administrator Stamford RAFFLES (1781–1826) founds Singapore.

1819 ZULU people under King SHAKA (1787–1828) establish control of the Natal region of South Africa.

1819 Carlsbad decrees impose strict censorship and control over university admissions throughout the German Confederation.

1819 Anti-Corn Law protesters are killed by troops at the Peterloo massacre in Britain.

THE AMERICAS

1815 US troops under General Andrew JACKSON (1767–1845) defeat the British at the battle of New Orleans.

1816 Argentines led by José de SAN MARTÍN (1778–1850) declare their independence from Spain.

1816 Spanish regain control of Mexico.

1816 James MONROE (1758–1831) is elected US president.

1816 Indiana becomes a state of the USA.

1817 Argentina annexes Uruguay.

1817 San Martín invades and liberates Chile.

1817 Mississippi becomes a state of the USA.

1818 Simón BOLÍVAR (1783–1830) leads a revolutionary army into Venezuela.

1818 USA and Britain agree on the 49th parallel as the Canadian boundary, with joint occupation of Oregon.

1818 Illinois becomes a state of the USA.

1818 Revolutionary leader Bernardo O'HIGGINS (1778–1842) becomes Supreme Director of Chile.

1818 Steamship service opens on the Great Lakes, central North America.

1819 USA purchases Florida from Spain.

1819 Bolívar defeats the Spanish and becomes president of Gran Colombia (present-day Venezuela, Ecuador and Colombia).

1819 Alabama becomes a state of the USA.

SCIENCE AND TECHNOLOGY

1815 German scientist Joseph von FRAUNHOFER (1787–1826) discovers black lines in the solar spectrum.

1816 Scottish scientist Robert Stirling (1790–1878) invents a closed-cycle external combustion engine.

1816 French hobbyist Nicéphore Niepce (1765–1833) begins experimenting with photography using a silver chloride solution.

▼ *Europe* The 1815 Congress of Vienna was convened to restore order in Europe after the Napoleonic Wars. The fear was that France might cause another European war so three buffer states were created to hinder her expansion eastward, as illustrated below. The Kingdom of Piedmont was strengthened. Belgium was joined with Holland in the Kingdom of the Netherlands. The Holy Roman Empire (consolidated by Napoleon into the Confederation of the Rhine) became the German Confederation – 39 states dominated by an Austrian president.

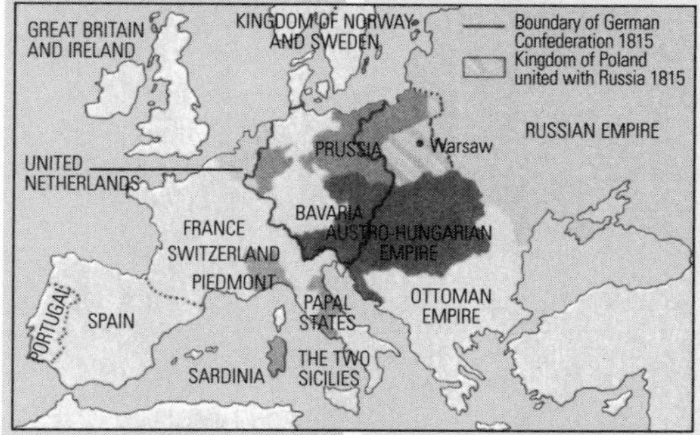

1819 French physician René Laennec (1781–1826) invents the stethoscope.

ARTS AND HUMANITIES

1816 Italian composer Gioacchino ROSSINI (1792–1868) writes his opera *The Barber of Seville.*

1816 German philosopher Georg HEGEL (1770–1831) introduces his dialectical system in *The Science of Logic.*

1817 British artist John CONSTABLE (1776–1831) paints his *View on the Stour.*

1817 British economist David Ricardo (1772–1823) publishes his *Principles of Political Economy and Taxation.*

1818 British novelist Mary Shelley (1797–1851) publishes her *Frankenstein.*

1819 German philosopher Arthur SCHOPENHAUER (1788–1860) publishes his pessimistic *The World as Will and Idea.*

1819 Austrian composer Franz SCHUBERT (1797–1828) writes his *Trout* quintet.

1819 Scottish poet Walter SCOTT (1771–1832) publishes his novel *Ivanhoe.*

1819 French artist Theodore Géricault (1791–1824) paints his *Raft of the Medusa.*

1815

1816

1817

1818

1819

ASIA AND AUSTRALASIA	AFRICA	EUROPE

1820

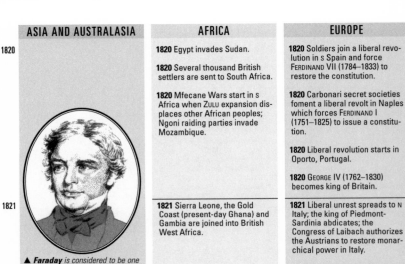

▲ **Faraday** is considered to be one of the world's greatest experimental scientists. He made fundamental contributions in electricity, magnetism and chemistry.

1820 Egypt invades Sudan.

1820 Several thousand British settlers are sent to South Africa.

1820 Mfecane Wars start in S Africa when ZULU expansion displaces other African peoples; Ngoni raiding parties invade Mozambique.

1820 Soldiers join a liberal revolution in S Spain and force FERDINAND VII (1784–1833) to restore the constitution.

1820 Carbonari secret societies foment a liberal revolt in Naples which forces FERDINAND I (1751–1825) to issue a constitution.

1820 Liberal revolution starts in Oporto, Portugal.

1820 GEORGE IV (1762–1830) becomes king of Britain.

1821

1821 Sierra Leone, the Gold Coast (present-day Ghana) and Gambia are joined into British West Africa.

1821 Liberal unrest spreads to N Italy; the king of Piedmont-Sardinia abdicates; the Congress of Laibach authorizes the Austrians to restore monarchical power in Italy.

1821 Greeks led by Alexander Ypsilante (1792–1828) revolt against Turkish rule and seize Bucharest.

1822 **1822** Burmese annex Assam.

1822 Liberia, on the coast of West Africa, is established as a colony for freed American slaves.

1822 Mfecane Wars spread to South Africa.

1822 Congress of Verona authorizes the French to intervene in Spain to restore the monarchy.

1822 Greeks declare independence; Turks invade and massacre the inhabitants of Chios, but fail to subdue the rebels.

1822 Egyptians occupy Crete.

1822 Portugal adopts a liberal constitution under King JOHN VI (1767–1826).

1823

1823 Egyptians found Khartoum as the capital of Sudan.

1823 John VI withdraws the Portuguese constitution; reactionaries led by his son start a civil war.

1823 French occupy Madrid, defeat the revolutionaries at the battle of the Trocadero, and restore Ferdinand VII.

1824 **1824** British declare war on Burma and capture Rangoon.

1824 Dutch cede Malacca to Britain in return for territory in Sumatra.

1824 British interference in West African affairs angers the ASHANTI people, who destroy a British force; start of the first Ashanti War.

1824 Omani governor of Mombasa dies and the British occupy the port.

1824 Greek rebels are divided by civil war.

1824 CHARLES X (1757–1836), becomes king of France and attempts to restore the power of the monarchy.

THE AMERICAS

1820 Missouri compromise prohibits slavery in the N part of the Louisiana purchase territory.

1820 Maine becomes a state of the USA.

1821 Aristocratic revolutionaries declare Mexican independence from Spain.

1821 Brazil incorporates Uruguay.

1821 US farmers begin to settle in Texas.

1821 José de SAN MARTÍN (1778–1850) and Simón BOLÍVAR (1783–1830) liberate Peru.

1821 Missouri becomes a state of the USA.

1822 Mexican general Agustín de ITURBIDE (1783–1824) is crowned Emperor Agustín I; Central American states become part of the Mexican empire.

1822 Brazil under Emperor PEDRO I (1798–1834) declares its independence from Portugal.

1823 Revolution overthrows the Mexican emperor.

1823 Guatemala, San Salvador, Nicaragua, Honduras and Costa Rica establish independence from Mexico and form the United Provinces of Central America.

1823 US president James MONROE (1758–1831) issues the Monroe doctrine forbidding European colonialism in the Americas.

1824 Mexico becomes a republic under President Guadalupe Vittoria (1768–1843).

SCIENCE AND TECHNOLOGY

1820 French physicians Pierre Pelletier (1788–1842) and Joseph Caventou (1795–1877) discover the antimalarial drug quinine.

1820 French physicist André AMPÈRE (1775–1836) establishes the science of electromagnetism.

1821 French physicist Augustin FRESNEL (1788–1827) finalizes his transverse wave theory of light.

1821 German physicist Thomas Seebeck (1770–1831) invents the thermocouple.

1821 British physicist Michael FARADAY (1791–1867) discovers electromagnetic rotation.

1822 French scientist and mathematician Jean Fourier (1768–1830) publishes his theory of heat conduction.

1822 French scholar Jean Champollion (1790–1832) translates Egyptian hieroglyphics.

1823 British mathematician Charles BABBAGE (1791–1871) begins building a working model of his difference engine calculating machine.

1824 British builder Joseph Aspidin (1779–1855) invents Portland cement.

1824 Scottish chemist Charles Macintosh (1766–1843) devises a method of bonding rubber to fabric for waterproof clothing.

1824 French engineer Sadi CARNOT (1796–1832) lays the foundations of thermodynamics in his *On the Motive Power of Fire*.

ARTS AND HUMANITIES

1820 Venus de Milo sculpture is discovered.

1820 French poet Alphonse Lamartine (1790–1869) publishes his *Poetic Meditations*.

1820 British poet John KEATS (1795–1821) publishes his *Ode to a Nightingale*.

1820 British poet Percy SHELLEY (1792–1822) publishes his *Prometheus Unbound*.

1821 French social reformer Claude de SAINT-SIMON (1760–1825) publishes his *Of the Industrial System*.

1822 German composer Carl von WEBER (1786–1826) writes his opera *Der Freischütz*.

1822 British writer Thomas De Quincey (1785–1859) publishes his *Confessions of an English Opium Eater*.

1822 Hungarian composer Franz LISZT (1811–86) makes his debut as a pianist.

1824 French artist Eugène DELACROIX (1798–1863) paints his *Massacre at Chios*.

1820

1821

1822

1823

1824

ASIA AND AUSTRALASIA	AFRICA	EUROPE

1825

1825 Persia attempts to recapture Georgia from Russia.

1825 King Radama I (1791–1828) evicts the French from Madagascar

1825 Egyptian army invades s Greece.

1825 ALEXANDER I (b.1777) of Russia dies; an attempted military coup (the Decembrists) fails; NICHOLAS I (1796–1855) becomes czar.

1826

1826 Anti-Sikh jihad is organized by Muslims in N India.

1826 Russians defeat Persians at the battle of Ganja and gain part of Armenia.

1826 Afghan chieftain Dost Muhammad (1789–1863) captures Kabul.

1826 King Rama III (d.1851) of Thailand signs a trade agreement with Britain.

1826 After defeating the Burmese, Britain gains Assam and part of the Malay peninsula by the treaty of Yandabu.

1826 British unite Penang, Singapore and Malacca into the Straits Settlements.

1826 Sultan MAHMUD II (1785–1839) massacres the Janisseries in Turkey.

1826 Dipo Negoro (c.1785–1855) leads a Javanese revolt against the Dutch.

1826 Boundary of Cape Colony is extended N to the Orange River.

1827 British defeat an ASHANTI invasion of the Gold Coast; end of the first Ashanti War.

1828 British evacuate Mombasa.

1828 Ranavalona I (1800–61) becomes Hova queen in Madagascar

1828 ZULU leader SHAKA (1787–1828) is assassinated by his brothers.

1826 Infant MARIA II (1819–53) becomes queen of Portugal.

1826 Turks capture the Greek stronghold of Missolongi.

1827 Turks capture the Acropolis in Athens.

1828 Force of British, French and Russian ships destroys the Egyptian fleet at the battle of Navarino; Egyptians evacuate Greece.

1828 Russians declare war on Turkey.

1828 British Corn Law is reformed.

1828 Portuguese regent Dom MIGUEL (1802–66) proclaims himself king.

1827

1828

1828 Russian forces capture Tehran; Persia cedes territory to Russia by the treaty of Turkmanchai.

1828 Dutch annex w New Guinea.

1829

1829 British claim the whole of Australia.

▶ *Adams was one of the most successful secretaries of state in US history. The Monroe Doctrine, which asserted US authority over the American continent and declared that European interference would be regarded as "dangerous to peace and safety", was largely formulated by Adams. His presidential administration was less successful.*

1829 South German state of Bavaria signs a trade tariff treaty with Prussia.

1829 London protocol establishes Greek independence under a monarchy.

1829 Russia gains the E coast of the Black Sea from the Turks under the treaty of Adrianople.

1829 Catholic Emancipation Act is passed in Britain.

1829 Ultraconservative Prince de POLIGNAC (1780–1847) becomes prime minister in France.

THE AMERICAS

1825 US House of Representatives elects John Quincy ADAMS (1767–1848) president.

1825 Erie canal is completed, linking New York City with the Great Lakes.

1825 Portugal recognizes the independence of Brazil.

1825 Bolivia under President Antonio de SUCRE (1795–1830) gains independence from Peru.

1825 Argentina sends troops to aid Uruguay against Brazil.

1827 Argentines defeat the Brazilians at the battle of Ituzaingo.

1828 Uruguay obtains independence from Brazil.

1828 General Andrew JACKSON (1767–1845) is elected US president.

1829 First US public railroad opens.

1829 Peru and Bolivia form a confederation.

1829 Mexican general Antonio de SANTA ANNA (1794–1876) defeats an attempted Spanish invasion.

1829 Workingmen's party is formed in the USA.

SCIENCE AND TECHNOLOGY

1825 George STEPHENSON (1781–1848) builds the first public railway between Stockton and Darlington.

1825 Danish physicist Hans Oersted (1777–1851) discovers how to produce aluminum metal.

1825 French engineer Marc Seguin (1786–1875) builds the first wire suspension bridge.

1827 German scientist Georg OHM (1787–1854) publishes his law of electrical voltage and current.

1827 Scottish scientist Robert Brown (1773–1858) observes the random movements of minute particles (Brownian motion).

1827 British chemist John Walker (c.1781–1859) invents friction matches.

1828 German chemist Friedrich Wöhler (1800–82) synthesizes urea.

1829 British chemist Thomas GRAHAM (1805–69) formulates his law of gas diffusion.

1829 French mathematician Gaspard de Coriolis (1792–1843) explains the effect that causes objects moving in the atmosphere to be deflected.

ARTS AND HUMANITIES

1825 Russian poet Alexander PUSHKIN (1799–1837) publishes his *Boris Godunov*.

1826 US novelist James Fenimore COOPER (1789–1851) publishes his *The Last of the Mohicans*.

1826 French poet and author Alfred de VIGNY (1797–1863) publishes his novel *Cinq-Mars*.

1827 German poet Heinrich HEINE (1797–1856) publishes his *The Book of Songs*.

1827 Italian poet and author Alessandro Manzoni (1785–1873) publishes his novel *The Betrothed*.

1828 American publisher Noah Webster (1758–1843) publishes the *American Dictionary of the English Language*.

1828 *Memoirs* of Giovanni Casanova (1725–98) are published.

1828 Italian violinist Niccolò Paganini (1782–1840) arrives in Vienna.

1829 French novelist Honoré de BALZAC (1788–1850) publishes *The Chouans* and begins *The Human Comedy*.

1829 Scottish philosopher James MILL (1773–1836) publishes his *An Analysis of the Phenomena of the Human Mind*.

1825
1826
1827
1828
1829

ASIA AND AUSTRALASIA	AFRICA	EUROPE

1830 **1830** Dutch suppress the Javanese revolt.

1830 French invade Algeria and occupy the cities of Algiers and Oran.

1830 WILLIAM IV (1765–1827) becomes king of Britain.

1830 Revolution in Paris overthrows CHARLES X (1757–1836); LOUIS PHILIPPE I (1773–1850) becomes king of France with a more liberal constitution.

▼ **Neoclassicism** *A movement of the late 18th and early 19th centuries, neoclassicism was inspired by the pure forms of Greek and Roman art. In architecture, the trend culminated with the Greek revival buildings of*

Karl Schinkel, such as the Old Museum (1822–30, illustrated below) in Berlin, built to house the art collection of the Prussian state. The style was characterized by solidity, severity and geometric clarity

1830 Revolutionaries in Brussels declare Belgian independence from the Netherlands.

1830 Rising in Warsaw led by Adam Jerzy CZARTORYSKI (1770–1861) establishes a Polish national government.

1830 German revolutionaries force the rulers of Saxony and Brunswick to abdicate.

1831 **1831** Muslims defeat the Sikhs at the battle of Balakot in NW India.

1831 Britain signs a peace treaty with the ASHANTI.

1831 Russian troops crush the Polish rebels.

1831 Mfecane Wars spread N to Zimbabwe.

1831 LEOPOLD I (1790–1865) becomes king of Belgium with a liberal constitution.

1831 French foreign legion is founded in Algeria.

1831 Nationalist risings in the Italian cities of Parma and Modena are suppressed by the Austrians.

1832 **1832** Ottoman governor MUHAMMAD ALI (1769–1849) invades Syria and Asia Minor and defeats the Turks at the battle of Konya.

1832 ABD AL-KADIR (1808–83) becomes leader of the Algerian resistance.

1832 Italian nationalist Giuseppe MAZZINI (1805–72) founds the Young Italy movement.

1832 Poland is made a province of Russia.

1832 British parliament is reformed.

1833 **1833** Russia sends ships to assist the Turks; France and Britain protest against Russian interference; Muhammad Ali gains control of Syria.

1833 German revolutionaries force the ruler of Hanover to issue a constitution.

1833 MARIA II (1819–53) is restored to the Portuguese throne.

1833 Infant ISABELLA II (1830–1904) becomes queen of Spain.

1834 **1834** Sikhs capture the Muslim city of Peshawar in present-day Pakistan.

1834 Slavery is abolished throughout the British Empire.

1834 German *Zollverein* (customs union) is formed under Prussian leadership.

1834 Muhammad Shah becomes ruler of Persia after the death of Fath Ali (b.1771).

1834 Isabella's brother Don CARLOS (1788–1845) claims the Spanish throne; start of the Carlist War.

1834 Republican revolts in French cities are repressed.

THE AMERICAS	SCIENCE AND TECHNOLOGY	ARTS AND HUMANITIES

THE AMERICAS

1830 Ecuador under President Juan Flores (1800–64) gains independence from Colombia.

1830 US Indian Removal Act organizes the removal of Native Americans to w of the River Mississippi.

1830 First American settlers arrive in California having crossed the Rocky Mountains.

1831 Nat TURNER (b.1800) is executed after leading a slave revolt in Virginia.

1831 PEDRO II (1825–91) becomes emperor of Brazil.

1833 Antonio de SANTA ANNA (1794–1876) is elected president of Mexico.

1833 Britain claims sovereignty over the Falkland Islands.

SCIENCE AND TECHNOLOGY

1830 British geologist Charles Lyell (1797–1875) publishes the first volume of his *Principles of Geology*.

1830 British engineer Joseph Whitworth (1803–87) introduces standardized screw threads.

1830 British physicist Michael FARADAY (1791–1867) discovers electromagnetic induction.

1831 British explorer James Ross (1800–62) reaches the N magnetic pole.

1831 British naturalist Charles DARWIN (1809–82) embarks on his round-the-world expedition on HMS *Beagle*.

1831 US physicist Joseph HENRY (1797–1878) publishes a description of his electric motor

1832 French instrument maker Hippolyte Pixii (1808–35) constructs a practical, heteropolar, electrical generator.

◀ *Darwin* is renowned for his theory of evolution based on natural selection. As well as The Origin of Species, Darwin published other books discussing evolution, including The Descent of Man.

1833 Steamship *Royal William* becomes the first to cross the Atlantic Ocean entirely by steam power.

1834 French teacher Louis Braille (1809–52) perfects his system of embossed dots that enable blind people to read.

1834 US farmer Cyrus McCormick (1809–84) invents the horse-drawn reaper-harvester.

ARTS AND HUMANITIES

1830 US religious leader Joseph SMITH (1805–44) publishes *The Book of Mormon*.

1830 French composer Hector BERLIOZ (1803–69) writes his *Symphonie fantastique*.

1830 French novelist Stendhal (Henry Beyle, 1783–1842) publishes his *Scarlet and Black*.

1830 French-born Polish composer Frédéric CHOPIN (1810–49) writes his first piano concerto.

1831 French Barbizon school of landscape painters exhibits at the Paris Salon.

1832 French novelist George Sand (1804–76) publishes her *Indiana*.

1832 US artist George Catlin (1796–1872) completes his portfolio of paintings of Native Americans.

1832 Military theories of Prussian general Carl von CLAUSEWITZ (1780–1831) are published posthumously as *On War*.

1833 Russian novelist and dramatist Nikolai GOGOL (1809–52) publishes his play *The Government Inspector*.

1833 Japanese artist Ando HIROSHIGE (1797–1858) publishes his woodcuts of the *Fifty-three Stages of the Tokaido*.

1830
1831
1832
1833
1834

ASIA AND AUSTRALASIA	AFRICA	EUROPE

1835

1835 Dost Muhammad (1789–1863) becomes ruler of all Afghanistan and establishes the Barakzai dynasty.

1835 Mfecane Wars spread further N to Zambia and Malawi.

1835 Turks overthrow the Karamanli dynasty in Tripoli and impose direct rule.

1835 AFRIKANERS (Boers) in South Africa begin the Great Trek to escape British repression.

1835 FERDINAND I (1793–1875) becomes Austrian emperor.

1836

1836 ABD AL-KADIR (1808–83) occupies the inland Algerian city of Mascara.

1836 Louis NAPOLEON (1808–73) attempts to seize power in France and is exiled to America.

1836 Rebellion in Spain forces the regent MARIA CHRISTINA (1806–78) to grant a new constitution.

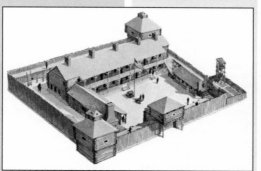

◄ **fort** In the early 19th century, the USA expanded westward. Forts were built along pioneer routes to protect scattered communities and to provide refuge from Native American attacks. Manned by US cavalry, forts were rectangular enclosures with high timber walls, plank walks for sentries and block-houses at diagonally opposite corners to provide defense.

1837

1837 Afrikaners establish the republic of Natal to the NE of the British Cape Colony.

1837 VICTORIA (1819–1901) becomes queen of Britain; Hanover is separated from Britain.

1837 Under Austrian influence, the constitution of Hanover is withdrawn.

1838

1838 Ismaili leader Aga Khan I (1800–81) flees to India after his rebellion against the shah of Persia is defeated.

1838 Afrikaners in Natal inflict a heavy defeat on the ZULUS.

1838 British advocates of free trade John BRIGHT (1811–89) and Richard COBDEN (1805–65) found the Anti-Corn Law league.

1838 Protestant cantons in Switzerland adopt more liberal constitutions.

1839

1839 British occupy the port of Aden in Yemen.

1839 Turks invade Syria and are defeated by the Egyptians at the battle of Nesib.

1839 British invade Afghanistan and overthrow Dost Muhammad.

1839 Chinese officials burn British opium in the port of Canton (Guangzhou).

▲ **Colt revolver** The Colt Navy revolver is probably the most famous percussion revolving pistol. As with most of Colt's revolvers, it was open-framed, having no strap over the top of the frame. It had a six-chambered cylinder and was of 0.36in caliber. Each chamber was normally loaded from the muzzle with powder and a ball or conical bullet.

1839 First Carlist War in Spain ends when Don CARLOS (1788–1845) leaves the country.

1839 Radical Chartists cause riots in Britain.

1839 The Netherlands recognizes the independence of Belgium and the grand duchy of Luxembourg by the treaty of London.

THE AMERICAS

1835 American settlers declare the independent republic of Texas.

1836 US congressman Davy CROCKETT (b.1786) and colonel Jim BOWIE (b.1796) are killed when Mexican troops defeat Texan rebels at the Alamo mission house; the Mexicans are decisively defeated at the battle of San Jacinto by Texans under General Sam HOUSTON (1793–1863).

1836 Martin VAN BUREN (1782–1862) is elected US president.

1836 Arkansas becomes a state of the USA.

1836 Settlers in California declare independence from Mexico.

1837 French-speakers in Lower Canada, led by Louis PAPINEAU (1786–1781), rebel against British administration; a similar revolt occurs in Upper Canada.

1837 Michigan becomes a state of the USA.

1838 British restore order in Canada.

1838 Underground Railroad is organized in the USA to smuggle slaves from the s states.

1838 Britain and France blockade the Argentine coast in a dispute over the Falkland Islands.

1839 Former slave-owners rebel against British rule in Jamaica.

1839 Chilean troops overthrow the Peru–Bolivia confederation.

SCIENCE AND TECHNOLOGY

1835 US inventor Samuel COLT (1814–62) patents his revolver handgun.

1836 British electrical engineer William Sturgeon (1783–1850) invents the moving-coil galvanometer.

1836 Belgian scientist Joseph Plateau (1801–83) invents the stroboscope.

1837 British educator Isaac Pitman (1813–97) invents his system of shorthand writing.

1837 US metalworker John Deere (1804–86) invents the steel plow.

1837 British physicists Charles WHEATSTONE (1802–75) and William Cooke (1806–79) jointly invent an electric telegraph.

1837 US inventor Samuel MORSE (1791–1872) devises an electric telegraph and a simple dot-dash message code.

1838 German astronomer Friedrich Bessel (1784–1846) discovers stellar parallax.

1839 German biologist Theodor Schwann (1810–82) publishes his cell theory.

1839 French artist Louis DAGUERRE (1789–1851) announces his invention of a photographic process for producing images on copper plates.

1839 British scientist William Talbot (1800–77) invents a process for making photographic negatives.

1839 US manufacturer Charles Goodyear (1800–60) discovers the process for vulcanizing rubber.

1839 Scottish engineer James Nasmyth (1808–90) invents the steam hammer.

1839 French physicist Anton Becquerel (1788–1878) invents a photoelectric cell.

ARTS AND HUMANITIES

1835

1835 French historian Alexis de TOCQUEVILLE (1805–1859) publishes his *Of Democracy in America*.

1835 Italian composer Gaetano Donizetti (1797–1848) writes his opera *Lucy of Lammermoor*.

1835 Danish writer Hans Christian ANDERSEN (1805–75) publishes his *Tales Told for Children*.

1836

1836 German composer Felix MENDELSSOHN (1809–47) writes his St. *Paul* oratorio.

1836 US writer Oliver Wendell HOLMES (1809–94) publishes his *Poems*.

1836 German theologian David Strauss (1808–74) treats the gospels as myth in *Life of Jesus*.

1836 US philosopher Ralph Waldo EMERSON (1803–82) introduces Transcendentalism in his collection of essays *Nature*.

1837

1838

1838 British novelist Charles DICKENS (1812–70) publishes his *Oliver Twist*.

1838 US artist John Audubon (1785–1851) publishes the fourth and final volume of illustrations for his *Birds of America*.

1839

1839 French socialist Louis Blanc (1811–82) publishes his *The Organization of Labor*.

1839 US poet Henry LONGFELLOW (1807–82) publishes his *Voices of the Night*.

ASIA AND AUSTRALASIA	AFRICA	EUROPE
1840		
1840 British colonists land in New Zealand; Maori chiefs cede sovereignty to Britain by the treaty of Waitangi.	**1840** Sultan of Oman, Sayyid Said (1791–1856), makes Zanzibar his capital.	**1840** FREDERICK WILLIAM IV (1795–1861) becomes king of Prussia.
1840 British occupy Chinese forts in Canton (Guangzhou).		**1840** Louis NAPOLEON (1808–73) attempts another coup in France and is imprisoned.
		1840 General Baldomero Espartero (1793–1879) makes himself dictator in Spain.
		1840 Britain, France and Russia agree to aid Turkey and send troops to Palestine.
1841		
1841 First Opium War starts when the British navy seizes ports along the Chinese coast.	**1841** Algerian leader ABD AL-KADIR (1808–83) is driven into Morocco by the French.	**1841** Straits Convention closes the Dardanelles (the entrance to the Black Sea) to non-Turkish warships.
1841 Afghans rebel against British occupation.		
1841 Sultan of Brunei cedes Sarawak to a British merchant.		
1841 European powers persuade Egypt to withdraw from Syria.		
1842		
1842 British are forced to withdraw from Afghanistan; Dost Muhammad (1789–1863) regains power.	**1842** French sign trade treaties with chieftains of the Ivory Coast in w Africa.	**1842** Rising in Barcelona, Spain, declares a republic, which is crushed by Espartero.
1842 Peace of Nanking ends the first Opium War; Britain obtains Hong Kong.		
1842 Tahiti becomes a French protectorate.		
1843		
1843 British conquer Sind in present-day sw Pakistan.	**1843** British conquer Natal from the AFRIKANERS.	**1843** Coup overthrows Espartero in Spain; Queen ISABELLA II (1830–1904) is declared of age.
1843 First Maori War breaks out over a land dispute.	**1843** Basutoland in s Africa comes under British protection	**1843** Revolution forces King OTTO I (1815–67) of Greece to grant a constitution.
1843 Chinese port of Shanghai is opened to foreign trade.	**1843** The Gambia is made a separate British colony.	
1843 Chinese emperor repeats his ban on opium smoking.		
1844		
1844 Cambodia comes under the control of Thailand.	**1844** French acquire Gabon in w central Africa.	**1844** Antiindustrial rebellion by Prussian weavers is suppressed by troops.
1844 Sayyid Ali Muhammad (c.1820–50) proclaims himself Bab and founds Babism in Persia.	**1844** French bombard Tangier in Morocco and defeat al-Kadir and his Moroccan allies at the battle of Isly.	

THE AMERICAS

1840 Confederation of Central American States breaks up.

1840 William HARRISON (1773–1841) is elected US president.

1840 Upper and Lower Canada are united and the country is granted self-governing status by the British.

1841 John TYLER (1790–1862) becomes US president.

1841 Peruvian attempt to annex Bolivia is defeated at the battle of Ingavi.

> "The history of the world is but the biography of great men."
>
> Thomas Carlyle (*On Heroes and Hero-worship*)

1842 Treaty between the USA and Britain settles the E stretch of the US–Canadian border.

1844 James POLK (1795–1849) is elected US president.

1844 Dominican Republic becomes independent of Haiti.

SCIENCE AND TECHNOLOGY

1840 German chemist Christian Schönbein (1799–1868) discovers ozone.

1840 Swiss geologist Louis Agassiz (1807–73) proposes his ice ages theory of global glaciation.

1840 "Needle-fire" breech-loading rifle, designed by German locksmith Nikolaus von Dreyse (1787–1867), is introduced into the Prussian army.

1841 German chemist Robert BUNSEN (1811–99) invents a zinc-carbon battery.

1841 US engineer John Roebling (1806–69) invents a machine for making wire rope.

1841 British paleontologist Richard Owen (1804–92) introduces the term "dinosaur".

1841 British astronomer John Couch ADAMS (1819–92) and French astronomer Urbain LEVERRIER (1811–77) independently predict the existence and position of the planet Neptune.

1842 Austrian physicist Christian DOPPLER (1805–53) discovers the change in frequency of sound waves from a moving source.

1842 US physician Crawford Long (1815–78) first uses ether as a surgical anesthetic.

1843 British physicist James JOULE (1818–89) establishes the first law of thermodynamics.

1844 US dentist Horace Wells (1815–48) first uses nitrous oxide as an anesthetic for tooth extraction.

1844 French scientist Lucien Vidi (1805–66) invents the aneroid barometer.

ARTS AND HUMANITIES

1840 French anarchist philosopher Pierre PROUDHON (1809–65) publishes his *What is Property?*

1840 German composer Robert SCHUMANN (1810–56) publishes his *Women's Love and Life* song-cycle.

1841 German educator Friedrich Froebel (1782–1852) opens the first kindergarten.

1841 German economist Friedrich List (1789–1846) publishes his *The National System of Political Economy.*

1841 Scottish historian Thomas CARLYLE (1795–1881) publishes his *On Heroes and Hero-worship.*

1843 Italian nationalist Vincenzo Gioberti (1801–52) publishes his *On the Moral and Civil Primacy of the Italians.*

1844 French writer Alexandre DUMAS (1802–70) publishes his novel *The Three Musketeers.*

1844 Danish philosopher Søren KIERKEGAARD (1813–55) publishes his *The Concept of Dread.*

1844 Italian composer Giuseppe VERDI (1813–1901) writes his opera *Ernani.*

1844 British artist Joseph TURNER (1775–1851) paints his *Rain, Steam and Speed.*

ASIA AND AUSTRALASIA	AFRICA	EUROPE

1845 **1845** Sikhs invade British territory in N India; start of the Anglo-Sikh War.

1845–46 Potato blight causes famine in Ireland.

1846 **1846** British conquer Kashmir from the Sikhs and sell it to a Hindu ruler.

1846 British defeat an incursion by the XHOSA people in South Africa.

1846 British corn laws are repealed by the government of Robert PEEL (1788–1850).

1846 Polish rising in Kraków is suppressed by Austria.

1847

1847 Liberia becomes an independent republic.

1847 ABD AL-KADIR (1808–83) surrenders to the French in Algeria.

1847 Protestant Swiss cantons defeat the Catholic Sonderbund.

1847 Unrest in N Italy is suppressed by Austria.

1848 **1848** Nasir al-Din (1829–96) becomes shah of Persia.

1848 Babists in Persia rebel and declare an independent state.

1848 Algeria becomes a part of France.

▼ *Revolutions of 1848* *Urban uprisings occurred in most European countries. They were caused by frustration with governing authorities and economic depression.*

1848 Revolution in France overthrows LOUIS PHILIPPE I (1773–1850) and forms a provisional government; Paris workers stage a rising; Louis NAPOLEON (1808–73) is elected president of the second French republic.

1848 Central and S Italian states receive constitutions; rebels drive Austrians from Milan; Venice declares a republic; Piedmont declares war on Austria.

1848 Switzerland adopts a new federal constitution.

1848 Rising in Berlin leads to a German national assembly meeting in Frankfurt.

1848 Denmark and Prussia go to war over Schleswig-Holstein.

1848 Rising in Vienna causes Klemens METTERNICH (1773–1859) to flee Austria; a constituent assembly meets; FRANZ JOSEPH I (1830–1916) becomes Austrian emperor; Hungarians establish a national government.

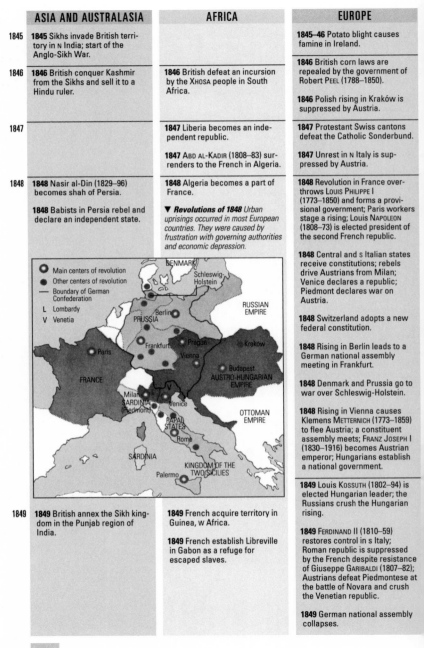

Main centers of revolution
Other centers of revolution
Boundary of German Confederation
L Lombardy
V Venetia

DENMARK
Schleswig-Holstein
RUSSIAN EMPIRE
Berlin
PRUSSIA
Frankfurt
Prague
Kraków
Paris
Vienna
Budapest
AUSTRO-HUNGARIAN EMPIRE
FRANCE
Milan
SARDINIA (Piedmont)
Venice
PAPAL STATES
Rome
OTTOMAN EMPIRE
SARDINIA
Palermo
KINGDOM OF THE TWO SICILIES

1849 Louis KOSSUTH (1802–94) is elected Hungarian leader; the Russians crush the Hungarian rising.

1849 **1849** British annex the Sikh kingdom in the Punjab region of India.

1849 French acquire territory in Guinea, W Africa.

1849 French establish Libreville in Gabon as a refuge for escaped slaves.

1849 FERDINAND II (1810–59) restores control in S Italy; Roman republic is suppressed by the French despite resistance of Giuseppe GARIBALDI (1807–82); Austrians defeat Piedmontese at the battle of Novara and crush the Venetian republic.

1849 German national assembly collapses.

THE AMERICAS	SCIENCE AND TECHNOLOGY	ARTS AND HUMANITIES	
1845 British and French ships blockade the River Plate during further disputes with Argentina. **1845** Florida becomes a state of the USA. **1845** Texas is annexed and becomes a state of the USA.	**1845** William McNaught builds the first compound (high-pressure/low-pressure) steam engine.	**1845** British politician and author Benjamin DISRAELI (1804–81) publishes his novel *Sybil*. **1845** German socialist Friedrich ENGELS (1820–95) publishes his *The Condition of the Working Classes in England*. **1845** US writer Edgar Allan POE (1809–49) publishes his *The Raven and Other Poems*.	**1845**
1846 Britain cedes Oregon to the USA; the 49th parallel becomes the w stretch of the US–Canadian border. **1846** USA declares war on Mexico. **1846** Iowa becomes a state of the USA.	**1846** US engineer Elias Howe (1819–67) invents the lockstitch sewing machine. **1846** Italian scientist Ascanio Sobrero (1812–88) invents nitro-glycerine. **1846** German astronomer Johann GALLE (1812–1910) makes the first sighting of the planet Neptune. **1846** Smithsonian Institution is founded in Washington, D.C.	**1846** Belgian musical instrument maker Adolphe Sax (1814–94) patents the saxophone.	**1846**
1847 US forces make an amphibious landing and capture Vera Cruz in Mexico. **1847** Brigham YOUNG (1801–77) founds Salt Lake City.	**1847** Scottish physician James Simpson (1811–70) first uses chloroform as an anesthetic for childbirth. **1847** US engineer Richard Hoe (1812–86) invents the rotary printing press.	**1847** British novelist Charlotte BRONTË (1816–55) publishes her *Jane Eyre*. **1847** British novelist Emily BRONTË (1818–48) publishes her *Wuthering Heights*.	**1847**
1848 Zachary TAYLOR (1785–1850) is elected US president **1848** Wisconsin becomes a state of the USA. **1848** California Gold Rush starts. **1848** US troops enter Mexico City; by the peace of Guadaloupe-Hidalgo, Mexico cedes all territory N of Rio Grande to the USA.	**1848** British mathematician George BOOLE (1815–64) introduces symbolic logic in his *The Mathematical Analysis of Logic*. **1848** British physicist William KELVIN (1824–1907) devises the absolute temperature scale. **1848** French physicist Armand Fizeau (1819–96) applies the Doppler effect to light waves.	**1848** British novelist William THACKERAY (1811–63) publishes his *Vanity Fair*. **1848** British artists form the Pre-Raphaelite Brotherhood. **1848** German socialists Karl MARX (1818–83) and Friedrich Engels issue their *Communist Manifesto*.	**1848**
	1849 French engineer Joseph Monier (1823–1906) invents rein-forced concrete. **1849** US inventor Walter Hunt (1796–1859) patents the safety pin. **1849** French army officer and engineer Claude Minié (1814–79) invents a rifle that fires expanding lead bullets.		**1849**

ASIA AND AUSTRALASIA	AFRICA	EUROPE

1850 **1850** Babist rebellion in Persia is crushed and the self-proclaimed Bab, Sayyid Ali Muhammad (b.*c.*1820), is executed.

1850 Quasi-Christian Taiping rebellion breaks out in SW China led by Hong Xiuquan.

1850 Britain's Australian colonies are granted self-government.

1850 Denmark sells its trading posts in W Africa to Britain

1850 German Confederation is restored under Austrian leadership.

1850 British gunboats blockade the Greek port of Piraeus.

1851 **1851** Colonists discover gold in Victoria, Australia.

▶ ***Franz Joseph*** *was the first leader of the Austro-Hungarian empire: he was emperor of the Austrian empire from 1848 and king of Hungary from 1867, granting Hungary coequal status in the Dual Monarchy. His long reign was beset by nationalist strife.*

1851 Austrian emperor, FRANZ JOSEPH I (1830–1916), withdraws the constitution.

1851 Louis Napoleon (1808–73) overthrows the French constitution.

1852 **1852** During the second Burmese War Britain annexes Pegu (S Burma); Mindon Min (1814–78) becomes king of N Burma.

1852 Fulani leader Al-Hadj Omar (*c.*1797–1864) launches a war of expansion against W African states.

1852 Louis Napoleon is declared Emperor NAPOLEON III.

1852 Camillo di CAVOUR (1810–61) becomes prime minister of Piedmont-Sardinia.

1852 Schleswig-Holstein comes under Danish protection.

1853 **1853** French annex the islands of New Caledonia in the S Pacific.

1853 Taiping rebels conquer the Chinese city of Nanjing and make it their capital.

1853 Heaven and Earth secret society captures the port of Shanghai in China.

1853 AFRIKANERS establish the independent republic of Transvaal.

1853 Ethiopian chieftain Ras Kasa (*c.*1818–68) reunifies the country and proclaims himself Emperor Tewodros II.

1853 Central and N German states renew the Zollverein agreement from which Austria is excluded.

1853 Russia invades Turkish-occupied Romania.

1854 **1854** US naval officer Matthew PERRY (1794–1858) forces Japan to open to limited foreign trade.

1854 British agree to the Afrikaners establishing an Orange Free State.

1854 Britain and France support Turkey against Russia in the Crimean War; British and French forces besiege the Russians at Sebastopol and win the battle of Balaclava; Florence NIGHTINGALE (1820–1910) nurses the British wounded.

1854 British and French ships occupy Piraeus to prevent Greece joining the war against Turkey.

1854 General Leopoldo O'Donnell (1809–67) leads a liberal revolution in Spain.

THE AMERICAS	SCIENCE AND TECHNOLOGY	ARTS AND HUMANITIES	
1850 USA and Britain agree by treaty the neutrality of a proposed canal construction zone across Panama.	**1850** US scientist Charles Page (1812–68) builds an electric locomotive.	**1850** US novelist Nathaniel HAWTHORNE (1804–64) publishes his *The Scarlet Letter*.	1850
1850 Millard FILLMORE (1800–74) becomes US president.	**1850** British physician Alfred Higginson (1808–84) introduces the use of the hypodermic syringe.	**1850** German composer Richard WAGNER (1813–83) writes his opera *Lohengrin*.	
1850 Clay Compromise abolishes the right of the US government to impose antislavery polices on new states.	**1850** German physicist Rudolf CLAUSIUS (1822–88) formulates the second law of thermodynamics.	**1850** French artist Gustave COURBET (1819–77) paints his *The Stone-Breakers*.	
1850 California becomes a state of the USA.	**1850** First submarine telegraph cable is laid (between Britain and France).		
1851 Spanish defeat a nationalist invasion of Cuba.	**1851** US manufacturer Isaac SINGER (1811–75) invents the single-thread domestic sewing machine.	**1851** US novelist Herman MELVILLE (1819–91) publishes his *Moby Dick*.	1851
	1851 German mathematician Bernhard Riemann (1826–66) proposes a general function theory.		
	1851 Great Exhibition, organized largely by Prince ALBERT (1819–61), opens in the specially built Crystal Palace in London, UK.		
1852 Franklin PIERCE (1804–69) is elected US president.	**1852** British chemist Edward Frankland (1825–99) proposes the theory of valency.	**1852** British artist William Holman Hunt (1827–1910) paints his *The Light of the World*.	1852
1852 Argentine dictator Juan de ROSAS (1793–1877) is overthrown after his defeat at the battle of Caseros.	**1852** French scientist Henri Regnault (1810–78) discovers a method for determining the density of a gas.	**1852** French philosopher Auguste COMTE (1798–1857) publishes his *System of Positive Polity*	
	1852 French physicist Jean FOUCAULT (1819–68) invents the gyroscope.	**1852** US author Harriet Beecher STOWE (1811–96) publishes her *Uncle Tom's Cabin*.	
1853 New York and Chicago are linked by rail.	**1853** British engineer Josiah Clark (1822–98) invents the pneumatic message tube.	**1853** French financier and administrator Georges Haussmann (1809–91) begins the rebuilding of Paris.	1853
1853 Buenos Aires breaks away from Argentina.	**1853** Swedish physicist Anders Ångström (1814–74) explains the formation of emission and absorption spectra.	**1853** Heinrich Steinway (1797–1871) opens a piano factory in New York.	
1854 US Kansas–Nebraska Act abolishes the Missouri compromise; the "War for Bleeding Kansas" starts between pro- and antislavery factions.	**1854** Canadian geologist Abraham Gesner (1797–1864) starts to manufacture kerosene.	**1854** British poet Alfred TENNYSON (1809–92) publishes his *The Charge of the Light Brigade*.	1854
	1854 Dutch physician Anthonius Mathijsen (1805–78) introduces the use of plaster of Paris for bone-setting.	**1854** French anthropologist Joseph de Gobineau (1816–82) publishes his racist *Essay on the Inequality of the Human Races*.	

ASIA AND AUSTRALASIA	AFRICA	EUROPE

1855

1855 Chinese troops prevent the Taiping rebels from capturing Beijing; imperial troops also recapture Shanghai with French assistance.

1855 ALEXANDER II (1818–81) becomes czar of Russia; Sebastopol falls to British and French troops.

1855 Lord PALMERSTON (1784–1865) becomes prime minister of Britain.

1856

1856 Ottoman sultan ABDUL MEDJID I (1823–61) approves the Hatt-i Humayun reforms, giving religious freedom to Christians.

1856 Britain annexes the Indian state of Oudh.

1856 Persians capture the Afghan city of Herat; Britain declares war on Persia.

1856 Chinese authorities arrest the British crew of the *Arrow* for smuggling; start of the second Opium War.

1856 Transvaal becomes the South African Republic, with Pretoria as its capital.

1856 David LIVINGSTONE (1813–73) completes the first E–W crossing of Africa by a European, having "discovered" and named the Victoria Falls.

1856 Peace of Paris ends the Crimean War; Russia loses the Danube delta region; the Black Sea is declared neutral; Britain and France guarantee the Ottoman Empire against further disintegration.

1857

1857 British and French troops capture Canton (Guangzhou), China.

1857 British forces occupy Bushire in Persia.

1857 French occupy Saigon in S Vietnam.

1857 Mandalay becomes the new capital of Burma.

1857 Sepoys (local troops) in India mutiny and massacre British civilians in many cities; British forces recapture Delhi.

1857 Fulani led by Al-Hadj Omar (*c.*1797–1864) besiege the French fort of Medine in Senegal.

1857 French found Dakar in Senegal.

1857 French forces conquer the BERBERS in S Algeria.

▶ **Brunel** *Isambard Kingdom Brunel and his father, Marc, revolutionized engineering in Britain. Isambard designed huge Atlantic-going ships, one of which was used to lay the first successful transatlantic telegraph cable.*

1858

1858 Indian Mutiny is completely suppressed; the British East India company is dissolved and India comes under the control of the British crown.

1858 Treaty of Tianjin opens more Chinese ports to foreign ships and legalizes the opium trade.

1858 China cedes N bank of Amur river to Russia by the treaty of Aigun.

1858 WILLIAM I (1797–1888) becomes regent of Prussia

1858 At a secret meeting at Plombiers, NAPOLEON III (1808–73) and Camillo di CAVOUR (1810–61) plan the unification of Italy.

1859

1859 Portuguese and Dutch agree to divide Timor.

1859 US ships assist the British and the French against the Chinese.

1859 Dispute over land sparks the second Maori War in New Zealand.

1859 Construction of the Suez canal begins under the direction of French engineer Ferdinand de LESSEPS (1805–94).

1859 Spanish troops invade Morocco in a dispute over the enclaves of Ceuta and Melila.

1859 During the Italian war of unification, Piedmontese armies defeat the Austrians at the battles of Magenta and Solferino; France captures Lombardy from Austria and cedes it to Piedmont in return for Savoy and Nice.

THE AMERICAS

1855 Antonio de SANTA ANNA (1794–1876) is overthrown in Mexico.

1856 US abolitionist John BROWN (1800–59) kills pro-slavers in Kansas at the Pottawatomie Creek massacre.

1856 US adventurer William WALKER (1824–60) seizes power in Nicaragua.

1856 James BUCHANAN (1791–1868) is elected US president.

1857 Dredd-Scott decision reinforces the rights of US slave-owners.

> "I am as content to die on the scaffold for God's eternal truth as in any other way."
>
> John Brown

1858 Minnesota becomes a state of the USA.

1858 Benito JUÁREZ (1806–72) is elected president of Mexico.

1858 Civil war breaks out in Mexico.

1858 Irish Republican Brotherhood (Fenians) is founded in New York.

1859 John Brown leads a raid on Harper's Ferry; he is caught and executed.

1859 Oregon becomes a state of the USA.

1859 Buenos Aires is compelled to rejoin Argentina.

SCIENCE AND TECHNOLOGY

1855 British chemist Alexander Parkes (1813–90) accidentally discovers celluloid.

1856 German engineer Werner von SIEMENS (1816–92) designs an improved armature for electrical generators.

1856 Fossil human bones are found in the Neanderthal valley in Germany.

1856 British engineer Henry Bessemer (1813–98) perfects his air-blast method of converting iron to steel.

1856 German anatomist Hermann Helmholtz (1821–94) publishes his *Handbook of Physiological Optics*.

1856 Swiss food technologist Henri Nestlé (1814–90) invents condensed milk.

1856 US inventor Elisha OTIS (1811–61) installs the first passenger safety elevator.

1856 British chemist William Perkins (1838–1907) produces aniline mauve, the first synthetic dye.

1857 German physicist Gustav KIRCHHOFF (1824–87) discovers emission spectroscopy.

1858 German chemist Friedrich Kekulé (1829–96) discovers that carbon atoms form chain molecules.

1858 British engineer Isambard Kingdom BRUNEL (1806–59) builds the *Great Eastern* steamship.

1858 First transatlantic telegraph cable goes into service.

1859 British naturalist Charles DARWIN (1809–82) publishes his *The Origin of Species by means of Natural Selection,* which proposes his theory of evolution.

1859 British naturalist Alfred WALLACE (1823–1913) independently develops a theory of evolution.

1859 First oil well is drilled in Pennsylvania, USA.

ARTS AND HUMANITIES

1855

1855 British poet Robert BROWNING (1812–89) publishes his *Men and Women*.

1855 US poet Walt WHITMAN 1819–92) publishes his *Leaves of Grass*.

1856

1856 French novelist Gustave FLAUBERT (1821–80) publishes his *Madame Bovary*.

1857

1857 French artist Jean-François Millet (1814–75) paints his *The Gleaners*.

1857 French poet Charles BAUDELAIRE (1821–67) publishes his *Les fleurs du mal*.

1857 British novelist Anthony TROLLOPE (1815–82) publishes his *Barchester Towers*.

1857 British poet (1806–61) Elizabeth Barrett BROWNING publishes her *Aurora Leigh*.

1858

1859

1859 French composer Jacques Offenbach (1819–80) writes his opera *Orpheus in the Underworld*.

1859 British philosopher John Stuart MILL (1806–73) publishes his essay *On Liberty*.

1859 French artist Édouard MANET (1832–83) paints his *The Absinthe Drinker*.

1859 French artist Jean-Baptiste Corot (1796–1875) paints his *Dante and Virgil*.

1860

1860 Irish explorer Robert Burke (1820–61) and English explorer William Wills (1834–61) lead the first expedition to cross Australia s-n.

1860 In s China, British and French troops defeat the Taiping rebels; in n China they capture the Dagu forts from the emperor; occupy Beijing and burn the summer palace; the treaty of Peking ends the second Opium War.

1860 Russia founds the port of Vladivostok.

1860 French troops land at Beirut (present-day Lebanon) to restore order.

1860 Japanese nationalists murder foreign sailors and officials.

1861

1862

1862 Tongzhi (1856–75) becomes emperor of China, with dowager empress Cixi (1835–1908) as regent.

1862 France annexes se Vietnam.

1862 Russia annexes parts of Turkistan.

1863

1863 Japanese forts fire at US, French and Dutch merchant ships.

1863 King Norodom (1838–1904) places Cambodia under French protection.

1863 Mercenary Ever-Victorious Army, led by British officer Charles Gordon (1833–85), liberates the city of Suzhou from the Taiping rebels.

1864

1864 Joint French, Dutch, British and US expedition destroys Japanese coastal forts.

1864 Imperial Chinese troops recapture Nanjing: end of the Taiping rebellion.

1860 German traders establish a settlement in Cameroon, w Africa.

1861 Zanzibar becomes independent of Oman.

1861 Britain acquires the Lagos coast of Nigeria.

1861 Fulani, under Al-Hadj Omar (c.1797–1864), conquer the kingdom of Segu.

1862 France purchases the port of Obock on the coast of Somalia, ne Africa.

1863 Ismail Pasha (1830–95) becomes ruler of Egypt.

1863 French establish a protectorate over Dahomey, w Africa.

1863 Madagascan chiefs overthrow pro-European king Radama II.

1864 Tewodros II (c.1818–68) of Ethiopia imprisons a British consul and merchants.

1860 France and Britain sign a free trade treaty.

1860 Giuseppe Garibaldi (1807–82) and his red shirts liberate Naples.

◄ *Lincoln, US president during the civil war, believed the country could not survive "half slave, half free" but was determined to prevent the breakup of the Union. He led the northern states (the Union) with firmness and urged fairness and charity after the southern states (the Confederacy) were defeated.*

1861 Victor Emmanuel II (1820–78) of Piedmont becomes king of a united Italy, with its capital at Turin.

1861 William I (1797–1888) becomes king of Prussia.

1861 Serfdom is abolished in Russia.

1862 Otto von Bismarck (1815–98) becomes prime minister of Prussia.

1862 Garibaldi marches on Rome but is defeated by Italian troops.

1863 Polish uprising torn by internal disputes is savagely repressed by Russian and Prussian troops.

1863 Christian IX (1818–1906) becomes king of Denmark.

1863 Prince William of Denmark becomes King George I (1845–1913) of Greece.

1864 Prussia makes war on Denmark and gains control of Schleswig-Holstein.

1864 Red Cross is established by the Geneva convention.

1864 Regional elected assemblies (*zemstvos*) are established in Russia.

1864 Britain cedes the Ionian Islands to Greece.

1864 Karl Marx (1818–83) organizes the First International Workingmen's Association in London.

THE AMERICAS

1860 Abraham LINCOLN (1809–65) is elected US president; South Carolina secedes from the Union.

1861 Kansas becomes a state of the USA.

1861 French, British and Spanish troops land in Mexico in a dispute over loan repayments.

1861 Confederate States of America is formed and Jefferson DAVIS (1808–89) is elected president; Confederate forces capture Fort Sumter and under Thomas "Stonewall" JACKSON (1824–63) defeat a Federal army at the first battle of Bull Run in Virginia.

1862 Nashville in Tennessee falls to Federal troops under Ulysses S. GRANT (1822–85); the Confederates, under commander-in-chief Robert E. LEE (1807–70), invade Maryland, fight the inconclusive battle of Antietam, and win the battle of Fredericksburg; Federal troops win the battle of Shiloh and take Memphis in Tennessee; US president Lincoln proclaims the emancipation of slaves.

1862 Slavery is abolished in Dutch West indies.

1863 West Virginia is created a state of the USA; Confederates win the battle of Chancellorsville in Virginia; Federal troops win the battle of Gettysburg in Pennsylvania; Grant captures Vicksburg in Mississippi.

1863 French troops enter Mexico City; MAXIMILIAN (1832–67) is declared emperor.

1863 US government decides upon the forcible removal of Native Americans from Kansas.

1864 Nevada is created a US state; Federal troops under William SHERMAN (1820–91) invade Georgia, destroy Atlanta, and capture Savannah; Lincoln is reelected US president.

1864 CHEYENNE Native Americans are defeated by US troops in Colorado.

SCIENCE AND TECHNOLOGY

1860 German metalworker Reinhard Mannesmann (1856–1922) invents a process for making seamless steel tubes.

1861 French anatomist Paul BROCA (1824–80) discovers the speech-center of the human brain.

1861 Belgian industrialist Ernest SOLVAY (1938–1922) invents a process for manufacturing soda ash.

1862 US engineer Richard Gatling (1818–1903) invents a rapid-fire, multibarreled, machine gun.

1862 US engineer Joseph Brown (1810–76) builds a universal milling machine.

1862 First engagement between iron-clad ships takes place when the Confederate *Merrimac* and the Federal *Monitor* exchange shots in the US Civil War.

1862 US industrialist John ROCKEFELLER (1839–1937) builds an oil refinery in Cleveland, Ohio.

1863 French engineer Pierre Martin (1824–1915) develops the open-hearth method of steel manufacture in France.

1863 London Underground Railway opens.

1864 Scottish mathematician James MAXWELL (1831–79) announces his equations that link light and electricity.

1864 French chemist Louis PASTEUR (1822–95) proves the existence of airborne microorganisms.

ARTS AND HUMANITIES

1860 British novelist George Eliot (1819–80) publishes her *The Mill on the Floss*.

1861 French artist Gustave Doré (1832–83) publishes his illustrations for Dante's *Inferno*.

1862 Russian author and dramatist Ivan TURGENEV (1818–83) publishes his novel *Fathers and Sons*.

1862 British artist Edward BURNE-JONES (1833–98) paints his *King Cophetua and the Beggar Maid*.

1862 French author and poet Victor HUGO (1802–85) publishes his novel *Les Miserables*.

1864 British theologian John NEWMAN (1801–90) explains his conversion to catholicism in his *Apologia pro vita sua*.

1864 Austrian composer Anton BRUCKNER (1824–96) writes his Mass No.1 in D minor.

1860

1861

1862

1863

1864

ASIA AND AUSTRALASIA	AFRICA	EUROPE

1865
1865 Muslim rebels set up an independent state in Chinese Turkistan.

1865 Russians occupy Tashkent in central Asia.

1865 Wellington is established as the capital of New Zealand.

1866
1866 Korean troops defeat a French military expedition marching on Seoul.

1867
1867 Last Japanese shōgun abdicates; Emperor Mutsuhito (1852–1912) takes personal control in the Meiji Restoration; Tokyo becomes the new capital.

1867 Turkish radicals form the Young Turks secret society.

1867 Last shipment of British convicts lands in Australia.

1868
1868 Muslim state in Chinese Turkistan is suppressed.

1869

1865 AFRIKANERS from a new Orange Free State defeat Basuto chief Moshoeshoe I (c.1786–1870), who cedes territory.

SWITZERLAND · AUSTRIA-HUNGARY · VENETIA · Rome · SARDINIA · KINGDOM OF THE TWO SICILIES

☐ Kingdom of Italy 1861
☐ Ceded to Italy 1866
☐ Added 1870

▲ *Italy Between 1859 and 1870 Italy was unified. In 1859 Cavour acquired much of N Italy in a war against Austria. In 1860 Garibaldi conquered Sicily and Naples, which he presented to Victor Emmanuel II in 1861. In 1866, when Italy joined Prussia in the Austro-Prussian war, it gained Venetia. Finally, in 1870, French troops withdrew from Rome in order to fight the Prussians.*

1868 British expedition to Ethiopia defeats Tewodros II (c.1818–68) at the battle of Arogee and frees British prisoners.

1868 British annex Basutoland (Lesotho) in South Africa.

1869 Suez canal opens, linking the Mediterranean with the Red Sea and the Indian Ocean.

◄ *Mendel laid the foundations of the modern science of genetics. The experiments that led to his discovery of heredity were begun in his monastery garden in 1856.*

1865 Otto von BISMARCK (1815–98) and NAPOLEON III (1808–73) meet at Biarritz and agree mutual neutrality in the event of war with Austria

1865 LEOPOLD II (1835–1909) becomes king of Belgium.

1866 Prussia and Italy declare war on Austria; the Austrians defeat the Italians at the battle of Custozza, but are defeated by the Prussians at the battle of Sadowa near Königgratz.

1866 Venice joins the kingdom of Italy.

1866 Cretans rise in revolt against the Turks.

1867 North German Confederation is formed under Prussian control.

1867 The Netherlands agrees to sell Luxembourg to France; the treaty of London establishes the independence and neutrality of Luxembourg.

1867 Turkish troops withdraw from Serbia.

1867 Giuseppe GARIBALDI (1807–82) again marches on Rome and is defeated by French troops at the battle of Mentana.

1867 Austria and Hungary become a joint monarchy.

1867 Cretan revolt is crushed.

1868 William GLADSTONE (1809–98) becomes prime minister of Britain.

1868 Revolution deposes Queen ISABELLA II (1830–1904) in Spain.

1869 Spanish parliament offers the throne to a German prince, provoking French hostility.

THE AMERICAS

1865 Federal army destroys Richmond, Virginia; Robert E. LEE (1807–70) surrenders at Appomattox court house, ending the Civil War; the 13th amendment to the US constitution prohibits slavery.

1865 Abraham LINCOLN (b.1809) is assassinated; Andrew JOHNSON (1808–75) becomes US president.

1865 Paraguay is invaded by the forces of Brazil, Argentina and Uruguay.

1865 Spain fights a naval war against Peru and other South American states.

1865 Klu Klux Klan is founded in Tennessee.

1866 Civil Rights Bill is adopted by the 14th amendment to the US constitution.

1866 France withdraws support for MAXIMILIAN (1832–67) in Mexico.

1866 Fenians from the US attack a British fort on the Canadian border.

1867 Maximilian is overthrown and executed.

1867 Canada becomes an independent dominion of the British Empire.

1867 Basic Reconstruction Act sets conditions for the readmission of Confederate states to the USA.

1867 USA purchases Alaska from Russia.

1867 Nebraska becomes a state of the USA.

1868 Paraguayan capital Asunción is captured.

1868 Ulysses S. GRANT (1822–85) is elected US president.

1869 First American transcontinental railroad is completed.

1869 Red River rebellion in central Canada establishes a short-lived provisional government.

SCIENCE AND TECHNOLOGY

1865 German botanist Julius von Sachs (1833–97) discovers chloroplasts in plant cells.

1865 Austrian monk Gregor MENDEL (1822–84) describes his experiments cross-breeding plants; the results suggest rules of heredity.

1865 US inventor Thaddeus Lowe (1832–1913) builds a compression ice machine.

1866 French scientist Georges Leclanché (1839–82) invents a zinc-carbon dry cell.

1867 French engineer Pierre Michaux manufactures the velocipede pedaled bicycle.

1867 Swedish industrialist Alfred NOBEL (1833–96) invents dynamite.

1867 British physician Joseph LISTER (1827–1912) introduces antiseptic surgery when he sprays phenol in an operating theater.

1867 US engineer Christopher Sholes (1819–90) invents a typewriter with a QWERTY keyboard.

1868 US engineer George Westinghouse (1846–1914) invents the air-brake.

1868 French paleontologist Édouard Lartet (1801–71) discovers the fossil bones of Cro-Magnon man.

1868 British astronomer William Huggins (1824–1910) measures the radial velocity of a star.

1869 Russian scientist Dmitri MENDELEYEV (1834–1907) publishes the periodic table of elements in his *Principles of Chemistry*.

1869 French scientist Hippolyte Mege-Mouries invents a process for making margarine.

1869 Irish physicist John Tyndall (1820–93) discovers that the scattering of light by atmospheric particles makes the sky blue.

ARTS AND HUMANITIES

1865 English mathematician Charles Dodgson (pen-name Lewis CARROLL, 1832–98) publishes *Alice in Wonderland*.

1866 Russian novelist Fyodor DOSTOEVSKY (1821–81) publishes his *Crime and Punishment*.

1867 French artist Edgar DEGAS (1834–1917) paints his *Mlle Fiocre in the Ballet "La Source"*.

1867 Norwegian dramatist Henrik IBSEN (1828–1906) writes his play *Peer Gynt*.

1867 German socialist Karl MARX (1818–83) publishes the first volume of *Das Kapital*.

1867 Austrian composer Johann STRAUSS (1825–99) writes his *The Blue Danube* waltz.

1868 German composer Johannnes BRAHMS (1833–97) writes his *German Requiem*.

1868 Norwegian composer Edvard GRIEG (1843–1907) writes his piano concerto in A minor.

1868 US writer Louisa May Alcott (1832–88) publishes her *Little Women*.

1869 French poet Paul VERLAINE (1844–96) publishes his *Fêtes Galantes*.

1869 French author Jules Verne (1828–1905) publishes his *20,000 Leagues under the Sea*.

1869 British poet and critic Matthew ARNOLD (1822–88) publishes his *Culture and Anarchy*.

1869 Russian novelist Leo TOLSTOY (1828–1910) publishes his *War and Peace*.

ASIA AND AUSTRALASIA	AFRICA	EUROPE
1870		
1870 Chinese mob massacres a French consul and missionaries in Tianjin.	**1870** Arab slave trader Tippu Tip (1837–1905) establishes himself as ruler in present-day Democratic Republic of Congo.	**1870** An Italian duke becomes King AMADEO I (1845–90) of Spain.
		1870 France declares war on Prussia and is defeated at the battle of Sedan; NAPOLEON III (1808–73) is overthrown and the third republic is declared; the Prussians besiege Paris.
		1870 International treaty establishes the neutrality of Belgium.
		1870 Vatican Council, convened by Pope PIUS IX (1792–1878) proclaims papal infallibility.
		1870 Italian troops occupy the papal states.
1871		
1871 US military expedition tries to force Korea to accept foreign trade, but is defeated.	**1871** Dutch cede their Gold Coast (present-day Ghana) forts and trading posts to Britain	**1871** Paris surrenders to Prussians; France cedes Alsace-Lorraine to Germany by the peace of Frankfurt; Paris Commune is declared and crushed; Louis THIERS (1797–1877) becomes president of France.
	1871 US journalist Henry STANLEY (1841–1904) finds British explorer David LIVINGSTONE (1813–73).	
	1871 British annex the diamond-producing area of the Orange Free State.	**1871** Germany is united into an empire under WILLIAM I (1797–1888) of Prussia.
	◀ *Edison patented his first invention – a mechanical vote recorder – at the age of 21. In 1876 he set up an "invention factory", where new inventions were patented at a prodigious rate.*	**1871** Rome becomes the capital of Italy; the Vatican state is established.
1872		**1871** Otto von BISMARCK (1815–98) begins the *Kulturkampf* struggle with the Roman Catholic church.
	1872 John IV (1831–89) becomes emperor of Ethiopia.	**1872** Austria, Prussia and Russian form the league of three emperors against France.
		1872 Civil war breaks out in Spain.
1873		
1873 French annex Hanoi and the Red River delta area of Vietnam.	**1873** Second ASHANTI War begins.	**1873** Amadeo I abdicates; a Spanish republic is established.
1873 Russia annexes Khiva in Uzbekistan.	**1873** Slave markets in Zanzibar are closed.	
1874		
1874 Turkish Ottoman Empire begins to disintegrate rapidly under economic pressure.	**1874** British forces destroy the Ashanti capital of Kumasi.	**1874** Benjamin DISRAELI (1804–81) becomes prime minister of Britain.
1874 British annex Fiji in the S Pacific.	**1874** British West Africa is broken up into separate colonies.	**1874** Group of Spanish generals declare ALFONSO XII (1857–85) king.
1874 Japanese expedition briefly captures Formosa (present-day Taiwan).	**1874** British officer Charles GORDON (1833–85) becomes governor of the Egyptian Sudan.	**1874** Universal postal union is formed in Berne, Switzerland.
1874 Russia conquers Kashgaria in Turkistan.		

THE AMERICAS

1870 Paraguay loses much territory after defeat by Brazil and Argentina.

1871 British Columbia becomes a part of Canada.

1871 Treaty of Washington settles outstanding differences with Britain over borders, fishing rights and war damage.

1871 US Indian Appropriations Bill abolishes the collective rights of Native American peoples.

SCIENCE AND TECHNOLOGY

1870 Belgian engineer Zénobe Gramme (1826–1901) invents the ring armature and constructs the first electrical generator to produce a constant flow of current.

1870 US inventor Rufus Gilbert (1832–85) patents an elevated railroad system.

1870 German mathematician Georg CANTOR (1845–1918) founds set theory.

▶ *Stanley emigrated to the USA from Britain at the age of 16. He served in the Confederate army and the US navy before becoming a journalist and being sent to central Africa to find David Livingstone.*

1871 British naturalist Charles DARWIN (1809–82) publishes his *The Descent of Man.*

1872 US inventor Thomas EDISON (1847–1931) patents an electric typewriter.

1873 Dutch physicist Johannes van der Waals (1837–1923) calculates intermolecular forces.

1873 US engineer Joseph Glidden (1813–1906) invents a machine for making barbed wire.

1874 US librarian Melvil Dewey (1851–1931) invents a decimal system for cataloguing books.

ARTS AND HUMANITIES

1871 US artist James WHISTLER (1834–1903) paints his *Arrangement in Gray and Black – the Artist's Mother.*

1871 British artist John MILLAIS (1829–96) paints his *The Boyhood of Raleigh.*

1871 *Aïda*, the opera by Italian composer Giuseppe VERDI (1813–1901), is premiered.

1872 British author Samuel Butler (1835–1902) publishes his novel *Erewhon.*

1872 German philosopher Friedrich NIETZSCHE (1844–1900) publishes his *The Death of Tragedy.*

1873 French poet Arthur RIMBAUD (1854–91) publishes his *A Season in Hell.*

1874 British novelist Thomas HARDY (1840–1928) publishes his *Far from the Madding Crowd.*

1874 First exhibition of Impressionist paintings is held in Paris.

1874 Russian composer Modest MUSSORGSKY (1839–81) writes his *Pictures at an Exhibition.*

1870

1871

1872

1873

1874

1875

1875 Infant Zai Tian (1871–1908) becomes Emperor Guangxu of China with the dowager empress CIXI (1835–1908) as regent.

1875 Russia cedes the Kuril Islands to Japan in return for part of Sakhalin Island.

1875 Britain, under prime minister Benjamin DISRAELI (1804–81), buys Egypt's shares in the Suez canal.

1875 Egypt invades Ethiopia and occupies the coastal region.

1875 Socialist congress at Gotha in Germany founds the Socialist Workingmen's Party.

1875 French third Republic is officially proclaimed with Marshal Patrice MacMahon (1808–93) as president.

1875 Kálmán Tisza (1830–92) becomes prime minister of Hungary and begins a program of Magyarization.

1876

1876 Japan occupies the Ryukyu Islands.

1876 Turkish chief minister Midhat Pasha (1822–84) replaces sultan Murad V (1840–1904) with ABDUL HAMID II (1842–1918) and issues a constitution.

1876 LEOPOLD II (1835–1909) of Belgium founds the International Association for the Exploration and Civilization of Africa.

1876 Ethiopian army defeats the Egyptians at the battles of Gura and forces them to withdraw.

1875 Anti-Turkish revolts break out in Bosnia and Herzegovina; Serbia and Russia support the rebels.

1876 Risings against the Turks in Bulgaria are brutally suppressed; Serbs declare war on Turkey and are defeated at the battle of Alexinatz.

1876 Mikhail BAKUNIN (1814–76) organizes the Land and Liberty secret society in Russia.

1877

1877 Turkish constitution is set aside by Sultan Abdul Hamid II.

1877 Saigo Takamori (1828–77) leads a samurai uprising (the Satsuma rebellion) against modernization in Japan.

1877 British annex the AFRIKANER South African republic.

1877 British annex Walvis Bay on the SW coast of Africa.

1877 Russia declares war and invades Turkey; Russian troops reach the walls of Istanbul.

1877 Queen VICTORIA (1819–1901) of Britain formally becomes Empress of India.

1877 President MacMahon's monarchist policies create a political crisis in France.

1878

1878 During the second Afghan War, the British invade and overthrow Sher Ali (1825–79).

1878 Chinese reconquer part of Turkistan from Islamic rebels.

▶ **Twain** was the first US author of world rank to write authentically colloquial novels employing a genuine American idiom. His work, which began as pure humor and developed to bitter satire, was marked by an egalitarian attitude and a strong desire for social justice.

1878 UMBERTO I (1844–1900) becomes king of Italy.

1878 Romania, Serbia and Montenegro become independent states by the treaty of San Stefano between Turkey and Russia.

1878 At the Congress of Berlin, Austria gains control of Bosnia and Herzegovina, Russia gains control of Bulgaria and Britain gains control of Cyprus.

1878 Anti-socialist laws are passed in Germany.

1879

1879 Abd Al-Rahman (c.1830–1901) becomes ruler of Afghanistan; the British gain control of the Khyber pass.

1879 ISMAIL PASHA (1830–95) is deposed as Egyptian ruler by the Ottoman sultan and replaced by Tewfik (1852–92).

1879 ZULUS under Cetewayo (1825–84) attack the British in South Africa; they win the battle of Isandhlwana but are defeated at the battle of Ulundi.

1879 Algeria comes under French civil government.

1879 Germany and Austria sign an alliance against Russia.

1879 Terrorist Will of the People secret society is founded by Russian radicals.

THE AMERICAS

1875 Fighting breaks out between SIOUX Native Americans and US prospectors in Dakota.

1876 Colorado becomes a state of the USA.

1876 US troops commanded by George CUSTER (1839–76) are massacred by Sioux and other Native American tribes led by chief SITTING BULL (1831–90) at the battle of the Little Big Horn in Dakota.

1876 US presidential election produces a disputed result.

1877 Sioux Native American chief CRAZY HORSE (1842–77) surrenders to US troops.

1877 Electoral commission decides that Rutherford HAYES (1822–93) becomes US president.

1877 Porfirio DÍAZ (1830–1915) becomes president of Mexico after leading a coup.

1878 Concession to construct a canal across Panama is granted to a French company.

1879 Chile wages war on Peru and Bolivia for control of the nitrate deposits in the Atacama region.

SCIENCE AND TECHNOLOGY

1876 British research ship HMS *Challenger* completes a three-year voyage that lays the foundations of oceanography.

1876 Nikolaus Otto (1832–91) builds a practical internal combustion gas engine.

1876 Scottish engineer Alexander Graham BELL (1847–1922) invents the telephone in the USA.

1876 German engineer Carl von Linde (1842–1934) patents the ammonia compression refrigerator.

1877 First telephone exchanged is installed in New Haven, USA.

1877 US inventor Thomas EDISON (1847–1931) invents the phonograph.

1877 Austrian physicist Ludwig BOLTZMANN (1844–1906) formulates his equations linking kinetic energy and temperature.

1877 Italian astronomer Giovanni Schiaparelli (1835–1910) announces his observation of "canals" on the surface of Mars.

1878 British scientist Joseph Swan (1828–1914) makes a carbon filament electric light.

1878 German chemist Adolf von Bayer synthesizes indigo dye.

1879 Russian psychologist Ivan PAVLOV (1849–1936) discovers how to produce a conditioned reflex in dogs.

1879 Edison patents an incandescent electric light bulb.

ARTS AND HUMANITIES

1875 French composer Georges BIZET (1838–75) writes his opera *Carmen*.

1875 US founder of the Christian Science movement Mary Baker EDDY (1821–1910) publishes her *Science and Health with Key to the Scriptures*.

1875 US author Mark TWAIN (1835–1910) publishes his *The Adventures of Tom Sawyer*.

1876 *The Ring of the Nibelungen* by German composer Richard WAGNER (1813–83) is given its first complete performance at the inaugural Bayreuth festival.

1876 French artist Auguste RENOIR (1841–1919) paints his *Le Moulin de la Galette*.

1876 French symbolist poet Stephane MALLARMÉ (1842–98) publishes his *The Afternoon of a Faun*.

1877 Russian composer Alexander BORODIN (1833–87) writes his Symphony No.2 in B minor.

1878 British social reformer William BOOTH (1829–1912) founds the Salvation Army in London.

*c.***1878** French artist Paul CÉZANNE (1839–1906) paints his *Still Life with a Fruit Dish*.

1878 British composers Arthur Sullivan (1842–1900) and William Gilbert (1836–1911) write their comic operetta *HMS Pinafore*.

1878 Russian composer Peter TCHAIKOVSKY (1840–93) composes his ballet *Swan Lake*.

1879 German socialist Albert Bebel (1840–1913) publishes his *Women and Socialism*.

ASIA AND AUSTRALASIA	AFRICA	EUROPE
1880 France annexes Tahiti. **1880** Outlaw Ned KELLY (b.1855) is executed in Australia.	**1880** French found Brazzaville in the Congo region of central Africa. **1880** AFRIKANERS in Transvaal, South Africa, revolt against British rule and declare a republic.	**1880** Otto von BISMARCK (1815–98) ends his *Kulturkampf* policy in Germany.
1881 China regains territory in Turkistan from Russia by the treaty of St. Petersburg. **1881** Russia annexes the entire Transcaucus region.	**1881** Henry STANLEY (1841–1904) founds Leopoldville in the Congo for LEOPOLD II (1835–1909) of Belgium. **1881** French invade Tunisia and declare a protectorate. **1881** Nationalist army officers stage a rising in Egypt. **1881** British grant limited independence to the Afrikaner South African republic.	**1881** Czar ALEXANDER II (b.1818) is assassinated; ALEXANDER III (1845–94) becomes ruler of Russia; the *Okhrana* political police are founded. **1881** Serbia places itself under Austrian protection by a secret treaty. **1881** Turks cede Thessaly to Greece but keep Macedonia.
1882 Korean nationalists attack Japanese officials in Seoul.	**1882** British bombard Alexandria, defeat the Egyptian army at the battle of Tel-el-Kebir, and occupy Cairo. **1882** Muhammad Ahmed (1840–85) declares himself MAHDI and starts an uprising in Sudan. **1882** Italy acquires the port of Assab in Eritrea.	**1882** Irish nationalists murder senior British officials in Phoenix Park, Dublin. **1882** Milan OBRENOVIĆ (1854–1901) declares himself king of Serbia. **1882** Italy, Germany and Austria sign the anti-French Triple Alliance.
1883 Treaty of Hué establishes a French protectorate over Annam (N Vietnam). **1883** Volcano on the island of Krakatoa erupts violently, causing great destruction.	**1883** Britain declares a protectorate over Egypt. **1883** British are defeated by the Mahdists at the battle of El Obeid. **1883** Paul KRUGER (1825–1904) becomes president of the South African republic. **1883** French go to war with the Hovas of Madagascar. **1883** French expand inland from the coast of Dahomey, W Africa.	**1883** Romania signs a secret anti-Russian treaty with Austria. **1883** Georgy PLEKHANOV (1857–1918) introduces Marxism to Russia.
1884 France and China go to war over control of the Gulf of Tonkin region. **1884** Russians conquer the city of Merv in central Asia. **1884** Chinese Turkistan becomes a province of China. **1884** Germany acquires Kaiser Wilhelmland in New Guinea; Britain annexes the SE part of island. **1884** Dowager empress CIXI (1835–1908) becomes the sole ruler of China. **1884** Chinese troops defeat a pro-Japanese coup in Korea.	**1884** Germany establishes colonies in Cameroon and Togo in W Africa and in SW Africa. **1884** Britain withdraws from Sudan. **1884** Britain establishes a protectorate over part of the Somali coast; French expand inland from Obock and establish French Somaliland.	**1884** Carl Peters (1856–1918) founds the society for German colonization. **1884** International conference in Berlin decides the future of Africa; Belgian king Leopold II's Congo state is recognized, and the principle of ownership through occupation of coastline is established; start of the "scramble for Africa".

THE AMERICAS

1880 After a brief civil war in Argentina, Buenos Aires becomes the federal capital.

1880 James GARFIELD (1831–81) is elected US president

1881 US outlaw William Bonney "BILLY THE KID" (b.1859) is shot dead in New Mexico.

1881 US marshal Wyatt EARP (1848–1929) wins a gunfight at the OK Corral in Tombstone, Arizona.

1881 Chester ARTHUR (1830–86) becomes US president.

1882 Chinese Exclusion Act prohibits Chinese immigration into the USA.

1882 US outlaw Jesse JAMES (b.1847) is shot dead in Missouri.

1883 Northern Pacific Railroad is completed.

1883 Slavery is abolished in the remaining Spanish colonies.

1884 Peru and Bolivia cede nitrate-rich territory to Chile; Bolivia becomes landlocked.

1884 Grover CLEVELAND (1837–1908) is elected US president.

SCIENCE AND TECHNOLOGY

1880 French chemist Louis PASTEUR (1822–95) discovers streptococcus bacteria.

1880 British engineer John Milne (1850–1913) invents an accurate seismograph.

1881 German scientist Karl Eberth (1835–1926) discovers the typhoid bacillus.

1881 First commercial electricity generating station is opened in New York, USA.

1882 German bacteriologist Robert KOCH (1843–1910) discovers the tuberculosis bacillus.

1882 St. Gotthard railroad tunnel through the Alps is opened.

1882 German scientist Walther Flemming (1843–1905) observes and describes cell division.

1883 First steel-frame skyscraper is built in Chicago.

1883 US engineer Hiram Maxim (1840–1916) invents the recoil-operated machine gun.

1884 US industrialist George EASTMAN (1854–1932) invents a roll film for cameras.

1884 British engineer Charles Parsons (1854–1931) patents a steam turbine.

ARTS AND HUMANITIES

1880 US artist John Singer Sargent (1856–1925) paints his portrait of Mrs. *Charles Gifford Dyer*.

1880 French artist Auguste RODIN (1840–1917) sculpts his statue *The Thinker*.

1880 French novelist Émile ZOLA (1840–1902) publishes his *Nana*.

1880 Swiss author Johanna Spyri (1827–1901) publishes her children's novel *Heidi*.

1881 French author known as Anatole France (1844–1924) publishes his novel *The Crime of Sylvester Bonnard*.

1881 US author Henry JAMES (1843–1916) publishes his novel *The Portrait of a Lady*.

1882 Indian author Bankim Chandra Chatterji (1838–94) publishes his novel *Anandamath*.

1883 Scottish author Robert Stevenson (1850–94) publishes his children's adventure *Treasure Island*.

1883 German philosopher Friedrich NIETZSCHE (1844–1900) publishes his *Thus Spake Zarathustra*.

1883 Spanish architect Antonio GAUDÍ (1852–1926) begins work on the church of the Holy Family in Barcelona.

1884 French artist Georges Seurat (1859–91) paints his *Bathers at Asnières*.

1884 French composer Jules Massenet (1842–1912) writes his opera *Manon*.

1885

1885 Dispute over the borders of Afghanistan takes Britain and Russia to the brink of war.

1885 Indian National congress is founded.

1885–86 Britain annexes the whole of Burma after the third Burmese War.

1886

▲ **Parnell** was a vigorous supporter of Home Rule for Ireland. He united all the Irish parties hostile to English rule. Parnell reached the zenith of his power in 1886 when British prime minister William Gladstone introduced the Home Rule Bill.

1885 Mahdists besiege and take Khartoum in Sudan and kill governor Charles GORDON (b.1833).

1885 British colonialist Cecil RHODES (1853–1902) gains control of Bechuanaland, S Africa.

1885 Spanish establish a protectorate over part of Guinea, W Africa.

1885 Congo Free State is established under the personal control of LEOPOLD II (1835–1909) of Belgium.

1885 French declare a protectorate over parts of the Congo region

1885 Germans establish a colony in Tanganyika (present-day Tanzania), E Africa.

1885 Italy occupies the port of Massawa and expands into Eritrea.

1886 Gold is discovered in the Transvaal; the city of Johannesburg is established.

1886 Britain acquires Kenya, E Africa.

1885 King ALFONSO XII (b.1857) of Spain dies; his wife Maria Christina becomes regent for her unborn child, the future ALFONSO XIII (1886–1941).

1885 Bulgaria annexes E Roumelia; Serbia declares war on Bulgaria; the Serbs are defeated at the battle of Slivnitza; Austria intervenes to prevent the invasion of Serbia.

1886 King LUDWIG II (1845–86) of Bavaria is declared insane and deposed.

1886 French minister of war General Georges BOULANGER (1837–91) becomes a national hero for his anti-German views.

1886 Influenced by Irish politician Charles PARNELL (1846–91), the British government, under William GLADSTONE (1809–98), attempts to introduce Home Rule in Ireland, but the bill is rejected by Parliament.

1887

1887 French organize their colonies in Vietnam and Cambodia into the Union of Indochina.

1887 Britain annexes Baluchistan in present-day W Pakistan.

1887 USA gains the use of Pearl Harbor in Hawaii as a naval base.

1888

1888 Britain establishes protectorates over Sarawak and N Borneo.

1888 First railroad in China is opened.

1889

1889 Constitution guaranteeing the rights of the emperor is issued in Japan.

1887 Henry STANLEY (1841–1904) leads an expedition to rescue Emin Pasha (1840–92), an Egyptian governor of the Sudan, from the Mahdists.

1887 Ethiopians attack the Italians and defeat them at the battle of Dogali.

1887 Britain establishes a protectorate over Nigeria.

1887 French expand into Djibouti

1887 Britain annexes Zululand.

1889 With Italian support MENELIK II (1844–1913) overthrows John IV (1831–89) and becomes emperor of Ethiopia; Italy annexes part of Somalia.

1889 French declare a protectorate over the Ivory Coast

1889 British grant Rhodes control of a large area of SE Africa.

1887 Francesco CRISPI (1819–1901) becomes Italian prime minister and pursues a policy of colonial expansion.

1888 WILLIAM II (1859–1941) becomes German emperor.

1889 Having failed to seize power, General Boulanger flees France.

1889 French Panama canal company collapses causing a financial scandal.

1889 International convention declares the Suez canal to be neutral and open to all ships in both peace and war.

1889 Heir to the Austrian throne Archduke Rudolf (b.1858) commits suicide at Mayerling.

THE AMERICAS

1885 Northwest rebellion is suppressed by Canadian troops; leader Louis RIEL (b.1844) is executed.

1885 President Justo Barrios (b.1835) of Guatemala leads an invasion of El Salvador but is defeated and killed at the battle of Chalchuapa.

1886 American Federation of Labor is formed under the leadership of Samuel GOMPERS (1850–1924).

1886 Statue of Liberty is erected at the entrance to New York harbor.

1886 Colombia adopts a centralized constitution.

1886 Apache Native American leader GERONIMO (1829–1908) surrenders to US troops.

1887 Canadian Pacific Railroad is opened.

1888 Slavery is abolished in Brazil.

1888 US Allotment Act allows for the dividing up of Native American reservations.

1888 Benjamin HARRISON (1833–1901) is elected US president.

1889 Revolution establishes a republic in Brazil.

1889 North Dakota, South Dakota, Washington and Montana become states of the USA.

1889 US Oklahoma territory is opened for settlement by a "land race".

1889 First Pan-American conference is held in Washington, D.C.

SCIENCE AND TECHNOLOGY

1885 German engineer Gottleib DAIMLER (1834–1900) patents the internal combustion gasoline engine and builds the first motorcycle.

1885 German engineer Karl BENZ (1844–1929) builds a prototype automobile with a four-stroke internal combustion engine.

1886 US scientist Charles Hall (1863–1914) develops a process for obtaining aluminum from bauxite by electrolysis.

1886 Construction starts on a hydroelectric power station at Niagara Falls.

1887 German physicist Heinrich HERTZ (1857–94) discovers the propagation of electromagnetic waves produced by electrical discharges.

1888 US engineer Nikola Tesla (1856–1943) invents an electric motor that runs on alternating current.

1888 US engineer William Burroughs (1857–98) patents a recording adding machine.

1888 Scottish inventor John Dunlop (1840–1921) develops the pneumatic tire.

1888 US industrialist George EASTMAN (1854–1932) perfects a hand-held (Kodak) camera.

1889 French engineer Gustave Eiffel (1832–1923) designs and builds a steel tower in Paris.

ARTS AND HUMANITIES

1885 French author Guy de Maupassant (1850–93) publishes his *Bel Ami*.

1885 British explorer and scholar Richard BURTON (1821–90) publishes the first volume of his translation of *The Arabian Nights*.

1885 French composer César Franck (1822–1890) writes his *Symphonic Variations*.

1885 US artist Winslow Homer (1836–1910) paints his *The Herring Net*.

1886 French composer Camille Saint-Saëns (1835–1921) writes his *Carnival of the Animals*.

1887 French poet Stephane MALLARMÉ (1842–98) publishes his *Poésies*.

1888 Dutch artist Vincent VAN GOGH (1853–90) paints his *Sunflowers*.

1888 Russian composer Nikolai RIMSKY-KORSAKOV (1844–1908) writes his *Sheherazade*.

1888 Swedish dramatist August STRINDBERG (1849–1912) writes his *Miss Julie*.

1889 Irish dramatist and critic George Bernard SHAW (1856–1950) edits a collection of *Fabian Essays*.

1889 French composer Gabriel Fauré (1845–1924) writes his song *Clair de lune*.

1889 Italian poet Gabriel D'ANNUNZIO (1863–1938) publishes the first volume of his *Romances of the Rose*.

ASIA AND AUSTRALASIA	AFRICA	EUROPE

1890

1890 Britain establishes a protectorate over Zanzibar.

1890 British force the Portuguese to abandon attempts to acquire territory linking Angola to Mozambique.

1890 Otto von BISMARCK (1815–98) is dismissed by the German emperor.

1890 Britain cedes the island of Heligoland to Germany in return for Zanzibar.

1890 Anti-socialist laws are repealed in Germany.

1890 Socialists in Europe initiate May Day celebrations.

1890 Luxembourg becomes independent of the Netherlands.

1890 WILHELMINA (1880–1962) becomes Queen of the Netherlands, with her mother, Emma (1858–1934), as regent.

1890 International convention in Brussels agrees on the suppression of the African slave trade.

► *Sun Yat-sen formed the Revive China Society in 1894 and, the following year, attempted to organize an uprising in Guangzhou (Canton). The uprising failed, and Sun Yat-sen was forced into exile for 16 years. On his return to China, he was part of the revolution that overthrew the Qing dynasty. He served as provisional president of the Chinese Republic from 1911 to 1912.*

1891

1891 Work starts on the trans-Siberian railroad.

1891 Italians defeat the Mahdists in Ethiopia.

1891 Belgium conquers the Katanga region of Congo.

1891 France and Russia sign a defensive entente.

1891 German Social Democratic party adopts Marxist policies under Karl Kautsky (1854–1938).

1892

1892 French defeat the FULANI in w Africa.

1892 Belgium defeats Arab slave-owners in the Congo.

1892 Ferdinand De LESSEPS (1805–94) goes on trial for his part in the Panama canal company scandal.

1892 German general Alfred von SCHLIEFFEN (1833–1913) devises a plan for the eventuality of war on two fronts against France and Russia.

1893

1893 Revolution overthrows Queen Lydia LILIUOKALANI (1838–1917) in Hawaii.

1893 King CHULALONGKORN (1853–1910) of Thailand recognizes a French protectorate over Laos by the treaty of Bangkok.

1893 France captures Timbuktu from the TUAREGS.

1893 French establish a colony in Guinea, w Africa.

1893 Corinth canal opens.

1893 Irish Home Rule bill is passed by the lower house of the British parliament, but is rejected by the upper house.

1894

1894 Republic of Hawaii is declared.

1894 Japan defeats China in a war for control of Korea.

1894 Turks massacre thousands of Armenians near the town of Sassun.

1894 SUN YAT-SEN (1866–1925) organizes a secret revolutionary society in Guangzhou (Canton), China.

1894 After victory in the third Ashanti War, Britain establishes a protectorate over Ghana.

1894 Britain establishes a protectorate over Uganda.

1894 British colonialist Leander Starr JAMESON (1853–1917) occupies Matabeleland, s Africa.

1894 Italians invade Ethiopia.

1894 French president Sadi CARNOT (b.1837) is stabbed to death by an Italian anarchist.

1894 French army officer Alfred DREYFUS (1859–1935) is court-martialed for treason and is sent to Devil's Island in French Guiana.

1894 NICHOLAS II (1868–1918) becomes czar of Russia.

THE AMERICAS

1890 Wyoming and Idaho becomes states of the USA.

1890 US troops massacre Native Americans at the battle of Wounded Knee.

1891 United States of Brazil is established.

1891 Civil war establishes parliamentary government in Chile.

1892 US reformer Susan ANTHONY (1820–1906) becomes president of the National American Women's Suffrage Association.

1892 Immigration facilities are opened at Ellis Island in New York harbor.

1892 Grover CLEVELAND (1837–1908) is again elected US president.

1893 US anarchist Emma GOLDMAN (1869–1940) is arrested in Philadelphia.

1893 Major rebellions are suppressed in s Brazil.

> "Science is nothing but trained and organized common sense."
>
> Thomas Huxley
> (*Collected Essays*)

SCIENCE AND TECHNOLOGY

1890 US engineer Emile Berliner (1851–1929) introduces the use of discs for sound recording.

1890 German bacteriologist Emil von BEHRING (1854–1917) discovers the viruses that cause diphtheria and tetanus.

1890 Electric chair is introduced as a method of capital punishment in New York.

1890 British mathematician John Venn (1834–1923) devises an overlapping diagram for depicting relationships between sets.

1892 German engineer Rudolf Diesel (1858–1913) patents his design for an engine that uses compression to ignite fuel oil.

1892 British scientist Charles Cross (1855–1935) invents the viscose method of making artificial fibers.

1892 Scottish chemist James Dewar (1842–1943) invents the silvered vacuum flask.

1892 French chemist Henri Moissan (1852–1907) invents the acetylene lamp.

1892 German engineer Leon Arons (1860–1919) invents the mercury vapor lamp.

1892 French engineer François Hennebique (1842–1921) invents prestressed concrete.

1893 British biologist Thomas HUXLEY (1825–95) publishes his *Evolution and Ethics*.

1893 US scientist Theobald Smith (1859–1934) shows that parasites such as ticks can spread disease.

1894 British scientists Lord RAYLEIGH (1842–1919) and William RAMSAY (1852–1916) discover the inert gas argon.

ARTS AND HUMANITIES

1890 British scholar James Frazer (1854–1951) publishes his *The Golden Bough; A Study in Magic and Religion.*

1890 Verse of US poet Emily DICKINSON (1830–86) is published posthumously.

1890 US historian Alfred Mahan (1840–1914) publishes his *The Influence of Sea Power on History.*

1890 Italian composer Pietro Mascagni (1863–1945) writes his opera *Cavalleria Rusticana.*

1891 French artist Paul GAUGIN (1848–1903) arrives in Tahiti.

1891 British writer Arthur Conan Doyle (1859–1930) publishes the first of his *Adventures of Sherlock Holmes.*

1891 Irish dramatist and poet Oscar WILDE (1854–1900) publishes his novel *The Picture of Dorian Gray.*

1891 French artist Henri ROUSSEAU (1844–1910) paints his *Surprised! (Tropical Storm with Tiger).*

1892 French artist Henri Toulouse-Lautrec (1864–1901) produces his poster advertising: *The Ambassadors: Aristide Bruant.*

1893 Antonín DVOŘÁK (1841–1904) writes his Symphony No.9 in E minor, "From the New World".

1893 Norwegian artist Edvard MUNCH (1863–1944) paints his *The Scream.*

1894 French composer Claude DEBUSSY (1862–1918) writes his *Prelude to the Afternoon of a Faun.*

1894 British poet and author Rudyard KIPLING (1865–1936) publishes his children's stories *The Jungle Book.*

ASIA AND AUSTRALASIA	AFRICA	EUROPE

1895

1895 China acknowledges Korean independence under Japanese influence by the treaty of Shimonseki; Japan also gains Formosa (present-day Taiwan) and other islands.

1895 British organize and name Rhodesia in SE Africa.

1895 British colonialist Leander Starr JAMESON (1853–1917) leads a British raid on the AFRIKANER (Boer) republic in South Africa.

1895 French conquer Madagascar.

1895 Kiel canal opens linking the North and Baltic seas.

1895 French trades unionists form the *Confederation Generale du Travail*.

1896

1896 Malay states form a federation under British control.

1896 Japan extends its control of Korea after the murder of Queen Min (b.1851).

1896 Turks again murder thousands of Armenians.

1896 British general Horatio KITCHENER (1850–1916) captures the Mahdist city of Dongola.

1896 Italians are routed at the battle of Adowa; the treaty of Addis Ababa secures Ethiopian independence.

1896 British bombard Zanzibar.

1896 Olympic Games are revived in Greece.

1896 Cretans revolt against Turkish rule.

1897

1897 Germans occupy Qingdao, N China.

1897 Slavery is abolished in Zanzibar.

1897 Greece declares war on Turkey and is heavily defeated.

1897 Rosa LUXEMBURG (1871–1919), leader of the Social Democratic Party of Congress in Poland, flees to Germany.

1898

1898 Russia obtains a lease on Port Arthur, N China.

1898 France obtains a lease on Leizhou Bandao in China; Britain gains Kowloon.

1898 USA captures Manila from the Spanish and gains the Philippines and Guam.

1898 USA formally annexes Hawaii.

1898 Influenced by reformer Kang Youwei (1858–1927), Chinese emperor Guangxu (1871–1908) begins the "100-days" reforms, which are quickly withdrawn by dowager empress CIXI (1835–1908) and Guangxu imprisoned.

1898 British defeat the Mahdists decisively at the battle of Omdurman; British and French troops confront each other at Fashoda; the French are forced to withdraw from Sudan.

1898 MENELIK II (1844–1913) brings all upland Ethiopia under his control.

1898 British and French agree the division of Nigeria.

1898 Bread riots occur in Milan and other Italian cities.

1898 French nationalists found the *Action Française* movement.

1898 German naval law is passed authorizing a larger navy as envisaged by admiral Alfred von TIRPITZ (1849–1930).

1898 Turks are forced to evacuate Crete, which is occupied by British, French, Italian and Russian troops.

1898 Empress ELIZABETH of Austria (b.1837) is assassinated in Switzerland by an Italian anarchist.

1898 Social Democratic party is founded in Russia.

1899

1899 George CURZON (1859–1925) becomes British viceroy of India.

1899 Huk insurrection against the USA breaks out in the Philippines.

1899 British sign a treaty with the sheikh of Kuwait.

1899 Concession to build the Berlin to Baghdad railroad is granted to a Germany company.

1899 Chinese court begins giving aid to the antiforeigner Society of Harmonious Fists.

1899 USA and Germany partition Samoa.

1899 British and French reach agreement over joint control of the Sudan.

1899 Germany takes control of Rwanda, E Africa.

1899 British lose the early battles of the South African War (Boer War); Afrikaner forces besiege Ladysmith and Mafeking.

1899 First Hague peace conference outlaws the use of poison gas and dum-dum bullets in warfare.

1899 French president pardons Alfred DREYFUS (1859–1935).

THE AMERICAS

1895 Nicaragua, El Salvador and Honduras form the Greater Republic of Central America.

1895 Antisaloon League starts a nation-wide antialcohol campaign in the USA.

1895 Britain clashes with Venezuela about the borders of British Guiana.

1895 Nationalist revolution occurs in Cuba.

1896 Gold is discovered in the Yukon region of Canada.

1896 Utah becomes a state of the USA.

1896 William McKINLEY (1843–1901) is elected US president.

1898 USS *Maine* is blown up in Havana harbor; USA declares war on Spain, wins the battles of San Juan Hill and Santiago, and invades Puerto Rico.

1898 Under the peace of Paris, Spain evacuates Cuba and the USA gains Puerto Rico.

1899 US secretary of state John HAY (1838–1905) proposes that the European powers adopt an "open door" policy allowing equal treatment of all foreign goods through treaty ports in China.

SCIENCE AND TECHNOLOGY

1895 Wilhelm RÖNTGEN (1845–1923) publishes his *A New Kind of Radiation*, in which he announces the discovery of X rays.

1895 French inventors Louis (1864–1948) and Auguste (1862–1954) LUMIÈRE give the first public cinema presentation in Paris.

1895 French mathematician Henri Poincaré (1854–1912) founds algebraic topology.

1895 Italian physicist Guglielmo MARCONI (1874–1937) invents the wireless telegraph.

1895 US industrialist King Gillette (1855–1932) invents the safety razor with disposable blades.

1896 Alfred NOBEL (1833–96) endows prizes for achievements in various branches of science.

1896 German pioneer of nonpowered flight Otto LILIENTHAL (b.1848) is killed in a glider crash.

1896 French physicist Henri BECQUEREL (1852–1908) discovers radioactivity in uranium compounds.

1897 British bacteriologist Ronald Ross (1857–1932) discovers the malaria parasite in mosquitoes.

1897 British physicist J.J. THOMSON (1856–1940) discovers the electron.

1897 German physicist Ferdinand Braun (1850–1918) invents the cathode-ray tube.

1897 German scientist Felix Hoffman discovers a method of producing pure aspirin.

1898 Danish engineer Valdemar Poulsen (1869–1942) invents magnetic sound recording on steel wire.

1898 Scientists Marie (1867–1934) and Pierre CURIE discover the radioactive elements radium and polonium.

1899 Aspirin goes on sale in Europe.

ARTS AND HUMANITIES

1895 Austrian composer Gustav MAHLER (1860–1911) writes his Symphony No.2.

1895 US author Stephen Crane (1871–1900) publishes his novel *The Red Badge of Courage*.

1896 French dramatist Alfred Jarry (1873–1907) writes his play *Ubu Roi*.

1896 Italian composer Giacomo PUCCINI (1858–1924) writes his opera *La Bohème*.

1896 Hungarian Zionist Theodor HERZL (1860–1904) publishes his *The Jewish State*.

1896 Nicaraguan poet Rubén Darío (1867–1916) publishes his *Profane Hymns*.

1896 British poet A.E. Housman (1859–1936) publishes his *A Shropshire Lad*.

1896 German composer Richard STRAUSS (1864–1949) writes his *Thus Spake Zarathustra*.

1897 Russian dramatist Anton CHEKOV (1960–1904) writes his play *Uncle Vanya*.

1897 French sociologist Emile DURKHEIM (1858–1917) publishes his *Suicide*, in which he outlines his theory of alienation.

1897 French author André Gide (1869–1951) writes his novel *The Fruits of the Earth*.

1897 French poet Edmond Rostand (1868–1918) writes his verse play *Cyrano de Bergerac*.

1898 Spanish novelist Vicente Blasco Ibáñez (1867–1928) publishes his *The Cabin*.

1898 French novelist Émile ZOLA (1840–1902) writes an open letter about the Dreyfus affair that begins "*J'accuse…*".

1898 British author H.G. WELLS (1856–1946) publishes his novel *The War of the Worlds*.

1899 Finnish composer Jean SIBELIUS (1865–1957) writes his *Finlandia*.

ASIA AND AUSTRALASIA	AFRICA	EUROPE

1900

1900 Foreign legations in Beijing are besieged by the society of Harmonious Fists in the Boxer Rebellion; the empress flees; the Russians annex Manchuria; an international military force restores order.

1900 Turks begin the construction of the Hejaz railroad to the holy places of Medina and Mecca in Arabia.

1901

1901 Boxer protocol imposes a huge fine on China.

1901 Britain grants the Commonwealth of Australia dominion status.

1902

1902 Chinese court returns to Beijing and begins reforms to strengthen the armed forces.

1902 Japan signs an alliance with Britain.

1902 Japanese raid the Russian base at Port Arthur in protest over the continuing occupation of Manchuria.

1903

1903 Trans-Siberian railroad is completed.

1903 British declare the Arabian Gulf to be within their sphere of control.

1904

1904 Japanese attack on Port Arthur starts the Russo-Japanese War; the Japanese win the battles of Yalu River and Liaoyang.

1904 British expedition occupies Lhasa, the capital of Tibet.

1900 British forces in South Africa under General Frederick ROBERTS (1832–1914) relieve Ladysmith and Mafeking, invade and annex the Orange Free State and Transvaal and capture Johannesburg and Pretoria; the AFRIKANERS adopt guerrilla warfare tactics.

1900 British suppress an ASHANTI uprising.

1900 France and Italy make a secret agreement giving France control of Morocco and Italy control of Libya.

1900 French defeat the African leader Rabeh Zobeir in the Lake Chad region.

1900 French capture the main Saharan oases s of Morocco and Algeria.

1901 British introduce concentration camps in South Africa for captured Afrikaner civilians.

1901 Britain annexes the Ashanti kingdom.

1902 Portuguese suppress a native rising in Angola.

1902 Peace of Vereeniging ends the South African War (Boer War) and Afrikaner (Boer) independence.

1902 Dam across the River Nile at Aswan is completed.

1903 Britain captures the cities of Kano and Sokoto, completing the conquest of N Nigeria.

1904 Spain and Morocco sign a treaty agreeing the division of Morocco.

1904 Herero people begin an insurrection in German Southwest Africa.

1900 Bernhard von BÜLOW (1849–1929) becomes chancellor of Germany.

1900 VICTOR EMMANUEL III (1869–1947) becomes king of Italy.

1900 Second German naval law proposes building a fleet to rival Britain's.

1901 EDWARD VII (1841–1910) becomes king of Britain.

1901 Violent street demonstrations are suppressed in St. Petersburg, Moscow and Kiev.

1902 ALFONSO XIII (1886–1941) becomes king of Spain.

> "... if civilization is to advance at all in the future, it must be through the help of women, women freed of their political shackles..."
>
> Emmeline Pankhurst
> (*My Own Story*)

1903 Serbian army officers murder King Alexander OBRENOVIĆ (b.1876) and set up King Peter I (1844–1921) as a puppet ruler.

1903 Russian Social Democratic party splits into minority Mensheviks and majority Bolsheviks under Vladimir Ilyich LENIN (1870–1924).

1903 Emmeline PANKHURST (1858–1928) founds the Women's Social and Political Union to campaign for female suffrage in Britain.

1904 Britain and France sign the Entente Cordiale.

THE AMERICAS

SCIENCE AND TECHNOLOGY

ARTS AND HUMANITIES

1900 German inventor Ferdinand von ZEPPELIN (1838–1917) builds a rigid airship.

1900 German physicist Max PLANCK (1858–1947) proposes that energy is radiated in discontinuous quanta and founds quantum theory.

1900 French physicist Paul Villard (1860–1934) discovers gamma rays.

1900 Austrian physician Karl Landsteiner (1868–1943) discovers the A, B and O blood groups.

1900 Austrian physician Sigmund FREUD (1856–1939) publishes his *The Interpretation of Dreams* and founds psychoanalysis.

1900 British archaeologist Arthur Evans (1851–1941) discovers the ruins of Minoan civilization in Crete.

1900 French author Colette (1873–1954) publishes the first of her *Claudine* novels.

1900 British novelist Joseph Conrad (1857–1924) publishes his *Lord Jim*.

1901 Theodore ROOSEVELT (1858–1919) becomes US president, following the assassination of William McKINLEY (b.1843).

1901 New Cuban constitution makes the country virtually a US protectorate.

1901 Italian physicist Guglielmo MARCONI (1874–1937) transmits a Morse code message across the Atlantic.

1901 Russian composer Sergei RACHMANINOV (1873–1943) writes his Piano Concerto No.2.

1902 Argentina obtains the greater part of Patagonia by agreement with Chile.

1902 European powers blockade Venezuela in a dispute over loan repayments.

1902 British scientist Oliver Heaviside (1850–1925) predicts the existence of an atmospheric layer that will reflect radio waves.

1902 Russian anarchist Peter KROPOTKIN (1842–1921) publishes his *Mutual Aid*.

1902 French artist Camille Pissarro (1830–1903) paints his *Louver from Pont Neuf*.

1902 US psychologist William JAMES (1842–1910) publishes his *Varieties of Religious Experience*.

1902 US ragtime composer Scott Joplin (1868–1917) writes his *The Entertainer*.

1902 Russian author Maxim Gorky (1868–1936) writes his play *The Lower Depths*.

▶ **Freud** was the founder of the psychoanalytic movement. His new methods of treating mental disorder, using free association and dream interpretation, were summarized in The Interpretation of Dreams.

1903 After a US-inspired coup Panama separates from Colombia.

1903 USA obtains perpetual rights to a canal zone across Panama.

1903 Alaska–Canada border is fixed.

1903 US inventors Orville (1971–1948) and Wilbur (1867–1912) WRIGHT make the first powered aircraft flight at Kitty Hawk in North Carolina, USA.

1903 Russian engineer Konstantin TSIOLKOVSKY (1857–1935) proposes multistage rockets for the exploration of space.

1903 US author Jack London (1876–1916) publishes his novel *Call of the Wild*.

1904 German sociologist Max Weber (1864–1920) publishes his *The Protestant Ethic and the Spirit of Capitalism*.

1904 Italian philosopher Benedetto CROCE (1866–1952) founds the review *La Critica*.

1904 Scottish artist and architect Charles Rennie MACKINTOSH (1868–1928) designs the Willow Tea Rooms in Glasgow.

1904 Roosevelt is elected president of the USA.

1904 Roosevelt warns European powers against further intervention in America.

1904 British engineer John Fleming (1849–1945) invents the diode thermionic valve.

1904 Scottish author James Barrie (1860–1937) writes his play *Peter Pan*.

1900

1901

1902

1903

1904

ASIA AND AUSTRALASIA	AFRICA	EUROPE

1905

1905 Japanese capture Port Arthur, defeat the Russians at the battle of Mukden and annihilate the Russian fleet at the battle of Tsushima Straits; the treaty of Portsmouth, New Hampshire, ends the Russo–Japanese War.

1905 Britain partitions the Indian state of Bengal.

1905 Papua New Guinea is joined to Australia.

1905 German emperor visits Tangier and provokes a crisis about French interests in Morocco.

1905 Emile Combes (1835–1921) introduces a bill that separates church and state in France.

1905 Norway under King HAAKON VII (1872–1957) becomes independent of Denmark.

1905 Dissent turns to revolution in Russia; the crew of the battleship *Potemkin* mutiny; Czar NICHOLAS II (1868–1918) issues his October manifesto granting a constitution; the suppression of the St. Petersburg *soviet* leads to a workers rising in Moscow.

1905 Popular risings occur in Poland and Finland.

1905 Serbia starts a tariff conflict (the "Pig War") with Austria.

1906

1906 Revolution in Persia (present-day Iran) compels the shah to issue a constitution.

1906 All-India Muslim league is formed.

1906 China acknowledges British control of Tibet.

1906 Egypt gains the Sinai peninsula from Turkey.

1906 Conference at Algerciras confirms Moroccan independence with an open door policy.

1906 Lagos is joined to the British colony of s Nigeria.

1906 Britain, France and Italy agree to respect the independence of Ethiopia.

1906 British Labor party is established under the leadership of Ramsay MACDONALD (1866–1937).

1906 Georges CLEMENCEAU (1841–1929) becomes prime minister of France.

1906 First Russian *duma* (parliament) meets.

1907

1907 Britain and Russia divide Persia into spheres of influence by the treaty of St. Petersburg

1907 Britain grants New Zealand dominion status.

1907 Dutch finally subdue the native revolt in Sumatra.

1907 Japan acquires a protectorate over Korea and disbands the Korean army, provoking rebellion.

1907 Proclamation of Mulay Hafid as sultan of Morocco leads to unrest; French bombard Casablanca and occupy the Atlantic coast region.

1907 Indian lawyer Mohandas GANDHI (1869–1948) leads a campaign of passive resistance against South African immigration policies.

1907 Nairobi becomes the capital of Kenya.

1907 Severe famine devastates Russia.

1907 Sinn Féin league is formed in Ireland.

1908

1908 Dutch take control of Bali.

1908 Henry PU YI (1906–67) becomes child emperor of China after the death of the dowager empress CIXI (b.1835) and grants a draft constitution.

1908 Persian shah Muhammad Ali withdraws the constitution and closes the national assembly; popular opposition causes Russian troops to invade N Persia in support of the shah.

1908 Rising by the Young Turks, supported by the military, restores the Turkish constitution.

1908 Oil is discovered in Persia.

1908 Congo Free State is annexed by Belgium.

1908 Herero rebellion in German Southwest Africa is finally suppressed, with genocidal ferocity.

1908 FERDINANO I (1861–1948) declares himself czar of an independent Bulgaria; Austria annexes Bosnia and Herzegovina; Serbia, backed by Russia, threatens war against Austria.

1908 Crete proclaims union with Greece.

1909

1909 MUHAMMAD V (1844–1918) becomes Turkish sultan; a new constitution removes almost all his powers.

1909 French complete the conquest of Mauritania.

1909 Spanish enclave of Melilla is attacked by Moroccans from the Rif mountains.

1909 Serbia is persuaded to back down; Italy and Russia sign the secret treaty of Raconnigi to maintain the status quo in the Balkans.

1909 Spanish priests and monks are massacred during a socialist uprising in Catalonia; the anarchist Francisco Ferrer (b.1849) is executed during the suppression.

THE AMERICAS

▲ **Einstein** published several papers of outstanding importance. His general theory of relativity, an extension of his special theory of relativity, led to a new era in cosmological research.

1906 US troops occupy Cuba after political unrest; William TAFT (1857–1930) declares himself governor.

1906 Massive earthquake and fire devastates San Francisco, USA.

1907 Nicaragua invades Honduras, installs a puppet ruler and prepares to invade El Salvador; it is forced to withdraw under US pressure.

1907 US army starts work on the construction of the Panama canal.

1907 Oklahoma becomes a state of the USA.

1908 William Taft is elected US president.

1909 Nationalist revolt in Honduras leads to civil war.

1909 US troops are withdrawn from Cuba; José Gómez (1858–1921) becomes president.

SCIENCE AND TECHNOLOGY

1905 French psychologist Alfred Binet (1857–1911) devises a practical intelligence test.

1905 German-born US physicist Albert EINSTEIN (1879–1955) publishes his special theory of relativity and introduces the concept of photons to quantum theory.

1905 German chemist Hermann Nernst (1864–1941) formulates the third law of thermodynamics.

1906 US scientist Lee DE FOREST (1873–1961) invents the amplifying audion triode valve.

1906 British launch HMS *Dreadnought*, the first big-gun battleship.

1906 US engineer Richard Fessenden (1866–1932) introduces music and speech on AM radio.

1907 German chemist Emil Fischer (1852–1919) discovers that proteins are made up of amino acids.

1908 US industrialist Henry FORD (1863–1947) announces the production of the Model T.

1908 German chemist Fritz Haber (1868–1934) invents a process for synthesizing ammonia.

1909 French aviator Louis BLÉRIOT (1872–1936) flies a monoplane across the English Channel.

1909 Belgian-born US chemist Leo Baekeland (1863–1944) invents Bakelite, a thermosetting plastic polymer.

ARTS AND HUMANITIES

1905 German artist Ernst Kirchner (1880–1938) founds *Die Brücke* ("The Bridge") group of expressionist artists.

1905 Spanish artist Pablo PICASSO (1881–1973) paints his *Acrobat and Young Harlequin*.

1905 French composer Claude DEBUSSY (1862–1918) writes his *La Mer*.

1906 British novelist John Galsworthy (1867–1933) publishes *The Man of Property*, the first volume of *The Forsyte Saga*.

1907 British ex-army officer Robert BADEN-POWELL (1857–1941) founds the Boy Scout youth movement.

1907 British writer Hilaire BELLOC (1870–1953) publishes his *Cautionary Tales* for children.

1907 Irish dramatist J.M. Synge writes his *The Playboy of the Western World*.

1908 Russian artist Marc Chagall (1887–1985) paints his *Nu Rouge*.

1908 US writer and educator Helen Keller (1880–1968) publishes her *The World I Live In*.

1908 French philosopher Georges Sorel (1847–1922) publishes his *Reflections on Violence*.

1908 Hungarian composer Béla BARTÓK (1881–1945) writes his String Quartet No.1.

1908 British author E.M. Forster (1879–1970) publishes his novel *A Room with a View*.

1909 US architect Frank Lloyd WRIGHT (1869–1959) designs the Robie house in Chicago.

1909 Indian poet Rabindranath TAGORE (1861–1941) publishes his *Gitanjali*.

1909 Italian poet Filippo MARINETTI (1876–1944) publishes his *First Futurist Manifesto*.

1905

1906

1907

1908

1909

ASIA AND AUSTRALASIA	AFRICA	EUROPE

1910

1910 Chinese invade Tibet.

1910 Anti-Turkish revolt in Albania is suppressed.

1910 National assembly meets in China and abolishes slavery.

1910 Japan annexes Korea, which is renamed Chosen.

1910 France takes control of the port of Agadir, Morocco.

1910 British grant the Union of South Africa dominion status; Louis BOTHA (1862–1919) is prime minister.

1910 French Congo is renamed French equatorial Africa.

1910 GEORGE V (1865–1936) becomes king of Britain.

1910 Portuguese king MANUEL II (1889–1932) flees after a revolution in Lisbon; a republic is proclaimed.

1911

1911 Military revolution breaks out in S China; the national assembly signs a truce and forms a provisional government.

1911 Russians invade and occupy Persia (present-day Iran).

1911 British reverse the partition of Bengal in India.

1911 Outer Mongolia becomes a Russian protectorate.

1911 Tibet declares independence from China.

1911 French troops occupy Fez; the Germans send the gunboat *Panther* to Agadir; France cedes parts of Congo to Germany in return for freedom of action in Morocco.

1911 Italy invades and annexes Tripoli in Libya, despite fierce Turkish resistance; a naval war develops between Italy and Turkey.

1911 British colony of Northern Rhodesia is created.

1911 Serbian army officers form the "Union or Death" (Black Hand) secret society to promote Serbian expansion.

1912

1912 Chinese emperor PU YI (1906–67) abdicates; end of the Qing dynasty.

1912 Albanian leader ESSAD PASHA (1864–1920) proclaims independence from Turkey.

1912 Sultan of Morocco is forced to accept a French protectorate.

1912 Italy bombards ports on the Dardanelles and conquers Rhodes and other Turkish islands; the treaty of Lausanne ends hostilities; Italy gains Libya.

1912 Spain and France sign a treaty dividing Morocco between them.

1912 Italian socialist leader Benito MUSSOLINI (1883–1945) becomes editor of the newspaper *Avanti*.

1912 Balkan crisis is provoked by Albanian independence; Serbia and Bulgaria form the Balkan league with Russian support and are joined by Greece and Montenegro; the league declares war on Turkey and wins the battles of Kumanovo and Lule Burgas; Italy and Austria oppose Serbian expansion in Albania.

1913

1913 YUAN SHIKAI (1859–1916) is elected president of China and purges the Kuomintang party, led by SUN YAT-SEN (1866–1925), from government.

1913 Young Turks, led by ENVER PASHA (1881–1922), seize power in Turkey and suppress opposition.

▶ *art nouveau* Flourishing in Europe and the USA from c.1890 to World War I, art nouveau focused mainly on the decorative arts. Its characteristic forms come from sinuous distortion of plant forms and asymmetrical lines. Examples are found in architecture and the applied arts, such as jewelry and glass design.

1913 Italians subdue the inland regions of Libya.

1913 Raymond POINCARÉ (1860–1934) becomes president of France.

1913 Treaty of London ends the first Balkan War; Bulgaria attacks Serbia, which is supported by Greece, Romania and Turkey; Austria threatens to intervene to aid Bulgaria; the peace of Bucharest ends the second Balkan War; Bulgaria loses most of Macedonia to Greece and Serbia.

172

1910 French scientist Georges Claude (1870–1960) invents neon lighting.

1910 US astronomer George Hale (1877–1945) invents the spectroheliograph.

1910 British author Arnold Bennett (1867–1931) publishes his novel *Clayhanger*.

1910 French artist Henri MATISSE (1869–1954) paints his *Dance II*.

1910 British composer Ralph VAUGHAN WILLIAMS (1872–1958) writes his *A Sea Symphony*.

1911 National Association for the Advancement of Colored People is founded in the USA.

1911 Mexican president Porfirio DÍAZ (1830–1915) is overthrown by a revolution led by Francisco MADERO (1873–1913).

1911 Polish biochemist Casimir Funk (1884–1967) discovers vitamins.

1911 Scottish physicist Charles Wilson (1869–1959) invents the cloud chamber.

1911 US composer Irving Berlin (1888–1989) writes his song "Alexander's Ragtime Band".

1911 Russian impresario Serge DIAGHILEV (1872–1929) forms the *Ballets Russes* in Paris.

1912 Woodrow WILSON (1856–1924) is elected US president.

1912 New Mexico and Arizona become states of the USA.

1912 *Titanic*, a liner, sinks off the coast of Newfoundland.

1912 German physicist Max von Laue (1879–1960) uses X-ray diffraction to study crystal structure.

1912 Austrian engineer Viktor Kaplan (1876–1934) invents a low-pressure water turbine.

1912 Swiss psychiatrist Carl JUNG (1875–1964) publishes his *The Psychology of the Unconscious*.

1912 US author Edgar Rice Burroughs (1875–1950) publishes his novel *Tarzan of the Apes*.

1912 British composer Frederick Delius (1862–1934) writes his *On Hearing the First Cuckoo in Spring*.

1912 French artist Marcel DUCHAMP (1887–1968) paints his *Nude Descending A Staircase, II*.

1912 Russian dancer Vaslav NIJINSKY (1880–1950) creates his ballet *Afternoon of a Faun*.

1912 German author Thomas MANN (1875–1955) publishes his novella *Death in Venice*.

▲ *Japanese territory* The expansion of Japanese territory at the end of the 19th and the beginning of the 20th century was the result of war and of treaties. In 1875 the Kurile Islands were acquired from Russia by treaty. Formosa (present-day Taiwan) was won in the Sino–Japanese War; South Sakhalin, the lease of Port Arthur and rights in south Manchuria were won in the Russo–Japanese war. Korea was annexed in 1910.

1913 Victoriano HUERTA (1854–1916) murders Francisco Madero and seizes power in Mexico.

1913 Danish physicist Niels BOHR (1885–1962) proposes a new model of atomic structure.

1913 British chemist Frederick SODDY (1877–1956) discovers isotopes.

1913 US astronomer Henry Russell (1877–1957) devises a diagram of the magnitude and temperature of stars; the diagram was independently conceived by Ejnar Hertzsprung (1873–1967).

1913 British mathematicians Bertrand RUSSELL (1872–1970) and Alfred WHITEHEAD (1861–1947) publish their *Principia Mathematica*.

1913 Russian composer Igor STRAVINSKY (1882–1971) writes his ballet *The Rite of Spring*.

1913 French author Marcel PROUST (1871–1922) publishes his novel *Swann's War*, the first volume of *Remembrance of Things Past*.

1913 French writer Henri Alain-Fournier (1886–1914) publishes his novel *Le Grand Meaulnes*.

1913 French artist Maurice Utrillo (1883–1955) paints his *Rue Saint-Vincent*.

1913 British author D.H. Lawrence (1885–1930) publishes his novel *Sons and Lovers*.

1914

1914 Japan declares war on Germany.

1914 Britain, France and Russia declare war on Turkey.

1914 British occupy Basra, present-day Iraq.

1914 New Zealand troops occupy German Samoa.

1914 Australian troops occupy German New Guinea.

▼ *Africa This map of Africa in 1914 shows how it had been partitioned among seven European countries. This partition had taken place rapidly in the last 20 years of the 19th century. Only Liberia and Ethiopia remained independent of European rule. Although some territories were termed protectorates (such as Uganda and Morocco) rather than colonies, Europeans were still firmly in control. The Union of South Africa had been formed in 1910, but it remained a British dominion. Colonial boundaries drawn up by Europeans were often merely straight lines on the map. These artificial boundaries have been the cause of many problems since African countries regained their independence.*

1914 British proclaim a protectorate over Egypt.

1914 Arab revolt against the Italians breaks out in Libya.

1914 Indian lawyer Mohandas GANDHI (1869–1948) leaves South Africa for India.

1914 British unite N and S Nigeria.

1914 British and French forces invade and occupy Cameroon and Togoland.

1914 British bombard Dar es Salaam, Tanganyika; a landing by British Indian troops is defeated by the Germans at the battle of Tanga.

1914 Heir to the Austrian throne archduke FRANZ FERDINAND (b.1863) is assassinated in Sarajevo by an agent of the Black Hand; Serbia rejects an Austrian ultimatum and gains Russian support; Austria declares war and Russia mobilizes; Germany declares war on Russia and France and invades Belgium; Britain issues Germany an ultimatum over Belgian neutrality and goes to war; Serbia declares war on Germany; Romania declares its neutrality.

1914 Germany signs an alliance with Turkey.

1914 German troops invade Luxembourg and Belgium and capture Brussels; British troops first encounter the Germans at the battle of Mons; British and French forces under the command of French general Joseph JOFFRE (1852–1931) halt the german advance on Paris at the battle of the Marne; Germans capture Ostend, Belgium, but are prevented from capturing further ports on the English Channel by the first battle of Ypres; the positions of the opposing armies become fixed with the Germans occupying *c.*10% of French territory; beginning of trench warfare.

1914 German aircraft attack Paris.

1914 St. Petersburg is renamed Petrograd.

1914 Britain sinks German ships in a raid on Heligoland Bight; German submarines sink British warships in the North Sea.

1914 Russian armies invade N and central Poland; in N Poland the Germans, under General Paul von HINDENBURG (1847–1934), win the battles of Tannenberg and the Masurian Lakes but fail to take Warsaw; an Austrian advance into central Poland fails to dislodge the Russians but prevents their capture of Kraków; two Austrian invasions of Serbia are repulsed; the Germans capture Łódź.

1914 Britain annexes Cyprus.

TANGIER
MOROCCO
TUNISIA
RIO DE ORO
ALGERIA
LIBYA
EGYPT
BRITISH SOMALILAND
FRENCH SOMALILAND
ERITREA
GAMBIA
SENEGAL
FRENCH WEST AFRICA
FRENCH EQUATORIAL AFRICA
ANGLO-EGYPTIAN SUDAN
PORTUGUESE GUINEA
IVORY COAST
NIGERIA
ETHIOPIA
SIERRA LEONE
GOLD COAST
CAMEROON
UGANDA
KENYA
LIBERIA
TOGOLAND
GABON
CONGO
GERMAN EAST AFRICA
ITALIAN SOMALILAND
SPANISH GUINEA
ANGOLA
RHODESIA
MOZAMBIQUE
MADAGASCAR
GERMAN SOUTH WEST AFRICA
SOUTH AFRICA
BECHUANALAND

POSSESSIONS
British
Spanish
French
Portuguese
German
Italian
Belgian
Independent states

THE AMERICAS

1914 Victoriano HUERTA (1854–1916) is ousted by Venustiano CARRANZA (1859–1920); civil war breaks out in Mexico.

1914 British warships win the naval battle of the Falklands.

1914 Panama canal opens.

1914 US marines seize Vera Cruz, Mexico.

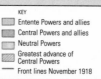

▲ **World War I** *Most of the fighting of World War I took place in Europe; the main battlefields were in N France and Belgium, Poland, Russia and Italy. Overseas campaigns were fought in Mesopotamia (present-day Iraq) and the Middle East and in the German colonies in Africa. The chief contestants were the Central Powers (Germany and Austria) and the Entente Powers (Britain, France and Russia).*

KEY

▢ Entente Powers and allies
▨ Central Powers and allies
▢ Neutral Powers
▨ Greatest advance of Central Powers
— Front lines November 1918

SCIENCE AND TECHNOLOGY

1914 US industrialist Henry FORD (1863–1947) introduces conveyor-belt production lines in his automobile factory.

ARTS AND HUMANITIES

1913 British architect Edwin Lutyens (1869–1944) designs the Viceroy's House in New Delhi, India.

1913 French poet and dramatist Guillaume APOLLINAIRE (1880–1918) attempts to define Cubism in his essay *Cubist Painters*.

1913 Italian artist Umberto Boccioni (1882–1916) creates his sculpture *Unique Forms of Continuity in Space*.

1914 British composer Gustav Holst (1872–1934) writes his orchestral suite *The Planets*.

1914 Scottish author Saki (Hector Munro, 1870–1916) publishes his collection of stories *Beasts and Superbeasts*.

1914 US poet Robert FROST (1874–1963) publishes his *North of Boston*.

1914 Irish poet and dramatist W.B. YEATS (1865–1939) publishes his collection of poems *Responsibilities*.

1914 US musician W.C. Handy (1873–1958) writes his "St Louis Blues".

1913 cont.

1914

▼ **German aircraft** *Gotha IIIs, as illustrated below, were used for armed reconnaissance over the battlefields as well as for bombing. They were developed to take over the Zeppelin's role in bombing English cities.*

ASIA AND AUSTRALASIA	AFRICA	EUROPE

1915

1915 China accepts 21 demands made by Japan that undermine Chinese sovereignty.

1915 British and Australian troops land at Gallipoli, Turkey, in an attempt to seize control of the Dardanelles.

1915 British capture Kut-el-Amra in Mesopotamia (present-day Iraq) from the Turks and occupy Bushehr in Persia (present-day Iran).

1915 South African forces under Louis BOTHA (1862–1919) defeat the Germans in Southwest Africa.

1915 Turks attempt to seize the Suez canal.

▼ *World War I In 1915 the Central Powers attacked Serbia, Austria and Germany from the north and Bulgaria from the east. The Serbian army was forced to retreat across the Albanian mountains in appalllling conditions.*

1915 Italy quits the Triple Alliance and attacks Austria.

1915 Bulgaria allies with Germany; German and Austrian forces invade Serbia and Montenegro.

1915 German Zeppelin airships make bombing raids on London.

1915 Second battle of Ypres results in German gains; French advance at the second battle of Artois; British successes at the third battle of Artois and the battle of Loos are not exploited; General Douglas HAIG (1861–1928) becomes British commander in chief.

1915 Germany orders a submarine blockade of Britain; the *Lusitania* is sunk off the Irish coast.

1915 Russian advance into Hungary is defeated; Germans advance into Lithuania; Austro-German offensive drives the Russians from central Poland and captures Warsaw, Vilna and Brest-Litovsk.

Central advance
Oct–Nov 1915
Serbian resistance
Nov 1915
Serbian retreat
Dec 1915–Feb 1916
French advance
Nov–Dec 1916
Allied front line
Dec 1915–Sept 1918

1916

1916 British troops are evacuated from the Turkish coast.

1916 Indian Hindus and Muslims make the pact of Lucknow, calling for independence.

1916 Russian forces invade Armenia.

1916 Civil wars break out in N China as rival warlords, with foreign support, battle for control of Beijing.

1916 HUSSEIN IBN ALI (1856–1931), the sharif of Mecca, is declared king of the Arabs; a general Arab revolt against the Turks begins.

1916 British troops surrender to the Turks at Kut el-Amra .

1916 British and French reach the Sykes Picot agreement over the future partition of the Ottoman Empire.

1916 Zauditu becomes empress of Ethiopia with RAS TAFARI MAKONNEN (1892–1975) as regent.

1916 AFRIKANER forces under Jan SMUTS (1870–1950) win control of Tanganyika (present-day Tanzania).

1916 South African and Portuguese troops capture Dar-es-Salaam, Tanganyika.

1916 Romania declares war on Austria; German and Austrian forces occupy Bucharest.

1916 Germany and Austria proclaim an independent Poland.

1916 Easter Rising by Irish nationalists in Dublin is crushed by British troops; its leaders, James CONNOLLY (b.1870) and Patrick PEARSE (b.1879), are executed.

1916 David LLOYD GEORGE (1863–1945) becomes British prime minister.

1916 Germans capture French fortresses protecting Verdun; British offensive at the battle of the Somme gains little ground at appalllling cost; French recapture Verdun forts; General Paul von HINDENBURG (1847–1934) takes overall control of German forces.

1916 British and German fleets fight the inconclusive battle of Jutland in the North Sea.

1916 German aircraft bomb London.

THE AMERICAS

1915 Klu Klux Klan is revived in the USA.

1915 American nations recognize Venustiano Carranza (1859–1920) as president of Mexico.

1915 US troops land in Haiti to restore order after political and financial instability.

SCIENCE AND TECHNOLOGY

1915 German-born US physicist Albert Einstein (1879–1955) publishes his general theory of relativity.

1915 German Fokker aircraft revolutionize aerial warfare with a machine gun synchronized to fire through the propeller.

1915 Poison gas (chlorine) is first used in warfare by the Germans, during the first battle of Ypres.

1915 German geologist Alfred Wegener (1880–1930) proposes his theory of continental drift.

ARTS AND HUMANITIES

1915 British poet Rupert Brooke (1887–1915) publishes his *1914 and Other Poems.*

1915 US poet Ezra Pound (1885–1968) publishes his *Cathay.*

1915 British author John Buchan (1875–1940) publishes his novel *The Thirty-Nine Steps.*

1915 Romanian artist Tristan Tzara (1896–1963) and Alsatian sculptor Jean Arp (1887–1966) found the Dada movement in Zurich.

1915 British author W. Somerset Maugham (1874–1965) publishes his novel *Of Human Bondage.*

1916 Denmark sells the Virgin Islands to the USA

1916 Mexican revolutionary Francisco ("Pancho") Villa (1877–1923) raids New Mexico; the USA sends a punitive expedition.

1916 US troops land in Cuba to suppress a liberal revolution.

1916 USA occupies the Dominican Republic and takes over the government.

1916 Newly invented tanks are used by the British at the battle of the Somme.

1916 German scientists develop mustard gas as a weapon.

1916 British poet Edith Sitwell (1887–1964) publishes her experimental anthology *Wheels.*

1916 Mexican artist José Orozco (1883–1949) completes his wash drawings *Mexico in Revolution.*

1916 French artist Claude Monet (1840–1926) paints his *Water Lilies* murals at the specially constructed musée d'orangerie in Paris.

1916 US artist Naum Gabo (1890–1977) creates his sculpture *Head No. 2.*

1916 Spanish dramatist Jacinto Benavente y Martínez (1866–1954) writes his play *La cuidad alegre y confiada.*

◀ *Villa* and Carranza became leaders of the Mexican revolution when they defeated Huerta. Rivalry between them, however, provoked Villa to murder US citizens in N Mexico and New Mexico. The US government sent troops, led by General Pershing, but failed to capture Villa.

1917

1917 Arab forces, led by T.E. LAWRENCE (1888–1935), capture Aqaba.

1917 British forces capture Baghdad and Jerusalem.

1917 Kuomintang forms a s Chinese government in Guangzhou (Canton) and appoints SUN YAT-SEN (1866–1925) commander in chief.

1917 China declares war on Germany.

1917 British foreign minister Arthur BALFOUR (1848–1930) declares his support for the settlement of Jews in Palestine.

1917 Germans invade Portuguese East Africa.

> "The Czar is not treacherous but he is weak. Weakness is not treachery, but it fulfills all its functions."
>
> German emperor William II, referring to Czar Nicholas II

1917 Germans withdraw to the Hindenburg Line; Canadian troops take Vimy Ridge during the battle of Arras; British take Messines Ridge but fail to make progress in the third battle of Ypres; US troops under General John PERSHING (1860–1948) arrive in France; Austrians and Germans defeat the Italians at the battles of the Caporetto.

1917 Germans capture Riga, Lithuania.

1917 Italy declares a protectorate over Albania.

1917 February revolution forces Russian czar NICHOLAS II (1868–1918) to abdicate; a provisional government shares power with the Petrograd *soviet*; Vladimir Ilyich LENIN (1870–1924) returns to Russia; Alexander KERENSKY (1881–1970) becomes prime minister and declares a republic; Bolsheviks establish a politburo which includes Lenin, Leon TROTSKY (1879–1940) and Joseph STALIN (1879–1953); Bolsheviks overthrow Kerensky in the October revolution; Congress of Soviets establishes a ruling Council of People's Commissars and takes Russia out of World War I; a constituent assembly is elected.

1917 Ukraine, Estonia and Moldavia declare their independence from Russia.

▲ *Bolsheviks* Following the 1917 October revolution, the Bolsheviks, led by Lenin, gained power. A significant element of support was provided by soldiers and sailors returning home from World War I, seen here at a rally in the Catherine Hall of the Tauride Palace, Petrograd.

1917 Finns under General Carl von MANNERHEIM (1867–1951) begin a war of independence against Russia.

1918

1918 British troops capture Damascus; French forces take Beirut.

1918 Britain occupies Persia after Russian troops are withdrawn.

1918 Armenia becomes an independent state.

1918 Germans invade Rhodesia.

1918 By the treaty of Brest-Litovsk, Russia recognizes Finland, Latvia, Lithuania, Estonia and Ukraine as independent states.

1918 "White" Russia declares independence and civil war breaks out.

1918 Bolsheviks order the Red Army to dissolve the constituent assembly; communist Central Committee is given supreme power; Russian Socialist Federative Soviet Republic is established; Nicholas II and his family are executed.

1917 USA declares war on Germany and Austria

1917 French scientist Felix d'Herelle (1873–1949) discovers bacteriophages.

▶ *East Africa campaign* Fighting in East Africa during World War I was protracted due to the military genius of the German commander, Paul von Lettow-Vorbeck. After the capture of the Tanganyika Central Railroad in 1916 by General Smuts, commander of the British forces in East Africa, Lettow-Vorbeck moved his troops south. Despite drastically outnumbered forces, he invaded Portuguese East Africa and N Rhodesia. He fought on until the Armistice, finally surrendering at Abercorn (present-day Mbala, Zambia) on 25 November 1918.

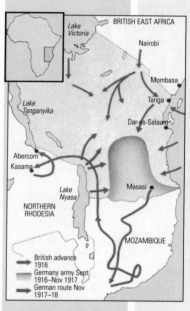

1918 US president Woodrow WILSON (1856–1924) proposes 14 points for a peace agreement.

1918 US astronomer Harlow Shapley (1885–1972) estimates the size and shape of our Galaxy.

1918 cont.

▲ League of Nations Set up as part of the Treaty of Versailles ending World War I, the League of Nations was formed to arbitrate over international disputes. Its original members were the 32 states that signed the Covenant and ratified it, and those states that joined by invitation. Other states were admitted at later dates by a two-thirds vote of the Assembly. The USA refused to participate and this lack of support weakened the League to the point that it was largely ineffectual as a forum for world peace.

KEY
☐ Original member states
☐ Later member states
☐ Nonmember states
☐ Colonies of member states
☐ Mandated territories

1918 Women get the vote in Britain.

1918 German offensive breaks through British and French lines at the second battle of the Somme; Ferdinand FOCH (1851–1929) is made French commander; French and US troops halt the Germans at the second battle of the Marne; allied counter attacks force the Germans to retreat into Belgium; Italians rout the Austrians at the battle of Vittorio Veneto.

1918 Revolutions occur in Munich and Berlin; the emperor goes into exile; a German republic is proclaimed.

1918 Revolution in Vienna dissolves the Austrian monarchy and dismantles the empire.

1918 Czechoslovakia and Hungary are proclaimed independent states; independent kingdom of the Serbs, Croats and Slovenes (later Yugoslavia) is established.

1918 Latvia and Lithuania declare their independence from Russia.

1918 Armistice stops the fighting on the Western Front.

1919

1919 Britain recognizes the independence of Afghanistan.

1919 Japan acquires from Germany Qingdao in China and the Marshall, Mariana and Caroline islands in the Pacific.

1919 British troops kill hundreds of Indian protesters at Amritsar.

1919 Belgium acquires Rwanda and Burundi from Germany.

1919 Britain gains Tanganyika from Germany and also shares Cameroon and Togo with France.

1919 South Africa gains a mandate over German Southwest Africa.

1919 International agreement limits the sale of alcohol and arms in Africa.

1919 French create the colony of Upper Volta (present-day Burkina Faso).

1919 Allied troops withdraw from Russia; Red armies, under Leon TROTSKY, defeat the Whites.

1919 Independent Polish republic is declared.

1919 Warfare breaks out in Ireland between nationalists and British forces.

1919 Radical Spartacists revolt in Berlin and Rosa LUXEMBURG (b.1871) is shot; republics are declared in Bavaria and Rhineland; Weimar constitution is adopted; German national assembly elects Friedrich EBERT (1871–1925) president.

1919 Peace conference in Paris establishes a league of nations.

1919 Under the treaty of Versailles, Germany has to cede territory, accept war guilt and occupation of the Saar district, and pay huge financial reparations.

KEY
- Russian empire 1914
- Germany 1914
- Austro-Hungarian empire 1914
- Ottoman Empire 1914
- boundaries 1920
- French mandate 1920
- British mandate 1920
- Emirate under British suzerainty 1923
- Serb-Croat-Slovene kingdom created 1918

▲ **Peace of Paris** At the Paris Peace Conference of 1919, the five leading victorious powers of World War I drew up a peace plan and established new national boundaries. New East European states emerged from the wreckage of the German, Austro-Hungarian and Russian empires. Although these states were founded on the basis of national self-determination, they also included alien minorities, such as the Germans in Czechoslovakia. Britain and France divided the former Ottoman Middle East between them. Both faced rising Arab nationalism and, in Britain's case, increasing Arab-Zionist conflict in Palestine. In the Ottoman Empire nationalists formally established the Republic of Turkey in 1923.

1919 British physicist Ernest RUTHERFORD (1871–1937) transmutes one element into another.

1919 British physicist Arthur EDDINGTON (1882–1944) observes the gravitational bending of light predicted by Einstein's theories.

1919 Austrian zoologist Karl von FRISCH (1886–1982) discovers the communication dance of honey-bees.

1919 British aviators John ALCOCK (1892–1919) and Arthur Brown (1886–1948) fly nonstop across the Atlantic Ocean from Newfoundland to Ireland

1918 Russian composer Sergei PROKOFIEV (1891–1953) writes his Symphony No.1 in D major, known as the "Classical".

1918 US poet Carl SANDBURG (1878–1967) publishes his *Cornhuskers*.

1918 German historian Oswald SPENGLER (1880–1936) publishes volume 1 of his *The Decline of the West*.

1918 Collected works of British poet Gerard Manley Hopkins (1844–89) are published posthumously.

1918 cont.

1919 Swiss theologian Karl BARTH (1886–1968) publishes his *The Epistle to the Romans*.

1919 German architect and designer Walter GROPIUS (1883–1969) founds the Bauhaus school of design, building and crafts in Weimar.

1919 US poet Amy Lowell (1872–1925) publishes her *Pictures of the Floating World*.

1919 US author Sherwood Anderson (1876–1941) publishes his collection of stories *Winesburg, Ohio*.

1919 British composer Edward ELGAR (1857–1934) writes his cello concerto.

1919 Italian nationalist poet Gabriel D'ANNUNZIO (1863–1938) seizes Fiume in Yugoslavia.

1919

1920

1920 France acquires a mandate over Syria and Lebanon.

1920 Britain acquires a mandate over Mesopotamia, renaming it Iraq, and Palestine.

1920 Britain annexes Kenya.

1920 Defeated White Russians withdraw from Crimea; end of the Russian civil war.

1920 League of Nations comes into existence.

1920 Poland in alliance with Ukraine invades S Russia and defeats a Russian counterattack outside Warsaw.

1920 Greece declares war on Turkey.

1921

1921 FAISAL I (1885–1933) is proclaimed king of Iraq.

1921 SUN YAT-SEN (1866–1925) is elected president of China.

1921 Cossack officer Reza PAHLAVI (1878–1944) stages a coup in Persia (present-day Iran) and becomes minister of war.

1921 Spanish are defeated by the peoples of the Rif, led by ABD EL-KRIM (d.1963), at the battle of Anual in Morocco.

1921 Mauritania and Niger are created as French colonies.

1921 Vladimir Ilyich LENIN (1870–1924) introduces the New Economic Policy in Russia.

1921 Peace of Riga fixes the Polish–Russian border.

1921 Adolf HITLER (1889–1945) becomes chairman of the National Socialist German Workers (Nazi) party.

1922

1922 Sultanate is abolished in Turkey.

1922 Kurds in Iraq begin an armed campaign for independence.

1922 Mohandas GANDHI (1869–1948) is arrested in India for civil disobedience.

1922 Egypt becomes a self-governing monarchy, the sultan becomes King FUAD I (1868–1936).

1922 Italy starts the conquest of S Libya.

1922 Ireland is partitioned; an independent Irish Free State is proclaimed; civil war breaks out.

1922 Italian fascists march on Rome; Benito MUSSOLINI (1883–1945) is asked to form a government.

1922 Union of Soviet Socialist Republics (USSR or Soviet Union) is formally established, joining Russia and Ukraine.

1923

1923 Treaty of Lausanne confirms the dismemberment of the Ottoman Empire and provides for compulsory population exchanges between Greece and Turkey.

1923 Mustafa KEMAL (1881–1938) is elected president of Turkey; Ankara becomes the capital.

1923 Earthquake devastates Yokohama and Tokyo.

1923 Transjordan is separated from Palestine.

1923 Southern Rhodesia becomes a British colony.

> "Fascism is a religion; the 20th century will be known in history as the century of Fascism."
>
> Benito Mussolini

1923 French and Belgian troops occupy Germany's Ruhr region.

1923 Nationalist and socialist risings take place in Germany, including Hitler's attempted putsch in Munich; martial law is declared.

1923 General PRIMO DE RIVERA (1870–1930) becomes dictator in Spain.

1923 Alexander Zankoff seizes power in Bulgaria following a military coup.

1924

1924 Chinese communists are admitted to the Kuomintang.

1924 Abdul Aziz Ibn SAUD (1880–1953) captures Mecca and Medina from HUSSEIN IBN ALI (1856–1931), sharif of Mecca.

1924 Mongol People's Republic is declared as a satellite of the Soviet Union.

1924 Slavery is abolished in Ethiopia.

1924 Rif uprising is revived against Spanish expansion in N Morocco.

1924 Joseph STALIN (1879–1953) takes control of the Soviet Union on Lenin's death.

1924 Albania and Greece become republics.

THE AMERICAS

1920 Transcontinental air-mail service begins in the USA.

1920 Women get the vote in the USA.

1920 US government refuses to join the League of Nations.

1920 Álvaro OBREGÓN (1880–1928) becomes Mexican president

1920 Warren HARDING (1865–1923) is elected US president.

1921 Washington conference limits the size of Pacific fleets and affirms the independence of China.

1921–22 Costa Rica, Guatemala, Honduras and El Salvador form the short-lived Federation of Central America.

1922 USA restores self-government to the Dominican Republic.

1923 Calvin COOLIDGE (1872–1933) becomes US president on the death of Warren Harding.

1924 US politician Charles DAWES (1865–1961) chairs a committee that devises a plan to collect German reparations.

1924 Coolidge is elected US president.

SCIENCE AND TECHNOLOGY

1920 US astronomer Edwin HUBBLE (1889–1953) discovers that the universe is expanding.

1920 Radio broadcasting begins in Pittsburgh, USA.

1920 US engineer John Thompson (1860–1940) designs a submachine gun.

1921 US scientist Albert Hull (1880–1966) invents the magnetron microwave-generating valve.

1921 US engineer Thomas Midgley (1889–1944) discovers the antiknock properties of tetraethyl lead.

1921 Canadian physician Frederick BANTING (1891–1941) isolates the hormone insulin.

1922 German engineer Herbert Kalmus invents Technicolor movie film.

1923 Spanish engineer Juan de le Cierva (1896–1936) invents the autogyro.

1924 French physicist Louis Victor de BROGLIE (1892–1987) proposes that electrons should sometimes behave as waves.

1924 South African anthropologist Raymond Dart (1893–1988) discovers the fossil remains of *Australopithecus*.

1924 US industrialist Clarence Birdseye (1886–1956) puts quick-frozen fish on sale.

ARTS AND HUMANITIES

1920 US author Sinclair Lewis (1885–1951) publishes his novel *Main Street*.

1921 German artist Max ERNST (1891–1976) paints his *The Elephant Celebes*.

1921 French artist Georges BRAQUE (1882–1963) paints his *Still Life with Guitar*.

1921 US novelist John Dos Passos (1896–1970) publishes his *Three Soldiers*.

1922 German poet Rainer Maria Rilke (1875–1926) publishes his *Sonnets to Orpheus*.

1922 German philosopher Ludwig WITTGENSTEIN (1889–1951) publishes his *Tractatus Logico-Philosophicus*.

1922 US photographer Man RAY (1890–1976) publishes *Delightful Fields*, an album of Rayographs.

1922 British archaeologist Howard Carter (1874–1939) discovers the tomb of Tutankhamun.

1922 British poet and critic T.S. ELIOT (1888–1965) publishes his poem *The Waste Land*.

1922 Irish author James JOYCE (1882–1941) publishes his novel *Ulysses*.

1923 Spanish artist Joan MIRÓ (1893–1983) paints his *Catalan Landscape*.

1923 British writer Walter De la Mare (1873–1956) publishes his poetry anthology *Come Hither*.

1924 US composer George GERSHWIN (1898–1937) writes his *Rhapsody in Blue*.

1924 French poet André Breton (1896–1966) writes the *Manifesto of Surrealism*.

1924 German artist Otto DIX (1891–1969) publishes his satirical etchings *The War*.

1924 Mexican artist Diego Rivera (1886–1957) paints murals for the ministry of education in Mexico City.

ASIA AND AUSTRALASIA	AFRICA	EUROPE

1925

1925 CHIANG KAI-SHEK (1887–1975) becomes head of the Kuomintang nationalist government in China.

1925 Reza PAHLAVI (1878–1944) becomes shah of Persia (present-day Iran).

1925–27 Druze rebel against French control in Lebanon and Syria.

▶ *Mao Zedong was a founder of the Chinese Communist Party in 1921. He soon became one of the foremost leaders in the world communist movement. Mao believed that the path to power lay through the mobilization of the peasantry.*

1925 At a conference in Locarno, France, Belgium and Germany sign treaties guaranteeing their mutual borders; France also signs treaties with Poland and Czechoslovakia.

1925 Paul von HINDENBURG (1847–1934) is elected president of Germany.

1925 President Ahmed Zogu (1895–1961) of Albania declares himself King ZOG.

1925 Joseph STALIN (1879–1953) removes Leon TROTSKY (1879–1940) from power in Russia.

1926

1926 Nationalists begin military campaigns to regain control of central and N China.

1926 Abdul Aziz Ibn SAUD (1880–1953) is proclaimed king of Hejaz and Nejd in Arabia.

1926 Communist-inspired revolt breaks out in the Dutch East Indies.

1926 Lebanon is established as an independent republic.

1926 International convention gives the League of Nations responsibility for the suppression of slavery.

1926 French and Spanish troops defeat the rebels, led by ABD EL-KRIM (d.1963), in N Morocco.

1926 Josef PILSUDSKI (1867–1935) seizes power in Poland.

1926 Military coup overthrows the Portuguese government.

1926 Antanas Smetona (1874–1944) seizes power in Lithuania and makes himself dictator.

1926 General strike afflicts British industry; Stanley BALDWIN (1867–1947) passes Trades Disputes Act (1927), which makes general strikes illegal.

1926 Italy establishes a virtual protectorate over Albania.

1927

1927 Communists are liquidated from the Kuomintang, which establishes a new government in Nanjing.

1927 Britain recognizes the independence of Iraq.

1928

1928 Transjordan becomes self-governing under Emir ABDULLAH IBN HUSSEIN (1882–1951).

1928 Chiang Kai-shek captures Beijing and reunites China under nationalist rule.

1928 Chinese communist Red Army is created by MAO ZEDONG (1893–1976).

1928 HIROHITO (1901–89) is crowned emperor of Japan.

1928 Ethiopian regent RAS TAFARI MAKONNEN (1892–1975) assumes the title Negus.

1928 Kellogg-Briand pact outlaws war and proposes international arbitration in cases of dispute.

1928 Stalin ends the New Economic Policy in Russia and introduces the first five-year plan.

1929

1929 Fighting breaks out between the Chinese and the Russians along the Manchurian border.

1929 Arabs attack Jewish settlements near Jerusalem.

1929 Lateran treaties between Italy and the papacy normalize relations and create Vatican City as an independent state.

1929 ALEXANDER I (1888–1934) declares his royal dictatorship over the country he officially renames Yugoslavia.

1929 Trotsky is forced into exile from Russia.

THE AMERICAS

1925 US aviator Charles LINDBERGH (1902–74) flies solo nonstop from New York to Paris.

1925 Scopes trial confirms the ban on the teaching of evolution in some US schools.

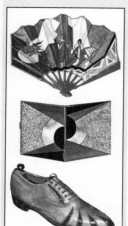

art deco *A fashionable style of design and interior decoration in the 1920s and 1930s, art deco is characterized by sleek forms, simplified lines and geometric patterns.*

1928 US secretary of state Frank KELLOGG (1856–1937) proposes the international renunciation of war.

1928 Herbert HOOVER (1874–1964) is elected US president.

1929 New York Stock Exchange slumps in the Wall Street Crash and causes financial collapse and economic depression around the world.

1929 US troops occupy Haiti to restore order after political unrest.

SCIENCE AND TECHNOLOGY

1925 US physicist Wolfgang PAULI (1900–1958) formulates his exclusion principle.

1925 Austrian physicist Erwin SCHRÖDINGER (1887–1961) establishes the study of quantum wave mechanics.

1925 British physicist Paul DIRAC (1902–84) independently formulates wave mechanics.

1926 Scottish engineer John Logie BAIRD (1888–1946) demonstrates television in London.

1926 US engineer Robert Goddard (1882–1945) launches the first liquid-fueled rocket.

1926 US aviator Richard Byrd (1888–1957) flies across the North Pole.

1927 French astrophysicist Georges LEMAÎTRE (1894–1966) formulates the Big Bang theory of the origin of the universe.

1927 German physicist Werner HEISENBERG (1901–76) formulates his uncertainty principle.

1927 German geneticist Hermann MULLER (1890–1967) induces mutations in fruit flies with X rays.

1927 First talking motion picture, *The Jazz Singer*, is released.

1928 US engineer Vladimir ZWORYKIN (1889–1982) patents a color television system.

1928 German physicist Hans Geiger (1882–1945) produces an improved version of his radiation counter.

1928 Scottish bacteriologist Alexander FLEMING (1881–1955) discovers the antibiotic properties of the penicillin mold.

ARTS AND HUMANITIES

1925

1925 Austrian composer Alban BERG (1885–1935) writes his opera *Wozzeck*.

1925 Adolf HITLER (1889–1945) publishes the first volume of his *Mein Kampf*.

1925 US author F. Scott FITZGERALD (1886–1940) publishes his novel *The Great Gatsby*.

1925 *Exposition des Arts Decoratifs* in Paris popularizes the Art Deco style.

1925 US author Theodore Dreiser (1871–1945) publishes his novel *An American Tragedy*.

1925 *The Trial* by German novelist Franz KAFKA (1883–1924) is published posthumously.

1925 Russian composer Dmitri SHOSTAKOVICH (1906–75) writes his Symphony No.1 in F minor.

1926

1926 Irish dramatist Sean O'Casey (1880–1964) writes his *The Plow and the Stars*.

1927

1927 German philosopher Martin HEIDEGGER (1889–1976) publishes his *Being and Time*.

1927 British author Virginia WOOLF (1882–1841) publishes her *To The Lighthouse*.

1928

1928 British writer Siegfried Sassoon (1886–1967) publishes his novel *Memoirs of a Fox-hunting Man*.

1929

1929 US author Ernest HEMINGWAY (1898–1961) publishes his *A Farewell to Arms*.

1929 Spanish philosopher José ORTEGA Y GASSET (1883–1955) publishes his *The Revolt of the Masses*.

1929 French artist and author Jean COCTEAU (1892–) publishes his novel *Les Enfants terribles*.

1929 German novelist Erich Remarque (1898–11970) publishes his *All Quiet on the Western Front*.

ASIA AND AUSTRALASIA

1930 Kurdish rising erupts on the Turkey–Persia border.

1930 Mohandas GANDHI (1869–1948) organizes and leads the salt march in India and is arrested and imprisoned.

1930 Three-way civil war breaks out in China.

1930 Vietnamese reformer HO CHI MINH (1880–1969) founds the Indochinese communist party.

1931 Japanese invade Manchuria.

▶ *Hailie Selassie I became emperor in 1930 after the death of Empress Zauditu, Menelik II's daughter. He became a focus for African nationalism and was vital to the establishment of the Organization of African Unity.*

1932 Military coup introduces representative government in Thailand.

1932 Sydney harbor bridge is opened.

1932 Indian National Congress is banned by the British.

1932 Kingdom of Saudi Arabia is formally established.

1932 Japanese declare Manchuria the independent state of Manchukuo.

1934 Saudi capture of Hodeida ends a border war with Yemen.

1934 Turkish president Mustafa Kemal (1881–1938) introduces the use of surnames and himself adopts the surname ATATÜRK, meaning father of the Turks.

1934 Chinese communist Red Army begins the Long March to evade nationalist forces.

1934 Former emperor of China Henry PU YI (1906–67) becomes Japanese puppet emperor of Manchukuo.

AFRICA

1930 Ras Tafari Makonnen (1892–1975) proclaims himself Emperor HAILE SELASSIE of Ethiopia.

1932 French complete their conquest of S Morocco.

> "I pledge you – I pledge myself – to a new deal for the American people."
>
> Franklin D. Roosevelt

1934 Italian and Ethiopian troops clash near Ethiopia's border with Italian Somaliland.

EUROPE

1930 London naval treaty limits the size of fleets.

1930 King CAROL II (1893–1953) returns to Romania and resumes the throne.

1930 Joseph STALIN (1879–1953) introduces the forced collectivization of farms in Russia.

1930 France starts to build the Maginot line of defenses against Germany.

1931 British Commonwealth of Nations is established.

1931 King ALFONSO XIII (1886–1941) flees Spain; a republic is declared.

1931 Bank failure in Austria starts a financial collapse in central Europe.

1932 Eamon DE VALERA (1882–1975) becomes prime minister of the Irish Free State.

1932 António SALAZAR (1889–1974) becomes prime minister of Portugal and introduces a new fascist-style constitution.

1932 Catalonia receives a degree of autonomy from Spain.

1933 Adolf HITLER (1889–1945) is elected chancellor of Germany; after the Reichstag fire he assumes emergency powers and declares the Third Reich.

1933 Austrian chancellor Engelbert DOLLFUSS (1892–1934) makes himself dictator.

1933 Nazis establish a concentration camp at Dachau.

1934 Dictatorships are established in Estonia and Latvia.

1934 Hitler purges the Nazi party in the "Night of the Long Knives" and declares himself Führer of Germany.

1934 Dollfuss is murdered during an attempted Nazi coup.

1934 Fascist coup takes power in Bulgaria.

THE AMERICAS

1930 Rafael Trujillo (1891–1961) makes himself president of the Dominican republic

1930 Army coup makes Getúlio Vargas (1883–1954) president of Brazil.

1931 US gangster Al Capone (1899–1947) is imprisoned.

1932 Bolivia and Paraguay go to war over control of the Chaco region.

1932 Franklin D. Roosevelt (1884–1945) is elected US president.

1933 US government introduces New Deal legislation to promote recovery from economic depression; Federal Emergency Relief Act establishes the Public Works Administration; National Industrial Recovery Act establishes the National Recovery Administration; Tennessee Valley Authority is formed.

1933 Fulgencio Batista (1901–73) leads a military coup in Cuba.

1934 Drought and bad farming techniques combine to form the "Dust Bowl" in the US Midwest.

1934 US troops withdraw from Haiti.

SCIENCE AND TECHNOLOGY

1930 US astronomer Clyde Tombaugh (1906–97) discovers the planet Pluto.

1930 Acrylic plastics Perspex and Lucite are invented.

1930 US engineer Eugene Houdry (1892–1962) invents the catalytic process of cracking crude oil.

1931 US physicist Ernest Lawrence (1901-58) invents the cyclotron particle accelerator.

1931 US physicist Robert Van de Graaff (1901–67) invents a high-voltage electrostatic generator.

1931 US mathematician Kurt Gödel (1906–78) publishes his proof that any system based on the laws of arithmetic must contain inaccuracies.

1931 Empire State Building is opened in New York.

1932 Swiss physicist Auguste Piccard (1884–1962) and an assistant ascend into the stratosphere in a balloon.

1932 US physicist Carl Anderson (1905–91) discovers positrons.

1932 US engineer Karl Jansky (1905–50) detects cosmic radio waves.

1932 US physicist Edwin Land (1909–91) invents polarized glass.

1932 German chemist Gerhard Domagk (1895–1964) discovers the first of the sulpha drugs.

1932 British physicist James Chadwick (1891–1974) discovers the neutron.

1932 Dutch complete the drainage of the Zuider Zee.

1933 US engineer Edwin Armstrong (1890–1954) invents FM radio transmission.

ARTS AND HUMANITIES

1930 Belgian artist René Magritte (1898–1967) paints his *The Key of Dreams*.

1930 British dramatist and composer Noel Coward (1899–1973) writes his play *Private Lives*.

1930 US poet Hart Crane (1899–1932) publishes his *The Bridge*.

1931 French novelist Antoine de Saint-Exupéry (1900–44) publishes his *Night Flight*.

1931 US dramatist Eugene O'Neill (1888–1953) writes his *Mourning Becomes Electra*.

1931 British composer William Walton (1902–83) writes his oratorio *Belshazzar's Feast*.

1931 Spanish artist Salvador Dalí (1904–89) paints his *The Persistence of Memory*.

1932 British novelist Aldous Huxley (1894–1963) publishes his *Brave New World*.

1933 French novelist André Malraux (1901–76) writes his *La condition humaine*.

1933 Spanish poet and dramatist Federico García Lorca (1898–1936) writes his play *Blood Wedding*.

1933 US author Gertrude Stein (1874–1946) publishes her *The Autobiography of Alice B. Toklas*.

1934 US composer Cole Porter (1891–1964) writes his musical *Anything Goes*.

1934 British poet and author Robert Graves (1895–1985) publishes his novel *I, Claudius*.

1934 US author Henry Miller (1891–1980) publishes his novel *Tropic of Cancer*.

1934 Russian novelist Mikhail Sholokhov (1905–84) publishes his *And Quiet Flows the Don*.

1930

1931

1932

1933

1934

ASIA AND AUSTRALASIA	AFRICA	EUROPE

1935

1935 New constitution establishes the Philippine Commonwealth as a semiindependent state; Manuel QUEZON (1878–1964) becomes president.

1935 Britain separates Burma and Aden from India and introduces a central legislature in Delhi.

1935 Benito MUSSOLINI (1883–1945) formally creates the Italian colony of Libya.

1935 Italy invades Ethiopia and captures the regional capital of Makale.

1935 Greek monarchy is restored under King George II (1890–1947).

1935 Saarland region is returned to Germany after a plebiscite.

1935 New constitution ends democratic government in Poland.

1935 Anti-Jewish Nuremberg laws are passed in Germany.

1935 Germany denounces the disarmament clauses of the Versailles treaty.

1936

1936 Jawaharlal NEHRU (1889–1964) is elected leader of the Indian National Congress.

1936 Britain sends reinforcements to Palestine to impose order on warring Jews and Arabs.

1936 Egypt becomes independent of Britain under King FAROUK (1920–65).

1936 Italians capture Addis Ababa and annex Ethiopia.

1936 Popular Front under Léon BLUM (1872–1950) forms a government in France.

1936 General Joannis METAXAS (1871–1941) becomes dictator in Greece.

1936 German troops occupy the demilitarized Rhineland.

1936 General Franciso FRANCO (1892–1975) leads a nationalist uprising in Spanish Morocco; he invades Spain and is proclaimed nationalist head of state; start of the Spanish civil war.

1936 Germany and Italy form the Rome-Berlin axis alliance.

1936 EDWARD VIII (1894–1972) becomes king of Britain and abdicates; GEORGE VI (1895–1952) becomes king.

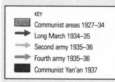

KEY
Communist areas 1927–34
Long March 1934–35
Second army 1935–36
Fourth army 1935–36
Communist Yan'an 1937

◀ *Long March (1934–35)* Led by Chu Teh and Mao Zedong, 90,000 communist troops, accompanied by 15,000 civilians, broke through a Nationalist encirclement of their headquarters and marched some 10,000km (6,000mi) from Jiangxi province, SE China, to Shanxi province in the NW. The communist 2nd and 4th armies also regrouped in N China. This enforced march prevented the extermination of the communist party.

1937

1937 Japanese forces invade NE China and capture Beijing, Shanghai and Nanjing; nationalist and communist Chinese leaders agree on joint defense.

1937 French suppress a nationalist uprising in Morocco.

1937 Italian troops and German aircraft provide military aid to the nationalists in Spain.

1937 Joseph STALIN (1879–1953) begins to purge the Soviet armed forces; many officers are executed.

1937 Irish Free State formally becomes Eire.

THE AMERICAS

1935 Chaco War ends with Paraguay gaining most of the disputed territory; Bolivia gains access to the sea.

1936 Fascist coup seizes power in Paraguay.

1936 Anastasio SOMOZA (1896–1956) makes himself dictator in Nicaragua

> "I have found it impossible to carry the heavy burden of responsibility and to discharge my duties as King as I would wish to do without the help and support of the woman I love."
>
> Edward VIII
> (abdication speech)

SCIENCE AND TECHNOLOGY

1935 British engineer Robert Watson-Watt (1892–1973) builds a radar system to detect aircraft.

1935 Fluorescent lighting and sodium vapor lamps are developed.

1935 US geologist Charles Richter (1900–85) devises a scale to measure the intensity of earthquakes.

1936 British mathematician Alan TURING (1912–54) develops the mathematical theory of computing.

1937 British engineer Frank WHITTLE (1907–96) builds a prototype jet engine.

1937 Nylon, invented by US chemist Wallace Carothers (1896–1937), is patented.

ARTS AND HUMANITIES

1935 British poet and critic T.S. ELIOT (1888–1965) writes his play *Murder in the Cathedral.*

1935 British artist Ben Nicholson (1894–1982) paints his *White Relief.*

1936 British economist John KEYNES (1883–1946) publishes his *General Theory of Employment, Interest and Money.*

1936 Dutch artist Piet Mondrian (1872–1944) paints his *Composition in Red and Blue.*

1936 US novelist William FAULKNER (1897–1962) publishes his *Absalom, Absalom!*.

◄ *Stalin* had become virtual dictator of Russia by 1927. He soon began a ruthless purge that eliminated possible rivals and resulted in a reign of terror (1936–39) in which millions perished. As premier from 1941, Stalin supervised Russia's participation in World War II.

1937 US sociologist Talcott Parsons (1902–79) publishes his *The Structure of Social Action.*

1937 Spanish artist Pablo PICASSO (1881–1973) paints his *Guernica* in protest at the German air-raid on that Spanish town.

1935

1936

1937

ASIA AND AUSTRALASIA	AFRICA	EUROPE

1938

Major areas of conflict
Extent of naval conflict
✦ Other engagements

▲ **World War II** *The war began in Europe but developed into a global conflict with campaigns in Africa, Asia and throughout the Pacific and Atlantic Oceans. Germany and Japan enjoyed a series of victories in the first three years. Thereafter, Allied* *superiority in potential manpower and industrial capacity steadily grew. It was a war of technology, with developments in tanks, aircraft, submarines, radar and eventually the atomic bomb, helping to influence strategic and tactical thinking.*

1938 German troops occupy Austria; Adolf HITLER (1889–1945) announces the Anschluss (union) of the two countries.

1938 British prime minister Neville CHAMBERLAIN (1869–1940) meets with Hitler to discuss German demands on Czechoslovakia.

1938 Conference of European leaders at Munich decides to appease German ambitions and to permit the annexation of the Sudetenland region of Czechoslovakia; Poland and Hungary also gain areas of Czech territory.

1938 Jewish shops and businesses are smashed during *Kristallnacht* in Germany.

1939

1939 Baron Hiranuma becomes Japanese prime minister.

1939 Faisal II (1935–58) becomes boy-king of Iraq.

1939 Soviet and Mongolian troops defeat the Japanese at the battle of Nomonhan.

1939 Turkey allies with France and Britain.

1939 Nazi-Soviet pact, signed by the respective foreign ministers Joachim von RIBBENTROP (1893–1946) and Vyacheslav MOLOTOV (1890–1986), agrees to partition Poland.

1939 Germany occupies the remainder of Czechoslovakia, annexes Memel in Lithuania and demands Danzig from Poland.

1939 Nationalist forces capture Barcelona and Madrid; end of the Spanish civil war.

1939 Italy invades Albania.

1939 Adolf Hitler and Benito MUSSOLINI (1883–1945) sign the "pact of steel".

1939 Germany invades Poland; Britain and France declare war; Russia invades Poland; the Poles surrender; Poland is partitioned; British troops are sent to France.

1939 German submarine sinks the British battleship *Royal Oak* in a Scottish harbor.

1939 Russian troops invade Finland and encounter strong resistance.

coelacanth *The coelacanth was thought to have become extinct 60 million years ago until its discovery* *in deep waters off the African coast in 1938. Its scales and bony plates are unlike those of modern fish.*

THE AMERICAS

1938 Mexico nationalizes US and British oil companies.

SCIENCE AND TECHNOLOGY

1938 Hungarian engineer Ladislao Biró (1899–1985) invents a ballpoint pen.

1938 US physicist Chester Carlson (1906–68) invents a process for photocopying documents.

1938 Coelacanth "living fossil" fish is caught in the Indian Ocean.

ARTS AND HUMANITIES

1938 British author Graham GREENE (1904–91) publishes his novel *Brighton Rock*.

1938 US actor Orson Welles (1915–85) panics radio audiences with his performance of *War of the Worlds*.

1939 German warship *Graf Spee* is scuttled after the battle of the River Plate.

1939 German chemist Otto HAHN (1879–1968) discovers atomic fission.

1939 Helicopter designed by US engineer Igor Sikorsky (1889–1972) goes into production.

1939 Swiss scientist Paul Müller (1899–1965) synthesizes DDT as an insecticide.

1939 British engineers John Randall (1905–84) and Henry Boot (1917–83) invent the cavity magnetron.

◄ *Hitler* proclaimed himself Führer of Germany in 1934, after Hindenburg's death. He remilitarized the Rhineland (1936), occupied Austria (1938) and Czechoslovakia (October 1938 and March 1939) and attacked Poland (September 1939). The invasion of Poland precipitated World War II.

1939 US author John STEINBECK (1902–68) publishes his novel *The Grapes of Wrath*.

1939 Irish author James JOYCE (1882–1941) publishes his novel *Finnegan's Wake*.

1939 US novelist Raymond Chandler (1888–1959) writes his *The Big Sleep*.

1939 British author Christopher Isherwood (1904–86) publishes his short story *Goodbye to Berlin*.

1939 French philosopher and author Jean-Paul SARTRE (1905–80) publishes his novel *Nausea*.

1939 US dramatist and author Lillian Hellman (1907–84) writes her play *Little Foxes*.

ASIA AND AUSTRALASIA	AFRICA	EUROPE

1940   **1940** Japan invades French Indochina and captures Saigon.

1940 British troops repel an Italian invasion of Egypt and advance into Libya.

1940 German troops occupy Denmark and invade Norway.

1941   **1941** British troops capture Damascus from Vichy French forces.

1940 Italians capture British Somaliland.

1940 Winston CHURCHILL (1874–1965) becomes British prime minister.

1941 British and Soviet troops occupy Tehran; Muhammad Reza PAHLAVI (1919–80) succeeds his father as shah of Iran.

1940 British warships destroy part of the French fleet at the Algerian port of Oran.

1940 Italy declares war on France and Britain.

1941 General Hideki TOJO (1885–1948) becomes Japanese prime minister.

1940 British and Free French forces attempt to capture Dakar in Senegal.

1940 Germany conquers the Netherlands, Belgium and Luxembourg, invades France and takes Paris; Marshal Henri PÉTAIN (1856–1951) surrenders; France is divided into occupied and unoccupied (Vichy) zones.

1941 Japanese aircraft make a surprise attack on US ships in Pearl Harbor, Hawaii; Japanese troops capture Wake Island and Guam.

1940 Germany begins a massive bombing campaign that leads to the battle of Britain.

1941 Thailand allies with Japan and declares war on Britain and the USA.

1940 Ion ANTONESCU (1882–1946) becomes dictator in Romania.

1941 Japanese forces invade the Philippines.

1940 Estonia, Lithuania and Latvia become part of the Soviet Union.

1941 Hong Kong surrenders to the Japanese.

1940 British occupy Iceland.

1942   **1942** Japanese take Kuala Lumpur in Malaya and invade Burma and Java; Singapore surrenders; British force the Japanese back from NE India into Burma.

1941 British capture Torbruk and Benghazi, Libya, from the Italians; German general Erwin ROMMEL (1891–1944) takes command; German Afrika Korps besieges the British at Torbruk.

1941 Germany invades Yugoslavia and Greece; German paratroops take Crete and British forces are evacuated.

1942 US forces surrender at Bataan and Corregidor fort in the Philippines; the Japanese take Manila.

1941 Ethiopian troops capture the Italian stronghold of Burye.

1941 German troops invade the Soviet Union, occupy Ukraine and besiege Leningrad, but fail to capture Moscow.

1941 British forces capture Mogadishu, in Italian Somaliland, and occupy Addis Ababa, Ethiopia.

1941 German minister Rudolf HESS (1894–1987) lands in Scotland on a peace mission.

1942 Allied victory in the naval battle of the Coral Sea prevents the Japanese invasion of Australia.

1941 Germany and Italy declare war on the USA.

1942 US fleet defeats the Japanese at the battle of Midway Island.

1942 German forces capture Torbruk; the British under General Bernard MONTGOMERY (1887–1976) halt the German advance on Cairo at the battle of El Alamein.

1942 Nazi Wannsee conference decides upon the "final solution"; Polish, Russian and French Jews are sent to death camps.

1942 US aircraft make a bombing raid on Tokyo.

1942 US and British troops land in Morocco and Algeria.

1942 Vidkun QUISLING (1887–1945) heads a collaborationist government in Norway.

1942 US troops capture the Henderson Field airstrip on Guadalcanal Island.

1942 Germans take Sebastopol and surround Stalingrad.

1942 Japanese are defeated by the nationalist Chinese at the battle of Changsha.

1942 Josip TITO (1892–1980) organizes the Yugoslavian resistance.

1942 Germans occupy Vichy France; the French navy is scuttled at Toulon.

THE AMERICAS

1940 Leon TROTSKY (b.1879) is assassinated in Mexico City.

1940 A Pan-American conference adopts joint trusteeship of European colonies in the Western hemisphere.

1941 US government passes the Lend-Lease Act enabling the supply of equipment to Britain.

1941 Franklin D. ROOSEVELT (1884–1945) and Winston Churchill issue the Atlantic charter setting out joint war aims.

1941 USA declares war on Japan after the attack on Pearl harbor.

1941 Manhattan project to build an atomic weapon is started in the USA.

1942 Inter-American conference at Rio de Janeiro agrees a joint position against Germany and Japan.

1942 Japan captures several of the Aleutian Islands.

1942 Japanese-Americans are relocated away from the w coast of the USA.

SCIENCE AND TECHNOLOGY

1940 British scientist Hans Krebs (1900–81) discovers the citric-acid cycle.

1940 Canadian scientist James Hillier (1915–) invents an electron microscope.

▲ *Fermi produced the first controlled, self-sustaining nuclear fission reaction – the key to a new and virtually inexhaustible source of energy. In 1942 he built the world's first nuclear reactor.*

1942 French divers Emile Gagnan and Jacques Cousteau (1910–97) devise the scuba aqualung.

1942 German Me 262 flies in combat as the first jet fighter.

1942 US physicist Enrico FERMI (1901–54) builds the world's first nuclear reactor, in Chicago.

1942 Team led by German engineer Wernher VON BRAUN (1912–77) designs the A4 (V2) rocket.

1943 German scientist Albert

ARTS AND HUMANITIES

1940 Russian artist Wassily KANDINSKY (1866–1944) paints his *Sky Blue*.

1940 US author Ernest HEMINGWAY (1898–1961) publishes his novel *For Whom the Bell Tolls*.

1940 Japanese artist Yasuo Kuniyoshi (1893–1953) paints his *Upside Down Table and Mask*.

1940 British author Graham GREENE (1904–91) publishes his novel *The Power and the Glory*.

1941 Illinois Institute of Technology, designed by German architect Ludwig MIES VAN DER ROHE (1886–1969), is completed.

1941 German poet and dramatist Berthold BRECHT (1898–1956) writes his play *Mother Courage and Her Children*.

1941 British composer Michael TIPPETT (1905–98) writes his oratorio *A Child of our Time*.

1942 French writer Albert CAMUS (1913–60) publishes his novel *The Stranger*.

1942 French philosopher Maurice MERLEAU-PONTY (1908–61) publishes his *The Structure of Behavior*.

1942 US artist Edward Hopper (1882–1967) paints his *Nighthawks*.

1940

1941

1942

ASIA AND AUSTRALASIA	AFRICA	EUROPE

1943

1943 At a conference in Tehran, Britain and the USA agree with Russia to open a second front against Germany by invading w Europe.

1943 Syria and Lebanon gain their independence from France.

1943 US troops retake the Kasserine Pass and join up with British troops in Tunisia; the German army in North Africa surrenders.

1943 Russians break the siege of Leningrad; German general Friedrich von Paulus (1890–1957) surrenders at Stalingrad; Russians retake Kiev and occupy Romania and Bulgaria.

1943 Jews in the Warsaw ghetto attempt an uprising against the Germans.

1943 British bombers fly the "dambusters" mission.

1943 US and British troops land in Sicily and occupy Messina; Benito MUSSOLINI (1883–1945) is overthrown; Allied troops take Naples; Italy surrenders; German troops occupy Rome; the Allied advance in Italy is halted by the German Gustav line.

1944

1944 USA starts a large-scale bombing campaign against Japan.

1944 US forces take the Marshall Islands, Guam and Saipan in the Marianas; landings at Leyte begin the recapture of the Philippines under General Douglas MACARTHUR (1880–1964).

1944 General Tojo resigns as Japanese prime minister.

1944 France promises its African colonies independence after the war.

▲ **De Gaulle** fought in World War I and was wounded and captured in 1916. He later served in the occupation of the Rhineland and in Lebanon. In 1940 he became brigadier general in charge of the 4th Armored Division. When the Vichy government was created, De Gaulle went to England as self-declared head of the French resistance.

1944 Allied troops break through at Monte Cassino and enter Rome.

1944 Allied forces under General Dwight EISENHOWER (1890–1969) invade Normandy, capture Cherbourg and break through German lines; Allied troops land in s France; Free French troops enter Paris; General Charles DE GAULLE (1890–1970) heads a provisional government; British troops liberate Brussels.

1944 Germans launch V1 and V2 rockets against European cities.

1944 Allied troops invade Germany; a German counter attack is defeated in the battle of the Bulge.

1944 Soviet troops capture Crimea, Minsk and Brest-Litovsk; Polish resistance attempts a rising in Warsaw; Soviet troops invade Czechoslovakia and Hungary.

1944 Attempt by German army officers to assassinate Adolf HITLER (1889–1945) fails.

1944 Iceland becomes an independent republic.

1944 Greece is liberated from the Germans; civil war starts between monarchists and communists.

1944 Yugoslav resistance and Russian troops jointly capture Belgrade.

THE AMERICAS

SCIENCE AND TECHNOLOGY

ARTS AND HUMANITIES

Hofman discovers the hallucinogenic drug LSD.

1943 Codebreakers at Bletchley Park, England, construct a programmable electronic computer.

1943 British artist Barbara Hepworth (1903–75) creates her sculpture *Wave*.

1943 US composers Richard Rodgers (1902–79) and Oscar Hammerstein (1895–1963) write their musical *Oklahoma*.

1943

1944 Conference at Bretton Woods in New Hampshire agrees the postwar establishment of a World Bank and an International Monetary Fund (IMF).

1944 Conference at Dumbarton Oaks agrees the postwar foundation of a United Nations Organization (UN) to replace the League of Nations.

1944 Roosevelt is elected for a fourth term as US president.

1944 US scientist Oswald Avery (1877–1955) discovers that DNA is the agent of inheritance.

1944 US astronomer Walter Baade (1893–1960) classifies stars into young Population I and old Population II.

1944 US dramatist Tennessee WILLIAMS (1911–83) writes his play *The Glass Menagerie*.

1944 US musician Glenn Miller (b.1904) is killed in an aircraft accident.

1944 French dramatist Jean ANOUILH (1910–87) writes his play *Antigone*.

1944

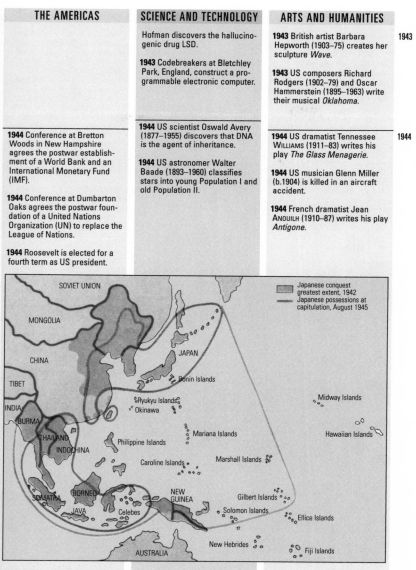

Japanese conquest greatest extent, 1942
Japanese possessions at capitulation, August 1945

SOVIET UNION

MONGOLIA

CHINA

TIBET

INDIA

BURMA

THAILAND

INDOCHINA

JAPAN

Bonin Islands

Ryukyu Islands
Okinawa

Philippine Islands

Mariana Islands

Caroline Islands

SUMATRA
BORNEO
JAVA Celebes

NEW GUINEA

Marshall Islands

Gilbert Islands

Solomon Islands

New Hebrides

AUSTRALIA

Midway Islands

Hawaiian Islands

Ellice Islands

Fiji Islands

▲ *World War II* By August 1942 Japan had seized a vast oceanic and continental empire, as illustrated on the map. It was not until early in 1944 that Allied sea power reversed these successes. While the Chinese nationalists and communists tied down large numbers of Japanese troops in a war of attrition and Allied supply lines were restored in Burma, American amphibious offensives in the Philippines and Gilbert Islands established bases from which air power could be brought to bear on Japan itself. In 1945, after atomic bombs had destroyed Hiroshima and Nagasaki, Japan agreed to an unconditional surrender.

1945

1945 Burma is liberated from the Japanese.

1945 US forces capture the islands of Iwo Jima and Okinawa.

1945 USA drops atomic bombs on Hiroshima and Nagasaki; Japan surrenders; US occupation forces land and establish a military government.

1945 HO CHI MINH (1880–1969) declares the independent republic of Vietnam.

1945 Cambodia declares its independence.

1945 Truce between nationalists and communists in China breaks down with fighting for control of Manchuria.

1945 Independent republics of Syria and Lebanon are established.

1945 Arab league is founded.

▲ **Ho Chi Minh** lived in France from 1917 to 1923. Returning to Vietnam in 1927, he presided over the founding of the Vietnamese Communist Party. Forced to flee, he moved to Russia and then China. On his return to Vietnam, he founded the Viet Minh to fight the Japanese and then the French.

1945 Warsaw and Kraków are liberated by Polish and Soviet troops.

1945 At a conference at Yalta in the Crimea, the USA and Britain tacitly agree to Soviet occupation of postwar Europe.

1945 Benito MUSSOLINI (b.1883) is shot dead by Italian resistance fighters; the German army in Italy surrenders.

1945 British air raid creates a firestorm in the city of Dresden.

1945 Soviet armies take Vienna; US and Soviet forces meet at the River Elbe; Russians under General Georgi ZHUKOV (1896–1974) take Berlin; Adolf HITLER (b.1889) commits suicide; Admiral DÖNITZ (1891–1980) surrenders; Germany and Austria are occupied in zones; the Potsdam conference agrees stringent controls on postwar Germany.

1945 Clement ATTLEE (1883–1967) is elected British prime minister.

1945 Republic of Austria is established under Karl Renner (1870–1950) .

1945 Josip TITO (1892–1980) declares the People's Republic of Yugoslavia.

1945 War crimes tribunal is set up at Nuremberg.

1946

1946 War crimes tribunal is set up in Tokyo.

1946 Jewish Irgun terrorists blow up the King David Hotel in Jerusalem.

1946 Jordan becomes an independent kingdom.

1946 French bombard the port of Haiphong while suppressing Vietnamese rebels.

1946 Republic of the Philippines becomes an independent state.

1946 USA tests atomic weapons at Bikini atoll.

1946 Charles DE GAULLE (1890–1970) resigns as president of France in protest against socialists.

1946 Communists win Czech elections.

1946 Albania becomes an independent republic under prime minister Enver HOXHA (1908–85).

1946 Italy becomes a republic under the leadership of Alcide DE GASPERI (1881–1954).

1946 British government nationalizes coal mines and lays the foundations of a welfare state.

THE AMERICAS

1945 Founding United Nations conference is held in San Francisco; Spain and Portugal are among the countries excluded from membership.

▼ *World War II These two maps illustrate the extent of Axis-controlled territory in 1942 (left) and 1945 (right). Axis conquests had reached their peak in November 1942. By May 1945 Russian counter-offensives and Allied landings in France and Italy had defeated Germany.*

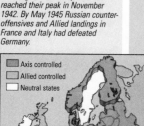

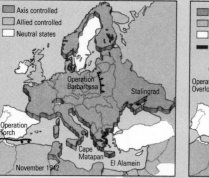

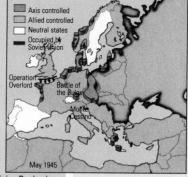

1946 Juan PERÓN (1895–1974) is elected president of Argentina.

SCIENCE AND TECHNOLOGY

1945 US scientists and engineers working at Los Alamos, New Mexico, under Robert OPPENHEIMER (1904–67) design and test an atomic bomb.

1945 US engineer Percy Spencer patents the microwave oven.

1946 US pediatrician Benjamin Spock (1903–98) writes his *The Common Sense Book of Baby and Child Care.*

1946 US chemist Willard LIBBY (1908–80) devises a method of radiocarbon dating.

1946 British engineer Maurice Wilkes (1913–) devises assembler computer-programming language.

ARTS AND HUMANITIES

1945 British artist Francis BACON (1909–92) paints his *Three Studies for Figures at the Base of a Crucifixion.*

1945 British philosopher Karl Popper (1902–94) publishes his *The Open Society and Its Enemies.*

1945 Italian author Carlo Levi (1902–75) publishes his novel *Christ Stopped at Eboli.*

1945 British novelist Evelyn Waugh (1903–66) publishes his *Brideshead Revisited.*

1945 British author J.B. Priestley (1894–1984) writes his play *An Inspector Calls.*

1945 British writer George ORWELL (1903–50) publishes his novel *Animal Farm.*

1946 French philosopher and author Jean-Paul SARTRE (1905–80) publishes his *Existentialism and Humanism.*

ASIA AND AUSTRALASIA	AFRICA	EUROPE

1947

1947 Britain grants the status of independent dominions to India and Pakistan (E and W); Jawaharlal NEHRU (1889–1964) becomes prime minister of India; Muhammad Ali JINNAH (1876–1948) becomes viceroy of Pakistan; millions die in factional fighting and there are massive population exchanges.

1947 New constitution is proclaimed in Japan.

1947 AUNG SAN (b.1914), president of the Anti-Fascist People's Freedom League in Burma, is assassinated by a political rival.

1947 Britain grants Nigeria limited self-government.

1947 All Algerians are granted French citizenship.

1947 Belgium, the Netherlands and Luxembourg form a customs union.

1947 Italy, Romania and Hungary lose small areas of territory under the Paris peace treaties.

1947 Communist coups seize power in Czechoslovakia, Hungary and Romania.

1948

1948 Burma becomes independent of Britain.

1948 Ceylon (present-day Sri Lanka) becomes a self governing British dominion.

1948 State of Israel is established and is attacked by the Egyptians and the Jordanian Arab Legion.

1948 Brussels treaty agreeing military and economic cooperation is signed by Britain, France, Belgium, the Netherlands and Luxembourg.

1948 JULIANA (1909–) becomes queen of the Netherlands.

1948 Russians blockade Berlin; an airlift is organized to keep the city supplied.

1949

1949 CHIANG KAI-SHEK (1887–1975) resigns as Chinese president following communist victories .

1949 Chinese nationalists evacuate to Formosa (present-day Taiwan); MAO ZEDONG (1893–1976) declares the People's Republic of China.

1949 Independent republics of North Korea, under president KIM IL SUNG (1912–94), and South Korea, under president Syngman RHEE (1875–1965), are established.

1949 Indonesia becomes independent under President Achmad SUKARNO (1901–70).

1949 France grants independence to Vietnam but does not recognize the regime of HO CHI MINH (1880–1969).

1949 Warfare between India and Pakistan over territory in Kashmir is ended by a UN ceasefire.

1949 Israel and Egypt agree an armistice.

1949 Cambodia becomes independent under King NORODOM SIHANOUK (1922–).

1949 South Africa passes legislation enforcing a policy of apartheid.

> "We are advocates of the abolition of war, we do not want war; but war can only be abolished through war, and in order to get rid of the gun it is necessary to take up the gun."
>
> Mao Zedong
> (*Quotations from Chairman Mao Zedong*)

1949 Republic of Ireland is declared.

1949 Soviet Union breaks off close relations with Yugoslavia.

1949 Council of Europe and the European Court of Human Rights are established.

1949 Federal Republic of (West) Germany, with its capital in Bonn, and the (East) German Democratic Republic are established.

1949 Greek civil war ends with a monarchist victory.

1949 Soviet Union tests an atomic bomb.

1949 Soviet Union and the communist-controlled countries of E Europe form the Comecon organization for economic cooperation.

THE AMERICAS

1947 US president Harry S. TRUMAN (1884–1972) pledges a doctrine of support for regimes threatened by communism.

1947 US secretary of state George MARSHALL (1880–1959) calls for a plan for European economic recovery.

1948 US government pledges massive financial aide to Europe for the implementation of the Marshall plan.

1948 Truman is elected US president.

1948 UN issues a declaration of human rights.

1949 North Atlantic Treaty Organization (NATO) is formed for mutual defense by the USA, Canada and w European states.

1949 Newfoundland becomes a part of Canada.

1949 Organization of American States (OAS) is established.

SCIENCE AND TECHNOLOGY

1947 Atomic power station opens at Harwell, England.

1947 US aviator Chuck Yeager (1923–) breaks the sound barrier in the Bell X1 rocket-powered aircraft.

1947 US engineers John BARDEEN (1908–91), Walter BRATTAIN (1902–87) and William SHOCKLEY (1910–89) invent the transistor.

1947 US engineer Buckminster Fuller (1895–1983) designs his geodesic dome.

1948 British physicist Dennis Gabor (1900–79) invents holography.

1948 US physicists Richard Feynman (1918–88) and Julian Schwinger (1918–94) formulate quantum electrodynamics.

▼ **Palestine** *Migration to Palestine began in the late 19th century as groups of Jews sought freedom from persecution. After the foundation of the World Zionist Organization (1897) more Jews arrived, buying land for collectives. Up to 1948 most arrivals were from Europe. After 1948, many Jews living in Arab countries migrated or fled to Israel. The Palestinians fled their homes in two waves, the majority (more than half a million) in 1948 and a second group of between 200,00 and 400,000 during the 1967 war.*

ARTS AND HUMANITIES

1947 Italian writer Primo LEVI (1919–87) publishes his *If This is a Man*.

1947 Italian artist Marino Marini (1901–80) creates his sculpture *Horseman*.

1947 British poet W.H. AUDEN (1907–73) publishes his *The Age of Anxiety*.

1948 US novelist Norman Mailer (1923–) publishes his *The Naked and the Dead*.

1948 US artist Jackson POLLOCK (1912–56) paints his *Composition No.1*.

1949 US dramatist Arthur MILLER (1915–) writes his play *Death of a Salesman*.

1949 French anthropologist Claude Lévi-Strauss (1908–90) publishes his *The Elementary Structures of Kinship*.

1949 French feminist and novelist Simone de BEAUVOIR (1908–86) publishes her *The Second Sex*.

1949 French author and dramatist Jean Genet (1910–86) publishes his novel *Diary of a Thief*.

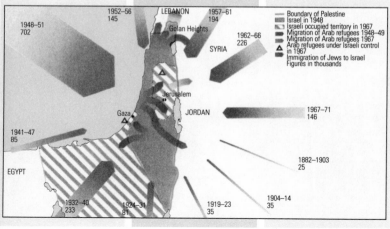

199

ASIA AND AUSTRALASIA	AFRICA	EUROPE
1950		
1950 India becomes a federal republic.		**1950** French foreign minister Robert Schuman (1886–1963) proposes a plan for the integration of the French and German coal and steel industries.
1950 Jordan annexes the West Bank and E Jerusalem.		**1950** GUSTAVUS VI (1882–1973) becomes king of Sweden.
1950 Soviet Union and China sign a treaty of alliance and cooperation.	**1951** Libya gains full independence under King IDRIS I (1890–1983).	**1951** West Germany is admitted to the Council of Europe.
1950 North Korean forces invade South Korea and start the Korean War; UN troops land at Ichon, liberate Seoul and invade North Korea; China sends troops to aid North Korea.	**1951** British troops occupy the Suez canal zone.	**1951** LEOPOLD III (1901–83) of Belgium abdicates in favor of his son BAUDOUIN (1930–93).
1950 Viet Minh forces under HO CHI MINH (1880–1969) defeat the French at the battle of Kaobang in Vietnam.		**1951** Marshall Plan economic aid to Europe ends.
1950 Chinese invade Tibet.		**1951** Winston CHURCHILL (1874–1965) is elected British prime minister.
1951	**1952** Mau Mau secret society starts a campaign of terrorism against British settlers in Kenya.	**1952** Swedish diplomat Dag HAMMARSKJÖLD (1905–61) is elected secretary-general of the United Nations (UN).
1951 North Korean and Chinese forces take Seoul; UN forces recapture the city and halt a communist offensive at the battle of Imjin River.	**1952** Eritrea becomes a part of Ethiopia.	**1952** European Coal and Steel community is formed.
1951 Iran under dictatorial prime minister Muhammad MUSSADEGH (1880–1967) nationalizes the oil industry and occupies the port of Abadan.	**1952** King FAROUK (1920–65).is overthrown in Egypt; King Fuad II becomes a figurehead for prime minister Muhammad Naguib.	**1952** ELIZABETH II (1926–) becomes queen of Britain.
1951 Colombo plan starts to distribute US aid to S Asian nations.		**1952** Greece and Turkey join NATO.
1952		
1953		
1953 HUSSEIN I (1935–99) becomes king of Jordan.	**1953** Britain establishes the federation of Rhodesia (Northern and Southern) and Nyasaland.	**1953** Josip TITO (1892–1980) is formally appointed president of the Federal People's republic of Yugoslavia.
1953 Laos gains full independence from France.	**1953** Berber rising overthrows the pro-French sultan.	**1953** Konrad ADENAUER (1876–1967) is reelected chancellor of West Germany.
1953 Shah of Iran dismisses Mussadegh.	**1953** Kenyan politician Jomo KENYATTA (1893–1978) is jailed by the British for involvement with the Mau Mau.	**1953** Nikita KHRUSHCHEV (1894–1971) becomes first secretary of the Communist Party in the Soviet Union after the death of Joseph STALIN (b.1879).
1953 Armistice signed at Panmunjom ends the Korean War.		
1954	**1954** Nigeria becomes a self-governing federation.	**1954** Greek nationalist EOKA movement carries out attacks on British troops in Cyprus.
1954 French forces in Vietnam surrender after defeat by the Viet Minh at the battle of Dien Bien Phu; the Geneva peace treaty splits Vietnam at the 17th parallel.	**1954** Gamal NASSER (1918–70) becomes prime minister of Egypt.	**1954** Italy and Yugoslavia reach agreement over the ownership of Trieste.
1954 Manila treaty establishes the South East Asian Treaty Organization (SEATO).	**1954** National Liberation Front (FLN) organizes an anti-French revolt in Algeria.	

1950 Chilean poet Pablo NERUDA (1904–73) publishes his epic *General Song*. **1950**

1950 British novelist Doris LESSING (1919–) publishes her *The Grass is Singing*.

1951 Twenty-second amendment to the US constitution limits presidents to two terms of office.

1951 US engineers John Eckert (1919–) and John Mauchly (1907–80) build UNIVAC I, the first commercial computer.

1951 US novelist J.D. SALINGER (1919–) publishes his *Catcher in the Rye*. **1951**

1951 US author Herman Wouk (1915–) publishes his novel *The Caine Mutiny*.

1952 Dwight EISENHOWER (1890–1969) is elected US president.

1952 Fulgencio BATISTA (1901–73) makes himself president of Cuba.

1951 British composer Benjamin BRITTEN (1913–76) writes his opera *Billy Budd*.

1951 French artist Fernand Léger (1881–1955) designs stained glass windows for the church of Sacre Coeur at Audicourt in France.

1952 Eva "Evita" PERÓN (b1919), the first wife of the Argentine president, dies.

1952 USA explodes a hydrogen bomb.

1952 British explode an atom bomb.

1952 British artist Henry MOORE (1898–1986) creates his sculpture *King and Queen*. **1952**

1952 US researcher Jonas SALK (1914–95) develops a vaccine against poliomyelitis.

1952 British Comet aircraft makes the first jet passenger flight.

1952 Alsatian humanitarian Albert SCHWEITZER (1987–1965) wins the Nobel peace prize.

1952 US composer John Cage (1912–92) conceives his *4'33"*.

Le Corbusier The chapel of Notre-Dame-du-Haut, Ronchamp, France, was built by Le Corbusier in 1955. The flowing, highly sculptural concrete structure deliberately resembles a nun's headdress. Set among hills, its design also echoes the forms of the surrounding landscape.

1953 US physicist Charles Townes (1915–) invents the maser.

1953 German chemist Karl Ziegler (1898–1973) invents a process for making high-density polyethene.

1953 British biophysicist Francis CRICK (1916–) and US biophysicist James WATSON (1928–) discover the helical structure of DNA.

1953 US engineer An Wang (1920–90) invents magnetic core computer memory.

1952 *Unité d'Habitation* designed by Swiss architect LE CORBUSIER (1887–1965) is opened in Marseilles, France.

1953 British scholar Michael Ventris (1922–56) deciphers Linear B as the Greek script of the Mycenaeans. **1953**

1953 US artist Willem DE KOONING (1904–97) paints his *Women*.

1954 British author and poet Dylan THOMAS (1914–53) writes his verse play *Under Milk Wood*. **1954**

1954 Anticommunist crusade of Senator Joseph MCCARTHY (1908–57) reaches a climax with televised hearings of his investigation committee.

1954 Swiss psychologist Jean Piaget (1896–1980) publishes his *The Origin of Intelligence in Children*.

1954 Chinese scientist Min-Chueh Chang (1909–91) and US biologists Gregory Pincus (1903–67) and Frank Colton (1923–) invent the contraceptive pill.

1954 British novelist William Golding (1911–93) publishes his *Lord of the Flies*.

1954 French author Françoise Sagan (1935–) publishes her *Bonjour Tristesse*.

1954 British novelist J.R.R. Tolkien (1892–1973) publishes the first volume of his *Lord of the Rings*.

ASIA AND AUSTRALASIA	AFRICA	EUROPE

1955

1955 After a civil war South Vietnam becomes a republic under President Ngo Dinh DIEM (1901–63).

1955 Turkey and Iraq sign the Baghdad Pact defense treaty.

1955 Twenty-nine nonaligned nations meet at Bandung in Indonesia.

1955 Allied occupation troops withdraw from West Germany, which joins Nato.

1955 Communist countries of E Europe form the Warsaw Pact with the Soviet Union.

1955 Austria, Spain, Italy, Portugal, Ireland, Bulgaria and Hungary are admitted to the UN.

1955 First summit conference of world leaders takes place in Geneva.

1956

1956 Islamic republic of Pakistan is declared.

1956 Solomon BANDARANAIKE (1899–1959) is elected prime minister of Ceylon (present-day Sri Lanka).

1956 France cedes its colonies on the subcontinent to India.

1956 Sudan and Morocco become independent.

1956 Gamal NASSER (1918–70) becomes president of Egypt and nationalizes the Suez canal; Israel invades Egypt; Britain and France send troops but withdraw under international pressure.

1956 British deport Archbishop MAKARIOS (1913–77) from Cyprus.

1956 Hungarian prime minister Imre NAGY (1896–1958) takes charge of an anticommunist uprising that is quickly crushed by Soviet troops; Nagy is replaced by János KÁDÁR (1912–89).

1957

1957 Malayan Federation gains independence.

1957 Israel evacuates the Gaza strip.

1957 NORODOM SIHANOUK (1922–) again becomes head of state in Cambodia.

1957 British colonies of the Gold Coast and Togoland are joined to form the independent state of Ghana.

1957 Habib BOURGUIBA (1903–) becomes president of the republic of Tunisia.

1957 Morocco becomes a kingdom under MUHAMMAD V (1909–61).

1957 Harold MACMILLAN (1894–1986) becomes British prime minister.

1957 Saar region is returned to West Germany.

1957 OLAF V (1903–91) becomes king of Norway.

1957 France, Belgium, the Netherlands, Luxembourg, Italy and West Germany sign the treaty of Rome establishing the European Economic Community (EEC) or Common Market.

1958

1958 Egypt and Syria form the United Arab Republic (UAR).

1958 Iraq and Jordan form a short-lived Arab Federation; the federation is ended by a military coup in Iraq, which becomes a republic.

1958 Chinese bombard the Quemoy islands off Formosa (present-day Taiwan).

1958 US troops intervene during elections in Beirut, Lebanon.

1958 After a military coup in Pakistan, Muhammad AYUB KHAN (1907–74) becomes president

1958 Niger, Upper Volta, Ivory Coast, Dahomey, Senegal, Mauritania, Congo and Gabon gain limited independence from France.

1958 Guinea becomes an independent republic.

1958 Mali and Senegal form the Federation of Mali.

1958 FLN rebels declare a provisional government in Algeria.

1958 Belgium, the Netherlands and Luxembourg become a single economic unit – Benelux.

1958 New constitution establishes the French fifth republic; Charles DE GAULLE (1890–1970) is elected president.

1958 Nikita KHRUSHCHEV (1894–1971) replaces Nikolai BULGANIN (1895–1975) as Soviet premier.

1959

1959 Singapore becomes an independent state.

1959 Antarctica is safeguarded by international treaty.

1959 Iraq leaves the Baghdad Pact, which becomes the Central Treaty Organization (CENTO).

1959 Chinese troops suppress a rising in Tibet, and the DALAI LAMA (1935–) flees.

1959 Pro-independence riots occur in Nyasaland.

1959 Rioting breaks out in Stanleyville in the Belgian Congo.

1959 Hutu people organize an uprising against the Tutsi in Rwanda.

1959 Ceasefire is agreed in the Algerian revolt.

1959 Eamon DE VALERA (1882–1975) is elected president of Ireland.

THE AMERICAS

1955 US supreme court rules that racial segregation in public schools must soon end.

1955 Juan PERÓN (1895–1974) is forced into exile from Argentina.

1955 General Alfredo STROESSNER (1912–) becomes president of Paraguay after a coup.

1955 US civil rights activist Rosa Parks (1913–) sits in a whites-only seat on a bus in Montgomery, Alabama.

1956 Revolutionary Fidel CASTRO (1926–) lands in Cuba.

1957 Jamaica becomes self-governing.

1957 François "Papa Doc" DUVALIER (1907–71) becomes president of Haiti.

1957 President EISENHOWER (1890–1969) states his doctrine to oppose communism in the Middle East.

1957 US Civil Rights Act appoints a commission to examine African-American voting rights.

1958 British form the Federation of the West Indies.

1958 Military coup overthrows President Pérez Jiménez (1914–) in Venezuela.

1958 US National Aeronautics and Space Administration (NASA) is established.

1959 Cuban revolutionaries capture Havana; Fulgencio BATISTA (1901–73) flees; Castro becomes prime minister.

1959 Alaska and Hawaii become states of the USA.

1959 St. Lawrence Seaway opens.

SCIENCE AND TECHNOLOGY

1955 British engineer Christopher Cockerell (1910–99) invents the hovercraft.

1955 US physicists Clyde Cowan (1919–) and Frederick Reines (1918–98) discover the neutrino.

1956 US engineer Alexander Poniatoff (1892–80) invents a video tape recorder.

1956 Implantable heart pacemaker is invented.

1956 US engineer Jack Backus leads a team that devises the FORTRAN computer programing language.

1957 Soviet Union launches an artificial satellite – *Sputnik I*.

1957 Soviet satellite *Sputnik II* carries the dog Laika into orbit.

1957 UN forms the International Atomic Energy Commission.

1957 Scottish virologist Alick Isaacs (1921–67) discovers interferon.

1957 International Geophysical Year promotes earth sciences.

1958 Nuclear-powered submarine USS *Nautilus* passes beneath the North Pole.

1958 British industrialist Alistair Pilkington (1920–95) invents the float-glass process for making plate glass.

1958 US satellite *Explorer I* discovers the Van Allen radiation belts around the Earth.

1958 Stereophonic music records go on sale in the USA.

1959 Soviet spaceprobe *Lunik 3* photographs the far side of the Moon.

ARTS AND HUMANITIES

1955 Irish dramatist and novelist Samuel BECKETT (1906–89) writes his play *Waiting for Godot*.

1955 French novelist Alain Robbe-Broilet (1922–) publishes his *nouveau roman Le Voyeur*.

1955 US novelist Vladimir NABOKOV (1899–1977) publishes his *Lolita*.

1955 US author James BALDWIN (1924–87) publishes his essays *Notes of a Native Son*.

1956 British dramatist John Osborne (1929–95) writes his play *Look Back in Anger*.

1956 US singer Elvis Presley (1935–77) releases his record *Heartbreak Hotel*.

1956 British philosopher A.J. AYER (1910–89) publishes his *The Problem of Knowledge*.

1956 US singer Frank Sinatra (1915–98) releases his record *Songs for Swinging Lovers*.

1957 US sculptor Alexander Calder (1898–1976) creates his *Mobile* for New York airport.

1957 US poet and novelist Jack KEROUAC (1922–69) publishes his *On the Road*.

1957 Australian novelist Patrick White (1912–90) publishes his *Voss*.

1958 US economist J.K. GALBRAITH (1908–) publishes his *The Affluent Society*.

1958 Russian poet and author Boris PASTERNAK (1890–1960) publishes his novel Dr. *Zhivago*.

1959 US novelist William S. Burroughs (1914–97) publishes his *The Naked Lunch*.

1959 German poet and author Günter GRASS (1927–) publishes his novel *The Tin Drum*.

1959 Irish author Brendan Behan (1923–64) writes the play *The Hostage*.

1960

1960 Ideological and political differences split the Soviet–Chinese alliance.

1960 Mrs. Sirimavo BANDARANAIKE (1916–) is elected prime minister of Ceylon (present-day Sri Lanka).

1960 Achmad SUKARNO (1901–70) assumes dictatorial powers in Indonesia.

1961

1961 India conquers the Portuguese colony of Goa.

1961 Nazi war criminal Adolf Eichmann is tried and sentenced to death in Israel.

1961 US military advisers group in Vietnam is enlarged.

1961 Coup in Syria breaks up the UAR.

1961 Burmese diplomat U THANT (1909–74) is elected secretary-general of the UN.

1962

1962 Western Samoa becomes independent.

1962 Military coup takes power in Thailand.

1962 Chinese troops invade N India, then withdraw to the disputed border.

1963

1963 Malaya, Northern Borneo, Sarawak and Singapore form the Federation of Malaysia.

1963 Military coup overthrows Ngo Dinh DIEM (1901–63) in South Vietnam.

1963 Arrest of Islamic reformer Ruhollah KHOMEINI (1900–89) sparks riots in Tehran.

1963 PARK CHUNG HEE (1917–79) becomes South Korean president.

1964

1964 Indonesian troops invade Malaysia.

1964 China explodes an atom bomb.

1964 Faisal (1905–75) becomes king of Saudi Arabia.

1960 French settlers in Algeria rebel against plans for independence.

1960 Kwame NKRUMAH (1909–72) becomes president of the independent republic of Ghana.

1960 South African troops kill demonstrators at Sharpeville.

1960 Nigeria, Upper Volta, Chad, Ivory Coast, Cameroon, Togo, Gabon, Congo, Mauritania, Somalia and the Malagassy republic become independent.

1960 Belgian Congo gains independence with Patrice LUMUMBA (1925–61) as prime minister; the Congo army mutinies; Belgian troops are sent; the province of Katanga declares independence; UN troops replace Belgian forces; Joseph MOBUTU (1930–97), commander-in-chief of the Congolese army, seizes power.

1961 South Africa becomes a republic and leaves the British commonwealth.

1962 Algeria becomes independent; the French nationalist OAS organizes a revolt.

1962 Uganda becomes independent.

1963 Organization of African Unity (OAU) is formed in Addis Ababa.

1963 Katanga surrenders to the Congo government.

1964 Tanganyika and Zanzibar unite to form Tanzania with Julius NYERERE (1922–) as president.

1964 ANC leader Nelson MANDELA (1918–) is sentenced to life imprisonment in South Africa.

1964 Zambia, formerly N Rhodesia, becomes independent under president Kenneth KAUNDA (1924–).

1964 Kenya becomes independent under President Jomo KENYATTA (1893–1978).

1960 Soviets shoot down a US U2 spyplane and capture pilot Gary Powers.

1960 NonCommon Market countries form the European Free Trade Association.

1960 Military coup takes power in Turkey.

1960 Cyprus becomes independent under President MAKARIOS (1913–77).

1960 USA and Canada join W European nations to form the Organization for Economic Cooperation and Development (OECD).

1961 Soviet authorities build a wall across the divided city of Berlin.

1961 Twenty-five countries attend a conference of non-aligned nations in Belgrade.

1962 Disarmament conference starts in Geneva.

1963 France vetoes the British application to join the Common Market.

1963 Britain, the Soviet Union and the USA sign a nuclear-test treaty banning all but underground explosions.

1964 UN troops are sent in response to fighting between Greeks and Turks in Cyprus.

1964 Harold WILSON (1916–95) is elected British prime minister.

1964 Malta gains its independence from Britain.

1964 Nikita KHRUSHCHEV (1894–1971) is deposed in the Soviet Union; Leonid BREZHNEV (1906–82) becomes first secretary and Aleksei KOSYGIN (1904–80) becomes prime minister.

1964 CONSTANTINE II (1940–) becomes king of Greece.

THE AMERICAS

1960 New city of Brasília becomes the capital of Brazil.

1960 US civil rights activist Martin Luther KING (1929–68) organizes a sit-in demonstration in Greensboro, North Carolina.

1960 USA embargoes exports to Cuba and cuts Cuban sugar quotas by 95%.

1960 Israeli agents kidnap Nazi war criminal Adolf EICHMANN (1906–62) in Argentina.

1960 John F. KENNEDY (1917–63) is elected US president.

1961 President Kennedy announces the formation of the Peace Corps.

1961 Cuban exiles in the USA attempt an invasion of Cuba at the Bay of Pigs.

1961 US civil rights activists organize "freedom rides" on segregated buses.

1962 Jamaica and Trinidad and Tobago become independent.

1962 Soviet Union attempts to install nuclear missiles in Cuba; the USA imposes a naval blockade.

1963 Hot-line is installed between the White House and the Kremlin.

1963 Martin Luther King leads a civil rights march to Washington, D.C.

1963 Kennedy is assassinated in Dallas, Texas; Lyndon JOHNSON (1908–73) becomes US president.

1964 Johnson is elected US president.

1964 Free Speech movement starts in US universities.

1964 US government passes the Gulf of Tonkin resolution authorizing military action in Southeast Asia.

SCIENCE AND TECHNOLOGY

1960 French explode an atom bomb.

1960 US chemist Robert Woodward (1917–79) synthesizes chlorophyll.

1960 US physicist Theodore Maiman (1927–) invents the laser.

1961 Soviet cosmonaut Yuri GAGARIN (1934–68) orbits the Earth.

1961 US astronaut Alan Shepard (1923–98) makes a suborbital flight.

1962 US astronaut John GLENN (1921–) orbits the Earth.

1962 US telecommunications satellite *Telstar* is launched.

1963 Soviet cosmonaut Valentina Tereshkova (1937–) orbits the Earth.

1963 US astronomer Maarten Schmidt (1929–) discovers quasars.

1964 US physicist Murray GELL-MANN (1929–) proposes the existence of quarks.

1964 Japanese railroads begin running high-speed "bullet" trains.

1964 US engineer Robert Moog (1934–) invents an electronic music synthesizer.

ARTS AND HUMANITIES

1960 Guggenheim Museum, designed by US architect Frank Lloyd WRIGHT (1869–1959), opens in New York.

1960 US author John Updike (1932–) publishes his novel *Rabbit Run*.

1960 French dramatist Eugène Ionesco (1912–94) writes his play *The Rhinoceros*.

1960 British author Elias Canetti (1905–94) publishes his *Crowds and Power*.

1961 British pop group The Beatles play their first performance at the Cavern Club in Liverpool.

1961 US novelist Joseph Heller (1923–) publishes his *Catch-22*.

1961 US singer-songwriter Bob Dylan (1941–) makes his debut performance in New York City.

1961 Soviet dancer Rudolf NUREYEV (1938–93) defects to the USA.

1962 US economist Milton FRIEDMAN (1912–) publishes his *Capitalism and Freedom*.

1962 British artist Graham Sutherland (1903–80) creates his *Christ in Glory* tapestry for the rebuilt Coventry cathedral.

1962 Soviet novelist Alexander SOLZHENITSYN (1918–) publishes his *One Day in the Life of Ivan Denisovich*.

1963 US artist Roy Lichtenstein (1923–97) paints his *Whaam!*.

1963 US environmentalist Rachel CARSON (1907–64) publishes her *Silent Spring*.

1964 Canadian academic Marshall McLuhan (1911–80) publishes his *Understanding Media*.

1964 US novelist Saul BELLOW (1915–) publishes his *Herzog*.

1964 US poet Robert Lowell 1917–77) publishes his *For the Union Dead*.

1960

1961

1962

1963

1964

ASIA AND AUSTRALASIA	AFRICA	EUROPE

1965

1965 USA begins a bombing campaign ("Rolling Thunder") against North Vietnam.

1965 Australian, New Zealand and South Korean troops are sent to Vietnam.

1965 Singapore becomes an independent republic.

1965 War breaks out between India and Pakistan.

1965 Gambia becomes independent.

1965 White settlers, led by Ian SMITH (1919–), opposed to black majority rule declare Southern Rhodesia independent (UDI).

1965 Houari BOUMÉDIENNE (1925–78) overthrows President Ahmed BEN BELLA (1916–) in Algeria.

1965 Charles DE GAULLE (1890–1970) defeats François MITTERRAND (1916–96) in the French presidential elections.

1966

1966 Indira GANDHI (1917–84) is elected prime minister of India.

1966 MAO ZEDONG (1893–1976) launches the Cultural Revolution in China; Red Guards are formed.

1966 Raden SUHARTO (1921–) seizes power in Indonesia.

1966 Indonesian-Malay conflict ends.

1966 Military coup overthrows President Nkrumah in Ghana.

1966 South African prime minister Hendrik VERWOERD (b.1901) is assassinated; Balthazaar VORSTER (1915–83) succeeds him.

1966 Colonel Jean BOKASSA (1921–96) leads a coup in the Central African Republic.

1966 Milton OBOTE (1924–) becomes president of Uganda.

1966 Bechuanaland becomes independent as Botswana; Basutoland becomes independent as Lesotho.

1966 France withdraws from NATO.

1967 Coup by Greek colonels takes power in Athens; King CONSTANTINE II (1940–) flees after a failed counter-coup.

1967 Nicolae CEAUŞESCU (1918–89) becomes head of state in Romania.

1967

1967 Israeli defeats its Arab neighbors in a six-day war; it recaptures the West Bank and E Jerusalem and occupies the Golan Heights.

1967 State of Biafra declares its independence and secedes from Nigeria; a civil war starts.

1967 Britain evacuates Aden; the People's Democratic Republic of Yemen is established.

1967 Forty-six nations sign the General Agreement on Trade and Tariffs (GATT) in Geneva.

1967 EEC becomes the European Community (EC).

1968

1968 North Vietnam launches the Tet offensive; the US bombing campaign is halted; US troops massacre villagers at Mai Lai.

1968 Ba'athist officers seize power in Iraq.

1968 Swaziland becomes an independent kingdom.

1968 equatorial Guinea gains independence from Spain.

1968 Famine conditions develop in Biafra.

1968 Students and workers build barricades in Paris; student leader Rudi Dutschke is shot in West Germany.

1968 Czech politician Alexander DUBČEK (1921–92) introduces reforms; a Soviet invasion ends the "Prague Spring".

1968 Albania withdraws from the Warsaw Pact.

1968 Spain closes its frontier with Gibraltar.

1969

1969 Yasir ARAFAT (1929–) is elected chairman of the Palestine Liberation Organization (PLO).

1969 Military coup seizes power in Pakistan.

1969 US troops begin withdrawing from Vietnam.

1969 Soviet and Chinese troops clash along their border.

1969 Ferdinand MARCOS (1917–89) is elected president of the Philippines.

1969 Golda MEIR (1898–1978) becomes prime minister of Israel.

1969 Dhofar rebellion starts in S Oman.

1969 Colonel Muammar al-QADDAFI (1942–) overthrows King IDRIS (1890–1983) in Libya.

1969 Left-wing coup seizes power in Sudan.

1969 Violence flares between Catholics and Protestants in Ulster.

1969 De Gaulle resigns; Georges POMPIDOU (1911–74) is elected French president.

1969 Willy BRANDT (1913–92) becomes chancellor of West Germany.

1969 Spanish dictator Franciso FRANCO (1892–1975) names Bourbon prince JUAN CARLOS (1938–) as his successor.

THE AMERICAS

1965 African-American activist MALCOLM X (b.1925) is assassinated in New York.

1965 Medicare and other welfare legislation is passed in the USA.

1965 Race riots erupt in the Watts district of Los Angeles.

1965 Military coup leads to widespread fighting in the Dominican Republic; US marines land and are then replaced by OAS forces.

1966 British Guyana and Barbados become independent.

1966 African-American activists Bobby Seale (1937–) and Huey Newton (1942–89) form the Black Panthers.

1967 US Court of Appeals orders the desegregation of Southern schools.

1967 Revolutionary Che GUEVERA (b.1928) is killed by Bolivian troops.

1968 Pierre TRUDEAU (1919–) becomes Canadian prime minister.

1968 UN approves a nuclear non-proliferation treaty.

1968 Student demonstrations disrupt the start of the Olympic Games in Mexico City.

1968 Martin Luther KING (b.1929) is assassinated in Memphis.

1968 Senator Robert KENNEDY (b.1925) is assassinated in Los Angeles.

1968 Antiwar protesters demonstrate outside the Democratic Party convention in Chicago.

1968 Richard NIXON (1913–94) is elected US president.

1969 War breaks out between Honduras and El Salvador.

SCIENCE AND TECHNOLOGY

1965 Soviet cosmonaut Alexei Leonov takes a "space walk" while in orbit.

1965 US spaceprobe *Mariner IV* orbits Mars and transmits photographs back to Earth.

1965 French launch an artificial satellite.

1965 US physicists Arno Penzias (1933–) and Robert Wilson (1936–) discover microwave cosmic background radiation.

1966 Soviet spaceprobe *Luna 9* makes a soft landing on the Moon.

1966 British engineers Charles Kao and George Hockham invent fiber-optic telephone cable.

1967 International treaty bans weapons of mass destruction from space.

1967 South African surgeon Christiaan BARNARD (1922–) performs a heart transplant.

1967 Chinese explode a hydrogen bomb.

1967 British astronomer Jocelyn Bell (1943–) discovers pulsars.

1968 US astronauts orbit the Moon in the *Apollo 8* spacecraft.

1969 Anglo-French Concorde supersonic passenger aircraft makes its first flight.

1969 US spacecraft *Apollo 11* lands on the Moon; astronaut Neil ARMSTRONG (1930–) takes the first steps.

1969 US engineer Douglas Engelbart (1925–) invents the "mouse" computer input device.

1969 DDT is banned in the USA.

ARTS AND HUMANITIES

1965 US author Truman Capote (1924–84) publishes his nonfictional *In Cold Blood*.

1965 US dramatist Neil Simon (1927–) writes his play *The Odd Couple*.

1965 US consumer lobbyist Ralph Nader (1934–) publishes his book *Unsafe at Any Speed*.

1966 Vatican abolishes the Inquisition.

1966 Japanese author Yukio MISHIMA (1925–70) publishes his novel *The Sailor Who fell from Grace with the Sea*.

1966 *Ariel* by US poet Sylvia PLATH (1932–63) is published posthumously.

1967 US artist Andy WARHOL (1928–87) publishes his print of *Marilyn Monroe*.

1967 British artist David HOCKNEY (1937–) paints his *A Bigger Splash*.

1967 The Beatles release their record *Sergeant Pepper's Lonely Hearts Club Band*.

1967 Colombian novelist Gabriel GARCÍA MÁRQUEZ (1928–) publishes his *One Hundred Years of Solitude*.

1967 British dramatist Tom Stoppard (1937–) writes his play *Rosencrantz and Guildenstern are Dead*.

1968 US psychologist Timothy Leary (1920–96) publishes his *The Politics of Ecstasy*.

1969 British novelist John Fowles (1926–) publishes his *The French Lieutenant's Woman*.

1969 US novelist Philip Roth (1933–) publishes his *Portnoy's Complaint*.

1969 US novelist Kurt Vonnegut Jr.(1922–) publishes his *Slaughterhouse Five*.

1969 US sculptor Claes Oldenburg (1929–) produces his *Lipstick*.

1970

1970 NORODOM SIHANOUK (1922–) is overthrown; communist guerrillas threaten Phnom Penh; Cambodia becomes the Khmer Republic.

1970 Sultan Qaboos (1940–) seizes power from his father in Oman.

1970 USA resumes bombing North Vietnam.

1970 Palestinians hijack passenger jets and blow them up at Dawson's Field in Jordan.

1970 Jordanian forces loyal to King Hussein evict the PLO in a brief civil war.

1970 Hafez al-ASSAD (1928–) seizes power and becomes president of Syria.

1971

1971 East Pakistan declares independence; West Pakistan declares war; India intervenes in the fighting; the republic of Bangladesh is established.

1971 Bahrain and Qatar become independent as does the newly formed United Arab Emirates.

1971 China is admitted to the UN; nationalist Taiwan is expelled.

1972

1972 Japanese Red Army terrorists kill passengers at Tel-Aviv airport.

1972 Ceylon becomes the independent republic of Sri Lanka.

1973

1973 Last US combat troops leave Vietnam.

1973 President Zulfikar Ali BHUTTO (1928–79) issues a new constitution in Pakistan.

1973 Arab countries attack Israel; Egyptian forces invade across the Suez canal but are defeated; Israel wins the war.

1973 Afghanistan becomes a republic after a coup.

1973 Arab states cut oil production and cause a worldwide energy crisis.

1974

1974 India explodes an atom bomb.

1970 Biafran War ends with victory for the federal government forces.

1970 Anwar SADAT (1918–81) becomes president of Egypt.

1970 Rhodesia declares itself a republic.

1970 New constitution restores the Moroccan parliament.

1971 Egypt, Libya and Syria form the federation of Arab republics.

1971 Former Belgian Congo is renamed Zaire.

1971 Army sergeant Idi AMIN (1925–) seizes power and becomes president of Uganda.

1972 Amin expels Asians from Uganda.

▲ *Sadat led Egypt into war with Israel in 1973, demanding the return of Egyptian land occupied by Israel in 1967. Five years later Sadat worked out peace terms with the Israeli premier Menachem Begin. They shared the 1978 Nobel Peace Prize for their attempts to end the lengthy Arab-Israeli conflict.*

1974 Ethiopian emperor HAILE SELASSIE (1892–1975) is deposed and a republic is declared.

1970 Strategic Arms Limitation Treaty (SALT) talks begin in Helsinki.

1970 Portuguese dictator António SALAZAR (b.1889) dies.

1971 Angry Brigade terrorists send letter bombs to British politicians.

1971 Austrian diplomat Kurt WALDHEIM (1918–) becomes UN secretary-general.

1972 Britain, Denmark and Ireland join the EC.

1972 Members of the terrorist Baader-Meinhof gang are arrested in West Germany.

1972 British impose direct rule in Ulster.

1972 Palestinian terrorists kidnap and kill Israeli athletes at the Munich Olympics.

1973 Paris peace agreement ends US involvement in Vietnam.

1973 "Cod war" breaks out between Iceland and Britain over fishing rights.

1973 Greece officially becomes a republic.

1973 British prime minister Edward HEATH (1916–) declares a state of emergency and a three-day working week because of strikes.

1974 Left-wingers seize power in a bloodless revolution in Portugal.

1974 Valéry GISCARD D'ESTAING (1926–) becomes president of France.

1974 Greek nationalists stage a coup in Cyprus and declare union with Greece; Turkish troops invade and conquer half the island.

1974 Junta of Greek colonels abdicates power.

1974 Illegal Irish Republican Army (IRA) intensifies its bombing campaign against British targets.

THE AMERICAS

1970 US National Guard soldiers kill four protesting students at Kent State university in Ohio.

1970 Weathermen radicals bomb a US Army research center.

1970 Salvador ALLENDE (1908–73) is elected president of Chile.

1970 French-speaking separatists in Quebec kidnap and murder a Canadian official.

1971 Tupamaros guerrillas kidnap foreign businessmen in Uruguay.

1971 US officer William Calley is found guilty of the Mai Lai massacre.

1972 Burglars are arrested in the Democratic Party election headquarters at the Watergate Hotel in Washington, D.C.

1973 US national security adviser Henry KISSINGER (1923–) is appointed secretary of state.

1973 Juan PERÓN (1895–1974) returns to Argentina and becomes president.

1973 British Honduras is renamed Belize.

1973 General Augusto PINOCHET (1915–) leads a military coup that seizes power in Chile.

1974 Isabel Perón (1931–) assumes the presidency of Argentina on her husband's death.

1974 US president Richard NIXON (1913–94) resigns over the Watergate scandal; Gerald FORD (1913–) becomes president.

SCIENCE AND TECHNOLOGY

1970 China launches an artificial satellite.

1970 Soviet space probe *Venera VII* soft-lands on Venus and sends information from the surface.

1970 Boeing 747 "Jumbo jet" enters service.

1971 US engineer Ted Hoff (1937–) invents the computer microprocessor ("chip").

1971 Electronic pocket calculator is invented.

1971 Soviet Union launches the *Salyut* space station into orbit.

1971 US paleontologist Stephen Jay GOULD (1941–) proposes his theory of punctuated equilibrium in evolution.

1972 US spaceprobe *Pioneer 10* is launched.

1973 US engineer Nolan Bushnell (1943–) invents the video game Pong.

1973 USA launches the *Skylab* space station.

1973 US biochemists Stanley Cohen (1935–) and Herbert Boyer (1936–) invent recombinant DNA genetic engineering when they use restriction enzymes to "cut and splice" DNA.

1974 US paleontologist Donald Johanson (1942–) discovers "Lucy" – a partial skeleton of *Australopithecus afarensis* – in Ethiopia.

1974 Bar codes are introduced in US shops.

ARTS AND HUMANITIES

1970 US revolutionary Jerry Rubin publishes his Yippie manifesto *Do It!*.

1970 Australian feminist Germaine GREER (1939–) publishes her *The Female Eunuch*.

1970 Complete *New English Bible* is published.

1970 British poet Ted HUGHES (1930–98) publishes his *Crow*.

1970 US musician Jimi Hendrix (b.1942) dies of a drug overdose.

1970 Italian dramatist Dario Fo (1926–) writes his *Accidental Death of an Anarchist*.

1971 Death of the US jazz musician Louis Armstrong (b.1900).

1972 Finnish architect Alvar AALTO (1898–1976) designs the North Jutland Museum in Denmark.

1972 US artist Christo Javaceff (1935–) erects his sculpture *Valley Curtain* in Colorado.

1972 British novelist Anthony Burgess (1917–93) writes his *A Clockwork Orange*.

1973 US novelist Thomas Pynchon (1937–) publishes his *Gravity's Rainbow*.

1973 German economist Ernst Shumacher (1911–77) publishes his *Small is Beautiful: A Study of Economics as if People Mattered*.

1974 Terracotta army buried with the first Chinese emperor is discovered.

1974 US poet and author Erica Jong (1942–) publishes her novel *Fear of Flying*.

1974 US author Robert Pirsig (1928–) publishes his *Zen and the Art of Motorcycle Maintenance*.

1974 US journalists Bob Woodward and Carl Bernstein publish their *All the President's Men*.

ASIA AND AUSTRALASIA	AFRICA	EUROPE

1975

1975 Clashes in Beirut between Palestinians and Christian Falangists start the Lebanese civil war.

1975 Cambodian Khmer Rouge guerrillas under POL POT (1928–98) capture Phnom Penh; "year zero" starts the systematic extermination of educated city dwellers.

1975 Saigon is occupied by North Vietnamese forces; end of the Vietnam War; Vietnam becomes one country with Hanoi as its capital.

1975 Papua New Guinea gains independence from Australia.

1975 Communists take control in Laos.

1976

1976 Deaths of MAO ZEDONG (b.1893) and prime minister ZHOU ENLAI (b.1898) cause a leadership crisis in China.

1977

1977 Menachem BEGIN (1913–92) becomes prime minister of Israel.

1977 General ZIA UL-HAQ (1924–88) seizes power in Pakistan.

1977 Chinese "Gang of Four", including Mao's wife, are expelled from power; DENG XIAOPING (1904–97) becomes Chinese premier.

1978

1978 Revolution overthrows the republic in Afghanistan.

1978 Vietnam invades Cambodia.

1979

1979 Vietnamese troops expel Pol Pot from Phnom Penh.

1979 Iranian shah Muhammad Reza PAHLAVI (1919–80) flees a revolution in Iran; Ayatollah KHOMEINI (1900–89) arrives from Paris; students storm the US embassy in Tehran and take the staff hostage.

1979 Soviet Union invades Afghanistan.

1979 SADDAM Hussein (1937–) seizes power in Iraq.

1975 Mozambique and Angola gain independence from Portugal.

1975 South Africa establishes Transkei as an "independent" black homeland.

1976 Schoolchildren demonstrating in Soweto are killed by South African security forces.

1976 Israeli commandos raid Entebbe airport in Uganda to free hijacked passengers.

1976 Seychelles becomes independent.

1977 German commandos free hijacked passengers at Mogadishu in Somalia.

1977 South African political activist Steve BIKO (b.1956) is murdered in police custody.

1977 Cuban troops assist Ethiopian forces against rebels in Eritrea.

1977 Jean BOKASSA (1921–96) proclaims himself emperor of a Central African Empire.

1978 French and Belgian paratroops try to restore order in Kolwezi after a secessionist rebellion in Zaire.

1979 Tanzanian troops invade Uganda and oust Idi AMIN (1925–).

1979 Conference in London ends the civil war in Rhodesia between guerrillas and the white minority government, and agrees majority rule.

1975 Helsinki accords on peace and human rights mark a major step in the process of détente between NATO and the Warsaw Pact.

1975 Britain becomes an oil-producing nation.

1975 Turkish Federated State of North Cyprus is established; UN forces maintain the border with the Greek sector of the island.

1975 Francisco FRANCO (b.1892) dies; JUAN CARLOS (1938–) becomes king of Spain.

1975 Terrorists led by "Carlos" take hostage members of the Organization of Gasolineeum Exporting Countries in Vienna.

1977 Czech political reformers form the Charter 77 organization.

1977 Dutch marines rescue hostages on a train hijacked by South Moluccan terrorists.

1977 Adolfo Suarez (1932–) is elected prime minister of Spain.

1978 Italian Red Brigade terrorists kidnap and murder politician Alberto Moro (b.1916).

1978 Group of Seven (G7) industrialized nations meet to discuss economic policy.

1979 Margaret THATCHER (1925–) is elected British prime minister.

THE AMERICAS

1975 Dutch Guiana becomes the independent state of Surinam.

1976 Coup overthrows Isabel Perón (1931–) in Argentina.

1976 Jimmy CARTER (1924–) is elected US president.

1977 USA and Panama sign a treaty for the return of the canal zone to Panama.

1978 Anwar SADAT (1918–81) and Menachem Begin meet at Camp David.

1978 Dominica gains independence from Britain.

1979 Israel and Egypt sign a peace treaty in Washington, D.C.

1979 Sandinista guerrillas capture Managua; President Anastasio SOMOZA (1925–80) flees Nicaragua; Daniel ORTEGA (1945–) forms a revolutionary government.

1979 Nuclear accident occurs at Three Mile Island power station in Pennsylvania.

1979 Hundreds of US cultists commit suicide in the People's Temple at Jonestown, Guyana.

SCIENCE AND TECHNOLOGY

1975 *Apollo* and *Soyuz* spacecraft link up while in orbit.

1975 Personal computer (PC) in kit form goes on sale in the USA.

1976 Legionnaire's disease is identified in the USA.

1976 US *Viking* probes send back pictures from the surface of Mars.

1977 British biochemist Frederick SANGER (1918–) discovers the full sequence of bases in DNA.

1977 US engineer Paul MacCready (1925–) designs a human-powered aircraft.

1977 Apple II personal computer is introduced.

1978 World Health Organization (WHO) announces that, apart from some laboratory samples, smallpox has been eradicated.

1978 First in-vitro fertilization baby is born in Britain.

1978 British paleontologist Mary LEAKEY (1913–96) discovers 3.5-million-year-old human footprints in Tanzania.

1979 US *Voyager* spaceprobes transmit close-up pictures of Jupiter and its moons.

1979 British scientist James Lovelock (1919–) proposes his Gaia theory.

1979 Liquid crystal display (LCD) television is developed in Japan.

ARTS AND HUMANITIES

1975 Mexican novelist Carlos FUENTES (1928–) publishes his *Terra Nostra*.

1975 US novelist E.L. Doctorow (1931–) publishes his *Ragtime*.

1975 Argentine writer Jorge Louis BORGES (1899–1986) publishes his *The Book of Sand*.

1976 US linguist Noam CHOMSKY (1928–) publishes his *Reflections on Language*.

1976 US author Alex Haley (1921–92) publishes his *Roots: The Saga of an American Family*.

1976 US novelist Paul Theroux (1941–) publishes his *The Family Arsenal*.

1977 Pompidou Center art gallery, designed by Richard Rogers (1933–) and Italian architect Renzo Piano (1937–), opens in Paris.

1977 British novelist Paul Scott (1930–78) publishes his *Staying On*.

1978 US novelist John Irving (1942–) publishes his *The World According to Garp*.

1978 British novelist A.S. BYATT (1936–) publishes her *The Virgin in the Garden*.

1978 US author Susan SONTAG (1933–) publishes her *Illness as Metaphor*.

1978 French philosopher Jacques DERRIDA (1930–) publishes his *Truth in Painting*.

1978 US author Armistead Maupin (1944–) publishes his *Tales of the City*.

1979 Czech novelist Milan Kundera (1929–) publishes his *The Book of Laughter and Forgetting*.

ASIA AND AUSTRALASIA	AFRICA	EUROPE

1980

1980 Opposition groups in the Syrian cities of Homs and Aleppo are ruthlessly suppressed by government forces.

1980 Attempt by US special forces to rescue hostages held in Tehran ends in disastrous failure.

1980 Iraq invades Iran in order to gain control of the Shatt al-Arab waterway.

1980 Rhodesia becomes independent as Zimbabwe; Robert MUGABE (1925–) is elected prime minister.

1980 Libya invades and occupies N Chad.

1980 Following the death of President TITO (b.1892), Yugoslavia comes under collective leadership.

1980 Polish shipyard workers led by Lech WALESA (1943–) form the Solidarity trades union.

1980 Greece joins the EC.

1981

1981 US hostages in Tehran are released.

1981 Chinese "Gang of Four" are convicted of treason.

1981 Israeli aircraft destroy an Iraqi nuclear reactor in a secret bombing raid.

1981 Anwar SADAT (1918–81) is assassinated; Hosni MUBARAK (1928–) becomes president Egypt.

1981 Nationalist civil guards attempt a coup in Spain.

1981 François MITTERRAND (1916–96) is elected president of France.

1981 Andreas PAPANDREOU (1919–96) is elected prime minister of Greece.

1981 Solidarity protests result in martial law being declared in Poland under General Wojciech Jaruzelski (1923–).

1982

1982 Israel invades Lebanon and forces the PLO to evacuate to Tunisia and Cyprus; S Lebanon comes under Israeli occupation; an international peacekeeping force arrives in Beirut.

1982 Iranian forces recapture port of Khurramshahr.

1982 Israel returns the Sinai peninsula to Egypt.

1982 Helmut KOHL (1930–) is elected German chancellor.

1983

1983 US and French troops are killed in bomb attacks in Beirut.

1983 Filipino politician Benigno Aquino (b.1932) is assassinated when he returns to Manilla.

1983 Yitzhak SHAMIR (1915–) becomes prime minister of Israel.

space shuttle Illustrated above is the first stage of a space shuttle flight – reaching orbit. The orbiter (1) is propelled upward by solid fuel boosters (2) and engines (3), fed with fuel from the external tank (4).

1983 Yuri ANDROPOV (1914–84) becomes president of the Soviet Union.

1983 Green party wins its first parliamentary seats in West German elections.

1983 Martial law ends in Poland.

1983 US cruise missiles are located at airbases in Britain.

1983 Turkish N Cyprus declares its independence under president Rauf Denktas.

1984

1984 Brunei becomes an independent sultanate.

1984 Indian troops storm Sikh protesters at the Golden Temple in Amriczar; Indira GANDHI (b.1917) is assassinated; Rajiv GANDHI (1944–91) becomes prime minister.

1984 Britain agrees to return Hong Kong to China.

1984 Chinese government introduces liberal economic reforms.

1984 Shimon PERES (1923–) becomes prime minister of Israel.

1984 South African president P.W. BOTHA (1916–) grants limited political rights to Asians and "coloreds".

1984 Konstantin CHERNENKO (1911–85) becomes president of the Soviet Union.

1980 Mount St. Helens erupts in Washington state.

1980 Ronald REAGAN (1911–) is elected US president.

1980 Ex-Nicaraguan president Anastasio SOMOZA (b.1925) is assassinated in Paraguay.

1980 US composer Philip GLASS (1937–) writes his opera *Satyagraha*.

1980 Former-Beatle John Lennon (b.1940) is murdered in New York.

1980

1981 Belize, Antigua and Barbuda gain independence from Britain.

1981 Peruvian diplomat Javier PÉREZ DE CUÉLLAR (1920–) becomes UN secretary-general.

1981 US space shuttle makes its first orbital flight.

1981 French high-speed train (TGV) service enters operation.

1981 IBM launch a PC using the Microsoft MS-DOS operating system.

1981 Disease Acquired Immune Deficiency Syndrome (AIDS) is identified.

1981 Italian author Umberto ECO (1932–) publishes his novel *The Name of the Rose*.

1981 US author Toni MORRISON (1931–) publishes her *Tar Baby*.

1981 Peruvian author Mario Vargas Llosa (1936–) publishes his novel *The War of the End of the World*.

1981 Death of the Jamaican musician Bob Marley (b.1945).

1981

1982 Argentine troops invade the Falkland Islands (Malvinas); British forces invade and recapture the islands.

1982 Compact music disks (CDs) are introduced.

1982 Genetically engineered insulin is produced for human use.

1982 Chilean novelist Isabel Allende (1942–) publishes her novel *The House of the Spirits*.

1982 Australian novelist Thomas Keneally (1935–) publishes his *Schindler's Ark*.

1982 US architect Maya Lin (1959–) designs the Vietnam Veterans' Memorial in Washington, D.C.

1982

1983 US president Ronald Reagan announces the development of a Strategic Defense Initiative (SDI) or "Star Wars" defense system; he also announces support for the Nicaraguan Contras.

1983 US marines invade Grenada and overthrow a revolutionary government.

1983 Martin Luther King Day is inaugurated in the USA.

1983 French physician Luc Montagnier (1932–) identifies the human immunodeficiency virus (HIV) as the infective agent that causes AIDS.

1983 *Pioneer 10* leaves the solar system.

1983 Italian novelist Italo Calvino (1923–85) publishes his Mr. *Palomar*.

1983 US poet and author Alice Walker (1944–) publishes her novel *The Color Purple*.

1983

1984 Canadian prime minister Pierre TRUDEAU (1919–) resigns.

1984 US troops are withdrawn from Lebanon.

1984 Daniel ORTEGA (1945–) is elected president of Nicaragua.

1984 Cellphone network is launched in Chicago, USA.

1984 British geneticist Alec JEFFREYS (1950–) devises a technique for genetic fingerprinting.

1984 Apple company launches the Macintosh computer featuring windows, icons, a mouse and pull-down menus.

1984 Scottish novelist Iain Banks (1954–) publishes his *The Wasp Factory*.

1984 British novelist J.G. Ballard (1930–) publishes his *Empire of the Sun*.

1984

1985	**1985** French secret agents blow up the Greenpeace ship *Rainbow Warrior* in New Zealand.	**1985** USA and the EC impose economic sanctions against South Africa. **1985** Famine in Ethiopia is partially alleviated by funds raised by the international Live Aid pop concert.	**1985** Spain re-opens its border with Gibraltar. **1985** Mikhail GORBACHEV (1931–) becomes general secretary of the Communist Party of the Soviet Union. **1985** Palestinian terrorist hijack the cruise ship *Achille Lauro* and attack Israeli airline desks at Rome and Vienna airports.
1986	**1986** Ferdinand MARCOS (1917–89) flees the Philippines; Cory AQUINO (1933–) becomes president. **1986** Iranian forces capture the Iraqi port of Al Faw.	**1986** US warplanes bomb Libya.	**1986** Spain and Portugal join the EC. **1986** Accident at the Chernobyl nuclear reactor in Ukraine releases a radioactive cloud over central and N Europe.
1987	**1987** Iran and Iraq use missiles to bombard each other's cities. **1987** Syrian troops enter Beirut to keep the peace. **1987** Indian troops impose a ceasefire in the conflict between the Tamil Tiger guerrillas and Sri Lankan government forces.	**1987** Chadian forces, assisted by the French foreign legion, expel the Libyans from N Chad.	**1986** Swedish prime minister Olaf Palme (1927–) is murdered. **1987** Gorbachev announces policies of *glasnost* and *perestroika* in the Soviet Union.
1988	**1988** Soviet republics of Azerbaijan and Armenia clash over the enclave of Nagorno-Karabakh. **1988** Iran-Iraq War ends in stalemate. **1988** General ZIA UL-HAQ (b.1924) is assassinated; Benazir BHUTTO (1953–) becomes prime minister of Pakistan. **1988** Soviet Union begins withdrawing troops from Afghanistan.	 ▲ *Milošević, a hardline Serbian nationalist, withdrew the status of Vojvodina and Kosovo as autonomous provinces when he became Serbian president. Opposed to the breakup of Yugoslavia, Milošević supported those who fought for a "Greater Serbia". In the late 1990s his attempt to ethnically "cleanse" Kosovo of its Albanian population provoked NATO attacks.*	**1988** USA and the Soviet Union agree to limit the number of missiles in Europe by the Intermediate-range Nuclear Forces (INF) treaty. **1988** US passenger jet is blown up by a terrorist bomb over Loccurbie in Scotland. **1989** Solidarity candidates win a majority in Polish elections. **1989** Hungary adopts a new constitution and opens its borders; popular protests in East Germany lead to the dismantling of the Berlin wall. **1989** Popular revolution overthrows Nicolae CEAUŞESCU (1918–89) in Romania.
1989	**1989** AKIHITO (1933–) becomes emperor of Japan. **1989** Chinese troops kill pro-democracy protesters in Tiananmen Square in Beijing. **1989** AUNG SAN SUU KYI (1945–), leader of the National League for Democracy in Burma, is placed under house arrest by the military junta.	**1989** Cuban troops are withdrawn from Angola; a ceasefire is declared in the civil war. **1989** F.W. DE KLERK (1936–) becomes president of South Africa.	**1989** Vaclav HAVEL (1936–) forms a democratic government in Czechoslovakia. **1989** Slobodan MILOŠEVIĆ (1941–) is elected president of Serbia. **1989** US and Soviet presidents officially declare the end of the Cold War.

THE AMERICAS

1985 Earthquake devastates Mexico City.

1986 Space shuttle Challenger explodes immediately after launch.

1986 Jean Claude "Baby Doc" DUVALIER (1951–) flees Haiti to exile in France.

1987 US colonel Oliver NORTH (1943–) is secretly authorized to sell weapons to Iran, the profits to be used to arm the antiSandinista Contras in Nicaragua; when revealed, the affair causes a major scandal in the USA.

1987 New York Stock Market crashes triggering a worldwide financial crisis; computerized dealing is blamed for the severity of the collapse.

1988 George BUSH (1924–) is elected US president.

1988 Sandinistas and Contras agree an armistice in Nicaragua.

1989 General Manuel NORIEGA (1934–) proclaims himself president of Panama; US troops invade.

1989 Alfredo STROESSNER (1912–) is overthrown by a coup in Paraguay.

1989 San Francisco suffers a major earthquake.

SCIENCE AND TECHNOLOGY

1985 International whaling commission (IWC) bans commercial whale hunts.

1986 European spaceprobe *Giotto* intercepts Halley's comet.

1986 *Voyager II* transmits pictures of Uranus.

1986 US aviators Jeana Yeager and Dick Rutan fly the aircraft *Voyager* nonstop around the world without refueling.

1987 International agreement is reached to limit the amounts of chlorofluorocarbons (CFCs) released into the atmosphere.

1987 Work starts on a tunnel between Britain and France.

1987 Supernova SN1987A is visible to the unaided eye.

1988 US scientists start a project to map the human genome.

1988 British mathematician and cosmologist Stephen HAWKING (1942–) publishes his *A Brief History of Time*.

1989 Convention on the International Trade in Endangered Species (CITES) imposes a worldwide ban on the sale of elephant ivory.

1989 *Voyager II* transmits pictures of Neptune.

ARTS AND HUMANITIES

1985 Headquarters of the Hong Kong and Shanghai Bank, designed by British architect Norman FOSTER (1935–), opens in Hong Kong.

1985 German novelist Patrick Süskind (1949–) publishes his *Perfume*.

1986 Japanese novelist Kazuo Ishiguro (1954–) publishes his *An Artist of the Floating World*.

1986 British composer Andrew Lloyd Webber (1948–) writes his musical *Phantom of the Opera*.

1987 US author Tom Wolfe (1931–) publishes his novel *Bonfire of the Vanities*.

1988 German composer Karlheinz STOCKHAUSEN (1928–) writes his *Montag aus Licht*.

1988 British author Salman RUSHDIE (1947–) publishes his *Satanic Verses*.

1988 Australian novelist Peter Carey (1943–) publishes his *Osautomobile and Lucinda*.

> "Democracy is the wholesome and pure air without which a socialist public organization cannot live a full-blooded life."
>
> Mikhail Gorbachev

ASIA AND AUSTRALASIA

1990 **1990** Benazir Bhutto (1953–) is dismissed as prime minister of Pakistan.

1990 Iraq invades and annexes Kuwait; the USA, EC countries and Arab nations form an opposing coalition.

1991 Warplanes commence "Desert Storm" bombing campaign against Iraq; Iraq launches
1991 Scud missiles against Israel and Saudi Arabia; a massive land invasion liberates Kuwait. Risings against Saddam Hussein (1937–) in N and S Iraq fail.

1992 **1992** Hindu extremists demolish the Ayodhya mosque igniting widespread violence across India.

1992 Afghan Islamic rebels capture Kabul and overthrow the communist government.

1995 Earthquake kills 5000 people in Kobe, Honshu, Japan.

1995 Israeli prime minister Yitzhak Rabin (b.1922) killed by a Jewish extremist. Binyamin Netanyahu (1949–) becomes prime minister at elections in 1996.

1993

1994

▲ ***Mandela*** *struggled for a democratic South Africa for much of*
1995 *his life, spending 27 years in prison charged with attempting to overthrow the government. He was primarily responsible for the immense and peaceful revolution that turned South Africa into a "rainbow republic". Mandela's charismatic personality and benevolence made him a figure of great moral stature.*

AFRICA

1990 Nelson Mandela (1918–) is released from prison in South Africa.

1990 Namibia becomes an independent republic.

1990 Robert Mugabe (1925–) is elected president of Zimbabwe.

1992 US troops arrive in Mogadishu, Somalia, to supervise food distribution.

1992 Algerian president Muhammad Boudiaf is assassinated by an Islamic extremist.

1992 Egyptian statesman Boutros Boutros-Ghali (1922–) becomes UN secretary-general.

1994 US troops withdraw from Somalia.

1994 Presidents of Burundi and Rwanda are killed in an air crash; intertribal violence and civil war erupt in Rwanda.

1994 African National Congress wins the South African elections; Nelson Mandela becomes president.

1994 Palestine National Authority takes control of the Gaza Strip and Jericho.

1994 Terrorist "Carlos" is arrested in Khartoum and taken to France for trial.

1995 Cameroon and Mozambique join the Commonwealth of Nations.

EUROPE

1990 Lithuania, Latvia and Estonia declare independence from the Soviet Union; Uzbekistan and Ukraine declare independence; Soviet troops occupy Lithuania and Latvia.

1990 Boris Yeltsin (1931–) is elected president of the Russian federation.

1990 East and West Germany are reunited.

1990 Margaret Thatcher (1925–) resigns; John Major (1943–) becomes British prime minister.

1991 Warsaw Pact is dissolved as a military alliance.

1991 Croatia and Slovenia declare independence from Yugoslavia; the Serb-dominated Yugoslav army invades Croatia.

1991 Army officers attempts a coup in Moscow; Mikhail Gorbachev (1931–) resigns; the Soviet Union ceases to exist; Russia, Belarus and Ukraine form the Commonwealth of Independent States (CIS) under President Yeltsin.

1992 Bosnia-Herzegovina declares independence from Yugoslavia; the Serbs attack Sarajevo.

1993 Czech and Slovak republics are established as separate states.

1994 Chechnia declares independence from Russia.

1995 Austria, Finland and Sweden join the European Union (EU).

1995 Russian troops capture Grozny, capital of Chechenia, but fail to defeat rebels. They are forced to withdraw in 1996. The war claims 100,000 lives.

1995 Bosnian Serb forces attack the 'safe haven' of Srebrenica. Muslims and Croats join forces and attack, forcing Bosnian Serbs to negotiate. The Dayton Accord ends the war in Bosnia.

1995 Jacques Chirac (1932–) elected president of France.

THE AMERICAS

1990 Manuel NORIEGA (1934–) is captured and taken to the USA to face charges of drug-dealing.

1991 Strategic Arms Reduction Talks (START) limit the size of US and Russian nuclear arsenals.

1991 Peace agreements ends an 11-year civil war in El Salvador.

1992 Bill CLINTON (1946–) is elected US president.

1992 Canada, the USA and Mexico form the North American Free Trade Association (NAFTA).

1992 Fernando Collor de Mello (1950–) resigns as president of Brazil.

1992 Abimael Guzman, leader of the Shining Path guerrillas, is arrested in Peru.

1992 UN organizes an environmental Earth Summit in Rio de Janeiro.

1993 Israel and the PLO reach a peace agreement in Washington.

1994 Zapatista National Liberation Army leads a revolt in Chiapas state in Mexico.

1994 US troops invade Haiti.

1995 Carlos Menem (1935–) reelected president of Argentina

1995 World Trade Organisation (WTO) succeeds GATT.

1995 Louis FARRAKHAN (1933–) leads up to 400,000 men on a march in Washington, D.C, calling for African-American unity.

1995 Bill CLINTON (1946–) reelected president of the United States.

1995 Québec narrowly rejects independence in referendum.

SCIENCE AND TECHNOLOGY

1990 US Hubble space telescope is carried into orbit by the space shuttle.

1990 US spaceprobe *Magellan* radar maps Venus.

1991 5000-year-old body is discovered preserved in ice on the Austrian-Italian border.

1991 Energy is experimentally produced by controlled nuclear fusion at the Joint European Torus in Britain.

1992 US COBE satellite discovers ripples in the microwave background that confirm the Big Bang origin of the universe.

1992 Propellerless ship powered by magnetohydrodynamics is launched in Japan.

1994 Fragments of comet Shoemaker-Levi impact on Jupiter.

1994 Rail tunnel opens between Britain and France.

1994 World Wide Web (WWW) is created.

1995 US scientists confirm the existence of the 'top quark'.

ARTS AND HUMANITIES

1990 US artist Jeff KOONS (1955–) creates his sculpture *Jeff and Ilona (Made in Heaven)*.

1990 British novelist Ian McEwan (1948–) publishes his *The Innocent.*

1991 British composer Harrison BIRTWISTLE (1934–) writes his opera *Sir Gawain and the Green Knight.*

1991 US composer Stephen SONDHEIM (1930–) writes his *Assassins.*

1991 British novelist Martin Amis (1949–) publishes his *Time's Arrow.*

1992 British artist Damien Hirst (1965–) creates his sculpture *The Physical Impossibility of Death in the Mind of Someone Living.*

1992 Chinese novelist Jung Chang (1952–) publishes her *Wild Swans.*

1992 Sri Lankan-born Canadian novelist Michael Ondaatje (1943–) publishes his *The English Patient.*

1993 Indian novelist Vikram SETH (1952–) publishes his *A Suitable Boy.*

1993 Polish composer Witold Lutoslawski (1913–94) writes his fourth symphony.

1995 Irish poet Seamus HEANEY (1939–) receives the Nobel Prize in literature.

1995 *The Ghost Road* by British novelist Pat Barker (1943–) wins the Booker Prize.

1990

1991

1992

1993

1994

1995

1996

1996 Yasir Arafat (1929–) elected president of the Palestinian National Authority.

1996 The Taliban capture Kabul, Afghanistan, and form a militant Islamic government.

1997

1997 China regains Hong Kong.

1997 Israeli troops withdraw from Hebron on the West Bank.

1997 Financial crisis in Japan leads to economic crisis throughout Southeast Asia.

1998

1998 Iraq refuses access to UN arms inspectors, the US attacks Iraqi military targets.

1999

1999 Hussein I of Jordan dies. His son, Abdullah (1962–), succeeds.

1999 Ehud Barak (1942–) defeats Netanyahu in Israeli elections.

1999 More than 15,000 die in earthquake centered on Izmit, Turkey.

1999 East Timor votes for independence from Indonesia.

2000

2001

2001 Ariel Sharon (1928–) elected prime minister of Israel after renewal of Palestinian Intifada. Sharon cuts off relations with the Palestinian Authority.

2001 Taliban regime in Afghanistan overthrown by Afghan opposition and US special forces backed by air power. Hamid Karzai (1957–) becomes interim leader.

1996 Renewed violence occurs between Hutus and Tutsis in Rwanda.

1996 Rebel forces, led by Laurent Kabila, exile Mobutu Sese Seko (1930–97), president of Zaire.

1997 Sierra Leone suspended from the Commonwealth of Nations after a military coup.

1997 Zaire renamed the Democratic Republic of the Congo (DRC).

1997 Ghanaian diplomat Kofi Annan (1938–) becomes UN secretary general.

1998 Thabo Mbeki (1942–) succeeds Nelson Mandela (1918–) as chairman of the African National Congress (ANC).

1999 Mbeki elected president of South Africa.

2000 British troops evacuate British citizens from Sierra Leone. They stay to train the army.

▲ *Bill and Hillary Clinton* Bill Clinton was only the second US president to be impeached (after Andrew Johnson). Hillary served as senator from 2001 and stood for the Democratic Party nomination in the 2008 presidential election.

1996 Yugoslavian war crimes tribunal in the Hague convicts a Serb of involvement in massacres at Srebrenica.

1997 Tony Blair (1953–) begins ten years in office as prime minister of Britain.

1997 Swiss banks agree to compensate Holocaust victims.

1997 Lionel Jospin (1937–) elected prime minister of France.

1998 Albanian separatists rebel against Serb rule in Kosovo.

1998 Gerhard Schröder (1944–) elected chancellor of Germany.

1998 Nationalists (led by John Hume), Republicans (led by Gerry Adams), Unionists (led by David Trimble), and the British and Irish governments, sign the Good Friday agreement in Northern Ireland. Trimble becomes first minister.

1999 Birth of single European currency (the euro)

1999 Commissioners of the EU, including the president Jacques Santer (1937–), resign en masse after accusations of corruption.

1999 Reports of atrocities by Serb forces in Kosovo prompts NATO air strikes against targets in Kosovo and Serbia. Tens of thousands of ethnic Albanians flee Kosovo. In June, after 11 weeks of NATO bombing, Serb forces withdraw.

2000 Vladimir Putin (1952–) becomes president of Russia.

2000 Russian troops renew war against Chechen separatists.

2000 Explosion aboard the *Kursk*, a Russian nuclear submarine, kills the entire crew of 118.

2000 Slobodan Milošević (1941–) forced from power. He is charged with war crimes in the Hague.

THE AMERICAS

1996 UN-negotiated peace agreement ends 36 years of civil war in Guatemala. The war claimed more than 200,000 lives.

1997 Tupac Amaru guerrillas killed to end siege of Japanese ambassador's residence in Lima, Peru.

1997 Jean Chrétien (1934–) reelected premier of Canada.

1998 US politics dominated by scandal over President Clinton's (1946–) purported sexual impropriety. He denies the affair and faces charges of perjury.

1998 Hurricane Mitch kills 11,000 in Honduras and Nicaragua.

1998 Fernando Cardoso (1931 –) reelected president of Brazil.

1998 General Augusto PINOCHET (1915–), former president of Chile, arrested in Britain for genocide.

1999 President Clinton acquitted in Senate impeachment trial.

1999 Inuit land of Nunavut created in Northwest Territories, Canada.

1999 Fernando de la Rúa (1935–) elected president of Argentina.

2000 Former president of Chile Augusto PINOCHET (1915–), considered too unwell to face a British trial for genocide, returns to Chile.

2001 George W. BUSH (1946–) is 43rd US president after a divisive 2000 election. A month of recounts were required, and his opponent Al Gore received over half a million more votes.

2001 On September 11, terrorists pilot two passenger aircraft into the towers of the World Trade Center in New York City. A third plane hits the Pentagon, Virginia. Almost 3000 people are killed. Afghanistan-based OSAMA BIN LADEN (1957–), head of al-Qaeda, is held responsible.

SCIENCE AND TECHNOLOGY

1996 US government bans the use of CFCs (chlorofluorocarbons).

1996 Physicists at CERN, Geneva, Switzerland create antimatter.

1997 The Roslin Institute, Edinburgh, clone an adult sheep.

1997 Comet Hale-Bopp comes within 200 million km (125 million mi) of Earth.

1997 'Deep Blue' computer defeats world chess champion Gary Kasparov (1963–).

1998 *Lunar Prospector* discovers water-ice near the Moon's poles.

2000 Scientists publish the rough draft of the sequence of the human genetic code.

2000 Launch of the International Space Station (ISS).

2000 The NEAR space probe enters orbit around Eros, a deep space asteroid.

2001 Mir space station drops out of orbit and burns up in Earth's atmosphere.

▲ *Dolly* Using nuclear-transfer technology, scientists produced an embryo from a single udder cell of a adult ewe and an unfertilized egg stripped of DNA. The embryo was implanted in a surrogate mother.

ARTS AND HUMANITIES

1996 Restored Globe Theater opens in London.

1997 Italian playwright Dario Fo (1926–) receives the Nobel Prize in literature.

1997 *The God of Small Things* by Arundhati Roy (1961–) wins the Booker Prize.

1997 New British Library opens in St. Pancras, London, UK.

1997 Guggenheim Museum opens in Bilbao, Spain, designed by Canadian Frank Gehry (1929–).

1998 Günter GRASS (1927–) earns the Nobel Prize in literature.

1998 *American Pastoral* by Philip Roth (1933–) wins the Pulitzer Prize in fiction.

1999 *Disgrace* by J.M. Coetzee (1940–) wins the Booker Prize.

2000 Gao Xiangjian (1940–) is the first Chinese writer to receive the Nobel Prize in literature.

2000 *The Blind Assassin* by Margaret Atwood (1939–) wins the Booker Prize.

2000 *American Beauty*, starring Kevin Spacey (1959–), wins Academy Awards for best picture and best actor.

WORLD EVENTS

2002 Euro notes and coins adopted in 12 European countries.

2003 US and British troops invade and swiftly conquer Iraq. Saddam Hussein is captured in December.

2003 In SE Iran, an earthquake strikes the town of Bam killing over 30,000 people.

2004 Ten more countries join the European Union.

2004 Disputed Ukrainian elections won by Victor Yushchenko after mass street demonstrations.

2004 Massive tsunami on December 26 hits countries around the Indian Ocean, killing more than 200,000.

2005 Israel withdraws from the Gaza Strip, forcibly removing Israeli settlers.

2006 After months of negotiations a coalition government is formed in Iraq, but it fails to prevent the country destabilising into civil war.

2006 Palestinian Hamas forces begin rocket bombardment of Israel. The Israeli army responds with an invasion and air raids but withdraws after a costly stalemate.

2006 North Korea unsuccessfully tests a nuclear weapon

2007 In Somalia, the Islamic Courts Union is defeated by transitional government and Ethiopian forces.

2007 Saddam Hussein is executed by the Iraqi government.

2007 Ban Ki-Moon becomes UN Secretary General.

2007 Fear of bad debt in the international banking system causes a global financial crisis.

2008 Kosovo, under UN administration since 1999, unilaterally declares its independence from Serbia to mixed response.

SCIENCE AND TECHNOLOGY

2002 Bonn Conference saves the Kyoto Protocol (1995) on climate change, without US participation.

2003 US space shuttle *Columbia* breaks up on re-entering Earth's atmosphere, killing all seven crew.

2003 China sends its first astronaut into space on *Shenzou 5*, making it the third nation to develop manned space capabilities.

2004 *SpaceShipOne* is the first private manned spacecraft and the winner of the Ansari X Prize.

2005 The Kyoto Protocol comes into effect, still without US support.

2006 The H5N1 strain of avian influenza causes fears of a devastating pandemic. It is later found unable to spread between humans, and deaths are few.

2007 Planets of Earthlike size and temperature are discovered around other stars.

▼ *September 11, 2001* *Terrorists pilot two hijacked passenger aircraft into the twin towers of the World Trade Center in New York City. The towers collapse, killing c.3000 people.*

ARTS AND HUMANITIES

2001 Archaeologists discover drawings more than 28,000 years old in a cave in Dordogne, France.

2001 *The Amazing Adventures of Kavalier and Clay* by Michael Chabon (1964–) gains the Pulitzer Prize for fiction.

2001 V.S. Naipaul (1932–) receives the Nobel Prize in literature.

2002 *The Amber Spyglass* by Philip Pullman (1946–) becomes the first children's book to win the Whitbread Prize.

2003 *Middlesex*, a novel by US writer Jeffrey Eugenides (1960–), wins the Pulitzer Prize for fiction.

2004 *The Lord of the Rings: The Return of the King* wins 11 Oscars, including best picture and best director for Peter Jackson (1961–).

2005 Harold Pinter (1930–) awarded Nobel Prize in literature.

2006 *Crash* wins three Oscars including that for best picture.

2007 Doris Lessing (1919–) receives Nobel Prize in literature.

2002

2003

2004

2005

2006

2007

A

Aalto, Alvar (1898–1976) Finnish architect, famous for imaginative handling of floor levels and use of natural materials and irregular forms. Aalto's work includes the Sanatorium at Paimio (1931) and Finlandia House, Helsinki (1967–71).

Abbas I (the Great) (1571–1629) Shah of Persia (1588–1629). The outstanding ruler of the SAFAVID DYNASTY, Abbas restored Persia as a great power, waging war successfully against the invading Uzbeks and Ottoman Turks and recapturing Hormuz from the Portuguese. Tolerant in religion, he encouraged Dutch and English merchants and admitted Christian missionaries.

Abbasid dynasty Muslim caliph dynasty (750–1258). They traced their descent from al-Abbas, the uncle of MUHAMMAD, and came to power by defeating the UMAYYADS. In 862 the Abbasids moved the caliphate from Damascus to Baghdad. From the 10th century Abbasid caliphs ceased to exercise political powers. After the family's downfall in 1258, following the fall of Baghdad to the Mongols, one member was invited by the sultan to Cairo, where the dynasty was recognized until the 16th century.

Abd al-Kadir (1808–83) Algerian leader and emir of Mascara. He displaced (1832–39) the French and Turks from N Algeria before launching a holy war against the French. In 1843 Abd al-Kadir was forced into Morocco where he enlisted the support of the sultan. He and his Moroccan forces were defeated at Isly (1844).

Abd el-Krim (1882?–1963) Moroccan BERBER resistance leader. In 1921 he led the Rif tribes to a famous victory against the Spanish. By 1925 he had advanced into French-held territory. In 1926 he was defeated by a French-Spanish force and sent into exile. In 1947 he escaped to Egypt and formed a liberation movement. In 1958 MUHAMMAD V proclaimed him a national hero.

Abdul Hamid II (1842–1918) Last OTTOMAN sultan (1876–1909). On his accession, Abdul Hamid suspended Parliament and the constitution. He concluded the disastrous Russo-Turkish Wars by ceding vast lands to Russia (1878). Abdul Hamid is remembered as the "Great Assassin" for his part in the Armenian massacres (1894–96). In 1908 the Young Turks forced him to reimplement the 1876 constitution and he was deposed shortly after.

Abdul Medjid I (1823–61) OTTOMAN sultan (1839–61). He carried on the program of reform begun by his father, MAHMUD II. He granted rights to his Christian subjects and made improvements in education. With the help of Britain and France, Abdul Medjid resisted Russian aggression in the Crimean War. The latter part of his reign was marked by increasing unrest among his subject peoples in the Balkans.

Abdullah ibn Hussein (1882–1951) King of Jordan (1946–51), son of HUSSEIN IBN ALI of the Hashemite family. In 1921, after aiding Britain in World War I, Abdullah became ruler of Transjordan. In 1928, when Transjordan became a constitutional monarchy, Abdullah became emir. Abdullah lost control of Hejaz to Ibn SAUD. In World War II he resisted the Axis. He fought against the creation of Israel, annexed Palestinian land and signed an armistice (1949). Abdullah was assassinated in Jerusalem.

Abélard, Pierre (1079–1142) French philosopher noted for his application of logic in approaching theological questions, as in his work *Sic et Non*. Abélard is known for his tragic love for his pupil Héloise. The affair scandalized his contemporaries. He was castrated and became a monk, and Héloise was forced to enter a convent. These events inspired his *Historia Calamitatum Mearum*.

Achaemenid dynasty Ruling dynasty of the first Persian empire, which stretched from the River Nile as far E as modern Afghanistan. The dynasty was founded (c.550 BCE) by CYRUS THE GREAT and named for its ancestor Achaemenes. DARIUS I (r.521–486 BCE) decentralized government administration. The last Achaemenid ruler, DARIUS III (r.336–330 BCE), was defeated by ALEXANDER THE GREAT. The dynasty was responsible for the spread of Zoroastrianism, and the remains at Persepolis are testimony to the splendor of Persian architecture at this time.

Adams, Gerry (1948–) Northern Irish politician, president of Sinn Féin (1983–). He was interned (1972–78) for involvement in the Irish Republican Army (IRA), before becoming vice-president (1978–83) of Sinn Féin. He served (1983–92, 1997–) as a member of parliament, but never took his seat at Westminster. Adams' negotiations with John HUME led to an IRA cease-fire (1994). He headed the Sinn Féin delegation in the 1997 peace talks.

Adams, John (1735–1826) Second US president (1797–1801). Influenced by his cousin Samuel ADAMS, he helped draft the Declaration of Independence (1776) and the Treaty of Paris (1783), ending the American Revolution. Adams was vice-president (1789–97) to George WASHINGTON. His presidency was marked by conflict between the Federalist Party led by Alexander HAMILTON and Thomas JEFFERSON's Democratic-Republican party.

Adams, John Couch (1819–92) British astronomer. Noting that Uranus' observed path was not in agreement with its calculated orbit, Adams believed that the discrepancies could be accounted for by the gravitational influence of an undiscovered planet. Neptune, as it was subsequently called, was discovered near a position predicted by Urbain LEVERRIER.

Adams, John Quincy (1767–1848) Sixth US president (1825–29), son of the second president, John ADAMS. He served in his father's administration, before acting (1803–08) as Federalist Party member in the Senate. Adams was secretary of state (1817–24) for James MONROE. He was largely responsible for formulating the Monroe Doctrine and negotiating the Adams-Onis Treaty (1819). Adams became president without an electoral majority, his appointment confirmed by the House of Representatives. His lack of a mandate and nonpartisan approach contributed to his defeat by Andrew JACKSON.

Adams, Samuel (1722–1803) American revolutionary leader. As a member and clerk of the Massachusetts legislature (1765–74), he was the chief spokesman for revolution. Adams helped form several radical organizations, led the Stamp Act protest in 1765, helped plan the Boston Tea Party of 1773, and was a signatory of the Declaration of Independence (1776). He was a delegate to the Continental Congress until 1781.

Adenauer, Konrad (1876–1967) German statesman, first chancellor of the Federal Republic of Germany (1949–63). He was twice imprisoned by the Nazis. Adenauer helped to create the Christian Democratic Union (CDU), West Germany's dominant postwar party, and was its leader (1946–66). He led West Germany into NATO (1955) and campaigned for the establishment of the European Economic Community (EEC).

Aeschylus (525–456 BCE) Earliest of the great Greek playwrights. Aeschylus is said to have been responsible for the development of tragedy as a dramatic form through his addition of a second actor, and for his reduction of the role of the chorus. His best-known work is the trilogy *Oresteia*, which comprises *Agamemnon*, *The Choephori* and *The Eumenides*.

Aesop (620–560 BCE) Semilegendary Greek fabulist. He was the reputed creator of numerous short tales about animals, all illustrating human virtues and failings.

Afrikaners (*Boer*, farmer) Descendants of the predominantly Dutch settlers in South Africa. Afrikaners settled around the Cape region in the 17th century. To avoid British control, they spread N and E from the Cape in the Great Trek (1835–40) and founded the independent South African Republic (Transvaal) and Orange Free State. Defeat in the South African Wars (1899–1902) led to the republics merging in the Union of South Africa (1910).

Agrippina II (15–59) Roman princess, daughter of Agrippina I and Germanicus; she was the mother of Emperor NERO. Agrippina married CLAUDIUS after he became emperor and persuaded him to make Nero his heir designate. She is believed to have murdered Claudius in 54 in order to hasten her son's succession to the throne. Agrippina was later murdered by Nero.

Ahmad Shah Durrani (1722–73) Emir of Afghanistan (1747–73), founder of the Durrani dynasty. He united the Afghan tribes and is known as the founder of modern Afghanistan.

Ahmose I King of ancient Egypt (r.1570–1546 BCE). Ahmose re-established Thebes as the center of government, reconquered Nubia and expelled the HYKSOS. He was Amenhotep I's father.

Akbar I (the Great) (1542–1605) Emperor of India (1556–1605). Regarded as the greatest ruler of the MUGHAL EMPIRE, Akbar assumed personal control in 1560 and set out to establish Mughal control of all of India, extending his authority as far s as Ahmadnagar. Akbar built a new capital at Fatehpur Sikri and endeavored to unify his empire by conciliation with Hindus.

Akhnaten (d. c.1362 BCE) (Akhenaten) Ancient Egyptian king of the 18th dynasty (r. c.1379–1362 BCE). He succeeded his father, Amenhotep III, as Amenhotep IV. In an attempt to counter the influence of the priests of the temple of Amon at Luxor, he renounced the old gods and introduced an almost monotheistic worship of the sun god, Aten. He adopted the name Akhnaten and established a new capital at Akhetaten. After his death TUTANKHAMUN reinstated Amon as the national god.

Akihito (1933–) Emperor of Japan (1989–). In 1959 Akihito married a commoner, Michiko Shoda, the first such marriage in the history of the imperial dynasty. He succeeded his father, HIROHITO.

Akkadians Inhabitants of the ancient region of Akkadia (Agade), Mesopotamia. From the mid 4th millennium BCE, Akkadians from the various regions fought each other, until SARGON united them in c.2340 BCE, forming the first empire of Babylonia.

Aksum (Axum) Powerful E African kingdom, which flourished from the 1st to 6th centuries CE. It was named for its capital, a town in N Ethiopia. Aksum was Christianized in the 4th century and became a major center of Ethiopian Christianity. According to tradition, Aksum's kings were descended from Menelik (legendary son of SOLOMON). Aksum was a rich trading center.

Alaric I (370–410) King of the VISIGOTHS (395–410). His forces ravaged Thrace, Macedonia and Greece and occupied Epirus (395–96). In 401 Alaric invaded Italy. Defeated by the Roman general Stilicho, he formed a pact with him. Emperor Honorius executed Stilicho for treason, and Alaric besieged (408) and captured Rome (410). He planned an invasion of Sicily and Africa, but his fleet was destroyed in a storm.

Alaungpaya (1711–60) (Alompra or Aungzeya) King of Burma (1752–60). Alaungpaya refused to become a vassal of the kingdom of Mon (in the Irrawaddy Delta) when Ava, the Burmese capital, was captured in 1752. He organized resistance, recaptured Ava in 1753 and took over the Mon capital, Pegu, in 1757. He tried to conquer Siam in 1760, but died with his army in retreat.

Albert II (1397–1439) King of Germany (1438–39), king of Bohemia and Hungary (1438–39); founder of the HAPSBURG succession. He succeeded his father as Albert V, duke of Austria (1404–39). His short reign as king was marked by unrest in Hungary and Bohemia and a war with the Turks in which he was killed.

Albert, Prince (1819–61) Consort of Queen VICTORIA. First cousin of the queen and prince of Saxe-Coburg-Gotha, he married Victoria in 1840. Albert was her chief adviser and was the principal organizer of the Great Exhibition of 1851. He took an active role in diplomatic affairs and called for moderation in the Trent Affair (1861) during the American Civil War.

Alberti, Leon Battista (1404–72) Italian architect, humanist and writer. Alberti's treatise *On Painting* (1435) was highly influential. His buildings include: the Rucellai Palace, Florence and the Church of San Andrea, Mantua.

Albuquerque, Afonso d' (1453–1515) Portuguese military commander, founder of the Portuguese Empire of the East Indies. After serving as a soldier in North Africa, Albuquerque became governor-general of the Portuguese settlements in W India. He established control over the spice trade by capturing Goa (1510), Malacca (1511), Calicut (1512) and the Malabar Coast.

Alcock, Sir John William (1892–1919) British airman who, with Arthur Whitten-Brown, was the first to fly nonstop across the Atlantic Ocean. The flight began in St. John's, Newfoundland, on 14 June 1919 and landed 16.5 hours later near Clifden, Ireland.

Alemanni (Alamanni) Loose confederation of ancient Germanic tribes. The Alemanni peoples were first mentioned in CE 213 as being attacked by the Romans between the Elbe and the Danube. During the 5th century they expanded into Alsace and N Switzerland. Conquered by the FRANKS in the early 6th century, they were absorbed into the Frankish kingdom.

Alembert, Jean le Rond d' (1717–83) French mathematician and philosopher, a leading figure in the Enlightenment. D'Alembert was DIDEROT's coeditor on the first edition of the *Encyclopédie* (1751) and contributed the "Preliminary Discourse".

Alexander I (1777–1825) Russian czar (1801–25). After repulsing NAPOLEON's attempt to conquer Russia (1812), Alexander led his troops across Europe and into Paris (1814). He helped form the Holy Alliance with other European powers. He was named constitutional monarch of Poland in 1815 and also annexed Finland, Georgia and Bessarabia to Russia.

Alexander II (1818–81) Russian czar (1855–81), known as "Czar Liberator" for his emancipation of the serfs in 1861. Alexander warred with Turkey (1877–78) and gained influence in the Balkans. He sold Alaska (1867) but expanded the Far Eastern and central Asian parts of the empire.

Alexander III (1845–94) Russian czar (1881–94). He introduced reactionary measures limiting local government; censorship of the press was enforced and arbitrary arrest and exile became common. He formed an alliance with France.

Alexander I (1888–1934) King of the Serbs, Croats and Slovenes (1921–29) and of Yugoslavia (1929–34). In his efforts to forge a united country from the rival national groups and ethnically divided political parties, he created an autocratic police state. Alexander was assassinated by a Croatian terrorist.

Alexander Nevski, Saint (1220–63) Russian ruler, Grand Duke of Novgorod and Grand Duke of Vladimir. He pragmatically submitted to MONGOL rule following their invasion of Russia, and the Great Khan appointed him Grand Duke of Kiev. He defeated the Swedes on the River Neva in 1240 (hence the name "Nevski") and the Teutonic Knights on Lake Peipus in 1242.

Alexander the Great (356–323 BCE) King of Macedonia (336–323 BCE, son of PHILIP II of Macedonia. Destroying rivals, Alexander rapidly consolidated Macedonian power in Greece. In 334 BCE he began his destruction of the vast ACHAEMENID EMPIRE, conquering W Asia Minor and storming Tyre in 332 BCE. Alexander subdued Egypt and occupied Babylon, conquering central Asia in 328 BCE. In 327 BCE he invaded India but was prevented from advancing beyond the Punjab by the threat of mutiny. Alexander died in Babylon, planning new conquests in Arabia. Although his empire did not outlive him, he was chiefly responsible for the spread of Greek civilization in the Mediterranean and W Asia.

Alexius I (1048–1118) (Alexius Comnenus) BYZANTINE emperor (1081–1118), founder of the Comnenian dynasty. He held off the Normans who threatened Constantinople and turned the armies of the First Crusade to his own advantage by using them to reconquer parts of Anatolia.

Alfonso XII (1857–85) King of Spain (1874–85). The son of ISABELLA II, he went into exile with her during the Carlist Wars. She abdicated in his favor in 1870, and in 1874 he was proclaimed king. His reign was marked by a considerable strengthening of the monarchy. He was succeeded by his son ALFONSO XIII.

Alfonso XIII (1886–1941) King of Spain (1886–1931). Alfonso was born after the death of his father, ALFONSO XII. His mother, Maria Christina, acted as regent until 1902. Alfonso could not satisfy the conflicting demands of nationalists, socialists, republicans and others. In 1923 he supported the establishment of a military dictatorship under Miguel PRIMO DE RIVERA.

Alfred the Great (849–99) King of Wessex (871–99). A warrior and scholar, Alfred saved Wessex from the Danes and laid the foundations of a united English kingdom. After the Danish invasion of 878, he escaped to Athelney in Somerset, returning to defeat the Danes at Edington and recover the kingdom. His pact with the Danish leader Guthrum roughly divided England in two; the Danelaw occupied the NE. Although he controlled only

Wessex and part of Mercia, Alfred's leadership was widely recognized throughout England after his capture of London (886).

Ali (*c.*600–61) Fourth Muslim caliph (656–61), cousin and son-in-law of the prophet MUHAMMAD. Ali was married to Fatima. He is regarded by the Shiites as the rightful heir of Muhammad. Ali succeeded Othman as caliph, despite opposition from Aishah and Muawiya. He was assassinated and his first son, Hasan, abdicated in favor of Muawiya, who founded the UMAYYAD DYNASTY. His second son, Husayn, led the insurrection against the Umayyads, but was killed at the battle of Karbala (680).

Ali Bey (1728–73) Ruler of Egypt (1768–72). As MAMELUKE chief (1750–68) of Ottoman-controlled Egypt, Ali Bey wielded great power. In 1768 he became sultan and declared independence from the Turks. He invaded and captured Syria and Mecca (1771) but was later betrayed and fled to Syria. Ali Bey tried to regain Egypt without success and died soon afterward.

Al-Khwarizmi (active 820) Persian mathematician. He is credited as being the first to solve the quadratic equation $ax^2 + bx + c = 0$. In his book *Calculation with Hindu Numerals* he described a number notation in use at the time. Following the translation of this work in the 13th century the Hindu number system was adopted in Europe.

Allen, Ethan (1738–89) US frontiersman and soldier. In *c.*1770 he became commander of the Green Mountain Boys, a volunteer militia. In the American Revolution, Allen and his troops captured Fort Ticonderoga (10 May 1775) and Crown Point (11 May 1775). During the invasion of Canada, he was captured (25 September 1775) and imprisoned in England until 1778.

Allende Gossens, Salvador (1908–73) Chilean statesman, president (1970–73). He was one of the founders of the Chilean Socialist Party (1933). Allende's narrow election victory led to the introduction of democratic socialist reforms, which antagonized the Chilean establishment. The nationalization of the US-owned copper industry resulted in a US trade embargo. The CIA began a covert campaign of destabilization. Allende was overthrown and died in a military coup led by General PINOCHET.

Almohad BERBER Muslim dynasty (1145–1269) in N Africa and Spain, the followers of a reform movement within Islam. It was founded by Muhammad ibn Tumart, who set out to purify Islam and oust the ALMORAVIDS from Morocco and eventually Spain. In 1212 Alfonso VIII of Castile routed the Almohads, and in 1269 their capital, Marrakesh, fell to the Marinids.

Almoravid BERBER Muslim dynasty (1054–1145) in Morocco and Spain. They rose to power under Abdullah ibn Yasin, who converted Saharan tribes in a religious revival. Abu Bakr founded Marrakesh as their capital in 1070; his brother Yusuf ibn Tashufin defeated Alfonso VI of Castile in 1086. Almoravid rule was ended by the rise of the ALMOHADS.

Alp Arslan (1029–72) Sultan of the SELJUK Turks (r.1063–72). He conquered Armenia, Syria, Cilicia and Cappadocia. In 1066 he attacked the BYZANTINE EMPIRE. His victory over the Byzantines at Manzikert in 1071 assured Turkish domination of Asia Minor.

Amadeo (1845–90) King of Spain (1870–73), son of VICTOR EMMANUEL II of Italy. After ISABELLA II of Spain was forced to abdicate in 1868, Amadeo was elected king by the Cortes. He reluctantly ruled for three years and abdicated after the Carlist Wars started again in 1873.

Ambrose, Saint (*c.*339–97) Bishop of Milan (374–97) and Doctor of the Church. The chief critic of Arianism, he persuaded Emperor Gratian to outlaw (379) all heresy in the ROMAN EMPIRE. His preaching and teachings were largely responsible for the conversion of Saint AUGUSTINE. His feast day is 7 December.

Amin, Idi (1925–2003) President of Uganda (1971–79). He gained power by a military coup in 1971, overthrowing Milton OBOTE. Amin established a dictatorship marked by atrocities and expelled *c.*80,000 Asian Ugandans in 1972. When Tanzanian forces joined rebel Ugandans in a march on Kampala, Amin fled to Libya.

Amorites Seminomadic people who dominated Mesopotamia, Syria and Palestine during the first half of the 2nd millennium

BCE. In the 18th century BCE their dynasty ruled in Babylon. The Amorites' greatest king was the lawgiver HAMMURABI. Descendants of the Amorites were living in Palestine when the Hebrews arrived and were gradually incorporated into the Israelites.

Ampère, André Marie (1775–1836) French physicist. Ampère founded electrodynamics and investigated the magnetic effects of electric currents. He proposed Ampère's law – a mathematical description of the magnetic force between two electric currents.

Anastasius I (d.518) BYZANTINE emperor (491–518). Before accession to the throne, Anastasius had been a court official responsible for the improvement of the monetary system and for the reorganization of the tax collecting process. As emperor, his interest in financial management led to large increases in the state treasury.

Andersen, Hans Christian (1805–75) Danish writer of some of the world's best-loved fairy tales. His humorous, delicate, but frequently also melancholy stories were first published in 1835. They include *The Ugly Duckling* and *The Emperor's New Clothes*.

Anderson, Carl David (1905–91) US physicist who shared the 1936 Nobel Prize for physics with Victor Hess for research into cosmic radiation. In 1932 he discovered the first known particle of antimatter – the positron. He later helped discover the muon.

Andropov, Yuri Vladimirovich (1914–84) Soviet statesman, president of the Soviet Union (1983–84), general secretary of the Communist Party (1982–84). He played a major role in the suppression of the Hungarian uprising (1956). As head of the KGB (1967–82), Andropov took a hard line against political dissidence, supporting Soviet intervention in Czechoslovakia (1968) and Poland (1981). In 1973 he joined the Politburo. Andropov succeeded Leonid BREZHNEV as leader.

Angles Germanic tribe from a district of Schleswig-Holstein now called Angeln. In the 5th century they invaded England with neighboring tribes, including JUTES and SAXONS. They settled in Northumbria and East Anglia.

Annan, Kofi (1938–) Ghanaian diplomat, seventh secretary-general (1997–2007) of the United Nations (UN). He was the first black African secretary-general. In 1993 Annan was elected under secretary-general for peacekeeping, handling the removal of UN troops from Bosnia.

Anne (1665–1714) Queen of Great Britain and Ireland (1702–14), second daughter of JAMES II. Anne succeeded WILLIAM III as the last STUART sovereign and, after the Act of Union (1707), was the first monarch of the United Kingdom of England and Scotland. The War of the Spanish Succession (1701–14) dominated her reign. Anne was the last English monarch to exercise the royal veto over legislation (1707), but the rise of parliamentary government was inexorable. The Jacobite cause was crushed when Anne was succeeded by GEORGE I.

Anouilh, Jean (1910–87) French playwright and screenwriter. Influenced by neoclassicism, he often reinterpreted Greek myth as a means of exploring oppression. *Antigone* (1944) is perhaps his most celebrated play. Other works include *Becket* (1959).

Anselm of Canterbury, Saint (1033–1109) English theologian, b. Italy. Anselm became Archbishop of Canterbury in 1093. His belief in the rational character of Christian belief led him to propose an ontological argument for the existence of God. His feast day is 21 April.

Anthony, Saint (*c.*250–*c.*355) Egyptian saint and first Christian monk. He withdrew into complete solitude at the age of 20 to practice ascetic devotion. By the time of his death, Christian monasticism was well established. His feast day is 17 January.

Anthony, Susan Brownell (1820–1906) US reformer and woman suffragist. With Elizabeth Cady Stanton, she cofounded the National Woman Suffrage Association (1869). It later became (1890) the National American Woman Suffrage Association, and she acted as president (1892–1900).

Antiochus III (242–187 BCE) King of Syria (223–187 BCE), son of Seleucus II. He invaded Egypt (212–202 BCE), seizing land from Ptolemy V with the help of Philip V of Macedon. He recaptured Palestine, Asia Minor and the Thracian Cheronese. The

Romans overwhelmed him at Thermopylae (191 BCE) and at Magnesia (190 BCE). The rebuilt SELEUCID EMPIRE shrank when he gave up all possessions w of the Taurus. Seleucus IV succeeded him.

Antiochus IV (215–164 BCE) King of Syria (175–164 BCE), son of ANTIOCHUS III. After his father's defeat by the Romans in 190 BCE, Antiochus was held hostage. On his release, he returned to claim the Syrian throne. His invasion of Egypt (168 BCE) was unsuccessful. He occupied Jerusalem but his attempts to Hellenize worship provoked the Jewish uprising of Judas MACCABAEUS.

Antonescu, Ion (1882–1946) Romanian fascist dictator. In 1938 he was imprisoned by CAROL II for leading an unsuccessful fascist coup. In September 1940, in the face of German aggression, Carol appointed Antonescu premier. Carol was forced to abdicate in favor of his son Michael, and Antonescu assumed dictatorial powers. Romania joined the Axis Powers. Antonescu unleashed pogroms against Jews. The Red Army invasion of Romania led to his arrest. He was executed for war crimes.

Antoninus Pius (86–161) Roman emperor (138–161). The adopted son of HADRIAN, he was made consul (120). His reign saw the promotion of art and science, the construction of fine buildings, legal reform and provisions for orphans. Antoninus' constant companion was MARCUS AURELIUS, who eventually became emperor himself.

Antony, Mark (82–30 BCE) (Marcus Antonius) Roman general and statesman. He fought in CAESAR's campaign (54–50 BCE) in Gaul. In 49 BCE he became tribune. After Caesar's assassination (44 BCE), Antony inspired the mob to drive the conspirators, Brutus and Cassius, from Rome. Octavian (later AUGUSTUS) emerged as Antony's main rival. Octavian and Brutus joined forces, and Antony retreated to Gaul. He sued for peace. Antony, Octavian and Lepidus formed the Second Triumverate, which divided up the ROMAN EMPIRE: Antony received Asia. He and CLEOPATRA, queen of Egypt, became lovers. In 40 BCE Antony married Octavian's sister Octavia but continued to live with Cleopatra in Alexandria and became isolated from Rome. In 32 BCE the senate deprived Antony of his posts. Defeated at the battle of Actium (31 BCE), Antony and Cleopatra committed suicide.

Apollinaire, Guillaume (1880–1918) (Wilhelm Apollinaris de Kostrowitzky) French experimental poet, essayist and playwright. Apollinaire's *Peintres Cubistes* (1913) was the first attempt to define cubism. His masterpiece was the wholly unpunctuated *Alcools* (1913), in which he relived the wild romances of his youth.

Apuleius, Lucius (c.125–c.170) Latin writer, b. North Africa. His narrative romance *Metamorphoses* (or *The Golden Ass*) is the only Latin novel to have survived in its entirety. A satire on contemporary vices, it relates the misadventures of a man turned into an ass and his restoration to human form by the goddess Isis.

Aquinas, Saint Thomas (1225–74) Italian theologian and philosopher, Doctor of the Church. St. Thomas is the greatest figure of scholasticism. His *Summa Theologiae* (Theological Digest, 1267–73) was declared (1879) by Pope Leo XIII to be the basis of official Catholic philosophy. His feast day is 7 March.

Aquino, (Maria) Cory (Corazon) (1933–) Philippine stateswoman, president (1986–92), b. Maria Corazon. In 1954 she married Benigno Aquino (1932–83), an outspoken opponent of the MARCOS regime. While he was in prison (1973–81), Cory campaigned for his release. Benigno was assassinated by Marcos' agents. Cory claimed victory over Marcos in the 1986 presidential election and accused the government of vote-rigging. A bloodless "people's revolution" forced Marcos into exile. Aquino's government was beset by economic obstacles.

Arafat, Yasir (1929–2004) Palestinian statesman, first president of Palestine (1996–2004), leader of the Palestine Liberation Organization (PLO). Arafat led the anti-Israel guerrilla organization Fatah. He sought the abolition of Israel and the creation of a secular Palestinian state. The Intifada in Israel's occupied territories prompted talks between Israel and the PLO. In 1993 Arafat and Yitzhak RABIN signed an agreement in which Arafat renounced

terrorism and recognized the state of Israel. In return, Rabin re ognized the PLO as the legitimate representative of Palestinia and agreed to a withdrawal of Israeli troops from parts of occupied territories. In 1994 the Palestinian National Authori headed by Arafat, assumed limited self-rule in the territories rel quished by the Israeli army. In 1996 Arafat became president.

Arcadius (c.377–408) First Eastern Roman empe (395–408). After the death of THEODOSIUS I, the ROMAN EMPI was split between his sons into separate states. The East was ru by Arcadius and the West by his brother Honorius. During Are dius' reign the government was controlled by the praetorian p fect Rufinus and later by the Empress Eudoxia.

Archimedes (287–212 BCE) Greek mathematician and en neer. His discoveries about the determination of areas and v umes led to a new method of measuring π (pi). In *On Floati Bodies* he stated Archimedes' Principle – the observation tha body immersed in a fluid is pushed up by a force equal to weight of the displaced fluid. He supposedly formulated t principle after stepping into a bath and watching it overflow.

Ardashir I King of Persia (r.224–41). Ardashir overthrew last Parthian king, Artabanus V, and re-united Persia. He four ed the SASSANIAN EMPIRE, establishing its capital at Ctesiph He established Zoroastrianism as the state religion. Ardas strengthened Persia by going to war against the Roman empe SEVERUS ALEXANDER. He was succeeded by Shapur I.

Ariosto, Ludovico (1474–1533) Italian Renaissance poet. 1503 he became a servant of Cardinal d'Este and from 15 served the duke of Ferrara. Ariosto's masterpiece, *Orlando Furio* (published 1532), was intended to glorify the Este family. *Orlan Furioso* follows several love stories from the era of Charlemagne

Aristarchus of Samos (310–230 BCE) Greek mathematici and astronomer. Aristarchus tried to calculate the distances the Sun and Moon from Earth, as well as their sizes. Although method was sound the results were inaccurate. He was the first propose that the Sun is the center of the Universe.

Aristophanes (448–380 BCE) Greek comic playwright. Of more than 40 plays, only 11 survive, and they are the only exta comedies from the period. All follow the same basic plan – cari tures of contemporary Athenians who become involved in abst situations. The importance of the chorus in the early works reflected in the titles, such as *The Wasps* (422 BCE), *The Bir* (414 BCE) and *The Frogs* (405 BCE).

Aristotle (384–322 BCE) Greek philosopher, b. Macedon Aristotle studied (367–347 BCE) under PLATO at the Academy Athens. After Plato's death he tutored the young ALEXANDER T GREAT before founding (337 BCE) the Lyceum. In direct oppo tion to Plato's idealism, Aristotle's metaphysics is based on t principle that all knowledge proceeds directly from observati of the particular. His principal works are the *Organon* (six tre tises on logic and syllogism), *Politics* (the conduct of the state *Poetics* (analysis of poetry and tragedy) and *Rhetoric*.

Arius (c.250–336) Christian theologian, b. Libya. Arius work in Alexandria, Egypt, where he developed the heretical doctri of Arianism. Rising to become the moral leader of Alexandria Christian community in the early 320s, Arius began to mal known his view that Christ was a perfect but less than divi being whom God had created and raised to the status of His So In 325 the Council of Nicaea condemned Arius as a heretic.

Arkwright, Sir Richard (1732–92) English inventor ar industrialist. Arkwright introduced powered machinery to t textile industry with his water-driven frame for spinning; patented his invention in 1769.

Armstrong, Neil Alden (1930–) US astronaut. Armstror was chosen as a NASA astronaut in 1962 and was the comman pilot for the Gemini 8 orbital flight in 1966. On 20 July 1969 became the first man to walk on the Moon, remarking that it w "one small step for man, one giant leap for mankind".

Arnold, Benedict (1741–1801) American colonial soldie During the Revolution, he was wounded at the battle of Saratog

(1777) and commanded Philadelphia (1778). In 1780 Arnold became commander of West Point, a fort he planned to betray to the British for money. After the plot was discovered, he fled to the British. His name has become proverbial for treachery.

Arnold, Matthew (1822–88) English poet and critic. His writings include literary criticism, such as *Essays in Criticism* (series 1, 1865; series 2, 1888), and social commentary, such as *Culture and Anarchy* (1869), as well as such classic Victorian poems as "Dover Beach" and "The Scholar Gypsy".

Arp, Jean (Hans) (1887–1966) Alsatian sculptor, painter and poet. He founded the Zurich Dada movement. Arp worked with the Blaue Reiter group and in the 1920s joined the surrealist movement. His works include *Navel Shirt and Head* (1926) and *Human Concretion* (1935).

Arthur, Chester Alan (1830–86) 21st US president (1881–85). In 1880 he was nominated by the Republican Party as vice-president. Arthur became president after the assassination of James GARFIELD and tried to reform the spoils system, in which incoming presidents replaced government staff with their own appointees. Suffering from incurable illness, he was not renominated (1884). He was succeeded by Grover CLEVELAND.

Ashanti Ethnic group and administrative region of central Ghana, W Africa. The capital is Kumasi. The Ashanti people (a matrilineal society) established a powerful empire based on the slave trade with the British and Dutch. In the 18th century their influence extended into Togo and the Ivory Coast. Conflicts with the British throughout the 19th century were finally resolved in 1902, when the Ashanti territories (a British protectorate since 1896) were declared a crown colony.

Ashoka (c.271–238 BCE) Indian emperor (r.264–238 BCE), greatest emperor of the MAURYA EMPIRE, Ashoka at first fought to expand his empire. He was disgusted by the bloodshed of war and, renouncing conquest by force, embraced Buddhism. He became one of Buddhism's most fervent supporters and spread its ideas through missionaries and edicts engraved on pillars. His empire encompassed most of India and Afghanistan.

Ashurbanipal (d. c.627 BCE) (Assurbanipal) Last great king (668–c.627 BCE) of the ASSYRIAN EMPIRE. The empire was at its height in Ashurbanipal's reign, reaching into Upper Egypt, before a rapid decline. Excavations at Nineveh have revealed an advanced civilization.

Assad, Hafez al- (1928–2000) Syrian statesman, president (1970–2000). He served as minister of defense (1965–70), before seizing power in a military coup. Assad was elected president in 1971. He took a hardline stance against Israel, and Syrian troops participated in the 1973 Arab-Israeli War. In 1976 Syrian troops were deployed in the Lebanese civil war. In 1987 the Syrian army moved into Beirut to restore order. In the 1990s Assad played a vital role in the Israeli-Palestinian peace negotiations.

Assassin (Arabic, users of hashish) Name given to a Muslim sect of Ismailis, founded c.1090 by Hasan ibn al-Sabbah. The Assassins fought against orthodox Muslims and Christian Crusaders and committed many political murders. They were defeated in the 13th century.

Assurdan II Ruler of the ASSYRIAN EMPIRE from 935 to 913 BCE. He briefly restored Assyrian military authority, but by his death the empire was at its smallest extent.

Assyrian empire Ancient empire of the Middle East. It took its name from the city of Ashur (Assur) on the River Tigris. The Assyrian empire was established in the 3rd millennium BCE and reached its zenith between the 9th and 7th centuries BCE, when it extended from the Nile to the Persian Gulf and N into Anatolia. Under ASHURBANIPAL, art and learning reached their peak. The luxuriance of Ashurbanipal's court at Nineveh was legendary. The capture of Nineveh in 612 BCE marked the decline of Assyria.

Atahualpa (1502–33) (Atabalipa) Last INCA ruler of Peru, the son of Huayna Capac. On his father's death Atahualpa inherited Quito, while his half-brother Huáscar controlled the rest of the Inca kingdom. In 1532 Atahualpa defeated Huáscar but his period of complete dominance was short-lived. In November 1532 Francisco PIZARRO captured Atahualpa, and he was later executed.

Atatürk, (Mustafa) Kemal (1881–1938) Turkish general and statesman, first president (1923–38) of the Turkish republic. He joined the Young Turks and was chief of staff to ENVER PASHA in the successful revolution (1908). During World War I he led resistance to the Allies' Gallipoli Campaign. The defeat of the OTTOMAN EMPIRE persuaded Mustafa Kemal to organize the Turkish Nationalist Party (1919). The harsh Treaty of Sèvres (1920) forced him on the offensive. His expulsion of the Greeks from Asia Minor (1921–22) led the sultan to flee Istanbul. The Treaty of Lausanne (1923) saw the creation of an independent republic. Kemal's dictatorship undertook reforms, transforming Turkey into a secular, industrial nation. In 1934 he adopted the title Atatürk (father of the Turks). He was succeeded by Ismet İnönü.

Attalus III Philometer (170–133 BCE) King of Pergamum (138–133 BCE), son of Eumenes II. He foresaw Roman expansion and bequeathed his kingdom to Rome. His legacy caused violent dissension in the Roman assembly when Tiberius GRACCHUS proposed that Attalus' wealth be used to finance agrarian reforms. In the resultant strife Tiberius and many followers were killed.

Attila (406–53) King of the HUNS (c.439–53), coruler with his elder brother until 445. Attila defeated the Eastern Roman emperor THEODOSIUS II, extorting land and tribute, and invaded Gaul in 451. Although his army suffered heavy losses, he invaded Italy in 452, but disease forced his withdrawal. Attila has a reputation as a fierce warrior but was fair to his subjects and encouraged learning. On his death the empire fell apart.

Attlee, Clement Richard, 1st Earl (1883–1967) British statesman, prime minister (1945–51). In 1935 Attlee became leader of the Labor Party. During World War II, he served in Winston CHURCHILL's cabinet. Attlee won a landslide victory in the 1945 general election. His administration was notable for the introduction of social reforms, such as the National Health Service (NHS) and the nationalization of the power industries, the railroads and the Bank of England. He granted independence to India (1947) and Burma (1948). Attlee was reelected in 1950, but was defeated by Churchill in the 1951 general election.

Auden, W.H. (Wystan Hugh) (1907–73) Anglo-American poet, b. England. His debut volume, *Poems* (1930), established him as the leading voice in a group of left-wing writers, which included Stephen Spender, Louis MacNeice, Cecil Day-Lewis and Christopher Isherwood. Auden and Isherwood collaborated on a series of plays, such as *The Ascent of F6* (1936). In 1939 Auden emigrated to New York. His volume *The Age of Anxiety* (1947) won a Pulitzer Prize.

Augustine, Saint (354–430) Christian theologian and philosopher. His *Confessions* describe a spirit in search of ultimate purpose, which he believed he found in his conversion to Christianity in 386. As Bishop of Hippo (396–430), North Africa, Augustine defended Christian orthodoxy against Manichaeism, Donatism and Pelagianism. Of the Four Fathers of the Latin Church, Augustine is considered the greatest. His feast day is 28 August.

Augustulus, Romulus (b.c.461) Western Roman emperor (r.475–76). Augustulus was given the throne by his father, Orestes, who had overthrown the Western emperor Julius Nepos. The Germanic mercenaries in Italy then mutinied, killed Orestes and forced Romulus to abdicate. ODOACER, leader of the Barbarian troops, assumed the title of king. The date 476 is therefore the traditional date for the fall of the Western ROMAN EMPIRE.

Augustus (63 BCE–CE 14) (Gaius Julius Caesar Octavianus) First Roman emperor (27 BCE–CE 14), also called **Octavian**. Nephew and adopted heir of Julius CAESAR, he formed the Second Triumvirate with Mark ANTONY and Lepidus after Caesar's assassination. They defeated Brutus and Cassius at Philippi in 42 BCE and divided the empire between them. Rivalry between Antony and Octavian was resolved by the defeat of Antony at Actium in 31 BCE. While preserving the form of the republic, Augustus held supreme power. He introduced peace and prosperity after years of civil war and built up the power and prestige of Rome. Augustus tried to arrange the succession to avoid future conflicts, but he had to acknowledge an unloved stepson, TIBERIUS, as his successor.

Augustus II (1670–1733) King of Poland (1697–1704, 1709–33) and, as Frederick Augustus I, elector of Saxony (1694–1733). He was elected by the Polish nobles in order to secure an alliance with Saxony, but the result was to draw Poland into the Northern War on the side of Russia. In 1704 Augustus was forced to give up the crown to Stanislas I Leszczyński. Civil war and invasion by CHARLES XII of Sweden weakened the Polish state. Augustus was restored to the throne after PETER THE GREAT defeated Sweden at the battle of Poltava in 1709.

Aung San (1914–47) Burmese politician who opposed British rule, father of AUNG SAN SUU KYI. Initially collaborating with the Japanese (1942), he later helped to expel the invaders. Aung San was assassinated shortly after his appointment as deputy chairman of the executive council.

Aung San Suu Kyi, Daw (1945–) Burmese civil rights activist, daughter of AUNG SAN. In 1989 she was placed under house arrest for leadership of the National League for Democracy, a coalition opposed to Myanmar's oppressive military junta. In 1991 she was awarded the Nobel Peace Prize and the European Parliament's Sakharov Prize for human rights.

Aurangzeb (1619–1707) Emperor of India (1659–1707). The last of the great MUGHAL emperors, he seized the throne from his father, SHAH JEHAN. Aurangzeb reigned over a great area and spent most of his reign defending it. He was a devout Muslim, whose intolerance of Hindus provoked long wars with the MARATHA.

Aurelian (c.215–75) Roman emperor. Having risen through the army ranks, Aurelian succeeded CLAUDIUS in 270. His victories against the Goths, reconquest of Palmyra and recovery of Gaul and Britain earned him the title "Restorer of the World". He built the Aurelian Wall and was assassinated in a military plot.

Austen, Jane (1775–1817) English novelist. Austen completed six novels of great art, insight and wit, casting an ironic but sympathetic light on the society of upper-middle-class England. Her novels are: *Northanger Abbey* (1818), a parody on the Gothic novel; *Sense and Sensibility* (1811); *Pride and Prejudice* (1813); *Mansfield Park* (1814); *Emma* (1816); and *Persuasion* (1818).

Avars Mongolian people who settled near the Volga River c.460. In the 6th century some Avars moved to the River Danube basin and occupied Dacia. Their domain extended from the Volga to the Baltic Sea, and they exacted tributes from the BYZANTINE EMPIRE. The Avars were crushed by CHARLEMAGNE in 796.

Averroës (Abu-al-Walid Ibn-Rushd) (1126–98) Leading Islamic philosopher in Spain. In 1182 Averroës became physician to the Caliph of Marrakesh, but in 1195 he was banished to Seville, Spain, for advocating reason over religion. His major work, *Incoherence of the Incoherence*, defends Neoplatonism and Aristotle.

Avicenna (979–1037) (Abu Ali al-Husayn ibn abd Allah ibn Sina) Persian physician and philosopher whose work influenced the science of medicine for many centuries. His *Canon Medicinae* became a standard work.

Avogadro, Amedeo, conte di Quaregna (1776–1856) Italian physicist and chemist. His hypothesis, Avogadro's law (1811), states that equal volumes of gases at the same pressure and temperature contain an equal number of molecules. This led later physicists to determine that the number of molecules in one gram molecule is constant for all gases. This number, Avogadro's constant, equals 6.02257×10^{23}.

Ayer, Sir A.J. (Alfred Jules) (1910–89) English philosopher. Building on the ideas of analytical philosophy from the Vienna Circle and of George BERKELEY, David HUME, Bertrand RUSSELL and Ludwig WITTGENSTEIN, Ayer introduced logical positivism into US and British philosophy. His works include *Language, Truth and Logic* (1936) and *Philosophy and Language* (1960).

Ayub Khan, Muhammad (1907–74) Pakistani general and statesman, president (1958–69). After the partition of India, he assumed control of the army in East Pakistan (now Bangladesh).

In 1958 he led the military coup that overthrew Iskander Mirza Ayub Khan was confirmed as president in a 1960 referendum. His administration was notable for its economic modernization and reforms to the political system. The failure of his regime to deal with poverty and social inequality forced him to resign.

Aztecs (Tenochca) Native American people of a civilization that rose to a position of dominance in the central valley of Mexico in c.1450. A warlike group, the Aztecs settled near Lake Texcoco in c.1325, where they founded their capital Tenochtitlán (now Mexico City). They established an empire that included most of present-day Mexico and extended S as far as Guatemala. The state was theocratic, with a number of deities whose worship included human sacrifice. The Aztecs built temples, pyramids and palaces and adorned them with stone images and symbolic carvings. At the time of the Spanish conquest, Aztec society was based on the exploitation of labor. As a result Hernán CORTÉS used disaffected tribesmen to help him defeat the Aztecs in 1521.

B

Babbage, Charles (1791–1871) English mathematician. Babbage compiled the first actuarial tables and planned a mechanical calculating machine, the forerunner of the modern computer. He failed to complete the construction of the machine because financial support was refused by the British government.

Babur (1483–1530) First Mughal emperor of India (1526–30, b. Zahir ud-Din Muhammad. Babur (Turk. tiger) became ruler of Fergana in 1495 and engaged in a long conflict for control of Samarkand but ultimately lost both territories. Raising an army he captured Kabul and carved out a new kingdom for himself in Afghanistan. From here he invaded India, gaining Delhi (1526) and Agra (1527) and conquering N India as far as Bengal.

Babylonia Ancient region and empire of Mesopotamia, based on the city of Babylon. The Babylonian empire was first established in the early 18th century BCE by HAMMURABI the Great but declined under the impact of HITTITES and KASSITES in c.1595 BCE. Babylonia eventually fell to the ASSYRIAN EMPIRE in the 8th century BCE. Babylon's greatness was restored and in c.625 BCE independence was won by Nabopolassar, who captured the Assyrian capital of Nineveh. This New Babylonian (Chaldaean) empire defeated Egypt and took the Jews to captivity in Babylon in 587 BCE. In 538 BCE it fell to the Persians.

Bach, Johann Sebastian (1685–1750) German composer. Bach brought contrapuntal forms to their highest expression and is unrivaled in his ability to interweave melodies within the exacting rules of baroque harmony and counterpoint. While at the court in Weimar (1708–17), Bach wrote many great organ works. At Köthen (1717–23), he wrote Book I of the *The Well-Tempered Clavier* and the six *Brandenburg Concertos*. As musical director of St. Thomas, Leipzig (1723–50), Bach wrote much church music including St. *Matthew Passion* (1729) and Mass in B Minor.

Bacon, Francis (1561–1626) English philosopher, statesman and advocate of the scientific method. He attempted to break the hold of Aristotelian logic and establish an inductive empiricism. Bacon entertained the idea of cataloguing all useful knowledge in his *Advancement of Learning* (1605) and *Novum Organum* (1620).

Bacon, Francis (1909–92) British painter, one of the most controversial artists of his generation, b. Ireland. Bacon changed the face of English painting in 1945 with his triptych *Three Studies for Figures at the Base of a Crucifixion*. The shock of the distorted representations of grieving people in his work stems from his violent handling of paint as much as from the subjects themselves.

Bacon, Roger (1220–92) English philosopher and scientist, strongly influenced by St. AUGUSTINE and medieval scholasticism. In 1247 Bacon became a Franciscan. His three best-known works, *Opus majus*, *Opus minor* and *Opus tertium*, were written (1267–68) for Pope Clement IV. His interest in alchemy and magic earned him the moniker "Doctor Mirabilis".

Baden-Powell of Gilwell, Robert Stephenson Smyth,

Baron (1857–1941) English soldier and founder of the Boy Scout movement. He held Mafeking against the Afrikaners (1899–1900).

Baffin, William (1584–1622) English navigator and explorer. Baffin took part in several expeditions (1612–16) in search of the Northwest Passage. He discovered the Canadian Arctic seaways, the island now named for him, and Lancaster Sound. He published a method of determining longitude by the stars, using nautical tables.

Baird, John Logie (1888–1946) Scottish electrical engineer. In 1926 Baird demonstrated the first working television. In 1928 he transmitted to a ship at sea, and in 1929 was granted broadcasting facilities by the British Broadcasting Corporation (BBC). His 240-line, part-mechanical television system was used for the world's first public television service by the BBC in 1936.

Bakunin, Mikhail Alexandrovich (1814–76) Russian political philosopher. Bakunin became a believer in violent revolution while in Paris in 1848. He was active in the first Communist International until expelled by Karl MARX in 1872. His approach, known as revolutionary anarchy, repudiates governmental authority as fundamentally at variance with human freedom and dignity.

Balboa, Vasco Núñez de (1475–1519) Spanish conquistador, the first European to see the Pacific Ocean. Balboa went to Hispaniola in 1500 and to Darién (Panama) ten years later. In September 1513 he crossed the isthmus and saw the Pacific, which he called the South Sea.

Baldwin I (1171–1205) Count of Flanders and Hainaut, first Latin emperor of Constantinople (1204–05). The capture of Constantinople by the Western armies of the Fourth Crusade led to the partition of the BYZANTINE EMPIRE, and Baldwin was elected ruler of the newly formed Latin state.

Baldwin, James (1924–87) US novelist and essayist. Baldwin's semiautobiographical first novel, *Go Tell It on the Mountain* (1953), has become an American classic. His prose is inflected with blues and gospel rhythms. His most celebrated novel is *Another Country* (1962).

Baldwin, Stanley, 1st earl of Bewdley (1867–1947) British statesman, prime minister (1923–24, 1924–29, 1935–37). Baldwin succeeded Bonar Law as Conservative prime minister. Baldwin responded to the General Strike (1926) by passing the Trades Disputes Acts (1927) which made any subsequent general strikes illegal. Baldwin opposed EDWARD VIII's marriage to Wallis Simpson and secured his abdication (1936). His appeasement of European fascism is often cited as a cause of Britain's lack of preparedness at the start of World War II.

Balfour, Arthur James Balfour, 1st Earl of (1848–1930) British statesman, prime minister (1902–05), b. Scotland. Balfour succeeded his uncle, the marquess of Salisbury, as prime minister. His government introduced educational reforms (1902), but the Conservative Party fractured over the tariff reform proposed by Joseph Chamberlain. Balfour resigned. He returned to the cabinet in the coalition governments of Herbert Asquith and David LLOYD GEORGE. As foreign secretary, Balfour issued the Balfour Declaration (1917), which was a letter written to the British Zionist Federation pledging cooperation for the settlement of Jews in Palestine.

Balzac, Honoré de (1799–1850) French novelist. Balzac's first success was *Les Chouans* (1829). More than 90 novels and short stories followed. Balzac organized these works into a grand fictional scheme intended as a realistic study of contemporary society, which he called *La Comédie Humaine*. Among his best-known novels are *Eugénie Grandet* (1833) and *Le Pére Goriot* (1835).

Bandaranaike, Sirimavo Ratwatte Dias (1916–2000) Sri Lankan stateswoman, prime minister (1960–65, 1970–77, 1994–2000). Following the assassination (1959) of her husband, Solomon BANDARANAIKE, she assumed control of the Sri Lanka Freedom Party and became the world's first woman prime minister. Her daughter, Kumaratunga, became president in 1994, and Sirimavo returned as prime minister.

Bandaranaike, Solomon West Ridgeway Dias (1899–1959) Ceylonese statesman, prime minister (1956–59). He made Sinhalese the official language and founded the Sri Lanka Freedom Party to unite nationalists and socialists. He was assassinated and his wife, Sirimavo BANDARANAIKE, succeeded him.

Banting, Sir Frederick Grant (1891–1941) Canadian physician. Banting shared, with J.J.R. Macleod, the 1923 Nobel Prize for physiology or medicine for his work in extracting the hormone insulin from the pancreas. This made possible the effective treatment of diabetes.

Barbarossa (1466–1546) (Redbeard) Name given by Christians to two Muslim privateers in the Mediterranean, **Aruj** (d.1518) and Khizr, or **Khayr ad-Din** (d.1546). Aruj was killed in battle against the Spanish. Khayr seized Algiers from Spain (1533), took Tunis (1534), raided Christian coasts and shipping, and gained control of the Barbary States. He acknowledged the Ottoman sultan as his overlord. From 1533 to 1544 Khayr was the commander of the fleet of SULEIMAN THE MAGNIFICENT. His forces were finally defeated by Spain and Italy in the famous naval battle of Lepanto (1571).

Bardeen, John (1908–91) US physicist. Bardeen won the Nobel Prize for physics twice: in 1956 he shared it with William SHOCKLEY and Walter BRATTAIN for their invention of the transistor, and in 1972 with Leon Cooper and John Schrieffer for their theory of superconductivity.

Barnard, Christiaan (1922–2001) South African surgeon. Barnard was the first to perform a human heart transplant (3 December 1967). In 1974 he was the first to implant a second heart into a patient and to link the circulations of the hearts so that they worked together as one.

Barth, Karl (1886–1968) Swiss theologian. Barth tried to lead theology back to the principles of the Reformation and emphasized the revelation of God through Jesus Christ. His school has been called dialectical theology.

Bartók, Béla (1881–1945) Hungarian composer. With Zoltán Kodály, Bartók amassed a collection of Hungarian folk music. His orchestral works include *Music for Strings, Percussion and Celesta* (1936). He wrote one opera, *Bluebeard's Castle* (1911). His compositions combine folk-music idioms with rhythmic energy.

Basil I (c.813–86) Byzantine emperor (r.867–86), founder of the Macedonian dynasty. Emperor Michael III assisted Basil in his rise to power. After Michael designated him coemperor, Basil had his former patron murdered. His most effective policies concerned the conversion of the Bulgars to Orthodox Christianity, military campaigns against the Paulician religious sect in Asia Minor and a revision of Roman legal codes.

Basil II (c.958–1025) Byzantine emperor (976–1025), surnamed Bulgaroctonus ("Bulgar-slayer"). One of Byzantium's ablest rulers, Basil reigned during the heyday of the empire. He is best known for his military victory over the Bulgarian czar Samuel in 1014, which brought the entire Balkan peninsula under Byzantine control.

Batista y Zaldívar, Fulgencio (1901–73) Cuban politician. In 1933 he led a successful military coup, and in 1940 he was elected president. In 1944 Batista retired and moved to Florida, but in 1952 a coup returned him to power. In 1959 he was overthrown by Fidel CASTRO.

Baudelaire, Charles Pierre (1821–67) French poet and critic. Baudelaire's collection of poems *Les Fleurs du Mal* (1857) represents one of the highest achievements of 19th-century French poetry. The poems were condemned by the censor and six were subsequently suppressed.

Baudouin (1930–93) King of Belgium (1951–93). During World War II he was interned by the Germans and after the war joined his father, LEOPOLD III, in exile (1945–50) in Switzerland. His father abdicated in 1951 and Baudouin became king. He granted independence to the Belgian Congo in 1960.

Bayle, Pierre (1647–1706) French philosopher. His major work was the *Historical and Critical Dictionary* (1697), a collection of biographies that examined philosophical and theological doctrines. A champion of religious toleration, Bayle was persecuted for his assertion that morality was independent of religion.

Beaker people People of the Neolithic culture known as the Beaker culture that spread throughout Europe in the late 3rd millennium BCE. Beaker culture is characterized by single-grave burials in round barrows, and a type of decorated, beaker-shaped pot accompanying the burial. It is likely that the diffusion of this culture represented a gradual spread of new ideas to existing groups, rather than the migration of large numbers of people.

Beauvoir, Simone de (1908–86) French novelist, and essayist. Her novels *She Came to Stay* (1943) and *The Mandarins* (1954) are portraits of the existentialist intellectual circle of which she and her lifelong companion, Jean-Paul SARTRE, were members. Her best-known work is the feminist treatise *The Second Sex* (1949).

Beckett, Samuel (1906–89) Irish playwright and novelist who wrote in both French and English. Beckett's reputation is largely due to his three full-length plays, *Waiting for Godot* (1952), *Endgame* (1957) and *Happy Days* (1961), which explore notions of suffering, paralysis and survival. His work is often linked to the Theater of the Absurd with its repetitive, inventive language and obsession with futility and meaninglessness. Beckett was awarded the 1969 Nobel Prize for literature.

Becquerel, (Antoine) Henri (1852–1908) French physicist. In 1896 Becquerel discovered radioactivity in uranium salts, for which he shared the 1903 Nobel Prize for physics with Pierre and Marie CURIE.

Bede, Saint (673–735) (Venerable Bede) English monk and scholar. Bede spent his life in the Northumbrian monasteries of Wearmouth and Jarrow. His most important work is the *Ecclesiastical History of the English People*, which remains an indispensable primary source for English history from 54 BCE to CE 697.

Beethoven, Ludwig van (1770–1827) German composer. Born in Bonn, Beethoven made Vienna his home from 1792. His early works, such as the piano sonatas *Pathétique* (1789) and *Moonlight* (1801), betray the influences of MOZART and HAYDN. The year 1801 marks the onset of Beethoven's deafness. His third symphony (*Eroica*, 1803) was a decisive break from the classical tradition. Beethoven's final period coincides with his complete loss of hearing (1817) and is marked by works of greater length and complexity, such as his ninth symphony (1817–23).

Begin, Menachem (1913–92) Israeli prime minister (1977–83), b.Poland. As commander of the paramilitary Irgun Zeva'i Leumi, Begin led resistance to British rule until Israeli independence in 1948. In 1973 he became leader of the Likud coalition. In 1977 Likud formed a coalition government with Begin as prime minister. Though a fervent nationalist, he sought reconciliation with Egypt and signed the Camp David Agreement with Anwar SADAT in 1979. In recognition of their efforts they shared the 1978 Nobel Peace Prize.

Behring, Emil Adolph von (1854–1917) German bacteriologist. Behring developed immunization against diphtheria (1890) and tetanus (1892) by injections of antitoxins. He was awarded (1901) the first Nobel Prize for physiology or medicine.

Belisarius (505–65) Byzantine general. Under JUSTINIAN I he waged campaigns against the Germanic tribes that threatened Byzantium on its W frontiers. He subjugated the VANDALS in N Africa and the OSTROGOTHS in Italy.

Bell, Alexander Graham (1847–1922) US inventor of the telephone, b. Scotland. He first worked with his father, inventor of a system for educating the deaf. The family moved to Canada in 1870. Bell's work on the transmission of sound by electricity led to the first demonstration of the telephone in 1876 and the founding of the Bell Telephone Company in 1877.

Bellini, Giovanni (*c.*1430–1516) Italian painter. Bellini single-handedly transformed Venice into a great center of the Renaissance. He is chiefly remembered as a religious painter. His pictures emphasize light and color as a means of expression. Many of the leading painters of Venice trained in his studio, including TITIAN.

Belloc, (Joseph) Hilaire (Pierre-René) (1870–1953) British writer, b. France. Belloc was a Liberal member of Parliament (1906–10). His work includes satirical novels, biographies and historical works. Belloc is best-known for his light verse, especially the children's classic, *Cautionary Tales* (1907).

Bellow, Saul (1915–2005) US novelist, b. Canada. His novels are concerned with the conflict between private and public, and the sense of alienation in urban life. Bellow won National Book awards for the picaresque *The Adventures of Augie March* (1953), the philosophical *Herzog* (1964), and *Mr. Sammler's Planet* (1970). He was awarded the 1976 Nobel Prize for literature.

Ben Bella, (Muhammad) Ahmed (1916–) Algerian statesman, prime minister (1962–63), president (1963–65). He was director (1952–56) of the *Front de Libération Nationale* (FLN). Imprisoned (1956–62) by the French, Ben Bella was released to become the first prime minister of an independent Algeria. He was deposed as president in a coup (1965) led by Houari BOUMÉDIENNE. After 15 years in prison, he went into exile (1980–90) in France where he formed the Movement for Democracy in Algeria.

Bentham, Jeremy (1748–1832) English philosopher and social reformer. In *Introduction to the Principles of Morals and Legislation* (1789), he developed the theory of utilitarianism, based on the premise that "the greatest happiness of the greatest number" should be the object of individual and government action.

Benz, Karl (1844–1929) German pioneer of the internal combustion engine. He built a four-stroke engine in 1885. Benz achieved great success when he installed the new engine in a four-wheel vehicle in 1893. Benz was the first to make and sell light, self-propelled vehicles built to a standardized pattern.

Berbers Caucasian Muslim people of N Africa and the Sahara. Some are herdsmen and subsistence farmers; others, like the TUAREG, roam the desert with their animal herds. Their stable culture dates back to before 2400 BCE. *See also* ALMOHAD; ALMORAVID

Berg, Alban (1885–1935) Austrian composer. A student of Arnold Schoenberg, Berg composed his later works in a complex individual style based on Schoenberg's twelve-tone technique *Wozzeck* (1925) is one of the masterpieces of 20th-century opera

Bering, Vitus Jonassen (1680–1741) Danish naval officer and explorer in Russian service who gave his name to the Bering Strait and Bering Sea. In 1728 he sailed N from Kamchatka, NE Siberia, to the Bering Strait to discover whether Asia and North America were joined. Bering turned back before he was certain but set out again in 1741, reaching Alaska. Returning, he was shipwrecked and died on what is now Bering Island.

Berkeley, George (1685–1753) Irish philosopher and clergy man. Drawing on the empiricism of John LOCKE, he argued tha there is no existence independent of subjective perception (*esse es percipi*). For Berkeley, the apparently ordered physical world is th work of God. This standpoint is often called subjective idealism.

Berlioz, (Louis) Hector (1803–69) French composer. Berlioz *Symphonie Fantastique* (1830) is a fine example of 19th-century romantic program music. His masterpiece is the cantata *L Damnation de Faust* (1846).

Bernadotte, Jean Baptiste *See* CHARLES XIV

Bernini, Gian Lorenzo (1598–1680) Italian architect an sculptor. Bernini's work combines astonishing, flamboyant ener gy with great clarity of detail. As the favorite of several pope Bernini was given many large-scale commissions in and aroun St. Peter's, including the *baldacchino* (canopy) above the hig altar (1633), Cathedra Petri (1657–66), and (from 165 onward) the great elliptical piazza and enclosing colonnades.

Bhutto, Benazir (1953–2007) Pakistani stateswoman, prim minister (1988–90, 1993–96), daughter of Zulfikar Ali BHUTT She was considered leader of the Pakistan People's Party but wa forced into exile. She returned in 1986. In 1988 she became Pak istan's first woman prime minister, but was removed from office c corruption charges. She was reelected in 1993 but again dismisse for corruption in 1996. In 2007 she returned to the country to con test planned 2008 elections, but was killed by a suicide bomber.

Bhutto, Zulfikar Ali (1928–79) Pakistani statesman, prime minister (1973–77), father of Benazir BHUTTO. He founded (1967) the Pakistan People's Party. In 1970 elections, Bhutto gained a majority in West Pakistan, but the Awami League controlled East Pakistan. Bhutto's refusal to grant autonomy to East Pakistan led to civil war (1971). Defeat led to the formation of Bangladesh, and Bhutto became Pakistan's president. He was overthrown in a military coup led by General ZIA. Bhutto was convicted of conspiracy to murder and executed.

Biko, Steve (Stephen) (1946–77) South African political activist. In 1969 Biko founded the South African Students Organization. In 1972 he cofounded the Black People's Convention, a black consciousness movement. In 1973 his freedom of speech and association were severely curtailed. He died in police custody at Port Elizabeth. Biko became a symbol of the cruelty of apartheid.

"Billy the Kid" (William H. Bonney) (1859–81) US frontier outlaw. Traditionally 21 murders are ascribed to him, but there is no evidence for this figure. In 1878 Billy the Kid killed a sheriff and led a gang of cattle rustlers. Sentenced in 1880, he escaped from jail but was caught and killed by Sheriff Pat Garrett.

Birtwistle, Harrison (1934–) English composer. Birtwistle has written a wide variety of works consolidating his position as a leading modern composer. His instrumental pieces include *The Triumph of Time* (1972). Birtwistle has written four operas: *Punch and Judy* (1967), *The Mask of Orpheus* (performed 1986), *Gawain* (1991) and *The Second Mrs. Kong* (1995).

Bismarck, Otto von (1815–98) German statesman responsible for 19th-century German unification. Bismarck first made an impression as a reactionary during the Revolutions of 1848. Keen to strengthen the Prussian army, WILLIAM I appointed (1862) him chancellor of Prussia. The status of Schleswig-Holstein enabled Bismarck to engineer the Austro-Prussian War (1866) and expel Austria from the German Confederation. Bismarck then provoked the Franco-Prussian War (1870–71) in order to bring the S German states into the Prussian-led North German Confederation. Victory saw Bismarck become (1871) the first chancellor of the empire. In 1882 he formed the Triple Alliance with Austro-Hungary and Italy. The rapid process of industrialization encouraged the building of a German empire. The accession (1888) of WILLIAM II saw the demise of Bismarck's political influence, and in 1890 he was forced to resign.

Bizet, Georges (1838–75) French composer. Bizet's opera *Carmen* (1875), although a failure at its first performance, has become one of the most popular operas. Bizet also composed other operas, notably *Les pêcheurs de perles* (1863), and orchestral works.

Black, Joseph (1728–99) British chemist, b. France. Rediscovering "fixed air" (carbon dioxide), Black found that this gas is produced by respiration, burning of charcoal and fermentation, that it behaves as an acid, and that it is found in the atmosphere.

Blair, Tony (Anthony Charles Lynton) (1953–) British statesman, prime minister (1997–2007). He entered Parliament in 1983 and joined the shadow cabinet in 1988. Blair was elected leader of the Labor Party after the death of John Smith (1994) and established himself as a moderator. His reform of the party's structure and constitution helped him achieve a landslide victory in the 1997 general election. His reforms as prime minister included giving the Bank of England independence in the setting of interest rates and devolution for Scotland and Wales.

Blake, William (1757–1827) English poet, philosopher and artist. A visionary, he attempted to create a visual symbolism to represent his spiritual visions. In the 1780s Blake worked as a commercial engraver, but from *c.*1787 he began printing his own illustrated poems in color. The first example was *Songs of Innocence* (1789). Among his productions were: *Songs of Experience* (1794); books portraying his private mythologies, such as *The Book of Urizen* (1794) and *The Four Zoas* (1797); and illustrations to *The Book of Job* and Dante's *Divine Comedy*.

Blériot, Louis (1872–1936) French aircraft designer and aviator. In 1909 Blériot became the first man to fly an aircraft across the English Channel. The flight from Calais to Dover took 37 minutes. As a designer, he was responsible for a system by which the pilot could operate ailerons by remote control.

Bligh, William (1754–1817) English naval officer. Bligh was captain of the *Bounty* in 1789, when his mutinous crew cast him adrift. With a few loyal companions, he sailed nearly 6,500km (4,000mi) to Timor. While governor of New South Wales (1805–08), he was arrested by mutineers and sent back to England. He was exonerated.

Blücher, Gebhard Leberrecht von (1744–1819) Prussian field-marshal. He distinguished himself during the Napoleonic Wars. Blücher led the Prussian troops at the battle of Lützen and helped defeat NAPOLEON I at Leipzig (1813). In 1815 he was defeated at Ligny but arrived at Waterloo in time to secure British victory.

Blum, Léon (1872–1950) French statesman, prime minister (1936–37). He served in the chamber of deputies (1919–40) as a leader of the Socialist Party. Blum formed the Popular Front, which became a coalition government. His administration embarked on a program of nationalization. Opposed by Conservatives, Blum was forced to resign. Interned by the Vichy government (1940–45), he briefly led a provisional government.

Boadicea (Boudicca) (d. CE 62) Queen of the Iceni in E Britain. She was the wife of King Prasutagus who, on his death, left his daughters and the Roman emperor as coheirs. The Romans seized his domain, and Boadicea led a revolt against them. After initial successes, during which her army is thought to have killed as many as 70,000 Roman soldiers, she was defeated and poisoned herself.

Boccaccio, Giovanni (1313–75) Italian poet, prose writer and scholar, one of the founders of the Italian Renaissance. Boccaccio is best known for the *Decameron* (1348–58). Ten prose stories with different narrators dealing with contemporary mores, it exercised a tremendous influence on the development of Renaissance literature.

Boethius (*c.*480–524) (Anicius Manlius Severinus) Roman statesman and philosopher under Emperor Theodoric. He attempted to eliminate governmental corruption but was imprisoned on a charge of conspiracy. In prison at Pavia, where he was subsequently executed, Boethius wrote *On the Consolation of Philosophy* (523).

Bohr, Niels Henrik David (1885–1962) Danish physicist, the first person to apply quantum theory successfully to atomic structure. In the 1920s Bohr helped to develop the "standard model" of quantum theory. During World War II he worked briefly on developing the atomic bomb in the USA. He later returned to Copenhagen and worked for international cooperation. Bohr was awarded the 1922 Nobel Prize for physics for his work on atomic structure and in 1957 received the first Atoms for Peace Award.

Bokassa, Jean Bédel (1921–96) Emperor of the Central African Empire (1977–79). Bokassa came to power in 1966 in a military coup. After serving as president (1966–77) of the Central African Republic, he crowned himself emperor. His regime was brutal. A 1979 coup removed Bokassa, who went into exile.

Bolívar, Simón (1783–1830) Latin American revolutionary leader, known as "the Liberator". Bolívar's victory at Boyacá led to the liberation of New Granada (later Colombia) in 1821. The liberation of Venezuela (1821), Ecuador (1822), Peru (1824) and Upper Peru (1825) followed, the latter renaming itself Bolivia in his honor. Despite the removal of Spanish hegemony from the continent, his hopes of uniting South America into one confederation were dashed by rivalry between the new states.

Boltzmann, Ludwig (1844–1906) Austrian physicist, acclaimed for his contribution to statistical mechanics and the kinetic theory of gases. Boltzmann's general law asserts that a system will approach a state of thermodynamic equilibrium. He introduced the "Boltzmann equation" (1877) relating the kinetic energy of a gas atom or molecule to temperature. In 1884 he derived a law, often termed the "Stefan-Boltzmann law", for black body radiation discovered by his Austrian teacher, Josef Stefan

(1835–93). Attacked for his belief in the atomic theory of matter, Boltzmann committed suicide.

Bonaparte, Joseph (1768–1844) King of Spain, b. Corsica. He was the eldest brother of NAPOLEON I. He served as diplomat for the First Republic of France. Napoleon made him king of Naples (1806), and he was also king of Spain (1808–13). After Napoleon's defeat at Waterloo, he resided in the USA (1815–32).

Boole, George (1815–64) English mathematician. Boole is remembered for his invention of Boolean algebra, commonly used in computers.

Boone, Daniel (1734–1820) US frontier pioneer. In 1775 he blazed the famous Wilderness Road from Virginia to Kentucky and founded the settlement of Boonesborough. During the American Revolution, Boone was captured by the SHAWNEE, but escaped and reached Boonesborough in time to prevent it from falling to the British and their Native-American allies.

Booth, William (1829–1912) English religious leader, founder and first general of the Salvation Army. A Methodist, Booth started his own revivalist movement, which undertook evangelistic and social work among the poor. It became known as the Salvation Army in 1878 and spread to many countries.

Borges, Jorge Luis (1899–1986) Argentinian short-story writer, poet and critic. Borges is best known for his short-story collections *Dreamtigers* (1960), *The Book of Imaginary Beings* (1967) and *Dr. Brodie's Report* (1970). Dreamlike and poetic, they established Borges as a significant literary talent.

Borgia, Cesare (1475–1507) Italian general and political figure, son of Pope Alexander VI. He was made a cardinal (1493) by his father, but forsook the church to embark on a military campaign (1498–1503) to establish his dominion in central Italy. Borgia's ruthless campaigns lend credence to the theory that he was the model for Machiavelli's *The Prince*. Imprisoned by Pope Julius II, Borgia escaped to Spain, where he was killed in battle.

Borodin, Alexander Porfirevich (1833–87) Russian composer and chemist. His works include the tone poem *In the Steppes of Central Asia* (1880) and the *Polovtsian Dances* from his opera *Prince Igor* (completed after his death by Glazunov and Rimsky-Korsakov).

Borromini, Francesco (1599–1667) Italian architect. Borromini's hallmark was a dynamic, hexagonal design, such as the spectacular Sant'Ivo della Sapienza, Rome (1642). His masterpieces include San Carlo alle Quattro Fontane (1638–41) and Sant'Agnese (1653–55), Rome.

Bosch, Hieronymus (c.1450–1516) Flemish painter, b. Jerome van Aken, in 's Hertogenbosch. His paintings of grotesque and fantastic visions based on religious themes led to accusations of heresy and influenced 20th-century surrealism. His surviving works include *The Temptation of St. Anthony* and *The Garden of Earthly Delights*.

Boswell, James (1740–95) Scottish biographer and author. He traveled widely in Europe, meeting VOLTAIRE and Jean-Jacques ROUSSEAU. An inveterate hero-worshiper, Boswell found his vocation as the friend and biographer of Samuel JOHNSON. His monumental *Life of Samuel Johnson* (1791) is regarded as one of the greatest biographies in English.

Botha, Louis (1862–1919) South African statesman and military leader. He was an outstanding commander during the South African War (1899–1902). A moderate, Botha advocated reconciliation with the British and in 1910 became first prime minister of the Union of South Africa.

Botha, P.W. (Pieter Willem) (1916–2006) South African statesman, the longest-serving member of the apartheid regime. As defense minister (1966–78), Botha was responsible for the military involvement in Angola. Botha became prime minister (1978) and undertook limited reform of apartheid. Botha established the Southwest Africa Territorial Force, as part of a destabilization policy of South Africa's neighbors. Botha became (1980) South Africa's first president. In 1989 he suffered a stroke and resigned. He was replaced by F.W. DE KLERK.

Botticelli, Sandro (1444–1510) (Alessandro di Mariano Filipepi) Florentine Renaissance painter. Botticelli was part of a movement that admired the ornamental, linear qualities of Gothic art. He is best known for his mythological allegories *Primavera* (c.1478), *The Birth of Venus* and *Pallas and the Centaur*. Botticelli was one of the few privileged to decorate the Sistine Chapel in Rome (1481). He was loved by the Pre-Raphaelite Brotherhood.

Boucher, François (1703–70) French painter, decorator and engraver. His style was the epitome of rococo frivolity. Boucher was immensely successful. He produced over 11,000 historical, mythological, genre and landscape paintings.

Bougainville, Louis Antoine de (1729–1811) French navigator. He commanded the first French naval force to circumnavigate the globe (1766–69). Important botanical and astronomical studies were made during the voyage, and Bougainville claimed many of the Pacific islands for France, rediscovering the Solomon Islands. He fought in the American Revolution but was disgraced by a French defeat (1782) in the Caribbean.

Boulanger, Georges Ernest Jean Marie (1837–91) French general and minister. Supported by the Bonapartists and royalists, he became a serious threat to the republican government in the 1880s. He committed suicide after being deported.

Boulton, Matthew (1728–1809) British engineer and manufacturer. In 1762 he built the Soho iron works near Birmingham. In 1775 he went into partnership with James WATT and began manufacturing Watt's steam engines on a commercial basis. In 1790 Boulton patented a steam-powered coining press.

Boumédienne, Houari (1925–78) President of Algeria. In the war for independence, Boumédienne commanded guerrilla forces. He served as vice-president from the achievement of independence in 1962 to 1965, when he overthrew President BEN BELLA and assumed authoritarian powers. He held office until his death.

Bourbon dynasty European dynastic family, descendants of the CAPETIANS. The ducal title was created in 1327 and continued until 1527. A cadet branch, the Bourbon-Vendôme line, won the kingdom of Navarre. The Bourbons ruled France from 1589 (when Henry of Navarre became HENRY IV) until the French Revolution (1789). Two members of the family, LOUIS XVIII and CHARLES X, reigned (1814–30) after the restoration of the monarchy. In 1700 the Bourbons became the ruling family of Spain when PHILIP V assumed the throne. His descendants most continued to rule Spain until 1931, when the Second Republic was declared. JUAN CARLOS I, a Bourbon, was restored to the Spanish throne in 1975.

Bourguiba, Habib (1903–2000) First president of Tunisia (1957–87). In 1954 he began the negotiations that culminated in Tunisian independence (1956). He became prime minister and, after the abolition of the monarchy, was elected president. In 1975 he was proclaimed president-for-life. Bourguiba maintained a pro-French, autocratic rule until he was overthrown in a coup led by Ben Ali.

Boutros-Ghali, Boutros (1922–) Egyptian politician, sixth secretary-general of the United Nations (1992–96). As Egypt's foreign affairs minister (1977–91), he was involved in much of the Middle East peace negotiations. Boutros-Ghali briefly served Egypt's prime minister (1991–92). As secretary general of the UN, he faced civil-war crises in the Balkans, Somalia and Rwanda.

Bowie, Jim (James) (1796–1836) US frontiersman. He moved to Texas from Louisiana in 1828 and married the daughter of the Mexican vice-governor. By 1832 he had joined the colonists, who opposed the Mexican government. Bowie was appointed a colonel in the Texas army (1835) and was killed at the battle of the Alamo (1836).

Boyle, Robert (1627–91) British chemist, b. Ireland. He researched air, vacuum, metals, combustion and sound. Boyle's *Sceptical Chymist* (1661) proposed an early atomic theory of matter. He made an efficient vacuum pump, which he used to establish (1662) Boyle's law. This law states that the volume of a gas at constant temperature is inversely proportional to the pressure.

Brahe, Tycho (1546–1601) Danish astronomer. He was expert in making accurate naked-eye measurements of the stars and planets. Brahe built an observatory on the island of Hven (1576) and calculated the orbit of the comet seen in 1577. This showed that ARISTOTLE was wrong in picturing an unchanging heaven. In Brahe's theory, the planets move around the Sun, and the Sun itself moves round the stationary Earth.

Brahms, Johannes (1833–97) German composer. Brahms used classical forms rather than the less-strict programmatic style that was popular, and he was a master of contrapuntal harmony. Brahms' major works are the *German Requiem* (1868), the Violin Concerto in D (1878) and four symphonies (1876–1885).

Bramante, Donato (1444–1514) Italian architect and painter, the greatest exponent of High Renaissance architecture. In 1506 he started rebuilding St. Peter's, Rome. His influence was enormous, and many Milanese painters took up his interest in perspective and *trompe l'oeil*.

Brandt, Willy (1913–92) German statesman, chancellor of West Germany (1969–74), b. Karl Herbert Frahm. An active Social Democrat, he fled Germany during the Nazi era. Brandt returned after World War II. As chancellor, he initiated a program of cooperation with the Communist bloc states, for which he was awarded the Nobel Peace Prize in 1971. Brandt resigned after a close aide was exposed as an East German spy.

Braque, Georges (1882–1963) French painter who created cubism with PICASSO. *Head of a Woman* (1909), *Violin and Palette* (1909–10) and *The Portuguese* (1911) show his transition through the early, analytical phases of cubism. Braque was wounded in World War I and afterward evolved a gentler style of painting which earned him enormous prestige.

Brattain, Walter Houser (1902–87) US physicist. He shared the 1956 Nobel Prize for physics with John BARDEEN and William SHOCKLEY for their development of the transistor and research into semiconductivity.

Brecht, Bertolt (1898–1956) German playwright, poet and drama theorist. In the 1920s, Brecht developed his theory of epic theater. It encouraged audiences to see theater as staged illusion via a range of "alienation" techniques. His major works were written in collaboration with composers: Kurt Weill, *The Threepenny Opera* (1928); Hanns Eisler, *The Mother* (1931); and Paul Dessau, *The Caucasian Chalk Circle* (1948). With the rise of Hitler, Brecht's Marxist views forced him into exile. While in USA, Brecht wrote *The Good Woman of Setzuan* (1943).

Brezhnev, Leonid Ilyich (1906–82) Soviet statesman, effective ruler from the mid1960s until his death. He rose through the Communist Party of the Soviet Union (CPSU) to become (1957) a member of the presidium (later politburo). In 1964 Brezhnev helped plan the downfall of Nikita KHRUSHCHEV and became party general secretary. In 1977 he became president of the Soviet Union. Brezhnev pursued a hard line against reforms at home and in Eastern Europe but also sought to reduce tensions with the West. After the Soviet invasion of Czechoslovakia (1968), he promulgated the "Brezhnev Doctrine" confirming Soviet domination of satellite states.

Bright, John (1811–89) British parliamentary reformer. A Quaker, he and his fellow radical, Richard COBDEN, were leaders of the Anti-Corn Law League. First elected to Parliament in 1843, Bright subsequently represented Manchester, the home of free trade. He lost his seat in 1857 after opposing the Crimean War but was reelected for Birmingham.

Britten, (Edward) Benjamin (1913–76) English composer. Britten is best known for his operas, which include *Peter Grimes* (1945), *Billy Budd* (1951), *The Turn of the Screw* (1954) and *Death in Venice* (1973). Other major works include the *Young Person's Guide to the Orchestra* (1945) and *War Requiem* (1962). In 1948 he established the music festival held annually at his hometown of Aldeburgh, E England. He was made a peer in 1976.

Broca, Paul (1824–80) French pathologist, anthropologist and neurosurgeon. Broca specialized in aphasia and located the brain center for articulate speech – the third convolution of the left frontal lobe (Broca's Area).

Broglie, Prince Louis Victor de (1892–1987) French physicist who theorized that all elementary particles have an associated wave. He devised the formula that predicts this wavelength, and its existence was proved in 1927. Broglie was awarded the 1929 Nobel Prize for physics.

Brontë, Charlotte (1816–55) English novelist and poet. Brontë suffered from poor health, and her mother, four sisters and dissolute brother Branwell died early. Her four novels, *The Professor* (1846), *Jane Eyre* (1847), *Shirley* (1849) and *Villette* (1853), are works of remarkable passion and imagination. Her writings initially appeared under the male pseudonym Currer Bell.

Brontë, Emily (1818–48) English novelist and poet. Like her sisters Charlotte and Anne, she wrote under a male pseudonym, Ellis Bell. Her love for the Yorkshire moors and insight into human passion are manifested in her poetry and her only novel, *Wuthering Heights* (1847).

Brown, John (1800–59) US antislavery crusader. In 1859, hoping to start a slave revolt, he led 21 men to capture the US arsenal at Harper's Ferry, Virginia. They were driven out by troops under Robert E. LEE. Brown was captured, charged with treason and hanged. The trial aggravated North–South tensions.

Browning, Elizabeth Barrett (1806–61) English poet. In 1846 she secretly married Robert BROWNING and, from 1847, the couple lived in Florence, Italy. *The Seraphim and Other Poems* (1838) and *Poems* (1844) established her popularity, confirmed by a collection of 1850, which included *Sonnets from the Portuguese*.

Browning, Robert (1812–89) English poet. "My Last Duchess" and "Soliloquy of the Spanish Cloister", both published in *Bells and Pomegranates* (1846), display his use of dramatic monologue. In 1846 he and Elizabeth Barrett (BROWNING) secretly married and moved to Italy. Browning published *Christmas Eve and Easter Day* (1850) and *Men and Women* (1855) before returning to London after Elizabeth's death. His popularity increased with *The Ring and the Book* (1868–69).

Bruckner, Anton (1824–96) Austrian composer. He wrote much church music and nine symphonies. Bruckner's compositions are noted for their massive scale.

Bruegel, Pieter the Elder (1525–69) Netherlandish landscape painter and draftsman. Bruegel traveled extensively in France and Italy. In 1563 he moved to Brussels. The characteristic rural scenes crowded with peasant figures of his early years gave way later to paintings with larger figures that illustrated proverbs.

Brunel, Isambard Kingdom (1806–59) English marine and railroad engineer who revolutionized British engineering. In 1829 he designed the Clifton Suspension Bridge (completed 1864). Brunel is also noted for his ships; *Great Western* (designed 1837), the first trans-Atlantic wooden steamship; *Great Britain* (1843), the first iron-hulled, screw-driven steamship; and *Great Eastern* (1858), the largest steamship of its era.

Brunelleschi, Filippo (1377–1446) Florentine architect, a pioneer of perspective. In 1420 he began to design the dome of Florence Cathedral, the largest since the Hagia Sophia. Other works include the Ospedale degl'Innocenti (1419–26) and the Basilica of San Lorenzo (begun 1421), both in Florence.

Buchanan, James (1791–1868) 15th US president (1857–1861). President POLK appointed him secretary of state (1845–49). Under President PIERCE, Buchanan served as minister to Great Britain (1853–56). His presidential administration was unpopular, and his attempt to compromise between pro- and antislavery factions floundered. His efforts to purchase Cuba and acceptance of a pro-slavery constitution in Kansas contributed to his defeat by Abraham LINCOLN. The Southern states seceded and, shortly after he left office, the Civil War began.

Buddha (Enlightened One) Title adopted by Gautama Siddhartha (*c.*563–*c.*483 BCE), the founder of Buddhism. Siddhartha was born in Lumbini, Nepal, and his early years were spent in luxury. At the age of 29, he realized that human life is little more than suffering. He gave up his wealth and comfort, deserted his wife and son, and took to the road as a wandering ascetic. He sought truth in a six-year regime of austerity. After abandoning asceticism as futile, he sought his own middle way toward enlightenment. The moment of truth came (*c*.528 BCE) as he sat beneath a banyan tree in the village of Buddha Gaya, Bihar, India. After this, he taught others about his way to truth.

Bülow, Bernhard, Prince von (1849–1929) Chancellor of the German empire (1900–09). His aggressive foreign policy left Germany isolated against the Triple Entente (Britain, France and Russia), heightening tensions in Europe before World War I. In 1908 he lost the favor of WILLIAM II and was forced to resign.

Bunsen, Robert Wilhelm (1811–99) German chemist. Working with organo-arsenic compounds, he discovered an arsenic poisoning antidote. With his assistant, Gustav KIRCHHOFF, he used spectroscopy to discover two new elements (cesium and rubidium). Bunsen invented various kinds of laboratory equipment. He also improved a gas burner that was later named for him.

Bunyan, John (1628–88) English preacher and author. During the English Civil War (1642–52) he fought as a Parliamentarian. In 1660 he was arrested for unlicensed preaching. Bunyan spent 12 years in prison, where he wrote the spiritual autobiography *Grace Abounding* (1666). In 1672 he was reimprisoned and started work on the Christian allegory *The Pilgrim's Progress* (1684).

Burgoyne, John (1722–92) British general during the American Revolution. He served as major-general in Canada (1776) and campaigned in New York State, securing Crown Point and Fort Ticonderoga. He was forced to surrender his troops at Saratoga in October 1777.

Burke, Edmund (1729–97) British statesman and writer, b. Ireland. He played a major part in the reduction of royal influence in the House of Commons and sought better treatment for Catholics and American colonists. He deplored the excesses of the French Revolution in *Reflections on the Revolution in France* (1790).

Burke, Robert O'Hara (1820–61) Irish explorer. In 1860 he led the first expedition to cross Australia from S to N. At the River Barcoo, Burke continued with only three companions. They reached N Australia in 1861. Only one of the group survived the return journey.

Burne-Jones, Sir Edward Coley (1833–98) English painter and designer. He was associated with the Pre-Raphaelite Brotherhood's romanticism and escapism. He was considered an outstanding designer of stained glass.

Burns, Robert (1759–96) Scottish poet. Burns is Scotland's unofficial national poet. *Poems, Chiefly in the Scottish Dialect* (1786) includes "The Holy Fair" and "To a Mouse". Other works include "Tam o'Shanter" (1790) and "Auld Lang Syne".

Burr, Aaron (1756–1836) US statesman, vice-president (1801–05). Burr was senator for New York (1791–97). His contribution to the formation of a Republican legislature in New York (1800) ensured the election of a Republican president. Burr was supposed to become vice-president, but confusion in the electoral college resulted in a tie for president between Burr and Thomas JEFFERSON. Jefferson was elected with the support of Alexander HAMILTON. Burr was an able vice-president. Hamilton led attacks on Burr's suitability, which resulted in a duel (1804). Burr killed Hamilton, effectively ending his own political career.

Burton, Sir Richard Francis (1821–90) English explorer and scholar. In 1853 he traveled in disguise to Medina and Mecca, one of the first Europeans to visit the holy cities. On his second trip to E Africa, with John Speke in 1857, Burton discovered Lake Tanganyika.

Bush, George Herbert Walker (1924–) 41st US president (1989–93). Bush served as a fighter pilot during World War II. In 1966 he entered Congress as a representative for Texas. Under President Gerald FORD, Bush was head (1976–77) of the Central Intelligence Agency (CIA). In 1980 he became vice-president (1981–88) to Ronald REAGAN. Iraq's invasion (1990) of Kuwait provided the first test of Bush's presidential administration. The Allied forces won the Gulf War (1991). At home, Bush was faced with a stagnant economy, high unemployment and a massive budget deficit. He was forced (1990) to raise taxes. This factor, combined with a split in the conservative vote, led to a victory for his Democratic successor Bill CLINTON.

Bush, George W. (Walker) (1946–) 43rd US president (2001–), son of the 41st president George Bush. He served as Republican governor of Texas (1995–2000). In the 2000 presidential elections, George W. Bush narrowly defeated the Democrat candidate Al Gore in a highly contentious ballot. Faced with economic recession, Bush passed a tax-cutting budget. After the terrorist attacks on the United States on September 11, 2001, Bush led the country into war in Afghanistan to topple the Taliban regime accused of supporting al-Qaeda. In 2003 he ordered the invasion of Iraq to topple the regime of SADDAM Hussein. Bush was reelected in 2004. The high cost of the ongoing Iraq and Afghan wars damaged the US economy.

Byron, George Gordon Noel Byron, 6th Baron (1788–1824) English poet. He became famous with the publication of the first two cantos of *Childe Harold's Pilgrimage* (1812). Byron's romantic image and reputation for dissolute living and sexual affairs vied with his poetic reputation. In exile, Byron wrote Cantos III and IV of *Childe Harold* (1816, 1818), and *Don Juan* (1819–24), an epic satire. In 1823 he went to fight for Greek independence against the Turks and died of fever at Missolonghi.

Byzantine Empire Christian, Greek-speaking, Eastern ROMAN EMPIRE. It outlasted the Roman Empire in the West by nearly 1000 years. Constantinople (Byzantium or Istanbul) was established by Roman Emperor CONSTANTINE I in CE 330. The area of the Byzantine Empire varied greatly, and its history from *c*.600 was marked by military crisis and heroic recovery. At its height, under JUSTINIAN I, in the 6th century, it controlled, as well as Asia Minor and the Balkans, much of the Near East and the Mediterranean coastal regions of Europe and North Africa. From 1204 to 1261 it was controlled by Crusaders from W Europe. Constantinople was recovered, but Byzantine territory shrank under pressure from the West and from the OTTOMAN Turks, who finally captured Constantinople in 1453, extinguishing the Byzantine Empire.

C

Cabot, John (*c*.1450–98) Italian navigator who made the first recorded European journey to the coast of North America since the Vikings. Supported by the English king Henry VII, Cabot sailed in search of a western route to India and reached New foundland (1497). His discovery served as the basis for English claims in North America.

Cabral, Pedro Alvares (1467–1520) Portuguese navigator who was the first European to discover Brazil. Supported by the Portuguese king Manuel I, Cabral led an expedition (1500) to the East Indies. To avoid the Gulf of Guinea, he sailed westward and reached Brazil, which he claimed for Portugal.

Cadillac, Antoine de la Mothe (1658–1730) French colonial administrator. He arrived in Canada in 1683. Cadillac became commander (1694–97) of the fur-trading post at Mackinac. He returned to France (1699) and received a grant to establish a colony. Cadillac founded Detroit (1701) and was governor of Louisiana (1713–16).

Caesar, (Gaius) Julius (100–44 BCE) Roman general and statesman. After the death of SULLA, Caesar became military tribune. In 63 BCE, as *pontifex maximus*, he directed reforms that resulted in the Julian calendar. In 60 BCE Caesar formed the First Triumvirate with POMPEY and CRASSUS. He conquered Gaul for Rome (58–49 BCE) and invaded Britain (54 BCE). Refusing Senate demands to disband his army, he provoked civil war with Pompey. Caesar defeated Pompey at Pharsalus (48 BCE) and pursued him to Egypt, where he made CLEOPATRA queen. He returned to Rome in 45 BCE and was received with unprecedented honors, culminating in the title of dictator for life. Caesar's power aroused resentment. He was assassinated in the Senate on 15 March by a con spiracy led by Cassius and Brutus. Octavian (later AUGUSTUS) and Mark ANTONY avenged his murder.

Caligula (CE 12–41) (Gaius Caesar) Roman emperor (37–41). Son of Germanicus Caesar, he became emperor after the death of TIBERIUS. Caligula was highly autocratic, made his horse a consul to mock the Senate, and was said to be insane. He was murdered by the Praetorian Guard and succeeded by his uncle, CLAUDIUS I.

Calvert, George, 1st Baron Baltimore (1580–1632) English colonizer. Calvert was secretary of state (1619–25) under James I, but resigned after converting to Roman Catholicism. In 1629 he sought a charter for a colony in what became Maryland.

Calvin, John (1509–64) French theologian. He prepared for a career in the Roman Catholic Church but in c.1533 became a Protestant and began work on *Institutes of the Christian Religion*. In this work he presented the basics of Calvinism. Rejecting papal authority and relying on the Bible, Calvinism stressed the sovereignty of God and predestination. Calvin went to live in Switzerland (1536), where he advanced the Reformation.

Camões, Luís vaz de (1524–80) Portuguese poet and soldier. In 1572 he published *The Lusiads*, which was adopted as Portugal's national epic and established him as the national poet.

Camus, Albert (1913–60) French novelist, playwright and essayist. An active figure in the French Resistance, Camus' first novel, *The Stranger* (1942) was permeated with the sense of individual alienation. His later works include the novels *The Plague* (1947) and *The Fall* (1956). He received the 1957 Nobel Prize in literature.

Canaletto (1697–1768) (Giovanni Antonio Canal) Italian painter of the Venetian School, famous for his perspectival views of Venice. Canaletto's early work is more dramatic and free-flowing than his smoother, accurate mature style. He used a camera obscura to make his paintings more precise.

Cantor, Georg (1845–1918) German mathematician, b. Russia. His work on infinity challenged the existing deductive process of mathematics. Cantor developed the set theory and provided a new definition of irrational numbers.

Canute (c.994–1035) King of Denmark (1014–28), England (1016–35) and Norway (1028–29). He accompanied his father, Sweyn, on the Danish invasion of England (1013). After his father's death (1014), Canute was accepted as joint king of Denmark with his brother and later became sole king. He invaded England again (1015) and divided it (1016) with the English king Edmund Ironside. Canute became king after Edmund's death. His rule was a just and peaceful one. His reign in Scandinavia was more turbulent. He conquered Norway (1028) made one son king of Denmark (1028) and another king of Norway (1029).

Capet, Hugh (938–96) King of France (987–96), founder of the CAPETIAN DYNASTY. Hugh inherited the title of duke of the Franks from his father, Hugh the Great, in 956. He allied himself (978–86) with the German emperors against the CAROLINGIAN king of France, Lothair. In 987 he was elected king of France on the death of Lothair's son Louis V. Although his election was disputed by Charles I of Lower Lorraine, Hugh was able to fix the succession on his son, who became Robert II.

Capetian dynasty French royal family forming the third dynasty. It provided France with 15 kings. The dynasty began (987) with Hugh CAPET, who succeeded Louis V, the last of the CAROLINGIAN DYNASTY. The Capetian dynasty dominated the feudal forces, extending the king's rule across the whole of France. The last Capetian king, Charles IV, was succeeded (1328) by Philip VI of the House of VALOIS.

Capone, Al (Alphonse) (1899–1947) US gangster of the prohibition era, b. Italy. He inherited a vast crime empire from Johnny Torio. Capone was suspected of many brutal crimes but was only ever convicted and imprisoned for income tax evasion (1931).

Caracalla (188–217) (Marcus Aurelius Antoninus) Roman emperor (211–17). Caracalla murdered his brother Geta (212). Excessive expenditure on war caused economic crisis. During his reign, Roman citizenship was extended to all free men in the empire. Caracalla was assassinated by his successor, Macrinus.

Caravaggio, Michelangelo Merisi da (1571–1610) Italian painter. His work brought a new, formidable sense of reality at a time when a feeble mannerism prevailed. The majestic *Supper at Emmaus* (c.1598–1600) shows him gaining confidence. His mature phase (1599–1606) began with two large-scale paintings of St. Matthew. The use of dramatic shadows and a living model show Caravaggio's revolutionary approach to religious themes.

Carlos (1788–1855) Spanish prince and pretender to the throne. His elder brother, FERDINAND VII, changed Spanish law so that his daughter ISABELLA II succeeded him (1833). Carlos was proclaimed king by the Carlists, and civil war ensued. Isabella won (1840), and Carlos went into exile. In 1845 he resigned his claim in favor of his son, Don Carlos II.

Carlyle, Thomas (1795–1881) Scottish philosopher, critic and historian. His most successful work, *Sartor Resartus* (1836), combined philosophy and autobiography. His histories include *The French Revolution* (1837). Influenced by romanticism, Carlyle was a powerful advocate of the significance of great leaders in history.

Carnot, Lazare Nicolas Marguerite (1753–1823) French general. He was the outstanding commander of the French Revolutionary wars, his strategy being largely responsible for French victories. Ousted in 1797, Carnot was recalled by NAPOLEON (1800), who made him minister of war.

Carnot, (Nicolas Léonard) Sadi (1796–1832) French engineer and physicist whose work laid the foundation for the science of thermodynamics. His *Réflexions sur la puissance motrice du feu* (1824) provided the first theoretical background for the steam engine and introduced the concept of the second law of thermodynamics, which was formulated later by Rudolf CLAUSIUS.

Carol II (1893–1953) King of Romania (1930–40), grandnephew of Carol I (the first king of Romania). In 1925 Carol renounced the throne. He returned in 1930 and supplanted his son, Michael, as king. He supported the fascist movement. German pressure forced him to abdicate in favor of Michael, leaving power in the hands of the fascist leader, Ion ANTONESCU.

Carolingian dynasty Second Frankish dynasty of early medieval Europe. Founded in the 7th century by Pepin of Landen, it rose to power under the weak kingship of the MEROVINGIAN DYNASTY. In 732 CHARLES MARTEL defeated the Muslims at Poitiers; in 751 his son, PEPIN III (THE SHORT), deposed the last Merovingian and became king of the Franks. The dynasty peaked under Pepin's son, CHARLEMAGNE. Charlemagne united the Frankish dominions and much of W and central Europe and was crowned Holy Roman emperor by the pope in 800. His empire was later broken up by civil wars. Carolingian rule ended in 987.

Carranza, Venustiano (1859–1920) Mexican statesman, president (1914). Carranza supported Francisco MADERO's revolution against Porfirio DíAZ. When Madero was overthrown by Victoriano HUERTA, Carranza joined Álvaro OBREGÓN, "Pancho" VILLA and Emiliano ZAPATA to defeat Huerta. Villa and Zapata's refusal to recognize Carranza's authority prolonged the civil war. Carranza's attempts to prevent the accession of Obregón led to a revolt. Carranza fled and was murdered.

Carroll, Lewis (1832–98) English mathematician, photographer and writer, b. Charles Lutwidge Dodgson. An Oxford don, much of whose output consisted of mathematical textbooks, Carroll is remembered for *Alice's Adventures in Wonderland* (1865) and its sequel, *Through the Looking Glass* (1872).

Carson, Rachel Louise (1907–64) US writer and marine biologist. Carson is best known for her books on marine ecology, such as *The Sea Around Us* (1951). *Silent Spring* (1962) was a pioneering work in the development of the environmental movement.

Carter, Jimmy (James Earl), Jr. (1924–) 39th US president (1977–81). He was a Democrat senator (1962–66) and governor (1971–74) for the state of Georgia. In 1976 Carter defeated President Gerald FORD. He had a number of foreign policy successes, such as the negotiation of the Camp David Agreement (1979), a significant step toward Arab-Israeli reconciliation. His successes were overshadowed by the disastrous attempt to free US hostages in Iran (April 1980). An oil price rise contributed to spiraling inflation, which was dampened only by a large increase in interest rates. In the 1980 election, Carter was easily defeated by Ronald REAGAN. Since then, he has acted as a international peace broker.

Cartier, Jacques (1491–1557) French navigator and explorer who discovered (1535) the St. Lawrence River. Cartier was sent (1534) to North America by Francis I. During this first voyage, he discovered the Magdalen Islands and explored the Gulf of St. Lawrence. In 1535–36 he sailed up the St. Lawrence River to the site of modern Quebec and continued on foot to Hochelaga. His discoveries laid the basis for French settlements in Canada.

Cartwright, Edmund (1743–1823) English inventor of the power loom. It was patented in 1785, but not used commercially until the early 19th century.

Cassiodorus, Flavius Magnus Aurelius (490–585) Roman writer and statesman. He served under THEODORIC and Athalaric and founded several monasteries. His major work, a history of the GOTHS, has been lost.

Castro, Fidel (1926–) Cuban revolutionary leader, premier (1959–2008). In 1953 he was sentenced to 15 years' imprisonment after an unsuccessful coup against the BATISTA regime. Two years later, Castro was granted an amnesty and exiled to Mexico. In January 1959 his guerrilla forces overthrew the regime. Castro instituted radical reforms, such as collectivizing agriculture and dispossessing foreign companies. In 1961 the USA organized the abortive Bay of Pigs invasion. Castro responded by allying with the Soviet Union. In 1962 the Cuban Missile Crisis, a confrontation over the installation of Soviet nuclear rockets in Cuba, saw the USA and Soviet Union on the brink of nuclear war. The collapse of Soviet communism and the continuing US trade embargo worsened Cuba's economic climate, forcing Castro to introduce economic reforms. He retired in 2007 due to failing health.

Castro, Raul (1931–) Cuban premier (2008–). The brother of Fidel CASTRO, Raul helped Fidel sieze power in 1959 and served as armed forces minister under his rule. When Fidel Castro stepped down in 2008 he appointed Raul to succeed him as president.

Catherine I (1684–1727) Empress of Russia (1725–27), b. Martha Skavronskaya. Of peasant origin, Catherine was captured (1702) by Russian soldiers and became the mistress of Alexander Menshikov and later of PETER I (THE GREAT), whom she married in 1712. Catherine was crowned in 1724 and after Peter's death (1725) was proclaimed empress, ruling through a council led by Menshikov. She was succeeded by PETER II.

Catherine II (the Great) (1729–96) Empress of Russia (1762–96), b. Germany, wife of PETER III. Peter succeeded to the throne in 1761. With the help of her lover, Grigori Orlov, Catherine overthrew her husband and shortly afterward he was murdered. Catherine began her reign as an "enlightened despot", with ambitious plans for reform, but after the peasants' revolt (1773–74), she became increasingly conservative. In 1785 Catherine extended the powers of the nobility at the expense of the serfs. Catherine's foreign policy, guided by POTEMKIN, extended Russian territory. In 1764 she secured the accession of her former lover to the Polish throne as Stanislaus II. Russia emerged from the first Russo-Turkish War (1768–74) as the dominant power in the Middle East. Crimea was annexed in 1783, and Alaska was colonized.

Catherine de' Medici *See* MEDICI, CATHERINE DE'

Catherine of Siena, Saint (1347–80) Italian nun of the Order of St. DOMINIC. In 1376 she went to Avignon to persuade Pope Gregory XI to return to Rome. She was canonized in 1461.

Cato the Elder (234–149 BCE) (Marcus Porcius) Roman leader. As censor from 184 BCE, Cato worked to restore old ideals of courage, honesty and simple living. He urged the Senate to destroy Carthage, precipitating the Third Punic War.

Cavendish, Henry (1731–1810) English chemist and physicist. He discovered hydrogen and the compositions of water and air. He estimated the Earth's mass and density by a method now known as the "Cavendish experiment". Cavendish also measured the specific gravity of carbon dioxide and hydrogen.

Cavour, Camillo Benso, conte di (1810–61) Piedmontese politician. From 1852 he was prime minister under VICTOR EMMANUEL II. Cavour engineered Italian liberation from Austria with French aid, expelled the French with the help of Giuseppe GARIBALDI and, finally, neutralized Garibaldi's influence. This led to the formation of the kingdom of Italy (1861).

Caxton, William (1422–91) First English printer. Following a period in Germany (1470–72), where he learned printing, Caxton set up his own press in 1476 at Westminster. Among his publications were editions of CHAUCER and MALORY.

Ceauşescu, Nicolae (1918–89) Romanian statesman, effective ruler from 1965 to 1989. He became general secretary of the Romanian Communist Party in 1965 and head of state in 1967. Ceauşescu promoted Romanian nationalism and pursued an independent foreign policy but instituted repressive domestic policies. He was deposed and executed in the December 1989 revolution.

Cellini, Benvenuto (1500–71) Italian sculptor, goldsmith and author. Cellini's autobiography (1558–62) is an important primary historical source on Renaissance Italy. Cellini entered the service of Pope Clement VII in 1519 and became the most skilled goldsmith of his generation.

Celsius, Anders (1701–44) Swedish astronomer who invented the Celsius, or centigrade, temperature scale in 1742. In this scale, the difference between the temperatures of the freezing and boiling points of water is divided into 100 degrees. The freezing point is 0°C and the boiling point is 100°C.

Celts People who speak one of the Celtic languages or who are descended from a Celtic language area. After 2000 BCE, early Celts spread from E France and W Germany over much of W Europe. They developed a village-based, hierarchical society headed by nobles and Druids. Conquered by the Romans, the Celts were pushed into Ireland, Wales, Cornwall and Brittany by Germanic peoples. Their culture remained vigorous, and Celtic churches were important in the early spread of Christianity in N Europe.

Cervantes, Miguel de (1547–1616) Spanish novelist, poet and dramatist. Cervantes published two volumes of his masterpiece, *Don Quixote de la Mancha* (1605; 1615). Don Quixote is a great archetype of Western fiction, the picaresque hero who misapplies the logic of high Romance to the situations of modern life.

Cézanne, Paul (1839–1906) French painter. He exhibited at the first impressionist show in 1874. Cézanne later moved away from impressionism in favor of a more analytical approach using color to express form. Figure paintings, such as *The Card Player* (1890–92) and *The Bathers* (1895–1905), and landscapes, such as *Mont Sainte Victoire* (1904–06), were painted on this principle.

Chadwick, Sir James (1891–1974) English physicist. He worked on radioactivity with Ernest RUTHERFORD. In 1920 Rutherford had predicted a particle without electric charge in the nucleus of an atom, and in 1932 Chadwick proved the neutron's existence and calculated its mass. He received the 1935 Nobel Prize for physics. During World War II, Chadwick headed British research for the Manhattan Project to develop the atomic bomb.

Chamberlain, (Arthur) Neville (1869–1940) British statesman, prime minister (1937–40). During the 1920s, he served as chancellor of the exchequer (1923–24, 1931–37) and minister of health (1924–29). He succeeded Stanley BALDWIN as prime minister and leader of the Conservative Party. Chamberlain approached Hitler with a policy of appeasement and signed the Munich Agreement (1938). After Hitler's invasion of Poland, he declared war in September 1939. After the loss of Norway, Chamberlain was replaced by Winston CHURCHILL in May 1940.

Champlain, Samuel de (1567–1635) French explorer, founder of New France (Canada). In 1603, following the discoveries of Jacques CARTIER, Champlain traveled up the St Lawrence River as far as Lachine. He explored the Atlantic coast from Cape Breton to Cape Cod, making the first detailed maps of the area, and in 1608 he founded Quebec. With the help of the HURON, he continued to explore the region.

Chandragupta Founder of the MAURYAN EMPIRE in India in

*c.*321–297 BCE), grandfather of ASHOKA. He seized the throne of Magadha and defeated SELEUCUS, gaining dominion over most of N India and part of Afghanistan. His reign was characterized by religious tolerance. He established a vast bureaucracy at Patna. He abdicated and, it is thought, become a Jain monk.

Chandragupta I Indian emperor (r.320–335), founder of the GUPTA DYNASTY. He inherited his kingdom from Ghatotkacha. He enlarged it through marriage to a princess of N Bihar.

Chandragupta II Emperor of N India (r. *c.*380–414). Grandson of CHANDRAGUPTA I, he increased his holdings southward through the marriage of his daughter to the Vakataka king Rudrasena II.

Charlemagne (742–814) King of the Franks (768–814) and Holy Roman emperor (800–14). The eldest son of PEPIN III (THE SHORT), Charlemagne inherited half the Frankish kingdom (768), annexed the remainder on his brother Carloman's death (771) and built a large empire. He invaded Italy twice and took the Lombard throne (773). Charlemagne undertook a long and brutal conquest of Saxony (772–804), annexed Bavaria (788) and defeated the Avars of the middle Danube (791–96, 804). He undertook campaigns against the Moors in Spain. In 800 Charlemagne was consecrated as emperor by Pope Leo II, thus reviving the concept of the Roman Empire and confirming the separation of the West from the Eastern, BYZANTINE EMPIRE. He encouraged the intellectual awakening of the Carolingian Renaissance. Charlemagne's central aim was Christian reform, both of church and laity.

Charles V (1500–58) Holy Roman emperor (1519–56), king of Spain as Charles I (1516–56). He ruled the Spanish kingdoms, S Italy, the Netherlands and the Austrian HAPSBURG lands by inheritance. When he succeeded his grandfather, MAXIMILIAN I, he headed the largest European empire since CHARLEMAGNE. In addition, the Spanish conquistadores made him master of a New World empire. Charles' efforts to unify his possessions were unsuccessful, largely due to the hostility of FRANCIS I of France, the Ottoman Turks in central Europe, and the advance of Lutheranism in Germany. The struggle with France was centered in Italy: Spanish control was largely confirmed by 1535, but French hostility was never overcome. The Turks were held in check but not defeated. In Germany, Charles, who saw himself as the defender of the Catholic Church, nevertheless recognized the need for reform and Lutheranism expanded. Charles increasingly delegated power in Germany to his brother FERDINAND I and in 1554–56 surrendered his other titles to his son, PHILIP II of Spain.

Charles VI (1685–1740) Holy Roman emperor (1711–40) and king of Hungary. His claim to the Spanish throne against the grandson of LOUIS XIV, PHILIP V, caused the War of the Spanish Succession. After his election as emperor, Charles gave up his Spanish claim. His reign was marked by the attempt to secure the succession of his daughter, MARIA THERESA.

Charles I (1600–49) King of England, Scotland and Ireland (1625–49), son of JAMES I. Charles' insistence on the "divine right of kings" provoked conflict with Parliament and led him to rule without it for 11 years (1629–40). With the support of the archbishop of Canterbury, William Laud, Charles enforced harsh penalties on nonconformists. When attempts to impose Anglican liturgy on Scotland led to the Bishops' War, Charles was obliged to recall Parliament to raise revenue. The Long Parliament insisted on imposing conditions. Relations worsened, and Charles' attempt to arrest five leading opponents in the Commons precipitated the Civil War. After the defeat of the Royalists, attempts by Oliver CROMWELL and other parliamentary and army leaders to reach a compromise with the king failed, and he was tried and executed.

Charles II (1630–85) King of England, Scotland and Ireland (1660–85). After the execution of his father, CHARLES I, he fled to France but in 1650 was invited to Scotland by the Covenanters and crowned king in 1651. Charles' attempted invasion of England was repulsed by Oliver CROMWELL. In 1660 Charles issued the Declaration of Breda, in which he promised religious toleration and an amnesty for his enemies. Parliament agreed to the Declaration, and Charles was crowned king in May 1660, ushering in the

Restoration. He attempted to preserve royal power, accepting subsidies from the French king LOUIS XIV in exchange for promoting Roman Catholicism. Conflict with Parliament was fueled by anti-Catholic feeling, manifest in the "Popish Plot" rumor and the Exclusion Crisis (1679–81), when attempts were made to exclude Charles' brother, the Catholic Duke of York (later JAMES II), from the succession. Unable to resolve his differences with Parliament, Charles dissolved it and ruled with support from Louis XIV. Charles had many mistresses but left no legitimate heir.

Charles V (the Wise) (1337–80) King of France (1364–80). He regained most of the territory lost to the English in the Hundred Years War. Charles strengthened royal authority by introducing a regular taxation system, a standing army and a powerful navy. He encouraged literature and art, and built the Bastille.

Charles VII (1403–61) King of France (1422–61). The son of Charles VI, he was excluded from the throne by the Treaty of Troyes (1420). When his father died, Charles controlled lands S of the River Loire, while the N remained in English hands. With the support of JOAN OF ARC, he checked the English at Orléans and was crowned king at Reims (1429). By 1453 the English had been driven out of most of France.

Charles VIII (1470–98) King of France (1483–98). He succeeded his father, LOUIS XI, and until 1491 was controlled by his sister Anne de Beaujeu. Charles invaded Italy in 1494, beginning the long Italian Wars. A league of Italian states, the papacy and Spain forced him to retreat. He was succeeded by his cousin, LOUIS XII.

Charles IX (1550–74) King of France (1560–74). Charles succeeded his brother Francis II; his mother, Catherine de' MEDICI, acted as regent. Her authority waned when, in 1571, the young king fell under the influence of Gaspard de Coligny, leader of the Huguenots. Coligny and thousands of his followers were slain in the Saint Bartholomew's Day Massacre (1572), ordered by Charles at the instigation of his mother.

Charles X (1757–1836) King of France (1824–30), brother of LOUIS XVI and LOUIS XVIII. He fled France at the outbreak of the French Revolution (1789) and remained in England until the BOURBON restoration (1814). Charles opposed the moderate policies of Louis XVIII. After the assassination of his son in 1820, his reactionary forces triumphed. In 1830 Charles dissolved the newly elected chamber of deputies. The people rebelled, and Charles was forced to abdicate.

Charles I (1226–85) King of Naples and of the Two Sicilies (1266–85), son of Louis VIII of France and Blanche of Castile. Charles was offered the throne by Pope Innocent IV and became one of the most powerful European rulers.

Charles III (1716–88) King of Spain (1759–88) and of Naples and Sicily (1735–59), son of Philip V and Elizabeth Farnese. Charles conquered Naples and Sicily in 1734 and inherited the Spanish crown in 1759. He handed Naples and Sicily to his son, Ferdinand. Charles was a highly competent ruler. He encouraged commercial and agrarian reform, and brought the Spanish Catholic Church under state control, expelling the Jesuits in 1767. He was succeeded by his son, CHARLES IV.

Charles IV (1748–1819) King of Spain (1788–1808), son and successor of CHARLES III. Unable to cope with the upheavals of NAPOLEON I, Charles virtually turned over government to his wife, Maria Luisa, and her lover, Manuel de Godoy. Spain was occupied by French troops in the Peninsular War. He was forced to abdicate in favor of his son, FERDINAND VII, who in turn was forced from the throne by Napoleon.

Charles IX (1550–1611) King of Sweden (1604–11), youngest son of Gustav I. He opposed his brother John III's Catholicism. At John's death Charles became regent (1599–1604) and established Lutheranism. John's son, Sigismund III, king of Poland, claimed the throne but was deposed by Charles. In 1600 Charles invaded Livonia, starting the 60-year conflict with Poland. He also embarked on the Kalmar War (1611–13) with Denmark.

Charles XII (1682–1718) King of Sweden (1697–1718), son and successor of Charles XI. He was one of the greatest military leaders in European history. Charles defeated Denmark, Poland, Saxony and Russia in a series of brilliant campaigns. He destroyed the army of PETER I (THE GREAT) at Narva (1700). In 1708 Charles renewed his assault on Russia, but his army was defeated at Poltava (1709). He fled to the Ottomans and persuaded the sultan to attack Russia (1711). The sultan turned against him and Charles escaped back to Sweden. He was killed fighting in Norway and was succeeded by his sister, Ulrika Eleanora.

Charles XIV (1763–1844) (Jean Baptiste Bernadotte) King of Sweden and Norway (1818–44), b. France. He fought in the French Revolution and in the battle of Austerlitz. In effective control of Sweden from 1810, he joined the Allies against NAPOLEON at the battle of Leipzig (1814) and forced Denmark to cede Norway to Sweden in the Treaty of Kiel (1814).

Charles, Jacques Alexandre César (1746–1823) French physicist, inventor and mathematician who was the first to use a hydrogen balloon. He discovered the law relating the expansion of a gas to its temperature rise.

Charles Martel (688–741) Frankish ruler, grandfather of CHARLEMAGNE. Charles seized power in a palace coup in Austria. He reconquered Neustria, Burgundy, Aquitaine and Provence and established the FRANKS as the rulers of Gaul. Charles defeated the Moors at the battle of Tours (732–33). His son succeeded him as PEPIN III (THE SHORT).

Charles the Bold (1433–77) Last reigning duke of Burgundy (1467–77), son and successor of PHILIP THE GOOD. Aligned with England by marriage to Margaret, Edward IV's sister (1468), Charles was ruler of the Low Countries, Luxembourg, Burgundy and Franche-Comté. He continued to conquer lands separating his possessions, and in 1475 he seized Lorraine, thereby alienating the Swiss. He was defeated and killed by the Swiss in 1477.

Chaucer, Geoffrey (1346–1400) English medieval poet. His writings are remarkable for their range, narrative sense, power of characterization and humor. Chaucer's most famous and popular work is *The Canterbury Tales* (c.1387–1400), an extraordinarily varied collection of narrative poems, each told by one of a group of pilgrims while traveling to the shrine of Thomas á Becket.

Chavín culture One of th earliest prehistoric culture periods in Peru, lasting from c.1200 to c.200 BCE. Named for the Chavín de Huántar in N Peru, the people of the culture developed excellent stone sculpture, goldwork and ceramics.

Chekhov, Anton Pavlovich (1860–1904) Russian dramatist who worked with Konstantin Stanislavsky at the Moscow Art Theater. His major plays, *The Seagull* (1896), *Uncle Vanya* (1897), *The Three Sisters* (1901) and *The Cherry Orchard* (1904), reveal a fine blend of comedy and tragedy.

Cheng Ho (1371–1433) Chinese admiral and diplomat. A member of a MONGOL family, he was captured, castrated and placed in the court of Emperor Yung Lo of the MING DYNASTY. In seven extensive voyages (1405–33), Cheng Ho helped to broaden Chinese influence throughout the regions of the Indian Ocean.

Cheops (Khufu) Ancient king of Egypt (active c.2600 BCE). He is remembered for his tomb, the Great Pyramid at Giza, near Cairo. It is the largest and most famous of the pyramids.

Chernenko, Konstantin Ustinovioch (1911–85) Soviet statesman, president (1984–85). A close ally of Leonid BREZHNEV, he joined the Politburo in 1978. Chernenko succeeded Yuri ANDROPOV as president and general secretary of the Communist Party of the Soviet Union (CPSU). He died after only 13 months in office and was succeeded by Mikhail GORBACHEV.

Cherokee Largest tribe of Native Americans in the USA, one of the Five Civilized Tribes. The Cherokee migrated S into the Appalllachian region of Tennessee, Georgia and the Carolinas. When gold was discovered on their land in Georgia in the 1830s, they were forced to move W. This tragic "Trail of Tears" (1838) reduced the population by 25%.

Cheyenne Native North American tribe. Tribal competition forced them to migrate W from Minnesota along the Cheyenne River. The tribe split (c.1830), with the Northern Cheyenne

remaining near the Platte River and the Southern Cheyenne settling near the Arkansas River. Following the Colorado Gold Rush (1858), they were restricted to a reservation. War broke out following a US army massacre of Cheyenne (1864). Colonel George CUSTER crushed the Southern Cheyenne, but the Northern Cheyenne helped in his eventual defeat at Little Bighorn. In 1877 the Cheyenne surrendered and were forced to move to Montana.

Chiang Kai-shek (1887–1975) (Jiang Jieshi) Chinese nationalist leader. After taking part in resistance against the QING DYNASTY, he joined the Kuomintang, succeeding SUN YAT-SEN as leader (1925). From 1927 he purged the party of communists and headed a nationalist government in Nanjing. During World War II Chiang led the fight against Japan. Civil war resumed in 1945. Chiang was elected president of China (1948), but in 1949 the communists led by MAO ZEDONG drove his government into exile in Taiwan. Here, Chiang established a dictatorship and maintained that the Kuomintang were the legitimate Chinese government.

Chimú Large pre-Columbian state in N Peru and its people. The Chimú capital was the great city of Chan Chan (near present-day Trujillo), which had a population of more than 100,000 inhabitants. From 1200 to 1465, when it was conquered by the INCA, Chimú was the most important kingdom in South America.

Chirac, Jacques René (1932–) French statesman, president (1995–2007). In 1974 Chirac was appointed prime minister by President GISCARD D'ESTAING. In 1976 he resigned and formed a new Gaullist party, the Rally for the Republic (RPR). He was again prime minister (1986–88), this time under President MITTERRAND. In 1995 Chirac succeeded Mitterrand as president.

Chola dynasty Rulers of S India from the 9th to the 13th centuries. Their territory expanded in the 10th century when they overthrew the PALLAVA DYNASTY. From 985 to 1026, they established an empire that included Sri Lanka, Bengal, parts of Sumatra and Malaysia. Its greatest ruler was Rajendra I (r.1016–44). It finally ended in 1279 with the rise of the Pandya dynasty.

Chomsky, (Avram) Noam (1928–) US professor of linguistics. In *Syntactic Structures* (1957), he developed the concept of a transformational generative grammar, embodying his theories about the relationship between language and the human mind and an underlying universal structure of language.

Chopin, Frédéric François (1810–49) French composer and pianist, b. Poland. His restrained and delicate style contrasted strongly with contemporary trends. Chopin composed almost exclusively for the piano. His major works include two piano concertos and three piano sonatas. He died of tuberculosis.

Christian I (1426–81) King of Denmark (1448–81), Norway (1450–81) and Sweden (1457–64). Christian was deposed in Sweden and his efforts to regain the throne ended in defeat (1471). His succession (1460) to Schleswig-Holstein formed the basis of future conflict between Denmark and Germany.

Christian IV (1577–1648) King of Denmark and Norway (1588–1648), son of Frederick II. Despite a costly war with Sweden (1611–13) and his disastrous participation (1625–29) in the Thirty Years War, Christian was a popular monarch. His reign brought culture and prosperity, and he founded Oslo, Norway.

Christian IX (1818–1906) King of Denmark (1863–1906), successor of Frederick VII. Christian lost Schleswig-Holstein in a war (1864) with Prussia and Austria. His reign brought reforms to the constitution and the gradual democratization of Danish society.

Chulalongkorn (1853–1910) King Rama V of Siam (1868–1910). He embraced Westernization in Siam (Thailand). Chulalongkorn abolished slavery, modernized the legal system, built railroads and advanced education and technology. His reforms ensured Siam's independence.

Churchill, Sir Winston Leonard Spencer (1874–1965) British statesman, son of Lord Randolph Churchill. Elected to Parliament in 1900 as a Conservative, Churchill joined the Liberals in 1904. In LLOYD GEORGE's cabinet, Churchill served as secretary of state for war (1918–21) and, as colonial secretary (1921–22), he oversaw the creation of the Irish Free State

Churchill returned to power as chancellor of the exchequer (1924–29) in Stanley BALDWIN's Conservative government. On the outbreak of World War II, he became first lord of the admiralty. In 1940 Churchill replaced Neville CHAMBERLAIN as prime minister. He proved an inspiring war leader. Cultivating close relations with President ROOSEVELT, Churchill was the principal architect of the grand alliance of Britain, the USA and the Soviet Union. In 1945 he was succeeded by Clement ATTLEE but was reelected in 1950. His extensive writings include the *History of the English-Speaking Peoples* (1956–58). Churchill was awarded the Nobel Prize for literature in 1953.

Cicero, Marcus Tullius (106–43 BCE) Roman politician, philosopher and orator. Cicero criticized Mark ANTONY, and when Octavian (later AUGUSTUS) came to power, Antony persuaded him to have Cicero executed. Among Cicero's greatest speeches were *Orations Against Catiline* and the *Phillipics*. His rhetorical and philosophical works include *De Amicitia*.

Cimon (d.449 BCE) Athenian statesman and general. He won many victories against the Persians, notably at Eurymedon (*c*.467 BCE). Leader of the aristocratic party in Athens, he helped Sparta in the revolt of the Helots, but subsequently lost favor.

Cixi (1835–1908) (Tz'u Hsi or Zi Xi) Empress Dowager of China. As mistress of the Emperor Xian Feng and mother of his only son, Cixi became coregent in 1861. She remained in power by arranging for the succession of her infant nephew in 1875 and displacing him in a coup in 1898. Ruthless and reactionary, she abandoned the modernization program of the "Hundred Days of Reform" and supported the Boxer Rebellion (1900).

Claude Lorrain (*c*.1604–82) (Claude Gellée) French landscape painter. He developed a style that combined poetic idealism with his own observations. His mature style explored the natural play of light on different textures.

Claudius I (10 BCE–CE 54) (Tiberius Claudius Nero Germanicus) Roman emperor (CE 41–54), nephew of TIBERIUS. As successor to CALIGULA, Claudius was the first emperor chosen by the army. He had military successes in Germany and conquered Britain in CE 43. AGRIPPINA the Younger (his fourth wife) supposedly poisoned him and made her son, NERO, emperor.

Clausewitz, Carl von (1780–1831) Prussian soldier and military theorist. He served in the Napoleonic Wars against France. In his theory of large-scale warfare, *On War* (1832), Clausewitz argued that war is simply an extension of politics by other means.

Clausius, Rudolf Julius Emanuel (1822–88) German physicist, regarded as the founder of thermodynamics. Clausius was the first to formulate the second law of thermodynamics – that heat cannot pass from a colder to a hotter object.

Clemenceau, Georges (1841–1929) French statesman, premier (1906–09, 1917–20). A moderate republican, he served in the Chamber of Deputies (1876–1893), favored compromise in the revolt of the Paris Commune (1871), and strongly supported DREYFUS. Concerned with the growing power of Germany, his first term as premier saw the strengthening of relations with Britain. After World War I, Clemenceau returned to power and led the French delegation at the Versailles peace conference.

Cleopatra (69–30 BCE) Queen of Egypt (51–48 BCE, 47–30 BCE). In 47 BCE she overthrew her husband, brother and coruler Ptolemy XIII with the aid of Julius CAESAR, who became her lover. Cleopatra went to Rome with Caesar, but after his assassination in 44 BCE, she returned to Alexandria, once again as queen. Mark ANTONY, who had become her lover, followed her to Egypt, and they married (37 BCE). The marriage infuriated Octavian (later AUGUSTUS), brother of Mark Antony's former wife. In 31 BCE Rome declared war on Egypt and defeated Antony and Cleopatra's forces at the battle of Actium. Mark Antony committed suicide. Cleopatra surrendered to Octavian but then killed herself.

Cleveland, (Stephen) Grover (1837–1908) 22nd and 24th US president (1885–89, 1893–97). He became the first Democratic president since the American Civil War. In his second term, he was faced with a monetary crisis (1893) and secured repeal of the

Sherman Silver Purchase Act. In 1895 Cleveland broadened the scope of the Monroe doctrine in response to Britain's boundary dispute with Venezuela. His attempt to maintain the gold standard angered radical Democrats, and Cleveland was not renominated.

Clinton, Bill (William Jefferson) (1946–) 42nd US president (1993–2001). Clinton was Democratic representative for Arkansas (1978–80, 1983–92). Economic recession and Clinton's reformist agenda led to an electoral victory (1992) over the incumbent president, George BUSH. His first term was dogged by the Whitewater investigation and the blocking of reforms and appointments by a Republican-dominated Congress. Despite allegations of financial and personal impropriety, a buoyant domestic economy secured Clinton's re-election. The priorities for his second term were education and welfare reforms. His second term was dogged by sexual scandal: Clinton was forced to admit that he had an improper relationship with a White House intern. In 1998, facing charges of perjury over the affair, he became only the second US president to be impeached. Clinton refused to resign and showed his ability to make tough political decisions by launching Operation Desert Fox (December 1998), a bombing campaign against Iraq for failing to comply with UN resolutions.

Clive, Robert, Baron Clive of Plassey (1725–74) British soldier and administrator. In 1743 he traveled to Madras, India, as an official of the British East India Company. Clive attracted attention for his masterly use of guerrilla warfare. In 1757 he recaptured Calcutta from the nawab of Bengal. As first governor of Bengal (1757–60), Clive established British supremacy in India but his administration was tarnished by corruption. After serving a second term as governor of Bengal (1765–67), he left for England. Clive faced charges of embezzling state funds, but was acquitted in 1773. He committed suicide.

Clotaire I (497–561) Frankish king. On the death of his father, CLOVIS I, in 511 Clotaire received a share of the Frankish kingdom. In 524 he divided the share of his deceased brother Clodomir with another brother, Childebert I. In 531 he conquered and divided Thuringia with his brother Theodoric. He and Childebert seized and divided Burgundy in 534. Clotaire became the sole king of the FRANKS after the death of Theodoric's heir (555) and of Childebert (558).

Clovis I (465–511) Frankish king of the MEROVINGIAN DYNASTY. He overthrew the Romanized kingdom of Soissons and conquered the ALEMANNI near Cologne. Clovis and his army later converted to Christianity in fulfillment of a promise made before the battle. In 507 he defeated the VISIGOTHS under Alaric II near Poitiers.

Cobden, Richard (1804–65) British Radical politician. With John BRIGHT he led the campaign for the repeal of the Corn Laws and was the chief spokesman in Parliament (1841–57, 1859–65) for the "Manchester School" of free trade. Cobden negotiated a major trading agreement with France (1860).

Cocteau, Jean (1889–1963) French writer and filmmaker, a leader of the French avant-garde. His works of surrealist fantasy include the novel, *Les Enfants terribles* (1929; filmed, 1950); the play, *Orphée* (1926; filmed 1950); and the films, *Le Sang d'un poète* (1930) and *La Belle et la bête* (1946).

Colbert, Jean Baptiste (1619–83) French statesman, the principal exponent of mercantilism. He came to prominence as an adviser to Cardinal MAZARIN. From 1661, when LOUIS XIV began his personal rule, Colbert controlled most aspects of government: reforming taxation and manufacturing, establishing commercial companies and strengthening the navy.

Coleridge, Samuel Taylor (1772–1834) English poet, critic and philosopher. In 1798 Coleridge and William WORDSWORTH published *Lyrical Ballads*. A fundamental work of romanticism, it opened with Coleridge's ballad "The Rime of the Ancient Mariner". *Christabel and Other Poems* (1816) included the ballad "Christabel" and the fragment "Kubla Khan".

Colt, Samuel (1814–62) US inventor. Colt patented (1835–36) the revolver, a single-barreled pistol with an automatic revolving set of chambers, brought into successive alignment. His Colt's

Patent Firearms Manufacturing Company at Hartford, Connecticut, was the first assembly-line in manufacturing.

Columbus, Christopher (1451–1506) Italian explorer credited with the discovery of America. Columbus believed he could establish a route to China and the East Indies by sailing across the Atlantic Ocean. In 1492 Columbus set out with three ships (*Niña, Pinta* and *Santa Maria*) and made landfall in the Bahamas, the first European to reach the Americas since the Vikings. On a second, larger expedition (1493), a permanent colony was established in Hispaniola. Columbus made two more voyages (1498 and 1502), exploring the Caribbean region. He never surrendered his belief that he had reached Asia. His discoveries laid the basis for the Spanish empire in the Americas.

Commodus, Lucius Aelius Aurelius (161–192) Roman emperor (180–192), son and successor of MARCUS AURELIUS. Commodus'profligate, perhaps insane, rule was spent organizing gladiatorial contests. He was assassinated by a wrestler.

Comte, Auguste (1798–1857) French philosopher, founder of positivism. He proposed a law of three stages (theological, metaphysical and positive) to represent the development of the human race. In the first two stages the human mind finds religious or abstract causes to explain phenomena, whereas in the third, explanation of a phenomenon is found in a scientific law. Comte's works include *System of Positive Polity* (1830–42).

Confucius (551–479 BCE) (K'ung-fu-tzu) Founder of Confucianism, a philosophy that dominated China until the early 20th century and that is still popular today. Born in Lu, Confucius was an excellent scholar and became an influential teacher of the sons of wealthy families. He is said to have been prime minister of Lu. In his later years he sought a return to the political morality of the early ZHOU DYNASTY.

Connolly, James (1870–1916) Irish nationalist leader. He went to the USA in 1903 and helped establish the Industrial Workers of the World (IWW). Returning to Ireland, he was a leader in the Easter Rising (1916) and was executed by the British authorities.

Conrad II (990–1039) Holy Roman emperor (1027–39), first of the Salian dynasty. Conrad became king of Germany in 1024. As emperor, he suppressed revolts in Lotharingia and Italy. In 1034 Conrad annexed Burgundy. His son succeeded him as Henry III.

Conrad III (1093–1152) First German king (1138–52) of the HOHENSTAUFEN DYNASTY. In 1128 Conrad was crowned as an antiking to Lothair II but was forced to submit in 1135. Upon Lothair's death, Conrad was officially crowned king. Anxious to deprive Lothair's son (Henry the Proud) of a power base, Conrad awarded Saxony to Albert the Bear. Henry's son, Henry the Lion, launched a civil war out of which emerged the rival factions of the GUELPHS and GHIBELLINES.

Conrad IV (1228–54) German king (1237–54), king of Sicily and Jerusalem (1250–54), son of FREDERICK II. The conflict between Frederick and Pope Innocent IV saw the election (1246) of an antiking, and Germany lurched into civil war. Conrad inherited Sicily and Jerusalem upon Frederick's death but was never crowned emperor. The pope excommunicated him in 1254.

Constable, John (1776–1837) English landscape painter. He attended (1795–1802) the Royal Academy and studied every effect of clouds and light on water. His first success came when *The Haywain* (1821) and *View on the Stour* (1817) were shown at the 1824 Paris Salon. Recognition in England came after his death.

Constans, Flavius Julius (*c.*323–50) Roman emperor (337–50). The youngest son of CONSTANTINE THE GREAT, he shared the title of Augustus with his two brothers. After the death of his brother Constantine II (340), Constans controlled both the central and western dioceses of the ROMAN EMPIRE.

Constantine I (the Great) (285–337) Roman emperor (306–37) and founder of the Christian empire. A series of feuds for control of Italy ended when Constantine defeated Maxentius (312). Constantine and LICINIUS signed the Edict of Milan (313), which extended tolerance to Christians throughout the empire. In 324 he defeated Licinius and became sole ruler. Constantine presided over the first council of the Christian church at Nicaea (325). He rebuilt (330) Byzantium as his capital and renamed it Constantinople (present-day Istanbul). Constantine centralized imperial power but divided the empire before his death.

Constantine II (1940–) King of Greece (1964–73). In 1967 a military junta seized power in Greece, and Constantine launched an abortive coup against the generals. He was forced into exile and was formally deposed in 1973.

Constantius II (317–61) Roman emperor. On the death of his father, CONSTANTINE THE GREAT, Constantius divided the empire with his brothers Constantine II and CONSTANS. While Constantius was away fighting the Persians, usurpers seized control of the ROMAN EMPIRE. Constans was killed and Constantius established sole control of the empire.

Cook, James (1728–79) British naval officer and explorer. In 1768–71 Cook led an expedition to investigate the strategic and economic potential of the South Pacific. He conducted a survey of the unknown coasts of New Zealand and charted the E coast of Australia, claiming it for Britain. On a second expedition to the S Pacific (1772–75), Cook charted much of the Southern Hemisphere and circumnavigated Antarctica. On his last voyage (1776–79) he discovered the Sandwich (Hawaiian) Islands, where he was killed in a dispute with the inhabitants.

Coolidge, (John) Calvin (1872–1933) 30th US President (1923–29). Stern action in the Boston police strike of 1919 earned him the Republican nomination as vice-president in 1920. He became president on the death of Warren HARDING in 1923. His administration was characterized by a laissez-faire approach, summed up by his phrase, "the business of America is business".

Cooper, James Fenimore (1789–1851) US novelist, one of the first to gain international recognition. Cooper's most successful works were the romantic "Leatherstocking Tales" about the frontier, of which the best known are *The Pioneers* (1823), *The Last of the Mohicans* (1826) and *The Deerslayer* (1841).

Copernicus, Nicolas (1473–1543) (Mikolaj Kopernik) Polish astronomer. Through his study of planetary motions, Copernicus developed a heliocentric (Sun-centered) theory of the universe in opposition to the accepted geocentric (Earth-centered) theory conceived by PTOLEMY 1,500 years before. An account of his work, *De revolutionibus orbium coelestium*, was published in 1543.

Corday, Charlotte (1768–93) French patriot. A noblewoman, she was one of the Girondins who disagreed with the radical policies espoused by the Jacobin Jean Paul MARAT. On 13 July 1793 Corday stabbed Marat to death and was guillotined on 17 July.

Corelli, Arcangelo (1653–1713) Italian composer and violinist. Corelli helped to develop the concerto grosso and did much to consolidate the principles behind modern violin playing.

Corneille, Pierre (1606–84) French dramatist. Corneille and RACINE are regarded as the masters of classical French tragedy. His masterpiece is the epic tragedy *Le Cid* (1637). His tragedies assert human will against fate in precise Alexandrine lines.

Cornwallis, Charles, 1st marquess (1738–1805) British general and statesman. In 1778 he became second in command of British forces in the American Revolution. In 1780 he took command of the Carolina Campaign. His surrender at the Siege of Yorktown (1781) signaled the end of the war. As governor-general of India (1786–93, 1805), he defeated TIPU SULTAN of Mysore. Cornwallis resigned as viceroy of Ireland (1798–1801) after GEORGE III refused to accept the Act of Catholic Emancipation.

Coronado, Francisco Vásquez de (1510–54) Spanish explorer. In 1540 he led an expedition in Mexico to locate the seven cities of Cibola, reportedly the repositories of untold wealth. He explored the W coast of Mexico, found the Colorado River and the Grand Canyon and headed N through the Texas Panhandle, Oklahoma and E Kansas.

Correggio (*c.*1490–1534) (Antonio Allegri) Italian painter from Correggio. His oil paintings and frescos produced daring foreshortening effects. Correggio was one of the first painters to experiment with the dramatic effects of artificial light.

Cortés, Hernán (1485–1547) Spanish conquistador. In 1518 he sailed from Cuba to Central America with 550 men. Cortés marched inland toward the AZTEC capital, Tenochtitlan, gaining allies among the subject peoples of the Aztec king, MONTEZUMA II. While he was absent conflict broke out. In 1521 Cortés recaptured the city after a siege, gaining the Aztec empire for Spain.

Coulomb, Charles Augustin de (1736–1806) French physicist. He invented the torsion balance that led to the discovery of Coulomb's law: the force between two point electric charges is proportional to the product of the charges, and inversely proportional to the square of the distance between them.

Courbet, Gustave (1819–77) French painter, the leading exponent of realism. Largely self-taught, Courbet rejected traditional subject matter and instead painted peasant groups and scenes from life in Paris. His nudes shocked contemporary society.

Coward, Sir Noel Pierce (1899–1973) English playwright, composer and performer. Coward was known for his urbane comedies such as *Hay Fever* (1925), *Private Lives* (1930) and *Blithe Spirit* (1941). His plays lampooned high-society etiquette. He wrote many songs, including "Mad Dogs and Englishmen".

Cranmer, Thomas (1489–1556) English prelate and religious reformer. Cranmer was appointed archbishop of Canterbury by HENRY VIII in 1533. He secured the annulment of Henry's marriage to Catherine of Aragón despite opposition from the pope. Cranmer promoted the introduction of Protestantism into England and compiled the first Book of Common Prayer in 1549. Following the accession of the Roman Catholic MARY I in 1553, Cranmer's reforms were halted. He was burned at the stake.

Crassus, Marcus Licinius (115–53 BCE) Roman political and military leader. He commanded an army for SULLA in 83 BCE and led the troops that defeated the slave rebellion of SPARTACUS in 71 BCE. With POMPEY and Julius CAESAR, Crassus formed (60 BCE) the First Triumvirate and became governor of Syria in 54 BCE.

Crazy Horse (1842–77) Chief of the Oglala SIOUX. A leader of Sioux resistance to the advance of white settlers in the Black Hills, Crazy Horse assisted SITTING BULL in the destruction of Colonel George CUSTER at the battle of Little Bighorn in 1876. Persuaded to surrender, he was killed a few months later.

Crick, Francis Harry Compton (1916–2004) English biophysicist. In the 1950s, with James WATSON and Maurice Wilkins, he established the double-helix molecular structure of deoxyribonucleic acid (DNA). The three shared the Nobel Prize for physiology or medicine in 1962.

Crispi, Francesco (1819–1901) Italian statesman, prime minister (1887–91, 1893–96). He served in GARIBALDI's army in 1860. A leftist and anticlericalist, Crispi served as president of the Chamber of Deputies (1876) and interior minister (1877–78) before becoming prime minister.

Croce, Benedetto (1866–1952) Italian philosopher and politician. When MUSSOLINI came to power, Croce retired from politics in protest against fascism. He re-entered politics following the fall of Mussolini in 1943. As leader of the Liberal Party, he played a prominent role in resurrecting Italy's democratic institutions.

Crockett, "Davy" (David) (1786–1836) US frontiersman and politician. He served in the Tennessee legislature (1821–26) and the US Congress (1827–31, 1833–35). A Whig, Crockett opposed the policies of Andrew JACKSON and the Democrats. He died at the battle of the Alamo between Mexico and the Republic of Texas.

Crompton, Samuel (1753–1827) English inventor of a spinning machine. His "spinning mule" of 1779 reduced thread-breakage and produced very fine yarn.

Cromwell, Oliver (1599–1658) Lord protector of England (1653–58). A committed Puritan, he entered Parliament in 1628 and was an active critic of CHARLES I in the Long Parliament (1640). In the first of the English Civil Wars, his Ironsides helped defeat the Cavaliers at Marston Moor (1644). In 1645 Cromwell helped to form the New Model Army. After a decisive victory at Naseby (1645), he emerged as the leading voice of the army faction. Cromwell favored a compromise with Charles I, but Charles'

duplicity convinced him of the need to execute the king. In the second civil war, Cromwell defeated the Scottish Royalists at Preston (1648). The Rump Parliament pressed for Charles' execution and established the Commonwealth republic (1649). Cromwell ruthlessly suppressed opposition in Ireland. The failure of Barebone's Parliament (1653) led to the establishment of the Protectorate. Cromwell became a virtual military dictator as "lord protector". The Humble Petition and Advice (1657) offered him the throne, but he refused. Cromwell's foreign policy was both anti-Stuart and pro-Protestant. The Dutch Wars (1652–54) and the war (1655–58) with Spain were financially exorbitant. He was succeeded by his son, Richard Cromwell.

Curie, Marie (1867–1934) Polish scientist. Marie and her husband **Pierre** Curie (1859–1906) worked on a series of radiation experiments. In 1898 they discovered radium and polonium. In 1903 they shared the Nobel Prize for physics with A.H. BECQUEREL. In 1911 Marie became the first person to be awarded a second Nobel Prize (this time for chemistry), for her work on radium and its compounds. She died of leukemia caused by radiation.

Curzon, George Nathaniel, 1st Marquess of Kedleston (1859–1925) British statesman. As viceroy of India (1899–1905), Curzon reformed administration and education and established (1901) the Northwest Frontier Province. He resigned after a dispute with Lord KITCHENER. During World War I Curzon served in the coalition cabinets of Herbert Asquith and LLOYD GEORGE. As foreign secretary (1919–24) in Bonar Law's government, he helped negotiate the Treaty of Lausanne.

Custer, George Armstrong (1839–76) US military leader. A flamboyant, headstrong character, Custer was the youngest Union general in the Civil War. Following the war he was posted to the frontier, but was court-martialed (1867) for disobeying orders. In 1868 he returned to service and led campaigns against the CHEYENNE. His decision to divide his regiment and attack a superior force of SIOUX at the battle of Little Bighorn (1876) resulted in the death of Custer and his entire regiment.

Cuvier, Georges, Baron (1769–1832) French geologist and zoologist, a founder of comparative anatomy and paleontology. His scheme of classification stressed the form of organs and their correlation within the body. Cuvier applied this system to fossils and came to accept the theory of catastrophic changes.

Cyrus II (the Great) (d.529 BCE) King of Persia (559–529), founder of the ACHAEMENID EMPIRE. He overthrew the Medes, then rulers of Persia, in 549 BCE, defeated King Croesus of Lydia (c.546 BCE) and captured Babylon (539 BCE) and the Greek cities in Asia Minor. His empire stretched from the Mediterranean to India. He delivered the Jews from their Babylonian captivity.

Czartoryski, Adam Jerzy (1770–1861) Polish politician. Czartoryski was responsible for the adoption (1815) of the Polish constitution. He opposed Czar NICHOLAS I's ambitions and, following an insurrection, headed (1830–31) a Polish provisional government. After its failure he was forced into exile in Paris.

D

Daguerre, Louis Jacques Mandé (1789–1851) French painter and inventor. In 1829 Daguerre and Niepce invented the daguerreotype, a photographic process in which a unique image is produced on a copper plate without an intervening negative.

Daimler, Gottlieb (1834–1900) German engineer and automobile manufacturer. In 1883, with Wilhelm Maybach, Daimler developed an internal combustion engine. He used this to power his first automobile (1886). In 1890 he founded the Daimler Motor Company, which made Mercedes automobiles and became Daimler-BENZ.

Dalai Lama (Grand Lama) Supreme head of the Yellow Hat Buddhist monastery at Lhasa, Tibet. The title was bestowed upon the third Grand Lama by the Mongol ruler Altan Khan (d.1583). In 1950–51, **Tenzin Gyatso** (1935–), 14th Dalai Lama, fled Tibet after it was annexed by the People's Republic of China. Following a brutally suppressed Tibetan uprising (1959), he went into exile in India. In Tibetan Buddhism the Dalai Lama is revered as the bodhisattva *Avalokitesvara*.

Dali, Salvador (1904–89) Spanish artist. His style, a blend of realism and hallucinatory transformations, made him an influential exponent of surrealism. His dreamlike paintings exploit the human fear of distortion, as in *The Persistence of Memory* (1931).

Dalton, John (1766–1844) English chemist, physicist and meteorologist. His study of gases led to Dalton's law of partial pressures: the total pressure of a gas mixture is equal to the sum of the partial pressures of the individual gases, provided no chemical reaction occurs. Dalton's atomic theory states that each element is made up of indestructible, small particles.

D'Annunzio, Gabriele (1863–1938) Italian writer and soldier. His masterpiece is the impressionistic collection *Halcyon* (1903). His rhetoric was instrumental in persuading Italy to join the Allies in World War I. D'Annunzio fought with spectacular bravery. He established personal rule (1919–21) of Fiume (Rijeka). D'Annunzio supported the rise of Mussolini's fascist movement.

Dante Alighieri (1265–1321) Italian poet. *The New Life* (*c.*1292) celebrates Dante's idealized love for Beatrice Portinari, the inspiration for much of his life's work. Dante's support for the moderate White GUELPHS against the papal faction of Black Guelphs led to his exile (1302). His allegorical masterpiece, *The Divine Comedy*, a three-book epic in *terza rima*, depicts the poet's spiritual journey through Hell, Purgatory and Paradise.

Danton, Georges Jacques (1759–94) French statesman, a leader of the French Revolution. He was instrumental in the arrest of LOUIS XVI (10 August 1792). Danton, DESMOULINS, ROBESPIERRE and MARAT formed a revolutionary tribunal. Danton dominated the Committee of Public Safety (April–July 1793) but was ousted by Robespierre and the Jacobins. He called for an end to the Reign of Terror and for leniency toward the Girondins. Danton was arrested for conspiracy, tried and guillotined.

Darius I (the Great) (*c.*558–486 BCE) King of Persia (521–486 BCE) of the ACHAEMENID DYNASTY. He extended the Persian empire through the conquests of Thrace and Macedonia. Darius divided the empire into provinces, made great improvements to transportation infrastructure, and was tolerant of religious diversity. He was defeated by the Greeks at Marathon in 490 BCE.

Darius III (380–330 BCE) King of Persia (336–330 BCE). By underestimating the strength of ALEXANDER THE GREAT, he brought about the demise of the ACHAEMENID DYNASTY. Defeated at Issus (333 BCE) and Gaugamela (331 BCE), Darius was forced to flee to Ecbatana and then to Bactria, where he was killed.

Darwin, Charles Robert (1809–82) English naturalist, who developed the organic theory of evolution. In 1831 he joined a five-year, round-the-world expedition on HMS Beagle. Observations made of the flora and fauna of South America (especially the Galápagos Islands) formed the basis of his work on animal variation. In 1859 he published *The Origin of Species*. Darwin argued that organisms reproduce more than is necessary to replenish their population, creating competition for survival. Opposed to the ideas of LAMARCK, Darwin argued that each organism was a unique combination of genetic variations. The variations that prove helpful in the struggle to survive are passed down to the offspring of survivors. He termed this process natural selection.

David (d. *c.*962 BCE) King of ancient Israel (*c.*1010–970 BCE), successor of Saul. David's military successes against the Philistines led Saul to plot his demise. As king, he united Judah and Israel. David captured Jerusalem, making it his capital and building his palace on Mount Zion. The later part of his reign was an era of decline, marked by the revolts of his sons Absalom and Adonijah. David was succeeded by SOLOMON, his son by Bathsheba.

David, Jacques Louis (1748–1825) French painter, a leader of neoclassicism. His output reflected his Jacobin views and support for Napoleon I. His most famous work is *Oath of the Horatii* (1784). Other works include *Death of Marat* (1793).

Davis, Jefferson (1808–89) American statesman, president of the Confederate States during the Civil War (1861–65). Davis

was elected to Congress in 1845 but resigned to fight in the Mexican War. He was a strong advocate for the extension of slavery. In 1857 he rejoined the Senate and acted as leader of the Southern bloc. He resigned when Mississippi seceded from the Union (1861) and was elected leader of the Confederacy. Following LEE's surrender, Davis was captured and imprisoned (1865–67).

Davy, Sir Humphry (1778–1829) English chemist, a founder of electrochemistry. In 1807, using electrolysis, Davy discovered potassium. In 1808 he isolated the elements sodium, barium, strontium, calcium and magnesium. His investigation into the conditions under which firedamp (methane and other gases) and air explode, led to his invention of the miner's safety lamp.

Dawes, Charles Gates (1865–1951) US statesman, vice-president (1925–29). He served (1897–1902) as comptroller of the currency under William MCKINLEY. Dawes was awarded the 1925 Nobel Peace Prize for his work that produced the Dawes Plan (1924) for stabilizing the German economy after World War I.

Debussy, Claude Achille (1862–1918) French composer. He explored new techniques of harmony and orchestral color to produce highly individual delicate music. His orchestral works include *Prélude à l'après-midi d'un faune* (1894), *Nocturnes* (1899) and *La Mer* (1905). His piano works include *Suite Bergamasque* (1890). His one opera is *Pelléas et Mélisande* (1902).

Decius, Gaius Messius Quintus Trajanus (CE 200–51) Roman emperor (249–51). In an attempt to strengthen the state religion Decius was responsible for especially cruel and methodical persecution of Christians.

Defoe, Daniel (1660–1731) English journalist and novelist. Defoe championed WILLIAM III in his first notable poem, *The True-born Englishman* (1701). A politically controversial journalist, he was twice imprisoned. Defoe's enduringly popular novels include *Robinson Crusoe* (1719) and *Moll Flanders* (1722).

De Forest, Lee (1873–1961) US inventor. In 1906 he invented the audion triode valve (electron tube). The triode could amplify signals and became essential in radio, television, radar and computer systems. In 1947 valves were replaced by the transistor.

Degas, (Hilaire Germain) Edgar (1834–1917) French painter and sculptor. After meeting Édouard MANET, Degas took part in exhibitions of impressionism. He differed from his colleagues in the stress he placed on composition, draftsmanship and the use of the studio. His favorite themes, ballet and horse racing, reveal his preoccupation with the depiction of movement.

De Gasperi, Alcide (1881–1954) Italian statesman, prime minister (1945–53). Born in Trentino, then under Austrian rule, De Gasperi struggled successfully for its reunification with Italy. A staunch antifascist, he was imprisoned in the 1920s. During World War II he founded the Italian Christian Democratic Party. De Gasperi was the chief architect of Italy's postwar recovery.

De Gaulle, Charles André Joseph Marie (1890–1970) French statesman, first president (1959–69) of the fifth republic. In 1940 he became undersecretary of war but fled to London after the German invasion. De Gaulle organized French resistance forces and in June 1944 was proclaimed president of the provisional French government. Following liberation he resigned, disenchanted with the political settlement. In 1958 De Gaulle emerged from retirement to deal with the war in Algeria. In 1962 he was forced to cede Algerian independence. In 1965 De Gaulle was reelected, but resigned after defeat in a 1969 referendum.

de Klerk, F.W. (Frederik Willem) (1936–) South African statesman, president (1989–94). He joined the cabinet in 1978. In 1989 de Klerk led a "palace coup" against P.W. BOTHA and became president and National Party leader. Following a narrow electoral victory, he began the process of dismantling apartheid. In 1990 the ban on the African National Congress (ANC) was lifted and Nelson MANDELA was released. In 1991 the main apartheid laws were repealed and victory in a 1992 whites-only referendum marked an end to white minority rule. In 1993 de Klerk shared the Nobel Peace Prize with Nelson Mandela. Following the 1994 elections, de Klerk became deputy president in

Mandela's government of national unity. In 1996 he resigned and led the Nationalists out of the coalition.

de Kooning, Willem (1904–97) US painter, b. Netherlands. In 1948 he became one of the leaders of abstract expressionism. He kept a figurative element in his work and shocked the public with violently distorted images, such as the *Women* series (1953). His emphasis on technique is known as action painting.

Delacroix, (Ferdinand Victor) Eugène (1798–1863) French painter. Opposed to the prevailing neoclassicism, he was inspired by history, politics, mythology and literature. *Massacre at Chios* (1824) and *Greece Expiring on the Ruins of Missolonghi* (1827) were inspired by the Greek War of Independence. In the 1830s his work underwent a change as he began to exploit divisionism.

Delhi Sultanate (1206–1526) Succession of ruling Muslim dynasties in India. In 1192 Muhammad of Ghur captured Delhi from the Hindus led by Prithvi Raj. In 1206 Qutb ud-Din proclaimed himself sultan of Delhi and established the so-called Slave dynasty. His successor, Iltutmish, made Delhi his permanent capital. In 1290 the Khaji dynasty came to power. By 1320, in the reign of Ala ud-Din Khaji, the sultanate's power extended as far as s India. In 1398 the empire fell to TAMERLANE.

Democritus (460–370 BCE) Greek philosopher and scientist. Democritus contributed to the theory of atomism, propounded by his teacher Leucippus, by suggesting that all matter consisted of tiny, indivisible particles.

Demosthenes (383–322 BCE) Athenian orator and statesman. In 351 BCE he delivered the first of his famous *Philippics*, urging the Greeks to resist PHILIP II of Macedon. The Greeks were defeated and Demosthenes put on trial. His defense, "On the Crown", is a masterpiece of political oratory. Demosthenes committed suicide after the failure of the Athenian revolt against Macedon.

Deng Xiaoping (1904–97) Chinese statesman. He took part in the Long March, served in the Red Army, and in 1945 became a member of the central committee of the Chinese Communist Party. After the establishment of the People's Republic (1949), Deng held several important posts, becoming general secretary of the party in 1956. During the Cultural Revolution, he was dismissed. Deng returned to government in 1973, was purged by the Gang of Four in 1976, but reinstated in 1977. Within three years he was paramount leader. Deng introduced economic modernization, encouraging foreign investment, but without social and political liberalization. He officially retired in 1987 but was still in control at the time of the Tiananmen Square massacre (1989).

Derrida, Jacques (1930–2004) French philosopher, b. Algeria. Derrida proposed a philosophy of deconstruction. He argued that Western philosophy is based on a series of metaphysical binary oppositions, such as speech/text. Derrida revealed the limits of these oppositions and sought to defer assimilation through an appeal to intertextuality, multiple meanings and free play of language. Derrida's writings include *Writing and Difference* (1967).

Descartes, René (1596–1650) French philosopher and mathematician. His philosophical principles are outlined in *Discourse on Method* (1637), *Meditations on the First Philosophy* (1641) and *Principles of Philosophy* (1644). He reached one indubitable proposition: "I am thinking", and from this concluded that he existed: *cogito ergo sum* (I think, therefore I am). Descartes founded analytic geometry, introducing the Cartesian coordinate system.

Desmoulins, Camille (1760–94) French revolutionary. His pamphlets, such as *Révolutions de France et de Brabant* (1789), were widely read, and he was responsible for inciting the mob to attack the Bastille on 12 July 1789, precipitating the French Revolution. Initially Desmoulins attacked the Girondins, but later urged moderation. He was arrested and guillotined.

De Soto, Hernando (1500–42) Spanish explorer. After taking part in the conquest of the INCA under Francisco PIZARRO, he was appointed governor of Cuba (1537) with permission to conquer the North American mainland. His expedition advanced as far north as the Carolinas and as far west as the Mississippi. The ruthless search for nonexistent treasure and extreme brutality toward

the native inhabitants led to a costly battle at Maubilia (1540). The explorers returned to the Mississippi, where De Soto died.

Dessalines, Jean Jacques (1758–1806) Haitian ruler. In 1802 he succeeded TOUSSAINT L'OUVERTURE as leader of the revolution. Having driven out the French, he declared independence in 1804, changing the country's name from St. Domingue to Haiti. As Emperor Jacques, he ruled despotically and was assassinated.

De Valera, Eamon (1882–1975) Irish statesman, prime minister (1932–48, 1951–54, 1957–59). He was active in the Irish independence movement. After the Easter Rising (1916), he was elected president of Sinn Féin while imprisoned in England. In 1924 De Valera founded Fianna Fáil. In 1959 he became president of the republic. De Valera retired in 1973.

Diaghilev, Sergei Pavlovich (1872–1929) Russian ballet impresario. He was active in the Russian avant-garde before moving to Paris, where he formed (1911) the Ballets Russes. Diaghilev was responsible for revolutionizing the world of ballet, integrating music and scene design with innovative choreography.

Diaz, Bartholomeu (*c*.1450–1500) Portuguese navigator, the first European to round the Cape of Good Hope. In 1487 Diaz sailed three ships around the Cape, opening the long-sought route to India. He took part in the expedition of CABRAL that discovered Brazil, but was drowned when his ship foundered.

Diaz, Porfirio (1830–1915) Mexican statesman, president (1876–80, 1884–1911). He supported Benito JUÁREZ in the war (1861–67) against Emperor MAXIMILIAN. Diaz refused to accept defeat in the 1871 and 1876 presidential elections and began a revolt that overthrew President Lerdo. Diaz's 35-year dictatorship was brutally effective. His fraudulent re-election (1910) sparked a uprising led by Francisco MADERO, and Diaz was forced into exile.

Dickens, Charles John Huffam (1812–70) English novelist. All of Dickens' novels first appeared in serial form. His early work includes *Oliver Twist* (1838), *Nicholas Nickleby* (1839) and *The Old Curiosity Shop* (1841). His mature novels included *David Copperfield* (1850), *Bleak House* (1853), *Hard Times* (1854) and *A Tale of Two Cities* (1859). Dickens' last novels, *Great Expectations* (1861) and *Our Mutual Friend* (1865), are bleak depictions of the destructive powers of money and ambition.

Dickinson, Emily Elizabeth (1830–86) US poet. From the age of 30 she lived in almost total seclusion in Amherst, Massachusetts. Dickinson wrote 1,775 short lyrics, only seven of which were published in her lifetime. *Poems by Emily Dickinson* appeared in 1890, and her collected works were not published until 1955. Her rich verse explores the world of emotion.

Diderot, Denis (1713–84) French philosopher and writer. He was chief editor of the *Encyclopédie* (1751–72), an influential publication of the Enlightenment. A friend of ROUSSEAU, Diderot broadened the scope of the *Encyclopédie* and, with d'ALEMBERT, recruited contributors, including VOLTAIRE. As a philosopher, Diderot progressed from Christianity through deism to atheism.

Diem, Ngo Dinh (1901–63) Vietnamese statesman, prime minister of South Vietnam (1954–63). In 1955 he formed a republic, forcing Emperor Bao Dai into exile. At first, Diem received strong US support but corruption and setbacks in the Vietnam War led to growing discontent. With covert US help, army officers staged a coup in which he was murdered.

Diocletian (245–313) Roman emperor (284–305). Diocletian reorganized the empire to resist the Barbarians, sharing power with Maximilian, Constantius I and Galerius. He ordered the last persecution of the Christians (303).

Diophantus (active CE 250) Greek mathematician, believed to have produced one of the earliest works in algebra. He is best known for his investigation and description of a set of algebraic equations now called Diophantine equations.

Dirac, Paul Adrien Maurice (1902–84) English physicist. In 1928 Dirac introduced a notation for quantum equations that combined SCHRÖDINGER's use of differential equations with HEISENBERG's use of matrices. In 1930 he applied EINSTEIN's theory of relativity to quantum mechanics in order to describe the spin of an electron. The resultant equation predicted the existence of antimatter. Dirac shared the 1933 Nobel Prize for physics with Schrödinger.

Disraeli, Benjamin, 1st earl of Beaconsfield (1804–81) British statesman and novelist, prime minister (1868, 1874–80). Disraeli was elected to Parliament in 1837. Following the split in the Tory Party over the repeal of the Corn Laws (1846), Disraeli became leader of the land-owning faction. His opposition to PEEL was rewarded when he became chancellor of the exchequer. Disraeli succeeded Derby as prime minister but was ousted by William GLADSTONE. His second term coincided with the greatest expansion of the second British Empire. Disraeli led Britain into the Zulu War (1879) and the second Afghan War (1878–79). In 1875 Britain purchased the Suez Canal from Egypt.

Dix, Otto (1891–1969) German painter and engraver. He was a pitiless satirist of inhumanity, notably in a series of 50 etchings called *The War* (1924). Dix attacked the corruption of post-World War I Germany and was jailed for an alleged plot to kill Hitler. After World War II, he concentrated on religious themes.

Dollfuss, Engelbert (1892–1934) Austrian chancellor (1932–34). Determined to preserve Austrian independence, he dissolved the National Socialist (Nazi) Party, which had demanded union with Germany (1933), and assumed authoritarian powers. He was assassinated by Austrian Nazis in an unsuccessful coup.

Domitian (CE 51–96) Roman emperor (81–96). A son of VESPASIAN, he succeeded his brother TITUS. His rule became increasingly tyrannical. After several attempts, he was assassinated. Domitian was partly responsible for building the Colosseum.

Donatello (c.1386–1466) Italian sculptor. His work marks a turning point in European sculpture, moving from a formulaic Gothic style to a more vital means of expression. After a visit to Rome (1430–32), his work, such as the bronze *David*, adopted a more classical feel. His late work, such as *Judith and Holofernes*, shows even greater emotional intensity.

Dönitz, Karl (1891–1980) German admiral, commander-in-chief (1943–45) of the German navy during World War II. On the death of HITLER, Dönitz became chancellor and negotiated the German surrender. He was imprisoned (1946–56) for war crimes.

Donne, John (1572–1631) English poet and cleric. Donne's metaphysical poetry is among the greatest work in English literature. His early poetry consists mainly of love poems, elegies and satires. *An Anatomy of the World* (1611) and *Of the Progress of the Soul* (1612) are more philosophical. Donne's rejection of Catholicism and conversion to Anglicanism is evident in the prose-work *Pseudo-Martyr* (1610).

Doppler, Christian Johann (1803–53) Austrian physicist and mathematician. Doppler is famous for his prediction (1842) of the Doppler effect – the change in frequency of a wave when there is relative motion between the wave source and the observer.

Dostoevsky, Fyodor Mikhailovich (1821–81) Russian novelist. He joined a revolutionary group and was arrested and sentenced to death (1849). He was reprieved at the eleventh hour, and his sentence was commuted to four years' hard labor. After *Crime and Punishment* was published (1866), Dostoevsky left Russia, partly to escape creditors. His last major work was his masterpiece, *The Brothers Karamazov* (1879–80).

Draco (active 7th century BCE) Athenian political leader and lawmaker. He drew up the first written code of laws in Athens. They were famous for their severity.

Drake, Sir Francis (c.1540–96) English mariner. In 1577–80 he circumnavigated the world in the *Golden Hind*, looting Spanish ships and settlements and claiming California for England. Drake was knighted by Elizabeth I on his return. His raid on Cádiz in 1587 postponed the Spanish Armada, which he helped to defeat in 1588. Drake died in a raid on the Spanish colonies.

Dreyfus, Alfred (1859–1935) French army officer. In 1894 Captain Alfred Dreyfus, a Jew, was convicted for treason on false evidence and transported to Devil's Island in French Guiana. A political crisis ensued. In 1898 Émile ZOLA published *J'accuse*, an

open letter in defense of Dreyfus, which provoked a bitter national controversy. Dreyfus later received a presidential pardon.

Dryden, John (1631–1700) English poet and playwright. He attracted attention for his *Heroic Stanzas* (1659) on the death of Oliver CROMWELL. His account of the events of 1666, *Annus Mirabilis* (1667), saw him become the first official poet laureate. For the next decade, Dryden concentrated on dramatic writing, such as *Tyrannic Love* (1669) and *Marriage à la mode* (1673).

Dubček, Alexander (1921–92) Czechoslovak statesman, Communist Party secretary (1968–69). Dubček was elected party leader at the start of the Prague Spring. His liberal reforms led to a Soviet invasion in August 1968. Dubček was forced to resign. Following the collapse of Czech communism, he was publicly rehabilitated and served as speaker (1989–92) of the parliament.

Duccio di Buoninsegna (c.1265–c.1319) Italian painter. He infused the rigid Byzantine style of figure painting with humanity and lyricism. Surviving works include *Rucellai Madonna* (1285) and the Maestà altarpiece (1308–11).

Duchamp, Marcel (1887–1968) French painter and theorist. His *Nude Descending a Staircase* outraged visitors to the 1913 Armory Show. Duchamp concentrated on abolishing the concept of esthetic beauty. His main work, *The Bride Stripped Bare by Her Bachelors, Even* (1915–23), is a "definitively unfinished" painting of metal collage elements on glass.

Dumas, Alexandre (1802–70) (*père*) French novelist and dramatist. He wrote popular swashbuckling novels, such as *The Three Musketeers* (1844–45) and *The Black Tulip* (1850).

Dumas, Alexandre (1824–95) (*fils*) French dramatist and novelist, illegitimate son of Alexandre DUMAS (*père*). His first great success was *La Dame aux Camélias* (1852), the basis of Verdi's opera *La Traviata*. His later plays, such as *Les idées de Madame Aubray* (1867), helped to provoke French social reform.

Dupleix, Joseph François (1697–1763) French colonial administrator, governor-general of the French East India Company (1742–54). As governor-general of Chandernagor from 1742, he controlled all French interests in India. Ambitious to expand the French Empire, Dupleix defended French possessions against the British in the 1740s and captured Madras (1746). He was frustrated by the successes of Robert CLIVE.

Dürer, Albrecht (1471–1528) German painter, engraver and designer of woodcuts. His synthesis of N and S European traditions deeply affected European art. His album of woodcuts *The Apocalypse* (1498) has remarkable paintlike tones.

Durkheim, Emile (1858–1917) French sociologist. He is considered (with Max Weber) a founder of sociology. In *The Division of Labor in Society* (1893) and the *Elementary Forms of Religious Life* (1912), Durkheim argued that religion and labor were basic organizing principles of society.

Duvalier, "Baby Doc" (Jean-Claude) (1951–) President of Haiti (1971–86). He succeeded his father, "Papa Doc" DUVALIER, as president-for-life. Although he introduced important reforms and disbanded the Tonton Macoutes, he retained his father's brutal methods. Civil unrest forced his exile to France in 1986.

Duvalier, "Papa Doc" (François) (1907–71) President of Haiti (1957–71). He declared himself president-for-life and relied on the feared Tonton Macoutes, a vigilante group, to consolidate his rule. Under Duvalier's ruthless regime, the longest in Haiti's history, the country's economy severely declined.

Dvořák, Antonín (1841–1904) Czech composer. He is best known for his orchestral works, which include nine symphonies and a cello concerto (1895). His stay in the USA (1892–95) inspired his Symphony in E minor ("From the New World").

E

Earp, Wyatt Berry Stapp (1848–1929) US law officer. In 1879 he became deputy sheriff of Tombstone, Arizona. In 1881 the Earp brothers and Doc Holliday fought the Clanton gang in the gunfight at the O.K. Corral.

Eastman, George (1854–1932) US inventor, industrialist and philanthropist who popularized the art of photography. Eastman invented (1879) a dry-plate process and began to mass produce photographic plates. In 1884 he designed a roll film. The first Kodak camera was produced in 1888.

Ebert, Friedrich (1871–1925) German statesman, first president of the Weimar Republic. He entered the Reichstag (parliament) as a member of the Social Democrat Party in 1912. He was elected president in 1919. His efforts to establish a parliamentary democracy in Germany after its defeat in World War I met strong opposition. During his period of office a series of political and economic crises encouraged the rise of extremist groups.

Eco, Umberto (1932–) Italian writer and academic. Eco's best-known work is the erudite philosophical thriller *The Name of the Rose* (1981). Other novels include *Foucault's Pendulum* (1989) and *The Island Before Time* (1994). He is a professor of semiotics.

Eddington, Sir Arthur Stanley (1882–1944) English astronomer and physicist. Eddington pioneered the use of atomic theory to study the internal constitution of stars. Among his discoveries were the mass-luminosity relationship. In 1919 he obtained experimental proof of Einstein's general theory of relativity by measuring stars close to the Sun during a solar eclipse.

Eddy, Mary Baker (1821–1910) US founder of Christian Science (1879). Her doctrine of healing based on the Bible was expounded in *Science and Health With Key to the Scriptures* (1875). In 1879 Eddy organized the Church of Christ, Scientist, and actively directed the movement until her death.

Edison, Thomas Alva (1847–1931) US inventor. Edison invented the carbon transmitter for telephones (1876) and the phonograph (1877). Using a carbon filament, he invented the first commercially viable electric light (21 October 1879). In New York City, he built (1881–82) the world's first permanent electric power plant for distributing electric light. In 1892 most of his companies were merged into the General Electric Company (GEC). In 1914 Edison developed an experimental talking motion picture. By the time of his death, he had patented over 1,300 inventions.

Edward I (1239–1307) King of England (1272–1307), son and successor of HENRY III. His suppression of the Barons'War (1263–65), led by Simon de Montfort, made him king in all but name. Edward joined the Ninth Crusade (1270) and was crowned on his return (1274). He conquered Wales and incorporated it into England (1272–84). In 1296 Edward captured the Scottish coronation stone from Scone, but William WALLACE and ROBERT I (THE BRUCE) led Scottish resistance. His reforms are central to Britain's legal and constitutional history. Edward's foreign ambitions led to the formation of the Model Parliament (1295). His son, EDWARD II, inherited the enmity of Scotland.

Edward II (1284–1327) King of England (1307–27), son and successor of EDWARD I. Edward's reliance on his friend and adviser Piers Gaveston alienated his barons. The barons drafted the Ordinances of 1311, which restricted royal power, and in 1312 they killed Gaveston. Renewing his father's campaign against the Scots, Edward was routed at Bannockburn (1314). In 1325 Edward's estranged queen, Isabella, went as envoy to France. In 1326 she formed an army with her lover, Roger Mortimer, which invaded England and forced Edward to abdicate in favor of his son, EDWARD III. Edward II was murdered.

Edward III (1312–77) King of England (1327–77), son and successor of EDWARD II. For the first three years of his reign, his mother, Isabella, and Roger Mortimer wielded all political power. In 1330 Edward mounted a successful coup. His reign was dominated by the outbreak of the Hundred Years War (1337). Edward won a famous victory at Crécy (1346), and claimed the title king of France, although only conquering Calais. In old age, his sons, EDWARD THE BLACK PRINCE and John of Gaunt, took over government. He was succeeded by his grandson, RICHARD II.

Edward VI (1537–53) King of England (1547–53), only legitimate son of HENRY VIII. He reigned under two regents, the dukes of Somerset (1547–49) and Northumberland (1549–53).

Edward died after willing the crown to Northumberland's daughter-in-law, Lady Jane Grey, to exclude his Catholic sister, MARY I.

Edward VII (1841–1910) King of Great Britain and Ireland (1901–10), son of VICTORIA. Edward's life style as prince of Wales led to his exclusion from government by his mother. As king, he restored court pageantry and contributed to the Entente Cordiale with France. He was succeeded by his son, GEORGE V.

Edward VIII (1894–1972) King of Great Britain and Ireland (1936), subsequently Duke of Windsor. Edward's proposed marriage to an American divorcee, Wallis Simpson, was opposed by Stanley BALDWIN's government. Edward refused to back down and was forced to abdicate after a 325-day reign.

Edward the Black Prince (1330–76) Prince of Wales (1343–76), son of EDWARD III of England. In the Hundred Years War, he distinguished himself at the battle of Crécy (1346) and captured John II of France at Poitiers (1356). As ruler (1362–71) of Aquitaine, Edward was responsible for the massacre at Limoges (1371). He ensured the accession of his son as RICHARD II.

Egyptians, ancient People of the civilization that flourished along the Nile River in NW Africa from *c.*3400 BCE–30 BCE. Ancient Egypt is divided into dynasties, numbered from 1 to 30. The kingdoms of Upper and Lower Egypt were united *c.*3100 BCE by the legendary MENES. Ancient Egyptian history is separated into a number of periods. The highlight of the **Old Kingdom** was the building of the pyramids of Giza during the 4th dynasty. After the death of Pepy II in the 6th dynasty, central government disintegrated. This was the **First Intermediate Period**. Central authority was restored in the 11th dynasty, and the capital was moved to Thebes (now Luxor). The **Middle Kingdom** (*c.*2040–1640 BCE) saw Egypt develop into a great power. Amenemhet I, founder of the 12th dynasty (*c.*1991 BCE), secured Egypt's borders and created a new capital. At the end of this Kingdom, Egypt again fell into disarray (**Second Intermediate Period**) and control was seized by the HYKSOS. The **New Kingdom** began *c.*1550 BCE and brought great wealth. Massive temples and tombs, such as TUTANKHÁMON's, were built. Wars with the HITTITES under RAMSES II weakened Egypt and led to the decline of the New Kingdom. The 21st to 25th dynasties (**Third Intermediate Period**) culminated in Assyrian domination. The Persians ruled from 525 until 404 BCE, when the last native dynasties appeared. In 332 BCE Egypt fell to the armies of ALEXANDER THE GREAT, who moved the capital to Alexandria. After Alexander's death, his general became ruler of Egypt, as PTOLEMY I. The Ptolemies maintained a powerful empire for three centuries. Roman power was on the ascendancy, and when Ptolemy XII asked POMPEY for aid in 58 BCE, it marked the end of Egyptian independence. CLEOPATRA tried to assert independence through associations with Julius CAESAR and Mark ANTONY but was defeated at Actium. Her son, Ptolemy XV (whose father was probably Julius Caesar), was the last Ptolemy; he was killed by Octavian (AUGUSTUS), and Egypt became a province of Rome.

Eichmann, (Karl) Adolf (1906–62) German Nazi, head of subsection IV-B-4 of the Reich Central Security Office in World War II. Eichmann supervised the fulfillment of the Nazi policies of deportation, slave labor and mass murder in the concentration camps. In 1945 he escaped to Argentina but was abducted (1960) by agents of Mossad, and tried and executed in Israel.

Einstein, Albert (1879–1955) US physicist, b. Germany. In 1905 Einstein published four papers that revolutionized physical science. "The Electrodynamics of Moving Bodies" announced his special theory of relativity. Drawing on the work of H.A. Lorentz, Einstein's **special theory** of relativity discarded the notion of absolute motion in favor of the hypothesis that the speed of light is constant for all observers in uniform motion. Measurements in one uniformly moving system can be correlated with measurements in another uniform system, if their relative velocity is known. It asserted that the speed of light was the maximum velocity attainable in the Universe. A corollary of this special theory – the equivalence of mass and energy ($E = mc^2$) – was put forward in a second paper. A third paper, on Brownian movement, confirmed the atomic theory of matter. Lastly, Einstein explained the photoelectric effect in terms of quanta or photons of light. For this insight, which forms the basis of modern quantum theory, Einstein received the 1921 Nobel Prize for physics. In 1911 he asserted the equivalence of gravitation and inertia. Einstein extended his special theory into a **general theory** of relativity (1916) that incorporated systems in nonuniform motion. He asserted that matter in space causes curvature in the space-time continuum, resulting in gravitational fields. This was confirmed (1919) by Arthur EDDINGTON's study of starlight.

Eisenhower, Dwight David ("Ike") (1890–1969) 34th US president (1953–61). As supreme commander of the Allied Expeditionary Force from 1943, Eisenhower was largely responsible for the integration of Allied forces in the liberation of Europe. In 1950 he became Supreme Allied Commander (Europe) and helped establish the North Atlantic Treaty Organization (NATO). In 1952 Eisenhower, a Republican, was elected president. He enforced a prompt end to the Korean War and established a staunchly anticommunist foreign policy. In 1956 Eisenhower was reelected. In 1957 he ordered Federal troops into Little Rock, Arkansas, to end segregation in schools. His second term was dominated by the Cold War. He was succeeded by John F. KENNEDY.

Elamites Inhabitants of the ancient country of Elam, Mesopotamia. Elamite civilization became dominant c.2000 BCE with the capture of Babylon. It flourished until the Muslim conquest in the 7th century. The capital of Elam, Susa, was an important center under the ACHAEMENID kings of Persia and contained a palace of DARIUS I. Archaeological finds include the stele of HAMMURABI, inscribed with his code of law.

Elgar, Sir Edward (1857–1934) English composer. His individual style is first evident in his set of 14 orchestral variations, the Enigma Variations (1899). Elgar's oratorio The Dream of Gerontius (1900) established him as a leading composer. Other works include a cello concerto (1919) and two symphonies.

El Greco See GRECO, EL

Eliot, T.S. (Thomas Stearns) (1888–1965) British poet and playwright, b. USA. His poem The Waste Land (1922) is a keystone of literary modernism. Later poems, notably Ash Wednesday (1930) and the Four Quartets (1935–43), concerned religious faith. Eliot also wrote verse plays, including Murder in the Cathedral (1935). He was awarded the 1948 Nobel Prize for literature.

Elizabeth (1709–62) Empress of Russia (1741–62), daughter of PETER I (THE GREAT). She came to the throne after overthrowing her nephew, Ivan VI. Elizabeth waged war (1741–43) against Sweden and annexed (1743) the southern portion of Finland. She was succeeded by her nephew, PETER III.

Elizabeth I (1533–1603) Queen of England (1558–1603), daughter of HENRY VIII and Anne Boleyn. During the reigns of her half-siblings, EDWARD VI and MARY I, she avoided political disputes. Once crowned, she re-established Protestantism. Various plots to murder Elizabeth and place the catholic MARY, QUEEN OF SCOTS, on the throne resulted in Mary's imprisonment and execution (1587). Elizabeth relied on a small group of advisers, such as Lord Burghley and Sir Francis Walsingham. For most of Elizabeth's reign, England was at peace, and commerce prospered. The expansion of the navy saw the development of the first British Empire and the defeat of the Spanish Armada (1588). Despite pressure to marry, Elizabeth remained single. She was the last of the TUDORS, and the throne passed to JAMES I, a STUART.

Elizabeth II (1926–) Queen of Great Britain and Northern Ireland and head of the Commonwealth of Nations (1952–), daughter of GEORGE VI. In 1947 she married Philip Mountbatten, with whom she had four children, Charles, Anne, Andrew and Edward. Popular and dutiful, Elizabeth has had to contend with scandals associated with the marriage failures in the royal family, particularly that of Charles and Diana, princess of Wales.

Emerson, Ralph Waldo (1803–82) US essayist, philosopher and poet. He was a minister in the Unitarian Church but became disillusioned and left (1832). Emerson settled in New England, where he formed a circle that included Nathaniel HAWTHORNE, Henry David Thoreau and Bronson Alcott. His essay Nature (1836) set out the principles of transcendentalism. In 1840 Emerson cofounded The Dial magazine.

Engels, Friedrich (1820–95) German political philosopher. Engels and MARX formulated the theory of dialectical materialism and cowrote the Communist Manifesto (1848). His materialist reworking of the dialectics of HEGEL is most evident in Socialism, Utopian and Scientific (1882). From 1870 Engels helped Marx with his writings, particularly Das Kapital.

Ennius, Quintus (239–169 BCE) Roman poet, sometimes known as the father of Latin poetry. He is best known for Annales, his epic history of Rome.

Enver Pasha (1881–1922) Turkish general and political leader. Involved in the Young Turk revolution (1908), he became virtual dictator after a coup (1913). Enver Pasha was instrumental in bringing Turkey into World War I as an ally of Germany. He was killed leading an antiSoviet expedition in Bukhara.

Epicurus (341–270 BCE) Greek philosopher, founder of Epicureanism. He began teaching philosophy at the age of 32. Epicureanism proposes that the sensations of pleasure and pain are the ultimate measures of good and evil. Epicurus embraced a theory of physics derived from the atomism of DEMOCRITUS.

Erasmus, Desiderius (1466–1536) (Gerhard Gerhards) Dutch scholar and teacher, considered the greatest of the Renaissance humanists. His Latin translation of the Greek New Testament revealed flaws in the Vulgate text. Erasmus had an early influence on Martin LUTHER but sought change from within the Catholic Church and disagreed with the course of the Reformation. In On Free Will (1524) he openly clashed with Luther.

Eratosthenes (c.276–c.194 BCE) Greek scholar who first measured the Earth's circumference by geometry. Eratosthenes administered the library of Alexandria.

Ernst, Max (1891–1976) German painter and sculptor, founder of Cologne Dada (1919). Ernst developed ways of using collage, photomontage and other radical pictorial techniques. His most important works include L'Eléphant Célèbes (1921) and Two Children Threatened by a Nightingale (1924).

Essad Pasha (1863–1920) Albanian political leader. He aided the Young Turks in their agitation of 1908 for reform of the OTTOMAN EMPIRE. Essad Pasha represented Albania in the new legislature but later turned against the Turks in search of Albanian independence. When this was achieved in 1913, he had a checkered career in the new state, finally being exiled when the Austrians invaded in 1916. He was assassinated in France.

Etruscans Inhabitants of ancient Etruria (modern Tuscany and Umbria), central Italy. Etruscan civilization flourished in the first millennium BCE. Their sophisticated society was influenced by Greece and organized into city-states. Etruscan civilization reached its peak in the 6th century BCE. Their wealth and power was based on their skill at ironworking and control of the iron trade. The Etruscan cult of the dead led them to produce elaborate tombs. From the 5th to the 3rd century BCE they were gradually overrun by neighboring peoples, particularly the ROMANS.

Euclid (c.330–c.260 BCE) Greek mathematician who taught at Alexandria, Egypt. Euclid is remembered for his classic textbook on geometry, Elements (Lat. pub. 1482). His axioms, that parallel lines never meet and the angles of a triangle always add up to 180°, remained the basis for geometry until the 18th century.

Euler, Leonhard (1707–83) Swiss mathematician. He is best known for his geometric theorem, which states that for any polyhedron $V - E + F = 2$, where V is the number of vertices, E the number of edges and F the number of faces.

Euripides (c.480–450 BCE) Greek playwright. Euripides' plays caused contemporary controversy, with their cynical depiction of human motivation. His works, such as Medea, Electra, Hecuba and Trojan Women, achieved great posthumous popularity.

Exiguus, Dionysius (500–50) Roman monk and theologian.

He worked out a method of calculating the date of Easter. This method was adopted by the Roman Church and is still in use. His collection of canon law was widely used in the early Middle Ages.

Eyck, Jan van (c.1390–1441) Flemish painter. His best-known work is the altarpiece for the Church of St. Bavon, Ghent, which includes the *Adoration of the Lamb* (1432) and the *Arnolfini Wedding* (1434). He perfected the manufacture of oil paint.

F

Fahrenheit, Gabriel Daniel (1686–1736) German physicist. He invented the alcohol thermometer (1709) and the first mercury thermometer (1714). He devised the Fahrenheit temperature scale, a system for measuring temperature based on the freezing point (32°F) and the boiling point (212°F) of water.

Faisal I (1885–1933) King of Iraq (1921–33). He joined T.E. LAWRENCE in the Arab revolt (1916) against the Turks. Faisal was installed as king by the British and helped Iraq achieve independence. His grandson ruled (1939–58) as **Faisal II**.

Faraday, Michael (1791–1867) English physicist and chemist. His early work was on the liquefaction of gases, and in 1825 he discovered benzene. After discovering (1832) the process of electrolysis, he went on to formulate the laws that control it. Faraday also discovered the relationship between electricity and magnetism, providing proof of electromagnetic induction. In 1831 he built the first electrical generator and the first transformer.

Farouk (1920–65) King of Egypt (1936–52), son of King FUAD I. He alienated many Egyptians by his personal extravagance and corruption. His ambitious foreign policy ended in defeat in the first Arab-Israeli War (1948). He was overthrown in a military coup, led by Gamal Abdel NASSER.

Farrakhan, Louis (1933–) US leader of the Nation of Islam, a black separatist organization. He was recruited into the Black Muslims in the 1950s by MALCOLM X. Farrakhan was a charismatic advocate of its racial exclusivity and in 1976 formed the Nation of Islam. He has been accused of inciting anger against other religions, particularly Jews. In 1995 Farrakhan assembled 400,000 men in a "Million Man March" on Washington.

Fatimid dynasty Shiite Islamic dynasty who claimed the caliphate on the basis of their descent from Fatima, daughter of MUHAMMAD. The dynasty was founded by Said ibn Husayn at the end of the 9th century. The Fatimids quickly overthrew the Sunni Islamic rulers in most of NW Africa. By Ibn Husayn's death (934), the Fatimid empire had expanded into S Europe, and in 969 they captured Egypt. By the end of the 11th century, Egypt was all that remained of the empire.

Faulkner, William Cuthbert (1897–1962) US novelist. *The Sound and the Fury* (1929) and *As I Lay Dying* (1930) utilize a stream of consciousness narrative. *Light in August* (1932) and *Absalom, Absalom!* (1936) examine racism in the Deep South. Faulkner was awarded the 1949 Nobel Prize for literature. He won Pulitzer prizes for *A Fable* (1951) and *The Reivers* (1962).

Ferdinand (1793–1875) Emperor of Austria (1835–48), king of Hungary (1830–48). A weak sovereign, he let Prince METTERNICH govern for him. Faced with revolutions in Hungary, Italy and Vienna, he was forced to abdicate and flee in 1848.

Ferdinand I (1503–64) Holy Roman emperor (1558–64), king of Bohemia and of Hungary (1526–64). His rule in Hungary was contested by John I, then by John II, both of whom were aided by the Turkish sultan. In Bohemia, Ferdinand secured the absolute rule of his HAPSBURG DYNASTY. In Germany, he helped defeat the Protestant Schmalkaldic League (1546–47). Although a devout Catholic, Ferdinand negotiated the Peace of Augsburg (1555) and worked for reconciliation between the two churches.

Ferdinand (1861–1948) Prince (1887–1908) and czar (1908–18) of Bulgaria. In 1908 he declared Bulgaria independent of the OTTOMAN EMPIRE. Ferdinand allied Bulgaria with Serbia, Greece and Montenegro in the first Balkan War (1912), but Bulgaria's territorial gains were largely lost in the second

war (1913) to its former allies. In a bid to regain territory, Ferdinand entered World War I on the side of the Central Powers. Further defeats saw him abdicate in favor of his son, Boris III.

Ferdinand III (1199–1252) Spanish king of Castile (1217–52) and León (1230–52). He was the son of Alfonso IX of León and Barengaria of Castile. His mother renounced her rights to Castile in his favor in 1217, and when he inherited León from his father in 1230, he permanently united the two kingdoms. Ferdinand spent most of his reign fighting the Moors. He expelled them from Córdoba, Jaén, Seville and Murcia. At his death all of Spain except for the kingdom of Granada had been Christianized.

Ferdinand V (1452–1516) (Ferdinand the Catholic) King of Castile and León (1474–1504), of Aragón (as Ferdinand II) (1479–1516), of Sicily (1468–1516), and of Naples (as Ferdinand III) (1504–16). Ferdinand became joint king of Castile and León after marrying ISABELLA I in 1469, and inherited Aragón from his father, John II, in 1479. After he and Isabella conquered the Moorish kingdom of Granada (1492), they ruled over a united Spain. They expelled the Jews from Spain, and initiated the Inquisition. After Isabella's death (1504), Ferdinand acted as regent in Castile for their insane daughter, Joanna, and then for her son, Charles I (later Holy Roman emperor CHARLES V).

Ferdinand VII (1784–1833) King of Spain (1808–33), son of CHARLES IV. As prince, excluded from government by Manuel de Godoy and his mother, Maria Luisa, he sought the support of NAPOLEON I. In 1808 a rising resulted in his father's abdication, but Napoleon began the Peninsular War, toppled Ferdinand and installed Joseph BONAPARTE. In 1812 Spain proclaimed a liberal constitution. Upon his restoration (1814), Ferdinand abolished the new constitution. Liberal opposition forced him to re-instate the constitution (1820). In 1823, with the help of French troops, Ferdinand crushed the liberals and revoked the constitution. During his reign Spain lost all of its North American colonies. He abandoned the Salic law so that his daughter, ISABELLA II, could succeed him. Conservatives (Carlists) supported the claim of Ferdinand's brother, Don CARLOS, and civil war ensued.

Ferdinand I (1751–1825) King of the Two Sicilies (1816–25), son of the future CHARLES III of Spain. He inherited the kingdoms of Naples and of Sicily on his father's accession (1759). In 1816 they were combined as the Kingdom of the Two Sicilies. Ferdinand's marriage (1768) to Marie Caroline, sister of MARIE ANTOINETTE, encouraged him to pursue pro-Austrian policies. He was driven from his throne by the French during the French Revolutionary Wars and Napoleonic Wars but was restored in 1815.

Ferdinand II (1810–59) King of the Two Sicilies (1830–59), son of Francis I. Originally a liberal, he came to be noted for his despotic rule. In 1849 he quelled a popular revolution begun in 1848, the first of many uprisings to sweep Europe that year. His authoritarian rule weakened the kingdom and led to its collapse and incorporation into a united Italy in 1860 after his death.

Fermat, Pierre de (1601–65) French mathematician. He is best known for his development of number theory. It was recently discovered that differential calculus, thought to be invented by Sir Isaac NEWTON, was communicated to him in a series of letters by Fermat. Fermat's last theorem was that for all integers $n > 2$, there are no natural numbers x, y and z that satisfy the equation $x^n + y^n = z^n$. Fermat wrote that he had found a proof, but died without revealing it. In 1993 Andrew Wiles announced a proof.

Fermi, Enrico (1901–54) US physicist, b. Italy. His early career was spent developing (independently of Paul DIRAC) a form of quantum statistics. Fermi-Dirac statistics assume that the subatomic particles known as fermions behave according to the exclusion principle outlined by Wolfgang PAULI. Fermi was awarded the 1938 Nobel Prize for physics for his work on the bombardment of uranium by neutrons. In 1940 Fermi produced the first synthetic transuranic element, neptunium. In 1942 he produced the first controlled nuclear chain reaction. Fermi worked on the Manhattan Project to develop the atomic bomb.

Fibonacci, Leonardo (c.1170–c.1240) Italian mathematician.

He wrote *Liber abaci* (c.1200), the first Western work to adopt the Arabic numerical system. Fibonacci produced the mathematical sequence named for him, in which each term is formed by the addition of the two terms preceding it. The sequence begins 0, 1, 1, 2, 3, 5, 8, 13, 21.... and so on.

Fielding, Henry (1707–54) English novelist and playwright. His first work of fiction, *An Apology for the Life of Mrs. Shamela Andrews* (1741), was a parody of Samuel RICHARDSON's *Pamela* (1740). Fielding strengthened the novel genre through his depiction of character and narrative sophistication. His masterpiece is the picaresque novel *Tom Jones* (1749). Fielding also founded Britain's first organized police force, the Bow Street Runners.

Fillmore, Millard (1800–74) 13th US president (1850–53). He served (1833–43) in the House of Representatives and in 1834 joined the newly formed Whig Party. In 1848 Fillmore was elected vice-president to Zachary TAYLOR and succeeded as president when Taylor died. In order to mediate between pro- and antislavery factions, he agreed to the Compromise of 1850. Fillmore failed to win renomination in 1852 and was succeeded by Franklin PIERCE. In the 1856 elections Fillmore stood for the Know-Nothing movement, but was defeated by Abraham LINCOLN.

Firdausi (935–1020) Persian poet. He wrote the *Shah-nameh* (*Book of Kings*), an epic poem about the history of Persia. The first major work in Persian literature, it was presented to Mahmud of Ghazni in 1010.

Fitzgerald, F. Scott (Francis Scott Key) (1896–1940) US author. *This Side of Paradise* (1920) and *The Beautiful and Damned* (1922) established him as a chronicler of what he christened the "Jazz Age". His masterpiece is *The Great Gatsby* (1925).

Flaubert, Gustave (1821–80) French novelist of the 19th-century realist school. Flaubert was a craftsmanlike and elegant writer. *Madame Bovary* (1857) represents the transition from romanticism to realism in the development of the novel.

Fleming, Sir Alexander (1881–1955) Scottish bacteriologist. In 1928, while conducting research on staphylococci, Fleming noticed that a mold, identified as *Penicillium notatum*, liberated a substance that inhibited the growth of some bacteria. He named it penicillin; it was the first antibiotic. Howard Florey and Ernst Chain refined the drug's production. In 1945 Fleming, Florey and Chain shared the Nobel Prize for physiology or medicine.

Fo, Dario (1926–) Italian playwright and director. Fo's drama incorporates elements of farce. His most famous works are *Accidental Death of an Anarchist* (1970) and *Can't Pay? Won't Pay!* (1975). In 1997 Fo was awarded the Nobel Prize for literature.

Foch, Ferdinand (1851–1929) French general. In World War I, he helped repel the German advance at Marne (1914), but the disastrous offensives at Ypres (1915) and the Somme (1916) led to his dismissal. In 1917 Foch returned as chief of the French general staff. As commander-in-chief of all Allied forces in France, he led the counter-offensive that ended in German surrender.

Ford, Gerald Rudolph (1913–2006) 38th US president (1974–77). Elected to the House of Representatives in 1948, he gained a reputation as an honest and hard-working Republican. He was nominated by President NIXON as vice-president (1973). When Nixon resigned, Ford became president – the only person to hold the office without winning a presidential or vice-presidential election. One of his first acts was to pardon Nixon. Renominated in 1976, he narrowly lost the election to Jimmy CARTER.

Ford, Henry (1863–1947) US industrialist. He developed a gas-engined automobile in 1892 and founded Ford Motors in 1903. In 1908 Ford designed the Model T. His introduction of an assembly line (1913) revolutionized industrial mass production. More than 15 million Model Ts were sold before it was discontinued in 1928.

Foster, Sir Norman (1935–) English architect. Foster's huge glass and steel exoskeletons exemplify modernist ideals of efficiency. His works include the Hong Kong Bank building (1986) and the Millenium Dome, Greenwich (2000).

Foucault, Jean Bernard Léon (1819–68) French physicist. He used a pendulum (Foucault's pendulum) to prove that the Earth spins on its axis. Foucault invented (1852) the gyroscope and devised a method to measure the absolute velocity of light (1850). With Armand Fizeau, he took the first clear photograph of the Sun. He also discovered eddy currents (Foucault currents).

Fourier, (François Marie) Charles (1772–1837) French socialist. He supported cooperativism and made detailed plans for the organization of communities (phalanxes). Fourier suggested that capital for the enterprise come from the capitalist, and he provided for payment to capital in his division of output.

Fox, George (1624–91) English religious leader, founder of the Quakers. In 1646 Fox embarked upon his evangelical calling. Imprisoned eight times between 1649 and 1673, he traveled to the Caribbean and America to visit Quaker colonists (1671–72). His *Journal* (1694) is a valuable record of the Quaker movement.

Foxe, John (1516–87) English Anglican clergyman and historian whose writings promoted Protestantism and influenced English people's perception of Roman Catholicism. Foxe wrote *Actes and Monuments of these latter and perillous Dayes*, better known as *Foxe's Book of Martyrs* (1563).

Francis II (1768–1835) Last Holy Roman emperor (1792–1806), first emperor of Austria, as Francis I (1804–35), and king of Bohemia and of Hungary (1792–1835). Francis was repeatedly defeated by the armies of NAPOLEON I in the French Revolutionary Wars. His territory steadily diminished, culminating in the rout at the battle of Austerlitz (1805) and the abolition of the Holy Roman Empire. In 1810 METTERNICH secured the marriage of Francis' daughter, MARIE LOUISE, to Napoleon. Austria was preserved by this alliance, and in 1813 Francis joined the coalition that defeated Napoleon. He formed the Holy Alliance.

Francis I (1494–1547) King of France (1515–47), cousin, son-in-law and successor of LOUIS XII. He is best remembered for his patronage of the arts and his palace at Fontainebleau. Persecution of the Waldenses, centralization of monarchical power and foolish financial policies made Francis unpopular. A struggle with Emperor CHARLES V over the imperial crown led to defeat at Pavia (1525). Francis was imprisoned and forced to give up Burgundy and renounce his claims to Italy. Two more wars (1527–29, 1536–38) ended ingloriously. In 1542 Francis concluded a treaty with SULEIMAN I and attacked Italy again. Charles, in alliance with Henry VIII, responded by invading France, and Francis lost further territory. He was succeeded by his son, Henry II.

Francis of Assisi, Saint (1182–1226) Italian founder of the Franciscans, b. Giovanni di Bernardone. In 1205 he renounced his worldly life for one of poverty and prayer. In 1209 Francis received permission from INNOCENT III to begin a monastic order. The Franciscans were vowed to humility, poverty and devotion to the task of helping people. In 1224, the stigmata wounds of the Crucifixion appeared on Francis' body. His feast day is 4 October.

Francis Xavier, Saint (1506–52) Jesuit missionary, often called Apostle of the Indies. Francis was an associate of St. IGNATIUS OF LOYOLA, with whom he took the vow founding the Society of Jesus (Jesuits). From 1541 he traveled through India, Japan and the East Indies, making converts. His feast day is 3 December.

Franco, Francisco (1892–1975) Spanish general and dictator (1939–75). He joined the 1936 uprising that led to the Spanish Civil War and assumed leadership of the fascist Falange. By 1939, with the aid of Nazi Germany and fascist Italy, Franco had won the war and become Spain's dictator. He kept Spain neutral in World War II, after which he presided over its economic development, while maintaining control over political expression. In 1947 Franco declared Spain a monarchy with himself as regent.

Franklin, Benjamin (1706–90) American statesman and scientist. His experiments in electricity, which he identified in lightning, were influential. Franklin was deputy paymaster general (1753–74) of the colonies. At the Albany Congress (1754), he proposed a union of the colonies. Franklin pressed for moderate opposition to the Stamp Act (1768). A leading delegate to the Continental Congress, he became an architect of the new republic. When war broke out, Franklin went to Paris and negotiated a treaty of alliance (1778). His peace proposals formed the basis of the final Treaty of Paris (1783) with Great Britain. As a member of the Constitutional Convention (1787), Franklin helped form the US Constitution.

Franks Germanic people who settled in the region of the River Rhine in the 3rd century. Under CLOVIS I in the 5th century, they overthrew Roman rule in Gaul and established the MEROVINGIAN empire. This was divided into the kingdoms of Austrasia, Neustria and Burgundy, but was reunited by the CAROLINGIANS, notably by CHARLEMAGNE. The partition of his empire into East and West Frankish kingdoms is the origin of Germany and France.

Franz Ferdinand (1863–1914) Archduke of Austria, nephew of FRANZ JOSEPH. He became heir apparent in 1889. On an official visit to Bosnia-Herzegovina, Franz Ferdinand and his wife were assassinated by a Serb nationalist in Sarajevo (28 June 1914). The incident led directly to the outbreak of World War I.

Franz Joseph (1830–1916) Emperor of Austria (1848–1916) and king of Hungary (1867–1916). He succeeded his uncle Ferdinand, who abdicated during the Revolutions of 1848. Franz Joseph brought the revolutions under control, defeating the Hungarians under Louis KOSSUTH in 1849. With the formation (1867) of the Austro-Hungarian empire, Franz Joseph was forced to grant Hungary coequal status. He died in the midst of World War I, two years before the collapse of the HAPSBURG EMPIRE.

Fraunhofer, Joseph von (1787–1826) German physicist, founder of astronomical spectroscopy. By studying the diffraction of light through narrow slits, he developed the earliest form of diffraction grating. He observed and began to map the dark lines in the Sun's spectrum (1814), now called Fraunhofer lines.

Frederick I (Barbarossa) (1123–90) Holy Roman emperor (1155–90) and king of Germany (1152–90); nephew and successor to Emperor CONRAD III. He hoped to end the division between the houses of HOHENSTAUFEN and GUELPH. In 1156 Frederick restored Bavaria to Henry the Lion. In 1158 he captured Milan and declared himself king of the Lombards. Frederick set up an antipope to Alexander III, who excommunicated him and formed the Lombard League. In 1176 Frederick was defeated at Legnano by the League and was forced to recognize Alexander as pope and make peace (1183) with the Lombards. In 1180 he defeated Henry the Lion and partitioned Bavaria. His son succeeded as HENRY VI.

Frederick II (1194–1250) Holy Roman emperor (1215–50) and German king (1212–20), king of Sicily (1198–1250) and king of Jerusalem (1229–50); son of Emperor HENRY VI. After his father's death, Germany was plunged into factional strife between the HOHENSTAUFENS, led by his uncle Philip of Swabia, and the GUELPHS led by OTTO IV. Otto prevailed, but his invasion of Italy prompted Pope INNOCENT III to promote Frederick. Frederick devoted himself to Italy and Sicily, and although he promised to make his son, Henry, king of Sicily, Frederick secured his election as king of Germany (1220) instead. His claims on Lombardy and postponement of a crusade angered Pope Honorius III, who excommunicated him. He finally embarked on a crusade in 1228 and proclaimed himself *stupor mundi* (wonder of the world). In Sicily, Frederick set up a centralized royal administration, while in Germany he devolved authority to the princes. The latter policy led Henry to rebel against his father. In 1235 Frederick imprisoned Henry, gave the German throne to CONRAD IV, and issued a land peace. In 1239 he captured most of the papal states. In 1245 Pope Innocent IV deposed him.

Frederick III (1415–93) Holy Roman emperor (1452–93) and German king (1440–93). He attempted to win the thrones of Bohemia and Hungary after the death of his ward, Ladislas V (1458). Instead, he lost Austria, Carinthia, Carniola and Styria to Matthias Corvinus of Hungary, only recovering them on Matthias' death (1490). By marrying his son Maximilian to Mary, heiress of Burgundy, in 1477, he acquired an enormous inheritance for the HAPSBURGS.

Frederick I (1657–1713) First king of Prussia (1701–13). He succeeded his father, FREDERICK WILLIAM, as Frederick III of Brandenburg. An ally of Emperor Leopold I, he gained the latter's approval of his assumption of the title "king in Prussia" in 1701. He promoted the cultural development of Brandenburg.

Frederick II (the Great) (1712–86) King of Prussia (1740–86). Succeeding his father, FREDERICK WILLIAM I, he made Prussia a major European force. In the War of the Austrian Succession (1740–48) against MARIA THERESA, Frederick gained the province of Silesia. During the Seven Years War (1756–63), his generalship preserved the kingdom from a superior hostile alliance. In 1760 Austro-Russian forces occupied Berlin, but Russia's withdrawal from the war enabled Frederick to emerge triumphant at the peace. He directed Prussia's remarkable recovery from the war. Gaining further territory in the first partition of Poland (1772), he renewed the contest against Austria in the War of the Bavarian Succession (1778–79). Artistic and intellectual, he built the palace of Sans Souci, and was a gifted musician.

Frederick William I (1688–1740) King of Prussia (1713–40), son and successor of FREDERICK I. He laid the basis for the rise of Prussia as a great power. Frederick William treated his son, the future FREDERICK II (THE GREAT), with brutality but bequeathed him a full treasury and the finest army in Europe.

Frederick William II (1744–97) King of Prussia (1786–97), nephew and successor of FREDERICK II (THE GREAT). He joined (1792) the alliance against France but made peace in 1795 in order to consolidate his acquisitions in the E as a result of the second (1793) and third (1795) partitions of Poland. He kept an extravagant court and left Prussia virtually bankrupt.

Frederick William III (1770–1840) King of Prussia (1797–1840), son and successor of FREDERICK WILLIAM II. He declared war on France (1806), suffered a disastrous defeat at Jena, and was forced to sign the Treaty of Tilsit (1807). In Prussia, some progressive reforms were made, but he later became increasingly reactionary. The reorganized Prussian army reentered the Napoleonic Wars in 1813 and played a major part in NAPOLEON I's eventual defeat.

Frederick William IV (1795–1861) King of Prussia (1840–61), son and successor of FREDERICK WILLIAM III. He granted a constitution in response to the Revolutions of 1848, but later amended it to eliminate popular influence. He refused the crown of Germany (1849) because it was offered by the Frankfurt Parliament, a democratic assembly. From 1858 the future Emperor WILLIAM I ruled as regent.

Frederick William (1620–88) (Great Elector) Elector of Brandenburg (1640–88). He inherited a collection of small and impoverished territories ravaged by the Thirty Years War. By the end of his reign, his organizational powers had created a unified state with a centralized tax system and a formidable standing army. The powers of the provincial estates (assemblies) were reduced. Frederick William acquired Eastern Pomerania at the Peace of Westphalia and, by his interventions in the war between Poland and Sweden (1655–60), gained sovereignty over Prussia.

Fresnel, Augustin Jean (1788–1827) French physicist. His work in optics was instrumental in establishing the wave theory of light. Fresnel researched the conditions governing interference phenomena in polarized light. He invented a convex lens (Fresnel lens) consisting of a series of stepped concentric rings.

Freud, Sigmund (1856–1939) Austrian physician, founder of psychoanalysis. With Josef Breuer he developed methods of treating mental disorders by free association and the interpretation of dreams. These methods derived from his theories of id, ego and superego, and emphasized the unconscious and subconscious as agents of human behavior. Freud developed theories of neuroses involving childhood relationships to one's parents and stressed the importance of sexuality in behavior. His works include *The Interpretation of Dreams* (1900), *The Psychopathology of Everyday Life* (1904) and *The Ego and the Id* (1923).

Friedman, Milton (1912–2006) US economist. He supported monetarism as the best means of controlling the economy. His works include: *A Monetary History of the United States 1867–1960*

(1963), a key book in monetary economics; *A Theory of the Consumption Function* (1957); and *Capitalism and Freedom* (1962). Friedman was awarded the 1976 Nobel Prize for economics.

Frisch, Karl von (1886–1982) Austrian zoologist. He shared the 1973 Nobel Prize for physiology or medicine with K. Lorenz and N. Tinbergen for his pioneering work in ethology. He deciphered the "language of bees" by studying their dance patterns (waggle dance), in which one bee tells others in the hive the direction and distance of a food source.

Frost, Robert Lee (1874–1963) US poet. Frost's first two volumes of lyric poems, *A Boy's Will* (1913) and *North of Boston* (1914), established his reputation. His best known poems include "The Road Not Taken" and "Mending Wall". Frost received the Pulitzer Prize for poetry (1924, 1931, 1937, 1943).

Fuad I (1868–1936) King of Egypt. Son of ISMAIL PASHA, he was sultan (1917–22) and first king of modern Egypt (1922–36). Fuad reigned under British influence and in conflict with the nationalist Wafd Party.

Fuentes, Carlos (1928–) Mexican novelist and short-story writer. His first two novels, *Where the Air is Clean* (1958) and *The Death of Artemio Cruz* (1962), share a critical view of Mexican society. Other fiction includes *The Hydra Head* (1978).

Fujiwara Strong, rich and cultured Japanese family, which between 857 and 1160 dominated the HEIAN period. By marrying Fujiwara women into the royal family they gained influence as "advisers" to the emperor. The family reached its peak of power under Michinaga Fujiwara (966–1027).

Fulani (Fulah or Fulbe) People of W Africa, numbering c.6 million. Their language belongs to the W Atlantic group of the Niger-Congo. Originally a pastoral people, they helped the spread of Islam in W Africa from the 16th century, establishing an empire that lasted until British colonialism in the 19th century.

G

Gaddi, Taddeo (c.1300–c.1366) Leading member in a family of Florentine artists. Taddeo served as an apprentice to GIOTTO. His best-known work is the fresco series *Life of the Virgin* (1338).

Gagarin, Yuri Alexseievich (1934–68) Russian cosmonaut, the first man to orbit the Earth. On 12 April 1961 he made a single orbit in 1 hour 29 minutes.

Gainsborough, Thomas (1727–88) English portrait and landscape painter. His style is remarkable for its characterization and use of color. Among his best landscapes is *The Watering Place* (1777). Gainsborough's portraits, such as *Viscount Kilmorey* (1768) and *Blue Boy* (c.1770), rivaled those of Joshua REYNOLDS.

Galbraith, J.K. (John Kenneth) (1908–2006) US economist, b. Canada. His famous works include *American Capitalism: The Concept of Countervailing Power* (1952) and *The New Industrial State* (1967). Galbraith takes the position that many accepted theories about the functioning of capitalist economies are outmoded. He advocates higher public spending on education and other services.

Galen (c.129–c.199) Greek physician, whose work provided the foundation for the development of medical practice. He made anatomical and physiological discoveries, including ones concerning heart valves, respiration and nervous function. He was among the first to study physiology by means of animal dissection.

Galerius (d.311) (Gaius Galerius Valerius Maximianus) Roman emperor (305–11). DIOCLETIAN appointed him caesar of the east in 293. He fought the Persians, losing in 296 but defeating them in 297. Originally he had urged Diocletian's persecution of Christians, but on his deathbed he issued an edict of toleration.

Galileo (1564–1642) (Galileo Galilei) Italian physicist and astronomer whose experimental methods laid the foundations of modern science. According to legend, Galileo observed that a hanging lamp in Pisa Cathedral took the same time to complete one oscillation however long the swing, and he suggested the pendulum could be used for timekeeping. He later studied falling bodies and disproved ARISTOTLE's view that they fall at different rates according to weight. In 1609 Galileo used one of the first astronomical telescopes to discover sunspots, lunar craters, Jupiter's major satellites and the phases of Venus. In *Sidereus Nuncius* (1610) he supported COPERNICUS' heliocentric system. Galileo was forbidden by the Roman Catholic Church to teach that this system represented physical reality, but in *Dialogue on the Two Great World Systems* (1632) he defied the pope by making his criticism of PTOLEMY's system even more explicit. As a result, Galileo was brought before the Inquisition and forced to recant.

Galle, Johann Gottfried (1812–1910) German astronomer, the first to observe and identify Neptune as a planet (1846). Galle also suggested a system for determining the scale of the Solar System based on the observation of asteroids.

Gallienus (Publius Licinius Valerianus Egnatius) (d.268) Roman emperor (253–68). He ruled with his father, VALERIAN, then alone. He ended his father's persecution of Christians.

Galvani, Luigi (1737–98) Italian physiologist. His experiments with frogs' legs indicated a connection between muscular contraction and electricity. He believed "animal electricity" was created in the muscle and nerve. His findings were disputed by VOLTA.

Gama, Vasco da (1469–1524) Portuguese navigator. He was charged with continuing Bartholomeu DIAZ's search for a sea route to India. Da Gama's successful expedition (1497–99) rounded the Cape of Good Hope and sailed across the Indian Ocean to Calicut. In 1502–03 he led a heavily armed expedition of 20 ships to Calicut and brutally avenged the killing of Portuguese settlers left there by CABRAL. Da Gama thereby secured Portuguese supremacy in the Eastern spice trade.

Gandhi, Indira (1917–84) Indian stateswoman, prime minister (1966–77, 1980–84), daughter of Jawaharlal NEHRU. She served as president of the Indian National Congress Party (1959–60) before becoming prime minister. In 1975, amid social unrest, Gandhi was found guilty of breaking electoral rules in the 1971 elections. She refused to resign, invoked emergency powers and imprisoned many opponents. In 1977 elections, the Congress Party suffered a heavy defeat and the party split. In 1980, leading a faction of the Congress Party, Gandhi returned to power. In 1984, after authorizing the use of force against Sikh dissidents in the Golden Temple at Amritsar, she was killed by a Sikh bodyguard. She was succeeded by her eldest son Rajiv GANDHI.

Gandhi, Mohandas Karamchand (1869–1948) Indian nationalist leader. In 1893 "Mahatma" (Sanskrit, Great Soul) Gandhi moved to South Africa and championed the rights of the Indian community. While in South Africa Gandhi launched (1907) his first noncooperation (*satyagraha*) campaign, involving nonviolent (*ahimsa*) civil disobedience. In 1914 he returned to India. Following the massacre at Amritsar (1919), Gandhi organized several campaigns of *satyagraha* and was imprisoned (1922–24). After his release, Gandhi served as president (1925–34) of the Indian National Congress. He campaigned for a free, united India. In 1930 he made his famous 400km (250mi) protest march against a salt tax. In 1942, after the British rejected his offer of cooperation in World War II if Britain granted immediate independence, Gandhi launched the Quit India movement. He was interned until 1944. Gandhi played a major role in the postwar talks with Nehru, Mountbatten and Muhammad Ali JINNAH that led to India's independence (1947). Gandhi opposed partition and the creation of a separate Muslim state. When violence flared between Hindus and Muslims, Gandhi resorted to fasts for peace. He was assassinated by a Hindu fanatic.

Gandhi, Rajiv (1944–91) Indian statesman, prime minister (1984–89), eldest son of Indira GANDHI. Rajiv became prime minister after his mother's assassination. He worked to placate India's Sikh extremists, but his reputation was tarnished by a bribery scandal. Defeated in the 1989 election, Rajiv was assassinated while campaigning for re-election.

García Márquez, Gabriel (1928–) Colombian novelist. His popular *One Hundred Years of Solitude* (1967) achieves a unique combination of realism, lyricism and mythical fantasy, making it a central text of magic realism. Later works include *Love in the Time of Cholera* (1985) and *The General in His Labyrinth* (1989). He was awarded the 1982 Nobel Prize for literature.

Garfield, James Abram (1831–81) 20th US President (1881). He served in the American Civil War until 1863. In 1876 he became the Republican leader of the house. In 1880 Garfield became the compromise presidential candidate. Garfield's four-month administration was characterized by party squabbles over federal jobs and political patronage. He was assassinated on 2 July 1881 and was succeeded by vice-president Chester A. ARTHUR.

Garibaldi, Giuseppe (1807–82) Italian patriot and soldier, who helped to achieve Italian unification. Influenced by MAZZINI, he participated in a republican rising (1834) and was forced into exile. Garibaldi returned to fight against the Austrians in the Revolutions of 1848 and in the unsuccessful defense of Rome against the French. In 1860 he led his 1,000-strong band of "Red Shirts"against the Kingdom of the Two Sicilies. Garibaldi handed his conquests over to King VICTOR EMMANUEL II, and they were incorporated into the new kingdom of Italy.

Gaudí (y Cornet), Antonio (1852–1926) Spanish architect. An idiosyncratic exponent of art nouveau, Gaudi employed sculptural, organic forms and ceramic ornamentation on buildings such as the unfinished church of the Sagrada Familia, Barcelona.

Gauguin, (Eugène Henri) Paul (1848–1903) French painter. In his early career, Gauguin exhibited (1881–86) with the impressionists in Paris. *The Vision After the Sermon* (1888) is a key work in Gauguin's break with the naturalism of impressionism. He developed a "synthetist"style of expressionism characterized by bold contours and large areas of unmodulated color. Inspired by"primitive"art, he left France for Tahiti in 1891. The late works convey a sense of mystery and myth. They include *Where do we come from? What are we? Where are we going?* (1897).

Gauss, Karl Friedrich (1777–1855) German mathematician. His *Disquisitiones Arithmeticae* (1798) was the first modern text on number theory. Gauss made many discoveries that were not credited to him, such as nonEuclidean geometry and quaternions. In 1801 he calculated the orbit of the asteroid Ceres. From 1821 he was involved in the first worldwide survey of the Earth's magnetic field, for which he invented a heliograph.

Gay-Lussac, Joseph Louis (1778–1850) French chemist and physicist. He discovered (1808) the law that gases combine in a simple ratio by volume (Gay-Lussac's law). Gay-Lussac also discovered the law of gas expansion, often attributed to J.A.C. CHARLES. He prepared (1808) the elements boron and potassium.

Gell-Mann, Murray (1929–) US theoretical physicist. In 1954 he introduced the concept of "strangeness"to account for the relative longevity of hadrons. In 1962 Gell-Mann predicted the existence of a new particle (omega-minus). In 1964 he coined the term"quark"to describe the basic constituent of the baryon and meson. He was awarded the 1969 Nobel Prize for physics.

Genghis Khan (*c*.1162–1227) Conqueror and founder of the MONGOL empire, b. Temüjin. In 1206, according to the *Secret History of the Mongol Nation* (*c*.1240), he united Mongolia and was proclaimed Genghis Khan (Universal Ruler). He turned his cavalry into a disciplined squadron (*ordus*, hence "hordes"), Genghis Khan demonstrated his military genius by capturing Beijing (1215) and subjugating most of N China. He went on to create one of the largest empires ever known, annexing Afghanistan, Iran, Uzbekistan and invading Russia as far as Moscow. On his death, the empire was divided among his sons.

Gentile da Fabriano (*c*.1370–1427) Italian painter. A leader of the international gothic style, he greatly influenced Florentine art with frescos and the *Adoration of the Magi* (1423) for the Church of Santa Trinita, Florence.

Geoffrey of Monmouth (*c*.1100–54) Welsh priest and chronicler, best known for his *History of the Kings of Britain* (*c*.1136). Though accepted as reliable until the 17th century, Geoffrey essentially told folk tales. His book was the chief source for the legend of King Arthur.

George I (1660–1727) King of Great Britain and Ireland (1714–27) and Elector of Hanover (1698–1727). A Protestant, he succeeded Queen ANNE as the first monarch of the House of Hanover. George favored the Whigs over the Tories, suspecting the latter of Jacobite sympathies. George preferred his native Hanover to England and spoke little English. As a result, power passed to Parliament and ministers such as Sir Robert WALPOLE.

George II (1683–1760) King of Great Britain and Ireland and Elector of Hanover (1727–1760), son of GEORGE I. He was more German than English, and Sir Robert WALPOLE dominated politics early in the reign. George was the last British king to lead his army in battle, at Dettingen (1746). British prosperity was growing, and George witnessed victories in the Seven Years War.

George III (1738–1820) King of Great Britain and Ireland (1760–1820) and King of Hanover (1760–1820), grandson of GEORGE II. He shared the blame with Lord NORTH for the loss of the American colonies in the American Revolution (1775–83). His reign witnessed the beginnings of the Industrial Revolution. In 1765 he suffered his first attack of apparent insanity, now known to be symptoms of porphyria. They grew worse, and in 1811 his son, the future GEORGE IV, was made prince regent.

George IV (1762–1830) King of Great Britain and Ireland (1820–30), son of GEORGE III. He served as regent for his father from 1811. Self-indulgent and extravagant, George was bored by government but was a strong patron of the arts. In 1785 he contracted a legally invalid marriage to Mrs. Fitzherbert. His marriage (1795) to Caroline of Brunswick was a source of scandal.

George V (1865–1936) King of Great Britain and Northern Ireland and Emperor of India (1910–36), the second son and successor of EDWARD VII. In 1893 he married Princess Mary of Teck. In 1917, during World War I, George changed the name of the royal house from the Saxe-Coburg-Gotha to Windsor.

George VI (1895–1952) King of Great Britain and Northern Ireland (1936–52) and Emperor of India (1936–47), son of GEORGE V. He became king when his brother, EDWARD VIII, abdicated. He remained with his family in London during the Blitz. In 1949 he became head of the newly formed Commonwealth.

George I (1845–1913) King of the Hellenes (1863–1913). Made king by Great Britain, France and Russia with approval of a Greek national assembly, he backed the constitution of 1864 giving power to an elected parliament. George gained territory for Greece in the Balkan Wars. Assassinated in 1913, he was succeeded by his son as Constantine I.

Geronimo (1829–1908) Chief of the Chiricahua Apache Native Americans. Escaping from a reservation into which he and his tribe were forced, he led a band of followers in raids against white settlers in Arizona for more than ten years. After surrendering in 1886, he was imprisoned. He became a national celebrity.

Gershwin, George (1898–1937) US composer and songwriter, b. Jacob Gershovitz. His brother, **Ira** Gershwin (1896–1983), mostly wrote the lyrics. Gershwin composed musicals, such as *Lady Be Good* (1924), a jazz opera *Porgy and Bess* (1935), and orchestral works, such as *Rhapsody in Blue* (1924).

Ghaznavid dynasty Muslim Turkish dynasty that ruled a region from E Iran to N India from 977 to 1186. They began as governors of Ghazni in Afghanistan, gaining independence when the Samanid emirs of Bukhara were overthrown. Mahmud Ghazni (r.998–1030) established Muslim rule in what is now Pakistan and made raids far into India. Thereafter, the dynasty declined through succession quarrels and attacks by the SELJUK Turks. The empire was reduced after the battle of Dandanqan (1040). Ghazni was sacked by the Ghuri in the 12th century, and the last Ghaznavid retreated to Lahore, which was lost in 1186.

Ghibelline Political faction in 13th-century Italy that supported the HOHENSTAUFEN DYNASTY of the HOLY ROMAN EMPIRE and opposed the pro-papal GUELPHS. During the struggles between FREDERICK II and the popes in the mid 13th century, Ghibellines came to designate those on the imperial side. They were defeated by the Guelphs in 1268, and the family went into decline.

Ghiberti, Lorenzo (1378–1455) Italian sculptor, goldsmith, architect, painter and writer, a major transitional figure between the late Gothic and Renaissance worlds. Ghiberti made two pairs of bronze doors for the Baptistery in Florence. One pair, the "Doors of Paradise"(1425–52), is considered his masterpiece.

Gibbon, Edward (1737–94) English historian. He conceived the idea of his great work, *The Decline and Fall of the Roman Empire* (1776–88), while among the ruins of ancient Rome.

Gilgamesh Hero of the great Assyro-Babylonian myth, the Epic of Gilgamesh. He went in search of the secret of immortality. Having overcome monsters and gods, Gilgamesh found the flower of immortality, only to have it snatched from him by a serpent.

Giorgione (*c.*1478–1510) Italian painter, b. Giorgio da Castlefranco. He had an enigmatic romantic style, as in *Tempest* (*c.*1505). His *Sleeping Venus* was probably completed by TITIAN.

Giotto (di Bondone) (*c.*1266–1337) Florentine painter. Giotto rejected the stylized form of Italo-Byzantine art in favor of a more realistic style, best represented by the frescos (*c.*1305–08) in the Arena Chapel, Padua. In 1334 he became architect of Florence and designed the campanile of the Duomo.

Giscard d'Estaing, Valéry (1926–) French statesman, president (1974–81). He served as finance minister (1962–66) under Charles DE GAULLE. After his dismissal, he formed the Independent Republican Party. Giscard d'Estaing returned as finance minister under Georges POMPIDOU. He defeated François MITTERRAND to become president, but lost to him in 1981. He has been leader of the Union for French Democracy (UDF) since 1988.

Gladstone, William Ewart (1809–98) British statesman, prime minister (1868–74, 1880–85, 1886, 1892–94). Elected to Parliament as a Tory in 1832, he served (1843–45) as president of the Board of Trade under Robert PEEL. Gladstone sided with the Peelites over the repeal of the Corn Laws. In 1867 Gladstone became leader of the Liberal Party. In his first term, he introduced the first Irish Land Act. In 1874 he was defeated by Benjamin DISRAELI. His criticism of Disraeli's imperialist tendencies won him the 1879 elections. In his second term, Gladstone passed a second Irish Land Act (1881) and several Reform Acts (1884, 1885) extending the franchise. Gladstone's last ministries were dominated by his advocacy of Home Rule for Ireland.

Glass, Philip (1937–) US composer. Glass's characteristic style is the hypnotic repetition of short motifs within a simple harmonic idiom. Glass's operas include *Einstein on the Beach* (1976), *Satyagraha* (1980) and *Akhnaten* (1984).

Glenn, John Herschel, Jr.(1921–) US astronaut. On 20 February 1962, aboard *Friendship 7*, he became the first person to orbit the Earth. Glenn became a US senator (Democrat). In 1998, at the age of 77, Glenn flew his second space mission, on the space shuttle *Discovery*, becoming the oldest person in space.

Glyn Dw̑r, Owain (Owen Glendower) (*c.*1359–1416) Welsh chief. A member of the house of Powys, he led a rebellion (1401) against HENRY IV. Proclaimed prince of Wales, Glyn Dw̑r allied himself with Henry's English enemies, Sir Henry Percy and the Mortimer family. By 1404 he had captured Harlech and Aberystwyth castles. By 1409 Glyn Dw̑r had lost both castles and retreated to the hills to maintain guerrilla warfare against the English.

Gobind Singh (1666–1708) Tenth and last Sikh guru, who laid the foundations of Sikh militarism. In 1699 he created the *Khalsa*, a military fraternity of devout Sikhs, which became the basis of the Sikh army he led against the MUGHAL empire.

Gödel, Kurt (1906–78) US logician. b. Moravia. He is known for his"undecidability"or"incompleteness"theorem, which states that any axiom-based mathematical system contains statements that can neither be proved nor disproved within the system.

Godfrey of Bouillon (*c.*1060–1100) French crusader, duke of Lower Lorraine (1089–95). He led the First Crusade (1096) and played a major role in the capture (1099) of Jerusalem. Elected king, he preferred the title Defender of the Holy Sepulcher.

Godunov, Boris (1551–1605) Czar of Russia (1598–1605). Chief minister and brother-in-law of IVAN IV (THE TERRIBLE), he

became regent to Ivan's imbecile son Fyodor. He was popularly supposed to have murdered Fyodor's brother and heir, Dmitri, in 1591. On Fyodor's death in 1598, Boris was elected czar. Godunov gained recognition for the Russian Orthodox Church as an independent patriarchate, but his suppression of the boyars led to the "Time of Troubles"(1604–12).

Goethe, Johann Wolfgang von (1749–1832) German poet, dramatist, novelist and statesman. Goethe's first play, *Götz von Berlichingen* (1773), was in the tradition of Sturm and Drang. His epistolary novel *The Sorrows of Young Werther* (1774) won him international fame. Goethe's most enduring work, the dramatic poem *Faust*, was published in two parts (1808, 1832).

Gogol, Nikolai Vasilievich (1809–52) Russian novelist and dramatist. His work marks the transition from romanticism to early realism. Gogol made his reputation with stories, such as *The Nose* (1835), and the drama *The Government Inspector* (1836).

Goldman, Emma (1869–1940) US anarchist and feminist, b. Lithuania. In New York she coedited (1906–17) the anarchist monthly *Mother Earth*. Goldman was imprisoned (1916, 1917) for advocating birth control and opposing conscription during World War I. In 1919 she was deported to Russia. Goldman was active in the Spanish Civil War.

Gompers, Samuel (1850–1924) US labor union leader, b. England. He helped to found the Federation of Organized Trades and Labor Unions. When it was reorganized as the American Federation of Labor (1886), Gompers became its first president, serving until his death except for the year 1895.

Gorbachev, Mikhail Sergeievich (1931–) Soviet statesman, president of the Soviet Union (1988–91) and general secretary of the Communist Party of the Soviet Union (1985–91). After succeeding Konstantin CHERNENKO as leader, Gorbachev embarked on a program of reform based on two principles: *perestroika* (restructuring) and *glasnost* (openness). He played a major role in the nuclear disarmament process, withdrew Soviet troops from Afghanistan and acquiesced to the demise of communist regimes in Eastern Europe (1989–90). In Russia the benefits of socioeconomic change were slow to take effect, and Gorbachev's popularity fell as prices rose. In August 1991 Communist hardliners mounted an unsuccessful coup. In December 1991 the Communist Party was abolished. Gorbachev was forced to dissolve the Soviet Union and hand power to his rival, Boris YELTSIN. He was awarded the Nobel Peace Prize in 1990.

Gordon, Charles George (1833–85) British soldier and administrator. He fought in the Crimean War and Opium War. He was governor-general of the Sudan (1877–80) and returned to Khartoum in 1884 to evacuate Egyptian forces threatened by the MAHDI. He was killed two days before the arrival of a relief force.

Goths Ancient Germanic people, groups of whom settled near the Black Sea in the 2nd and 3rd centuries CE. The VISIGOTHS were driven westward into Roman territory by the HUNS in 376, culminating in their sacking Rome under ALARIC in 410. They settled in SW France, then, driven out by the Franks in the early 6th century, in Spain. Some groups united to create the OSTROGOTHS, who conquered Italy under THEODORIC THE GREAT (489). They held Italy until conquered by the Byzantines.

Gould, Stephen Jay (1941–) US paleontologist. Gould's theory of punctuated equilibrium suggested that sudden accelerations in the evolutionary process could produce rapid changes in species over the comparatively short time of a few hundred thousand years. His popular science books include *Hen's Teeth and Horses' Toes* (1983) and *Bully for Brontosaurus* (1992).

Goya (y Lucientes), Francisco José de (1746–1828) Spanish painter and engraver. A severe illness (1791) provoked a vein of fantastic works, one of the most sinister of which is *Los Caprichos*, a series of 82 engravings published in 1799. Goya enjoyed the royal patronage of CHARLES IV despite mercilessly realistic paintings such as *The Family of Charles IV* (1800). His bloody scenes, *The Second of May, 1808* and *The Third of May, 1808*, portray the Spanish resistance to the French invasion.

Gracchus, Gaius Sempronius (*c*.153–121 BCE) Roman statesman. As tribune (123–121 BCE) he continued to implement the social reforms of his brother **Tiberius** (*c*.163–133 BCE), who was killed for attempting to reform agrarian law to benefit the poor. Gaius sought to check the power of the Senate by uniting the plebeians and the equites. These reforms were short-lived; he was defeated in the election of 121 and killed in the ensuing riots.

Graham, Thomas (1805–69) Scottish chemist. He is best remembered for Graham's law, which states that the diffusion rate of a gas is inversely proportional to the square root of its density. Graham also discovered dialysis.

Grant, Ulysses S. (Simpson) (1822–85) US Civil War general and 18th US President (1869–77). In command of the Vicksburg Campaign (1862–63). In 1864 Abraham LINCOLN gave him overall command of the Union forces. He coordinated the final campaigns and accepted the surrender of Robert E. LEE (1865). As president, Grant achieved foreign policy successes but failed to prevent the growth of domestic corruption.

Grass, Günter Wilhelm (1927–) German novelist, poet and playwright. His prose combines evocative description with historical documentation. He used powerful techniques to grotesque comic effect in *The Tin Drum* (1959) and *Cat and Mouse* (1961), and he satirized the Nazi era in *Dog Years* (1963).

Greco, El (1541–1614) Cretan painter, b. Domenikos Theotokopoulos. By 1577 El Greco had settled in Toledo, N Spain. His characteristically elongated and distorted figures disregard normal rules of perspective. His later paintings, such as *Burial of Count Orgasz* (1586), *Agony in the Garden* (1610) and *Assumption* (1613), express his profound religious conviction.

Greeks, ancient Inhabitants of classical Greece, from the period beginning with the defeat of the second Persian invasion in 479 BCE to the death of ALEXANDER THE GREAT in 323 BCE. During this period, warring city-states flourished as centers of trade. Athens, the most wealthy and powerful, developed a democratic system under the guidance of PERICLES. Its main rival was the military state of Sparta. Classical Greece was the birthplace of many ideas in art, literature, philosophy and science.

Greene, (Henry) Graham (1904–91) English novelist, journalist, travel writer and dramatist. Guilt and the search for redemption are consistent themes in Greene's novels. His psychological thrillers are among the most popular works of 20th-century fiction. His works include *Brighton Rock* (1938), *The Power and the Glory* (1940) and *The Honorary Consul* (1973).

Greer, Germaine (1939–) Australian feminist and writer. Her book *The Female Eunuch* (1970) challenged the misrepresentation of female sexuality by a patriarchal society. Other works include *Sex and Destiny: the Politics of Human Fertility* (1984) and *The Change: Women, Aging and the Menopause* (1991).

Gregory I (the Great), Saint (*c*.540–604) Pope (590–604), last of the Latin Fathers of the Church. He devoted himself to alleviating poverty and hunger among the Romans. Gregory was responsible for enforcing the spiritual supremacy of the papacy and establishing the temporal independence of the pope. Gregory sent Saint Augustine to England to convert the Anglo-Saxons. His feast day is 12 March.

Gregory of Tours, Saint (538–94) Bishop and historian of Frankish Gaul. His *History of the Franks* consists of three separate sections on current affairs. He also wrote on miracles, martyrs and some of the Fathers of the Church.

Gregory XIII (1502–85) Pope (1572–85), b. Ugo Buoncompagni. He promoted church reform and sought to carry out the decrees of the Council of Trent. He is best known for his reform of the Julian calendar (1582).

Grieg, Edvard Hagerup (1843–1907) Norwegian composer. He used Norwegian folk themes in many of his compositions. Grieg wrote the incidental music for IBSEN's play *Peer Gynt* (1876). Other major works include the Piano Concerto (1868).

Grimm brothers German philologists and folklorists. **Jakob Ludwig Karl** (1785–1863) formulated Grimm's law, which

detailed the regular shifting of consonants in Indo-European languages. He and his brother, **Wilhelm Karl** (1786–1859), are popularly known for their enduring collection of folk tales, *Grimm's Fairy Tales* (1812–15). It was a major text of romanticism.

Gropius, Walter (1883–1969) German-US architect. Gropius transformed the Weimar School of Art into the Bauhaus, which was relocated (1926) to his newly designed buildings in Dessau. Gropius pioneered functionalism and the International style. The results of his cooperative, group-work design methods can be seen in the Harvard Graduate Center (1949).

Guelph Political faction in medieval Italy, opposed to the GHIBELLINE. The two factions were linked to rival families contending for the HOLY ROMAN EMPIRE in the 12th century. In 1198 OTTO IV (a Guelph) became Holy Roman emperor. In the battle for control of Italy, the Guelphs took the side of the papacy, whereas the Ghibellines backed the emperor FREDERICK II. The Ghibellines were defeated (1268) by the Guelphs at Tagliacozzo.

Guevara, "Che" (Ernesto) (1928–67) Argentine revolutionary leader. Guevara became associated with Fidel CASTRO in Mexico and returned with him to Cuba to play a leading role in the Cuban revolution (1956–59). Guevara became a minister in Castro's government. In 1965 he disappeared from public view. Two years later he was captured and killed while trying to establish a communist guerrilla base in Bolivia.

Guillaume de Lorris (1210–37) French romance writer. He wrote the earlier part of the *Roman de la Rose* (*c*.1230), an allegory in which a courtly lover becomes enamored of a rosebud. Guillaume died before it was finished, and Jean de Meung composed the second part.

Gupta dynasty (*c*.CE 320–*c*.550) Ruling house whose kingdom covered most of N India. Founded by CHANDRAGUPTA I, the Gupta dynasty embraced Buddhism and is seen as a golden age. It reached its greatest extent at the end of the 4th century but declined at the end of the 5th century under attack from the HUNS.

Gustavus I (Vasa) (1496–1560) King of Sweden (1523–60) and founder of the Vasa dynasty. In 1520 he led a victorious rebellion against the invading Danes. In 1523 Gustavus was elected king. During his reign Sweden gained independence.

Gustavus II (Adolphus) (1594–1632) King of Sweden (1611–32). His reign was distinguished by constitutional and educational reforms. Gustavus ended war with Denmark (1613) and Russia (1617). Hoping to increase Sweden's control of the Baltic, he entered the Thirty Years War (1618–48). He was killed during the Swedish victory at the battle of Lützen.

Gustavus III (1746–92) King of Sweden (1771–92). During his reign, known as the Gustavian Enlightenment, he instituted financial reforms, religious toleration, a free press and a strong navy. He was a gifted writer and patron of the arts.

Gustavus VI (1882–1973) King of Sweden (1950–73). He succeeded Gustavus V and was the last Swedish king to hold political power. His grandson Carl Gustavus (b.1946) succeeded him.

Gutenberg, Johann (1400–68) German goldsmith and printer, credited with inventing printing from movable metallic type. He produced the first printed Bible, known as the *Gutenberg Bible* or *Mazarin Bible* (*c*.1455).

H

Haakon VII (1872–1957) King of Norway (1905–57). He was elected king when Norway regained its independence from Sweden. In 1940 Haakon was forced into exile by the German invasion and led a government-in-exile (1940–45) in London, UK.

Hapsburg dynasty (Hapsburg dynasty) Austrian royal dynasty, a leading ruling house in Europe from the 13th to 19th century. It became a major force when RUDOLF I was elected (1273) king of the Germans. He established the core of the Hapsburg dominions in Austria, Styria and Carniola. FREDERICK III arranged the marriage (1477) by which his son, Maximilian, gained Burgundy, the Netherlands and Luxembourg. MAXIMILIAN I extended his father's marriage diplomacy to his own son, Philip, who acquired (1496) Castile, Aragón, Granada, Spanish America, Naples, Sicily and Sardinia. When CHARLES V became emperor in 1519, he ruled over the largest European empire since Charlemagne. His brother, FERDINAND I, gained Hungary and Bohemia through marriage. In 1556 Charles abdicated, leaving his Spanish titles to his son, PHILIP II, and his Austrian titles to Ferdinand I. In 1700 the Spanish line ended and in the subsequent War of the Spanish Succession (1703–13) power passed to the BOURBON DYNASTY. In 1740 the male line of the Austrian branch ended, but MARIA THERESA re-established the house as that of Hapsburg-Lorraine. At the end of the Napoleonic Wars (1803–15) the Hapsburgs lost the Austrian Netherlands and the title of Holy Roman Emperor, but continued to control Austria. By 1867 the Hapsburg empire was reduced to the Austro-Hungarian empire. FRANZ JOSEPH saw the disintegration of his empire in World War I. It finally broke up in 1918, when Charles I was deposed.

Hadrian, Publius Aelius (CE 76–138) Roman emperor (117–138). Nephew of Emperor TRAJAN, Hadrian adopted a policy of imperial retrenchment, discouraging new conquests and ordering the construction of Hadrian's Wall in Britain. One of the most cultured Roman emperors, he erected many fine buildings and rebuilt the Pantheon. The erection of a shrine to Jupiter on the site of the Temple in Jerusalem provoked a Jewish revolt (132–135), which was ruthlessly suppressed.

Hahn, Otto (1879–1968) German physical chemist. He worked on radioactivity with William RAMSAY and Edward RUTHERFORD. In 1917 he and Lise Meitner discovered the radioactive element protactinium. Assisted by Fritz Strassmann, Hahn and Meitner investigated Enrico FERMI's work on the neutron bombardment of uranium. In 1938 Hahn and Strassmann discovered nuclear fission. Hahn was awarded the 1944 Nobel Prize for chemistry.

Haig, Douglas, 1st Earl (1861–1928) British field marshal. During World War I he served as commander-in-chief of British forces in France. Haig's policy of attrition inflicted appalling losses among British troops, particularly in the campaigns of the Somme and Passchendaele. Under the supreme command of Marshal FOCH, he led the final assault on the Hindenburg line.

Haile Selassie I (1892–1975) (Ras Tafari Makonnen) Emperor of Ethiopia (1930–74). When Italy invaded Ethiopia in 1935, he was forced into exile (1936). In 1941 Haile Selassie drove out the Italians with British aid. Subsequently he became a leader among independent African nations, helping to found (1963) the Organization of African Unity (OAU). Unrest at corruption and lack of reform led to his overthrow by a military coup in 1974.

Halley, Edmond (1656–1742) English astronomer and mathematician, Astronomer Royal (1720–42). Halley's most famous discovery (1696) was that comets have periodic orbits. In 1705 he accurately predicted the return of the comet now known as Halley's Comet in 1758. Halley charted variations in Earth's magnetic field and established the magnetic origin of the aurora borealis.

Hamilcar Barca (d.228 BCE) Carthaginian commander. Initially successful in the first of the Punic Wars, he was defeated in 241 BCE. Hamilcar suppressed a revolt of Carthaginian mercenaries in 238 BCE and the following year conquered much of Spain. He was the father of HANNIBAL and Hasdrubal Barca.

Hamilton, Alexander (1755–1804) US statesman. During the American Revolution he served as George WASHINGTON's aide-de-camp and secretary. After the war he became a member of the Continental Congress and a delegate to the Constitutional Convention. Hamilton was the principal contributor to The Federalist Papers (1788), advocating the new US Constitution. As the first secretary of the treasury (1789–95), he established the Bank of the United States (1791). In 1800 he alienated many within the Federalist Party by supporting Thomas JEFFERSON's bid for presidency. In 1804 he thwarted Aaron BURR's campaign for governor of New York. Burr challenged him to a duel and killed him.

Hammarskjöld, Dag (1905–61) Swedish diplomat, second secretary-general (1953–61) of the United Nations (UN). He

brought great moral authority to the office. In 1956 Hammarskjöld played a leading role in resolving the Suez Crisis. He sent a UN peacekeeping force to the Congo. He died in an air crash over Zambia while on a mission to the Congo. He was posthumously awarded the 1961 Nobel Peace Prize.

Hammurabi (d. c.1750 BCE) King of BABYLONIA (c.1792–c.1750 BCE). By conquering neighbors, such as Sumeria, he extended his rule in Mesopotamia. He reorganized the empire under the series of laws known as the Code of Hammurabi.

Han dynasty Imperial Chinese dynasty (202 BCE–CE 220). It was founded by a rebellious peasant, Liu Bang, who overthrew the QIN DYNASTY. Under the Han, Confucianism became the state philosophy. China achieved unprecedented power, prosperity, technological invention and cultural growth, especially under Wu Ti in the 2nd century BCE. A usurper, WANG MANG, interrupted the dynasty between CE 8 and 25; the dynasty is divided by that period into the Former Han and Later Han.

Handel, George Frideric (1685–1759) English composer, b. Germany. In 1712 he moved to England. Handel wrote (c.1717) the Water Music to serenade GEORGE I's procession down the River Thames. From 1729 to 1734 he wrote a series of operas for the Kings Theater, London, including Orlando (1733). From 1739 Handel concentrated on oratorios, producing such masterpieces as Saul (1739) and Messiah (1742).

Hannibal (247–183 BCE) Carthaginian general in the second of the Punic Wars, son of HAMILCAR BARCA. In 218 BCE he invaded N Italy after crossing the Alps with 40,000 troops and a force of elephants. Hannibal won a series of victories but was unable to capture Rome. Recalled to Carthage to confront the invasion of SCIPIO AFRICANUS, he was defeated at Zama (202 BCE). After the war, as chief magistrate of Carthage, he alienated the nobility by reducing their power. They sought Roman intervention, and Hannibal fled to the Seleucid kingdom of ANTIOCHUS III. He fought against the Romans, was defeated and committed suicide.

Harding, Warren Gamaliel (1865–1923) 29th US President (1921–23). He was the Republican compromise candidate to run for president in 1920. Harding's campaign for a return to "normalcy" easily defeated the Democratic challenge. He left government to his cabinet and advisers. This administration, known as the "Ohio Gang", was one of the most corrupt in US history. The Teapot Dome Scandal forced a Congressional investigation. Harding died before the worst excesses became public knowledge. He was succeeded by the vice-president, Calvin COOLIDGE.

Hardouin-Mansart, Jules (1646–1708) French architect to LOUIS XIV. His small baroque style can be best seen in the Palace of Versailles, notably the Hall of Mirrors (1678–84).

Hardy, Thomas (1840–1928) English novelist and poet. His birthplace, Dorset, SW England, formed the background for most of his writing. His often tragic tales include Far from the Madding Crowd (1874), The Mayor of Casterbridge (1886), Tess of the d'Urbervilles (1891) and Jude the Obscure (1895). The latter was attacked for its immoral tone, and thereafter Hardy devoted himself to poetry, such as Wessex Poems (1898).

Hargreaves, James (1722–78) English inventor and industrialist. In 1764 he invented the spinning jenny. This machine greatly speeded the spinning process of cotton by producing eight threads simultaneously. In 1768 local spinners destroyed the jenny, fearing that it threatened their jobs.

Harrison, Benjamin (1833–1901) 23rd US President (1889–93), grandson of William Henry HARRISON. After one term in the US Senate, he was selected (1888) as the Republican presidential nominee against Grover CLEVELAND. As president, he signed into law the Sherman Antitrust Act and the McKinley Tariff Act (both 1890). He was defeated by Cleveland in 1892.

Harrison, John (1693–1776) British horologist. In 1753 he made a marine chronometer for which he was awarded a Government-sponsored prize of £20,000.

Harrison, William Henry (1773–1841) Ninth US President (1841). He is remembered chiefly for his military career, especially his victory at Tippecanoe over Native Americans (1811). He was elected president in 1840, with John Tyler as vice-president, under the famous slogan "Tippecanoe and Tyler too". Harrison died after one month in office.

Harun al-Rashid (764–809) ABBASID caliph of Baghdad (786–809). His reign has gained romantic luster from the stories of the *Arabian Nights*. He engaged in successful war with the BYZANTINE EMPIRE, but his effort to reconcile competing interests by dividing the empire between his sons led to civil war.

Hastings, Warren (1732–1818) British colonial administrator, first British governor general of India (1774–85). Hastings reformed the administration and finances of the British East India Company and consolidated Britain's military control of India. He made many enemies and returned to England to face charges of corruption. He was acquitted, but his career was ruined.

Hatshepsut (d.1482 BCE) Queen of Egypt (c.1494–1482 BCE). Daughter of Thutmose I, she married Thutmose II. After his death (c. 1504 BCE), she ruled first as regent for her nephew and then in her own right, the only woman to rule as pharaoh.

Hausa Mainly Muslim people, inhabiting NW Nigeria and S Niger. Hausa society is feudal and based on patrilineal descent. Its language is the lingua franca of N Nigeria and a major trading language of W Africa.

Havel, Vaclav (1936–) Czech statesman and dramatist. He wrote a series of plays, such as *The Garden Party* (1963), that were highly critical of Czechoslovakia's communist regime. Havel was imprisoned (1979–83) by the regime. In 1989 he served another brief spell in prison before founding the Civic Forum. Following the "Velvet Revolution" (December 1989) Havel was elected president of Czechoslovakia. He resigned (1992) in protest at the partition of Czechoslovakia, but returned by popular demand. He served as president of the Czech Republic until 2003.

Hawking, Stephen William (1942–) English theoretical physicist. He used the general theory of relativity and quantum mechanics to produce theories on the Big Bang and the formation of black holes. Hawking wrote the popular science bestseller *A Brief History of Time* (1988). Since the 1960s he has suffered from a progressive motor neurone disease.

Hawkins, Sir John (1532–95) English naval commander. He led two lucrative expeditions to Africa and the West Indies (1562–63, 1564–65). On his third expedition (1567–69) the Spanish destroyed most of his ships. He played an important role in the defeat of the Spanish Armada in 1588.

Hawthorne, Nathaniel (1804–64) US novelist. His works include *The House of the Seven Gables* (1851) and *The Snow Image and Other Twice-Told Tales* (1851). Much of his work is set in Puritan New England and examines the conflict between emotion and repressive social strictures.

Hay, John Milton (1838–1905) US secretary of state (1898–1905) under Presidents McKINLEY and Theodore ROOSEVELT. His "open-door policy" was a demand for equal trading status for foreign powers in China. He negotiated the Hay-Pauncefote Treaty ensuring US control of the Panama Canal.

Haydn, Franz Joseph (1732–1809) Austrian composer. Haydn wrote more than 100 symphonies, notably the *Military*, the *Clock* and the *London* (all 1793–95). His most famous choral works are the oratorios *The Creation* (1798) and *The Seasons* (1801). He also wrote string quartets, chamber works, concertos and masses.

Hayes, Rutherford Birchard (1822–93) 19th US President (1877–81). As governor of Ohio, he won the Republican nomination for president in 1876. Some of the electoral votes were disputed, but an electoral commission awarded all of them to Hayes. As president, Hayes removed all federal troops from the South and tried to promote civil-service reform.

Heaney, Seamus (1939–) Irish poet, b. Northern Ireland. His works, such as *North* (1975), *Field Work* (1979) and *Station Island* (1984), examine the political and historical connotations of words. Heaney won the Whitbread Prize for *The Spirit Level* (1996). He was awarded the 1995 Nobel Prize for literature.

Heath, Sir Edward Richard George (1916–2005) British statesman, prime minister (1970–74). In 1965 Heath succeeded Alec Douglas-Home as leader of the Conservative Party. He defeated Harold WILSON in the 1970 general election. As prime minister, Heath secured (1973) Britain's membership of the European Community (EC), but poor industrial relations led to a bitter miners' strike and the "three-day week" (1974) to conserve energy. He was replaced (1975) as Conservative leader by Margaret THATCHER. Heath was a staunch critic of "Thatcherism" and an outspoken advocate of European integration.

Hegel, Georg Wilhelm Friedrich (1770–1831) German philosopher, whose method of dialectical reasoning influenced his successors, notably Karl MARX. He developed a metaphysical system that traced the self-realization of spirit by dialectical movements toward perfection. Hegel wrote two major books, *Phenomenology of Mind* (1807) and *Science of Logic* (1812–16).

Heian Period of rule in Japanese history from c.794 to 1185, centered on the city of Heian, now Kyoto. Under the FUJIWARA dynasty the period was marked by great advances in Japanese civilization, above all in poetry and prose. Some of the most important developments of Japanese Buddhism occurred at this time.

Heidegger, Martin (1889–1976) German philosopher, a founder of existentialism and a major influence on modern philosophy. Influenced by hermeneutics, phenomenology and Christian ontology, his most important work was *Being and Time* (1927).

Heine, Heinrich (1797–1856) German poet and prose writer. The *Book of Songs* (1827), a collection of verse, is his best-known work. It was followed by the four-volume *Pictures of Travel* (1826–31). SCHUMANN and SCHUBERT set his lyrics to music.

Heisenberg, Werner Karl (1901–76) German physicist and philosopher. In 1926 Heisenberg developed a form of quantum theory based on matrix algebra. In 1927 Heisenberg published his famous uncertainty principle, which stated that the momentum and position of a subatomic particle cannot be measured at the same time because the act of measuring disturbs the system. He was awarded the 1932 Nobel Prize for physics.

Helvétius, Claude Adrien (1715–71) French philosopher and educator. His best-known work, *De L'Esprit* (1758), attacked the religious basis of morality, arousing great opposition. Helvétius claimed that everybody is intellectually equal but some have less desire to learn than others. This led him to claim, in *De l'homme* (1772), that all human problems could be solved by education.

Hemingway, Ernest Millar (1899–1961) US writer. He was a war correspondent in the Spanish Civil War and World War II. His works include *A Farewell to Arms* (1929), *For Whom the Bell Tolls* (1940) and the novella *The Old Man and the Sea* (1952). Hemingway was awarded the 1954 Nobel Prize for literature. Prone to severe depression, he committed suicide.

Henry I (the Fowler) (c.876–936) King of the Germans (918–36). Duke of Saxony, he was elected to succeed Conrad I as king. He asserted authority over the German princes and reconquered Lotharingia (925). In 933 he defeated Magyar raiders. He was succeeded by his son, OTTO I, first Holy Roman emperor.

Henry VI (1165–97) German king (1190–97) and Holy Roman emperor (1191–97), son of FREDERICK I (BARBAROSSA). In 1186 he married Constance, heiress of the kingdom of Sicily, and much of his reign was devoted to securing that inheritance. After 1194, the empire was at the height of its power. Although he failed to make the empire hereditary in the HOHENSTAUFEN line, his infant son, FREDERICK II, was accepted as his successor.

Henry II (1133–89) King of England (1154–89), son of Geoffrey of Anjou and Matilda (daughter of Henry I). He inherited the Angevin lands and obtained Aquitaine by marrying Eleanor in 1152. He re-established stable royal government in England. His efforts to extend royal justice to priests led to his quarrel with Thomas à Becket. His later reign was troubled by the rebellions of his sons, including two future kings, RICHARD I and JOHN.

Henry III (1207–72) King of England (1216–72). The influence of foreigners on his administration antagonized the nobles. He was forced to accept the Provisions of Westminster (1259), giving more power to his councillors, but renounced them in 1261, provoking the Barons'War. The leader of the barons, Simon de Montfort, was defeated at Lewes (1264) by Henry's son, the future Edward I, who thereafter ruled on his father's behalf.

Henry IV (1367–1413) King of England (1399–1413), son of John of Gaunt. Henry Bolingbroke was exiled in 1399 by RICHARD II. He returned and overthrew Richard, claiming the crown for himself. As a usurper Henry had to overcome revolts, notably by Owain GLYN Dŵr and Sir Henry Percy.

Henry V (1387–1422) King of England (1413–22), son of HENRY IV. Henry renewed English claims against France in the Hundred Years War and won a victory at Agincourt in 1415. Further conquests in 1417–19 resulted in the Treaty of Troyes (1420), when Charles VI of France recognized him as his heir.

Henry VII (1457–1509) King of England (1485–1509), founder of the TUDOR DYNASTY. Having come to the throne by defeating RICHARD III in the final battle of the Wars of the ROSES at Bosworth Field (1485), Henry united the houses of LANCASTER and YORK by marrying the Yorkist heiress, Elizabeth. His financial acumen restored England's fortunes after the devastation of civil war. He secured the succession of his son HENRY VIII.

Henry VIII (1491–1547) King of England (1509–47), second son of HENRY VII. He became heir on the death of his brother Arthur. His aggressive foreign policy depleted the royal treasury. Henry, supported by Thomas Cromwell, presided over the first stages of the English Reformation, brought about largely because the pope refused to grant Henry a divorce from Catherine of Aragón. With the legislation in place, Henry divorced Catherine and married Anne Boleyn (1533), mother of the future ELIZABETH I. In 1535 Anne was executed for adultery. Thomas MORE, Henry's former chancellor, was executed for refusing to accept Henry as head of the church. Henry then married Jane Seymour, who died after the birth of the future EDWARD VI. His next marriage, to Anne of Cleves, ended in divorce (1540). Shortly after, he married Catherine HOWARD (executed 1542) and finally Catherine Parr (1543), who survived him. Henry's reign will also be remembered for the Dissolution of the Monasteries (1536–40), which brought temporary relief from financial problems.

Henry III (1551–89) King of France (1574–89). As duke of Anjou, he fought against the Huguenots in the Wars of Religion. By making peace with the Huguenots (1576), he antagonized extremist Roman Catholics, who formed the Catholic League led by the House of Guise. After the League provoked a revolt in 1588, Henry had the Guise leaders killed and made an alliance with the Huguenot, Henry of Navarre (later HENRY IV). The king was assassinated by a member of the league.

Henry IV (1553–1610) King of France (1589–1610), first of the BOURBON dynasty. From a Protestant upbringing, he was recognized as leader of the Huguenots. Henry's marriage to Margaret of Valois was marred by the Saint Bartholemew's Day Massacre (1572). Henry survived, but was forced to convert to Roman Catholicism. In 1584 he became legal heir to HENRY III. He ended the French Wars of Religion by the Edict of Nantes (1598), but remained sympathetic to Protestantism, secretly supporting the revolt of the Protestant Netherlands against Spain. A popular king, with a keen sense of social justice, he was assassinated.

Henry the Navigator (1394–1460) Portuguese prince, son of JOHN I. Henry sponsored Portuguese voyages to the Atlantic coast of Africa, which later led to the discovery of the route to India via the Cape of Good Hope.

Henry, Joseph (1797–1878) US physicist, whose work on electromagnetism was essential for the development of the telegraph. His work on induction led to the production of the transformer.

Heraclius (575–641) Byzantine emperor (610–41). An outstanding military leader, Heraclius came to power at a time of crisis. He re-established government and army, defeated the Persians and took the BYZANTINE EMPIRE to unrivaled power. By his death, however, the Arabs had conquered much of the empire.

Herder, Johann Gottfried von (1744–1803) German philosopher. He believed human society to be an organic, secular totality that develops as the result of a historical process. *Outlines of a Philosophy on the History of Man* (1784–91) is his masterpiece.

Herodotus (*c.*485–*c.*425 BCE) Greek historian. His *Histories* are the first great prose works in European literature. His main theme was the struggle of Greece against the Persian empire, but he also provides an insight into contemporary Mediterranean life.

Herod the Great (73–04 BCE) King of Judaea (37–04 BCE). Supported by Mark ANTONY and AUGUSTUS, he endeavored to reconcile Jews and Romans. He was responsible for many public works, including the rebuilding of the Temple in Jerusalem. Herod later became cruel and tyrannical. According to the New Testament, he was king of Judaea when JESUS was born.

Hero of Alexandria (b. *c.*CE 20) Greek engineer who built an early steam turbine, called an aeolipile. He also devised mechanisms to control doors automatically.

Herschel, Sir William (1738–1821) English astronomer, b. Germany. He discovered Uranus (1781) and later two satellites of Uranus (1787) and two of Saturn (1789). Herschel observed many double stars and more than 2,000 nebulae and clusters. In 1800 he discovered and investigated infrared radiation.

Hertz, Heinrich Rudolf (1857–94) German physicist. In 1888 Hertz discovered, broadcast and received the radio waves predicted by James Clerk MAXWELL. He also demonstrated that heat and light are kinds of electromagnetic radiation.

Herzl, Theodor (1860–1904) Jewish leader and founder of Zionism, b. Budapest. In 1897 Herzl became president of the World Zionist Organization, which worked throughout Europe to establish a Jewish national home in Palestine.

Hesiod (active 8th century BCE) Greek poet. Little is known of his life; he seems to have lived slightly later than HOMER. Hesoid's two major works are *Theogony*, which presents a genealogy of the gods, and *Works and Days*, containing advice for farmers.

Hess, Rudolf (1894–1987) German Nazi leader. He joined the Nazi Party in 1921 and took part in the abortive Munich Putsch. Hess was the nominal deputy leader under HITLER from 1933. In 1941 he flew to Scotland in a mysterious one-man effort to make peace with the British. In 1945 Hess was sentenced to life imprisonment at the Nuremberg trials.

Hidalgo y Costilla, Miguel (1753–1811) Mexican priest and revolutionary. He was a priest in Dolores, Guanajuato, where he plotted a revolt against Spain. With an untrained army of 80,000, he captured Guanajuato and Valladolid. Defeated at Calderón Bridge, Hidalgo fled but was captured and executed.

Hindenburg, Paul Ludwig Hans von Beneckendorf und von (1847–1934) German statesman and general, president (1925–34). Commanding the army on the E front in World War I, he defeated the Russians in the battle of Tannenberg. In 1916 Hindenburg became supreme commander and directed the German retreat on the Western Front. As president of the Weimar Republic, he reluctantly appointed HITLER as chancellor in 1933.

Hipparchus (active 2nd century BCE) Greek astronomer. He estimated the distance of the Moon from the Earth and drew the first accurate star map. He developed an organization of the Universe that, although it had the Earth at its center, provided for accurate prediction of the positions of the planets.

Hippocrates (*c.*460–*c.*377 BCE) Greek physician, often called "the father of medicine". He emphasized clinical observation and provided guidelines for surgery. He is credited with the Hippocratic oath, a code of professional conduct followed by doctors.

Hirohito (1901–89) Emperor of Japan (1926–89). Although he exercised little political power, Hirohito persuaded the government to surrender to the Allies in 1945. Under the constitution of 1946, he lost all power and renounced the claim of the Japanese emperors to be divine. He was succeeded by his son AKIHITO.

Hiroshige, Ando (1797–1858) Japanese master of the ukiyo-e (colored woodcut). Hiroshige is best known for his landscapes, such as *Fifty-Three Stages of the Tokaido Highway* (1833).

Hitler, Adolf (1889–1945) German fascist dictator (1933–45), b. Austria. He served in the German army during World War I. In 1921 Hitler became leader of the small National Socialist Workers' Party (Nazi Party). While imprisoned for his role in the failed Munich Putsch, he set out his extreme racist and nationalist views in *Mein Kampf* (1925). Economic distress and dissatisfaction with the Weimar Republic led to electoral gains for the Nazis and, by forming an alliance with orthodox Nationalists, Hitler became chancellor in January 1933. He made himself dictator of a one-party state in which all opposition was ruthlessly suppressed by the SS and Gestapo. The racial hatred he incited led to a policy of extermination of Jews and others in the Holocaust. Hitler pursued an aggressive foreign policy aimed at territorial expansion. The invasion of Poland finally goaded Britain and France into declaring war on Germany in September 1939. Hitler himself played a large part in determining strategy during World War II. In April 1945, with Germany in ruins, he committed suicide.

Hittites People of Asia Minor who controlled a powerful empire in the 15th–13th centuries BCE. They founded a kingdom in Anatolia in the 18th century BCE; their capital was Hattusas. They expanded E and S in the 15th century BCE and conquered N Syria before being checked by the Egyptians. Under attack from the ASSYRIAN EMPIRE, the Hittite empire disintegrated *c*.1200 BCE.

Hobbes, Thomas (1588–1679) English philosopher. In *De Corpore* (1655), *De Homine* (1658) and *De Cive* (1642), he maintains that matter and its motion comprise the only valid subjects for philosophy. In *Leviathan* (1651) he argues that man is inherently selfish but obeys a social contract to maintain civilized society.

Ho Chi Minh (1890–1969) (Nguyen That Thanh) Vietnamese statesman, president of North Vietnam (1954–69). He founded the Vietnamese Communist Party in 1930. Forced into exile, he returned to Vietnam in 1941 to lead the Viet Minh against the Japanese. In 1945 Ho Chi Minh declared Vietnamese independence and led resistance to French forces. After the French defeat at Dien Bien Phu (1954), Vietnam was partitioned and Ho Chi Minh became president of North Vietnam. He organized and supported the Viet Cong against South Vietnam and committed North Vietnamese forces against the USA in the Vietnam War.

Hockney, David (1937–) English painter. He made his name with pop art paintings such as *Flight into Italy–Swiss Landscape* (1962). In the 1960s and 1970s, Hockney developed a more realistic, classical style, with pictures such as *A Bigger Splash* (1967).

Hogarth, William (1697–1764) English painter and engraver. He established his reputation with *A Harlot's Progress* (1731–32), the first in a series of "modern moral subjects". Hogarth painted narrative pictures that satirically exposed the vices of his age. He is best known for *Marriage à la Mode* (1743–45).

Hohenstaufen dynasty German dynasty that exercised great power in Germany and the HOLY ROMAN EMPIRE from 1138 to 1254. It is named for the castle of Staufen, built by Frederick, Count of Swabia, whose son became CONRAD III of Germany and Holy Roman emperor in 1138. From Conrad III to CONRAD IV, the family occupied the Imperial throne, except between 1209 and 1215 (when OTTO IV, a GUELPHS, was emperor). The greatest of the dynasty was FREDERICK II.

Hohokam culture Farming culture of the S Arizona desert, North America, arising in the last centuries BCE and surviving until *c*.CE 1400. Sophisticated irrigation systems were the basis of Hohokam prosperity, and sizable settlements were founded.

Holbein, Hans, the Younger (1497–1543) German painter. Holbein's portraits of ERASMUS earned him the patronage (1526–28) of Sir Thomas MORE. In 1532 he settled in London and became (1536) court painter to HENRY VIII. Holbein's masterpieces include *The Ambassadors* (1533) and portraits of *Christina of Denmark, Duchess of Milan* (1538) and *Anne of Cleves* (1540).

Holmes, Oliver Wendell (1809–94) US author and physician. His best literary work takes the form of humorous table talk, such as *The Professor at the Breakfast Table* (1860) and *The Poet at the Breakfast Table* (1872).

Holy Roman Empire European empire centered on Germany (10th–19th centuries), which echoed the empire of ancient Rome. It was founded (962) when the German king OTTO I (THE GREAT) was crowned in Rome, although some historians date it from the coronation of CHARLEMAGNE in 800. The emperor, who was elected by the German princes, claimed to be the temporal sovereign of Christendom, ruling in cooperation with the spiritual sovereign, the pope. However, the empire never encompassed all of western Christendom and relations with the papacy were often difficult. From 1438 the title was virtually hereditary in the HAPSBURG DYNASTY. After 1648 the empire became little more than a loose confederation, containing hundreds of virtually independent states. It was abolished by NAPOLEON I in 1806.

Homer (active 8th century BCE) Greek poet. Homer is traditionally considered to be the author of the epics of Greek literature, the *Iliad* and the *Odyssey*. The *Iliad* relates the siege of Troy in the Trojan War. The *Odyssey* tells of the wanderings of Odysseus.

Hoover, Herbert Clark (1874–1964) 31st US President (1929–33). He was secretary of commerce under presidents HARDING and COOLIDGE. After winning the Republican nomination for president in 1928, Hoover defeated Alfred E. Smith. During his first year in office, the economy was shattered by the Wall Street Crash and the ensuing Great Depression. With his belief in individual enterprise and distrust of government interference, Hoover failed to provide sufficient government resources to deal with the Depression. In 1932 he was resoundingly defeated by Franklin ROOSEVELT's promise of a New Deal.

Hopewell culture Culture centered in Ohio and Illinois, North America, that reached its peak in the last centuries BCE and the first four centuries CE. Hopewell people were efficient farmers, built complex earthworks, such as the Great Serpent Mound of Ohio, for ceremonial and business purposes, and traded widely.

Horace (65–08 BCE) Roman poet, b. Quintus Horatius Flaccus. His first *Satires* appeared in *c*.35 BCE and were followed by *Epodes* (*c*.30 BCE), *Odes* (*c*.23 BCE) and *Ars Poetica* (*c*.19 BCE). His simple Latin lyrics provided a vivid picture of the Augustan age.

Houston, Sam (Samuel) (1793–1863) US military and political leader. He became commander in chief of the army when Texas rebelled against Mexican rule (1835). He was the first president of the Republic of Texas (1836–38, 1841–44). When Texas was annexed by the USA, he served in the Senate and as governor. Isolated by his support for the Union and for Native Americans, he was forced out of office when Texas voted to secede (1861).

Hoxha, Enver (1908–85) Albanian statesman, prime minister (1946–54), first secretary of the Communist Party (1954–85). In 1941 he founded the Albanian Communist Party and led the resistance to Italian occupation during World War II. In 1946 the Republic of Albania was established and Hoxha became prime minister. His dictatorial control of party, army and state led to accusations of Stalinism. In 1961 Hoxha withdrew from the Warsaw Pact. After breaking with Beijing, Albania became isolated and economically impoverished.

Hubble, Edwin Powell (1889–1953) US astronomer. In 1925 he published his classification of galaxies. Hubble measured the distance to the Andromeda Galaxy. He attributed the red shift of the spectral lines of galaxies to the recession of galaxies and hence to the expanding universe. In 1929 he proposed a linear relation between the distance of a galaxy from Earth and their velocity of recession (Hubble's law).

Hudson, Henry (d.1611) English maritime explorer. Employed by the Dutch East India Company (1609), Hudson crossed the Atlantic to search for a Northwest Passage, becoming the first European to sail up the Hudson River. In 1610 he embarked on another voyage to discover the Northwest Passage and reached Hudson Bay. Forced by ice to winter in the bay, his crew set him adrift to die in an open boat.

Huerta, Victoriano (1854–1916) Mexican statesman and general, president (1913–14). Instructed by President Francisco MADERO to suppress the revolt led by Félix Díaz, Huerta instead joined forces with the rebels. Madero was arrested and killed, and Huerta became president. Defeated by the Constitutionalists led by Venustiano CARRANZA, Huerta fled to the USA.

Hughes, Ted (Edward James) (1930–98) English poet. He succeeded John Betjeman as poet laureate in 1984. Hughes focused on the raw, primal forces of nature. Collections include *Crow* (1970), *Moortown* (1979) and *Wolfwatching* (1989). His creative translation of *Tales from Ovid* (1997) won the Whitbread Prize. Hughes was married (1956–62) to Sylvia PLATH. His last volume, *Birthday Letters* (1998), was a reflection on their relationship and posthumously won him a Whitbread Prize.

Hugo, Victor Marie (1802–85) French poet, dramatist and novelist. He received a pension from Louis XVIII for his collection of *Odes* (1822). He presented his manifesto of romanticism in the preface to his play *Cromwell* (1827). Later works include the plays *Hernani* (1830) and *Ruy Blas* (1838) and the novels *The Hunchback of Notre Dame* (1831) and *Les Misérables* (1862).

Hulegu Khan (1217–65) Mongol leader, grandson of GENGHIS KHAN. He quelled an uprising in Persia and annihilated the ASSASSIN sect. He sacked Baghdad (1258) and seized Aleppo in Syria (1260). The Mongol advance under his command was checked by the MAMELUKES, an Egyptian military caste.

Hume, David (1711–76) Scottish philosopher, historian and man of letters. Hume's publications include *A Treatise of Human Nature* (1739–40), *History of England* (1754–63) and various philosophical "inquiries". He was widely known for his humanitarianism and philosophical skepticism.

Hume, John (1937–) Northern Irish politician, leader (1983–) of the nationalist Social Democratic Labor Party (SDLP). Hume entered Parliament in 1983. His commitment to peace in Northern Ireland helped secure an IRA cease-fire. Hume shared the 1998 Nobel Peace Prize with David TRIMBLE.

Huns Nomadic people of Mongol or Turkic origin who expanded from central Asia into E Europe. Under ATTILA, they overran large parts of the ROMAN EMPIRE in 434–53, exacting tribute, but after his death they disintegrated.

Huron Confederation of Iroquoian-speaking tribes of Native Americans who once occupied the St. Lawrence Valley E of Lake Huron. In wars for control of the fur trade with the IROQUOIS CONFEDERACY (1648–50), the Huron population was reduced from 15,000 to c.500. After a period of wandering, they settled in Ohio, the Great Lakes area and Kansas.

Hurrians Ancient people of Mesopotamia. They established a kingdom to the N of the SUMERIANS by 2000 BCE. By 1500 BCE this had become organized into the kingdom of Mitanni, which established an empire in Syria. The power of the Hurrians was destroyed by the ASSYRIANS in c.1200 BCE, but they had considerable influence over HITTITE culture. They used a cuneiform script.

Hus, Jan (1369–1415) Bohemian religious reformer. Influenced by the writings of John WYCLIFFE, Hus was excommunicated in 1411. In *De Ecclesia* (1412), he outlined his case for reform of the Church. He was tried by the Council of Constance (1415) and burned at the stake as a heretic. His followers, known as Hussites, launched a civil war against the Holy Roman Empire.

Hussein I (1935–99) Hashemite king of Jordan (1953–99). He sought to maintain good relations with the West while supporting the Palestinians' cause in the Arab-Israeli Wars. In 1967 Hussein led Jordan into the Six Day War, losing the West Bank and East Jerusalem to Israel. In 1970 he ordered his army to suppress the activities of the Palestine Liberation Organization (PLO) in Jordan. In 1974 Hussein relinquished Jordan's claim to the West Bank to the PLO. In the 1990s he supported efforts to secure peace in the Middle East, signing a treaty with Israel in 1994. He was succeeded by his son Abdullah (1962–).

Hussein Ibn Ali (1856–1931) Arabian leader. After 1908 he reigned over Mecca and the Hejaz, then controlled by Turkey. He revolted successfully against the Turks (1916) and made himself king of Arabia, but Ibn SAUD, ruler of Nejd, defeated him and forced him to abdicate in 1924.

Huxley, Aldous Leonard (1894–1963) English novelist, grandson of Thomas HUXLEY. Huxley began his career as a journalist and published several volumes of poetry before his default novel, *Crome Yellow* (1921). *Point Counter Point* (1928) satirized the hedonism of the 1920s. His best-known work, *Brave New World* (1932), presents a nightmarish vision of a future society. *Island* (1962) evokes a Utopian community. *Eyeless in Gaza* (1936) and *The Doors of Perception* (1954) explore his interest in mysticism and states of consciousness.

Huxley, Thomas Henry (1825–95) English biologist. Huxley was an early champion of Charles DARWIN's theory of evolution. His works include *Zoological Evidences as to Man's Place in Nature* (1863), *Manual of Comparative Anatomy of Vertebrated Animals* (1871) and *Evolution and Ethics* (1893).

Huygens, Christiaan (1629–95) Dutch astronomer. He developed improved telescope eyepieces, and in 1655 discovered Saturn's rings and its largest satellite, Titan. In 1656 Huygens built the first pendulum clock. In 1678 he presented his wave theory of light to explain reflection and refraction.

Hyder Ali (1722–82) Sultan of Mysore (1761–82). An able general, he commanded the Mysore army from 1749. His expansionist policies led to confrontation with the British, whom he defeated in 1767 and 1780. In 1781 he was defeated by British forces under Eyre Coote in a series of battles.

Hyksos Name used for a people who took power in Egypt in the 17th century BCE. They probably originated in Palestine. The Hyksos are attributed with the first use of horse-drawn chariots, and introduced these to Egypt along with the recurve bow. They ruled northern and central Egypt from c.1674 to 1567 BCE as the 15th and 16th dynasties, while the south of the country remained in the hands of native rulers governing from Thebes. The Theban rulers of the 17th dynasty reconquered the entire country, ending Hyksos rule and inaugurating the era of Egyptian unity and expansion known as the New Kingdom.

Hypatia (370–415) Egyptian Neoplatonist teacher, philosopher and mathematician. She was the first woman known to have made a major contribution to science and mathematics. Although her works are lost, it is thought that she wrote critiques on the *Arithmetica* of DIOPHANTUS and on PTOLEMY's astronomical canon. Hypatia, a pagan, was accused of interfering in politics to limit the power of the church, and was murdered by a Christian mob.

I

Ibn Batuta (1304–68) Arab traveler and writer. Born in Tangier, Morocco, he began his adventures in c.1325 with a pilgrimage to Mecca by way of Egypt and Syria. Travel occupied the next 30 years of his life, with visits to Africa, Asia and Europe. In 1349 he returned to Morocco to write an account of his travels.

Ibn Khaldun (1332–1406) Philosopher and scholar, the greatest Arab historian of the Middle Ages. Born in Tunis, N Africa, he abandoned politics in order to write the *Muqaddimah* ("Introduction to History"). In this work he put forward a cyclical view of history, in which civilizations alternate between growth and decay. He also wrote a history of Muslim North Africa.

Ibrahim Pasha (1789–1848) Egyptian general and governor son of MUHAMMAD ALI. He campaigned (1816–18) against the Wahhabis of Arabia and fought the Greek insurgents until the Ottoman defeat at Navarino (1827). When his father defied Ottoman supremacy, Ibrahim conquered Syria (1832–33) and became its governor until forced to withdraw in 1841.

Ibsen, Henrik Johan (1828–1906) Norwegian playwright and poet. He came to international attention for the drama *Peer Gynt* (1867). The naturalism of his presentation of social issues in tragedies such as *A Doll's House* (1879), *Ghosts* (1881) and *Hedda Gabler* (1890) established his reputation.

Idris I (1890–1983) King of Libya (1951-69). Head of the Cyrenaican government and leader of the Islamic Sanusi sect, he sided with the British in World War II, and was ruler of Libya when it became independent in 1950. In 1969 Idris was deposed by a military junta dominated by Muammar al-QADDAFI.

Ignatius of Loyola, Saint (1491–1556) Spanish soldier, churchman and founder of the Jesuits. In 1534 he made vows of poverty, chastity and obedience. Ignatius was ordained in 1537 and moved to Rome where, in 1540, Pope Paul III approved his request to found the Society of Jesus. He spent the rest of his life supervising the growth of the order, which was to become the leading force in the Counter-Reformation. His feast day is 31 July.

Imhotep (active 27th century BCE) Egyptian architect. He is often credited with designing the step pyramid at Saqqara for Pharaoh Zoser in the Third Dynasty of the Old Kingdom. He was later deified as the patron of scribes and the son of Ptah, the builder god of Memphis.

Inca South American people who migrated (*c.*CE 1250) from the Peruvian highlands into the Cuzco area. The Incas conquered and assimilated the CHIMÚ. They consolidated their empire slowly until the reigns of Pachacuti (r.1438–71) and his son Topa (r.1471–93), when Inca dominance extended over most of the continent w of the Andes. Although highly organized, the Inca empire collapsed when the Spanish invasion (1532) led by PIZARRO coincided with a civil war between ATAHUALPA and Huáscar.

Ingres, Jean Auguste Dominique (1780–1867) French painter, one of the great figures of French neoclassicism. Ingres was an outstanding portraitist, especially of women in high society, such as *Madame d'Haussonville* (1845). He also produced sensual nudes, such as *Bather of Valpinçon* (1808).

Innocent III (1161–1216) Pope (1198–1216), b. Lotario di Segni. He extended the temporal and spiritual power of the papacy. Innocent successfully intervened in the dispute over the imperial crown, backing the claim of FREDERICK II over OTTO IV. He regained control of the Papal States. Innocent excommunicated King JOHN of England for refusing to recognize Stephen Langton as Archbishop of Canterbury. He condemned PHILIP II of France and proclaimed the fourth Crusade (1204). The fourth Lateran Council (1215) defined the doctrine of the Eucharist, establishing the concept of transubstantiation.

Iroquois Confederacy League of Native Americans occupying the Mohawk Valley and the Lakes area of New York state. They called themselves Oñgwanósioñi (Hodinonhsioni), "people of the long house", after the shape of their bark dwellings. The original tribes were the Mohawk, SENECA, Onondaga, Cayuga and Oneida. The Tuscarora joined later. The Iroquois had a highly developed political system and were renowned warriors. Their total number has halved since 1600; in the mid1990s they numbered *c.*10,000, living in New York, Wisconsin, Oklahoma and Canada.

Isabella I (1451–1504) Queen of Castile (1474–1504), whose marriage to Ferdinand II of Aragón (FERDINAND V of Castile and León) led to the unification of Spain. Daughter of John II, she won a dispute over the succession and married Ferdinand (1469). Isabella was responsible for the Spanish Inquisition (1487) and the expulsion of the Jews (1492). Her popularity was enhanced by the conquest of Granada (1492). Isabella supported the voyages of COLUMBUS.

Isabella II (1830–1904) Queen of Spain (1833–68), daughter of FERDINAND VII. She was challenged by her uncle, Don CARLOS, resulting in the first Carlist civil war. In 1868 a liberal revolt led by army officers forced her into exile, and in 1870 she abdicated in favor of her son, ALFONSO XII.

Isidore of Seville, Saint (*c.*560–636) Spanish ecclesiastic, last of the western Fathers of the Church. In c.600 he became Archbishop of Seville. Isidore is famous for his encyclopedia of knowledge, *Etymologies*. His feast day is 4 April.

Ismail (1486–1524) Shah of Persia (1501–24), founder of the SAFAVID DYNASTY. He re-established Persian independence and established Shiite Islam as the state religion. He warred successfully against the Uzbeks in 1510 but was defeated by the Ottoman sultan, SELIM I, at the battle of Chaldiran (1514).

Ismail Pasha (1830–95) **Vice**roy of Egypt (1863–79), grand-

son of MUHAMMAD ALI. In 1867 he received the title of khedive from the Ottoman sultan. Ismail built extensively in Alexandria and Cairo but later financial difficulties forced him to sell Egypt's share in the Suez Canal Company to Britain. He was forced to resign in favor of his son, Tewfik Pasha.

Itúrbide, Agustín de (1783–1824) Mexican general and politician. He helped Mexico achieve independence (1821) and was emperor (1822–23). Dissent crystallized when SANTA ANNA and Guadalupe Victoria called for the creation of a republic. Itúrbide abdicated and was exiled. Early in 1824 he returned to Mexico and was promptly arrested and shot.

Ivan III (the Great) (1440–1505) Grand Duke of Moscow (1462–1505). He laid the foundations of the empire of Russia. By 1480 Moscow's northern rivals were absorbed by conquest or persuasion, domestic rebellion was crushed, and the Tatar threat was ended permanently. Ivan's later years were troubled by conspiracies over succession. He began to use the title *czar* ("caesar").

Ivan IV (the Terrible) (1530–84) Grand Duke of Moscow (1533–84) and first czar of Russia (1547–84). In 1547 he married Anastasia, a ROMANOV. At first, Ivan was an able and progressive ruler. He established trade with w European states and began Russian expansion into Siberia. Defeat by the Poles in the Livonian War (1558–82) left Russia financial crippled. After his wife's death in 1560, Ivan became increasingly unbalanced, killing his own son in a rage. He established a personal dominion, the *oprichnina*, inside Russia and created a military force, the *oprichniki*, which pursued a reign of terror against the boyars.

J

Jackson, Andrew (1767–1845) Seventh US president (1829–37). He became a hero in the War of 1812 when he defeated the British at New Orleans. His popular appeal narrowly failed to defeat John Quincy ADAMS in the 1824 presidential election. His supporters built the basis of the Democratic Party, and in 1928 Jackson was elected. He faced staunch opposition from the establishment and set up a spoils system of political appointments. Jackson faced conflict over states' rights and the expansion of the frontier. He was succeeded by Martin VAN BUREN.

Jackson, "Stonewall" (Thomas Jonathan) (1824–63) Confederate general in the American Civil War. His stand against overwhelming odds at the first battle of Bull Run (1861) gained him the nickname "Stonewall". He fought in the Shenandoah Valley (1862) and played an important part in the Confederate victories after the second battle of Bull Run. Jackson was accidentally shot and killed by his own men at the battle of Chancellorsville.

James I (1566–1625) King of England (1603–25) and, as James VI, king of Scotland (1567–1625). Son of MARY, QUEEN OF SCOTS, and Lord Darnley, he acceded to the Scottish throne as an infant on his mother's abdication. In 1603 James inherited the English throne on the death of ELIZABETH I. He supported the Anglican Church and sponsored the publication (1611) of the Authorized, or King James, Version of the Bible. The Gunpowder Plot (1605) was foiled and James cracked down heavily on Catholics. In 1607 the first English colony in America (Jamestown) was founded. James' insistence on the divine right of kings brought conflict with Parliament. In 1611 he dissolved Parliament, and (excluding the 1614 Addled Parliament) ruled without one until 1621. He was succeeded by his son, CHARLES I.

James II (1633–1701) King of England (1685–88), second son of CHARLES I. After the second English Civil War (1648) James escaped to Holland. At the Restoration (1660) of his brother CHARLES II, James was appointed lord high admiral. In 1669 he converted to Roman Catholicism and was forced to resign his offices. On his accession, James was confronted by the Duke of Monmouth's Rebellion (1685). His pro-Catholic policies and the birth of a son (James Edward STUART) to his second wife provoked the Glorious Revolution (1688–89). His daughter Mary, from his first marriage, and her husband, WILLIAM OF ORANGE, assumed the crown and James fled to France. He invaded Ireland but was defeated at the battle of the Boyne (1690).

James, Henry (1843–1916) US novelist, short-story writer and critic, brother of William JAMES. James' early masterpiece, *The Portrait of a Lady* (1881), features a recurrent theme – the conflict between the values of American and European society. Later novels, such as *The Wings of the Dove* (1902) and *The Golden Bowl* (1904), show his mastery of the psychological novel.

James, Jesse Woodson (1847–82) US outlaw. He fought for the Confederacy during the US Civil War. In 1867 they formed an outlaw band and terrorized the frontier, robbing banks and trains in Missouri and neighboring states. He was shot dead by Robert Ford, a member of his own gang, for a reward.

James, William (1842–1910) US philosopher and psychologist, elder brother of Henry JAMES. He held that the feeling of emotion is based on the sensation of a state of the body; the bodily state comes first and the emotion follows. His most famous works are *The Principles of Psychology* (1890) and *Varieties of Religious Experience* (1902).

Jameson, Sir Leander Starr (1853–1917) South African statesman, b. Scotland. In 1878 he emigrated to South Africa. In 1895, supported by Cecil RHODES, he led an abortive raid on the Afrikaner republic of Transvaal and was imprisoned. After his release, he served as prime minister (1904–08) of Cape Colony.

Jansky, Karl (1905–50) US engineer. In 1931 he discovered unidentifiable radio signals from space. Jansky concluded they were stellar in origin and that the source lay in the direction of Sagittarius. His discovery was the beginning of radio astronomy.

Jefferson, Thomas (1743–1826) Third US president (1801–09), vice-president (1797–81). Jefferson was a leading member of the Continental Congress and the primary author of the Declaration of Independence (1776). His governorship of Virginia (1779–81) was ended by the American Revolution. Jefferson was persuaded by George WASHINGTON to serve as his first secretary of state (1789–93). Disagreements with Alexander HAMILTON saw the formation of the precursor of the Democratic Party. The landmarks of his first administration (1801–05) were the Louisiana Purchase (1803) and the Lewis and Clark Expedition (1804–06). During his second term (1805–09), he managed to avoid war with Britain, passing an Embargo Act (1807). He was a slave owner, although in principle opposed to slavery.

Jeffreys, Alec John (1950–) British geneticist. He discovered particular elements of DNA that enabled genetic fingerprinting to be used as an accurate method of identification.

Jenner, Edward (1749–1823) English physician who pioneered vaccination. In 1796, aware that cowpox (a minor disease) seemed to protect people from smallpox, Jenner inoculated a healthy boy with cowpox from the sores of an infected dairymaid. The boy was later found to be immune to smallpox.

Jerome, Saint (*c.*CE 342–420) Doctor of the Church, b. Dalmatia as Eusebius Hieronymus. He studied in Rome before traveling to Antioch. Jerome lived as a hermit in the desert before returning to Rome. He acted as papal secretary (382–85) to Pope Damasus I. In 386 Jerome settled in Jerusalem, where he founded a monastery and compiled the Latin Vulgate version of the Bible. His feast day is 30 September.

Jesus Christ (active 1st century CE) Hebrew preacher who founded the religion of Christianity, hailed and worshiped by his followers as the Son of God. Knowledge of Jesus' life is based on the biblical gospels of St. Matthew, St. Mark and St. Luke. The date of Jesus' birth in Bethlehem, Judaea, is conventionally given as *c.*4 BCE. Mary, believed by Christians to have been made pregnant by God, gave birth to Jesus. The birth was said to have taken place in a stable and been attended by the appearance of a bright star and other unusual events. In *c.*CE 27 Jesus was baptized by John the Baptist. Thereafter Jesus began his own ministry, preaching to large numbers as he wandered the country. He also taught a special group of 12 of his closest disciples, who were later sent out as his Apostles to bring his teachings to the Jews.

Jesus' basic teaching was to "love God and love one's neighbor" He also taught that salvation depended on doing God's wi rather than adhering to the letter of the Torah. Such a precep angered the hierarchy of the Jewish religion. In *c.*CE 30 Jesus an his disciples went to Jerusalem. His reputation as preacher an miracle-worker preceded him, and he was acclaimed as the Mess ah. A few days later Jesus gathered his disciples to partake in th Last Supper. At this meal, he instituted the Eucharist. Jesus wa arrested by agents of the Hebrew authorities, accompanied b Judas Iscariot, and summarily tried by the Sanhedrin, th Supreme Council of the Jews. He was handed to the Roma procurator PONTIUS PILATE on a charge of sedition. Roman so diers crucified Jesus. After his death, Jesus' body was buried in sealed rock tomb. Two days later, according to the gospels, he ros from the dead and appeared to his disciples and to others. Fort days after his resurrection, he is said to have ascended into heaver

Jinnah, Muhammad Ali (1876–1948) Indian statesmar founder of Pakistan. He joined the Indian National Congress i 1906 but left it in 1920 when his demand for a separate Muslir electorate was rejected. Jinnah led the Muslim League in cam paigning for political equality for Indian Muslims, while contin uing to seek agreement with Hindus. By 1940 he had adopted th aim of a separate Muslim state. This was realized when India wa partitioned in 1947.

Joan of Arc, Saint (*c.*1412–31) (Jeanne d'Arc) French sair and national heroine. She claimed to hear heavenly voices urgin her to save France during the Hundred Years War. In 1429 Joan o Arc led French troops in breaking the English siege of Orléans She drove the English from the Loire towns and persuaded th indecisive dauphin to have himself crowned as CHARLES VII o France at Reims. In 1430 Joan of Arc was captured and hande over to the English. Condemned as a heretic, she was burned a the stake. Her feast day is 30 May.

Joffre, Joseph Jacques Césaire (1852–1931) French mar shal. He was commander-in-chief (1914–16) of the Frenc armies during World War I. Determined to take the offensive, Jol fre was forced to retreat but recouped his forces, and his reputa tion, in the first battle of the Marne (September 1914). Afte heavy losses at Verdun and the Somme (both 1916), he resigned.

John (1167–1216) King of England (1199–1216), youngest so of HENRY II and Eleanor of Aquitaine. He ruled during RICHAR I's absence on the Third Crusade. Disgraced for intriguing agains Richard, John nevertheless succeeded him as king. He waged wa (1204–05) against PHILIP II of France, losing territories i France. In 1209 he was excommunicated by INNOCENT III for refus ing to accept Stephen Langton as Archbishop of Canterbury. I 1214 his ally Emperor OTTO IV was defeated by Philip II. Joh attempted to collect further tax from the nobles to finance war. I 1215 he was compelled by his barons to sign the Magna Carta. H disregard of the terms led to the first Barons'War (1215–17).

John I (1357–1433) King of Portugal (1385–1433). After th death of his half-brother, Ferdinand I, he resisted the propose regency of Ferdinand's daughter, Beatrice of Castile, and wa elected king. In 1415 John captured Ceuta, Morocco, the firs European possession in Africa.

John VI (1767–1826) King of Portugal (1816–26). Because o the insanity of his mother, Queen Maria, he was effectively sover eign from 1792, officially regent from 1799. In 1807 he fled t Brazil to escape the invading army of NAPOLEON I and did no return to claim the throne until 1822, when he accepted the con stitutional government proclaimed in 1820.

Johnson, Andrew (1808–75) 17th US president (1865–69 vice-president (1864–65). A Democrat governor (1853–57) an senator (1857–62) for Tennessee, he was the only Southerner t remain in the Senate after the outbreak of the Civil War. Johnson was elected with the incumbent Republican president Abraham LINCOLN on a National Union ticket and became president wher Lincoln was assassinated. His policy of Reconstruction saw the restoration of civil government to the South. The hostility of th

predominantly Republican congress to his support for the southern states led to his impeachment trial in the Senate for "crimes
and misdemeanors". Johnson was acquitted by one vote.

Johnson, Lyndon Baines (1908–73) 36th US president
(1963–69), vice-president (1960–63). He represented Texas as a
Democrat in the Senate (1948–60). Johnson served as vice-president to John F. KENNEDY and became president after Kennedy's
assassination (1963). He showed considerable skill in securing
passage of the Civil Rights Act (1964) and was overwhelmingly
reelected in 1964. Johnson carried out an ambitious domestic
reform program, but its success was overshadowed by the escala-
tion of the Vietnam War, which, together with severe race riots
between 1965 and 1968, dissuaded him from seeking re-election.

Johnson, Samuel (1709–84) English lexicographer, poet and
critic. His reputation was established by the masterly *Dictionary
of the English Language* (1755). Other works include the essay
collection *The Idler* (1758–61) and the critical *Lives of the Poets*
(1779–81). A trenchant conversationalist, Johnson cofounded
(1764) "The Club", later known as "The Literary Club". In 1773
he toured Scotland with his biographer James BOSWELL.

Jolliet, Louis (1646–1700) French explorer, b. Quebec, Canada. In 1673 Jolliet and Jacques Marquette became the first Europeans to travel the Mississippi River, from its confluence with the
Wisconsin River to the mouth of the Arkansas River.

Jones, Inigo (1573–1652) English architect and painter. He
introduced England to a pure classical style based on the work of
PALLADIO. His noted buildings include the Queen's House, Greenwich (1616–35), and Banqueting House, Whitehall (1619–21).

Jones, John Paul (1747–92) American naval officer in the
American Revolution, b. Scotland as John Paul. In 1775 he
joined the Continental navy. With his flagship *Bonhomme
Richard* he engaged the British ship *Serapis* in an epic battle off
the coast of England (1779). He boarded and captured the *Serapis* while his ship burned and then sank.

Jonson, Ben (1572–1637) English dramatist, poet and actor.
In 1598 he killed an actor in a duel. Jonson's major works are the
four comedies *Volpone* (1606), *Epicoene* (1609), *The Alchemist*
(1610) and *Bartholomew Fair* (1614). He collaborated on several
masques for the court of James I and became the first poet laureate. His verse includes *Epigrams* (1616) and *The Forest* (1616).

Joseph II (1741–90) Holy Roman emperor (1765–90), king of
Hungary and Bohemia (1780–90), son of MARIA THERESA and
Emperor Francis I. Until 1780 he ruled the HAPSBURG lands
jointly with his mother. As sole ruler, Joseph introduced sweeping
liberal and humanitarian reforms, including the abolition (1781)
of serfdom. His radical program required autocratic means and
the support of ministers such as KAUNITZ. The scale of change led
to revolts in Hungary and the Austrian Netherlands.

Jospin, Lionel (1937–) French statesman, prime minister
(1997–2002). In 1995 he succeeded François MITTERRAND as
leader of the French Socialist Party (PS) but lost the ensuing
presidential election to Jacques CHIRAC. In the 1997 prime ministerial elections, Jospin won a surprise victory against Alain Juppé.

Josquin Desprez (1445–1521) Flemish composer. He wrote
three books of masses, more than 100 motets and many secular
songs. The expressiveness and inventiveness of his music mark him
as the most prominent composer of Renaissance Europe.

Joule, James Prescott (1818–89) English physicist. He
showed that heat is a form of energy (the first law of thermodynamics) and established the mechanical equivalent of heat. In
1841 he measured the heat loss of an electric current due to the
resistance of the wire. The SI unit of energy is named for him.

Joyce, James (1882–1941) Irish novelist. Joyce's experiments
with narrative form and stream of consciousness place him at the
center of literary modernism. His first work was the short-story
collection *Dubliners* (1914). *A Portrait of the Artist as a Young
Man* (1916) was a fictionalized autobiography of Stephen
Daedalus. His masterpiece, the novel *Ulysses* (1922), presents a
day (16 June 1904) in the life of Leopold Bloom.

Juan Carlos (1938–) King of Spain (1975–), grandson of
ALFONSO XIII. He succeeded FRANCO and set about the democratization of Spanish society.

Juárez, Benito Pablo (1806–72) Mexican statesman, president (1858–62, 1867–72). Elected governor of Oaxaca in 1847,
he was exiled (1853–55) by SANTA ANNA. As president, Juárez
won a victory over conservatives in the "War of Reform". He
headed resistance to the French invasion (1862) until the fall of
MAXIMILIAN (1867).

Jugurtha (156–104 BCE) King of Numidia (108–106 BCE). He
divided Numidia with a brother. In 112 BCE he attacked and
seized Cirta, his brother's capital; a number of Romans were
killed. In retaliation Rome invaded Numidia (111 BCE), beginning the Jugurthine War. Jugurtha made peace and was ordered
to Rome. While in Rome, he had a potential rival murdered. War
broke out again. Jugurtha defeated a Roman force in 110 BCE
with the aid of Bocchus of Mauretania. In 106 BCE Bocchus
turned Jugurtha over to the Romans. He died in a Roman prison.

Julian (the Apostate) (331–63) Roman Emperor (361–63).
He achieved power on the death of Constantine II. He tried to
restore paganism, without persecuting Christians.

Juliana (1909–2004) Queen of The Netherlands (1948–80).
She succeeded to the throne upon the abdication of her mother,
Wilhelmina. Married in 1937 to the German prince Bernhard,
she retained the loyalty of the Dutch during World War II. She
abdicated in 1980 in favor of her eldest daughter, Beatrix.

Jung, Carl Gustav (1875–1961) Swiss psychiatrist. He worked
closely (1907–13) with Sigmund FREUD but disagreed that sexuality was the prime cause of neurosis. Jung founded analytical psychology. He argued that the unconscious had two dimensions – the
personal and archetypes of a collective unconscious. Jung believed
introversion and extroversion to be basic personality types.

Justinian I (482–565) Byzantine Emperor (527–565), sometimes called "the Great". His troops, commanded by Belisarius,
regained much of the old Roman Empire, including Italy, North
Africa and part of Spain. A longer-lasting achievement was the
Justinian Code, a revision of the whole body of Roman law.

Jutes Germanic people who invaded Britain in the 5th century
along with ANGLES, SAXONS and others. They settled mainly in
Kent and the Isle of Wight.

Juvenal, Decimus Junius (CE 55–140) Roman poet. His 16
Satires (*c*.98–128) denounced the immorality of Roman society
under Emperor DOMITIAN. Juvenal contrasted the decadence in
imperial Rome with the virtues of the republic.

K

Kádár, János (1912–89) Hungarian statesman, premier
(1956–58, 1961–65) and first secretary of the Hungarian
Socialist Workers' Party (1956–88). He fought in the resistance
during World War II. In 1956 Kádár replaced Imre NAGY as premier after crushing the Hungarian uprising. In 1968 he gave military support to the Soviet invasion of Czechoslovakia.

Kafka, Franz (1883–1924) German novelist, b. Czechoslovakia.
He suffered from intense self-doubt, publishing only essays and
short stories, such as *Metamorphosis* (1916), during his lifetime.
Kafka requested that his friend Max Brod destroy his works after
his death. Brod overrode his wishes and published the trilogy of
unfinished novels for which Kafka is best known today: *The Trial*
(1925), *The Castle* (1926) and *Amerika* (1927).

Kalidasa (active 5th century CE) Indian dramatist and poet.
Kalidasa is regarded as the major figure in classical Sanskrit literature. He is chiefly remembered for his play *Sakuntala*, the love
story of King Dushyanta and the nymph Sakuntala.

Kandinsky, Wassily (1866–1944) Russian painter and theorist, a founder of abstract art. His early paintings, including the
many numbered *Compositions*, express great lyricism. From 1911
Kandinsky was an active member of der Blaue Reiter. *White Line*
(1920) and *In the Black Circle* (1921) demonstrate the begin-

nings of a refinement of geometrical form that developed during his years (1922–33) at the Bauhaus.

Kant, Immanuel (1724–1804) German metaphysical philosopher. His philosophy of idealism, outlined in *Critique of Pure Reason* (1781), sought to discover the nature and boundaries of human knowledge. Kant's system of ethics, described in the *Critique of Practical Reason* (1790), places moral duty above happiness and asserts the existence of an absolute moral law. His views on esthetics are embodied in his *Critique of Judgment* (1790).

Karageorge (1766–1817) (George Petrović) Leader of the Serbs in their fight for independence from Turkey. In 1804 he launched a successful war of independence, with token support from Russia. In 1812 Russia concluded a treaty with Turkey giving Turkey a free hand in Serbia, but the Serbs rose again in 1815. Karageorge returned from exile in Russia in 1817 but was murdered by Milos Obrenović, the new leader.

Karim Khan (1705–79) Ruler of Persia (1750–79), founder of the Zand dynasty. He seized control, ruled peacefully as Vakil Al-Roaya ("Regent of the People") and beautified his capital, Shiraz. His dynasty was overthrown in 1794 by the Qajars.

Kassites (Cassites) Ancient people, possibly of Persian origin, who rose to importance in the 3rd millennium BCE. By the middle of the 18th century BCE they were impinging on BABYLONIA. Their system of government was policed by a small feudal aristocracy of warriors who used the innovatory horse-drawn chariot. The ASSYRIANS eventually forced the Kassites to withdraw to the Zagros Mountains in Iran during the 1st millennium.

Kaunda, Kenneth David (1924–) Zambian statesman, president (1964–91). In 1959 he was imprisoned for membership of the banned Zambia African National Congress. In 1960 Kaunda became leader of the United National Independence Party (UNIP). Kaunda led Northern Rhodesia to independence as Zambia, becoming its first president. In 1972 he imposed single-party rule. Kaunda was a staunch opponent of apartheid. In 1991 economic problems and political unrest forced him to allow multiparty elections in which he was defeated by Frederick Chiluba. In 1997, following a failed military coup, Kaunda was imprisoned. In 1998 he was released and resigned as leader of UNIP.

Kaunitz, Wenzel Anton, count von (1711–94) Austrian statesman. In 1748 he negotiated the treaty ending the War of the Austrian Succession. As chancellor and foreign minister (1753–92) under MARIA THERESA and JOSEPH II, Kaunitz favored France over Austria's traditional ally, Prussia. His defensive alliance with France and Russia (1756) precipitated the Seven Years War (1756–63). In 1772 Kaunitz secured Austria a share in the partition of Poland. The French Revolution (1789) destroyed the French alliance.

Kay, John (1704–64) British engineer. In 1733 he patented his famous flying shuttle which, by enabling a weaver to throw the shuttle automatically from side to side across the warp of a loom, doubled output. His invention was seen as a threat to handloom weavers and he was forced to emigrate to France.

Keats, John (1795–1821) English poet. His first volume, *Poems* (1817), included "On First Looking into Chapman's Homer". *Lamia, Isabella, The Eve of St. Agnes and Other Poems* (1820) included the magnificent lyrics "Ode on a Grecian Urn", "Ode to a Nightingale" and "Ode to Fall".

Kellogg, Frank Billings (1856–1937) US diplomat. He is celebrated chiefly for his negotiation, with French foreign minister Aristide Briand, of the Kellogg-Briand Pact (1928). This pact renounced war as a means of settling international disputes. Kellogg received the Nobel Peace Prize in 1929.

Kelly, Ned (Edward) (1855–80) Australian bushranger (outlaw). From 1878 he led a gang which carried out a series of robberies in Victoria and New South Wales. He was captured and hanged after a siege in Glenrowan township.

Kelvin, William Thomson, 1st Baron (1824–1907) Scottish physicist and mathematician after whom the absolute scale of temperature is named. The Kelvin temperature scale has its zero point at absolute zero and degree intervals the same size as the degree Celsius. The freezing point of water occurs at 273K (0°C or 32°F) and the boiling point at 373K (100°C or 212°F).

Kemal Atatürk *See* ATATÜRK, KEMAL

Kennedy, John Fitzgerald (1917–63) 35th US president (1961–63). He was elected to Congress as a Democrat from Massachusetts in 1946, serving in the Senate from 1953 to 1960. Kennedy gained the presidential nomination in 1960 and narrowly defeated Richard NIXON. He adopted an ambitious and liberal program and embraced the cause of civil rights. In foreign policy, Kennedy founded the "Alliance for Progress" to improve the image of the USA abroad. Adopting a strong anticommunist line, he outfaced KHRUSHCHEV in the Cuban Missile Crisis, which was followed by a US-Soviet treaty banning nuclear tests. He increased military aid to South Vietnam. Kennedy was assassinated in Dallas, Texas, on 22 November 1963.

Kennedy, Robert Francis (1925–68) US lawyer and politician. In 1960 he managed the successful presidential campaign of his brother John F. KENNEDY. He became US attorney general (1961–64), vigorously enforcing civil rights laws and promoting the Civil Rights Act of 1964. After his brother's assassination, he left the cabinet and was elected (1964) senator for New York. While a candidate for the Democratic presidential nomination he was assassinated (4 June) in Los Angeles.

Kenyatta, Jomo (1893–1978) Kenyan statesman, president of Kenya (1964–78). A Kikuyu, he led the struggle for Kenyan independence from 1946. Kenyatta was imprisoned (1952–61) by the British colonial authorities for alleged involvement in the Mau Mau uprising. As leader of the Kenya African National Union (KANU), he became the first president of an independent Kenya. Although Kenyatta suppressed domestic opposition, he presided over a prosperous economy and followed prowestern policies.

Kepler, Johannes (1571–1630) German mathematician and astronomer. He supported the heliocentric theory of COPERNICUS. Kepler succeeded Tycho BRAHE as imperial mathematician to Emperor Rudolf II. From Brahe's observations, he concluded that Mars moves in an elliptical orbit, and he went on to establish his three famous laws of planetary motion.

Kerensky, Alexander Feodorovich (1881–1970) Russian moderate political leader. He became prime minister of the provisional government in July 1917, shortly after the overthrow of the Czar. Deposed by the Bolsheviks, he fled to France.

Kerouac, Jack (1922–69) US poet and novelist. *On the Road* (1957) established Kerouac as the leading novelist of the beat movement. Later works include *The Dharma Bums* (1958) and *Desolation Angels* (1965).

Keynes, John Maynard (1883–1946) English economist. In *The General Theory of Employment, Interest and Money* (1936) Keynes established the foundation of modern macroeconomics. He advocated the active intervention of government in the economy to stimulate employment and prosperity. He took a leading role in the Bretton Woods Conference of 1944, which aimed to establish a system of preventing severe financial crises.

Khoisan Group of South African peoples and their languages. The Khoikhoi (or Hottentot) and San (or Bushmen) are the two largest groups. Khoikhoi, who were traditionally nomadic, are now almost extinct. Many of them were displaced or exterminated by Dutch settlers, and their descendants have mostly been absorbed into the South African population. The San until recently had a hunting and gathering culture. About half still follow the traditional ways, mostly in the Kalahari region of Botswana and Namibia.

Khomeini, Ruhollah (1900–89) Iranian ayatollah (religious leader). An Islamic scholar with great influence over his Shiite students, he published (1941) an outspoken attack on Reza PAHLAVI and remained an opponent of his son, Muhammad Reza PAHLAVI. Exiled in 1964, Khomeini returned to Iran in triumph after the fall of the Shah in 1979. His rule was characterized by strict religious orthodoxy and elimination of political opposition. In 1989

Khomeini issued a *fatwa* (death order) against author Salman RUSHDIE. He was succeeded by Hojatoleslam Rafsanjani.

Khoshru I (d. CE 579) Persian king (r.531–79) of the SASSANIAN DYNASTY. He extended his empire and expanded commerce.

Khoshru II (d.628) Persian king (r.591–627) of the SASSANIAN DYNASTY, grandson of KHOSHRU I. He was overthrown by Bahram, the Usurper, but regained the throne. He seized Syria, Palestine and Egypt but lost them to HERACLIUS. He was executed after a revolution and his son, Sheroe, succeeded to the throne.

Khrushchev, Nikita Sergeievich (1894–1971) Soviet statesman, first secretary of the Communist Party (1953–64) and Soviet prime minister (1958–64). Noted for economic success and ruthless suppression of opposition in the Ukraine, he was elected to the Politburo in 1939. After STALIN died, Khrushchev made a speech denouncing him and expelled his backers from the central committee. Favoring detente with the West, he yielded to the USA in the Cuban missile crisis. Economic setbacks led to his replacement by Leonid BREZHNEV and Aleksei KOSYGIN in 1964.

Kierkegaard, Søren (Aaby) (1813–55) Danish philosopher, regarded as the founder of modern existentialism. He believed that the individual must exercise free will, making deliberate decisions about the direction of their life. He considered that religious faith was blind obedience to an irrational God. His books include *Either/Or* (1843) and *Philosophical Fragments* (1844).

Kim Il Sung (1912–94) Korean statesman, first premier of North Korea (1948–72) and president (1972–94). He joined the Korean Communist Party in 1931. In 1950 Kim led a North Korean invasion of South Korea, precipitating the Korean War (1950–53). Chairman of the Korean Workers' Party from 1948, his government suppressed opposition and pursued strictly orthodox communist policies. He was succeeded by his son, Kim Jong Il.

King, Martin Luther, Jr. (1929–68) US Baptist minister and civil rights leader. In 1956 he led the boycott of segregated public transportation in Montgomery, Alabama. As founder (1960) and president of the Southern Christian Leadership Council (SCLC), he became a national figure. King opposed the Vietnam War and demanded measures to relieve poverty, organizing a huge march on Washington (1963) where he made his most famous ("I have a dream...") speech. In 1964 he became the youngest person to be awarded the Nobel Peace Prize. He was assassinated (4 April 1968) in Memphis, Tennessee.

Kipling, (Joseph) Rudyard (1865–1936) British author, b. India. His *Barrack Room Ballads and Other Verses* (1892), which include the poems "If" and "Gunga Din", is a classic text of colonialist literature. He also wrote many children's stories, including *The Jungle Book* (1894) and *Just So Stories* (1902). Kipling was awarded the Nobel Prize for literature (1907).

Kirchhoff, Gustav Robert (1824–87) German physicist. With Robert BUNSEN, he developed the spectroscope, with which they discovered cesium and rubidium in 1860. He is famous for two laws that apply to multiple-loop electric circuits.

Kissinger, Henry Alfred (1923–) US statesman, secretary of state (1973–77), b. Germany. In 1969 he became NIXON's chief adviser on foreign policy, helping to establish the Strategic Arms Limitation Talks (SALT) with the Soviet Union. As secretary of state, Kissinger shared the Nobel Peace Prize (1973) with Le Duc Tho for his part in negotiating a cease-fire in the Vietnam War. His "shuttle diplomacy" brought a cease-fire agreement between Egypt and Israel in the 1973 Yom Kippur War.

Kitchener, Horatio Herbert, 1st Earl (1850–1916) British field marshal and statesman. He took part in the unsuccessful relief of General GORDON at Khartoum (1883–85), but reconquered Sudan in 1898 and became its governor-general. Kitchener served as chief of staff in the second of the South African Wars (1900–02). After service in India and Egypt, he was appointed secretary of state for war at the outbreak of World War I.

Klee, Paul (1879–1940) Swiss painter and graphic artist. In 1912 he joined KANDINSKY's Blaue Reiter group. Klee evolved his own pictorial language based on correspondences between line,

color and plane. Some of his images are entirely abstract, but some are recognizable figures. His works include *Graduated Shades of Red-Green* (1921) and *Revolutions of the Viaducts* (1937).

Knox, John (1514–72) Leader of the Protestant Reformation in Scotland. Ordained a Catholic priest, he was later converted to Protestantism. Captured by French soldiers in Scotland, he was imprisoned in France (1547), then lived in exile. In 1559 Knox returned to Scotland, where he continued to promote the Protestant cause. In 1560, the Scottish Parliament, under Knox's leadership, made Presbyterianism the state religion.

Koch, Robert (1843–1910) German bacteriologist. He was awarded the 1905 Nobel Prize for physiology or medicine for his discovery of the bacillus that causes tuberculosis.

Kohl, Helmut (1930–) German statesman, chancellor (1982–98). Between 1976 and 1982 he led the Christian Democratic Union (CDU) Party opposition to Helmut Schmidt. Kohl succeeded Schmidt as chancellor. His conservative approach advocated strong support for NATO. Kohl strongly supported closer integration in the European Union (EU). In 1990 he presided over the reunification of East and West Germany and was elected as the first chancellor of the unified Germany. Reelected in 1994 and 1996, Kohl lost the 1998 election to Gerhard SCHRÖDER.

Kongo, Kingdom of the African state from the 14th century to about 1700, occupying the area now included in the Democratic Republic of Congo and Angola. It was ruled by a king, or *manikongo*. The kingdom began trade with Portugal in 1483. The Portuguese brought Christianity, which Manikongo Afonso I tried to spread. Afonso was hampered by the greed of the Portuguese, who carried on a brisk slave trade. Under continued depredations by the Portuguese and repeated attacks from interior tribes, the kingdom collapsed, and Portugal took control.

Koons, Jeff (1955–) US sculptor. He burst onto the art scene in the 1980s with a series of sexually explicit pieces. Other exhibits, such as his vacuum cleaners in clear plastic cases, comment on consumer society and have their roots in the 1960s pop art movement.

Kościuszko, Thaddeus (1746–1817) Polish general and patriot. After the second partition of Poland in 1793, he led a movement to regain Polish independence. It was initially successful, but the invading armies of Russia and Prussia proved too strong, and Kościuszko was imprisoned (1794–96) and exiled.

Kossuth, Lajos (1802–94) Hungarian statesman. In 1848 Kossuth led the Hungarian Revolution against HAPSBURG rule and was appointed provisional governor of the independent republic. In 1849 the Russians crushed the uprising, forcing him to flee. From exile, Kossuth continued to champion Hungarian independence but the Compromise of 1867, which created the Dual Monarchy of the Austro-Hungarian empire, ended his hopes.

Kosygin, Aleksei Nikolaievich (1904–80) Soviet statesman, premier (1964–80). He was elected to the Communist Party Central Committee in 1939 and the Politburo in 1948. Kosygin served as an economics expert to Joseph STALIN. He was removed on the accession of Nikolai KHRUSHCHEV, but returned to share power with Leonid BREZHNEV.

Kropotkin, Peter Alexeievich (1842–1921) Russian anarchist. He was jailed for seditious propaganda in 1874 but escaped into exile in 1876. Living mostly in Britain, Kropotkin became one of the most important theorists of anarchist socialism, criticizing the centralizing tendencies of Marxism.

Kruger, Paul (Stephanus Johannes Paulus) (1825–1904) South African statesman and soldier, president (1883–1902) of the South African Republic. In the 1830s he took part in the Great Trek. In 1877 Britain annexed Transvaal and Kruger led the fight for independence. He fought in the first of the South African Wars and was elected the first president of the South African Republic. His refusal to grant equal status to non-AFRIKANER (Boer) settlers precipitated the second South African War. Kruger was forced into exile. He died in Switzerland.

Kublai Khan (1215–94) MONGOL Emperor (1260–94). Grandson of GENGHIS KHAN, he completed the conquest of China in

1279, establishing the YUAN DYNASTY, which ruled until 1368. He conquered the Southern SONG DYNASTY and extended operations into SE Asia, although his attempt to invade Japan was thwarted by storms. He conducted correspondence with European rulers and apparently employed Marco POLO.

Kush Former kingdom in Nubia. Lasting from c.1000 BCE to c.CE 350, it conquered Egypt in the 7th–8th centuries BCE. It was later defeated by the Assyrians and moved its capital to Meroë in the Sudan. After Roman and Arab attacks, Meroë was captured by the Aksumites c.CE 350. The Kushites are thought to have fled west.

Kushan dynasty Rulers over much of N India, Afghanistan and parts of Central Asia from c.CE 50 to c.400. Descended from nomads who ruled over Bactria, they were wealthy traders. The decline of Kushan rule followed the rise of the SASSANIAN DYNASTY in Persia.

L

Lafayette, Marie Joseph Gilbert de Motier, marquis de (1757–1834) French general and statesman. He fought for the colonists in the American Revolution. Returning to France, Lafayette presented the Declaration of the Rights of Man to the States General (1789). After the storming of the Bastille, he commanded (1789–91) the National Guard in the first phase of the French Revolution. In 1791 Lafayette lost popular support by ordering his troops to fire on a riotous crowd. In 1792, hounded by the Jacobins, he deserted to the Austrians. In 1799 Lafayette was rehabilitated by Napoleon and returned to France. He played a major role in the July Revolution (1830) that installed LOUIS PHILIPPE as king of France.

Lamarck, Jean-Baptiste Pierre Antoine de Monet, chevalier de (1744–1829) French biologist. His theories of evolution, according to which acquired characteristics are inheritable, influenced evolutionary thought throughout most of the 19th century but were disproved by Charles DARWIN.

Lancaster dynasty English royal dynasty. The first earl of Lancaster was Edmund "Crouchback" (1245–96), son of HENRY III. In 1361 the title and lands passed to John of Gaunt via his wife. Their son became HENRY IV in 1399. During the Wars of the Roses in the 15th century, the royal houses of Lancaster and YORK, both PLANTAGENETS, contended for the crown.

Langland, William (1331–99) English poet. His poem *Piers Plowman* (c.1367–70), a late flowering of the alliterative tradition in English verse, is considered one of the most important works of medieval literature.

Lao Tzu (Laozi) (active 6th century BCE) Chinese philosopher, credited as the founder of Taoism. According to tradition he was a contemporary of CONFUCIUS and developed Taoism as a mystical reaction to Confucianism. He is said to have written *Tao Te Ching*, the sacred book of Taoism.

Laplace, Pierre Simon, marquis de (1749–1827) French astronomer and mathematician. He made significant advances in probability theory. His application of NEWTON's theory of gravitation to the Solar System was summarized in his book *Celestial Mechanics* (1798–1827). Laplace proposed that the Solar System had condensed out of a vast, rotating gaseous nebula.

La Salle, (René) Robert Cavelier, sieur de (1643–87) French explorer. In 1668 he sailed for Canada to make his fortune in the fur trade. He explored the Great Lakes area and was governor of Fort Frontenac on Lake Ontario (1675). On his greatest journey, he followed the Mississippi to its mouth (1682), naming the land Louisiana and claiming it for France.

Las Casas, Bartolomé de (1474–1566) Spanish missionary, known as Apostle of the Indies. He went to Hispaniola in 1502 and spent his life trying to help Native Americans. His *History of the Indies* documents their persecution by Spanish colonists.

Lavoisier, Antoine Laurent (1743–94) French chemist. He demolished the phlogiston theory by demonstrating the function of oxygen in combustion. Lavoisier named oxygen and hydrogen

and showed how they combined to form water. In collaboration with Berthollet, he published *Methods of Chemical Nomenclature* (1787), which laid down the method of naming substances.

Law, John (1671–1729) French financier, b. Scotland. His banking and stock-market schemes created a boom in France, where he founded a state bank in 1716. His "Mississippi Scheme" (1717) attracted huge investment in French Louisiana and, as the Company of the Indies (1719), took over all other trading companies. Appointed controller-general of finance (1720), he merged all his interests into one organization. Within months a dip in public confidence caused heavy selling and the whole scheme collapsed. Law died in exile, a bankrupt.

Lawrence, Ernest Orlando (1901–58) US physicist. In 1930 he built the first cyclotron, a subatomic particle accelerator. He received the 1939 Nobel Prize for physics.

Lawrence, T.E. (Thomas Edward) (1888–1935) (Lawrence of Arabia) British soldier. He joined the army in World War I and in 1916 led the Arab revolt against the Turks. He was a successful guerrilla commander, leading (October 1918) Arab forces into Damascus, Syria. In 1926 he published his remarkable account of the Arab revolt, *The Seven Pillars of Wisdom*.

Leakey, Mary (1913–96) English archaeologist and anthropologist. From 1931 she researched Olduvai Gorge in Tanzania with her husband, Louis Leakey (1903–72).

Le Corbusier (1887–1963) French architect, b. Switzerland as Charles Édouard Jeanneret. His early work exploited the qualities of reinforced concrete in cubelike forms. His Unité d'Habitation, Marseilles (1946–52), was a modular design widely adopted for modern mass housing. Later, Le Corbusier evolved a more poetic style, of which the highly sculptural chapel of Notre-Dame-du-Haut at Ronchamp (1955) is the finest example.

Lee, Ann (1736–84) British mystic, member of the United Society of Believers in Christ's Second Appearing, popularly called the Shakers. The Shaker sect was persecuted in Britain, and in 1774 Lee and eight others fled to the American colonies.

Lee, Robert Edward (1807–70) Commander of the Confederate forces in the American Civil War. In 1862 he was appointed commander of the main Confederate force, the Army of Virginia. Lee won the second battle of Bull Run (1862) and defeated the Union forces at Fredericksburg (1862) and Chancellorsville (1863). In July 1863 his invasion of the North ended in decisive defeat at Gettysburg. In April 1965 Lee was finally trapped and forced to surrender by Ulysses S. GRANT.

Leeuwenhoek, Anton van (1632–1723) Dutch scientist. He built simple single-lensed microscopes that were so accurate they had better magnifying powers than the compound microscopes of his day. He investigated and described many microorganisms.

Leibniz, Gottfried Wilhelm (1646–1716) German philosopher and mathematician. In 1684 he published his discovery of differential and integral calculus, made independently of Sir Isaac NEWTON. His philosophy that the Universe comprises a hierarchy of constituents with God at the top asserting a divine plan was satirized in VOLTAIRE's *Candide* (1759). His major works include *New Essays Concerning Human Understanding* (1704).

Lemaître, Abbé Georges Édouard (1894–1966) Belgian astrophysicist who formulated the Big Bang theory for the origin of the Universe. He saw the Universe as originally analogous to a radioactive atom, with all the energy and matter concentrated into a kernel that he called the "primeval atom". Lemaître argued that an expanding universe would have originated in the explosion of that primeval atom.

Lenin, Vladimir Ilyich (1870–1924) Russian revolutionary and statesman, b. Vladimir Ilyich Ulyanov. He evolved a revolutionary form of socialism (Marxism-Leninism) that emphasized the need for a vanguard party to lead the revolution. In 1900 Lenin went into exile, founding (1903) what became the Bolsheviks. After the first part of the Russian Revolution of 1917, he returned to Russia. Lenin denounced the liberal government of KERENSKY and demanded armed revolt. After the Bolshevik revo lution (November 1917), he became the head of state. Lenin withdrew Russia from World War I. With the help of TROTSKY, Lenin's government survived famine and the Russian Civil War (1918–22) by instituting a centralized command economy. In 1921 the New Economic Policy (NEP) marked a return to a mixed economy. In 1922 Lenin became head of the newly formed Soviet Union. In 1923 a new constitution established the supremacy of the Communist Party. Lenin's authority was unchallenged until he was crippled by a stroke in 1922. After his death, a power struggle ensued between Trotsky and STALIN.

Leo III, Saint (c.750–816) Pope (795–816). With the help of CHARLEMAGNE, Leo imposed his rule on Rome and crowned Charlemagne emperor on Christmas Day, 800. This strengthened papal authority in Rome and led to recognition of the pope and emperor as religious and secular leaders of Western Christendom.

Leo X (1475–1521) Pope (1513–21), b. Giovanni de' Medici, son of Lorenzo de' MEDICI. He presided over the Fifth Lateran Council, which failed to enact church reforms. Martin LUTHER was excommunicated by Leo in 1521. He gave HENRY VIII the title Defender of the Faith.

Leonardo da Vinci (1452–1519) Florentine painter, sculptor, architect, engineer and scientist. Leonardo was the founder of the High Renaissance style. By the 1470s he had developed his characteristic style of painting figures who seem rapt in sweet melancholy. In c.1482 Leonardo moved to Milan where he worked mainly for Ludovico SFORZA. He painted the *Last Supper* (c.1498) on the walls of Santa Maria delle Grazie, Milan. From 1500 to 1506 Leonardo created his finest easel paintings, including the enigmatic *Mona Lisa* (c.1504–05). His 19 notebooks contain detailed scientific drawings, including plans for a helicopterlike flying machine, a tank and a submarine.

Leopold I (1790–1865) First king of independent Belgium (1831–65). Son of the duke of Saxe-Coburg-Saalfield, he became a British subject after marrying the daughter of the future King GEORGE IV (1816). An important influence on Queen VICTORIA, his niece, he was responsible for her marriage to ALBERT.

Leopold II (1835–1909) King of Belgium (1865–1909). He initiated colonial expansion and sponsored the expedition of Henry STANLEY to the Congo (1879–84). In 1885 Leopold established the Congo Free State under his own personal rule. In 1908 he was forced to cede the Congo to the Belgian state.

Leopold III (1901–83) King of Belgium (1934–51). When the Germans invaded Belgium (1940) during World War II, he surrendered. He remained in Belgium during the war, until removed to Germany in 1944. On his return, he encountered such fierce opposition that he abdicated in favor of his son, BAUDOUIN.

Lepidus, Marcus Aemilius (d.13 BCE) Roman statesman. He served as consul with Julius CAESAR, as triumvir with Mark ANTONY and Octavian (AUGUSTUS), and again as consul, governing Rome during the Philippi campaign. Octavian forced him from his offices, except that of pontifex maximus.

Lesseps, Ferdinand Marie, vicomte de (1805–94) French diplomat and engineer. He conceived the idea of a canal through the isthmus of Suez, linking the Red Sea with the Mediterranean. He formed the Suez Canal Company, securing finance from the French government. Digging began in 1859, and the canal was opened in November 1869. In 1879 he launched a scheme to construct the Panama Canal but it was abandoned in 1886.

Lessing, Doris May (1919–) British novelist, b. Persia, who was brought up in Rhodesia. Her first novel, *The Grass Is Singing* (1950), is a story of racial hatred. Her *Children of Violence* quintet (1952–69) explores the social position of women; *The Golden Notebook* (1962) is a key feminist text.

Leverrier, Urbain Jean Joseph (1811–77) French astronomer. In 1846 he successfully predicted that an unknown planet (Neptune) was responsible for discrepancies between the calculated and observed orbital motion of Uranus.

Levi, Primo (1919–87) Italian writer. A Jew, he joined a guerrilla movement in World War II. He was captured and sent to Auschwitz. Levi survived but was haunted by the Holocaust. His books, such as *If This is a Man* (1947) and *The Periodic Table* (1984), attempt to come to terms with the experience.

Lewis, Meriwether (1774–1809) US explorer. An army officer, he was secretary to Thomas JEFFERSON, who chose him to lead the Lewis and Clark expedition (1804) to seek a route by water from the Mississippi to the Pacific Ocean.

Libby, Willard Frank (1908–80) US chemist. From 1941 to 1945 he worked on the separation of isotopes for the atomic bomb. In 1960 Libby was awarded the Nobel Prize for chemistry for his development of carbon dating.

Licinius, Valerius Licinianus (c.270–325) Roman emperor (311–23). In 313 Licinius, together with CONSTANTINE THE GREAT, issued the "Edict of Milan", legislation that favored Christians in the empire. A few years later Licinius reversed his position and resumed attacks on the Christians.

Lilienthal, Otto (1849–96) German engineer and pioneer of glider design. In 1891 Lilienthal became the first person to control a glider in flight. He made c.2,500 more flights.

Liliuokalani, Lydia Kamekeha (1838–1917) Last sovereign ruler of Hawaii (1891–93). She resisted US dominance and tried to restore powers lost to the crown in the constitution of 1887. Overthrown in a rebellion (1893), she later abdicated.

Limbourg, Pol de (active 1380–1416) Franco-Flemish manuscript illustrator. Pol and his brothers, Jan and Hermann, were court painters to Jean, duc de Berry. Their masterpiece is the book of hours *Les Très Riches Heures du Duc de Berry* (1413–15).

Lincoln, Abraham (1809–65) 16th US President (1861–65). He was elected to the Illinois legislature for the Whig Party in 1834 and served (1847–49) in the House of Representatives. He was Republican candidate for president in 1860. Lincoln's victory made the secession of the Southern, slave-owning states inevitable, and his determination to defend Fort Sumter began the Civil War. In September 1862 he issued the Emancipation Proclamation and in November 1863 delivered his famous Gettysburg Address. In 1864 Lincoln was reelected and saw the war to a successful conclusion. On 14 April 1865, five days after the surrender of Robert E. LEE, Lincoln was shot by John Wilkes Booth, a Southern sympathizer. He died the next day.

Lindbergh, Charles Augustus (1902–74) US aviator. He became an international hero when, in *The Spirit of St. Louis*, he made the first nonstop transatlantic solo flight, from New York to Paris (1927) in 33 hours 30 minutes.

Linnaeus, Carolus (1707–78) (Carl von Linné) Swedish botanist and taxonomist. His *Systema Naturae* (1735) laid the foundation of the modern science of taxonomy by including all known organisms in a single classification system. He devised the system of binomial nomenclature.

Li Po (CE 701–62) Chinese poet of the TANG DYNASTY. The influence of Taoism can be seen in the sensual and spiritual aspects of his work. He is said to have drowned while drunk.

Lippi, Fra Filippo (1406–69) Florentine painter. His most characteristic subject was the Virgin and Child. His finest fresco cycle (1452–64) depicts the lives of St. Stephen and St. John in Prato Cathedral, Florence.

Lister, Joseph, 1st Baron (1827–1912) English surgeon who introduced the principle of antisepsis. Using carbolic acid as the antiseptic agent, in conjunction with heat sterilization of instruments, he brought about a decrease in postoperative fatalities.

Liszt, Franz (1811–86) Hungarian composer and pianist. Liszt's many challenging compositions for piano include *Transcendental Studies* (1851). He also wrote orchestral works, notably symphonic poems such as *Mazeppa* (1851), and choral music.

Livingstone, David (1813–73) Scottish explorer of Africa. In 1841 he went to South Africa as a missionary and became famous through his account of a journey (1853–56) across Africa from Angola to Mozambique. In 1866 he set off to find the source of the Nile. Livingstone disappeared and was found in 1871 by Henry Morton STANLEY on Lake Tanganyika.

Livy (59–17 BCE) (Titus Livius). One of the greatest Roman historians. He began his *History of Rome c.*28 BCE. Of the original 142 books, 35 have survived in full.

Lloyd George, David (1863–1945) British statesman, prime minister (1916–22). A Liberal, he entered Parliament in 1890. As chancellor of the exchequer (1908–15), Lloyd George increased taxation to pay for social measures such as old-age pensions. His "People's Budget" (1909) provoked a constitutional crisis that led to a reduction of the powers of the House of Lords. In 1916 he led a cabinet rebellion to dislodge the prime minister, Herbert Asquith. Lloyd George led a coalition government for the rest of the war. In 1918 he won an electoral victory and was a leading figure at the peace conference at Versailles. In 1921 he negotiated with Sinn Féin to create the Irish Free State.

Locke, John (1632–1704) English philosopher. He is chiefly remembered for his political theory of liberalism expounded in *Two Treatises on Civil Government* (1690). Locke argued that all men had equal rights to "life, health, liberty or possessions". He rejected the divine right of kings, advocating that the state, guided by natural law, be formed by social contract.

Lombards Germanic peoples who inhabited the area E of the lower River Elbe until driven W by the Romans in CE 9. In 568 they invaded N Italy under Alboin and conquered much of the country, adopting Catholicism and Latin customs. The Lombard kingdom reached its peak under Liutprand (d.744). It went into decline after defeat by the FRANKS under CHARLEMAGNE (775).

Longfellow, Henry Wadsworth (1807–82) US poet. He is chiefly remembered for his narrative poems, such as *Evangeline* (1847), *The Song of Hiawatha* (1855), *The Courtship of Miles Standish* (1858) and *Tales of a Wayside Inn* (1863), which includes "Paul Revere's Ride".

Lorca, Federico García (1898–1936) Spanish poet and dramatist. His poetry, ranging from *Gypsy Ballads* (1928) to *The Poet in New York* (1940), was internationally acclaimed. In the theater, his early farces gave way to tragedies such as *Blood Wedding* (1933), *Yerma* (1935) and *The House of Bernarda Alba* (1936). He was killed by nationalists in the Spanish Civil War.

Louis VI (1081–1137) King of France (1108–37). He succeeded his father, Philip I. He increased the authority of the royal courts and enjoyed the strong support of the church. In 1137, he secured the marriage of his heir, LOUIS VII, to Eleanor of Aquitaine.

Louis VII (*c.*1120–80) King of France (1137–80). His marriage to Eleanor of Aquitaine extended the French crown's lands to the Pyrenees. Returning from the Second Crusade, he divorced Eleanor for alleged infidelity. She married HENRY II of England, whose French territories then became greater than those of Louis. Louis retaliated by supporting the rebellions of Henry's sons.

Louis IX (1214–70) King of France (1226–70), later known as St. Louis. His mother, Blanche of Castile, was regent from 1226 to 1236 and during his absence from France (1248–54). In 1242 Louis defeated the English at Taillebourg. He was captured on the Sixth Crusade.

Louis XI (1423–83) King of France (1461–83), son of CHARLES VII. He rebelled against his father and was driven out of his province of the Dauphiné in 1456. As king, he suppressed rebellious nobles. His greatest rival was Charles the Bold of Burgundy, but after Charles' death (1477), Louis gained Burgundy and also, after another convenient death, Anjou.

Louis XII (1462–1515) King of France (1498–1515). On becoming king, he had his first marriage annulled in order to wed Anne of Britanny, resulting in the incorporation of Britanny in France. He succeeded his cousin, CHARLES VIII, and was involved in the dynastic wars arising from Charles' invasion of Italy in 1494. Louis was defeated by the Holy League and forced to surrender all his Italian acquisitions (1513).

Louis XIII (1601–43) King of France (1601–43), son of Henry IV and Marie de MÉDICI. In 1617 he ended his mother's regency. He relied on Cardinal RICHELIEU, who exercised total authority from 1624. Louis approved the crushing of the Huguenots at home but made alliances with Protestant powers abroad, in opposition to the Hapsburgs, during the Thirty Years War.

Louis XIV (1638–1715) King of France (1643–1715). His early reign was dominated by Cardinal MAZARIN. From 1661 Louis ruled personally as the epitome of absolute monarchy, becoming known as the "Sun King" for the luxury of his court. His ministers included COLBERT. Louis' wars of aggrandisement in the Low Countries drained the treasury. His revocation of the Edict of Nantes drove Huguenots abroad, weakening the economy. In the War of the Spanish Succession, the French armies were defeated.

Louis XV (1710–74) King of France (1715–74), grandson and successor of LOUIS XIV. He failed to arrest France's slow decline. Disastrous wars, especially the War of the Austrian Succession and the Seven Years War, resulted in financial crisis and the loss of most of the French Empire. The monarchy became unpopular.

Louis XVI (1754–93) King of France (1774–92), grandson and successor of LOUIS XV. In 1770 he married the Austrian archduchess MARIE ANTOINETTE. Louis' lack of leadership allowed the *parlements* (supreme courts) and aristocracy to defeat the efforts of government ministers, such as Jacques NECKER, to carry out vital economic reforms. The massive public debt forced Louis to convoke the States General to raise taxation. His indecisiveness on the composition of the States General led the third (popular) estate to proclaim itself a National Assembly, signaling the start of the French Revolution. The dismissal of Necker led to the storming of the Bastille (14 July 1789). In October 1789 the royal family was confined to the Tuileries palace. Early French defeats in the war against Austria and Prussia led to the declaration of a republic. Louis was tried for treason by the Convention and found guilty. He was guillotined on 21 January 1793.

Louis XVIII (1755–1824) King of France (1814–24), brother of LOUIS XVI. He fled from the French Revolution to England. Louis was restored to the throne in 1814 but was forced to flee again during the Hundred Days until NAPOLEON I's final defeat at Waterloo (1815). He agreed to a constitution providing for parliamentary government and a relatively free society.

Louis I (the Great) (1326–82) King of Hungary (1342–82) and Poland (1370–82). The son of Charles I, Louis was appointed king of Poland by Casimir III. Louis had control of one of the largest realms in Europe. He encouraged commerce and science.

Louis II (1506–26) King of Hungary (1516–26), son and dissolute successor of Ladislas II. In 1521 the Turks captured Belgrade; in 1526 they crushed the Hungarians at the battle of Mohács in which Louis and 20,000 others perished.

Louis Philippe (1773–1850) King of France (1830–48). In 1814 he returned to France from exile. In 1830 Louis gained the throne after the July Revolution. Although known as the "Citizen King", he retained much power. The February Revolution (1848) forced him to abdicate and the Second Republic was declared.

Lucretius (*c.*95–*c.*55 BCE) (Titus Lucretius Carus) Latin poet and philosopher. His six-volume poem *On the Nature of Things* is based on the philosophy of EPICURUS.

Ludwig II (1845–86) King of Bavaria (1864–86), a member of the Wittelsbach family, which had a history of insanity. Ludwig spent his time building extravagant castles. His neglect of affairs of state was one of the reasons for Bavaria's political decline. In 1871 it was absorbed into the German Empire.

Lull, Ramón (*c.*1235–1315) Catalan scholastic philosopher, known as "Doctor Illuminatus" ("Bright Teacher"). His youthful exuberance was transformed into a life devoted to converting Muslims to Christianity. His most notable theological work, the *Ars Magna*, formed the basis of his arguments against Islam.

Lully, Jean-Baptiste (1632–87) French composer, b. Italy. In 1652 he joined the court musicians to Louis XIV. After collaborating with MOLIÈRE on comedies such as *Le Bourgeois Gentil homme* (1670), Lully turned to opera. His *Cadmus and Hermione* (1673) has been called the first French lyrical tragedy.

Lumière Two French brothers, **Louis Jean** (1864–1948) and **Auguste** (1862–1954), pioneers of cinematography. They invent ed a combination of motion-picture camera and projector called the "Cinématographe". Their film *Lunch Break at the Lumière Factory* (1895) is considered to be the first motion picture.

Lumumba, Patrice Emergy (1925–61) Congolese statesman, prime minister (1960–61) of Congo. Leader of the Congolese nationalist movement against the Belgians, he became first premier of the independent Republic of the Congo. The country was plunged into civil war when the province of Katanga tried to secede. Lumumba appealed to the United Nations for assistance. Lumumba was dismissed and imprisoned by MOBUTU. He escaped, but was recaptured and killed.

Luther, Martin (1483–1546) German Christian reformer, a founder of Protestantism. In 1517 he affixed his 95 Theses to the door of the Schlosskirche in Wittenberg. This was a document that attacked, among other things, the sale of indulgences. This action led to a quarrel between Luther and the pope. Luther decided that the Bible was the true source of authority and renounced obedience to Rome. In 1521 Luther was excommunicated at the Diet of Worms. His view that salvation could not be attained by good works was a free gift of God's grace led to a rift with ERASMUS. In 1529 Luther defended consubstantiation against ZWINGLI. Although Luther initially merely sought to reform the Catholic Church his approval of MELANCHTHON's Augsburg Confession (1530) established Lutheranism.

Luxemburg, Rosa (1871–1919) German revolutionary, b. Poland. In 1893 she founded the Polish Communist Party. In 1915 Luxemburg was imprisoned for her opposition to World War I. While in prison, she and Karl Liebknecht founded (1916) the socialist and pacifist Spartacist League (the Spartacists). In 1918 she formed the German Communist Party. In 1919 she and Liebknecht were murdered after an abortive uprising in Berlin.

M

MacArthur, Douglas (1880–1964) US general. A division commander in World War I, he became army chief of staff in 1930, retiring in 1937. He was recalled in 1941. As supreme Allied commander in the SW Pacific (1942–45), he directed the campaigns that led to Japanese defeat. In 1950 he was appointed commander of UN forces in the Korean War. Autocratic and controversial, he was relieved of his command by TRUMAN in 1951.

Maccabaeus, Judas (d.161 BCE) Jewish warrior who led a revolt against the forces of King Antiochus IV Epiphanes, the SELEUCID ruler of Syria. Antiochus sought to impose Hellenistic culture upon Judaea by defiling the Temple in Jerusalem. Maccabaeus used guerrilla tactics to defeat four Syrian armies, and in 165 BCE he recaptured, purified and reconsecrated the Jerusalem Temple. The festival of HANUKKAH celebrates his achievement.

McCarthy, Joseph Raymond (1908–57) US Republican senator, leader of the crusade against alleged communists in the US government. Taking advantage of anticommunist sentiment in the Cold War, he widened his attack to other sectors of public life. During the period of "McCarthyism" many of those accused of communism were blacklisted. In 1954 his House Un-American Activities Committee (HUAC) turned its attention to the army. McCarthy's accusations were shown to be baseless.

MacDonald, (James) Ramsay (1866–1937) British statesman, prime minister (1924, 1929–31, 1931–35), b. Scotland. He became leader of the Labor Party in 1911. His opposition to Britain's participation in World War I lost him the leadership in 1914 and his seat in 1918. Reelected in 1922, he regained the party leadership and became Britain's first Labor prime minister. His minority government fell within months when the Liberals withdrew their support. In 1929 he became prime minister again, but the Great Depression led to the collapse of the Labor government (1931). MacDonald remained as prime minister at the head of a Conservative-dominated national government. He was succeeded by Stanley BALDWIN.

Machiavelli, Niccolò (1469–1527) Florentine statesman and

political theorist. He served (1498–1512) as an official in the republican government of Florence but lost his post when the MEDICI family returned to power. His famous work, *The Prince* (1513), offered advice on how the ruler of a small state might best preserve his power. The term "Machiavellian", to describe immoral political behavior, arose from Machiavelli's ideas.

McKinley, William (1843–1901) 25th US president (1897–1901). In 1896 McKinley defeated William Jennings BRYAN in the presidential election. A strong and effective president, he was largely preoccupied by foreign affairs. McKinley gained the support of Congress for the Spanish-American War (1898) and sanctioned US participation in suppression of the Boxer Rebellion in China (1900). McKinley declared that isolationism was "no longer possible or desirable". Reelected in 1900, he was shot dead by an anarchist on 6 September 1901.

Mackintosh, Charles Rennie (1868–1928) Scottish architect, artist and designer. He was one of the most gifted exponents of art nouveau. His buildings, such as the Glasgow School of Art (1898–1909), were notable for their simplicity of line.

Macmillan, (Maurice) Harold (1894–1986) British statesman, prime minister (1957–63). Macmillan held a succession of Conservative cabinet posts including minister of defense (1954–55) and chancellor of the exchequer (1955–57), before succeeding Anthony Eden as prime minister. Macmillan improved Anglo-American relations and sought a *rapprochement* between Moscow and Washington. His attempt to lead Britain into the European Economic Community (EEC) faltered in the face of Charles DE GAULLE's opposition. Macmillan's campaign on the theme of domestic prosperity ("you've never had it so good") won him a landslide victory in the 1959 general election. His second term was beset by recession and scandal.

Madero, Francisco Indalecio (1873–1913) Mexican statesman, president (1911–13). In 1910 Madero was imprisoned for his opposition to the dictatorship of Porfirio DÍAZ and was forced to flee to Texas. With the aid of "Pancho" VILLA and Emiliano ZAPATA, Madero overthrew Díaz. Madero was a weak president, and the revolutionary movement fragmented. He was murdered during a coup led by his former general Victoriano HUERTA.

Madison, James (1751–1836) Fourth US President (1809–17). Madison was a close adviser to George WASHINGTON until, dismayed by the growing power of the executive, he broke with the Federalist Party. Madison became associated with Thomas JEFFERSON and succeeded him in the presidency. As president Madison was unable to avoid the War of 1812 with Britain, which provoked threats of secession in New England. The successful conclusion of the war restored national prosperity, and Madison, the "Father of the Constitution", retired.

Magadha Kingdom in ancient India that comprised the present-day Gaya and Patna districts of Bihar. Between the 6th century BCE and the 8th century CE Magadha was the focus of larger empires or kingdoms. Strategically located in the Ganges valley, it had control of river trade and communications. Its capital was originally at Rajgir, but was later removed to Pataliputra.

Magellan, Ferdinand (1480–1521) Portuguese explorer, leader of the first expedition to circumnavigate the globe. He took service with Spain, promising to find a route to the Moluccas via the New World and the Pacific. In 1519 Magellan set out with five ships and nearly 300 men. He found the waterway near the S tip of South America that is now named Magellan's Strait. After severe hardships, the expedition reached the Philippines, where Magellan was killed in a local conflict. Only one ship, the *Victoria*, completed the round-the-world voyage.

Magnus VII (1316–74) King of Sweden and Norway (1319–65). Crowned at the age of three, Magnus united Sweden and Norway because he was heir to both thrones. In 1365 he was defeated by his nephew, Albert of Mecklenburg, who then became king of Sweden, while Magnus retired to Norway.

Magritte, René (1898–1967) Belgian painter. Influenced by Dada, his *The Menaced Assassin* (1926) is a landmark in the development of surrealism. Magritte concentrated on the analysis of pictorial language, placing familiar objects in incongruous surroundings and disturbing the link between word and image.

Magyars People who founded the kingdom of Hungary in the late 9th century. From their homeland in NE Europe, they moved south and occupied the Carpathian basin in 895. Excellent horsemen, they raided the German lands to the west until checked by OTTO I in 955. They adopted Christianity and established a powerful state that included much of the N Balkans, but lost territory to the Ottoman Turks after the battle of Mohács (1526). The remainder of the kingdom fell to the HAPSBURG DYNASTY.

Mahdi Messianic Islamic leader. The title usually refers to Muhammad Ahmad (1844–85) of Sudan, who declared himself to be the Mahdi (the Rightly Guided One) in 1882 and led an attack on Khartoum (1885). He set up a great Islamic empire with its capital at Omdurman. His reign lasted less than six months as he died in June 1885. His followers were defeated (1898).

Mahler, Gustav (1860–1911) Austrian composer and conductor. His nine symphonies (the unfinished tenth was left as a sketch) expanded the size of the orchestra. His second, fourth and eighth symphonies feature choral parts. Other works include the song cycles *Das Lied von der Erde* (1908) and *Kindertotenlieder* (1902).

Mahmud II (1785–1839) Sultan of the OTTOMAN EMPIRE (1808–39) whose reign saw conflict with Greece, Russia and Egypt. He was initially successful in the Greek War of Independence, but Russian and British intervention forced him to capitulate and started the Russo-Turkish war (1828–29). Mahmud lost the support of the viceroy of Egypt, MUHAMMAD ALI, which led to the invasion of Turkey, precipitating Egyptian independence.

Major, John (1943–) British statesman, prime minister (1990–97). In 1989 Margaret THATCHER made him foreign secretary then chancellor of the exchequer. Following Thatcher's resignation, Major emerged as her compromise successor. He led the Conservative Party to a surprise victory in the 1992 general election. The catastrophic events of "Black Wednesday" (16 September 1992) forced Britain to withdraw from the European Monetary System (EMS) and devalue the pound. The issue of Europe fractured the Conservative Party. Political scandals and sleaze contributed to Tony BLAIR's victory in the 1997 general election.

Makarios III (1913–77) Greek-Cypriot leader. In 1950 Makarios was appointed Greek Orthodox archbishop of Cyprus and led the movement for *enosis* (union with Greece). In 1959 he became the first president of an independent Cyprus. In 1974 he was briefly overthrown by Greek Cypriots still demanding *enosis*. The coup provoked unrest among Turkish Cypriots and led to a Turkish invasion. Makarios was unable to prevent the subsequent partition of Cyprus into Greek and Turkish sections.

Malcolm X (1925–65) US African-American nationalist leader, b. Malcolm Little. He joined the Black Muslims while in prison and, after his release, became their leading spokesman. Following an ideological split with the founder of the movement, Elijah Muhammad, he made a pilgrimage to Mecca, became an orthodox Muslim and formed a rival group. He was assassinated.

Mallarmé, Stephane (1842–98) French poet, leading exponent of symbolism. His allusive style defies definitive statement in favor of sound associations. Mallarmé's best known poems are *Hérodiade* (1869) and *L'Après-Midi d'un faune* (1876).

Malory, Sir Thomas (d.1471) English writer. His major work, *Le Morte d'Arthur*, is a seminal text of Arthurian romance. It was printed by Caxton in 1485.

Malthus, Thomas Robert (1766–1834) English economist. In his famous *Essay on Population* (1798), Malthus argued that population increases geometrically but food supply can increase only arithmetically, so that population must eventually pass it, with famine, war and disease as consequences.

Mamelukes (Arabic, slaves) Military elite in Egypt and other Arab countries. In 1250 the Mamelukes of Egypt overthrew the Ayyubid dynasty. They halted the MONGOLS, defeated the Crusaders and crushed the ASSASSINS. In 1517 Egypt was conquered

by the OTTOMAN Turks, but the Mamelukes continued to control Egypt until suppressed by MUHAMMAD ALI in 1811.

Mandela, Nelson Rolihlahla (1918–) South African statesman, president (1994–99). He joined the African National Congress (ANC) in 1944, and led the campaign of civil disobedience against South Africa's apartheid government. Following the Sharpeville Massacre (1960), Mandela formed *Umkhonte We Sizwe* (Spear of the Nation), a paramilitary wing of the ANC. In 1961 the ANC was banned. In 1964 Mandela was sentenced to life imprisonment for political offenses. He spent the next 27 years in prison, becoming a symbol of resistance to apartheid. International sanctions forced F.W. DE KLERK to begin dismantling apartheid. In 1990 Mandela was released and resumed his leadership of the newly legalized ANC. In 1993 Mandela and de Klerk shared the Nobel Peace Prize. In 1994 Mandela gained two-thirds of the vote in South Africa's first multiracial democratic elections. A strong advocate of the need for reconciliation, he made de Klerk deputy president in his government of national unity. In 1997 Mandela was replaced as president of the ANC by Thabo MBEKI. In 1999 Mbeki became president of South Africa.

Manet, Édouard (1832–83) French painter. The famed *L Déjeuner sur l'Herbe* (1863) was attacked by critics for its realistic depiction of the female nude. Manet finally achieved recognition with later works, such as *Le Bar aux Folies-Bergère* (1881).

Mani (216–76) Persian prophet, founder of Manichaeism. As a youth he saw a vision of an angel, which was himself, and several years later, when the vision returned, he believed that he was the prophet of a new religion. Although he was martyred, his ideas spread throughout Europe, Africa and Chinese Turkistan.

Mann, Thomas (1875–1955) German novelist and essayist. His works include the novella *Death in Venice* (1912) and the autobiographical essay *Reflections of a Nonpolitical man* (1918). The *Magic Mountain* (1924) is acclaimed as his masterpiece. *Mario and the Magician* (1930) was an allegorical critique of fascism. In 1933 Mann left Germany, moving to Switzerland then the USA. He was awarded the 1929 Nobel Prize for literature.

Mannerheim, Carl Gustav Emil, baron von (1867–1951) Finnish field marshal, president (1944–46). In 1918 he led the anti-Bolshevik forces to victory in the Finnish Civil War and became regent of independent Finland. In 1919 he retired after defeat in presidential elections. In 1931, as head of the defense council, he planned the Mannerheim Line across Karelia. He commanded Finnish forces in the Finnish-Russian War (1939–40, 1941–44) and led the postwar Finnish administration.

Mansa Musa (d.1337) Muslim emperor of Mali (1312–37). His reign marked Mali's greatest period of economic and cultural dominance. His impressive displays of the golden wealth of the imperial treasury, such as his pilgrimage to Mecca (1324–25) and his lavish gifts to Egypt, gained Mali wide recognition.

Mantegna, Andrea (1431–1506) Italian painter and engraver. In 1460 he became court painter to the Gonzaga family in Mantua and decorated the bridal chamber in the Ducal Palace. The murals on the ceiling of the room are the first example of illusionist architecture to have been created since antiquity. Mantegna's other great work was *The Triumph of Caesar* (c.1480–95).

Manuel II (1889–1932) King of Portugal (1908–10). He became king when his father, Carlos I, and older brother were assassinated. In 1910 he was dethroned by a revolution and a republic was established. He was the head of the house of Braganza and Portugal's last king. He spent his exile in England.

Mao Zedong (1893–1976) Chinese statesman, founder and chairman (1949–76) of the People's Republic of China. In 1921 Mao helped found the Chinese Communist Party. After the nationalist Kuomintang, led by CHIANG KAI-SHEK, dissolved the alliance with the communists in 1927, Mao helped established rural soviets. In 1931 he was elected chairman of the Soviet Republic of China, based in Jiangsu. The advance of nationalist forces forced Mao to lead the Red Army on the Long March (1934–35) NW to Shanxi. In 1937 the civil war was suspended as communists and nationalists combined to fight the second Sino–Japanese War. The communists' brand of guerrilla warfare gained hold of much of rural China. Civil war restarted in 1945, and by 1949 the nationalists had been driven out of mainland China. Mao became chairman of the People's Republic. ZHOU ENLAI acted as prime minister. In 1958 Mao launched the Great Leap Forward, which ended in mass starvation. The Cultural Revolution was an attempt by Mao and his wife, Jiang Qing, to reassert Maoist ideology. Political rivals were dismissed, and Mao became supreme commander of the nation and army (1970). Mao and Zhou Enlai's death created a power vacuum. A struggle developed between the Gang of Four, Hua Guofeng and DENG XIAOP-ING. *Quotations from Chairman Mao Zedong* ("The Little Red Book", 1967) is a worldwide bestseller.

Marat, Jean Paul (1743–93) French revolutionary, b. Switzerland. A physician, he founded *L'Ami du Peuple*, a vitriolic journal that supported the Jacobins. His murder by Charlotte CORDAY, a member of the Girondins, was exploited for propaganda by the Jacobins and contributed to the ensuing Reign of Terror.

Maratha (Mahratta) Hindu warrior people of w central India, who rose to power in the 17th century. They extended their rule throughout w India by defeating the MUGHAL EMPIRE and successfully resisting British supremacy in India during the 18th century. They were finally defeated in 1818.

Marconi, Guglielmo (1874–1937) Italian physicist who developed radio. By 1897 Marconi was able to demonstrate radio telegraphy over a distance of 19km (12mi) and established radio communication between France and England in 1899. By 1901 radio transmissions were being received across the Atlantic Ocean. In 1909 Marconi was awarded the Nobel Prize for physics.

Marcos, Ferdinand Edralin (1917–89) Philippine statesman, president (1965–86). He was elected to the Philippine Congress in 1949. As president, Marcos received support from the USA for his military campaigns (1969) against communist guerrilla. Continued civil unrest led to the imposition of martial law in 1972. A new constitution (1973) gave Marcos authoritarian powers. His regime acquired a reputation for corruption, symbolized by the extravagance of his wife, Imelda (1930–). In 1983 his main rival, Benigno Aquino, was assassinated and political opposition coalesced behind Benigno's widow, Cory AQUINO. Marcos appeared to win the 1986 general election, but allegations of vote-rigging forced him into exile. In 1988 US authorities indicted both him for fraud. Ferdinand was too ill to stand trial and died in Hawaii.

Marcus Aurelius Antoninus (CE 121–180) Roman emperor (161–180) and philosopher of the Stoic school. Between 161 and 169 he ruled as coemperor with his adoptive younger brother Lucius Aurelius Verus (d.169). His only surviving work, the much-admired *Meditations*, is a collection of philosophical thoughts and ideas that occurred to him during his campaigns.

Maria II (1819–53) Queen of Portugal (1833–53). She was the daughter of Peter I, who abdicated in her favor when he became emperor of Brazil (PEDRO I). She was betrothed to her uncle, Dom MIGUEL, but attempted to usurp the crown, thereby setting off the Miguelist Wars. Maria's forces defeated Miguel in 1834.

Maria Christina (1806–78) Queen of Spain, consort of FERDINAND VII. At her behest Ferdinand named their daughter ISABEL-LA II as heir. She was regent to Isabella after Ferdinand's death and marshaled Isabella's forces against the Carlists, the supporters of Don CARLOS, the pretender to the throne. Forced from the regency in 1840, she returned in 1843 and thereafter played a major role in the political intrigues that marked Isabella's reign.

Maria Theresa (1717–80) Archduchess of Austria, ruler of the HAPSBURG EMPIRE (1740–80). She succeeded her father, the Emperor CHARLES VI, but was challenged by neighboring powers in the War of the Austrian Succession (1741–48), losing Silesia to Prussia but securing the imperial title for her husband, Francis I. Count von KAUNITZ negotiated an alliance with France, but failed to regain Silesia in the Seven Years War (1756–63). From 1765 she ruled with her son, JOSEPH II.

Marie Antoinette (1755–93) Queen of France, daughter of Emperor Francis I and MARIA THERESA of Austria, she married the future LOUIS XVI in 1770. Her life of pleasure and extravagance contributed to the outbreak of the French Revolution in 1789. She initiated the royal family's attempt to escape in 1791, was held prisoner and finally guillotined.

Marie de Médicis *See* MEDICI, MARIE DE

Marie Louise (1791–1847) French Empress, daughter of Emperor FRANCIS II. In 1810 she married NAPOLEON I. In 1811 she gave birth to the future Napoleon II. Alienated from him by 1814, she was made duchess of Parma.

Marinetti, Filippo Tommaso (1876–1944) Italian poet, novelist, dramatist and founder of futurism. In such works as *Futurismo e Fascismo* (1924), Marinetti embraced fascism and advocated the glorification of machinery, speed and war.

Marius, Gaius (157–86 BCE) Roman general and politician. His policy of recruiting poor men contributed to the bond between Roman troops and their commanders. He also revised army training and equipment. His rivalry with SULLA forced him out of Rome, but he raised an army and recaptured the city (87 BCE).

Marlborough, John Churchill, 1st duke of (1650–1722) English general. In 1685 he helped JAMES II defeat Monmouth, but switched allegiance in support of the Protestant Glorious Revolution (1688). Marlborough was appointed Captain-General of the Allied armies in the War of the Spanish Succession. His strategic skill gained great victories at Blenheim (1704), Ramillies (1706), Oudenaarde (1708) and Malplaquet (1709). Churchill was rewarded with a dukedom and Blenheim Palace. When his wife lost the Queen ANNE's favor, Marlborough was dismissed (1711) and went into exile.

Marlowe, Christopher (1564–93) English dramatist and poet. He helped make blank verse the vehicle of Elizabethan drama. Much of Marlowe's success derives from his ability to humanize his overreaching heroes, as in *Tamburlaine the Great* (1590) and *The Tragical History of Doctor Faustus* (1604). His masterpiece is *Edward II* (1592). Marlowe's greatest poems are *Hero and Leander* (1598) and *The Passionate Shepherd* (1599).

Marquette, Father Jacques (1637–75) French Jesuit missionary and explorer in North America. In 1666 Marquette arrived in Quebec as a missionary priest. In 1673 Marquette and Louis JOL-LIET led the first European expedition along the upper Mississippi River, exploring it as far as the mouth of the Arkansas River.

Marshall, George Catlett (1880–1959) US statesman, secretary of state (1947–49) and defense secretary (1950–51). He served as US chief of staff (1939–45) during World War II. He initiated the Marshall Plan of economic assistance for postwar Europe and was awarded the 1953 Nobel Peace Prize.

Marx, Karl Heinrich (1818–83) German social philosopher, political theorist and founder (with Friedrich ENGELS) of international communism. He produced his own philosophical approach of dialectical materialism. Marx proclaimed that religion was "the opium of the people". In Brussels he joined the Communist League and wrote with Engels the epoch-making *Communist Manifesto* (1848). Marx took part in the revolutionary movements in France and Germany, then went to London (1849) where he lived until his death. He produced a stream of writings, including *Das Kapital* (3 vols, 1867, 1885, 1894). In 1864 the International Workingmen's Association (the First International) was formed, and Marx became its leading figure.

Mary I (1516–58) (Mary Tudor) Queen of England (1553–58), daughter of HENRY VIII and Catherine of Aragón. During the reign of her half-brother, EDWARD VI, she remained a Catholic. On Edward's death, the Duke of Northumberland arranged the brief usurpation of Lady Jane Grey, but Mary acceded with popular support. In 1554 a Spanish alliance was secured by her marriage to the future King PHILIP II of Spain. Mary's determination to re-establish papal authority saw the restoration of heresy laws. The resultant execution of *c*.300 Protestants earned her the epithet "Bloody Mary". She was succeeded by ELIZABETH I.

Mary, Queen of Scots (1542–87) Daughter of James V, she succeeded him as queen when one week old. She was sent to France and married the future Francis II of France in 1558. On his death in 1560 she returned to Scotland, where, as a Catholic, she came into conflict with Protestant reformers. Her marriage to Lord Darnley was also resented and soon broke down. After Darnley's murder (1567), she married James Bothwell, possibly her husband's murderer, which alienated her few remaining supporters. Following a rebellion of Scottish nobles, she was forced to abdicate in favor of her infant son, James VI (later JAMES I of England). Mary fled to England. Kept in captivity, she became involved in plots against ELIZABETH I and was executed.

Masaccio (1401–28) Florentine painter of the early Renaissance, b. Tommaso Giovanni di Mone. His most important surviving works are: a polyptych (1426) for the Carmelite Church, Pisa; a fresco cycle that he created with Masolino portraying the life of St. Peter, in the Brancacci Chapel, Florence (c.1425–28); and the *Trinity* fresco in Santa Maria Novella, Florence (c.1428).

Masinissa (238–149 BCE) Numidian king. He fought against the Romans in the second Punic War, but changed sides in 206 BCE and helped in the downfall of Carthage. He was supported in his North African kingdom by the Romans and annexed Carthaginian lands. His reign greatly organized the Numidian people.

Mather, Cotton (1663–1728) Puritan minister in colonial Massachusetts. He supported the Salem witch trials, though not the subsequent executions, yet was sympathetic to scientific and philosophical ideas. He was a founder of Yale University.

Matisse, Henri Emile Benoït (1869–1954) French painter, sculptor, graphic artist and designer. He developed the style of painting that became known as fauvism. After a relatively brief flirtation with cubism, Matisse turned back to the luminous and sensual calmness that typified his art. One of his greatest works is the design of the Chapel of the Rosary at Venice (1949–51).

Mauryan empire (321–185 BCE) Ancient Indian dynasty and state founded by CHANDRAGUPTA (r. c.321–c.297 BCE). His son Bindusara (r. c.291–c.268 BCE) conquered the Deccan, and all N India was united under ASHOKA (r. c.264–c.238 BCE), Chandragupta's grandson. After Ashoka's death the empire broke up, the last emperor being assassinated in c.185 BCE.

Maximilian I (1459–1519) Holy Roman emperor (1493–1519), son and successor of FREDERICK III. Maximilian was one of the most successful members of the HAPSBURG DYNASTY. He gained Burgundy and the Netherlands by marriage and defended them against France. His involvement in the Italian Wars led to his defeat by the Swiss (1499). Maximilian strengthened the Hapsburg heartland in Austria and, through arranged marriages, ensured that his grandson, CHARLES V, inherited a vast empire.

Maximilian, Ferdinand Joseph (1832–67) Emperor of Mexico (1864–67), brother of FRANZ JOSEPH. An Austrian archduke, he was offered the throne of Mexico after the French invasion (1862). When the French withdrew in 1867, Maximilian was overthrown by the liberal forces of Benito JUÁREZ and executed.

Maxwell, James Clerk (1831–79) Scottish mathematician and physicist. His outstanding theoretical work revealed the existence of electromagnetic radiation. Maxwell used the theory of the electromagnetic field for Maxwell's equations, which provided a unified theory of light, electricity and magnetism.

Maya Outstanding culture of classic American civilization. Occupying S Mexico and N Central America, it was at its height from the 3rd to 9th centuries. The Maya built great temple-cities with buildings surmounting stepped pyramids. They worshiped gods and ancestors, and blood sacrifice was an important element of religion. Maya civilization declined after c.900, and much was destroyed after the Spanish conquest in the 16th century. Modern Maya, numbering c.4 million, live in the same area.

Mazarin, Jules (1602–61) French statesman and Roman Catholic cardinal, b. Italy. He was the protégé of Cardinal RICHELIEU. During the Fronde rebellions (1648–52), Mazarin played off the various factions and, though twice forced out of France,

emerged in control. As a former papal diplomat, he was a skillful negotiator of the treaties that ended the Thirty Years War.

Mazzini, Giuseppe (1805–72) Italian patriot and theorist of the Risorgimento. A member of the *Carbonari* (republican underground) from 1830, he founded the "Young Italy" movement dedicated to the unification of Italy. He fought in the Revolutions of 1848 and ruled in Rome in 1849, but was exiled. Unlike GARIBALDI or CAVOUR, Mazzini remained committed to republicanism.

Mbeki, Thabo (1942–) South African statesman, president (1999–). In 1990 he returned from exile to become chairman of the African National Congress (ANC). In 1997 Mbeki succeeded Nelson MANDELA as president of the ANC.

Medes Group of ancient Iranian tribes from around the Elburz Mountains. They frequently clashed with Assyrians during the 9th century BCE and were conquered by SCYTHIANS in the 7th century. The Median king Cyaxares drove out the Scythians and also helped the Babylonians destroy the ASSYRIAN EMPIRE; this period (c.615–c.585 BCE) saw the greatest extent of Median power. CYRUS THE GREAT defeated the last Median king in 550 BCE).

Medici, Catherine de' (1519–89) Queen of France, wife of Henry II, daughter of Lorenzo de'MEDICI. She exerted political influence after her husband's and first son's deaths in 1559. In 1560 Catherine became regent for her second son, CHARLES IX, and remained principal adviser until his death (1574). Her tolerance of the Huguenots turned to enmity at the beginning of the French Wars of Religion. Catherine's concern for preserving the power of the monarchy led to a dependence on the Catholic House of Guise. Fearing the decline of her own importance at court, she planned the Saint Bartholomew's Day Massacre (1572). When her third son, HENRY III, acceded to the throne in 1574, her effectiveness in policy-making had been compromised.

Medici, Cosimo de' (the Elder) (1389–1464) Ruler of Florence (1434–64). With the Medici banking fortune, he led the oligarchy that was expelled from Florence in 1433 but returned to rule permanently the next year. He increased the Medici fortune, strengthened Florence by alliance with Milan and Naples and was a great patron of the artists of the early Renaissance.

Medici, Lorenzo de' (the Magnificent) (1449–92) Ruler of Florence, grandson of Cosimo de'MEDICI (the Elder). Lorenzo's grip on power worried Pope Sixtus IV who instigated a coup led by the rival Pazzi family. Lorenzo survived an assassination attempt and ruthlessly clamped down on his enemies. His patronage of Renaissance artists drained the Medici coffers.

Medici, Marie de' (1573–1642) Queen of France. Daughter of the Grand Duke of Tuscany, she married HENRY IV of France (1600). He was assassinated, possibly with her connivance, the day after she was crowned queen in 1610. As regent for her son, LOUIS XIII, she relied on Italian advisers and reversed Henry's anti-Hapsburg policy. She was constantly at odds with Louis after 1614 and antagonized Cardinal RICHELIEU. Failing to have him dismissed in 1630, she was forced to leave France.

Meir, Golda (1898–1978) Israeli stateswoman, prime minister (1969–74), b. Ukraine as Golda Mabovitch. In 1906 her family emigrated to the USA, and she became active in Zionism. In 1921 Meir emigrated to Palestine. After Israeli independence, Meir became minister of labor (1949–56) and foreign minister (1956–66). She succeeded Levi Eshkol as prime minister. Meir was forced to resign following criticism of the government's lack of preparedness for the 1973 Arab–Israeli War.

Melanchthon, Philip (1497–1560) German theologian and educator, considered with Martin LUTHER as a founder of Protestantism. In 1930 Melanchthon wrote the Augsburg Confession, statement of Protestant beliefs.

Melville, Herman (1819–91) US novelist. He became a sailor in 1839 and joined a whaling ship in 1841. *Moby Dick*, an allegorical story of the search for a great whale, was written in 1851. Melville's work was neglected during his lifetime, but *Moby Dick* is now regarded as a classic.

Menander (342–292 BCE) Greek playwright. He wrote more

than 100 comedies of which only one survives in full. As the outstanding exponent of the New Comedy of Hellenistic times, he is regarded as the founder of the comedy of manners.

Mencius (*c.*372–289 BCE) (Mengzi) Chinese philosopher. He held that human beings are basically good but require cultivation to bring out the goodness. His teachings were recorded in the *Book of Mencius*, one of the canonical writings of Confucianism.

Mendel, Gregor Johann (1822–84) Austrian naturalist. He discovered the laws of heredity and in so doing laid the foundation for the modern science of genetics. His study of the inheritance of characteristics was published in *Experiments with Plant Hybrids* (1866). It was rediscovered in 1900.

Mendeleyev, Dmitri Ivanovich (1834–1907) Russian chemist who devised the periodic table. He demonstrated that chemically similar elements appear at regular intervals if the elements are arranged in order by atomic weights. Mendeleyev classified the 60 known elements and left gaps in the table, predicting the existence and properties of several elements later discovered.

Mendelssohn (-Bartholdy), (Jakob Ludwig) Felix (1809–47) German composer and conductor. His performance (1829) of the St. *Matthew Passion* revived interest in J.S. BACH. His orchestral works include a violin concerto (1845) and five symphonies. His two oratorios, St. *Paul* (1836) and *Elijah* (1846), are considered to be among the greatest of the 19th century. His compositions were often inspired by extra-musical associations.

Menelik II (1844–1913) Emperor of Ethiopia (1889–1913). He became emperor with Italian support, succeeding John IV. He defeated an Italian invasion in 1896, securing Ethiopian independence. Having proved himself an able king, he expanded and modernized his empire, establishing a capital at Addis Ababa.

Menes Egyptian king (*c.*3100 BCE) regarded as the first king of the 1st dynasty. He unified Upper and Lower Egypt, establishing the Old Kingdom with its capital at Memphis.

Menuhotep (*c.*2060–2010 BCE) Egyptian king of the 11th dynasty. Establishing central control, he reunified Egypt, initiating the Middle Kingdom (*c.*2040–1640 BCE). Menuhotep oversaw many building projects, including a temple complex at Thebes.

Mercator, Gerardus (1512–94) Flemish cartographer. His huge world map of 1569 employed the system of projection now named for him, in which lines of longitude, as well as latitude, appear as straight, parallel lines.

Merleau-Ponty, Maurice (1908–61) French philosopher. He contributed greatly to phenomenology, especially in *The Phenomenology of Perception* (1945). In 1945, with Jean-Paul SARTRE and Simone de BEAUVOIR, he founded the journal *Les Temps Modernes*.

Merovingian (476–750) Frankish dynasty. It was named for Merovech, a leader of the Salian FRANKS, whose grandson CLOVIS (r. *c.*481–511) ruled over most of France and converted to Christianity. The last Merovingian king was overthrown by PEPIN III, founder of the CAROLINGIAN DYNASTY.

Metaxas, Joannis (1871–1941) Greek general and statesman, prime minister (1936–41). Metaxas was dismissed for pro-German leanings during World War I. As prime minister, Metaxas dissolved parliament and ruled as a virtual dictator. Despite fascist leanings, he led resistance to MUSSOLINI's imperialism.

Metternich, Klemens Wenzel Lothar, Prince von (1773–1859) Austrian statesman. As foreign minister (1809–48) and chancellor (1821–48), Metternich was the leading statesman of the post-Napoleonic era. After NAPOLEON I's retreat from Moscow (1812), Metternich formed the Quadruple Alliance (1813), which led to Napoleon's defeat. He was the dominant figure at the Congress of Vienna (1814–15). In 1815 Metternich secured peace in Europe. He became increasingly autocratic, pressing for intervention against any revolutionary outbreak, and was ousted in the Revolution of 1848.

Michelangelo Buonarroti (1475–1564) Florentine sculptor, painter, architect and poet, one of the outstanding figures of the High Renaissance. He spent five years in Rome where he made his name with a statue of *Bacchus* (1497) and the *Pietà* (1499). In 1501 he returned to Florence where he carved the gigantic *David*.

In 1505 Pope Julius II called him to Rome, where he created the vast painting for the Sistine Chapel ceiling (1508–12), his most sublime achievement. He added *The Last Judgment* later (1536–41). Michelangelo created the magnificent cathedral of St. Peter's, Rome, but died before completing it.

Mies van der Rohe, Ludwig (1886–1969) US architect, b. Germany, a pioneer of modernism. Mies attracted attention in the 1920s with his designs for glass and steel skyscrapers. His German pavilion at the 1929 International Exposition is regarded as one of the most pure examples of geometric architecture. Mies was the last director (1930–33) of the Bauhaus. In 1938 he emigrated to the USA. Mies planned (1942–58) the new campus of the Illinois Institute of Technology, Chicago.

Miguel (1802–66) Portuguese prince and pretender to the throne, younger brother of Peter I. When Peter abdicated (1826) in favor of his infant daughter, MARIA II, he made an agreement with Dom Miguel whereby Miguel would marry Maria and act as her regent. Miguel tried to usurp the throne, beginning the Miguelist Wars. In 1833 Maria's forces finally defeated Miguel. He went into exile and renounced his claims to the throne.

Mill, James (1773–1836) Scottish philosopher, father of John Stuart MILL. He became a friend of Jeremy BENTHAM, and together they evolved the doctrine of utilitarianism. Mill wrote an *Analysis of the Phenomena of the Human Mind* (1829).

Mill, John Stuart (1806–73) Scottish philosopher, son of James MILL. He defended empiricism and inductive logic in *System of Logic* (1843). Mill is chiefly remembered for *On Liberty* (1859), a classic exposition of liberalism. In *Utilitarianism* (1861) he outlined a humanist version of utilitarianism.

Millais, Sir John Everett (1829–96) English painter and illustrator, a founder member of the pre-Raphaelite Brotherhood. His pre-Raphaelite works, such as *Christ in the House of his Parents* (1850), show the Brotherhood's liking for righteous subjects. Later, Millais turned to sentimental subjects, such as *Bubbles* (1886), used as an advertisement by Pears Soap Company.

Miller, Arthur (1915–2005) US dramatist. His Pulitzer Prize-winning play *Death of a Salesman* (1949) is a masterpiece of 20th-century theater. *The Crucible* (1953) is both a dramatic reconstruction of the Salem witch trials and a parable of the McCARTHY era. Miller won a second Pulitzer Prize for *A View From the Bridge* (1955). Married (1955–61) to Marilyn Monroe, he wrote the screenplay for her film *The Misfits* (1961).

Milošević, Slobodan (1941–2006) Serbian statesman, president of Serbia (1989–97), president of Yugoslavia (1997–2000). In 1986 he became head of the Serbian Communist Party. As Serbian president, Milošević confronted the breakup of Yugoslavia. After re-election in 1992, he gave support to the Serb populations in Croatia and Bosnia-Herzegovina, who fought for a Greater Serbia. In November 1995 he signed the Dayton Peace Accord to end the war in former Yugoslavia. In 1998 Milošević ordered Serbian forces to crush a rebellion in the province of Kosovo. In 1999 his refusal to grant autonomy to the majority Albanian population in Kosovo led to NATO air strikes, and the consequent withdrawal of Serb forces from Kosovo. Forced from office in 2000, Milošević war crimes charges at a tribunal in the Hague but died before his trial could be completed.

Milton, John (1608–74) English poet. He was committed to reform of the Church of England, and his pamphlet *Of Reformation in England* (1641) attacked episcopacy. Milton's defense of regicide in *The Tenure of Kings and Magistrates* (1649) earned him a position in Oliver CROMWELL's Commonwealth government. He was forced into hiding after the Restoration (1660). *Paradise Lost*, perhaps the greatest epic poem in English, was first published in 10 books (1667). In 1674 he produced a revised edition in 12 books. Written in blank-verse, it relates the theological stories of Satan's rebellion against God, and Adam and Eve in the Garden of Eden. Its sequel, *Paradise Regained* (1671), was published in four books, and describes Christ's temptation.

Ming dynasty (1368–1644) Imperial Chinese dynasty. It was founded by Chu Yuan-chang (r.1328–98), who expelled the Mongol YUAN dynasty and unified China by 1382. Under the despotic rule of the early Ming emperors, China experienced a period of great artistic and intellectual distinction and economic expansion. Decline began in the late 16th century, and in 1644 a rebel leader took Beijing. A Ming general summoned aid from the MANCHU, who overthrew the dynasty and established their own.

Minoan civilization (c.3000–c.1100 BCE) Ancient Aegean civilization that flourished on Crete, named for the legendary King Minos. The Minoan period is divided into three parts – Early (c.3000–c.2100 BCE), Middle (c.2100–c.1550 BCE) and Late (c.1550–c.1100 BCE). In terms of artistic achievement, Minoan civilization reached its height in the Late period. The prosperity of Bronze Age Crete is evident from the palaces excavated at Knossos and other sites. It was based on trade and seafaring.

Minuit, Peter (1580–1638) First governor of New Netherland, b. Netherlands. He bought Manhattan Island (1626) for the Dutch West India Company from Native Americans for US$24 worth of trinkets.

Miranda, Francisco de (1750–1816) Venezuelan revolutionary. Miranda served in the Spanish army but fled to the USA after accusations of financial irregularities. He gained limited English and Russian support for a rebellion against Spanish rule in Central and South America. In1806 he led an uprising against Spanish rule in Venezuela but was forced to turn back. Returning to Venezuela, he declared its independence in 1811. Forced to negotiate with the Spanish, Miranda was arrested and died in prison.

Miró, Joan (1893–1983) Spanish painter and graphic artist. His *Catalan Landscape* (1923) shows an affinity with abstract art and primitivism. In 1924 he became a member of the surrealism movement, with works such as *Dog barking at the moon* (1926).

Mishima, Yukio (1925–70) Japanese writer. His *Confessions of a Mask* (1949) is a semiautobiographical study of homosexuality. His final work, the four-volume *The Sea of Fertility* (1965), is an epic of modern Japan. He committed ritual suicide at Tokyo's military headquarters, which he had occupied with his private army.

Mithridates VI (132–63 BCE) King of Pontus (120–63 BCE). He attempted to extend his rule southward but was repeatedly defeated by the Romans. He was overwhelmed by the forces of SULLA in the war of 88–85 BCE and lost his kingdom in a second campaign in 83–82. He reconquered it in 74 but was defeated by POMPEY in 66 and fled to the Bosporus. He was planning an invasion of Italy when his troops mutinied, and he committed suicide.

Mitterrand, François Maurice Marie (1916–96) French statesman, president (1981–96). He united the parties of the left. In 1981 Mitterrand defeated the incumbent GISCARD D'ESTAING. He was reelected in 1988. Mitterrand introduced reforms, including the abolition of capital punishment, and favored state intervention in the economy. In the 1980s he changed course. Nationalization ceased and some industries returned to private ownership. He was forced further right after 1986, when he had to cooperate with Gaullist prime minister Jacques CHIRAC. Mitterrand was a supporter of the European Union (EU).

Mobutu Sese Seko (1930–97) Zairean statesman, president (1970–97), b. Joseph-Désiré Mobutu. He was defense minister under Patrice LUMUMBA. In 1960 he deposed Lumumba. In 1965 Mobutu seized power in a military coup. His calls for Africanization were largely publicity stunts. The reality of his autocratic rule was a state founded on corruption. Mobutu amassed a huge personal fortune, while Zaireans became increasingly impoverished. With the support of France, the CIA and the criminal activities of his security forces, Mobutu maintained his dictatorship for more than 30 years. In May 1997 he was deposed in a Tutsi-dominated revolt, led by Laurent Kabila. He died in exile.

Mochica Ancient civilization of N Peru, sometimes called "Early Chimú". It dates from the latter part of the Early Intermediate Period (c.200 BCE–CE 600). Named for their home area in the Moche Valley, the people were famous for their pottery.

Molière (1622–73) French playwright, b. Jean-Baptiste Poquelin. An accurate observer of contemporary manners, he is regarded as the founder of modern French comedy. Molière's best-known comedies include *Tartuffe* (1661), *The Misanthrope* (1667) and *The Miser* (1668).

Molotov, Vyacheslav Mikhailovich (1890–1986) Soviet statesman, premier (1930–41) and foreign minister (1939–49, 1953–56). A loyal ally of STALIN, he became a full member of the Politburo in 1926. As foreign minister, Molotov signed the Nazi-Soviet Pact (1939) with RIBBENTROP. His enthusiastic use of the veto in the UN Security Council contributed to the Cold War. He lost favor under Nikita KHRUSHCHEV and was expelled from the Communist Party in 1962. Molotov was readmitted in 1984.

Monet, Claude (1840–1926) French painter. A founder of impressionism, Monet's piece *Impression, Sunrise* (1872) gave the movement its name. During the 1860s he studied in Paris with RENOIR, Sisley and Bazille. The group painted directly from nature, recording the transient effects of light. Monet often painted the same scene several times, such as the *Gare St-Lazare* (1876–78) and *Rouen Cathedral* (1892–94). Monet's last series, *Water Lilies* (1906–26), is his most vibrant.

Mongols Nomadic people of E central Asia who overran a vast region in the 13th–14th centuries. The different tribes in the area were united by GENGHIS KHAN in the early 13th century and conquered an empire that stretched from the Black Sea to the Pacific Ocean and from Siberia to Tibet. Genghis Khan's possessions were divided among his sons and developed into four khanates, one of which was the empire of KUBLAI KHAN, which included China. In the 14th century TAMERLANE conquered the Persian and Turkish khanates and broke up the Golden Horde. By the end of the century the true Mongol khanates had disappeared.

Monroe, James (1758–1831) Fifth US President (1817–25). He fought in the American Revolution. A friend of Thomas JEFFERSON, he served him loyally in the Senate (1790–94). Monroe helped to negotiate the Louisiana Purchase (1803). He was secretary of state (1811–16) under James MADISON, before becoming president. His first term was marred by disputes over slavery, which resulted in the Missouri Compromise. His foreign policy successes included an agreement with Britain on the US-Canada border. He is chiefly remembered for the Monroe Doctrine, asserting US authority over the American continent.

Montcalm, Louis-Joseph de Montcalm-Gozon, marquis de (1712–59) French general in North America. Commander in chief of the French army in Canada (1756– 59), he won several victories against the British. In 1759 he held Quebec against a British siege for several months, but when the British, under James WOLFE, climbed the cliffs from the St. Lawrence River to the Plains of Abraham, he was taken by surprise. Both he and Wolfe were killed in the battle.

Monteverdi, Claudio (1567–1643) Italian composer, the last and greatest master of the madrigal. Monteverdi introduced greater dramatic power and characterization to the opera form. His surviving operas include *Orfeo* (1607) and *The Coronation of Poppea* (1642). He is also remembered for his *Vespers* (1610).

Montezuma I AZTEC emperor (r.1440–69). During his reign, he increased the Aztec empire by conquest.

Montezuma II (1466–1520) Last AZTEC emperor (r.1502–20). He allowed the Spaniards under Hernán CORTÉS to enter his capital, Tenochtitlán, unopposed in 1519 and became their captive.

Montgolfier, Joseph Michel (1740–1810) and **Jacques Étienne** (1745–99) French inventors of the hot-air balloon. In 1782 the brothers experimented with paper and linen balloons filled with hot gases collected over a fire. In November 1783 the Montgolfier brothers launched the first balloon to carry humans.

Montgomery, Bernard Law, 1st Viscount Montgomery of Alamein (1887–1976) British field marshal. As commander of the British Eighth Army in World War II, he defeated ROMMEL and the Afrika Korps at El Alamein. He led the invasion of Sicily and Italy. "Monty"helped to plan the Normandy landings (1944) and, under the overall command of General EISENHOWER, led the Allied forces in the initial stages.

Moore, Henry (1898–1986) English sculptor and graphic artist. The most characteristic features of his art are hollowed-out or pierced spaces, such as *Reclining Figure* (1938). One of his favorite themes was the mother and child.

More, Sir Thomas (1478–1535) English scholar and statesman. He was a leading exponent of humanism. More's most famous work, *Utopia* (1516), portrays an ideal state founded on reason. In 1529 More succeeded Cardinal Wolsey as lord chancellor. In 1532 he resigned, unhappy at Henry VIII's break with the pope. More enraged the king by refusing to subscribe to the Act of Supremacy (1534), making the king head of the English Church, and he was executed for treason.

Morrison, Toni (1931–) US writer, b. Chloe Anthony Wofford. Her chronicles of African-American experience in the rural South include *Song of Solomon* (1977) and *Tar Baby* (1981). *Beloved* (1987), a powerful indictment of slavery, won a Pulitzer Prize. In 1993 she was awarded the Nobel Prize for Literature.

Morse, Samuel Finley Breese (1791–1872) US inventor of the Morse code. A successful artist, he became interested in developing a practical electric telegraph in *c.*1832. His receiver was based on an electromagnet. Using a simple system of dots and dashes, now known as the Morse code, he set up the first US telegraph from Washington to Baltimore in 1844.

Mozart, Wolfgang Amadeus (1756–91) Austrian composer. A child prodigy on the piano, Mozart was taken by his father, Leopold, on performing tours in Europe (1762–65), during which he composed his first symphonies. In the 1770s he worked at the prince archbishop's court in Salzburg. Masses, symphonies and his first major piano concerto date from this time. In the 1780s he moved to Vienna, becoming court composer to the Austrian emperor in 1787. In this decade, he composed his greatest piano concertos, the last eight of his 41 symphonies and the brilliant comic operas *Le Nozze di Figaro* (1786), *Don Giovanni* (1787) and *Così fan tutti* (1790). In the last year of his life, Mozart wrote the operas *Die Zauberflöte* and *La Clemenza di Tito*, the clarinet concerto and the *Requiem* (completed by a pupil).

Mubarak, Hosni (1928–) Egyptian statesman, president (1981–). He was vice-president (1975–81) under Anwar SADAT and became president on his assassination. Mubarak continued Sadat's moderate policies, improving relations with Israel and the west. In 1989 he gained Egypt's readmission to the Arab League. Mubarak struggled to contain the rise of Islamic fundamentalism.

Mugabe, Robert Gabriel (1925–) Zimbabwean statesman, prime minister (1980–), president (1987–). In 1961 he became deputy secretary-general of the Zimbabwe African People's Union (ZAPU). In 1963 Mugabe was forced into exile and cofounded the Zimbabwe African National Union (ZANU). He was imprisoned (1964–74) by Ian Smith's white minority Rhodesian regime. After his release, he agitated for majority rule from Mozambique. In 1976 ZAPU and ZANU merged to form the Patriotic Front, which became the first black majority government. During the 1980s Mugabe shifted away from communism. He succeeded Canaan Banana as president. Mugabe won Zimbabwe's first multiparty elections (1990).

Mughal empire (1526–1857) Muslim empire in India. It was founded by BABUR, who conquered Delhi and Agra (1526). The Mughal empire reached its height (1542–1605) under AKBAR I (THE GREAT), Babur's grandson, when it extended from Afghanistan to the Bay of Bengal and as far south as the Deccan. Religious tolerance encouraged by Akbar was reduced under his successors, Jahangir (r.1605–27), SHAH JAHAN (1627–58) and AURANGZEB (1658–1707). Mughal art and architecture reached a peak under Shah Jahan, builder of the Taj Mahal. By the death of Aurangzeb, the power of the Mughal dynasty was being supplanted by the Hindu MARATHAS. In 1858 the last Mughal emperor was deposed by the British after the Indian Mutiny.

Muhammad (*c.*570–632) Arab prophet and inspirational religious leader who founded Islam. He was born in the Arabian city of Mecca. At the age of 25, he began working as a trading agent for Khadijah, a wealthy widow of 40, whom he married. For 25 years, she was his closest companion and gave birth to several children. Only one brought him descendants – his daughter Fatima, who became the wife of his cousin, ALI. In *c.*610 Muhammad had a vision while meditating. A voice commanded him to "recite" and he heard the words of the first of many revelations that came to him in several similar visions. The revelations came from Allah, or God, and Muhammad's followers believe that they were passed to him through the angel Gabriel. At the core of his new religion was the doctrine that there is no God but Allah and His followers must submit to Him – the word *islam* means "submission". Muhammad gained followers but also many enemies among the Meccans. In 622 he fled to Medina. Muslims, followers of Islam, later took this *Hejira* as initiating the first year in their calendar. Muhammad organized rules for the proper worship of Allah and for Islamic society. He made war against his enemies and conquered Mecca in 630. In Medina, he married Aishah, the daughter of Abu Bakr, one of his supporters. Muhammad never claimed supernatural powers and is not held to be divine.

Muhammad Ali (1769–1849) Albanian soldier who founded an Egyptian dynasty. In 1798 he took part in an OTTOMAN expeditionary force sent to Egypt to drive out the French. He was unsuccessful but after the departure of the French quickly rose to power. In 1805 he was proclaimed the Ottoman sultan's viceroy. In 1811 he defeated the MAMELUKES. He put down a rebellion in Greece in 1821, but his fleet was later destroyed by the European powers at the battle of Navarino in 1827. Muhammad challenged the sultan and began the conquest of Syria in 1831. European powers again intervened, and he was forced to withdraw.

Muhammad V (1909–61) Sultan (1927–57) and King of Morocco (1957–61). A member of the Filali dynasty, he sympathized with those who wanted freedom from the French. Deposed and exiled by the French in 1953, he returned in 1955 and was recognized as sultan. He adopted the title of king in 1957.

Muller, Hermann Joseph (1890–1967) US geneticist. He found that he could artificially increase the rate of mutations in the fruit fly (*Drosophila*) by the use of X-rays. He thus highlighted the human risk in exposure to radioactive material. In 1946 he was awarded the Nobel Prize for physiology or medicine.

Munch, Edvard (1863–1944) Norwegian painter and printmaker. He inspired expressionism with his tortured, isolated figures and violent coloring. He compiled a series of studies of love and death entitled *Frieze of Life*; it included *The Scream* (1893).

Murasaki, Shikibu (978–1014) Japanese diarist and novelist. She is best known for her novel *The Tale of Genji* (c.1000), which is one of the first works of fiction written in Japanese.

Murat, Joachim (1767–1815) French general, king of Naples (1808–15). He helped bring NAPOLEON to power in the coup of 1799. In 1808 he succeeded Joseph Napoleon as king of Naples. A brilliant cavalry commander, Murat played an important part in Napoleon I's victories but in 1813 came to an agreement with the Austrians to protect his own throne. When the Austrians turned against him, he was defeated, captured and shot.

Mussadegh, Muhammad (1880–1967) Iranian statesman. He served in various public offices but retired when Reza PAHLAVI rose to dictatorial power in 1925. Mussadegh resumed government service in 1944, becoming prime minister in 1951. Political and economic crises caused his downfall in 1953. He was imprisoned (1953–56) then placed under house arrest for the rest of his life.

Mussolini, Benito (1883–1945) Italian fascist dictator, prime minister (1922–43). Mussolini founded the Italian fascist movement in 1919. In 1922 the fascists' march on Rome secured his appointment as prime minister. Mussolini imposed one-party government with himself as *Il Duce*, or dictator. His movement was a model for Adolf HITLER's Nazi Party, with whom Mussolini formed an alliance in 1936. Imperial ambitions led to the conquest of Ethiopia (1935–36) and the invasion of Albania (1939). Mussolini delayed entering World War II until a German victory seemed probable in 1940. A succession of defeats led to his fall from power. In April 1945, fleeing Allied forces, he was captured and killed by Italian partisans.

Mussorgsky, Modest Petrovich (1839–81) Russian composer, one of the "Russian Five" who promoted nationalism in Russian music. His finest work is the opera *Boris Godunov* (1868–69).

Mycenaean civilization Ancient Bronze age civilization (c.1580–1120 BCE) centered around Mycenae, s Greece. The Mycenaeans entered Greece from the N, bringing with them advanced techniques, particularly in architecture and metallurgy. By 1400 BCE, having invaded Crete and incorporated much of MINOAN CIVILIZATION, the Mycenaeans became the dominant power in the Aegean. It is uncertain why the Mycenaean civilization collapsed, but it was most likely due to invasion by the Dorians.

N

Nabokov, Vladimir (1899–1977) US novelist, b. Russia. In 1919 he left Russia and settled in Germany. The rise of fascism forced him to flee to France then the USA (1940). Nabokov's best-selling novel, *Lolita* (1955), is a controversial, lyrical novel about an old man's desire for a 12-year old "nymphette".

Nadir Shah (1688–1747) Ruler of Persia (1736–47). After seizing the throne he embarked upon a series of wars against neighboring states. Nadir invaded India and conducted campaigns against Russia and Turkey. Nadir's ceaseless warring ruined Persia's economy. He was assassinated by his own soldiers.

Nagy, Imre (1896–1958) Hungarian statesman, premier (1953–55, 1956). He enacted liberal reforms. Under pressure from the Soviet Union, Nagy was dismissed from the Hungarian Communist Party. The Hungarian Revolution (1956) led to his reinstatement as premier. Soviet tanks crushed the uprising and handed power to János Kádár. Nagy was executed for treason.

Nanak (1469–1539) Indian spiritual teacher, founder and first guru of Sikhism. He preached a monotheistic religion that combined elements from both Hinduism and Islam. In 1519 Nanak built the first Sikh temple in Kartarpur, Punjab. His teachings are contained in a number of hymns in the Adi Granth.

Napoleon I (1769–1821) (Napoléon Bonaparte) Emperor of the French (1804–15), b. Corsica, one of the greatest military leaders of modern times. In 1796 Napoleon married Joséphine de Beauharnais and was given command in Italy, where he defeated the Austrians and Sardinians. In 1798 he launched an invasion of Egypt, but was defeated by NELSON at the battle of Aboukir Bay. In 1799 Napoleon returned to Paris, where his coup of 18 Brumaire (9 November) overthrew the Directory and set up the Consulate. As First Consul, he enacted domestic reforms such as the Code Napoléon, while defeating the Austrians at Marengo (1800) and making peace with the British at Amiens (1802). Efforts to extend French power led to the Napoleonic Wars (1803–15). After the battle of Trafalgar (1805) Britain controlled the seas, but Napoleon's Grand Army continued to score notable land victories at Austerlitz (1805) and Jena (1806). The Continental System attempted to defeat Britain by a commercial blockade. In 1810, after obtaining a divorce from Joséphine, Napoleon married MARIE LOUISE. In 1812 Napoleon invaded Russia with a million-man army. Forced to retreat by hunger, more than 400,000 soldiers perished. In 1813 Napoleon was routed by a European coalition at Leipzig. In March 1814 Paris was captured and Napoleon was exiled to Elba. In March 1815 he escaped and returned to France, overthrowing LOUIS XVIII. The Hundred Days of his return to power ended with defeat at the battle of Waterloo (June 1815). Napoleon was exiled to St. Helena.

Napoleon III (1808–73) (Louis Napoleon) Emperor of the French (1852–70), nephew of NAPOLEON I. He twice attempted a coup in France (1836, 1840). Returning from exile after the February Revolution (1848), Napoleon was elected president of the Second Republic. In 1851 he assumed autocratic powers and established the Second Empire (1852), taking the title Napoleon III. His attempt to establish a Mexican empire under Archduke

MAXIMILIAN ended in disaster. In 1870 Napoleon was provoked by BISMARCK into the Franco-Prussian War (1870–71). Defeat at Sedan was followed by a republican rising that ended his reign.

Nash, John (1752–1835) English architect and town planner, an important figure in the Regency style. Nash designed Regent's Park and Regent Street, London, enlarged Buckingham Palace, and rebuilt the Royal Pavilion, Brighton (1815–23).

Nasser, Gamal Abdel (1918–70) Egyptian soldier and statesman, prime minister (1954–56) and first president of the republic of Egypt (1956–70). Nasser led the 1952 army coup against King FAROUK. He ousted the nominal prime minister Muhammad Neguib and assumed presidential powers. In 1956 the nationalization of the Suez Canal prompted an abortive Anglo-French and Israeli invasion. Nasser emerged as champion of the Arab world. He formed the short-lived United Arab Republic (1958–61) with Syria. Nasser briefly resigned after Israel won the Six Day War (1967). The crowning achievement of his brand of Arab socialism was the completion of the Aswan dam (1970).

Natchez Tribe of Muskogean-speaking Native Americans of the southern Mississippi region. Today, only a handful of Natchez people survive in Oklahoma.

Nazca Native American civilization that flourished in coastal valleys of s Peru between 200 BCE and CE 600. It is noted for enigmatic lines and figures marked out on desert plateaus.

Nebuchadnezzar II (c.630–562 BCE) Second and greatest king of the Chaldaean (New Babylonian) empire (r.605–562 BCE). He subjugated Syria and Palestine but was defeated by Egyptian forces (601). Nebuchadnezzar occupied Judah, capturing Jerusalem (597) and installing Zedekiah on the throne. In 586, after Zedekiah's rebellion, Nebuchadnezzar destroyed the city and Temple of Jerusalem and deported the Jews to Babylon (the start of the Babylonian Captivity). Nebuchadnezzar launched a major building program in Babylon. According to legend, he built the famous Hanging Gardens for his Median wife.

Necker, Jacques (1732–1804) French financier and statesman, b. Switzerland. He was finance minister (1776–81) under LOUIS XVI. Dismissed, he was recalled to deal with a financial crisis in 1788 and advised calling the States General. The political demands of the Third Estate caused Necker's second dismissal, but the consequent riots, leading to the storming of the Bastille, forced Louis XVI to reappoint him. Unable to prevent the French Revolution, he resigned in 1790.

Nehru, Jawaharlal (1889–1964) Indian statesman, prime minister of India (1947–64), father of Indira GANDHI. He succeeded his father Motilal Nehru (1861–1931) as president of the Congress Party in 1929. Nehru and "Mahatma" GANDHI led nationalist opposition to British rule in India. Nehru was imprisoned nine times for noncooperation with the British. He played a leading role in the negotiations with Mountbatten and Jinnah that led to the independence of India and Pakistan. As the first prime minister of an independent India, Nehru became a respected leader of the Third World.

Nelson, Horatio, Viscount (1758–1805) British admiral. Nelson fought in the American Revolution. At the start of the French Revolutionary Wars, he was given command (1793) of the *Agamemnon*. In 1794 Nelson lost the sight of his right eye in the capture of Calvi, Corsica. In 1797 he defeated the Spanish fleet at the battle of Cape St. Vincent (1797). Nelson lost his right arm in battle at Santa Cruz. In 1798 he commanded the squadron that pursued NAPOLEON Bonaparte's expedition to Egypt. Nelson's victory at the battle of Aboukir Bay (1798) destroyed Napoleon's hopes of capturing Britain's eastern empire. Nelson received a hero's welcome at Naples and began his long love affair with Lady Hamilton, wife of the British ambassador. He crushed the Danish fleet at the battle of Copenhagen (1801). At the start of the Napoleonic Wars, he was given command (1803) of the fleet in the Mediterranean. In the *Victory*, Nelson defeated the combined French and Spanish navies at the battle of Trafalgar (21 October, 1805). He died in the process of securing a brilliant victory.

Nero, Claudius Caesar (CE 37–68) Roman emperor (54–68), b. Lucius Domitius Ahenobarbus. In CE 49 his mother, AGRIPPINA, married her uncle Emperor CLAUDIUS and persuaded him to adopt Nero as his successor. In 54 Claudius and his natural son, Britannicus, were murdered. Under the guidance of SENECA, Nero pursued moderate policies and his early reign was heralded as a new golden age. In 59 he ordered the murder of his mother. Nero neglected government affairs in favor of sex, poetry, sport, music and cult practices. In 65 a plot to overthrow him (Conspiracy of Piso) was foiled. In 68 he established the worship of Apollo and freed the slaves. Nero failed to quell a series of revolts and his Praetorian Guard abandoned him. He committed suicide.

Neruda, Pablo (1904–73) Chilean poet, b. Neftalí Ricardo Reyes. He identified with the impoverished masses and was active in politics. His best-known work is the epic *Canto General* (1950). In 1971 Neruda was awarded the Nobel Prize for literature.

Nerva, Marcus Cocceus (*c.*CE 30–98) Roman emperor (CE 96–98). He denounced his predecessor, DOMITIAN, as a tyrant. Nerva reformed the agrarian laws and ensured the smooth accession of his successor, TRAJAN.

Netanyahu, Binyamin (1949–) Israeli statesman, prime minister (1996–99). He served as a permanent representative to the UN (1984–88). In 1993 Netanyahu became leader of the rightwing Likud Party. After the assassination of Yitzhak RABIN, Netanyahu was elected prime minister of a coalition government. His uncompromising leadership and Likud's opposition to the Israeli-Palestinian Accord threatened to disrupt the peace process. In 1999 elections Netanyahu was defeated.

Newcomen, Thomas (1663–1729) English engineer. In 1712 he constructed the first practical steam engine, consisting of a piston moved by atmospheric pressure within a cylinder in which a partial vacuum had been created by condensing steam.

Newman, John Henry (1801–90) English cardinal. As leader of the Oxford Movement (1833–45), Newman had a powerful effect on the Church of England, equaled only by the shock of his conversion to Roman Catholicism (1845). He is remembered especially for his autobiography, *Apologia pro vita sua* (1864).

Newton, Sir Isaac (1642–1727) English scientist. In *Philosophiae Naturalis Principia Mathematica* (1687), Newton outlined his three laws of motion and proposed the principle of universal gravitation. In *Opticks* (1704), he proposed his particle theory of light. In the 1660s he devised a system of calculus but did not publish it until Gottfried LEIBNIZ had published his own system in 1684. In *c.*1671 he built the first reflecting telescope. In 1705 Newton became the first person to be knighted for scientific work. His theory of celestial mechanics remained unchallenged until EINSTEIN's theory of relativity and quantum mechanics.

Nicholas I (1796–1855) Czar of Russia (1825–55). As czar, he was confronted by the Decembrist revolt, during which a secret society of officers and aristocrats assembled some 3,000 troops in St. Petersburg, demanding a representative democracy. Having crushed the rebels, Nicholas suppressed rebellion in Poland and assisted Austria against the Hungarian Revolutions of 1848. His pressure on Turkey led to the Crimean War (1853–56).

Nicholas II (1868–1918) Last czar of Russia (1894–1917). Torn between the autocracy of his father, ALEXANDER III, and the reformist policies of his ministers, he lacked the capacity for firm leadership. Defeat in the Russo-Japanese War was followed by the Russian Revolution of 1905. Nicholas agreed to constitutional government but removed most of the powers of the Duma. A succession of defeats in World War I provoked the Russian Revolution (1917). Nicholas was forced to abdicate, and in July 1918 he and his family were executed by the Bolsheviks.

Nietzsche, Friedrich Wilhelm (1844–1900) German philosopher who rejected Christianity and the morality of his time and emphasized people's freedom to create their own values. In *Thus Spake Zarathustra* (1883–91), Nietzsche presented his notion of the *Übermensch* (superman), the idealized man, strong, positive, and able to impose his wishes upon the weak and worth-

less. The concept was distorted by the Nazis to justify their notion of Aryan superiority. Other works include *Beyond Good and Evil* (1886). In 1889 Nietzsche was declared insane.

Nightingale, Florence (1820–1910) British nurse, b. Italy. She founded modern nursing and became known as the "lady of the lamp" for her activities in the Crimean War. In 1854 Nightingale took a unit of 38 nurses to care for wounded British soldiers.

Nijinsky, Vaslav (1890–1950) Russian ballet dancer and choreographer. In 1909 Nijinsky joined DIAGHILEV's Ballets Russes. Michel Fokine choreographed *The Specter of the Rose* and *Petrushka* (both 1911) for him. Nijinsky's radical choreography of Stravinsky's *The Rite of Spring* (1913) outraged audiences.

Nixon, Richard Milhous (1913–94) 37th US President (1969–74). He came to prominence as a member of the House Un-American Activities Committee (HUAC). Nixon was vice-president under Dwight D. EISENHOWER (1953–61) but lost the presidential election of 1960 to John F. KENNEDY. In 1968 he narrowly defeated his Democrat challenger. As president, he adopted a policy of *détente* with the Soviet Union and opened US relations with communist China. Overwhelmingly reelected in 1972, he withdrew US troops from the Vietnam War (1973). Nixon was personally implicated in the obstruction of justice in the Watergate affair (1972–74) and resigned to avoid impeachment. He was pardoned by his successor, Gerald FORD.

Nkrumah, Kwame (1909–72) Ghanaian statesman, prime minister (1957–60) and president (1960–66). He was the leading postcolonial proponent of Pan-Africanism. In 1949 Nkrumah formed the Convention People's Party in the Gold Coast. He was imprisoned (1950–52) by the British, but released when his party won the general election. He led the Gold Coast to independence (1957) and became prime minister. In 1960 Gold Coast became the Republic of Ghana and Nkrumah was made president. Nkrumah gradually assumed absolute power and, following a series of assassination attempts, Ghana became a one-party state (1964). He was deposed in a military coup (1966).

Nobel, Alfred Bernhard (1833–96) Swedish chemist, engineer and industrialist. In 1866 Nobel invented dynamite. In 1876 he patented a more powerful explosive, gelignite. With the fortune he made from explosives, he founded the Nobel prizes.

Noriega, Manuel Antonio Morena (1934–) Panamanian statesman and general, head of state (1983–89). In 1963 he became head of Panama's National Defense Forces. Recruited as a CIA operative by the USA, Noriega became an important backstage powerbroker. For most of the 1980s he was effectively Panama's paramount leader. In 1987 evidence emerged of Noriega's criminal activities, and the USA withdrew its support. In 1988 he was indicted by a US court on drug-connected charges and accused of murder. In December 1989 US troops invaded Panama and installed a civilian government. Noriega surrendered. In April 1992 he was sentenced to 40 years in prison.

Norodom Sihanouk (1922–) Cambodian statesman, king (1941–55, 1993– 2004), prime minister (1955–60) and head of state (1960–70, 1975–76, 1991–93). In 1955 he abdicated to become head of a socialist government. In 1960 Sihanouk became head of state. In 1970 he was deposed by Lon Nol in a right-wing military coup. In 1975 he returned from exile when the Khmer Rouge took over, first supporting, then opposing their regime. In 1979, after the Vietnamese invasion, Sihanouk formed a government-in-exile. In 1993 UN peacekeepers withdrew from Cambodia and Sihanouk was reinstated as a constitutional monarch. In 2004 he abdicated in favor of his son Norodom Sihamoni.

North, Frederick, Lord (1732–92) British statesman, prime minister (1770–82). North was lord of the treasury (1770–82) and chancellor of the exchequer (1767–70) before becoming prime minister under GEORGE III. His repressive measures against the North American colonies, particularly the Intolerable Acts (Coercive Acts), have been blamed for precipitating the American Revolution. He was forced to resign in 1783.

North, Oliver Laurence (1943–) US marine lieutenant

colonel. In 1987 a Congressional committee named North as the central figure in the Iran-Contra Affair – a secret agreement to sell weapons to Iran via Israel in order to secure the release of US hostages. Funds from the sale were diverted to support the Nicaraguan Contras bid to overthrow Daniel ORTEGA. North was convicted of three criminal charges, including obstructing Congress. In 1992 North was pardoned by President George BUSH.

Nureyev, Rudolf (1938–93) Russian ballet dancer and choreographer. In 1961, while on tour in Paris, he defected from the Soviet Union. Nureyev was noted for his spectacular technical virtuosity and dramatic character portrayal.

Nurhachi (1559–1626) Organizer and creator of the Manchu state in China. In 1615 Nurhaci welded related tribes into a powerful unit, creating the Manchu military banner organization for control and mobilization. He also introduced a writing system.

Nyerere, Julius Kambarage (1922–99) Tanzanian statesman, first president of Tanzania (1964–85). In 1961 Nyerere led Tanganyika to independence. In 1964 he negotiated the union between Tanganyika and Zanzibar that created Tanzania. Nyerere established a one-party state. In 1979 Nyerere sent troops into Uganda to topple the regime of Idi AMIN. Economic setbacks led to calls for greater democracy and he was forced to retire.

O

Obote, (Apollo) Milton (1924–2005) Ugandan statesman, prime minister (1962–66) and president (1967–71, 1981–85). In 1962 he became the first prime minister of an independent Uganda. In 1966 Obote became president of a more centralized state. In 1971 he was ousted by his army chief, Idi AMIN. Obote returned to power after Amin was overthrown. In 1985 he was overthrown in a further military coup.

Obregón, Álvaro (1880–1928) Mexican statesman, president (1920–24). Obregón supported Francisco MADERO's revolution against Porfirio DÍAZ. When Madero was overthrown by Victoriano HUERTA, Obregón joined forces with Venustiano CARRANZA, "Pancho" VILLA and Emiliano ZAPATA to defeat Huerta. A capable president, he enacted some notable reforms. In 1928 Obregón was reelected but assassinated before he could take office.

Obrenović dynasty (1815–42, 1858–1903) Serbian ruling family. In 1815 Miloš Obrenović (1780–1860) led the Serbian revolt against the Turks. In 1817 the murder of KARAGEORGE was probably instigated by Miloš. In 1839 he was succeeded as prince of Serbia by his son, **Michael Obrenović** (1823–68). In 1842 Michael was deposed by Alexander Karageorge. In 1858 Miloš returned to the throne. He was again succeeded by Michael, who completed the liberation of Serbia. Michael was assassinated and his nephew, **Milan Obrenović** (1854–1901), succeeded. At the Congress of Berlin (1878) Milan obtained recognition of Serbian independence. In 1878 he declared himself King of Serbia. The failure of the war against Bulgaria (1878) increased his unpopularity and he abdicated (1889) in favor of his son, **Alexander Obrenović** (1873–1903). Alexander was assassinated in a military coup. PETER Karageorge succeeded as PETER I.

Odoacer (c.435–93) (Odovacar) Chief of the Germanic Heruli people and conqueror of the West ROMAN EMPIRE. The Heruli were Roman mercenaries until 476, when they declared Odoacer king of Italy. In 489 the Ostrogoths, led by THEODORIC, invaded. Odoacer was murdered at a banquet given by Theordoric.

Oglethorpe, James Edward (1696–1785) English general and colonist. In 1732 Oglethorpe received a charter to establish a colony for debtors in America. In 1733 he set sail with 116 debtors, who settled in Savannah and founded the colony of Georgia. In 1742 he defeated his Spanish neighbors in Florida.

O'Higgins, Bernardo (1778–1842) South American revolutionary leader and ruler of Chile. He commanded the Chilean army against the Spanish. Defeated in 1814, he joined José de SAN MARTÍN in Argentina to defeat the Spanish at Chacabuco (1817). Appointed"supreme director"of Chile, he declared independence in 1818 but resigned in 1823.

Ohm, Georg Simon (1787–1854) German physicist. In 1827 Ohm proposed a rule linking current, electromotive force and resistance in an electric circuit. Ohm's law is expressed mathematically as $V = IR$, where V = voltage, I = current and R = resistance. The SI unit of electrical resistance is named for him.

Olaf II (995–1030) King of Norway (1015–29). His introduction of Christianity prompted a revolt of chiefs, backed by CANUTE II of Denmark. Olaf was forced into exile and killed in battle. In 1164, following reports of miracles at his grave, he was made patron saint of Norway.

Olaf V (1903–91) King of Norway (1957–91), son and successor of HAAKON VII. During World War II he played an active role in the liberation of Norway from Nazi occupation.

Olmec Early civilization of Central America, which flourished between the 12th and 4th centuries BCE. Its heartland was the S coast of the Gulf of Mexico, but its influence spread widely. From the 9th century BCE the Olmec center was La Venta. Olmec art included high-quality carving of jade and stone. The Olmec heritage can be traced through later civilizations, notably the MAYA.

Omar (581–644) (Umar) Second caliph. In 618 he was converted to Islam and became a counselor of MUHAMMAD. In 632 Omar helped chose the first caliph, ABU BAKR. In 634 he succeeded Abu Bakr. Under Omar's rule, Islam spread by into Syria, Egypt and Iran, and the foundations of an empire were laid.

Omar Khayyám (1048–1131) Iranian poet, mathematician and astronomer. His fame in the West is due to a free-verse translation of his epigrammatic lyrics, *The Rubáiyát of Omar Khayyám* (1859), by Edward Fitzgerald.

O'Neill, Eugene Gladstone (1888–1953) US dramatist. His first full-length play, *Beyond the Horizon* (1920), won a Pulitzer Prize, as did *Anna Christie* (1921). O'Neill won a third Pulitzer Prize for *Strange Interlude* (1928). In 1936 he was awarded the Nobel Prize in literature. O'Neill won a posthumous Pulitzer Prize for *Long Day's Journey into Night* (1956).

Oppenheimer, (Julius) Robert (1904–67) US nuclear physicist. As director (1943–45) of the Los Alamos laboratory in New Mexico, Oppenheimer headed the Manhattan Project to develop the atomic bomb. He argued for joint US-Soviet control of nuclear weapons. In 1949 he opposed the making of the hydrogen bomb.

Ortega (Saavedra), Daniel (1945–) Nicaraguan statesman, president (1984–90, 2006–). In 1966 he became leader of the Sandinistas (FSLN). In 1979 Ortega led the revolution that toppled the SOMOZA regime and formed a socialist government. Elected president in 1984, his Sandinista government was destabilized by the US-backed Contra rebels. Violeta Chamorro defeated Ortega in 1990 elections but lost to him in 2006.

Ortega y Gasset, José (1883–1955) Spanish philosopher and humanist. Ortega's most famous work, *The Revolt of the Masses* (1929), advocated government by an intellectual élite. Other works include *Man and People* (1957) and *Man and Crisis* (1956).

Orwell, George (1903–50) British novelist and essayist, b. India as Eric Arthur Blair. Autobiographical works include *Down and Out in Paris and London* (1933), *The Road to Wigan Pier* (1937) and *Homage to Catalonia* (1938). Orwell, however, is best-known for his fictions on totalitarianism: the satirical fable *Animal Farm* (1945) and the dystopic novel *1984* (1949).

Osama bin Laden (1957–) Saudi dissident, leader of al-Qaeda (Arabic, 'the base'), a loose network of terrorist groups. He commanded a group of Arab *mujaheddin* against Soviet troops in Afghanistan. Expelled by the Saudi government in 1991, after denouncing the presence of US soldiers in Saudi Arabia during the Gulf War (1991), bin Laden went first to the Sudan and then to Afghanistan. Linked to several terrorist attacks, in 1998 he called for a religious war against the US. Later that year, he was named as the architect of the bomb attacks on the US embassies in Kenya and Tanzania. The US responded with missile attacks against suspected bases in Sudan and Afghanistan. In 2000 the US accused him of instigating the suicide bomb attack on a US destroyer in Yemen. In 2001 the US linked him to the terrorist attacks on the World Trade

Center, New York City, and the Pentagon, Washington, D.C., which claimed more than 3000 lives. The US declared war on al-Qaeda and the Taliban regime in Afghanistan.

Osman I (1258–1326) Founder of the OTTOMAN EMPIRE. As ruler of the Osmanli, or Ottoman, state in NW Anatolia, he declared independence from the SELJUK sultan in c.1290. Osman expanded his territory in wars against the BYZANTINE EMPIRE.

Ostrogoths Eastern division of the GOTHS. The Ostrogoths settled in the Ukraine, whereas the VISIGOTHS moved west. From c.374 to the death of ATTILA (453) the Ostrogoths were subject to the HUNS. In 493 the Ostrogoths, led by THEODORIC (THE GREAT), assassinated ODOACER and established a kingdom in Italy. In 535, Byzantine general BELISAURUS reconquered Italy.

Otis, Elisha Graves (1811–61) US inventor. In 1856 Otis designed and installed the first passenger lift, in a New York department store.

Otis, James (1725–83) American statesman. In 1761 he was elected to the Massachusetts Assembly. Otis led resistance to the Stamp Act (1765) and the Townshend Acts (1767).

Ottawa Group of Algonquian-speaking Native Americans from the Great Lakes region. The Ottawa controlled trade with French settlers. Their alliance with the French and Huron led to conflict with the IROQUOIS and the Ottawa were dispersed. In 1670, with French protection, they returned to Lake Huron.

Otto I (the Great) (912–73) First Holy Roman Emperor (962–73) and king of the Germans (936–73), son of HENRY I (THE FOWLER). In 941 he defeated the rebellious princes and their ally, Louis IV of France. Otto curbed the power of the nobles by forming a close alliance with the Church. In 951 he invaded Italy to aid Queen Adelaide of Lombardy, married her and became King of Lombardy. In 955, he crushed the MAGYARS at Lechfeld. In 962 Otto entered Rome and was crowned emperor.

Otto IV (1174?–1218) (Otto of Brunswick) Holy Roman Emperor (1198–1215). A member of the GUELPH family, Otto antagonized the Pope INNOCENT III by his invasion of Italy against the HOHENSTAUFEN king Frederick I (later Emperor FREDERICK II). With Innocent's support, Frederick was elected king by the German princes (1212) and supported by PHILIP II of France. Otto was defeated by Philip at Bouvines (1214) and forced to retire.

Otto I (1815–67) First king of the Hellenes (1832–62), son of Louis I of Bavaria. He was chosen by European leaders to become king of an independent Greece. Otto ruled in an autocratic manner until a military coup (1843) forced him to accept a constitution limiting royal powers. He was deposed in 1862.

Ottoman Empire Former Turkish state that controlled much of SE Europe, the Middle East, and North Africa between the 14th and 20th centuries. It was founded by OSMAN I (r.1290–1326). He ruled a small principality in Anatolia, which he greatly enlarged at the expense of the BYZANTINE EMPIRE. The contest with the Byzantines ended with the capture of Constantinople (now Istanbul), which became the Ottoman capital in 1453. Under SULEIMAN I (THE MAGNIFICENT) (r.1520–66), the Ottoman Empire controlled the Arab lands of the Middle East and North Africa, SE Europe, and the E Mediterranean. The decline of Ottoman power began before 1600, and thereafter Ottoman territory was reduced in wars with its European neighbors. After World War I, when Ottoman land was reduced to roughly the Turkish borders, nationalists led by ATATÜRK deposed the last Ottoman sultan and created the modern Turkish republic (1923).

Ovid (43 BCE–CE 18) (Publius Ovidius Naso) Roman poet. Ovid's poems, mainly elegaics, fall into three categories: love poetry, such as *Amores* and *Ars Amatoria*; poems of exile, such as *Tristia*; and mythological poetry, such as his masterpiece, *Metamorphoses*, written in hexameters.

Owen, Robert (1771–1858) Welsh industrialist and social reformer. He believed that better conditions for workers would lead to greater productivity. He put these beliefs into practice at his textile mills in Scotland. Owen attempted to establish a self-contained cooperative community in New Harmony, Indiana, USA. His ideas provided the basis for the cooperative movement.

P

Pahlavi, Muhammad Reza (1919–80) Shah of Iran (1941–79), son of Reza PAHLAVI. With receipts from oil exports, Pahlavi encouraged economic development and social reforms. The westernization of Iran, combined with a repressive regime and social inequalities, aroused discontent among religious fundamentalists. In 1979 a theocratic revolution, led by Ayatollah KHOMEINI, forced him into exile.

Pahlavi, Reza (1878–1944) Shah of Iran and founder of the modern Iranian state. In 1921 he took part in a nationalist coup and built up a modern army as defense minister and prime minister. In 1925 Pahlavi deposed Ahmad Shah and assumed the crown. He enforced extensive social and legal reforms, crushed tribalism and ended the influence in Iran of Britain and the Soviet Union. In 1941, when British and Soviet forces occupied Iran, he abdicated in favor of his son, Muhammad PAHLAVI.

Paine, Thomas (1737–1809) Anglo-American political writer. In 1754 he emigrated from England to Pennsylvania. His pamphlet *Common Sense* (1776) demanded independence for the North American colonies. In 1787 Paine returned to England and published *The Rights of Man* (1791–92), a defense of the French Revolution.

Palladio, Andrea (1508–80) Italian architect. Palladio studied Roman architecture and published his neoclassical designs and drawings of Roman ruins in *Four Books of Architecture* (1570).

Pallava dynasty Rulers of S India from the 4th to the 8th century CE; their capital was at Kanchipuram. Celebrated for its Dravidian architecture, the Pallavas were supplanted by the CHOLA DYNASTY.

Palmerston, Henry John Temple, 3rd Viscount (1784–1865) British statesman, prime minister (1855–58, 1859–65). He entered Parliament as a Tory in 1807, but defected to the Whigs in 1830. As prime minister, Palmerston vigorously prosecuted the Crimean War. In 1856 he initiated the second Opium War against China. In 1858 he ordered the suppression of the Indian Mutiny. Palmerston supported the Confederacy in the US Civil War, but maintained British neutrality. He opposed political reform in Britain.

Pandya dynasty Tamil rulers of S India from the 1st century BCE to the 16th century CE; their capital was at Madurai. In the 9th century the Pandya and the CHOLA combined to defeat the PALLAVA dynasty. The Pandya were the major force in s India during the reign of Jatavarman Sundara (1251–68). In 1311 Madurai was captured by the DELHI SULTANATE and the dynasty waned.

Pankhurst, Emily (Emmeline Goulden) (1858–1928) English leader of the suffragette movement. In 1903 Pankhurst set up the Women's Social and Political Union, supported by her daughters, Christabel (1880–1958) and Sylvia (1882–1960). Their militant tactics courted prosecution, and they gained further publicity in prison by hunger strikes.

Papandreou, Andreas (1919–96) Greek statesman, prime minister (1981–89, 1993–96). He founded the Pan-Hellenic Socialist Movement (PASOK), becoming Greece's first socialist prime minister in 1981. Implicated in a financial fraud, he failed to form a government following the 1989 elections and resigned. Cleared of fraud, Papandreou was reelected in 1993. Costas Simitis succeeded him.

Papineau, Louis Joseph (1786–1871) French-Canadian political leader. His quarrels with Britain, which rejected his plan for greater French-Canadian autonomy, incited his followers to rebellion (1837). He escaped arrest by fleeing to the USA, then to France. Granted an amnesty (1847), he returned to Canada and was a member of the unified legislature (1848–54).

Pappus of Alexandria (active c. CE 300) Greek mathematician. His *Mathematical Collection* (8 vols) is an early commentary on EUCLID and PTOLEMY. He extended PYTHAGORAS' theorem to any triangle.

Paracas Ancient Native American culture of S Peru. There are three distinctive phases (900 BCE–CE 400): Cavernas, Pinilla and Necropolis. Influenced by the CHAVÍN culture, the Paracas produced fine pottery and textiles.

Paracelsus (1493–1541) Swiss physician and alchemist, b. Philippus Aureolus Theophrastus Bombast von Hohenheim. According to Paracelsus, the human body is primarily composed of salt, sulfur and mercury, and it is the separation of these elements that causes illness. He introduced mineral baths.

Paris, Matthew (d.1259) English historian and monk. In c.1236 he succeeded Roger of Wendover as historiographer of the monastery of St. Albans. His *Chronica majora* is an important primary source for the history of the world between 1235 and 1259.

Park Chung Hee (1917–79) South Korean general and statesman, president (1963–79). In 1961 he seized power in a military coup. In 1963 Park was elected president and was reelected in 1967 and 1971. Park was assassinated by the head of the South Korean Central Intelligence Agency.

Parmigiano (1503–40) Northern Italian painter and graphic artist, b. Francesco Mazzola. He was a master of mannerism. Among his best-known works are *Madonna with St. Zachary* (c.1530) and *Vision of St. Jerome* (c.1527).

Parnell, Charles Stewart (1846–91) Irish nationalist leader. In 1875 he entered the British Parliament. Parnell led the parliamentary movement for Irish Home Rule. In 1879 he became president of the National Land League. He was imprisoned in 1881–82. In 1886 he supported GLADSTONE's introduction of the Home Rule Bill. In 1889 his career collapsed when he was cited as corespondent in the divorce of William O'Shea.

Parthians Seminomadic peoples of Persia. In c.248 BCE, led by the Arsacid dynasty, they rebelled against the SELEUCID empire. At its peak, in the 1st century BCE, the Parthian empire extended from the River Euphrates to the Indus. In CE 224 the Parthians were defeated by the SASSANIDS and the empire crumbled.

Pascal, Blaise (1623–62) French scientist and mystic. Pascal and Pierre de FERMAT laid the foundations of the theory of probability. Pascal also contributed to hydrodynamics, devising (1647) a law of fluidic pressure. In 1655 Pascal retired from science to concentrate on his philosophical and religious writing.

Pasternak, Boris (1890–1960) Russian novelist and poet. After the death of STALIN, Pasternak began work on *Dr. Zhivago* (1957). Its themes offended officials, and he was expelled from the Soviet Writers Union. Pasternak was compelled by official pressure to retract his acceptance of the 1958 Nobel Prize for literature.

Pasteur, Louis (1822–95) French chemist. In 1862 his work on bacteria led to the "germ theory" of infection. Pasteur discovered that microorganisms can be destroyed by heat, a technique now known as pasteurization. He also found that he could weaken certain disease-causing microorganisms and then use the weakened culture to provide immunity. In 1881 Pasteur produced the first vaccines against anthrax.

Pauli, Wolfgang (1900–58) US physicist, b. Austria. In 1925 he formulated the exclusion principle that states that no two electrons in an atom can possess the same energy and spin. Pauli received the 1945 Nobel Prize for physics for his contribution to quantum theory. In 1931 he predicted the neutrino's existence.

Pavlov, Ivan Petrovich (1849–1936) Russian neurophysiologist. He received the 1904 Nobel Prize for physiology or medicine for his work on the physiology and neurology of digestion. Pavlov is best known for his studies of conditioning of behavior in dogs. His works include *Conditioned Reflexes* (1927).

Pearse, Patrick Henry (1879–1916) Irish author and political figure. He headed the revival of interest in Gaelic culture. Pearse led the insurgents in the Easter Rising (1916) and was court-martialed and executed by the British authorities.

Pedro I (1798–1834) Emperor of Brazil (1822–31), son of the future King JOHN VI of Portugal. In 1807 he fled with the royal family to Brazil. When his father reclaimed the Portuguese crown (1821), Pedro became prince regent of Brazil and declared it an independent monarchy (1822). His reign was marked by military failure. Pedro abdicated and returned to Portugal, where he secured the succession of his daughter, MARIA II, to the throne.

Pedro II (1825–91) Emperor of Brazil (1831–89). He reigned under a regency until 1840. Pedro's rule was marked by internal unrest and external threats from Argentina and Paraguay. In 1888 slavery was abolished. Pedro's policy was generally

reformist, antagonizing the military. In 1889 he was forced to resign and retire to Europe, while Brazil became a republic.

Peel, Sir Robert (1788–1850) British statesman, prime minister (1834–35, 1841–46). As Tory home secretary, he created (1829) the first modern police force, the Metropolitan Police. Peel was chiefly responsible for passage of the Catholic Emancipation Act (1829). He became converted to the doctrine of free trade, and the Irish famine convinced him of the need to repeal the Corn Laws. The proposal split the Tory Party and Peel resigned. In his second term, he carried through the repeal.

Penn, William (1644–1718) English Quaker leader and founder of Pennsylvania. He was imprisoned four times for his advocacy of religious freedom. In 1681 he persuaded King CHARLES II to honor an unpaid debt by granting him wilderness land in America to be settled by the Quakers and others seeking refuge from religious persecution. The colony was named the Commonwealth of Pennsylvania in his honor.

Pepin II (d.714) Mayor of the palace (680–714) of the Frankish kingdom of Austrasia, father of CHARLES MARTEL. His defeat of the Neustrians at the battle of Tertry (687) marked the ascendancy of the CAROLINGIANS over the MEROVINGIANS.

Pepin III (the Short) (c.714–68) First CAROLINGIAN king of the Franks (750–68), son of CHARLES MARTEL. In 750 he deposed the last MEROVINGIAN king, Childeric III. Pepin defeated the LOMBARDS in 754 and 756. He ceded the conquered territories (the future Papal States) to the papacy in the Donation of Pepin. He was succeeded by his son CHARLEMAGNE.

Pepys, Samuel (1633–1703) English diarist. Pepys' *Diary* (1660–69) describes his private life and contemporary English society. It includes a vivid account of the Restoration, the plague and the Great Fire of London (1666).

Peres, Shimon (1923–) Israeli statesman, prime minister (1984–86, 1995–96), president (2007–), b. Poland. In 1968 Peres helped found the Labor Party and became party leader in 1977. He held ministerial posts under Golda MEIR and Yitzhak RABIN. In 1992, losing the party leadership to Rabin, Peres played a vital role in the Palestinian peace process. On Rabin's assassination (1995), he returned as prime minister but was defeated by NETANYAHU. He became president in 2007 elections.

Pérez de Cuéllar, Javier (1920–) Peruvian diplomat, fifth secretary-general of the United Nations (UN) (1982–91). He emerged as a successful compromise candidate following opposition to the re-election of Kurt WALDHEIM. He earned a reputation for skillful diplomacy in the cease-fire agreements at the end of the Falklands War (1982) and the Iran–Iraq War (1980–88).

Pericles (490–429 BCE) Athenian statesman. He dominated Athens from c.460 BCE to his death, overseeing its golden age. Pericles is associated with achievements in art and literature, including the building of the Parthenon, while strengthening the Athenian empire and government. He initiated the Peloponnesian Wars (431–404 BCE) but died of plague at the outset.

Perón, Eva Duarte de (1919–52) Argentine political leader, first wife of Juan PERÓN. Known as "Evita", she administered Argentina's social welfare agencies. Eva's popularity contributed to the longevity of the Peronist regime.

Perón, Juan Domingo (1895–1974) Argentine statesman, president (1946–55, 1973–74). He was the leading figure in the military junta (1943–46). Perón earned support from the poor by social reforms, greatly assisted by his wife "Evita" PERÓN. He won the 1946 presidential election. Perón's populist program was nationalist and totalitarian. Changing economic circumstances reduced Perón's popularity, and he was overthrown in 1955. He retired to Spain, but returned to regain the presidency.

Perry, Matthew Calbraith (1794–1858) US naval officer. In 1837 he commanded the first steam vessel in the US Navy, the *Fulton*. He was responsible for opening up Japan to the West.

Pershing, John Joseph (1860–1948) US general. In 1916 he led a punitive expedition against "Pancho" VILLA in Mexico. Pershing was commander (1917–19) of the American Expeditionary

Force (AEF) during World War I. He later served as army chief of staff (1921–24).

Pétain, Henri Philippe (1856–1951) French general and political leader. In World War I he led the defense of Verdun (1916) made him a national hero. In 1917 Pétain was appointed commander-in-chief. With the defeat of France in 1940, Pétain was recalled as prime minister. He signed the surrender and became head of the collaborationist Vichy regime. He was charged with treason after the liberation of France in 1945 and died in prison.

Peter I (the Great) (1672–1725) Russian czar (1682–1725). After ruling with his half-brother Ivan (1682–89), he gained sole control in 1689. Peter employed foreign experts to modernize the army, transportation and technology. He compelled the aristocracy and the church to serve the interests of the state, eliminating ancient tradition in favor of modernization. In the Great Northern War (1700–21), Russia replaced Sweden as the dominant power in N Europe and gained land on the Baltic, where he built his capital, St. Petersburg. In the E, he initiated the exploration of Siberia.

Peter III (1728–62) Russian czar (1762). During his six-month reign, he returned East Prussia voluntarily to FREDERICK II, whom he admired, thus losing all the territory that Russia had gained during the Seven Years War. Peter was dethroned and murdered in a conspiracy led by the brothers Orlov and probably encouraged by his wife and successor, CATHERINE II (THE GREAT).

Peter I (1844–1921) King of Serbia (1903–18) and king of the Serbs, Croats and Slovenes (1918–21), son of Alexander Karajordjević. He was brought up in exile while the OBRENOVIĆ DYNASTY ruled Serbia. Peter became king of Serbia after the assassination of Alexander Obrenović. He reformed Serbian social and political institutions. Peter became the first king of the new kingdom of Serbs, Croats and Slovenes.

Petrarch (1304–74) Italian poet and humanist, b. Francesco Petrarca. In 1327 he met Laura, the inspiration for some of literature's greatest love lyrics. In 1341 Petrarch was crowned laureate. He was a master of the sonnet form.

Phidias (c.490–c.430 BCE) Greek sculptor. No surviving originals can be definitely attributed to him. Phidias is celebrated for two gigantic chryselephantine statues, one of *Athena* for the Parthenon and the other of *Zeus* for the temple at Olympia.

Philip II (Augustus) (1165–1223) King of France (1180–1223). He increased the royal domain by marriage and by war. His main rival was HENRY II of England. Philip supported the rebellions of Henry's sons, fought a long war against RICHARD I, and during the reign of JOHN, occupied Normandy and Anjou. He won a decisive victory over the English at the battle of Bouvines (1214). Philip persecuted Jews and Christian heretics and opened the crusade against the Albigenses.

Philip IV (the Fair) (1268–1314) King of France (1285–1314). Partly to pay for wars against Flanders and England, he expelled the Jews (1306), confiscating their property. Claiming the right to tax the clergy involved him in a long quarrel with Pope Boniface VIII. He used assemblies later called the States General to popularize his case. After the death of Boniface (1303), Philip secured the election of a French pope, Clement V, based at Avignon. Philip suppressed the Knights Templar.

Philip VI (1293–1350) King of France (1328–50). First of the house of VALOIS, he was chosen to succeed his cousin, CHARLES IV, in preference to the rival claimant, EDWARD III of England. After the outbreak of the Hundred Years War (1337), many of his vassals supported Edward. Philip suffered serious defeats in the naval battle of Sluys (1340) and at Crécy (1346).

Philip II (382–336 BCE) King of Macedonia (359–336 BCE). He conquered neighboring tribes and extended his rule over the Greek states, defeating the Athenians at Chaeronea (338 BCE) and gaining reluctant acknowledgment as king of Greece. Philip was preparing to attack the Persian empire when he was assassinated, leaving the task to his son, ALEXANDER THE GREAT.

Philip II (1527–98) King of Spain (1556–98), king of Naples and Sicily (1554–98) and king of Portugal as Philip I

(1580–98), son of Emperor CHARLES V. He was married (1554–58) to MARY I of England. The war with France was ended by the Treaty of Cateau-Cambrésis (1559) and the HAPSBURG-VALOIS rapprochement was sealed by Philip's marriage to Elizabeth of Valois. Philip led the Counter-Reformation. He attempted to quell the Protestant revolt in the Netherlands. English support for the Dutch rebels led Philip to launch the ill-fated Armada (1588). In 1580 Spanish forces, led by the duke of Alba, conquered Portugal. The demands of war, colonial expansion and Philip's authoritarianism destabilized Spain.

Philip III (1578–1621) King of Spain, Naples and Sicily (1598–1621) and king of Portugal as Philip II (1598–1621), son of PHILIP II of Spain. He left government to his favorite, the duke of Lerma. In 1620 Spain entered the Thirty Years War.

Philip V (1683–1746) King of Spain (1700–46). Because he was a grandson and possible successor of LOUIS XIV of France, his accession to the Spanish throne provoked the War of the Spanish Succession (1701–14). Philip was the first BOURBON king of Spain. At the Treaty of Utrecht (1713) he kept the Spanish throne by exclusion from the succession in France and the loss of Spanish territories in Italy and the Netherlands.

Phoenicians Semitic peoples of an ancient region bordering the E Mediterranean coast. The Phoenicians were famous as merchants and sailors and never formed a single political unit. Phoenicia was dominated by Egypt before c.1200 BCE and by successive Near Eastern empires from the 9th century BCE. The Phoenician city-states, such as Tyre, Sidon and Byblos, reached the peak of their prosperity in the intervening period. The Phoenicians dominated trade in the Mediterranean during the Bronze Age. They founded colonies in Spain and North Africa, notably Carthage. In 332 BCE ALEXANDER THE GREAT captured Tyre and subsumed Phoenicia into the Hellenistic empire.

Picasso, Pablo (1881–1973) Spanish painter, sculptor, graphic artist and designer. During his "Blue" and "Rose" periods (1900–07), Picasso turned from portrayals of poor and isolated people to representations of harlequins, acrobats and dancers in warmer colors. His *Les Demoiselles d'Avignon* (1907) is a watershed in the development of contemporary art. The fragmentary forms heralded cubism. Other paintings include *Guernica* (1937).

Piccard, Auguste (1884–1962) Swiss physicist. In 1931 Piccard made the first ascent into the stratosphere in a hydrogen balloon. In 1953 Piccard and his son, **Jacques Piccard** (1922–) descended in the bathyscaphe *Trieste* to a depth of c.3,100m (10,000ft). In 1960 he submerged to 10,900m (35,800ft).

Pierce, Franklin (1804–69) 14th US President (1853–57). He gained the Democratic presidential nomination as a compromise candidate and was elected in 1852. The most notable feature of his presidency was his endorsement of the Kansas-Nebraska Act (1854), which resulted in near-civil war in Kansas between pro- and antislavery settlers.

Piero della Francesca (1415–92) (Piero dei Francheschi) Italian painter. He created a monumental, deeply reflective style. His most important work is the fresco series depicting the *Legend of the True Cross* (c.1465) for the choir of San Francesco, Arezzo.

Pilsudski, Józef (1867–1935) Polish marshal and statesman. During World War I he led Polish forces against Russia, hoping to establish a Polish state. After independence, Pilsudski became head of state. His attempt to create a larger Polish state during the Polish–Soviet War failed, although he inflicted an astonishing defeat on the invading Russians in 1920. In 1926 Pilsudski established a dictatorship that lasted until his death.

Pindar (522–438 BCE) Greek poet known for his choric lyrics and triumphal odes. Of the 17 volumes of Pindar's works known to his contemporaries, only 44 odes survive.

Pinochet (Ugarte), Augusto (1915–2006) Chilean general and statesman, president (1973–89). He led the military coup that overthrew Salvador ALLENDE. Pinochet established a military dictatorship that enforced social control through routine torture and murder. In 1989 he was forced to permit democratic elections. He retained command of the armed forces until 1998. In 1998, while undergoing hospital treatment in England, he was arrested for crimes against humanity. The Law Lords ruled that Pinochet could be extradited for crimes committed since 1988.

Pisano, Nicola (c.1225–c.1278) Italian sculptor. His first masterpiece was the pulpit for the Baptistry in Pisa (1260). In his work on the cathedral pulpit in Siena (1265–68), Pisano was aided by his son, **Giovanni Pisano** (c.1250–c.1320).

Pitt, William, 1st earl of Chatham (1708–78) (Pitt the Elder) British statesman, known as "the Great Commoner". Pitt was noted for his opposition to the foreign policies of prime ministers WALPOLE and Carteret and King GEORGE II. The crisis at the start of the Seven Years War (1756–63) made him effective head of the government. Widespread criticism of Pitt's dismissal (1757) brought about his reappointment as head of a coalition government. His ministry was a brilliant one, preserving and consolidating Britain's old empire and gaining a new one. In 1761 he resigned after GEORGE III refused to declare war on Spain. After the war he spoke out against the imposition of the Stamp Act (1765) on the American colonies. Created Earl Chatham in 1766, he retired to the House of Lords in 1768. There he spoke out against repression of the American colonies and in favor of any peace settlement that stopped short of granting independence.

Pitt, William (1759–1806) (Pitt the Younger) British statesman, prime minister (1783–1801, 1804–06), second son of William PITT, earl of Chatham. He became chancellor of the exchequer in 1782 and shortly after became Britain's youngest prime minister, aged 24. Pitt's reputation rests on his financial and commercial reforms, which restored British prosperity and prestige after defeat in the American Revolution. During his first administration, the India Act (1784), the Constitutional Act (1791) dividing Canada into French and English provinces, and the Act of Union with Ireland (1800) were passed. Pitt resigned in the face of GEORGE III's refusal to consider Catholic emancipation. In 1804 he returned to power and continued to hold office until his death. His second ministry was marked by the coalition with Russia, Sweden and Austria against NAPOLEON I.

Pius IX (1792–1878) Pope (1846–78), b. Giovanni Maria Mastai-Ferretti. Pius fled from Rome (1848–50) in the Revolutions of 1848 but was restored by NAPOLEON III. In 1860 the Papal States were seized by the Italian nationalists. Pius refused to acknowledge the new kingdom of Italy and remained a voluntary "prisoner" within the walls of the Vatican until his death. He defined the dogma of the Immaculate Conception (1854). In 1869 Pius convened the First Vatican Council, which proclaimed the principle of Papal Infallibility.

Pizarro, Francisco (c.1476–1541) Spanish *conquistador* of the INCA empire of Peru. He served under CORTÉS and led expeditions to South America (1522–28). In 1531, having gained the support of CHARLES V, Pizarro and Diego de Almagro sailed from Panama to Peru. They captured and later murdered the Inca leader ATAHUALPA, and took the capital, Cuzco, in 1534. Pizarro acted as governor of the conquered territory.

Placidia, Galla (c.388–450) Roman empress of the West, daughter of THEODOSIUS I. In 410 she was captured by the VISIGOTHS and compelled to marry (414) the chieftain Ataulf. In 416 Placidia was returned to her brother Emperor Honorius. In 425 she became regent for her son, Valentinian III.

Planck, Max Karl Ernst Ludwig (1858–1947) German physicist. In 1900 he came to the conclusion that the frequency distribution of black-body radiation could only be accounted for if the radiation was emitted in separate "packets" (quanta), rather than continuously. His equation, relating the energy of a quantum to its frequency, is the basis of quantum theory. In 1918 Planck was awarded the Nobel Prize for physics.

Plantagenet (Angevin) English royal dynasty descended from Geoffrey of Anjou and Matilda, daughter of HENRY I. In 1154 Henry II became the first Plantagenet king. His successors were RICHARD I, JOHN, HENRY III, EDWARD I, EDWARD II, EDWARD III.

After Richard II the dynasty split into the rival houses of LANCASTER and YORK.

Plath, Sylvia (1932–63) US poet. Her verse includes *The Colossus* (1960) and *Ariel* (1965). Plath wrote one novel, *The Bell Jar* (1963). Her work is characterized by personal, confessional elements. Plath was married (1956–62) to fellow poet Ted HUGHES.

Plato (c.427–347 BCE) Greek philosopher and writer. From c.407 BCE he was a disciple of SOCRATES. In Athens, Plato set up his Academy (c.387 BCE), where he taught ARISTOTLE. Plato wrote in the form of dialogues, in which Socrates genially interrogates another person, demolishing their arguments. All of Plato's 36 works survive. His most famous dialogues include *Gorgias* (on rhetoric as an art of flattery), *Phaedo* (on death and the immortality of the soul) and the *Symposium* (a discussion on the nature of love). Plato's greatest work was the *Republic*, a dialogue on justice, in which he outlined his view of an ideal state.

Plautus, Titus Maccius (254–184 BCE) Roman dramatist. His farces, such as *Miles Gloriosus*, were modeled on Greek originals. SHAKESPEARE'S *The Comedy of Errors* (1593) derives from Plautus' *Menaechmi*.

Plekhanov, Georgi Valentinovich (1857–1918) Russian revolutionary. After leading populist demonstrations, he was exiled and adopted Marxism. As leader of the Mensheviks, Plekhanov worked with LENIN until the split (1903) with the Bolsheviks. In 1917 he returned and died shortly after the Russian Revolution.

Pliny the Elder (CE 23–79) (Gaius Plinius Secundus) Roman scholar. His one major surviving work, *Historia Naturalis*, covers a vast range of subjects, mixing fact and fiction.

Plotinus (205–70) Egyptian philosopher, founder of Neoplatonism. In c.244 he opened a school in Rome. Plotinus conceived of the universe as a hierarchy proceeding from matter, through soul and reason, to God. Porphyry compiled and edited Plotinus' writings into six books, known as the *Enneads*.

Plutarch (c.CE 46–120) Greek biographer and essayist. His best known work is *The Parallel Lives*, which consists of biographies of soldiers and statesmen.

Poe, Edgar Allan (1809–49) US poet and short-story writer. His finest poetry, such as *The Raven* (1845), deals with horror in the tradition of the Gothic novel. Other works include stories *The Fall of the House of Usher* (1839), *The Murders in the Rue Morgue* (1841) and *The Pit and the Pendulum* (1843).

Poincaré, Raymond Nicolas Landry (1860–1934) French statesman, president (1913–20) and prime minister (1912–13, 1922–24, 1926–29). An ardent nationalist and conservative, he accepted his opponent Georges CLEMENCEAU as premier in 1917, in the cause of national unity. In 1923 Poincaré ordered the occupation of the Ruhr to force German payment of reparations.

Polignac, Jules Armand, prince de (1780–1847) French statesman. A leader of the ultraroyalists in the reigns of LOUIS XVIII and CHARLES X, he was appointed premier in 1829. Polignac's autocratic regime precipitated the July Revolution (1830). He was sentenced to life imprisonment, but released in 1836.

Polk, James Knox (1795–1849) 11th US President (1845–49). During his administration, California and New Mexico were acquired as a result of the US victory in the Mexican War (1846–48). He gained Oregon through the Oregon Treaty (1846).

Pollock, Jackson (1912–56) US painter, a leading figure in abstract expressionism. In 1947 he started to experiment with dripping paint onto enormous canvases. Sometimes he applied paint straight from the tube, other times he used knives to create patterns. His energetic approach became known as "action painting". His works include *Black and White* (1948) and *One* (1950).

Polo, Marco (1254–1324) Venetian traveler in Asia. In 1274 he embarked on a trading mission to the court of KUBLAI KHAN, the Mongol emperor of China. According to Marco Polo's account, he remained in the Far East for more than 20 years, becoming the confidant of Kublai Khan and traveling throughout China. His *The Description of the World* was the chief source of European knowledge of China until the late 19th century.

Pol Pot (1928–98) Cambodian ruler. In 1975 he led the communist Khmer Rouge in the overthrow of the US-backed government of Lon Nol. Pol Pot instigated a reign of terror in Cambodia (renamed Kampuchea). Intellectuals were massacred and city dwellers were driven into the countryside. Estimates suggest that *c.*2 million Cambodians were murdered. In 1979 Pol Pot was overthrown by a Vietnamese invasion. He continued to lead the Khmer Rouge. In 1998 Pol Pot died of heart failure.

Pombal, Sebastião José de Carvalho e Mello, marquês de (1699–1782) Portuguese statesman. As chief minister, Pombal was virtual ruler of Portugal from 1756 until the death of King Joseph in 1777. He increased royal power at the expense of the nobility, the Inquisition and the JESUITS, whom he expelled in 1759. An "enlightened despot", Pombal reformed the administration, economy and army, and encouraged trade with Brazil.

Pompadour, Jeanne-Antoinette Poisson, marquise de (1721–64) French mistress and confidante of LOUIS XV after 1745. She was a great patron of the arts, befriending DIDEROT and encouraging publication of the *Encyclopédie*.

Pompey (106–48 BCE) (Gnaeus Pompeius Magnus) Roman general. In 83 BCE he fought for SULLA and campaigned in Sicily, Africa and Spain. In 70 BCE Pompey was named consul with CRASSUS and fought a campaign (66 BCE) against MITHRIDATES VI of Pontus. In 59 BCE he formed the first triumvirate with Crassus and his rival, Julius CAESAR. After the death of Crassus, Pompey joined Caesar's enemies, and civil war broke out (49 BCE). Driven out of Rome by Caesar's advance, Pompey was defeated at Pharsalus (48 BCE) and fled to Egypt, where he was murdered.

Pompidou, Georges Jean Raymond (1911–74) French statesman, prime minister (1962, 1962–66, 1966–67, 1967–68) and president (1969–74). In 1958 he helped Charles DE GAULLE draft the constitution of the Fifth Republic. In 1961 Pompidou negotiated a settlement to the war in Algeria. He succeeded De Gaulle as president. Pompidou died in office.

Ponce de León, Juan (1460–1521) Spanish explorer. He conquered Puerto Rico for Spain (1508–09) and in 1513 led an expedition to explore rumored islands north of Cuba. He reached land near what is now St. Augustine, Florida. In 1521 he returned but received an arrow wound from which he later died.

Pontiac (d.1769) Ottawa chief who led a loose association of allies hostile to the British takeover of Quebec (1760). In the rebellion (1763–66) a number of outposts in the Great Lakes region were overrun. News of the French withdrawal from North America fatally weakened the campaign, which soon collapsed.

Pontius Pilate (active 1st century CE) Roman prefect. In *c.*26 Emperor TIBERIUS appointed him procurator of Judaea. Pilate is noted for his order to crucify JESUS CHRIST. In *c.*36 he was recalled to Rome after sanctioning the massacre of Samaritans.

Pope, Alexander (1688–1744) English poet. His philosophical poem *Essay on Man* (1733–34) was complemented by the satire *The Dunciad* (1728–43). *Epistle to Dr. Arbuthnot* (1735) was a stinging attack on his critics. Pope also made popular translations of Homer's *Iliad* (1715–20) and *The Odyssey* (1726–26).

Pound, Ezra Loomis (1885–1972) US poet, founder of imagism and vorticism. In 1907 Pound emigrated to England. In 1924 he moved to Italy, and during World War II he made pro-fascist, anti-Semitic broadcasts to the USA. In 1945 he was escorted back to the USA and indicted for treason. Pound was judged mentally unfit to stand trial and confined in a mental hospital (1946–58). His masterpiece is the epic *Cantos* (1925–60).

Poussin, Nicolas (1594–1665) French painter who worked mainly in Rome. At first inspired by mannerism, Poussin turned to more elaborate Old Testament and historical themes, such as *The Eucharist* (1644–48) and *The Seven Sacraments* (1648).

Priestley, Joseph (1733–1804) English chemist and clergyman. In 1774 Priestley discovered oxygen. He also found a number of other gases, including ammonia and oxides of nitrogen.

Primo de Rivera, Miguel (1870–1930) Spanish general. In 1923 he staged a coup with the support of ALFONSO XIII. He dissolved parliament and established a military dictatorship modeled on the government of MUSSOLINI. He restored order and helped to end the revolt of Abd-el-Krim in Morocco (1926). The parlous state of the economy forced him to resign in 1930.

Prokofiev, Sergei (1891–1953) Russian composer. His style is characterized by biting dissonances within rich harmony. His works include the ballets *Romeo and Juliet* (1935) and *Cinderella* (1944); the *Classical* (first) symphony (1918); *Peter and the Wolf* (1936); and the comic opera *The Love for Three Oranges* (1921).

Proudhon, Pierre Joseph (1809–65) French political theorist. His anarchist theories of liberty, equality and justice conflicted with the communism of Karl MARX. In *What is Property?* (1840), Proudhon famously argued that "property is theft".

Proust, Marcel (1871–1922) French novelist. In 1912 Proust produced *Swann's Way*, the first section of a semiautobiographical cyclical novel collectively entitled *À la recherche du temps perdu*. The series offers an insight into the relationship between psyche and society, and the distortions of time and memory.

Ptolemy I (367–283 BCE) (Ptolemy Soter) King of ancient Egypt, first ruler of the Ptolemaic dynasty that ruled Egypt for nearly 300 years (323–30 BCE). A leading Macedonian general of ALEXANDER THE GREAT, Ptolemy I was granted Egypt in the division of the empire upon Alexander's death (323 BCE). In 305 BCE he assumed the title of king. During Ptolemy's reign Egypt prospered through its control of trade in much of the E Mediterranean region. He established his former soldiers as settlers in Egypt and endeavored to unite the country through the cult of Serapis, although he also supported traditional Egyptian religion. He made his capital at Alexandria, where he created the library. In 284 BCE he abdicated in favor of his son, PTOLEMY II.

Ptolemy II (*c.*308–246 BCE) (Ptolemy Philadelphus) King of ancient Egypt (284–246 BCE), son of PTOLEMY I. He built Alexandria into the cultural and commercial center of the Greek world, attracting poets such as Callimachus and Theocritus, and expanding the collection of books in the Library of Alexandria.

Ptolemy (CE 90–168) (Claudius Ptolemaeus) Greek astronomer and geographer. He worked at the library of Alexandria, Egypt. Ptolemy's chief astronomical work, the *Almagest*, drew heavily on the work of HIPPARCHUS. In *c.*CE 140 he proposed his geocentric system. The resulting model reproduced the apparent motions of the planets so well that it remained unchallenged until the revival of the heliocentric theory in the 16th century.

Puccini, Giacomo (1858–1924) Italian composer. His operas combine dramatic libretti with expressive music. His best-known works are *La Bohème* (1896), *Tosca* (1900), *Madam Butterfly* (1904) and his last opera (left incomplete) *Turandot* (1926).

Pugachev, Emelian Ivanovich (1726–75) Russian Cossack leader. In 1773 he claimed to be Peter III and promised freedom from serfdom, taxes and military service, and the elimination of landlords and other officials. Pugachev led a massive popular revolt against CATHERINE II (THE GREAT). In 1774 he was betrayed, taken to Moscow for trial and executed.

Purcell, Henry (1659–95) English composer. He was organist for Westminster Abbey (1679–95) and the Chapel Royal (1682–95). Purcell is chiefly celebrated for his church music. He also composed the first English opera, *Dido and Aeneas* (1689).

Pushkin, Alexander Sergeievich (1799–1837) Russian poet and novelist. In 1820 he was exiled for his political beliefs. His tragedy *Boris Godunov* (1826) reveals the influence of BYRON. Pushkin's masterpiece was the verse novel *Eugene Onegin* (1833). Other works include the short story *The Queen of Spades* (1834).

Pu Yi, Henry (1906–67) (Hsuan Tung) Last Emperor of China (1908–11). Deposed after the formation of the Chinese republic, Pu Yi was rescued from obscurity to become president of the Japanese puppet state of Manchukuo in 1932. Captured by Soviet forces (1945), he was delivered to MAO ZEDONG and imprisoned (1949–59). He later worked as a gardener in Beijing.

Pythagoras (*c.*580–500 BCE) Greek philosopher and founder of the Pythagorean school. The Pythagoreans were bound to their teacher by rigid vows and were ascetic in their way of life. The famous theorem, that the square of the hypotenuse of a right-angled triangle equals the sum of the squares of the other two sides, is named for him, but was already known to the Egyptians and Babylonians. His school was suppressed at the end of the 6th century, but its doctrines were revived by the Romans.

Q

Qaddafi, Muammar al- (1942–) Libyan commander-in-chief and chairman of the Revolutionary Command Council. In 1969 he led the coup that toppled King Idris I. As head of state, Qaddafi sought to remove all vestiges of Libya's colonial past. He shut down US and British bases, nationalized oil assets, and encouraged a return to Islamic law. In 1986 the USA bombed Libya in an attempt to stop its support of international terrorist organizations. In 1999 Qaddafi handed over for trial two Libyans suspected of the bombing of Pan-Am flight 103 over Scotland.

Qin dynasty (formerly Ch'in) Imperial dynasty of China (221–206 BCE). Originating in NW China, the Qin emerged after the collapse of the ZHOU DYNASTY; its founder was QIN SHI-HUANGDI. The first centralized imperial administration was established. Uniformity was encouraged in every sphere. The Great Wall took shape during this period.

Qing dynasty (formerly Ch'ing) Imperial Manchurian dynasty of China (1644–1911). It was established (1636) by NURHACHI following the collapse of the MING DYNASTY, but it was not until the fall of Beijing that the Qing became the official ruling dynasty. By 1800 the Qing exercised control over an area stretching from Siam (Thailand) and Tibet to Mongolia and the River Amur. The dynasty was weakened by internal struggles, such as the Taiping Rebellion (1851–64), and the increase of foreign influence after the Opium Wars (1839–42). It ended with the abdication of PU YI in 1911 and the establishment of the Chinese republic.

Qin Shihuangdi (259–210 BCE) Emperor of China (221–210 BCE). The first emperor of the QIN DYNASTY, he reformed the bureaucracy and consolidated the Great Wall. In the 1970s excavations of his tomb on Mount Li, Xian, NW China, revealed an "army" of c.7,500 life-size terracotta guardians.

Quezon, Manuel Luis (1878–1944) Philippine statesman, first president of the Commonwealth of the Philippines (1935–44). In 1901 he was imprisoned for his part in the revolt against US rule. After his release, Quezon became leader of the Nationalist Party and secured the passage of the Tydings-McDuffie Bill (1934), which paved the way for independence. An autocratic president, Quezon instigated administrative reforms. His strengthening of Philippine defenses failed to prevent Japan's invasion. Quezon formed a government-in-exile in the USA.

Quisling, Vidkun (1887–1945) Norwegian fascist leader. He founded the National Union Party (1933), based on the German Nazi Party. In 1940 Quisling collaborated with the invading Germans, and they set him up as a puppet ruler during their occupation of Norway. After World War II he was shot as a traitor.

R

Rabelais, François (1494–1553) French satirist and humanist. He is famed for his classic series of satires, now known collectively as *Gargantua and Pantagruel*. The series itself consists of *Pantagruel* (1532), *Gargantua* (1534), *Le Tiers Livre* (1546), *Le Quart Livre* (1552) and *Le Cinquième Livre* (1564).

Rabin, Yitzhak (1922–95) Israeli statesman, prime minister (1974–77, 1992–95). As chief of staff (1964–68), he directed Israeli operations in the Six Day War (1967). Rabin was ambassador to the USA (1968–73) before becoming prime minister. As minister of defense (1984–90), he directed operations against the Palestinian intifada. In 1993 Rabin and Yasir ARAFAT signed the Israeli-Palestinian Accord, which promised progress toward

Palestinian autonomy in the occupied territories. In November 1995 Rabin was assassinated by an Israeli extremist.

Rachmaninov, Sergei (1873–1943) Russian composer. His most popular works include Piano Concerto No. 2 (1901), *Rhapsody on a Theme of Paganini* (1934) and Symphony No. 2 (1907).

Racine, Jean Baptiste (1639–99) French dramatist. He is regarded as the greatest tragedian of the French classical period. His major verse tragedies are *Andromaque* (1667), *Britannicus* (1669) *Bérénice* (1673), *Bajazet* (1672) and *Phèdre* (1677).

Raffles, Sir Thomas Stamford (1781–1826) British colonial administrator, founder of Singapore, b. Jamaica. When Java returned to Dutch rule (1816), Raffles bought the island of Singapore for the British East India Company (1819). Under his guidance it developed rapidly into a prosperous free port.

Rajput Hindi warrior caste from NW India. They became powerful in the 7th century CE, gaining control of an historic region named Rajputana. After the Muslim conquests in the 12th century, they retained their independence but by the early 17th century had submitted to the MUGHAL EMPIRE. In the early 18th century they extended their control. In the 19th century most of their territorial gains were lost to the MARATHAS, Sikhs and the British Empire. During the colonial period much of Rajputana retained its independence under princely rule. After Indian independence in 1947, most of the princes lost their powers.

Raleigh, Sir Walter (1552–1618) English soldier, explorer and writer. A favorite courtier of ELIZABETH I, Raleigh organized expeditions to North America. On JAMES I's ascension to the throne, Raleigh was imprisoned for treason (1603–16). He gained release in order to lead an expedition to Guiana in search of the gold of El Dorado. He was betrayed to the Spanish authorities, returned to prison and later executed for treason.

Ramsay, Sir William (1852–1916) Scottish chemist. In 1894 Ramsay and Lord RAYLEIGH discovered argon in air. Ramsay later discovered helium, neon, krypton, xenon and radon. In 1904 he was awarded the 1904 Nobel Prize for chemistry.

Ramses II Egyptian king of the 19th dynasty (r. c.1290–1224 BCE). He reigned during a period of unprecedented prosperity. His efforts to confirm Egypt's dominant position in Palestine led to a clash with the HITTITES at Kadesh (c.1285 BCE). In 1269 BCE a truce was agreed, and Ramses married a Hittite princess. He built many monuments, including the temple at Abu Simbel.

Ranjit Singh (1780–1835) Indian maharaja, founder of the Sikh kingdom of the Punjab. At the age of 12, he became the ruler of a small territory in NW India. Ranjit absorbed neighboring states, and in 1799 established his capital at Lahore. In 1803 he took possession of the Sikh holy city of Amritsar. Turning his attention to the W and N, he captured Peshawar and Kashmir. His kingdom collapsed after his death.

Ras Tafari Makonnen *See* HAILE SELASSIE

Rasputin, Grigori Yefimovich (1872–1916) Russian mystic. He exercised great influence at the court of NICHOLAS II because of his apparent ability to cure the crown prince Alexis' hemophilia. Rasputin attracted suspicion because of his advocacy of sexual ecstasy as a means of salvation. In 1916 he was poisoned by a group of nobles, and when this failed, he was shot and drowned.

Ray, Man (1890–1976) US photographer, painter, sculptor and film-maker. He cofounded the New York Dada movement. Ray is best known for photographs produced without a camera by placing objects on light-sensitive paper and exposing them to light.

Rayleigh, John William Strutt, Lord (1842–1919) English physicist. His work was concerned with various forms of wave motion. Rayleigh was awarded the 1904 Nobel Prize for physics for his discovery (with William RAMSAY) of the noble gas argon.

Reagan, Ronald Wilson (1911–2004) 40th US President (1981–89). A well-known film actor, he joined the Republican Party in 1962. Nominated as presidential candidate in 1980, he defeated Jimmy CARTER. In 1981 Reagan survived an assassination attempt. As president, he introduced large tax cuts and reduced public spending, except on defense. By the end of Reagan's second term, budget and trade deficits had reached record heights. Fiercely anticommunist, he adopted strong measures against opponents abroad, invading Grenada (1983) and undermining Daniel ORTEGA's regime in Nicaragua. While pursuing his Strategic Defense Initiative (SDI), Reagan reached a historic nuclear disarmament treaty (1987) with Mikhail GORBACHEV, signaling an end to the Cold War. The last year of his presidency was overshadowed by the Iran-Contra affair. He was succeeded by his vice-president George BUSH.

Réaumur, René Antoine Ferchault de (1683–1757) French physicist. Réaumur is chiefly remembered for his thermometer scale, which designates 0° as the freezing point of water and 80° as its boiling point.

Rembrandt Harmenszoon van Rijn (1606–69) Dutch painter and graphic artist. In 1632 Rembrandt settled in Amsterdam. By 1636 he was painting in a richly detailed baroque style, typified by the *Sacrifice of Abraham* (1636). In 1642 Rembrandt finished his famous group portrait *The Corporalship of Captain Frans Banning Cocq's Civic Guards* (or *The Night Watch*). In his later years Rembrandt produced some of his greatest works, such as *Jacob Blessing the Sons of Joseph* (1656) and *The Jewish Bride* (late 1660s). His works total more than 300 paintings.

Renoir, (Pierre) Auguste (1841–1919) French painter. In 1874 he contributed to the first exhibition of impressionism; masterpieces of this period include *Le Moulin de la Galette* (1876). In the early 1880s Renoir became interested in the human figure with such works as *Bathers* (1884–87) and *After the Bath* (c.1895).

Reynolds, Sir Joshua (1723–92) English portrait painter and writer on art. In 1768 he espoused the principles of the "Grand Manner" style in his annual *Discourses* (1768–90) to the Royal Academy. His portraits, such as *Mrs. Siddons as the Tragic Muse* (1784), are remarkable for their individuality and sensitivity.

Rhee, Syngman (1875–1965) Korean statesman, first president (1948–60) of South Korea. He was imprisoned (1898–1904) for his opposition to Japanese rule before living (1912–45) in exile in the USA. After World War II he was leader of US-occupied South Korea. His presidency was marked by the Korean War (1950–53). Rhee's regime became increasingly authoritarian and corrupt. Accusations of vote-rigging sparked riots, and Rhee was forced to resign.

Rhodes, Cecil John (1853–1902) South African statesman, b. Britain. In 1870 Rhodes emigrated to Natal and made a fortune in the diamond mines. In 1880 he founded the De Beers Mining Company. In 1885 Rhodes persuaded the British government to form a protectorate over Bechuanaland. In 1889 he founded the British South Africa Company, which occupied Mashonaland and Matabeleland, thus forming Rhodesia (now Zambia and Zimbabwe). Rhodes was prime minister (1890–96) of Cape Colony. The discovery of his role in Leander JAMESON's attempt to overthrow Paul KRUGER in the Transvaal led to his resignation.

Ribbentrop, Joachim von (1893–1946) German diplomat and politician. In 1932 he joined the Nazi Party and became foreign affairs adviser to Adolf HITLER in 1933. Ribbentrop negotiated the secret Nazi-Soviet Pact (1939) with MOLOTOV but steadily lost influence during World War II. At the Nuremberg Trials (1946), he was convicted of war crimes and hanged.

Richard I (1157–99) King of England (1189–99), known as Richard the Lion-heart. He was involved in rebellions against his father, HENRY II. A leader of the Third Crusade (1189–92), Richard won several victories but failed to retake Jerusalem. Between 1192 and 1194 he was held prisoner by Emperor Henry VI. Meanwhile, his brother JOHN conspired against him in England, while in France PHILIP II invaded Richard's territories. The English revolt was contained, and from 1194 Richard endeavored to restore the Angevin empire in France.

Richard II (1367–1400) King of England (1377–99), son of EDWARD THE BLACK PRINCE. Richard succeeded his grandfather, EDWARD III, and was faced with the Peasants' Revolt (1381). His reign was marked by conflict with the barons. On the orders of

the "lords appellant", the "Merciless Parliament" (1388) executed many of Richard's supporters. Richard reasserted control and reigned ably until he began to assume authoritarian powers. In 1397–98 he exacted his revenge on the lords appellant by having the duke of Gloucester murdered and the duke of Hereford banished. Hereford led a revolt and was crowned HENRY IV. Richard was imprisoned and died in mysterious circumstances.

Richard III (1452–85) King of England (1483–85). As Duke of Gloucester, he ably supported his brother, Edward IV, in N England. When Edward died, Richard became protector and had the young King Edward V declared illegitimate and took the crown himself. Edward and his younger brother subsequently disappeared. Richard's numerous enemies supported the invasion of Henry Tudor (HENRY VII) in 1485. Richard's death at the battle of Bosworth ended the Wars of the Roses.

Richardson, Samuel (1689–1761) English novelist. He wrote his first work of fiction, the novel *Pamela* (1740–41), after the age of 50. It was followed by two more epistolary novels, *Clarissa* (1747–48) and *Sir Charles Grandison* (1753–54).

Richelieu, Armand Jean du Plessis, duc de (1585–1642) French cardinal and statesman. A protégé of Marie de MÉDICI, he became chief of the royal council in 1624. Richelieu suppressed the military and political power of the Huguenots but tolerated Protestant religious practices. He alienated many powerful Catholics by his policy of placing the interests of the state above all else. In the Thirty Years War, Richelieu formed alliances with Protestant powers against the HAPSBURGS.

Riel, Louis (1844–85) French-Canadian revolutionary, leader of the *métis* (people of mixed French and native descent) in the Red River rebellion in Manitoba (1869–70). In 1884 Riel led resistance to Canada's policies in Saskatchewan and set up a rebel government in 1885. He was captured and executed for treason.

Rimbaud, Arthur (1854–91) French anarchic poet who influenced symbolism. He had a stormy relationship with Paul VERLAINE, under whose tutelage he wrote *The Drunken Boat* (1871). In 1873 they separated and *A Season in Hell* appeared. In 1886 *Les Illuminations* was mischievously published by Verlaine as the work of the late Arthur Rimbaud.

Rimsky-Korsakov, Nikolai Andreievich (1844–1908) Russian composer. His operas include *The Snow Maiden* (1881) and *The Golden Cockerel* (1907), and among his most popular orchestral works are *Sheherazade* (1888), *Capriccio espagnole* (1887) and *The Flight of the Bumblebee* (1900).

Robert I (the Bruce) (1274–1329) King of Scotland (1306–29). He was descended from a prominent Anglo-Norman family with a strong claim to the crown. In 1296 Robert swore fealty to EDWARD I of England but in 1297 joined a Scottish revolt against the English. After killing a powerful rival, Robert had himself crowned king of Scotland but, defeated at Methven (1306) by the English, he fled the kingdom. Returning on Edward's death (1307), the Bruce renewed the struggle with increasing support. In 1314 he won a famous victory over the English at Bannockburn. The battle secured Scottish independence, finally recognized in the Treaty of Northampton (1328).

Roberts, Frederick Sleigh, 1st earl of Kandahar (1832–1914) British field marshal. He distinguished himself in the Indian Mutiny (1857–58) and in the relief of Kandahar in the second Afghan War (1878–80). He and KITCHENER directed British forces in the South African War (1899–1900).

Robespierre, Maximilien François Marie Isidore de (1758–94) French revolutionary leader. Elected to the National Assembly in 1789, he advocated democracy and liberal reform. In 1791 he became leader of the Jacobins. With the king and the Girondins discredited, Robespierre led the republican revolution of 1792 and was elected to the National Convention. His election to the Committee of Public Safety (June 1793) heralded the Reign of Terror. Ruthless methods seemed less urgent after French victories in war, and Robespierre was arrested in the coup of 9th Thermidor (27 July) 1794 and executed.

281

Rockefeller, John D. (Davison) (1839–1937) US industrialist and philanthropist. In 1863 Rockefeller built an oil refinery that was incorporated (1870) into the Standard Oil Company of Ohio. On retirement, Rockefeller devoted his attention to charitable corporations. In 1913 he founded the Rockefeller Foundation.

Rodin, Auguste (1840–1917) French sculptor. His first major work, *The Age of Bronze* (exhibited in 1878), caused a scandal because the naked figure was so naturalistic. His next great project was *The Gates of Hell*, unfinished studies for a bronze door for the *Musée des arts décoratifs*, Paris. It provided him with the subjects for further great sculptures, including *The Thinker* (1880), *The Kiss* (1886) and *Fugit Amor* (1897).

Rodney, George Brydes Rodney, 1st Baron (1719–92) British admiral. In the Seven Years War he captured (1762) Martinique. Rodney's defeat of a Spanish fleet off Cape St. Vincent in 1780 and a French fleet off Dominica in 1782 made him a hero.

Rollo (c.860–c.932) Viking chief who formed a settlement at the mouth of the Seine. By the Treaty of Saint-Clair-sur-Epte (911) Rollo was granted the fiefdom by Charles III of France in return for Rollo being baptized and swearing his allegiance to the French crown. The land expanded into the duchy of Normandy.

Roman Empire Mediterranean empire formed (c.27 BCE) by AUGUSTUS after the assassination (c.44 BCE) of Julius CAESAR. Its power center was ancient ROME. The Romans adopted the culture of the ancient GREEKS, but their empire was based on military power and Roman law. By the death of Augustus (CE 14), the empire included most of Asia Minor, Syria, Egypt and the whole North African coast. In the 1st and 2nd centuries Britain was conquered; in the E, Roman rule extended to the Caspian Sea and the Persian Gulf, and further territory, including Dacia, was added in SE Europe. The empire was at its greatest extent at the death of TRAJAN (CE 117), when it included all the lands around the Mediterranean and extended to N Britain, the Black Sea and Mesopotamia. HADRIAN (r.117–138) called a halt to further expansion. Rome reached the height of its power during the first 150 years of imperial rule, becoming a city of grand, monumental buildings with c.1 million inhabitants. In the 3rd century pressure from Germanic tribes and the Persians, plus economic difficulties, contributed to the breakdown of government. DIOCLETIAN restored order, and from his time the empire tended to be split into E and W divisions. In 330 CONSTANTINE I founded an E capital at Constantinople. Rome was increasingly challenged by different peoples, such as the GOTHS who sacked the city in 410. By 500 the Roman Empire in the west had ceased to exist. The Eastern or BYZANTINE EMPIRE survived until 1453.

Romanov Russian imperial dynasty (1613–1917). Michael, the first Romanov czar, was elected in 1613. His descendants, especially PETER I (THE GREAT) and CATHERINE II (THE GREAT), a Romanov by marriage, transformed Russia into the world's largest empire. The last Romanov emperor, NICHOLAS II, abdicated in 1917 and was later murdered by the BOLSHEVIKS.

Romans, ancient According to tradition, Rome was founded in 753 BCE by ROMULUS AND REMUS. By 509 BCE the Latin-speaking Romans had thrown off the rule of ETRUSCAN kings and established an independent republic dominated by an aristocratic elite. By 340 BCE Rome controlled Italy S of the River Po. By the 3rd century BCE the plebeian class had largely gained political equality. The Punic Wars gave Rome dominance of the Mediterranean in the 2nd century BCE, when major eastward expansion began with the conquest of the Greek Aegean. The republican constitution was strained by social division and military dictatorship. SPARTACUS's slave revolt was crushed by POMPEY, who emerged as SULLA's successor. Pompey and Julius CAESAR formed the First Triumvirate (60 BCE). Caesar's assassination led to the formation of the ROMAN EMPIRE under AUGUSTUS (27 BCE).

Rommel, Erwin (1891–1944) German general. He led the Afrika Korps in a victorious campaign in North Africa until defeated by the British at El Alamein (1942). Transferred to France in 1943, he was unable to repel the invasion of Normandy and was wounded. Implicated in the plot against Hitler in July 1944, he was forced to commit suicide by drinking poison.

Romulus and Remus In Roman mythology, founders of Rome. Twin brothers, they were said to be sons of Mars. Amulius, who had usurped the throne, ordered the babies to be drowned in the Tiber. They survived and were suckled by a wolf. They built a city on the site of their rescue.

Röntgen, Wilhelm Konrad (1845–1923) German physicist. He conducted research on electricity, the specific heats of gases and the conductivity of crystals. In 1895 Röntgen discovered X rays. He was awarded the first Nobel Prize for physics (1901).

Roosevelt, Franklin Delano (1882–1945) 32nd US President (1933–45). He served in the New York State Senate as a Democrat and was vice-presidential candidate in 1920. He was governor of New York (1928–32) and won the Democratic candidacy for president in 1932. As president, Roosevelt was faced by the Great Depression. He launched the "New Deal" program of federal expenditure on public works to foster social and economic reconstruction. Roosevelt was reelected in 1936 and won a third term in 1940 and a fourth in 1944. When World War II broke out in Europe, he gave as much support to Britain as a neutral government could, until the Japanese attack on Pearl Harbor ended US neutrality. Roosevelt was succeeded by Harry S. TRUMAN.

Roosevelt, Theodore (1858–1919) 26th US President (1901–09), fifth cousin of Franklin D. ROOSEVELT. He became Republican governor of New York in 1899 and vice-president in 1901. The assassination of President MCKINLEY (1901) made him president. A progressive, Roosevelt moved to regulate monopolies through antitrust legislation. Abroad, he expanded US power and prestige, gaining the Panama Canal. His mediation after the Russo-Japanese war won him the Nobel Peace Prize (1905). In 1912 he challenged William TAFT for the presidency as leader of his National Progressive Party (Bull Moose Party). The Republican split resulted in a Democratic victory.

Rosas, Juan Manuel de (1793–1877) Argentine dictator, governor of Buenos Aires (1829–32, 1835–52). Assisted by the *Mazorca* (secret police), Rosas waged a campaign of terror throughout Argentina. His dispute with Britain over the rights of the Falkland Islands led to economic blockades of Argentina. In 1852 Rosas was overthrown in a provincial revolt.

Rossini, Gioacchino Antonio (1792–1868) Italian opera composer. His comic operas, including *The Barber of Seville* (1816) and *Cinderella* (1817), demonstrate his wit and sense of melody. His serious operas include *William Tell* (1829).

Rousseau, Henri (1844–1910) French painter. Rousseau is celebrated for his scenes from an imaginary jungle, such as *Surprised! (Tropical Storm with Tiger)* (1891) and *The Dream* (1910).

Rousseau, Jean Jacques (1712–78) French philosopher. His social theories helped to shape the political events that resulted in the French Revolution. In the 1740s he contributed articles on music to the *Encyclopédie* of DIDEROT and won fame for his essay *Discourses on Science and the Arts* (1750). In *The Social Contract* (1762), Rousseau argued that man had been corrupted by civilization. His ideas on individual liberation from the constraints of society were developed in the novel *Émile* (1762).

Rubens, Peter Paul (1577–1640) Flemish painter, engraver and designer. He gained an international reputation with his huge, vigorous triptychs *Raising of the Cross* (1610–11) and *Descent from the Cross* (1611–14). Rubens worked for many of the royal families of Europe, and his most notable commissions included 25 gigantic paintings of Marie de'MEDICI.

Rudolf I (1218–91) German king (1273–91), founder of the HAPSBURG DYNASTY. His election as king ended a period of anarchy (1250–73). Rudolf set out to restore the position of the monarchy and won the duchies of Austria, Styria and Carniola from Ottokar II of Bohemia (1278). He was never crowned emperor and failed to persuade the electors to confirm his son, Albert I, as his successor, although in 1298 Albert eventually succeeded to the German throne.

Rurik (d. *c*.879) Semilegendary leader of the Varangians (VIKINGS) in Russia, first Prince of Novgorod. In *c*.862 he established his rule, a date usually taken as marking the beginning of the first Russian state. The capital was moved to KIEV under Rurik's successor, Oleg, and members of his dynasty ruled there and in Moscow until the 16th century.

Rushdie, (Ahmed) Salman (1947–) British novelist, b. India. His early works, including the Booker Prize-winning *Midnight's Children* (1981), were eclipsed by *Satanic Verses* (1988). This novel incited the condemnation of Islamic extremists who perceived the book as blasphemy, and he was sentenced to death by KHOMEINI. In 1998 the Iranian government revoked the death sentence.

Russell, Bertrand Arthur William, 3rd Earl (1872–1970) Welsh philosopher, mathematician and social reformer. His most influential work, the monumental *Principia Mathematica* (1910–13), written in collaboration with A.N. Whitehead, set out to show how mathematics was grounded in logic. Russell's commitment to pacifism led to his imprisonment in 1918. He supported, however, the antifascist aims of World War II. Russell's *History of Western Philosophy* (1946) was a popular bestseller. In 1950 he was awarded the Nobel Prize for literature.

Rutherford, Ernest, Lord (1871–1937) British nuclear physicist, b. New Zealand. Rutherford and Frederick SODDY formed the theory of atomic disintegration. In 1907 he devised the nuclear theory of the atom and, with Niels BOHR, the idea of orbital electrons. Rutherford received the 1908 Nobel Prize for chemistry. In 1919 his research team became the first to split the nucleus of an atom. Rutherford predicted the existence of the neutron, later discovered by James CHADWICK.

S

Sadat, (Muhammad) Anwar (al-) (1918–81) Egyptian statesman, president (1970–81). A close associate of NASSER, he succeeded him as president. In the Yom Kippur War (1973) Egypt and Syria were defeated by Israel. In 1978 Sadat and Israeli leader Menachem BEGIN signed the Camp David Agreement. Sadat was assassinated by Islamic fundamentalists.

Saddam Hussein (1937–2006) Iraqi statesman, president of Iraq (1979–2003). In 1959 he was forced into exile for his part in an attempt to assassinate the Iraqi prime minister. In 1963 Saddam returned and was imprisoned in 1964. After his release, he played a prominent role in the 1968 coup led by the Ba'ath Party. In 1979 Saddam took control of the party and country. His invasion of Iran led to the Iran-Iraq War (1980–88). At home, Saddam ruthlessly suppressed all opposition. His 1990 invasion of Kuwait provoked worldwide condemnation, and a multinational force expelled the Iraqi forces. Further uprisings by Kurds and Iraqi Shiites were ruthlessly suppressed. He was deposed by a US-led invasion in 2003. The Iraqi interim government put Saddam on trial for crimes against humanity, and executed him in 2006.

Safavid dynasty (1501–1722) Persian ruling family who established the territorial and Shiite theocratic principles of modern Iran. The dynastic founder, Shah ISMAIL, claimed descent from a Sufist order, and the state adopted Shi'a as the state religion. His successor, ABBAS I, accepted the Ottoman occupation of w Iran and concentrated on subduing the threat to Iran's E borders. Shah Husayn's concentration on the capture of Bahrain enabled Afghan troops to overrun the country. His forced abdication in 1722 marked the end of Safavid rule.

Saint-Just, Louis Antoine Léon de (1767–94) French revolutionary. A leading Jacobin, he helped in the downfall of the Girondins (June 1793) and was a member of the Committee of Public Safety during the Reign of Terror. Saint-Just was executed with ROBESPIERRE after the coup of 9 Thermidor (27 July 1794).

Saladin (1138–93) (Salah ad-din) Muslim general and founder of the Ayyubid dynasty. From 1152 he was a soldier and administrator in Egypt. Appointed grand vizier in 1169, Saladin overthrew the FATIMIDS in 1171 and made himself sultan. After con-

quering most of Syria, he gathered widespread support for a *jihad* to drive the Christians from Palestine (1187). Saladin reconquered Jerusalem, provoking the Third Crusade (1189). His rule restored Egypt as a major power.

Salazar, António de Oliveira (1889–1970) Portuguese dictator (1932–68). In 1933 he imposed a constitution that established an authoritarian state. At the expense of economic progress, Salazar maintained power through the army and secret police. He supported FRANCO in the Spanish Civil War (1936–39).

Salinger, J.D. (Jerome David) (1919–) US novelist. He achieved fame with his only novel, *Catcher in the Rye* (1951). The story of a tortured teenager, it is recounted in modern speech, and its style influenced a generation of US writers. Other works are collections of short stories, including *Franny and Zooey* (1961).

Salk, Jonas Edward (1914–95) US medical researcher. In 1952 he developed the first vaccine against poliomyelitis, using inactivated poliomyelitis virus as an immunizing agent.

Samnites Ancient warlike people of s central Italy, probably descendants of the Sabines, who formed a Samnite confederation in the s Apennines. After being defeated by the Romans in the Samnite Wars (343–41, 316–04, 298–90 BCE) and again by SULLA in the civil war (82 BCE), they were eventually Romanized.

Sandburg, Carl (1878–1967) US poet and biographer. He received Pulitzer prizes for *Cornhuskers* (1918), *Complete Poems* (1950) and the biography *Abraham Lincoln: The War Years* (1939).

Sanger, Frederick (1918–) English biochemist, the first person to win two Nobel prizes for chemistry. Sanger was awarded his first prize (1958) for finding the structure of insulin. He shared the 1980 Nobel Prize for chemistry for his work on the chemical structure of nucleic acid.

Sankara (active 8th century CE) Indian philosopher and theologian. He founded the Advaita (Sanskrit, "nonduality") school of Vedanta Hinduism. Shankara systematized the teachings of the Upanishads, stressing the indivisibility of Brahman and atman.

San Martín, José de (1778–1850) South American revolutionary. He led revolutionary forces in Argentina, Peru and Chile, gaining a reputation as a bold commander and imaginative strategist. After defeating the Spaniards in Argentina, San Martín gained the element of surprise in Chile (1817–18) by crossing the Andes. He captured Peru (1821) after an unexpected naval attack. In 1822 San Martín surrendered his effective rule of Peru to Simón BOLÍVAR and retired to Europe.

Santa Anna, Antonio López de (1794–1876) Mexican general and dictator. He was the dominant political figure in Mexico from 1823 to 1855. In 1836 Santa Anna led the forces that captured the Alamo, but failed to subdue the rebellion in Texas. He regained power after gallant action against a French raid on Vera Cruz (1838). After his failure in the Mexican War (1846–48), Santa Anna went into exile. He returned to power in 1853 but was overthrown in 1855.

Santer, Jacques (1937–) Luxembourg statesman, prime minister of Luxembourg (1984–94), president of the European Commission (1994–99). In 1999, following charges of corruption, Santer and all the European commissioners resigned.

Sappho (active 6th century BCE) Greek poet. Her passionate love poetry, written on the island of Lesbos was regarded by PLATO as the expression of "the tenth Muse".

Sargon King of Akkad (r.c.2334–c.2279 BCE). One of the first of the great Mesopotamian conquerors, he was a usurper who founded his capital at Agade (Akkad). Sargon conquered Sumeria and upper Mesopotamia and extracted tribute from lands as far w as the Mediterranean. *See also* AKKADIANS; SUMERIANS

Sartre, Jean-Paul (1905–80) French philosopher and writer, the leading advocate of existentialism. His major philosophical work is *Being and Nothingness* (1943). His complex relationship with Marxism is explored in *Critique of Dialectical Reason* (1960). Sartre refused the 1964 Nobel Prize for literature on "personal" grounds but is later said to have accepted it. He had a long-term relationship with Simone de BEAUVOIR.

Sassanian dynasty Ruling family of Persia (CE 224–651). Founded by ARDASHIR I (r.224–241), the Sassanians revived the native Persian traditions of the ACHAEMENID DYNASTY, confirming Zoroastrianism as the state religion. There were c.30 Sassanian rulers, the most important after Ardashir being Shapur II (309–379), KHOSHRU I and KHOSHRU II. The latter's conquest of Syria, Palestine and Egypt marked the height of the dynasty's power. The Sassanian dynasty was overthrown by the Arabs.

Saud, Abdul Aziz ibn (1880–1953) Founder and first king of Saudi Arabia (1932–53). As leader of the Saudi dynasty, he was forced into exile (1891) by the rival Rashid dynasty. He returned in 1902 and extended his authority, driving out the Turks and the Hashemites and founding the modern Saudi state in 1932. Ibn Saud was succeeded by his sons, **Ibn Abdul Aziz Saud** (r.1953–64) and **Faisal ibn Abd al Aziz** (r.1964–75).

Savonarola, Girolamo (1452–98) Italian religious reformer. His sermons attacked the corruption and decadence of the papacy and the state of Florence. After the death of Lorenzo de' MEDICI (1494), Savonarola became leader of the city. His support for the invasion of CHARLES VIII of France infuriated Pope Alexander VI, who excommunicated him in 1497. Public hostility to his regime intensified. Savonarola was hanged for heresy.

Saxons Ancient Germanic people. By the 5th century they had settled in NW Germany, N Gaul and S Britain. In Germany they were subdued by CHARLEMAGNE. In Britain, along with other Germanic tribes, they evolved into the English.

Schiller, Johann Christoph Friedrich von (1759–1805) German dramatist, historian and philosopher. His early blank verse plays, such as *The Robbers* (1781) and *Don Carlos* (1787), are classics of the *Sturm und Drang* period. Schiller's esthetic and philosophical ideas were influenced by the idealism of KANT. His masterpiece is the trilogy *Wallenstein* (1800).

Schlieffen, Alfred, graf von (1833–1913) German field marshal. As chief of the German general staff (1891–1905) Schlieffen designed a plan to wage war on two fronts against France and Prussia. The Schlieffen Plan advocated an all-out attack in the W, which would rapidly defeat the French, enabling Germany to transfer its full force to the E against Russia, whose mobilization would be slower. A modified version was put into effect in 1914.

Schopenhauer, Arthur (1788–1860) German philosopher whose exposition of the doctrine of the will opposed the idealism of HEGEL and influenced NIETZSCHE, WAGNER and others. Schopenhauer's system, described in *The World as Will and Idea* (1819), was an intensely pessimistic one.

Schröder, Gerhard (1944–) German statesman, chancellor (1998–2005). In 1998 he defeated Oskar Lafontaine to become leader of the Social Democratic Party (SPD). Schröder defeated Helmut KOHL in the ensuing general election and formed a coalition with the Green Party.

Schrödinger, Erwin (1887–1961) Austrian physicist. He established the science of wave mechanics as part of quantum theory. Schrödinger formulated an equation that established a relationship between wave function, mass and energy. He shared the 1933 Nobel Prize for physics with Paul DIRAC.

Schubert, Franz Peter (1797–1828) Austrian composer. Among his most popular works are symphonies such as the Eighth (*Unfinished*, 1822) and the Ninth in C major (1825). Schubert wrote more than 600 *lieder* to the lyrics of such poets as Heinrich HEINE and Friedrich von SCHILLER; these include the cycles *Die schöne Müllerin* (1823) and *Winterreise* (1827).

Schumann, Robert Alexander (1810–56) German composer. Schumann's piano compositions include *Kinderszenen* (1838) and *Waldscenen* (1848–49). Among his song cycles is *Frauenliebe und Leben* (1840). His "Spring" Symphony (1841) and Piano Concerto (1841–45) are among his best-known orchestral works.

Schweitzer, Albert (1875–1965) Alsatian medical missionary, philosopher, theologian and musician. He was a gifted organist and wrote an influential biography on J.S. Bach. Schweitzer spent most of his life in Gabon (then French equatorial Africa).

Scipio Africanus Major (236–183 BCE) (Publius Cornelius Scipio) Roman general in the second of the Punic Wars. He defeated the Carthaginian forces in Spain (209 BCE). Elected consul in 205, he invaded North Africa and defeated HANNIBAL at Zama (202 BCE), earning the honorary surname Africanus.

Scott, Sir Walter (1771–1832) Scottish novelist and poet. His first historical novel, *Waverley* (1814), was an immediate success and was followed by other Scottish novels.

Scythians Nomadic people who inhabited the steppes N of the Black Sea in the 1st millennium BCE. In the 7th century BCE their territory extended into Mesopotamia, the Balkans and Greece. Powerful warriors, their elaborate tombs contain evidence of great wealth. Pressure from the Sarmatians confined them to the Crimea (c.300 BCE), and their culture eventually disappeared.

Seleucid dynasty Hellenistic ruling family founded (c.300 BCE) by SELEUCUS I, a former general of ALEXANDER THE GREAT. Centered on Syria, it included most of the Asian provinces of Alexander's empire, extending from the E Mediterranean to India. War with Egypt and later the Romans, steadily reduced its territory. In 63 BCE it became the Roman province of Syria.

Seleucus I (c.355–281 BCE) King of ancient Syria, founder of the SELEUCID DYNASTY. He was a trusted general of ALEXANDER THE GREAT. By 281 BCE Seleucus had secured control of Babylonia, Syria and all of Asia Minor, founding a western capital at Antioch to balance the eastern capital of Seleucia. He appeared to be on the brink of restoring the whole of Alexander's empire under his rule when he was murdered.

Selim I (the Grim) (1467–1520) Ottoman sultan (1512–20). He forced the abdication of his father, Bayazid II. In 1514 Selim defeated Shah ISMAIL of Persia. He added Syria and Egypt to the OTTOMAN EMPIRE by defeating the MAMELUKES (1516–17). Selim made himself caliph, ensuing that his successors were both temporal and spiritual rulers of Mecca and Medina. His son, SULEIMAN I (THE MAGNIFICENT), succeeded him.

Selim II (c.1524–74) Ottoman sultan (1566–74), son and successor of SULEIMAN I (THE MAGNIFICENT). He was dominated by his grand vizier Sokolli. In 1569 the Ottomans regained Tunis from Spain and captured Cyprus from Venice. Spain and Venice allied to defeat Selim at the naval battle of Lepanto (1571).

Seljuks Nomadic tribesmen from central Asia who adopted Islam in the 7th century and founded the Baghdad sultanate in 1055. Their empire included Mesopotamia, Syria and Persia. Under Alp Arslan, they defeated the Byzantines (1071), which led to their occupation of Anatolia. They revived Sunni administration and religious institutions, checking the spread of Shi'a Islam and laying the basis for the Ottoman administration. In the early 12th century the Seljuk empire began to disintegrate, and the Seljuk states were conquered by MONGOLS in the 13th century.

Seneca (Lucius Annaeus) (CE 4–65) Roman Stoic philosopher, b. Spain. Seneca's nine tragedies, such as *Phaedra*, *Medea* and *Oedipus*, have had a lasting impact on European literature.

Seth, Vikram (1952–) Indian writer. His epic *A Suitable Boy* (1993) is one of the longest novels in English.

Severus, (Marcus Aurelius) Alexander (205–35) Roman emperor (222–35), successor of Heliogabulus. In 232 he defeated ARDASHIR I of Persia. Severus was murdered by his troops.

Severus, Lucius Septimius (146–211) Roman emperor (193–211). He was proclaimed emperor by his troops, who marched on Rome and persuaded the Senate to confirm him. Severus dissolved the Praetorian Guard, replacing it with his own men. He divided Britain into two provinces and launched a campaign to conquer Scotland. Repulsed, he died at York.

Shah Jahan (1592–1666) Mughal emperor of India (1628–58), son of Jahangir. He secured his succession by killing most of his male relatives. Shah Jahan subsumed most of the Deccan plateau into the MUGHAL EMPIRE and regained (1638–49) Kandahar from the Persians. Although relatively tolerant of Hinduism, he made Islam the state religion. Shah Jahan was responsible for building the Taj Mahal in Agra.

Shaka (1787–1828) King of the Zulu. In *c*.1816 he claimed the throne, forming a powerful Zulu army and extending his control over all of what is now KwaZulu-Natal. Shaka maintained good relations with the white government in the Cape, but his harsh rule provoked opposition and he was killed by his half brother.

Shakespeare, William (1564–1616) English poet and dramatist. In 1599 he became a partner in the Globe Theater, London, where his plays were presented. In *c*.1613 Shakespeare retired to Stratford-upon-Avon. His 154 *Sonnets* (1609) stand among the finest works in English literature. His history plays include *Richard III* (1592–93), *Henry IV* (parts 1 and 2, 1596–97), *Henry V* (1599) and *Julius Caesar* (1599). Shakespeare's tragedies are *Romeo and Juliet* (1595–96), *Hamlet* (1600–01), *Othello* (1604), *King Lear* (1605–06) and *Macbeth* (1605–06). His comedies include *A Midsummer Night's Dream* (1595), *The Merchant of Venice* (1596–98) and *Twelfth Night* (1600–02). His plots are generally drawn from existing sources.

Shamir, Yitzhak (1915–) Israeli statesman, prime minister (1983–84, 1986–92). He was the leader (1940–48) of the Stern Gang of Zionist guerrillas against the British mandate in Palestine. Shamir became head (1955–65) of Mossad, Israel's secret service. He succeeded Menachim Begin as prime minister and head of the right-wing Likud Party. In 1986 he succeeded Shimon Peres as head of a coalition government. Shamir oversaw the Jewish settlement of the West Bank and Gaza Strip. In 1992 he was defeated by Yitzhak Rabin.

Shang dynasty (Yin) Early Chinese dynasty (*c*.1523–*c*.1027 BCE). Successor to the Xia dynasty, the Shang was based in the valley of the Huang He (Yellow River). During the Shang period, the Chinese written language was perfected, techniques of irrigation were practiced, and artifacts were made in cast bronze.

Shaw, George Bernard (1856–1950) Irish dramatist, critic and member of the Fabian Society. *Arms and the Man* (1894) was his first publicly performed play. *Man and Superman* (1905) and *Major Barbara* (1905) were first performed at the Royal Court, London. *Pygmalion* (1913) was turned into the musical *My Fair Lady* (1956). Shaw received the 1925 Nobel Prize for literature.

Shawnee Algonquian-speaking tribe of Native Americans. In the mid18th century the tribe was reunited in Ohio, where they fiercely resisted white settlement. At the battle of Tippecanoe (1811), William Henry Harrison defeated the Shawnee, led by Shawnee Prophet (*c*.1775–*c*.1837) and Tecumseh. Today, *c*.5,000 Shawnee live on reservations in Oklahoma.

Shelley, Percy Bysshe (1792–1822) English poet. His radical pamphlets forced him into hiding in Wales, where he wrote *Queen Mab* (1813). *Alastor* (1816) reflects his political idealism. The Peterloo Massacre (1819) prompted *The Mask of Anarchy*. *Prometheus Unbound* (1820), a four-act lyrical drama, is a masterpiece of romanticism. Smaller poems include "Ode to the West Wind"(1819) and "To a Skylark"(1820).

Sherman, William Tecumseh (1820–91) Union general in the American Civil War. He took part in the first battle of Bull Run (21 July 1861) and in the capture of Vicksburg (1863). He won the battle of Atlanta and led the "March to the Sea" from Atlanta to Savannah in 1864.

Shockley, William Bradford (1910–89) US physicist. In 1947 Shockley, John Bardeen and Walter Brattain invented the transistor. They shared the 1956 Nobel Prize for physics.

Shostakovich, Dmitri Dmitrievich (1906–75) Russian composer. His use of contemporary western musical developments in his compositions did not conform with Soviet socialist realism. His opera *The Lady Macbeth of the Mtsensk District* (1934) was criticized in *Pravda*. Other works were deliberately more conventional. He composed 15 symphonies, 13 string quartets, ballets, concertos, piano music, film music and vocal works.

Sibelius, Jean Julius Christian (1865–1957) Finnish composer. His work represents the culmination of nationalism in Finnish music. His orchestral works include seven symphonies, a violin concerto (1903–05) and the tone poem *Finlandia* (1899).

Siemens, Ernst Werner von (1816–92) German electrical engineer. In 1849 he developed an electric telegraph system. With **Karl** (1829–1906), he set up subsidiaries of the family firm in London, Vienna and Paris. **Friedrich** (1826–1904) and **Karl Wilhelm** (later William) (1823–83) developed a regenerative furnace that led to the open-hearth process used in the steel industry.

Sièyes, Emmanuel Joseph (1748–1836) French revolutionary. His pamphlet *What is the Third Estate?* (1789) was influential at the start of the French Revolution. In 1790 Sièyes became president of the States-General and helped formulate a new constitution. As a member of the Convention, he voted for the execution of Louis XVI. In 1799 Sièyes entered the Directory but conspired with Napoleon Bonaparte in the coup of 18 Brumaire.

Sigismund (1368–1437) Holy Roman emperor (1411–37) and king of Germany (1410–37), Hungary (1387–1437) and Bohemia (1419–37). As king of Hungary, he was defeated by the Ottoman Turks in 1396 and 1427. In Bohemia he was challenged by the Hussite revolt. Sigismund secured the succession on Albert II, his son-in-law, the first ruler of the Hapsburg dynasty.

Singer, Isaac Merrit (1811–75) US manufacturer. He invented a rock drill (1839) and a single-thread sewing machine (1852).

Sioux (Dakota) Group of seven Native American tribes inhabiting Minnesota, Nebraska, North and South Dakota and Montana. In the 18th century they numbered *c*.30,000. They opposed US forces in the American Revolution and the War of 1812. The tribes concluded several treaties with the US government (1815, 1825, 1851) and finally agreed in 1867 to settle on a reservation in SW Dakota. The discovery of gold in the Black Hills and the rush of prospectors brought resistance from Sioux chiefs such as Sitting Bull and Crazy Horse. In 1876 they defeated General Custer at the battle of Little Bighorn. The last confrontation was the Massacre at Wounded Knee (1890), which resulted in the massacre of more than 200 Sioux.

Sitting Bull (1831–90) Native American leader, chief of the Sioux. With others, he led the attack on General Custer's cavalry at the battle of Little Bighorn (1876). In 1881 Sitting Bull was captured and imprisoned for two years. Later, he joined the Wild West Show of "Buffalo Bill". He was killed resisting arrest.

Smith, Adam (1723–90) Scottish philosopher, regarded as the founder of modern economics. His book *The Wealth of Nations* (1776) was enormously influential in the development of Western capitalism. In place of mercantilism, Smith proposed the doctrine of laissez–faire: that governments should not interfere in economic affairs and that free trade increases wealth.

Smith, John (1580–1631) English soldier and colonist. He was instrumental in establishing the first English colony in North America at Jamestown (1607). Exploring Chesapeake Bay, Smith was captured by Powhatan and possibly saved from death by Powhatan's daughter, Pocahontas.

Smith, Joseph (1805–44) US religious leader. In 1830 he founded the Mormon Church of Jesus Christ of the Latter Day Saints. His *Book of Mormon* (1830) was based on writings he claimed were given to him on golden plates by a heavenly messenger named Moroni. In 1844 he was jailed on a charge of treason at Carthage, Illinois, where he was murdered by a mob.

Smuts, Jan Christiaan (1870–1950) South African statesman, prime minister (1919–24, 1939–48). He was a guerrilla commander during the South African Wars (1899–1902) but afterward worked with Louis Botha to establish the Union of South Africa (1910). During World War I Smuts commanded British forces in East Africa. Upon Botha's death, he succeeded as prime minister. Smuts formed a second administration after James Hertzog opposed entry into World War II. After the war, he was defeated by the apartheid policies of the Nationalist Party.

Snorri Sturluson (1179–1241) Icelandic poet and historian. His *Prose Edda* is a collection of Norse mythology and a discussion of the art of poetry. *Heimskringla*, sagas of the Norwegian kings to 1184, mingles Norse literature, history and legend.

Socrates (469–399 BCE) Greek philosopher. Information about his life and philosophy is found in the writings of PLATO. For Socrates, knowledge and virtue were synonymous. His criticism of tyranny attracted powerful enemies, and he was charged with impiety and corrupting the young. Condemned to death, he drank the poisonous draft of hemlock required by law.

Soddy, Frederick (1877–1956) English chemist. Soddy was awarded the 1921 Nobel Prize for chemistry for his studies of radioactive isotopes. Soddy and Ernest RUTHERFORD worked out an explanation of radioactive decay.

Solomon (d.922 BCE) King of Israel (c.972–922 BCE), son of DAVID and Bathsheba. His kingdom prospered, thanks partly to economic relations with the Egyptians and Phoenicians, enabling Solomon to build the Temple in Jerusalem. His reputation for wisdom reflected his interest in literature, although the works attributed to him were probably written by others.

Solon (c.639–c.599 BCE) Athenian political reformer. In c.594 BCE, during an economic crisis, he was elected archon (chief magistrate). Solon carried out drastic economic and constitutional reforms, laying the foundations of Athenian democracy.

Solvay, Ernest (1838–1922) Belgian industrial chemist. In 1861 he patented a technique for preparing soda from sodium chloride (common salt) and calcium carbonate.

Solzhenitsyn, Alexander (1918–) Russian novelist. Sentenced to a forced labor camp in 1945 for criticizing Stalin, he was subsequently exiled to Ryazan but was officially rehabilitated in 1956. His novels include *One Day in the Life of Ivan Denisovich* (1962), *Cancer Ward* (1968) and *August 1914* (1971). He was awarded the 1970 Nobel Prize for literature.

Somoza García, Anastasio (1896–1956) Nicaraguan dictator, president (1937–47, 1950–56). In 1936 Somoza led a coup against the liberal President Sacasa. In 1947 he installed a puppet president. In 1950 he reestablished his dictatorship, maintaining close links with the USA. He was assassinated and was succeeded in office by his two sons, Luis and Anastasio. In 1979 the Somoza dynasty was overthrown by Daniel ORTEGA.

Sondheim, Stephen (1930–) US composer and lyricist. Sondheim made his mark on Broadway in 1957 with the lyrics for *West Side Story*. His success as a lyricist-composer was established in *Sunday in the Park with George* (1984) and *Assassins* (1991).

Song dynasty (960–1279) (Sung) Chinese imperial dynasty (960–1279). The period is divided into the Northern (960–1126) and, after the N was overrun by Jurchen tribes, the Southern (1127–1279) Song. The Song dynasty was notable for a deliberate reduction in military might and the development of a powerful civil service. The Southern Song, with its capital at Hangzhou, was overrun by the MONGOLS.

Songhai West African empire, founded c.CE 700. In 1468 Sonni Ali captured the market city of Timbuktu, and the Songhai empire acquired control of most of the trade in w Africa. Sonni was succeeded by Askia Muhammad I, who further increased the Songhai stranglehold on trade routes. The empire began to disintegrate because of factional in-fighting. The Songhai peoples still control much of the trans-Saharan trade.

Sontag, Susan (1933–2004) US writer, critic and essayist. Her works of cultural criticism include *Against Interpretation* (1966), *Illness as Metaphor* (1978) and *Aids and its Metaphors* (1986).

Sophocles (496–406 BCE) Greek dramatist. Of his 100 plays, only seven tragedies and part of a Satyr play remain. These include *Antigone* (c.442–441 BCE), *Electra* (409 BCE) and *Oedipus Rex* (c.429 BCE).

Spartacus (d.71 BCE) Thracian gladiator in Rome who led a slave revolt known as the Third Servile (Gladiatorial) War (73–71 BCE). His soldiers devastated the land and then moved s toward Sicily, where they were eventually defeated by CRASSUS with POMPEY's aid. Spartacus died in battle.

Spengler, Oswald (1880–1936) German philosophical historian. In *The Decline of the West* (1918–22), he expounded his theory that all civilizations are subject to a process of growth and decay, concluding that Western civilization was ending.

Spenser, Edmund (1552–99) English poet. His poetry includes the pastoral *The Shepheardes Calender* (1579). His masterpiece was *The Faerie Queene* (1589–96), a moral allegory.

Spinoza, Baruch (1632–77) Dutch-Jewish rationalist philosopher. He argued that all mind and matter were modes of the one key substance, which he called either God or Nature. In *Ethics* (1677), he held that free will was an illusion that would be dispelled by man's recognition that every event has a cause.

Staël, (Anne-Louise-Germaine), madame de (1766–1817) French writer. She published two proto-feminist novels, *Delphine* (1802) and *Corinne* (1807), but is best known for works of social philosophy including *A Treatise on the Influence of the Passions upon the Happiness of Individuals and of Nations* (1796).

Stalin, Joseph (1879–1953) (Iosif Vissarionovich Dzhugashvili) Leader of the Soviet Union (1924–53). He supported LENIN and the Bolsheviks from 1903, adopting the name Stalin ("man of steel"). Exiled to Siberia (1913–17), he returned to join the Russian Revolution (1917) and became secretary of the central committee of the party in 1922. On Lenin's death in 1924, he achieved supreme power. He outmaneuvered rivals, such as TROTSKY, driving him from power. From 1929 he was virtually dictator. He enforced collectivization of agriculture and industrialization, brutally suppressing all opposition. In the 1930s he exterminated all opponents in a series of purges. During World War II Stalin controlled the armed forces and negotiated skillfully during the Yalta Conference with CHURCHILL and ROOSEVELT. After the war he reimposed severe repression and forced puppet communist governments on the states of Eastern Europe.

Stanley, Sir Henry Morton (1841–1904) British-US explorer of Africa, b. Wales. He emigrated to the USA at the age of 16. He was commissioned by the *New York Herald* to lead an expedition in search of David LIVINGSTONE in E Africa. They met in 1871. On a second expedition, Stanley led a large party from the E African lakes down the River Congo to the W coast. He returned to the area (1880) as an agent for King LEOPOLD II.

Steinbeck, John (1902–68) US novelist. Early successes included his novella *Of Mice and Men* (1937). Later novels include *Cannery Row* (1945), *East of Eden* (1952) and *The Grapes of Wrath* (1939), which earned him a Pulitzer Prize. He was awarded the 1962 Nobel Prize for literature.

Stephen, Saint (977–1038) Stephen I of Hungary (r.1000–38), the first king of the Árpád dynasty. His chief work was to continue the Christianization of Hungary begun by his father, by endowing abbeys, inviting in foreign prelates and suppressing paganism. He was canonized in 1083.

Stephenson, George (1781–1848) English engineer. He built his first locomotive, *Blucher*, in 1814. His most famous locomotive, *Rocket* (1829), ran on the Liverpool to Manchester line, one of the many railroad lines that he engineered.

Stockhausen, Karlheinz (1928–2007) German composer and theorist, the most successful exponent of electronic music. An example of his work is *Kontakte* (1960), which uses instruments with tape. His seven-part opera, *Licht*, was begun in 1977.

Stowe, Harriet Beecher (1811–96) US writer, best known for *Uncle Tom's Cabin* (1851–52), a powerful antislavery novel.

Strabo (c.63 BCE–c.CE 24) Greek historian and geographer. He traveled widely, collecting material for *Historical Sketches*, most of which have been lost. His *Geographical Sketches*, containing geographical and historical information of the ancient world, has survived almost intact.

Stradivari, Antonio (1644–1737) Italian violin maker. His instruments remain unsurpassed in brilliance of tone.

Strauss, Johann (the Younger) (1825–99) Austrian composer and conductor. He became extremely popular for his waltzes, such as *The Blue Danube* and *Tales from the Vienna Woods*. Strauss also composed operettas, notably *Die Fledermaus* (1874).

Strauss, Richard (1864–1949) German composer and conductor. His symphonic poems, such as *Don Juan* (1888), *Till Eulenspiegel* (1895) and *Also sprach Zarathustra* (1896), use brilliantly colored orchestration for characterization. His early operas, *Salome* (1905) and *Elektra* (1908), deal with female obsession.

Stravinsky, Igor Feodorovich (1882–1971) Russian composer. His early ballets, *The Firebird* (1910) and *Petrushka* (1911), were commissioned by DIAGHILEV for his Ballets Russes. The première of the ballet *The Rite of Spring* (1913) caused a riot because of its dissonance and unfamiliar rhythms. Stravinsky turned to neoclassicism in *Pulcinella* (1920). In 1939 he moved to the USA, collaborating with Balanchine on the abstract ballet *Agon* (1957). He also experimented with twelve-tone music.

Strindberg, Johan August (1849–1912) Swedish dramatist and novelist. His major dramatic theme was subjective, psychological experience. After suffering a mental breakdown, he produced *A Dream Play* (1902) and *The Ghost Sonata* (1907), both of which prefigure the Theater of the Absurd and expressionism.

Stroessner, Alfredo (1912–2006) Paraguayan statesman, president (1954–89). As commander-in-chief of the armed forces, he led the coup that overthrew the regime of Federico Chavez. His rule was essentially totalitarian but, using foreign aid, he introduced development programs, building roads, bridges and schools.

Stuart, Charles Edward (1720–88) Scottish prince, known as "Bonnie Prince Charlie" or the "Young Pretender". A grandson of the deposed James II, he led the Jacobites in the rebellion of 1745 on behalf of his father, James, the "Old Pretender". Landing in the Scottish Highlands, he gained the support of many clan chiefs, defeated government troops at Prestonpans, E central Scotland, and marched on London. Lacking widespread support in England, he turned back at Derby. The following year his largely Highland force was decimated in the battle of Culloden. He escaped to the continent and lived in exile until his death.

Stuart dynasty Scottish royal house, which inherited the Scottish crown in 1371 and the English crown in 1603. The Stuarts descended from Alan, whose descendants held the hereditary office of steward in the royal household. Walter (d.1326) married a daughter of King Robert I, and their son, Robert II, became the first Stuart king (1371). The crown descended in the male line until the death of James V (1542), who was succeeded by his daughter, MARY, QUEEN OF SCOTS. In 1603 her son, James VI, succeeded ELIZABETH I of England as JAMES I. In 1649 James's son, CHARLES I, was executed following the Civil War, but the dynasty was restored on the Restoration of CHARLES II in 1660. His brother, JAMES II, lost the throne in the Glorious Revolution (1685) and was replaced by the joint monarchy of WILLIAM III and Mary II, James's daughter. On the death (1714) of ANNE, James's daughter, without an heir, the House of Hanover succeeded. The male descendants of James II made several attempts to regain the throne, culminating in the Jacobite rebellion of 1745.

Stuyvesant, Peter (1610–72) Dutch colonial administrator. He became governor of the Caribbean islands of Curaçao, Bonaire and Aruba in 1643, and in 1647 he became director-general of all the Dutch territories, including New Amsterdam (later New York City). In 1655 he ended Swedish influence in Delaware.

Sucre, Antonio José de (1795–1830) South American revolutionary leader and first president of Bolivia (1826–28). He joined the fight for independence in 1811 and played a key role in the liberation of Ecuador, Peru and Bolivia. With Simón BOLIVAR's support, Sucre became the first elected president of Bolivia, but local opposition forced his resignation.

Suetonius (Gaius Suetonius Tranquillus) (c.CE 69–c.140) Roman author. A lawyer and secretary to Emperor HADRIAN, Suetonius is best remembered as a biographer. Two collections of his work survive: parts of *De viris illustribus* ("On Famous Men") and *De vita Caesarum* ("The Lives of the Caesars").

Suevi (Suebi) Germanic peoples, including the Marcomanni, Quadi, Hermunduri, Semnones and Langobardi (LOMBARDS). They occupied the area around the River Elbe until driven out by the HUNS in the early 5th century. Suevi settled in N Spain, where their influence spread to the Roman provinces. Their territory was finally conquered by Visigoth king Leovigild in 583.

Suharto, Raden (1921–2008) Indonesian general and statesman, president (1967–98). Suharto seized power from President SUKARNO, averting an alleged communist coup, in 1966. He was formally elected president in 1968 and was reelected (unopposed) five times. Under Suharto, Indonesia experienced rapid economic development, but his autocratic rule was criticized for abuses of human rights. In 1997 economic collapse destabilized Suharto's government, and in 1998 he was ousted after rioting.

Sui dynasty (581–618) Chinese dynasty, the two rulers (Yang Jian and Yangdi) of which re-established strong central rule in China following more than 250 years of division. The Grand Canal was completed, the Great Wall refortified and many towns beautified, all at great human cost in taxation and forced labor. After defeat at the hands of Eastern Turks (615), the Sui dynasty was overthrown and succeeded by the TANG.

Sukarno, Achmad (1901–70) Indonesian statesman, first president of independent Indonesia (1947–67). Founder of the Indonesian Nationalist Party (1927), he led opposition to Dutch rule. At the end of World War II he declared Indonesian independence and became president. In the 1950s his rule became dictatorial. He dissolved the parliament, declared himself president for life (1963) and aligned himself with the communists. The failure of a communist coup against the leaders of the army in 1965 weakened Sukarno's position. He was forced out of power by the generals, led by SUHARTO, who replaced him as president.

Suleiman I (the Magnificent) (1494–1566) OTTOMAN sultan (1520–66). He succeeded his father, SELIM I. He captured Rhodes from the Knights Hospitallers and launched a series of campaigns against the HAPSBURGS, defeating the Hungarians at Mohács (1526). His troops besieged Vienna (1529), and his admiral, BARBAROSSA, created a navy that ensured Ottoman control of much of the North African coastal region. In the east he won victories against the SAFAVIDS and conquered Mesopotamia.

Sulla, Lucius Cornelius (138–78 BCE) Roman dictator (82–81 BCE). Elected consul in 88 BCE, he defeated MITHRIDATES VI in spite of the opposition of MARIUS, Cinna and their supporters in Rome. Invading Italy, he captured Rome in 82 BCE and massacred his antipatrician enemies.

Sumerians People of Sumeria, the world's first civilization, dating from before 3000 BCE in S Mesopotamia. The Sumerians are credited with inventing cuneiform writing, many sociopolitical institutions and a money-based economy. Major cities were Ur, Kish and Lagash. During the third millennium it built up a large empire. In c.2340 BCE the AKKADIANS conquered Mesopotamia, and by c.1950 BCE the civilization had disintegrated.

Sun Yat-sen (1866–1925) Chinese nationalist leader, first president of the Chinese Republic (1911–12). After the revolution of 1911 he became provisional president, but soon resigned in favor of the militarily powerful YUAN SHIKAI. When Yuan turned autocratic, Sun gave his support to the Kuomintang, or Nationalist Party, formed to oppose Yuan.

Swedenborg, Emanuel (1688–1772) Swedish scientist, philosopher, theologian and mystic. After a glittering scientific career, he turned to theological teaching after a spiritual crisis. His writings include *Heavenly Arcana* (1749–56), *The New Jerusalem* (1758) and *True Christian Religion* (1771).

Swift, Jonathan (1667–1745) Irish satirist and poet. He was ordained an Anglican priest and became dean of St. Patrick's Cathedral. His best-known work, *Gulliver's Travels* (1726), is a satire on human follies. He wrote many works criticizing England's treatment of Ireland, including *A Modest Proposal* (1729).

T

Tacitus, Cornelius (CE 55–120) Roman historian. His crisp style and reliability make him one of the greatest of ancient historians. His major works, the *Annals* and *Histories*, exist only in fragmentary form.

Taft, William Howard (1857–1930) 27th US President

(1909–13) and tenth chief justice of the Supreme Court (1921–30). After a distinguished legal career, he entered the cabinet of Theodore ROOSEVELT. In 1908 Taft won the Republican nomination for president. His lack of political experience and his tendency to side with the conservatives caused dissension. In 1912 Roosevelt, having failed to regain the presidential nomination, set up his own Progressive Party. With the split in the Republican vote, the Democrat, Woodrow WILSON, won the election.

Tagore, Rabindranath (1861–1941) Indian poet and philosopher. He wrote novels, essays, plays and poetic works in colloquial Bengali. His best-known work is *Gitanjali* (1912), a volume of spiritual poetry. In 1913 Tagore became the first Asian writer to be awarded the Nobel Prize for literature.

Talleyrand (-Périgord), Charles Maurice de (1754–1838) French statesman and diplomat. As foreign minister under the Directory (1797–99), he participated in the coup that brought NAPOLEON to power. In 1807, concerned about the growing power of Napoleon, Talleyrand resigned as foreign minister. In 1814 he negotiated the restoration of the BOURBON monarchy. As foreign minister to LOUIS XVIII, Talleyrand represented France at the Congress of Vienna (1814–15). He was LOUIS PHILIPPE's chief adviser in the July Revolution (1830).

Tamerlane (1336–1405) (Turkish *Timur Leng*, Timur the Lame) Mongol conqueror, b. Uzbekistan. He claimed descent from GENGHIS KHAN. By 1369 Tamerlane had conquered present-day Turkistan and established Samarkand as his capital. He extended his conquests to the region of the Golden Horde between the Caspian and Black seas. In 1398 Tamerlane invaded NW India and defeated the DELHI SULTANATE. He then turned toward the MAMELUKE empire, capturing Syria and Damascus. In 1402 he captured the Ottoman sultan, Beyazid I, at Angora. His death, at the head of a 200,000-strong invasion force of China, enabled the reopening of the Silk Road.

Tang dynasty (T'ang dynasty) Chinese imperial dynasty (618–907). The early period was a golden age of China, when it was by far the largest, richest and culturally most accomplished society in the world. Tang armies carried Chinese authority to Afghanistan, Tibet and Korea. During the 8th century the dynasty was submerged in civil conflict.

Tao Ch'ien (365–427) Chinese poet, one of the greatest of the Chinese tradition. His verse, which has a predominantly Taoist outlook, often extols the pleasures of nature and wine.

Tarquin Superbus ("Tarquin the Proud") (r.534–510 BCE) Etruscan king, traditionally the seventh and last king of Rome. Largely known only in legend, he is said to have been a despot, whose cruelty provoked an uprising that led to his expulsion from Rome and the abolition of the Roman monarchy.

Tartaglia, Niccoló Fontana (1499–1557) Italian mathematician, the first to obtain a general solution to the cubic equation of the form $x^3 + ax^2 + bx + c = 0$. He published *Nova Scientia* (1537) and *Trattato di numeri et misure* (1556–60).

Tasman, Abel Janszoon (1603–59) Dutch maritime explorer. On his voyage of 1642–43 he discovered Tasmania. Tasman reached New Zealand but was attacked by Maoris. He landed on Tonga and Fiji and sailed along the coast of New Ireland. Although he circumnavigated Australia, he never sighted it.

Taylor, Zachary (1784–1850) 12th US President (1849–50). He fought in the War of 1812. In 1845 Taylor was ordered to occupy Texas, recently annexed, which set off the Mexican War. He emerged from the war as a popular hero. Taylor won the Whig nomination for president and the subsequent election (1848) but died suddenly after only 16 months in office.

Tchaikovsky, Peter Ilyich (1840–93) Russian composer. His gift for melody and expressiveness is apparent in all his works. Tchaikovsky's popular ballets include *Swan Lake* (1876), *The Sleeping Beauty* (1889) and *The Nutcracker* (1892). Other famous works include his first Piano Concerto (1875), the *1812* overture (1880) and the sixth (*Pathétique*) symphony (1893).

Tecumseh (1768–1813) Native American leader. A SHAWNEE

chief, he worked with his brother, known as the Prophet, to uni Native Americans of the West and resist white expansion. Aft the Prophet's defeat, Tecumseh joined the British in the War 1812. He was killed in Upper Canada.

Tennyson, Alfred, 1st Baron (1809–92) (Alfred Lord Te nyson) English poet. He became poet laureate in 1850. His oe vre includes such patriotic classics as "Ode on the Death of th Duke of Wellington" (1852) and "The Charge of the Lig Brigade"(1855). Tennyson also wrote deeply personal utterance such as "Crossing the Bar" (1889). Other notable works inclu "The Lady of Shalott" and the epic *Idylls of the King* (1872–7)

Terence (*c*.190–159 BCE) (Publius Terentius Afer) Roma author. He was a slave in Rome where he was educated and subs quently freed by his master. Six of his comedies survive and inclu *Andria* (*c*.166 BCE), *Hecyra* (*c*.165 BCE) and *Phormio* (*c*.161 BCE)

Teresa of Avila, Saint (1515–82) (Teresa de Cepeda y Ahum da) Spanish Carmelite nun and mystic. From 1558 she set abo reforming the Carmelite order for women. Her literary work including an autobiography and the meditative *Interior Cas* (1577), as well as her monastic reforms, led to her canonization

Thackeray, William Makepeace (1811–63) British noveli b. India. His best-known novel is *Vanity Fair* (1847–48), a sati on 19th-century upper-class London society. Other novels inclu *Pendennis* (1848–50) and *The Virginians* (1857–59). Thacker was the founding editor (1860–75) of the *Cornhill Magazine*.

Thales (636–546 BCE) Greek scientist and philosopher. He ma discoveries in geometry, such as that the angles at the base of a isosceles triangle are equal. Thales predicted the eclipse of th Sun that took place in 585 BCE.

Thant, U (1909–74) Burmese diplomat, third secretary-gener (1962–72) of the United Nations (UN). He was acting secretar general from 1961 before being elected in his own right. Than helped to settle several major disputes, including the civil wars the Congo (Zaire) in 1963 and Cyprus in 1964.

Thatcher, Margaret Hilda, Baroness (1925–) Britis stateswoman, prime minister (1979–90). She was secretary state for education and science (1970–74) under Edward HEATI whom she defeated for the party leadership in 1975. In 1979 sh became Britain's first woman prime minister. Her governme embarked on a radical free-market program, which becam known as "Thatcherism". Her monetarist policies, especially cu in public spending, provoked criticism, but her popularity w restored by victory in the Falklands War (1982). Thatcher's dete mination to curb the power of labor unions provoked a bitt miners' strike (1983–84). In 1987 Thatcher won a third term, b clashed with colleagues over her hostile attitude to the Europea Union (EU). A poll tax (1989) was widely seen as unfair, and sh was forced to resign. Thatcher was succeeded by John MAJOR.

Theodoric the Great (*c*.454–526) King of the OSTROGOTI and ruler of Italy. He drove ODOACER from Italy (488) an attempted to recreate the Western Roman Empire with himself emperor. Religious differences and political rivalries frustrate his empire-building, and his kingdom was destroyed by JUSTINIA after his death.

Theodosius I (*c*.347–395) Roman emperor (379–95), the la to rule both Eastern (from 379) and Western (from 392) ROMA EMPIRES. A champion of orthodox Christianity, he summoned th first ecumenical council of Constantinople (381) to solve the rel gious dispute over the doctrine of Arianism. He ended the wa with the VISIGOTHS. After 392 he briefly reunited the empire aft defeating a pretender, but left the two parts separately to his son

Theodosius II (401–450) Eastern Roman emperor (408–50 He was dominated by ministers. His armies repelled Persian inva sions, and the fortifications of Constantinople were strength ened. He promulgated the Theodosian Code of laws (438).

Thespis (6th century BCE) Greek writer, according to traditio the inventor of tragedy. He is also said to have introduced a cha acter separate from the chorus, who provided dialogue b responding to the chorus' comments.

Thiers, Louis Adolphe (1797–1877) French politician and historian. He was twice foreign minister under Louis Philippe and led Liberal opposition to Napoleon III from 1863 to 1870. Thiers was first president of the Third Republic (1871–73). He wrote a 10-volume *History of the French Revolution* (1823–27).

Thomas, Dylan Marlais (1914–53) Welsh poet and short-story writer. His flamboyant alcoholic life style contributed to the popularity of his meticulously crafted verse. His *Collected Poems* was published in 1953. Many of his best short stories appear in *Portrait of the Artist as a Young Dog* (1940). The "play for voices" *Under Milk Wood* (1952) is his best-known work.

Thomson, Sir Joseph John (1856–1940) British physicist, b. Belfast. His discovery (1897) of the electron is regarded as the birth of particle physics. He established that cathode rays consisted of a stream of particles. Thomson went on to prove that the electron was negatively charged and that its mass was *c.*2,000 times smaller than the smallest atom (hydrogen). He was awarded the 1906 Nobel Prize for physics.

Thucydides (*c.*460–*c.*400 BCE) Greek historian. He was a commander in the Peloponnesian Wars. His *History of the Peloponnesian War* is a determined attempt to write objective history.

Tiberius (42 BCE–CE 37) (Tiberius Julius Caesar Augustus) Roman emperor (CE 14–37). He was the stepson of Augustus, who adopted him as his heir (CE 4). Initially, his administration was just and moderate, but he became increasingly fearful of conspiracy and had many people executed for alleged treason.

Tintoretto (1518–94) Italian painter, b. Jacopo Robusti. Among his most notable works are *The Finding of the Body of St. Mark* (1562) and the *Paradiso* (1588–90) in the Doge's Palace, Venice.

Tippett, Sir Michael Kemp (1905–98) English composer. His music incorporates apparently disparate musical forms and social themes of justice, pacifism and humanism. Tippett's oratorio *A Child of our Time* (1941) was a response to the 1938 Kristallnacht in Nazi Germany. His operas include *The Midsummer Marriage* (1952), *King Priam* (1962) and *New Year* (1988).

Tipu Sultan (1749–99) Indian ruler, sultan of Mysore (1782–99). He fought the Maratha and the British in the service of his father, Hyder Ali, but concluded peace with the British in 1784. His negotiations with the French provoked a British invasion of Mysore in 1799, and Tipu was killed.

Tirpitz, Alfred von (1849–1930) German admiral. Tirpitz was chiefly responsible for the buildup of the German navy before World War I. Frustrated by government cut-backs and restrictions on submarine warfare, he resigned in 1916.

Titian (1485–1576) Venetian painter, b. Tiziano Vecellio. He combined the balance of High Renaissance composition with a new dynamism. His finest mythological paintings include *Bacchanal* (*c.*1518) and *Bacchus and Ariadne* (1522–23). In 1533 Titian was appointed court painter to Emperor Charles V. From 1550 Titian produced erotic mythologies for Philip II of Spain, such as *The Rape of Europa* (1562). His last work was the powerful *Pietà*, which he designed for his own tomb.

Tito (1892–1980) Yugoslav statesman, b. Croatia as Josip Broz. A soldier in the Austro-Hungarian army, he was captured by the Russians (1915) but released by the Bolsheviks in 1917. He helped to organize the Yugoslav Communist Party. He led the Partisans' successful campaign against the Germans during World War II. In 1945 Tito established a communist government and was prime minister (1945–53) and thereafter president, although virtually a dictator. Soviet efforts to control Yugoslavia led to a split between the two countries in 1948. Tito sought to balance the deep ethnic and religious divisions in Yugoslavia and to develop an economic model of communist "self-management". His greatest achievement was to hold the Yugoslavian federation together.

Titus (CE 39–81) Roman emperor (r.79–81), eldest son of Vespasian. He captured and destroyed Jerusalem in CE 70 after a Jewish revolt. As emperor, Titus stopped persecutions for treason, completed the Colosseum and provided aid for the survivors after the eruption of Vesuvius (79). He was succeeded by Domitian.

Tocqueville, Alexis de (1805–59) French historian. Sent to the USA by the French government, he produced *Of Democracy in America* (1835), an in-depth study of the US political system. His later work includes *L'Ancien Régime et la Révolution* (1856).

Tojo, Hideki (1885–1948) Japanese statesman and general, prime minister (1941–44). He was chief of staff (1937–40) in Manchuria and minister of war (1940–41). As prime minister, he approved the attack on Pearl Harbor and was responsible for the war effort. In 1944 he resigned. In 1945 he was arrested by the Allies, tried for war crimes, found guilty and hanged.

Tokugawa Ieyasu (1543–1616) Japanese leader. He completed the unification of Japan and established the Tokugawa shogunate. This dynasty ruled Japan from 1603 to 1867 through the shogun. It controlled much of Japan's wealth as well as the emperor and priests. The Tokugawa shogunate banned Christianity and Western trade, revived Confucianism, and isolated Japan from the rest of the world. The regime declined during the 19th century. The last Tokugawa shogun was overthrown before the Meiji Restoration (1867).

Tolstoy, Leo Nikolaievich, Count (1828–1910) Russian novelist, moralist and mystic. His masterpiece, *War and Peace* (1865–69), is an epic account of the Napoleonic Wars. Tolstoy's most popular work, *Anna Karenina* (1875–77), is a tragic love story. In his *Confession* (1879), Tolstoy outlines his conversion to an extreme form of Christian anarchism.

Toltecs (Nuhuatl, master builder) Native American people of an ancient civilization, the capital of which was Tollán (Tula), Mexico. The Toltec were the dominant people in the region from CE 900 to 1200. Their architecture is characterized by pyramid building. Although theirs was considered a polytheistic culture, images of Quetzalcóatl predominate. In the 12th century the Toltecs were gradually supplanted by the Aztecs.

Tombaugh, Clyde William (1906–97) US astronomer. In 1930, during a search based on predictions by Percival Lowell, he discovered the planet Pluto. He also discovered star clusters, clusters of galaxies, a comet and hundreds of asteroids.

Tone, (Theobald) Wolfe (1763–98) Irish revolutionary leader. In 1791 Tone, who wanted the Irish to sink religious differences and unite for independence, founded the United Irishmen. He promoted the Catholic Relief Act (1793). After visiting America in 1795, Tone masterminded an abortive French invasion of Ireland in 1796. He committed suicide after being captured.

Torquemada, Tomás de (1420–98) Spanish churchman and grand inquisitor. A Dominican priest and confessor to Ferdinand V and Isabella I, he was appointed head of the Spanish Inquisition (1483). Torquemada was noted for the severity of his judgments. He was responsible for *c.*2,000 burnings.

Torricelli, Evangelista (1608–47) Italian physicist. He is credited with the first manufactured vacuum (the Torricellian vacuum) and the invention of the mercury barometer (1643).

Toussaint L'Ouverture, Pierre Dominique (1744–1803) Haitian revolutionary leader. In 1790 he took part in the slave revolt in Haiti, joined the Spaniards when they attacked the French in 1793, but fought for the French (1794) when they promised to abolish slavery. By 1801 Toussaint had gained control of virtually the whole of Hispaniola. In 1802 Napoleon sought to restore French control. Toussaint died a prisoner in France.

Trajan (CE 53–117) Roman emperor (98–117), b. Spain. He distinguished himself as a general and administrator and was made junior coemperor by Nerva in 97. With army support, he became emperor on Nerva's death. He conducted major campaigns in Dacia (101–102, 105–106) and against the people of Parthia (113–117), enlarging the Roman Empire to its greatest extent.

Trevithick, Richard (1771–1833) English engineer. In 1801 he built a steam-powered road vehicle. In 1802 Trevithick patented a high-pressure steam engine, his most important invention. In 1803 he built the first steam railroad locomotive.

Trimble, David (1944–) Northern Irish statesman, first minister of Northern Ireland (1998–2001). He entered the British

Parliament in 1990. In 1995 he succeeded James Molyneaux as leader of the Ulster Unionists. Following the Good Friday Agreement (10 April 1998), he became first minister. In 1998 Trimble and John HUME shared the Nobel Peace Prize for their efforts to find a peaceful solution to the conflict in Northern Ireland.

Trollope, Anthony (1815–82) English novelist. His reputation as a writer is founded chiefly on a series of six novels, chronicling rural Victorian life in the imaginary county of Barsetshire. The series included *The Warden* (1855) and *Barchester Towers* (1857).

Trotsky, Leon (1879–1940) Russian revolutionary leader and theoretician, b. Lev Davidovich Bronstein. A Marxist revolutionary from 1897, he headed the workers' soviet in St. Petersburg in the Russian Revolution of 1905. Arrested, Trotsky escaped abroad and embarked on the work that made him, with LENIN, the leading architect of the Russian Revolution of 1917. He returned to Russia after the March revolution (1917) and joined the Bolsheviks. As chairman of the Petrograd Soviet, Trotsky set up the Military Revolutionary Committee to seize power for the Bolsheviks. After the Bolshevik success, he negotiated the peace of Brest-Litovsk, withdrawing Russia from World War I. As commissar of war (1918–25), Trotsky created the Red Army, which won the civil war. He criticized the growth of bureaucracy in the party and the lack of democracy. Trotsky disapproved of Lenin's dictatorial tendencies. He objected to STALIN's adoption of a policy of "socialism in one country", rather than the world revolution in which Trotsky believed. He was driven from power, from the party, and from the country.

Trudeau, Pierre Elliott (1919–2000) Canadian statesman, prime minister (1968–79, 1980–84). Trudeau promoted the economic and diplomatic independence of Canada, reducing US influence. He resisted Quebec separatism, imposing martial law to combat separatist terrorism in 1970. Defeated in the elections of 1979, he returned to power in 1980. Autonomy for Quebec was rejected in a referendum (1980), and Trudeau succeeded in winning agreement for a revised constitution (1981).

Trujillo Molina, Rafael Leonidas (1891–1961) Dominant figure of the Dominican Republic from 1930 until his death. Initially installed as chief executive by a revolutionary coup, Trujillo was several times reelected. As president or maker-of-presidents, Trujillo controlled the nation's institutions.

Truman, Harry S. (1884–1972) 33rd US President (1945–53). He won election to the Senate in 1934. In 1944 he was Franklin ROOSEVELT's running mate. Truman became president on Roosevelt's death and was faced with many difficulties abroad. He approved the use of the atomic bomb to force Japanese surrender (1945), ending World War II, and adopted a robust policy toward the Soviet Union during the Cold War. Truman approved the Marshall Plan (1947) and the creation (1949) of the North Atlantic Treaty Organization (NATO). In the Korean War, Truman was forced to dismiss the US commander, General MACARTHUR. Truman was succeeded by Dwight D. EISENHOWER.

Tsiolkovsky, Konstantin Eduardovich (1857–1935) Russian aeronautical engineer. In 1898 he became the first person to stress the importance of liquid propellants in rockets. He also proposed the idea of using multistage rockets to overcome gravitation.

Tuaregs Fiercely independent BERBERS of Islamic faith who inhabit the desert regions of N Africa. Their matrilineal, feudal society is based on nomadic pastoralism. Tuareg males wear blue veils, whereas the women are unveiled. About half the population is no longer nomadic, and there have been demands for the Tuareg to have their own homeland.

Tudors English royal dynasty (1485–1603). Of Welsh origin, they were descended from Owen Tudor (d.1461), who married the widow of HENRY V. Owen Tudor's grandson defeated RICHARD III at Bosworth in 1485 to win the English throne as HENRY VII. The dynasty ended with the death of ELIZABETH I in 1603.

Tu Fu (712–70) Chinese poet of the TANG DYNASTY. His poetry reflects his troubled personal life and laments the corruption and cruelty that prevailed at court.

Tull, Jethro (1674–1741) English agriculturalist. He influenced agricultural methods through his invention (1701) of a mechanical seed drill. The drill reduced the labor involved in weeding.

Tupac Amaru (c.1742–81) (José Gabriel Condorcanqui) Native American leader in Peru. Tupac Amaru led (1780–81) an army of more than 10,000 Native Americans in a revolt against Spanish colonial rule. The revolt was quashed and its leader executed.

Turgenev, Ivan Sergeievich (1818–83) Russian novelist, playwright and short-story writer. His novels often opposed social and political evils and attracted official disapproval. His play *A Month in the Country* (1855) is often considered the first psychological drama of the Russian theater. After the publication of *Fathers and Sons* (1862), he left Russia permanently.

Turing, Alan Mathison (1912–54) English mathematician. In 1937 he invented the Turing machine, a hypothetical machine that could modify a set of input instructions. It was the forerunner of the modern computer. During World War II Turing played a major role in deciphering the German "Enigma" code. In 1950 he devised the Turing test, which paved the way for the foundation of artificial intelligence (AI).

Turner, Joseph Mallord William (1775–1851) English landscape painter. His paintings were revolutionary in their representation of light, especially on water. His style changed dramatically in his late works, such as *The Slave Ship* (1840) and *Rain, Steam and Speed* (1844), in which the original subjects are almost obscured in a hazy interplay of light and color.

Turner, Nat (1800–31) US revolutionary. A slave in Virginia, he believed that he was called by God to take violent revenge on whites and win freedom for blacks. With c.70 followers, he was responsible for the death of more than 50 whites before the revolt was crushed. Turner was captured and hanged.

Tutankhamun (c.1341–1323 BCE) Egyptian pharaoh (r.1333–1323 BCE) of the New Kingdom's 18th dynasty (1550–1307 BCE). The revolutionary changes made by his predecessor, AKHNATEN, were reversed during his reign. The capital was re-established at Thebes (Luxor) and worship of Amon reinstated. Tutankhamun's fame is due to the discovery of his tomb by Howard Carter in 1922. It contained magnificent treasures.

Twain, Mark (1835–1910) US writer, journalist and lecturer, b. Samuel Langhorne Clemens. Twain was among the first to write novels in the American vernacular, such as *The Adventures of Tom Sawyer* (1876) and *The Adventures of Huckleberry Finn* (1884).

Tyler, John (1790–1862) Tenth US President (1841–45). He served in Congress (1811–16) and as governor of Virginia (1825–27). Tyler was a supporter of states' rights. The Whigs chose him as vice-presidential candidate with William H. HARRISON, and he succeeded to the presidency on Harrison's death. He came into conflict with the nationalist Whigs in Congress.

Tyler, Wat (d.1381) English leader of the Peasants' Revolt (1381). He was chosen as leader of the rebels in Kent, SE England, and led their march on London. Tyler was eventually killed by the lord mayor of London while parleying with RICHARD II.

U

Umayyad dynasty (Omayyad dynasty) Dynasty of Arabian Muslim caliphs (661–750). From their capital at Damascus, the Umayyads ruled an empire that stretched from Spain to India. They made little effort to convert conquered peoples to Islam, but there was great cultural exchange. Arabic became established as the language of Islam. They were overthrown by the ABBASIDS.

Umberto I (1844–1900) King of Italy (1878–1900). Son and successor of Italy's first king, VICTOR EMMANUEL II, he approved the Triple Alliance (1882) with Germany and Austria.

Urban II (c.1035–99) Pope (1088–99), b. Odo of Châtillon-sur-Marne. He carried on the reforms begun by Gregory VII. In 1095 at the Council of Clermont, Urban preached the First Crusade. His work as a reformer encouraged the development of the Curia Romana and the formation of the College of Cardinals.

V

Valens (c.328–78) Roman emperor (364–78). He was appointed coemperor by his older brother, VALENTIAN I. Ruling the Eastern ROMAN EMPIRE, Valens spent his entire reign defending his territory from VISIGOTHS and SASSANIANS.

Valentinian I (321–75) Roman emperor (364–75). Proclaimed emperor by his troops, he assigned the eastern half of the empire to his brother VALENS. Valentinian ably defended the frontiers in Gaul and Britain. A Christian, he promoted religious toleration.

Valerian, Publius Licinius (died c.269) Roman emperor (253–60). In 257 he revived the persecution of the Christians that had begun under Emperor DECIUS. Christians were required to perform public acts of worship to the state gods. The persecution ended when Valerian was captured by the Persians in 260 while attempting to halt their invasion of Syria and Armenia.

Valois Royal dynasty that ruled France from the accession (1328) of PHILIP VI to the death (1589) of HENRY III (1589), when the throne passed to the BOURBONS. *See also* CHARLES VIII; FRANCIS I; LOUIS XI; LOUIS XII

Van Buren, Martin (1782–1862) Eighth US President (1837–41). He served (1921–28) in the US Senate. As Andrew JACKSON's secretary of state, Van Buren's opposition to nullification earned him the vice-presidency (1832–36) and the Democratic nomination. Van Buren was an advocate of states' rights, and his presidency was plunged into crisis by the lack of federal intervention in the economic depression (1837). In foreign affairs, Van Buren sought conciliation with Great Britain over the Aroostook War. He was defeated by William H. HARRISON in 1840.

Vandals Germanic tribe who attacked the Roman Empire in the 5th century. They looted Gaul and invaded Spain in 409. Defeated by the GOTHS, they moved south and invaded North Africa (429), establishing a kingdom from where they controlled the w Mediterranean. They sacked Rome in 455. The Vandal kingdom was destroyed (533–34) by the Byzantine general BELISARIUS.

Van Dyck, Sir Anthony (1599–1641) Flemish artist. His portraits of the aristocracy, such as *Marchesa Elena Grimaldi* (c.1625), were widely copied. In 1632 Van Dyck was invited to England by Charles I, who made him court painter.

Van Gogh, Vincent (1853–90) Dutch painter, a leading exponent of expressionism. Van Gogh's early works, such as *The Potato Eaters* (1885), are studies of working-class life. In 1886 he left Holland for Paris, where his palette was transformed by postimpressionism. In 1888 Van Gogh moved to Arles, Provence. Suffering from mental illness, he cut off part of his left ear after a quarrel with GAUGUIN. Van Gogh's paintings from this period include the *Sunflower* series (1888) and the *Night Café* (1888).

Vargas, Getúlio Dornelles (1883–1954) Brazilian statesman, president (1930–45, 1951–54). He led a successful revolt after being defeated in presidential elections. Vargas' autocratic regime was bolstered by the army. He established a corporative state. His refusal to grant elections led to a military coup. Vargas' second term was tainted by scandal and he was forced to resign.

Vasari, Giorgio (1511–74) Italian painter, architect and biographer. His fame now rests on his history of Italian art, *The Lives of the most excellent Painters, Sculptors and Architects* (1550). In architecture he is noted for his design for the Uffizi.

Vaughan Williams, Ralph (1872–1958) English composer. His interest in English folk music is apparent in the instrumental arrangement *Fantasia on Greensleeves*. Vaughan Williams wrote nine symphonies, the best known of which is the *Sinfonia Antarctica* (1952). Other works include *The Lark Ascending* (1914).

Vega Carpio, Félix, Lope de (1562–1635) Spanish poet and dramatist. Vega Carpio was a prolific writer, but only c.300 of his works survive. These include the plays *Peribáñez and the Commander of Ocaña* (c.1610) and *All Citizens Are Soldiers* (c.1613).

Velázquez, Diego Rodríguez de Silva y (1599–1660) Spanish painter. He developed a personal style that combined naturalism with a deep spirituality. He painted dignified genre paintings,

notably *The Old Woman Cooking Eggs* (1618). In 1623 Velázquez became court painter to Philip IV of Spain. During the 1630s and 1640s he produced a series of royal and equestrian portraits. Velázquez's late works include *The Maids of Honor* (c.1656).

Verdi, Giuseppe (1813–1901) Italian composer. His early operas display a sense of the dramatic. Up to 1853 his masterpieces were *Rigoletto* (1851), *Il trovatore* (1853) and *La traviata* (1853). With Verdi's last three operas, *Don Carlos* (1884), *Otello* (1887) and *Falstaff* (1893), Italian opera reached its greatest heights. Among other compositions are the *Requiem* (1874).

Verlaine, Paul (1844–96) French poet. His early poetry, *Poèmes Saturniens* (1866) and *Fêtes Galantes* (1869), was influenced by BAUDELAIRE. An intense relationship with RIMBAUD ended violently. While in jail (1874–75), he wrote *Songs Without Words* (1874), an early work of symbolism.

Vermeer, Jan (1632–75) Dutch painter. Early mythological and religious works gave way to a middle period featuring the serene domestic scenes for which he is best known. The compositions are extremely simple and powerful. He treated light and color with enormous delicacy, as in *View of Delft* (c.1660).

Veronese, Paolo Caliari (1528–88) Italian painter. He excelled at painting large scenes featuring flamboyant pageants. He also painted religious and mythological themes. The Inquisition objected to his irreverent treatment of *The Last Supper* (1573) so he renamed it *The Feast in the House of Levi*.

Verwoerd, Hendrik Frensch (1901–66) South African statesman, prime minister (1958–66), b. Netherlands. A vocal advocate of apartheid, he promoted the policy of "separate development" of the races. In 1961 Verwoerd led South Africa out of the British Commonwealth. He was assassinated by a white extremist.

Vesalius, Andreas (1514–64) Belgian physician. His *On the Structure of the Human Body* (1543) was the first anatomy book to make use of accurate illustrations based on dissections.

Vespasian (CE 9–79) (Titus Flavius Vespasianus) Roman emperor (69–79). A successful general and administrator, he was leading the campaign against the Jews in Palestine when he was proclaimed emperor by his soldiers. Vespasian proved a capable ruler, extending and strengthening the empire, rectifying the budget deficit and adding to the monumental buildings of Rome.

Vespucci, Amerigo (1454–1512) Italian maritime explorer. He was possibly the first to realize that the Americas constituted new continents, which were named for him by the German cartographer Martin Waldseemüller in 1507.

Vico, Giambattista (1668–1744) Italian historian. In his *New Science* (1725), he advanced the arguments of historicism, that all aspects of society and culture are relevant to the study of history and that the history of any period should be judged according to the standards and customs of that time and place.

Victor Emmanuel II (1820–78) King of Italy (1861–78). In 1849 he succeeded his father, Charles Albert, as king of Piedmont-Sardinia. From 1852, guided by CAVOUR, he strengthened his kingdom, formed a French alliance and defeated Austria (1859–61). In 1861 he assumed the title of king of Italy. Rome became his new capital after French troops withdrew (1870).

Victor Emmanuel III (1869–1947) King of Italy (1900–46). In 1922 he appointed Benito MUSSOLINI as prime minister. Although Mussolini established a dictatorship, the king retained the power to dismiss him and did so in 1943. He abdicated in 1946.

Victoria (1819–1901) Queen of Great Britain and Ireland (1837–1901) and empress of India (1876–1901). A granddaughter of GEORGE III, she succeeded her uncle, WILLIAM IV. In 1840 Victoria married her cousin, Prince ALBERT of Saxe-Coburg-Gotha. During her reign, the role of the monarchy was established as a ceremonial, symbolic institution with virtually no power but much influence. After Albert's death (1861) she went into seclusion and her neglect of public duties aroused republican sentiments. Victoria's domestic popularity was restored when she became Empress of India. Victoria reigned over an empire containing 25% of the world's people and 30% of its land.

Vigny, Alfred de (1797–1863) French poet, dramatist and novelist. His work often emphasizes the lonely struggle of the individual in a hostile universe, as in *Chatterton* (1853). Vigny's best poems are contained in *Poems Ancient and Modern* (1826). His fiction includes the pioneering historical novel *Cinq-Mars* (1826).

Vikings Scandinavian, seaborne marauders, traders and settlers, who spread throughout much of Europe and the North Atlantic region between the 9th and 11th centuries. The remarkable Viking expansion was made possible by their advanced maritime technology, which enabled them to cross N European waters in a period when other sailors feared to venture out of sight of land. Although they first appeared in their greatly feared "longships" as raiders on the coasts of NW Europe, later groups came to settle. Swedes, known as Varangians, founded the first Russian state at Novgorod and traded via the River Volga in Byzantium and Persia. Danes conquered much of N and E England. Norwegians created kingdoms in N Britain and Ireland; they also colonized Iceland and established settlements in Greenland. A short-lived settlement, Vinland, was established (*c.*1003) in North America by Leif Ericsson. In the early 10th century, the Vikings settled in Normandy. Anarchic conditions in 10th-century Scandinavia resulted in the formation of larger, more powerful kingdoms, and Viking expansion declined. It was renewed in a different form with the conquest of England by King Sweyn of Denmark in 1013 and the Norman Conquest of 1066.

Villa, "Pancho" (Francisco) (1877–1923) Mexican revolutionary leader. He joined the forces of Francisco MADERO (1909) during the Mexican Revolution. Villa sided with Venustiano CARRANZA but later supported Emiliano ZAPATA. Angered by US recognition of Carranza's government, he murdered US citizens in N Mexico and New Mexico. In 1920 Villa was pardoned in return for agreeing to retire from politics. He was assassinated.

Villon, François (1430–1463) French lyric poet, b. François de Montcorbier or François des Loges. He led a troubled life after killing a priest in 1455. Villon wrote the famous *Ballad of a Hanged Man* while awaiting execution in 1462 (the sentence was later commuted to banishment). Among his other major works are *Le Petit Testament* and *Le Grand Testament*.

Virgil (70–19 BCE) (Publius Vergilius Maro) Roman poet. He gained a high reputation in Rome with the *Eclogues* (42–37 BCE) and the *Georgics* (37–30). Virgil's greatest work was the *Aeneid*, which established him as an epic poet. Unfinished at his death, it was published at the command of Emperor AUGUSTUS.

Visigoths Western division of the GOTHS. They settled in parts of the Roman Empire after 378 and founded kingdoms in Portugal, Spain and Gaul. They were at their most powerful in the 6th century. Visigothic culture declined after the Arab conquests of their territory in 711–18. *See also* OSTROGOTHS

Vitruvius (active early 1st century CE) Roman architect and engineer. His *De Architectura* (before CE 27) covers almost every aspect of ancient architecture. It is the only work of its type to survive from the ancient world.

Vivaldi, Antonio (1675–1741) Italian composer. A master of the concerto and a virtuoso violinist, he helped to standardize the three-movement concerto form and to develop the *concerto grosso*. His best-known work is *The Four Seasons* (1725).

Vladimir I (the Great) (956–1015) Grand Duke of Kiev and first Christian ruler of Russia (980–1015). Vladimir raised an army of VIKING mercenaries in 979 and conquered Polotsk and Kiev. Proclaimed prince of all Russia, he extended Russian territories, conquering parts of Poland and Lithuania. He became a Christian. St. Vladimir, as he is also called, established the Greek Orthodox Church in Russia.

Volta, Count Alessandro Giuseppe Antonio Anastasio (1745–1827) Italian physicist. His investigations into electricity led him to interpret correctly Luigi GALVANI's experiments with muscles, showing that the metal electrodes generated the current.

Voltaire (1694–1778) French philosopher, historian, dramatist and poet, b. François Marie Arouet. Voltaire spent much of his life combating intolerance and injustice and attacking institutions, such as the Church. While in the Bastille (1717), Voltaire wrote his first tragedy *Oedipe* (1718). Voltaire's eulogy *Philosophical Letters* (1734) provoked official censure. He contributed to DIDEROT's *Encyclopédie*. His best-known work, the philosophical romance *Candide* (1759), was published anonymously.

Von Braun, Wernher (1912–77) US engineer, b. Germany. In World War II he was responsible for building the V-2 rocket. In 1945 he went to the USA, where he developed the Jupiter rocket that took the first US satellite, Explorer 1, into space (1958).

Vorster, Balthazar Johannes (1915–83) South African statesman, prime minister (1966–78). Imprisoned during World War II as a Nazi sympathizer, he was a staunch advocate of apartheid under Hendrik VERWOERD and succeeded him as prime minister and Nationalist Party leader. Vorster suppressed the Soweto uprising (1976). He invaded Angola to try to prevent Namibian independence. In 1978 Vorster became president, but corruption charges forced his resignation in 1979.

W

Wagner, Richard (1813–83) German composer. His works consist almost entirely of operas, for which he provided his own libretti. *Tristan and Isolde* (1865) and the four-part *Der Ring des Nibelungen* (1851–76) display the genius of Wagner. His rich, chromatic style lends emotional depth, and a web of leitmotifs propels the drama. Other operas include *Parsifal* (1882).

Waldemar IV (1320–75) (Waldemar Atterday) King of Denmark (1340–75). He restored the Danish kingdom by a mixture of force, diplomacy and persuasion. In 1367 his enemies, including the Hanseatic League, united to drive him from Denmark. He regained the throne at the Peace of Stralsund (1370).

Waldheim, Kurt (1918–2007) Austrian statesman, fourth secretary-general of the United Nations (1972–81). He succeeded U THANT as secretary general, but proved to be a weak appeaser of the major powers. Waldheim's tenure was tainted by revelations about his Nazi war record; he was replaced by PÉREZ DE CUÉLLAR.

Walesa, Lech (1943–) Polish statesman, labor leader, president (1990–95). In August 1980 he organized Solidarity, an independent labor union. A general strike took place, and in December 1980 Polish administrators agreed to give workers the right to organize freely. In 1981 the government outlawed Solidarity, and Walesa was interned until late 1982. In 1983 he was awarded the Nobel Peace Prize. Following reforms in the Soviet Union, Solidarity was legalized and won free elections in 1989. In 1990 the Communist Party was disbanded and Walesa became president.

Walker, William (1824–60) US adventurer in Central America. He led an armed band that attempted to seize land in Mexico in 1853. He made a similar invasion of Nicaragua in 1855 and set himself up as president (1856) but was expelled in 1857. In 1860 he made a sortie into Honduras but was captured and shot.

Wallace, Alfred Russel (1823–1913) English naturalist. He developed a theory of natural selection concurrently with, but independent of, DARWIN. Wallace's *Contributions to the Theory of Natural Selection* (1870) outlines his theory of evolution.

Wallace, Sir William (1270–1305) Scottish nationalist leader. He led resistance to the English king, EDWARD I. Wallace defeated an English army at Stirling Bridge (1297). The English were driven from Scotland, and Wallace pursued them over the border. He was confronted by Edward with a large army at Falkirk in 1298 and was defeated. He went into hiding, but was eventually captured (1305) and executed.

Walpole, Sir Robert, 1st earl of Orford (1676–1745) British politician. Although he resigned as chancellor of the exchequer in 1717, he restored order after the South Sea Bubble crisis in 1720. He returned as chancellor of the exchequer and first lord of the Treasury in 1721. He was forced to resign in 1742 because of opposition to his foreign policy.

Wang Mang (33 BCE–CE 23) Emperor of China. He overthrew

the HAN DYNASTY and proclaimed the Hsin (New) dynasty in CE 8. Opposition from landowners and officials forced him to withdraw his reforms, and his one-emperor dynasty, which divides the Former Han from the Later Han, ended in his assassination.

Warhol, Andy (1928–87) US painter, printmaker and filmmaker, innovator of pop art. He achieved fame with his stencil pictures of Campbell's soup cans and his sculptures of Brillo soap pad boxes (1962).

Washington, George (1732–99) Commander in chief of the Continental army in the American Revolution and first president of the USA (1789–97). In 1775 Washington was chosen as commander in chief by the Continental Congress. With victory achieved, he resigned (1783) but was recalled from retirement to preside over the Constitutional Convention at Philadelphia (1787). In 1789 Washington was elected, unopposed, as president of the new republic. He was unable to heal the divisions between his secretary of state, Thomas JEFFERSON, and his secretary of the treasury, Alexander HAMILTON. The Federalist Party and the Democratic Republican Party emerged from this split. In 1793 Washington was reelected. In 1796 he declined a third term.

Watson, James Dewey (1928–) US geneticist and biophysicist. He is known for his role in the discovery of the molecular structure of deoxyribonucleic acid (DNA), and he shared the 1962 Nobel Prize for physiology or medicine with Francis CRICK and Maurice Wilkins.

Watt, James (1736–1819) Scottish engineer. In 1765 he invented the condensing steam engine. In 1782 Watt invented the double-acting engine in which steam pressure acted alternately on each side of a piston. He coined the term "horsepower".

Wayne, Anthony (1745–96) American Revolutionary general. He was called "Mad Anthony Wayne" because of his daring tactics. In 1777 he was made brigadier general and joined George WASHINGTON's army. He led a division at the battle of Brandywine. In 1779 Wayne led the successful night attack on Stony Point, New York. He also fought in the Siege of Yorktown and occupied Charleston. In 1792 he became commander in chief in the Northwest Territory and defeated the Ohio tribes in the battle of Fallen Timbers (1794). Wayne secured the Treaty of Greenville (1795), the first to recognize Native American title to US lands.

Weber, Carl Maria von (1786–1826) German composer, conductor and pianist. He helped establish a German national style in his operas *Der Freischütz* (1821) and *Euryanthe* (1823).

Wellesley, Arthur *See* WELLINGTON, ARTHUR WELLESLEY, DUKE OF

Wellington, Arthur Wellesley, duke of (1769–1852) British general and statesman, prime minister (1828–30). He was knighted for his defeat of the Marathas in India (1803). In 1809 Wellesley became commander of allied forces in the Peninsular War. Wellington's victory at the battle of Toulouse (1814) precipitated NAPOLEON I's abdication. Wellesley was created duke of Wellington. While representing Britain at the Congress of Vienna (1814–15), he learned of Napoleon's escape from Elba. Wellington resumed command of allied troops and, with General von BLÜCHER, defeated Napoleon at the battle of Waterloo (1815). As prime minister, Wellington grudgingly accepted the passage of the Act of Catholic Emancipation (1829).

Wells, H.G. (Herbert George) (1866–1946) English writer. His reputation was established with the science fiction novels *The Invisible Man* (1897) and *The War of the Worlds* (1898). Later novels include *Kipps* (1905), *Tono-Bungay* (1909) and *The History of Mr. Polly* (1910).

Wesley, John (1703–91) English theologian and evangelist, founder of Methodism. With his brother Charles Wesley, he founded (1729) the Holy Club at Oxford. In 1735 the brothers traveled as missionaries to the USA. In 1738, during a Moravian meeting, Wesley underwent a religious experience that laid the foundation upon which he built the Methodist movement.

Wheatstone, Sir Charles (1802–75) English physicist and inventor. In 1843, with William Cooke, he improved the Wheat-stone bridge, a device for measuring electrical resistance. In 1837 they patented an electric telegraph.

Whistler, James Abbott McNeill (1834–1903) US painter. For Whistler, the artist's duty was to select elements from nature to create a harmonious composition that existed for its own sake. His most famous painting is the portrait of his mother entitled *Arrangement in Gray and Black* (1872).

Whitehead, A.N. (Alfred North) (1861–1947) English philosopher and mathematician. In his "philosophy of organism" he attempted a synthesis of modern science and metaphysics. The system is presented in his *Process and Reality* (1929). His three-volume *Principia Mathematica* (1910–13) is an important work in the study of logic.

Whitman, Walt (Walter) (1819–92) US poet. In 1855 he published at his own expense *Leaves of Grass*, a volume of 12 poems that included "Song of Myself". Later works include *Drum-Taps* (1865) and *Sequel to Drum-Taps* (1865–66), which includes his famous elegies to Abraham Lincoln, "When Lilacs Last in the Dooryard Bloom'd" and "O Captain! My Captain!".

Whitney, Eli (1765–1825) US inventor. Whitney invented (1793) the cotton gin, which revolutionized cotton culture in the South and turned cotton into a profitable export.

Whittle, Sir Frank (1907–96) English inventor. In 1930 he patented the first turbojet (gas turbine) engine for aircraft. Whittle developed the engine while a test pilot in the Royal Air Force (RAF). By 1941 his first jet plane was flying, and the first jets entered service with the RAF in 1944.

Wilde, Oscar (1854–1900) (Oscar Fingal O'Flahertie Wills) Irish dramatist, poet, prose writer and wit. A leader of the Aesthetic Movement, he wrote only one novel, *The Picture of Dorian Grey* (1891). Wilde is best known for his drama, which combines social criticism with epigrammatic wit. His plays include *Lady Windermere's Fan* (1892) and his masterpiece, *The Importance of Being Earnest* (1895). In 1895 Wilde was convicted of homosexual practices and sentenced to two years' hard labor.

Wilhelmina (1880–1962) Queen of the Netherlands (1890–1948). She kept the country neutral in World War I and often intervened in political affairs. During World War II, she led the government in exile in England. In 1848 she abdicated in favor of her daughter, Juliana.

William I (1797–1888) King of Prussia (1861–88) and emperor of Germany (1871–88). He was regent for his brother, FREDERICK WILLIAM IV, from 1858. His suppression of revolution in 1848–49 earned him a reputation as a reactionary, but as king he followed the advice of his chief minister, Otto von BISMARCK. William supported the unification of Germany but accepted his proclamation as emperor reluctantly.

William II (1859–1941) Emperor of Germany (1888–1918). He modeled himself on his grandfather, WILLIAM I, but lacked his good sense. In 1890 he dismissed BISMARCK and assumed leadership of the government. His aggressive foreign policy, including the construction of a navy, antagonized Britain, France and Russia. Many regard his policies as largely responsible for the outbreak of World War I (1914). William abdicated after the armistice (November 1918).

William I (the Conqueror) (1027–87) King of England (1066–87) and Duke of Normandy (1035–87). Supported initially by Henry I of France, he consolidated his position in Normandy against hostile neighbors. On the death of Edward the Confessor (1066), he claimed the English throne, having allegedly gained the agreement of King Harold in 1064. He defeated and killed Harold at the battle of Hastings (1066) and enforced his rule over the whole kingdom. He rewarded his followers by grants of land, eventually replacing almost the entire feudal ruling class. He invaded Scotland (1072) and Wales (1081). He ordered the survey known as the Domesday Book (1086).

William III (of Orange) (1650–1702) King of England, Scotland and Ireland (1689–1702). He was born after the death of his father, William II, Prince of Orange, and succeeded him as ruler in effect of the United Provinces (Netherlands) in 1572. In 1677 he married Mary, daughter of JAMES II of England, and following the Glorious Revolution (1688), he and Mary, strong Protestants, replaced the Catholic James II. They ruled jointly until her death in 1694. In 1699 he organized the alliance that was to defeat the French in the War of the Spanish Succession.

William IV (1765–1837) King of Great Britain and Ireland and elector of Hanover (1830–37). Third son of GEORGE III, he succeeded, unexpectedly, aged 65 after a long career in the navy. Nicknamed "Silly Billy", he was well-meaning though unkingly. He assisted the passage of the Great Reform Bill (1832).

William I (the Silent) (1533–84) Prince of Orange, leader of the revolt of the Netherlands against Spanish rule. In 1572 he became the leader of a broad coalition in the Low Countries that opposed Spanish rule on the principle of religious tolerance. It broke down in 1579, when the Catholic S provinces broke away. William continued as stadholder of Holland and leader of the N provinces until he was assassinated in Delft.

William of Occam (1285–1349) English scholastic philosopher. Contributing to the development of formal logic, he employed the principle of economy known as Occam's Razor; that is, a problem should be stated in its most basic terms.

Williams, Roger (1603–83) English Puritan minister. In 1631 he emigrated to the Massachusetts Bay colony. His radical politics and theology antagonized the Puritan authorities. In 1636 Williams founded Providence, the first settlement in Rhode Island. He returned to England and acquired a charter. Williams served (1654–57) as president of Rhode Island colony.

Williams, Tennessee (Thomas Lanier) (1911–83) US playwright. His first Broadway play, *The Glass Menagerie* (1945), was awarded the New York Drama Critic's Circle Award. He received Pulitzer prizes for *A Streetcar Named Desire* (1947) and *Cat on a Hot Tin Roof* (1955). Many of his plays were set in the South, in a repressive environment that reflected the plight of the characters.

Wilson, Sir (James) Harold (1916–95) (Baron Wilson of Rievaulx) British statesman, prime minister (1964–70, 1974–76). Wilson entered Parliament in 1945. In 1963 he succeeded Hugh Gaitskell as Labor leader. In 1964 he won a narrow general election victory. His administration was faced with Rhodesia's unilateral declaration of independence and domestic recession. Wilson was forced to impose strict price and income controls and devalue sterling. In the 1970 general election he was defeated by Edward HEATH. In 1974 Wilson returned to power at the head of a minority Labor government. In 1976 he resigned and was succeeded by Jim Callaghan.

Wilson, (Thomas) Woodrow (1856–1924) 28th US president (1913–21). In 1912 he gained the Democratic nomination. His "New Freedom" reforms included the establishment of the Federal Reserve System (1913). Several amendments to the US Constitution were introduced, including prohibition (18th, 1919) and the extension of the franchise to women (19th, 1920). The Mexican Revolution brought instability to the S border. Wilson's efforts to maintain US neutrality at the start of World War I aided his re-election in 1916. The failure of diplomacy forced Wilson to declare war (April 1917) on Germany. His Fourteen Points (January 1918) represented US war aims and became the basis of the peace negotiations at the Versailles peace conference (1919). Wilson was forced to compromise in the settlement but succeeded in securing the establishment of the League of Nations. The Republican-dominated Senate rejected it. In October 1919 Wilson suffered a stroke and became an increasingly marginal figure for the remainder of his term.

Wittgenstein, Ludwig (1889–1951) Austrian philosopher. His masterwork, *Tractatus Logico-philosophicus* (1921), influenced logical positivism, positing the strict relationships between language and the physical world. After 1929 he criticized this hypothesis, and these second thoughts were posthumously published in *Philosophical Investigations* (1953).

Wolfe, James (1727–59) British general. He commanded the force that captured Quebec by scaling the cliffs above the St. Lawrence River and defeating the French, under MONTCALM, on the Plains of Abraham (1759). This victory resulted in Britain's acquisition of Canada. Wolfe's death in action made him a hero.

Wolfram von Eschenbach (1170–1220) German poet. His only complete work is the Middle High German epic *Parzival*. It introduced the Grail legend into German.

Wollstonecraft, Mary (1759–97) English writer, mother of Mary Shelley. Wollstonecraft's *Vindication of the Rights of Women* (1792) is often regarded as the first great work of feminism.

Woolf, Virginia (1882–1941) English novelist and critic. Her novels, which often use the stream of consciousness style associated with modernism, include *Mrs. Dalloway* (1925), *To the Lighthouse* (1927), *Orlando* (1928) and *The Waves* (1931). A member of the Bloomsbury Group, her long essay *A Room of One's Own* (1929) is a key text of feminist criticism.

Wordsworth, William (1770–1850) English poet. He collaborated with Samuel Taylor COLERIDGE on *Lyrical Ballads* (1798). The collection concluded with his poem "Tintern Abbey". Wordsworth's preface to the second edition (1800) outlined the aims of English romanticism. In 1799 he and his sister Dorothy moved to the Lake District; his poetry was always bound up with a love of nature. After *Poems in Two Volumes* (1807), which includes "Ode: Intimations of Immortality", it is recognized that his creativity declined. In 1843 he became poet laureate.

Wren, Sir Christopher (1632–1723) English architect. He designed more than 50 new churches in the city of London based on syntheses of classical, Renaissance and Baroque ideas; the greatest of these is St. Paul's Cathedral.

Wright, Frank Lloyd (1869–1959) US architect, regarded as the leading modernist designer of private housing. His distinctive "organic" style of low-built, prairie-style houses was designed to blend in with natural contours and features. Notable buildings include Robie House, Chicago (1909); "Fallingwater", Bear Run, Pennsylvania (1936–37); and the Guggenheim Museum, New York (1946–59).

Wright brothers US aviation pioneers. Wilbur Wright (1867–1912) and Orville Wright (1871–1948) assembled their first aircraft in their bicycle factory. In 1903 Orville made the first piloted flight in a power-driven plane at Kitty Hawk, North Carolina. This flight lasted just 12 seconds.

Wycliffe, John (1330–84) English religious reformer. He attacked corrupt practices in the church and the authority of the pope. His criticism became increasingly radical, questioning the authority of the pope and insisting on the primacy of scripture, but he escaped condemnation until after his death.

X

Xerxes I (519–465 BCE) King of Persia (486–465 BCE). Succeeding his father, DARIUS I, he regained Egypt and crushed a rebellion in Babylon before launching his invasion of Greece (480 BCE). After his fleet was destroyed at the battle of Salamis (480), he retired. The defeat of the Persian army in Greece at the battle of Plataea (479) ended his plans for conquest.

Xhosa (Xosa) Group of related Bantu tribes. The Xhosa moved from E Africa to the vicinity of the Great Fish River, S Africa, in the 17th and 18th centuries. In 1835 they were defeated by the Europeans, after which they came under European rule. In culture they are closely related to the ZULU.

Y

Yaroslav I (980–1054) Grand Duke of Kiev (1019–54), known as "the Wise". He used Viking mercenaries to defeat his brother Sviatopolk the Accursed in 1019. He codified Russian law, rebuilt Kiev and developed close relations with the rest of Europe.

Yeats, W.B. (William Butler) (1865–1939) Irish poet and dramatist. In 1094 he and Lady Gregory founded the Abbey

Theater, Dublin, as an Irish national theater. Yeats'plays *On Baile's Strand* (1905) and *Cathleen Ni Houlihan* (1902) were on the first bill. The poetry in *Responsibilities* (1914) acted as social commentary. His mature poetry includes *Michael Robartes and the Dancer* (1921, which contains "The Second Coming" and "Easter 1916"). Yeats received the 1923 Nobel Prize for literature.

Yeltsin, Boris Nikolayevich (1931–2007) Russian statesman, first democratically elected president of the Russian Federation (1991–1999). He was Communist Party leader in Ekaterinburg (Sverdlovsk) before joining (1985) the reforming government of Mikhail GORBACHEV. His blunt criticism of the slow pace of *perestroika* led to demotion in 1987, but his immense popularity gained him election as president of the Russian Republic in 1990. His denunciation of the 1991 attempted coup against Gorbachev established his ascendancy. Elected president of the Russian Federation, he presided over the dissolution of the Soviet Union and the termination of Communist Party rule. Economic disintegration and internal conflicts, notably in Chechenia, damaged his popularity, and failing health reduced his effectiveness. Nevertheless, he was reelected in 1996. In 1998 he twice sacked the entire cabinet in the face of economic crisis. In 1999 Yeltsin again dismissed the cabinet.

York, House of English royal house, a branch of the PLANTA-GENETS. During the Wars of the Roses, rival claimants from the houses of York and LANCASTER contended for the crown. The Yorkist claimant, Richard, duke of York, was a great-grandson of EDWARD III. His son gained the crown as Edward IV. The death of Edward's brother, RICHARD III, by HENRY VII in 1485 brought the brief Yorkist line to a close. *See also* TUDORS

Young, Brigham (1801–77) US religious leader, founder of Salt Lake City. An early convert to the Church of Jesus Christ of Latter-Day Saints (Mormons), Young took over the leadership when Joseph SMITH, the founder, was killed by a mob in 1844. Young led the group's westward migration (1846–47) to Utah, where he organized the settlement that became Salt Lake City.

Yuan dynasty (1246–1368) MONGOL dynasty in China. Continuing the conquests of GENGHIS KHAN, KUBLAI KHAN established his rule over China, eliminating the last SONG claimant in 1279. He returned the capital to Beijing and promoted construction and commerce. Native Chinese were excluded from government, and foreign visitors were encouraged. Among the Chinese, resentment of alien rule was aggravated by economic problems. The less competent successors of Kublai were increasingly challenged by rebellion, culminating in the victory of the MING DYNASTY.

Yuan Shikai (1859–1916) Chinese military commander in the last days of the QING DYNASTY. He became the first president of the Chinese Republic in 1913 when SUN YAT-SEN resigned, but his attempt to start a new dynasty and make himself emperor was thwarted shortly before his death.

Z

Zapata, Emiliano (1880–1919) Mexican revolutionary leader. He became leader of the growing peasant movement in 1910. His demands for radical agrarian reform led to the Mexican Revolution. In pursuit of "Land and Liberty", he opposed, successively, Porfirio DÍAZ, Francisco MADERO, Victoriano HUERTA and (with "Pancho" VILLA) Venustiano CARRANZA. His guerrilla campaign ended with his murder.

Zapotec Native American group that inhabits part of the Mexican state of Oaxaca. The Zapotec built great pre-Columbian urban centers at Mitla and Monte Albán and fought to preserve their independence from the rival Mixtecs and AZTECS.

Zenger, John Peter (1697–1746) US journalist, b. Germany. Editor of the *New York Weekly Journal*, he attacked Governor William Cosby and was jailed for libel in 1734. He was later tried by a jury and acquitted. His case established truth as a defense for libel and made Zenger a symbol of the freedom of the press.

Zeno of Citium (*c.*334–*c.*262 BCE) Greek philosopher and founder of the Stoics. Proceeding from the Cynic concept of self-

sufficiency, he stressed the brotherhood of men living in harmony with the cosmos. He claimed virtue to be the only good, and wealth, illness and death to be of no human concern.

Zeppelin, Ferdinand, Count von (1838–1917) German army officer and inventor. He served in the armies of Württemburg and Prussia. While an observer with the Union army during the American Civil War, he made his first balloon ascent. In 1900 he invented the first rigid airship, called Zeppelin after him.

Zhou dynasty Chinese dynasty (1030–221 BCE). After the nomadic Zhou overthrew the SHANG DYNASTY, Chinese civilization spread to most parts of modern China, although the dynasty never established effective control over the regions. The Late Zhou, from 772 BCE, was a cultural golden age, marked by the writings of CONFUCIUS and LAO TZU. As the provincial states grew in power, the Zhou dynasty disintegrated.

Zhou Enlai (1898–1976) Chinese statesman. Zhou was a founder of the Chinese Communist Party. As a member of the Communist-Kuomintang alliance (1924–27), he directed the general strike in Shanghai. When CHIANG KAI-SHEK broke the alliance, Zhou joined the Long March (1934–35). He was the chief negotiator of a renewed peace (1936–46) with nationalist forces. After the establishment of a communist republic, Zhou became prime minister (1949–76) and foreign minister (1949–58).

Zhukov, Georgi Konstantinovich (1896–1974) Soviet military commander and politician. In World War II he led the defense of Moscow (1941) and defeated the German siege of Stalingrad and Leningrad (1943). In 1945 he led the final assault on Berlin. After STALIN's death, he became defense minister (1955). Although supportive of Nikita KHRUSCHEV's reforms, he was removed from office in 1957. He was rehabilitated in the 1960s.

Zia ul-Haq, Muhammad (1924–88) Pakistani general and statesman, president (1978–88). In 1976 he was appointed chief of staff of the army by Zulfikar BHUTTO. In 1977 Zia ousted Bhutto in a coup, establishing Pakistan's fourth military dictatorship since 1947. As president, he imposed martial law and banned political opposition. In 1979 Zia authorized the hanging of Bhutto. In 1984 Zia was reelected and lifted martial law. He died in a air crash, possibly caused by sabotage.

Zog I (1895–1961) King of Albania (1928–39), b. Ahmed Bey Zogu. Premier of Albania (1922–24), Zog was elected president in 1925 when Albania was proclaimed a republic. In 1928 he proclaimed himself King. As head of state, he championed modernization and reforms. His rule became autocratic, however, and he was powerless to resist the Italian invasion in 1939.

Zola, Émile Edouard Charles Antoine (1840–1902) French novelist. For years he worked on the Rougon-Macquart sequence (1871–93), a 20-novel cycle telling the story of a family during the Second Empire. The sequence includes *The Drunkard* (1877), *Germinal* (1885) and *The Human Animal* (1890). In 1898 he wrote a famous letter, beginning "*J'Accuse*", which denounced the punishment of Alfred DREYFUS.

Zulu Bantu people of S Africa, most of whom live in KwaZulu-Natal. They are closely related to the Swazi and the XHOSA. The Zulus have a patriarchal, polygamous society, with a strong militaristic tradition. In the 19th century, under their leader SHAKA, they resisted colonialism. The predominant religion is now Christianity, although ethnic religions are still common.

Zwingli, Ulrich (1484–1531) Swiss Protestant theologian and reformer. He was ordained a Roman Catholic priest in 1506, but his studies of the New Testament in ERASMUS's editions led him to become a reformer. By 1522 he was preaching reformed doctrine in Zurich, a center of the Reformation. More radical than LUTHER, he saw communion as symbolic and commemorative.

Zworykin, Vladimir Kosma (1889–1982) US physicist and inventor, b. Russia. In 1929 he joined the Radio Corporation of America (RCA). Zworykin and his colleagues developed the iconoscope, the forerunner of the modern television camera tube, and the kinescope, a cathode-ray tube for television sets. In 1928 he patented a color television system.

battle of 1402
An Lushan revolt 755
Anna Comnena 1153
Annam 111 BCE, 1428, 1431, 1471,
  1802, 1883
ANNAN, KOFI 1997
ANNE, queen of Britain 1702, 1714
Anschluss 1938
Antarctica 1959
Antequerra, Jose de 1721, 1731
ANTHONY, SUSAN 1892
ANTHONY the Hermit 305
antibiotics 1928
Antietam, battle of 1862
Antigua and Barbuda 1981
antimatter 1996
Antioch 540, 253, 1268
ANTIOCHUS III, Seleucid king 196
  BCE
ANTIOCHUS IV, Seleucid king 168
Anti-Saloon League 1895
antiseptics 1867
ANTONESCU, ION 1940
ANTONINUS PIUS, Roman emperor
  138, 161
ANTONY, MARK 43 BCE, 30 BCE
Antwerp, sack of 1576
Anual, battle of 1921
An Wang 1953
Apache 1886
Apartheid 1949, 1984
Aphilas, king of Aksum 285
APOLLINAIRE, GUILLAUME 1913
Apollo spacecraft 1968, 1969, 1975
Appert, Nicholas 1810
APULEIUS 165
aquaducts 310 BCE, 25 BCE
aqualung 1942
AQUINAS, THOMAS 1273
Aquino, Benigno 1983
AQUINO, CORY 1986
Arab empire 632, 636, 639, 642,
  650, 652, 670, 673, 700, 702,
  705, 713, 739, 753, 823, 825,
  839, 961, 1061
  Abbasid dynasty 744, 750, 762,
    820, 945, 971
  battle of Tours 732
  sack of Rome 846
  Seljuks capture Baghdad 1055
  Umayyad dynasty 656, 740,
    750, 1008
Arab Federation 1958
Arabia (Roman province) 106
Arab-Israeli conflict 1948, 1949,
  1967, 1973, 1978, 1979, 1993,
  1997
Arab League 1945
Arab Revolt 1916, 1917
ARAFAT, YASIR 1969, 1996
Aragón 1235
  united with Castile 1479
Aranyakas 900 BCE
ARCADIUS, emperor 395
archaeology 1738
Archaic Period Mesoamerica 7000
  BCE
ARCHIMEDES 212 BCE
Arcot 1751
ARDASHIR, king of Persia 224
Ardebil, Holy Carpet 1540
Argentina 1683, 1816, 1817, 1827,
  1845, 1852, 1853, 1859, 1880,
  1902, 1955, 1973
  Falklands War 1982
  Paraguayan War 1865–70
argon, discovery 1894
Argos 750 BCE, 669 BCE
Arguim Island 1448
Arguin 1621
Arian heresy 325
ARIOSTO, LUDOVICO 1516
ARISOPHANES 405 BCE
ARISTARCHUS 275 BCE
ARISTOTLE 337 BCE
ARISTOTLE 480, 1120, 1198
ARIUS 325
Arizona 1912
Arkansas 1836
ARKWRIGHT, RICHARD *1769*
Armenia 190 BCE, 114, 244, 1064,

1826, 1918, 1988
Armenians, Turkish massacre 1896
Armstrong, Edwin 1933
Armstrong, Louis 1970
ARMSTRONG, NEIL 1969
ARNOLD, BENEDICT 1780
ARNOLD, MATTHEW 1869
Arogee, battle of 1868
Arons, Leon 1892
ARP, JEAN 1915
Arras, battle of 1917
Arsacid dynsaty 53
Artaxiad I, king of Armenia 190 BCE
art deco style *1925*
ARTHUR, CHESTER 1881
Aryabhata 499
Aryan peoples 1600 BCE, 1200 BCE
ASHANTI 1745, 1824, 1900, 1901
Ashanti Wars 1824, 1827, 1873,
  1874, 1894
Ashoka 256 BCE, 240 BCE
Ashraf, shah of Persia 1726
asiento 1702, 1713
Aslanduz, battle of 1812
Aspidin, Joseph 1824
aspirin 1897, 1899
Assab 1882
ASSAD, HAFEZ AL- 1970
As Saheli *1324*
Assam 1229, 1826
ASSASSINS 1256
Assaye, battle of 1803
assaying 1556
ASSURDAN II, king of Assyria 935
  BCE
astrolabe 1003
astronomy 929, *987*, 1054, 1437
  Copernicus 1510, 1543
  expanding universe 1920
  Kepler's laws of planetary
    motion 1619
  Messier's star catalogue 1771
  Moon's surface mapped 1647
  Population I and II stars 1944
  Ptolemy *160*
  radial velocity of stars 1868
  stellar parallax 1838
Asunción 1537, 1868
Aswan Dam 1902
ATAHUALPA, Inca king 1525, 1532,
  1533
ATATÜRK 1923, 1934
Athens 621 BCE, 594 BCE, 499 BCE,
  449 BCE, 460 BCE, 445 BCE, 415
  BCE, 267, 582
  Academy 387 BCE
  Corinthian War 396 BCE–386
    BCE
  Council of Four Hundred 411
    BCE
  democracy 507 BCE, 461 BCE
  empire 477 BCE
  Lyceum 337 BCE
  Parthenon *445* BCE
  Peloponnesian Wars 461 BCE,
    431 BCE, 421 BCE, 404 BCE
  Turkish capture 1456
Atlanta 1864
Atlantic Charter 1941
atomic energy 1942, 1947, 1957,
  1958, 1981
  1979, 1986
atomic fission 1939
atomic structure 1913
atomic weapons 1941, 1945, 1946,
  1949, 1952, 1960, 1962, 1964,
  1967, 1974, 1983, 1985
  treaties and talks 1968, 1970,
    1988, 1991
ATTALUS III, king of Pergamum 133
  BCE
ATTILA 434, 451, 452, 453
ATTLEE, CLEMENT 1945
AUDEN, W.H. 1947
Audubon, John 1838
Auerstadt, battle of 1806
Augsburg 1331
  Peace of 1555

War of the League of 1686–97
AUGUSTINE of Hippo 397
AUGUSTULUS, Roman emperor 476
AUGUSTUS II, king of Poland 1733
AUGUSTUS, Roman emperor 31 BCE,
  27 BCE, 14
AUNG SAN 1947
AUNG SAN SUU KYI 1989
AURANGZEB, Mughal emperor 1685,
  1707
AURELIAN 273
Aurelian, Roman emperor 274
AUSTEN, JANE 1813
Austerlitz, battle of 1805
Australia 1606
  British 1770, 1788, 1829, 1850,
    1901
  circumnavigation *1803*
  convict colonies 1788, 1867
  dominion status 1901
  free settlers 1793
  gold 1850
  interior explored 1860
  Rum Rebellion 1808
  self-government 1850
  Vietnam War 1965
  World War I 1915
  World War 2 1942
Australopithecus 1924, 1974
Austria 1261, 1278, 1315, 1664,
  1714
  Anschluss 1938
  Austro-Prussian (Seven
    Weeks') War 1866
  Belgium 1746, 1787, 1789
  Dollfuss 1933, 1934
  French Revolutionary Wars
    1792–95
  Holy Alliance 1684, 1699, 1815
  Italy 1815, 1831, 1847, 1848,
    1859
  Napoleonic Wars 1796–97,
    1800, 1801, 1805, 1809,
    1813
  Polish partitions 1772, 1795,
    1846
  Quadruple Alliance 1718
  republic 1945
  Russo-Turkish Wars 1781, 1789
  Serbia 1736, 1789
  serfdom abolished 1781
  Seven Years War 1756–63
  War of the Austrian Succession
    1740–48
  War of the Bavarian Succession
    1778
  War of the Polish Succession
    1733–38
Austria-Hungary 1808, 1818, 1867
  Balkan Wars 1912, 1913
  Congress of Berlin 1878
  League of Three Emperors
    1872
  Pig War 1905
  Triple Alliance 1882
  World War I *1914*–18
Austrian Succession, War of the
  1740–48
autogyro 1923
AVARS 375, 557, 582, 626, 796, 850
AVERROËS 1111, 1198
Avery, Oswald 1944
AVICENNA 1037, 1111
Avignon, papacy 1309, 1352, 1377
AVOGADRO, AMEDEO 1811
Awole, king of Oyo 1789
axis alliance 1936
AYER, A.J. 1956
AYUB KHAN, MUHAMMAD 1958
Ayutthaya 1347
AYYUBID DYNASTY 1171
Azerbaijan 1590, 1988
Azes I, Saka king 58 BCE
Azores 1430
Azov 1696, 1711, 1736
AZTECS 1190, 1325, 1370, 1426,
  1440, 1441, 1502, 1519

B

Baade, Walter 1944
Baader-Meinhof gang 1972
Ba'athists 1968

BABBAGE, CHARLES 1823
Babists 1844, 1848, 1850
BABUR 1504, 1523, 1526
BABYLONIA 1830 BCE, 1800 BCE,
  1595 BCE, 538 BCE
  Babylonian Captivity 1309, 1377
BACH, JOHANN SEBASTIAN 1721,
  1734
Backus, Jack 1956
BACON, FRANCIS 1605, 1945
Bacon, Nathaniel 1676
BACON, ROGER 1266
bacteria 1680, 1880
bacteriophages 1917
Bactria 329 BCE, 250 BCE, 171 BCE
Badajoz 1810
Badarian culture 5000 BCE
BADEN-POWELL, ROBERT 1907
Baekeland, Leo 1909
BAFFIN, WILLIAM 1616
Baffin Bay 1616
Baghavand, battle of 1735
Baghdad 762, 945, 1258, 1603,
  1609, 1638, 1917
  House of Wisdom 825
  Pact 1955
  Seljuk capture 1055
Baghdad Pact 1955, 1959
Bagyidaw, king of Burma 1819
Bahadur, Mughal emperor 1712
Bahamas 1492, 1667
Bahia 1549, 1624
Bahrain 1971
Bahri dynasty 1250, 1382
BAIRD, JOHN LOGIE 1926
Bakelite 1909
Baku 1723, 1813
BAKUNIN, MIKHAIL 1876
Balaclava, battle of 1854
Balacot, battle of 1831
BALBOA, VASCO NÚÑEZ DE 1513
BALDWIN, king of Jerusalem 1100
BALDWIN, JAMES 1955
BALDWIN, STANLEY 1926
BALFOUR, ARTHUR 1917
Bali 1908
Balkan League 1912
Balkan Wars 193, 1912
Ballard, J.G. 1984
balloon flight *1783*, 1797
ballpoint pen 1939
Baluchistan 1887
BALZAC, HONORÉ DE 1829
BALZAC, HONORE DE 1829
Ban Chao 90
BANDARANAIKE, SIRIMAVO 1960
BANDARANAIKE, SOLOMON 1956
Bangkok 1782
Bangladesh 1971
banking 1397
Banks, Iain 1984
Bannockburn, battle of 1314
Bantam 1808
BANTING, FREDERICK 1921
Bantu peoples 400 BCE, 200, 500
Ban Zhou 114
Barakzai dynasty 1835
Barbados 1625, 1966
BARBAROSSA (Khayr ad-Din) 1535
barbed wire 1873
Barbizon school of painters 1831
Barcelona 1842, 1883, 1939
bar coding 1974
BARDEEN, JOHN 1947
Barker, Pat 1995
barley 6000 BCE
BARNARD, CHRISTIAAN 1967
barometer 1643, 1844
baroque style 1575, 1696
Barovier, Anzolo 1460
Barrie, James 1904
Barrios, Justo, president of
  Guatemala 1885
BARTH, KARL 1919
BARTÓK, BÉLA 1908
Bartolommeo, Michelozzi di 1444
Bartolus of Sassoferrato 1357
Bashō, Matsuo 1694
BASIL I, Byzantine emperor 868
BASIL II, Byzantine emperor 1014
Baskar, battle of 1764
Basketmaker culture 1

Basle, Peace of 1795
Basra 1770, 1775, 1914
Bassein, Treaty of 1802
Basutoland 1843, 1865, 1868, 1966
Batavia 1619
Batavian Republic 1795
Baths of Caracalla 216
BATISTA, FULGENCIO 1933, 1952, 1959
battery 1800, 1841
BAUDELAIRE, CHARLES 1857
BAUDOUIN, king of Belgium 1951
Bauer, Georg (Agricola) 1556
Bavaria 1646, 1829, 1886, 1919
Bavarian Succession, War of the 1778
Baybars 1250
Bayer, Adolf von 1878
Bayeux tapestry 1070
BAYLE, PIERRE 1697
Bay of Pigs invasion 1961
BEAKER PEOPLE 2400 BCE
bean, cultivation 7000 BCE, 800
Beatles, The 1961, 1967, 1980
Beaufort, Francis 1806
Beaufort scale 1806
BEAUVOIR, SIMONE DE 1949
Bebel, Albert 1879
Becan 425
Bechuanaland 1885, 1966
BECKETT, SAMUEL 1955
Becquerel, Anton 1839
BECQUEREL, HENRI 1896
BEDE 731
beer 7500 BCE
BEETHOVEN, LUDWIG VAN 1802, 1808
BEGIN, MENACHEM 1977, 1978
Behan, Brendan 1959
BEHRING, EMIL VON 1890
Beijing 1267, 1420, 1855, 1902, 1928
   Forbidden City 1406
   Summer Palace 1860
Beirut 1918, 1958
   French 1860
   Israeli invasion 1982
   Lebanese civil war 1982, 1987
Bejing 1916
Belarus 1991
Belém 1616
Belgium
   Austrian control 1746, 1787, 1789, 1794
   British conquest 1706
   French control 1683, 1746, 1792
   French Revolutionary Wars 1793–95
   Germany invasion 1940
   independence 1830, 1831, 1839
   Kingdom of the Netherlands 1815
   Locarno Treaty 1925
   neutrality 1870, 1914
   Spanish control 1579, 1678
   World War I 1914–18
   see also Flanders; Low Countries
Belgrade 1688, 1717, 1789, 1944
BELISARIUS 533
Belize 1973, 1981
BELL, ALEXANDER GRAHAM 1876
Bell, Jocelyn 1967
Bellay, Joachim du 1549
BELLINI, GIOVANNI 1472
BELLOC, HILAIRE 1907
BELLOW, SAUL 1964
BEN BELLA, AHMED 1965
Benelux 1958
Bengal 1338, 1576, 1700, 1742, 1756, 1757, 1764, 1773, 1905, 1911
Bengel, Johann 1752
Benin 1300
Bennett, Arnold 1910
BENTHAM, JEREMY 1789
Benyowski, Maritius 1775, 1786
BENZ, KARL 1885
BERBERS 740, 1054, 1086, 1143, 1857, 1953
BERG, ALBAN 1925

Bergamo 1427
BERING, VITUS 1728
Bering ice bridge 8500 BCE
Bering Strait 1728
BERKELEY, GEORGE 1710
Berlin 1760, 1848, 1918
   Academy of Sciences 1701
   blockade and air lift 1948
   Conference 1884
   Congress of 1878
   Spartacists 1919
   Wall 1961, 1989
Berlin, Irvine 1911
Berliner, Emile 1890
BERLIOZ, HECTOR 1830
Berlusconi, Silvio 1994
Bermuda 1612
BERNADOTTE, JEAN 1813, 1818
BERNINI, GIANLORENZO 1633
Bernoulli, Daniel 1738
Bernoulli, Jakob 1698
Bernstein, Carl 1974
Berthollet, Claude 1785
Berzelius, Jons 1814
Bessarabia 1812
Bessel, Friedrich 1838
Bessemer, Henry 1856
Bethlehem 1228
BHUTTO, BENAZIR 1988, 1990
BHUTTO, ZULFIKAR ALI 1973
Biafra 1967, 1968, 1970
Bible
   Gutenberg Bible 1455
   Luther 1534
   New English Bible 1970
   translations 341, 385, 1380, 1525, 1534
   Tyndale 1525
   Vulgate 385
   Wycliffe 1380
bicycle 1867
Bidur 1429
Big Bang theory 1927, 1992
Bikini atoll 1944
BIKO, STEVE 1977
"BILLY THE KID" (William Bonney) 1881
Biloxi 1699
Bimbisara, king of Magadha 545 BCE
Bindusara, king 280 BCE
Binet, Alfred 1905
Bird, John 1758
Birdseye, Clarence 1924
Biringuccio, Vannoccio 1540
Biró, Ladislao 1938
BIRTWISTLE, HARRISON 1991
Bishapur 265
BISMARCK, OTTO VON 1862, 1865, 1871, 1880, 1890
BIZET, GEORGES 1875
BLACK, JOSEPH 1763
Black Death 1335, 1341, 1346, 1347, 1348, 1358, 1361
Black Hand 1911, 1914
Black Panthers 1966
BLAIR, TONY 1997
Blanc, Louis 1839
Blanche of Castile 1226
blast furnace 1709
Blenheim, battle of 1704
BLÉRIOT, LOUIS 1909
BLIGH, WILLIAM 1789, 1808
BLÜCHER, GEBHARD 1814, 1815
BLUM, LÉON 1936
BOADICEA, queen of the Iceni 60
BOCCACCIO, GIOVANNI 1358
Boccioni, Umberto 1913
Bodawpaya, king of Burma 1793
BODIN, JEAN 1576
Boerhaave, Hermann 1732
Boers see Afrikaners
Boer War 1899–1902
BOETHIUS 480
Bogotá 1538
Bohemia 973, 1261, 1278, 1433, 1515
   battle of the White Mountain 1620
   Habsburg dynasty 1438
   Hussites 1413, 1415, 1419,

1434
   Hussite Wars 1419, 1420, 1430, 1434
   Protestantism 1618
   Seven Years War 1756–63
Bohemian War 1618
BOHR, NIELS 1913
BOKASSA, JEAN 1966, 1977
BOLÍVAR, SIMÓN 1812, 1813, 1818, 1819, 1821
Bolivia 1841
   Chaco War 1932, 1935
   independence 1825
   Peruvian confederation 1829, 1839
   War of the Pacific 1879–84
Bologna 1088
Bolsheviks 1903, 1917
BOLTZMANN, LUDWIG 1877
Bombay 1661
Bombelli, Raffaele 1572
BONAPARTE, JOSEPH 1806, 1808
Bonaparte, Napoleon see Napoleon Bonaparte
Bonney, William, (Billy the Kid) 1881
book-keeping 1270
BOOLE, GEORGE 1848
BOONE, DANIEL 1769
Boot, Henry 1939
BOOTH, WILLIAM 1878
Bordeaux 1814
BORGES, JORGE LUIS 1975
BORGIA, CESARE 1499
boring machine 1774
Borneo 1888
   Northern 1963
BORODIN, ALEXANDER 1877
Borodino, battle of 1812
BORROMINI, FRANCESCO 1638
BOSCH, HIERONYMUS 1495
Bosnia and Herzegovina 1878, 1908, 1992, 1995
Boston 1700, 1721, 1765, 1768, 1775
   Massacre 1770
   siege 1775, 1776
   Tea Party 1773
BOSWELL, JAMES 1791
Bosworth, Battle of 1485
botany 1542
   binomal nomenclature 1735
Botany Bay 1770
BOTHA, LOUIS 1910, 1915
BOTHA, P.W. 1984
Botswana 1966
BOTTICELLI, SANDRO 1478
BOUCHER, FRANÇOIS 1742
BOUGAINVILLE, LOUIS DE 1768, 1772
BOUILLON, GEDFREY OF 1099
BOULANGER, GEORGES 1886, 1889
BOULTON, MATTHEW 1785, 1790
BOUMÉDIENNE, HOUARI 1965
Bounty mutiny 1789
BOURBON DYNASTY 1589, 1700
   Family Compacts 1733, 1743, 1761
Bourse 1309
BOUTROS-GHALI, BOUTROS 1992
Bouvines, battle of 1214
bow and arrow 15,000 BCE, 2500 BCE, 900 BCE
BOWIE, JIM 1836
Boxer Protocol 1901
Boxers (Harmonious Fists) 1899, 1900
Boyar revolt 1564
Boyer, Herbert 1973
BOYLE, ROBERT 1662
Boyne, battle of the 1690
Boy Scout movement 1907
Bradley, James 1728
BRAHE, TYCHO 1576, 1576
Brahmagupta 628
Brahmanas 900 BCE
BRAHMS, JOHANNES 1868
Braille, Louis 1834
BRAMANTE, DONATO 1502
Brandenburg 1404
Brandt, Sebastian 1494
BRANDT, WILLY 1969

Brandywine, battle of 1777
BRAQUE, GEORGES 1921
Brasilia 1960
BRATTAIN, WALTER 1947
Braun, Ferdinand 1897
Brazil 1500, 1827, 1828, 1831
   Capture and ransom of Rio de Janeiro 1711
   de Silva revolt 1789
   Dutch colonies 1630, 1645, 1654
   French colonies 1555, 1567, 1612, 1616
   French invasion 1807
   independence 1822, 1825
   Paraguayan War 1865–70
   Paulistas 1708
   Portuguese 1530, 1549, 1554, 1567, 1616, 1630, 1645, 1654, 1680, 1708, 1710, 1750, 1807
   republic 1889
   slavery 1888
   United States 1891, 1893
   Vargas 1930
   War of the Emboabas 1708
   War of the Mascates 1710
Brazzaville 1884
breadfruit 2600 BCE
BRECHT, BERTHOLD 1941
Breda, Treaty of 1667
breech-loading rifle 1840
Breitenfeld, battle of 1631
Breslau and Berlin, Treaty of 1742
Brest-Litovsk 1915, 1944
   Treaty of 1918
Bretigny, Peace of 1360
Breton, André 1924
Breton Woods Conference 1944
BREZHNEV, LEONID 1964
bricks 8500 BCE, 2600 BCE
bridges 1377
   suspension 1800, 1825
BRIGHT, JOHN 1838
Brighton, Royal Pavilion 1810
Britain
   Angles, Saxons and Jutes 420
   Black Death 1347
   Roman 43, 60, 83, 121
   trade 1600, 1717, 1770, 1773
Britain, battle of 1940
British Africa Company 1723
British Columbia 1871
British Guiana 1895
British Guyana 1966
British Honduras 1973
British Somaliland 1940
British West Africa 1821, 1874
BRITTEN, BENJAMIN 1951
BROCA, PAUL 1861
BROGLIE, VICTOR DE 1924
BRONTË, CHARLOTTE 1847
BRONTË, EMILY 1847
bronze 4200 BCE, 3200 BCE, 2000 BCE
Bronze Age 3200 BCE, 2750 BCE, 2300 BCE
Brooke, Rupert 1915
broomcorn 6000 BCE
Brown, Arthur 1919
BROWN, JOHN 1856, 1859
Brown, Joseph 1862
Brown, Robert 1827
Brownian motion 1827
BROWNING, ELIZABETH BARRETT 1857
BROWNING, ROBERT 1855
BRUCE, ROBERT 1314
Brücke, Die 1905
BRUCKNER, ANTON 1864
Bruni, Leonardo 1445
Brunswick 1830
Brussels 1914
   Treaty of 1948
Buchan, John 1915
BRUNEI 1841, 1984
BRUNEL, ISAMBARD KINGDOM 1858
BRUNELLESCHI, FILIPPO 1420
BRUEGEL, PIETER (THE ELDER) 1563
Bruges
   Bourse 1309
   school of painting 1370

right to feud abolished 1471
Schmalkaldic League 1531, 1546
Social Democrats 1891
Swabian League 1331, 1367, 1372, 1376
Third Reich 1932
Thirty Years War 1620, 1625, 1629–35, 1646
Triple Alliance 1882
War of the League of Augsburg 1686–97
Weimar Constitution 1919
West *see* Federal Republic of Germany
World War 1 *1914*–18
World War 2 *1939*–45
Zollverein 1834, 1853
see also Holy Roman Empire
GERONIMO 1886
Gershwin, George 1924
Gerstenberg, Heinrich 1766
Gesner, Abraham 1854
Gesner, Konrad 1542
Geta, Roman emperor 211
Gettysburg, battle of 1863
Ghana 550, 753, 1076, 1203, 1240, 1471, 1482, 1894, 1957, 1960
military coup 1966
GHAZNAVID DYNASTY 998, 1000, 1048, 1160
Ghent 1678
Treaty of 1814
GHIBELLINES 1218, 1277
GHIBERTI, LORENZO 1425
GIBBON, EDWARD 1776
Gibraltar 1968
British control 1704, 1779, 1985
siege 1779
Gide, Andre 1897
Gideon Tapestries 1449
Gilbert, Rufus 1870
Gilbert, William 1600, 1878
GILGAMESH, king of Uruk 2700 BCE
Gilgamesh, Epic of 1900 BCE
Gillette, King 1895
Gioberti, Vincenzo 1843
GIORGIONE 1505
GIOTTO DI BONDONE 1304, 1334
Giotto space probe 1986
GISCARD D'ESTAING, VALÉRY 1974
Giza pyramids *2550* BCE
GLADSTONE, WILLIAM 1868
glasnost 1987
glass 2600 BCE, 1500 BCE, 50 BCE, 1010, 1291, 1300, 1460, 1932, 1958
GLASS, PHILIP 1980
Glendower, Owen *see* Glyn Dwr, Owain
GLENN, JOHN 1962
Glidden, Joseph 1873
Glorious Revolution (Britain) 1688
Glorious Revolution (Spain) 1868
Gluck, Christoph 1762
GLYN DWR, OWAIN 1400
Goa 1510, 1752, 1961
GOBIND SINGH 1708
Gobineau, Joseph de 1854
Gobir 1791
Go-daigo 1333
Goddard, John 1926
GÖDEL, KURT 1931
GODUNOV, BORIS, tsar of Russia 1598
GOETHE, JOHANN 1774, 1808
GOGOL, NIKOLAI 1833
Gogra River, battle of the 1529
Golan Heights 1967
gold 4000 BCE
Gold Coast 1821, 1827, 1871, 1957
Golden Hind 1578
Golden Horde, khanate of the 1237, 1325, 1388, 1408, 1462
Golding, William 1954
GOLDMAN, EMMA 1893
Goldoni, Carlo 1745
Gold Rush 1848
Goldsmith, Oliver 1766
Gómez, José 1909
GOMPERS, SAMUEL 1886

Good Friday agreement 1998
Goodyear, Charles 1839
goosegrass 2200 BCE
GORBACHEV, MIKHAIL 1985, 1987, 1989, 1991
Gordion knot 333 BCE
GORDON, CHARLES 1863, 1874, 1885
Gordon Riots 1780
Goree 1621
Gorky, Maxim 1902
Gothic alphabet 341
Gothic architecture 1220, *1248*
GOTHS 260, 267, 409
see also Ostrogoths; Visigoths
GOULD, STEPHEN JAY 1971
GOYA, FRANCISCO 1795, 1810
Graaft, Robert Van de 1931
GRACCHUS, GAIUS 122 BCE
GRACCHUS, TIBERIUS *133* BCE
GRAHAM, THOMAS 1829
Gramme, Zénobe 1870
Granada
Alhambra *1248*
Christian reconquest 1492
emirate of 1232, 1492
Gran Colombia 1819
Grand Alliance 1701, 1702, 1704, 1706, 1709, 1713
Grand Canyon 1540
GRANT, ULYSSES S. 1862, 1863, 1868
GRASS, GÜNTER 1959
Gravelines, battle of 1588
Graves, Robert 1934
gravity 1665, 1774
Great Britain 1707
Act of Union 1801
American Revolution (War of Independence) 1774–83
Anglo-Afghan Wars 1839, 1841, 1842, 1878, 1879
Anglo-Sikh War 1845, 1846, 1849
Ashanti Wars 1824, 1827, 1873, 1874, 1894
Boer War 1899–1902
Catholic Emancipation Act 1829
Chartists 1839
Commonwealth of Nations 1931
Corn Laws 1815, 1819, 1828, 1838, 1846
Crimean War 1854–56
Entente Cordiale 1904
French and Indian War 1755–63
French Revolutionary Wars 1794–95
General Strike 1926
Grand Trunk Canal 1770
Gurkha War 1814
Hanoverian dynasty 1714
India Act 1784
Indian (Sepoy) Mutiny 1857, 1858
Ireland 1171, 1763
Jacobite rebellions 1715, *1745*, 1746
King Philip's War 1675
Labour Party 1906
Lord Dunmore's War 1774
Luddites 1811
Maori Wars 1843, 1859
Maratha Wars 1775, 1779–82, 1803, 1817
Napoleonic Wars 1793–*1815*
natonalization 1946
Opium Wars 1841, 1842, 1856–60
Parliamentary reforms 1832
Peterloo massacre 1819
prime minister 1721
Quadruple Alliance 1718
Seven Years War 1756–63
Straits Settlement 1826
War of Jenkin's Ear 1739
welfare state 1946
World War 1 *1914*–18
World War 2 *1939*–45
Zulu War 1879
see also England; Scotland;

Wales
Great Eastern 1858
Greater Republic of Central America 1895
Great Exhibition 1851
Great Fear 1789
Great Northern War 1700, 1702, 1720
Great Schism (Orthodox/Catholic split) 1054
Great Schism (papal) 1378, 1417
Great Swabian League 1488
Great Wall of China 214 BCE
Great Zimbabwe *1440*
GRECO, EL 1586
Greece 1330, 1829, 1923
Balkan Wars 1912, 1913
civil wars 1824, 1944, 1949
Crimean War 1854
Metaxas dictatorship 1936
military junta 1967, 1974
monarchy restored 1935
republic 1924, 1973
revolution and constitution 1843
War of Independence 1821, 1822, 1825–29
war with Turkey 1920
World War 2 1941, 1944
Greek fire 675
Greek Orthodox Church 1589
GREEKS 2000 BCE, 1050 BCE, 540 BCE
alphabet 700 BCE
art orientalized 730 BCE
city-states 750 BCE, 66CE, 338 BCE
classical period of art 490 BCE
coinage 700 BCE
colonies 700 BCE, 650 BCE, 600 BCE
Corinthian War 396 BCE-386 BCE
democracy 507 BCE
Hellenistic period 330 BCE
hoplites 750 BCE
Macedonian control 338 BCE
Olympic Games 776 BCE
Peloponnesian Wars 461 BCE, 431 BCE, 421 BCE, 404 BCE
Persian invasions 512 BCE
Persian Wars 490 BCE, 480 BCE, 479 BCE
philosophy 585 BCE, 387 BCE
Phoenician alphabet 800 BCE
pottery 900 BCE, 720 BCE, 550 BCE
rising against Roman rule 146 BCE
theatre 534 BCE, 487 BCE, 430 BCE, 350 BCE
Trojan War 1225 BCE
see also Athens; Sparta
GREENE, GRAHAM 1938, 1940
Greenland 982
Green Party 1983
Greenpeace 1985
Greenwich Royal Observatory 1675
GREER, GERMAINE 1970
Gregorian calendar 1582, 1700, 1752
Gregorian chant 600
Gregory XIII, Pope *1582*
GREGORY THE GREAT, Pope 600
GREGORY OF TOUR 590
Grenada 1983
GRIEG, EDVARD 1868
GRIMM, JAKOB AND WILHELM 1812
Grimmelshausen, Hans von 1669
GROPIUS, WALTER 1919
Grotius, Hugo 1625
Group of Seven (G7) 1978
Grünewald, Mathias 1515
Guadalajara 1548
Guadalcanal 1942
Guadeloupe 1635, 1759
Guadeloupe-Hidalgo, Peace of 1848
Guam 1898, 1944
Guangxu, emperor of China 1875, 1898
Guangzhou 1917
see also Canton

Guarino da Verona 1429
Guatemala 1823, 1885, 1921
Gudea, king of Lagash 2130 BCE
Gudit, Falasha queen 960
GUELPHS 1198, 1218, 1227, 1260, 1381
Guericke, Otto von 1650
Guernica 1937
GUEVARA, CHE 1967
GUILLAUME DE LORRIS 1230
Guinea 1595, 1683, 1849, 1893, 1958
Gujarat 1297, 1538, 1573
Gulf of Tonkin 1884
Gulf of Tonkin Resolution 1964
Gulf War 1990–91
Gulistan, Treaty of 1813
Gumelnita culture 4400 BCE
gunpowder 850, 1250
Gunpowder Plot 1605
GUPTA DYNASTY 320, 360, 375, 395, 405, 450, 495, 535
Gura, battle of 1876
Gurkha War 1814
Gustav line 1943
GUSTAVUS I, king of Sweden 1523
Gustavus II, king of Sweden 1621, 1630, 1632
GUSTAVUS III, king of Sweden 1772
GUSTAVUS VI, king of Sweden 1950
GUTENBERG, JOHANN 1445, 1455
Gutenberg Bible 1455
Guti people 2190 BCE
Guyana 1979
Guzman, Abimael 1992
gyroscope 1852

H

HAAKON VII, king of Norway 1905
Haber, Fritz 1908
HABSBURG DYNASTY 1278, 1291, 1438, 1452, 1479, *1486*, 1519
Burgundy 1493
Hungary 1526
Low Countries 1477, 1479, 1556
Portugal 1580
Pragmatic Sanction 1713, 1740
Spain 1515, 1556, 1580, 1700
Swabian War 1499
Hadley, John 1730
Hadrian, Roman emperor 117
Hadrian's Wall 121
Hafsid dynasty 1228
Hague peace conferences 1899
Hague war crimes tribunal 1996
HAHN, OTTO 1939
HAIG, DOUGLAS 1915
HAILE SELASSIE *1930*, 1974
Haiphong 1946
Haiti 1655, 1748, 1808, 1844, 1915, 1929, 1934, 1986, 1994
independence 1804
slave revolt 1791, 1798
Toussaint L'Ouverture 1798
Hale, George 1910
Hales, Stephen 1727
Haley, Alex 1976
Halifax (Nova Scotia) 1749
Hall, Charles 1886
HALLEY, EDMOND 1682
Halley's Comet 1682, 1986
Hals, Frans 1624
Halstatt 750 BCE, 800 BCE
Hamburg 1259
Hamilca 480 BCE
HAMILCAR BARCA 235 BCE
HAMILTON, ALEXANDER 1791, 1804
HAMMARSKJOLD, DAG 1952
Hammerstein, Oscar 1943
HAMMURABI, Babylonian king 1800 BCE, 1780 BCE, 1530 BCE
HANDEL, GEORGE FRIDERIC 1705, 1717, 1741
Handy, W.C. 1914
HAN DYNASTY 1, 20, 190, 220
HANNIBAL 218-211 BCE
Hanno 470 BCE
Hanoi 1873, 1975
Hanover
constitution of 1833, 1837
Napoleonic invasion 1803

Hanoverian dynasty 1714
Hansa ports 1259
Hanseatic League 1332, 1356, 1361, 1427, 1512
Han Yu 824
Harappa 2600 BCE
Hardenberg, Friedrich von (Novalis) 1800
HARDING, WARREN 1920, 1923
HARDOUIN-MANSART, JULES 1678
HARDY, THOMAS 1874
HARGREAVES, JAMES 1764
Harmonious Fists see Boxers
Harper's Ferry raid 1859
Harriot, Thomas 1631
HARRISON, BENJAMIN 1888
HARRISON, JOHN 1759
HARRISON, WILLIAM 1840
Harsha 620
HARUN AL-RASHID, caliph 820
Harvey, William 1628
Hastings, battle of 1066
HASTINGS, WARREN 1774
HATSHEPSUT, queen of Egypt 1490 BCE
Hattusas 1700 BCE
HAUSA states 1517, 1804
Haussmann, George 1853
HAVEL, VACLAV 1989
Hawaii 600, 1778, 1898, 1959
HAWKING, STEPHEN 1988
HAWKINS, JOHN 1568
Hawkwood, John 1436
HAWTHORNE, NATHANIEL 1850
HAY, JOHN 1899
HAYDN, FRANZ 1755
HAYES, RUTHERFORD 1877
HEANEY, SEAMUS 1996
heart pacemaker 1956
heat
  Boltzmann equations 1877
  conduction 1822
  kinetic theory 1798
  latent 1763
HEATH, EDWARD 1973
Heaven and Earth society 1853
Heaviside, Oliver 1902
Heaviside Layer 1902
Hebron 1997
HEGEL, GEORG 1816
HEIAN period 794, 1156
HEIDEGGER, MARTIN 1927
Heidelberg university 1385
HEINE, HEINRICH 1827
HEISENBERG, WERNER 1927
Hejaz 1926
Hejira 622
helicopter 1500, 1939
Heligoland 1890
Heligoland Bight 1914
heliots 669 BCE
Hellenistic period 330 BCE
Heller, Joseph 1961
Hellman, Lillian 1939
Helmholtz, Hermann 1856
Helsinki accords 1975
HELVETIUS, CLAUDE 1758
HEMINGWAY, ERNEST 1929, 1940
Hendrix, Jimi 1970
Henlein, Peter 1505
Hennebique, François 1892
HENRY I (THE FOWLER), king of Germany 919
HENRY VI, Holy Roman emperor 1198
HENRY II, king of England 1154, 1171
HENRY III, king of England 1242, 1258
HENRY IV, king of England 1399
HENRY V, king of England 1413, 1415
HENRY VII, king of England 1485
HENRY VIII, king of England 1511, 1534, 1553
HENRY III, king of France 1589
HENRY IV, king of France 1589, 1610
HENRY THE NAVIGATOR 1419
HENRY, JOSEPH 1831
Henry, William 1803
Henry Pu Yi, emperor of China

1908
Henry (son of Frederick II) 1232
Hepthalites 450, 484, 495, 535, 562, 747
Hepworth, Barbara 1943
HERACLIUS, Byzantine emperor 628
Herat 1717, 1856
Herculaneum 79, 1738
HERDER, JOHANN 1775
Herero 1904, 1908
HERO OF ALEXANDRIA 60
HEROD THE GREAT 37 BCE
HERODOTUS 425 BCE
Herrera, Juan de 1563
HERSCHEL, WILLIAM 1781, 1800
HERTZ, HEINRICH 1887
Hertzsprung, Ejnar 1913
HERZL, THEODOR 1896
HESIOD 700 BCE
HESS, RUDOLF 1941
Heumac, Toltec king 1156
Hevelius, Johannes 1647
HIDALGO, MIGUEL 1810
Hideoshi, Toyotomi 1584, 1590
hieratic script 2000 BCE
hieroglyphic writing 3000 BCE, 250 BCE, 1822
Higginson, Alfred 1850
hijacks 1970, 1976, 1977
Hillier, James 1940
HINDENBURG, PAUL VON 1914, 1916, 1925
Hindenburg Line 1917
Hinduism 1200 BCE, 900 BCE, 600 BCE 747, 780, 1330, 1336
HIPPOCRATUS 130 BCE
HIPPOCRATES of Kos 377 BCE
Hirado 1609
Hiranuma, baron 1939
HIROHITO, emperor of Japan 1928
HIROSHIGE, ANDO 1833
Hiroshima bomb 1945
Hirst, Damien 1992
Hispaniola 1492, 1496
HITLER, ADOLF 1921, 1923, 1925, 1933, 1938, 1939, 1944, 1945
HITTITES 1700 BCE, 1600 BCE, 1595 BCE, 1350 BCE, 1200 BCE
HOBBES, THOMAS 1651
HO CHI MINH 1930, 1945, 1949, 1950
Hockham, George 1966
HOCKNEY, DAVID 1967
Hodeida 1934
Hoe, Richard 1847
Hoff, Ted 1971
Hoffman, Albert 1943
Hoffman, Felix 1897
HOGARTH, WILLIAM 1735
Hohenlinden, battle of 1800
HOHENSTAUFEN DYNASTY 1138, 1198, 1254
Hohokam 900
Hojo clan 1219
Holbach, Paul 1770
HOLBEIN, HANS, the younger 1533
Holland see Netherlands
HOLMES, OLIVER WENDELL 1836
Holocaust 1942, 1997
holography 1948
Holst, Gustav 1914
Holy Alliance (against the Turks) 1684, 1699
Holy Alliance (Russia, Austria, Prussia, France) 1815, 1818
Holy League 1511
HOLY ROMAN EMPIRE 800, 804, 812, 962, 1033, 1138, 1153, 1154, 1167, 1556
  dissolution 1806
HOMER 750 BCE
Homer, Winslow 1885
Homs 1980
Honduras 1720, 1823, 1895, 1907, 1921, 1969
  civil war 1909
Hong Kong 1941, 1984, 1985, 1997
Hong-wu, emperor of China 1355, 1368
Hong Xiuquan 1850
Honorius, emperor 395
HOOVER, HERBERT 1928

HOPEWELL CULTURE 200 BCE, 100, 401
Hopkins, Gerard Manley 1918
hoplites 750 BCE
Hopper, Edward 1942
HORACE 24 BCE
Hormuz 1515, 1621
horse 8000 BCE, 2500 BCE, 1700 BCE, 1000 BCE
  cavalry 900 BCE
  chariot 1800 BCE, 1600 BCE
  collar 400 BCE
  domestication 4200 BCE
  saddle 900 BCE
  stirrup 375
horticulture 7000 BCE
Hot-line (White House/Kremlin) 1963
Houdry, Eugene 1930
Housman, A.E. 1896
HOUSTON, SAM 1836
Hovas 1810, 1828, 1883
hovercraft 1955
Howe, Elias 1846
HOXHA, ENVER 1946
Huari 500, 600, 750, 800
Huáscar 1525
Huayna Capac, Inca king 1520, 1525
HUBBLE, EDWIN 1920
Hubble space telescope 1990
HUDSON, HENRY 1609, 1610
Hudson Bay 1610
Hudson River 1609
Hudson's Bay 1674
Hué, Treaty of 1883
HUERTA, VICTORIANO 1913, 1914
Huggins, William 1868
HUGH CAPET, king of France 987
HUGHES, TED 1970
HUGO, VICTOR 1862
Huguenots 1562, 1572, 1598, 1625, 1628, 1688
Huk 1899
HULEGU 1253
Hull, Albert 1921
human genome project 1988
human immunodeficiency virus (HIV) 1971
humanism 1325, 1396, 1402, 1409, 1445, 1486, 1494
human rights
  European Court of 1949
  UN declaration 1948
HUME, DAVID 1739, 1757
HUME, JOHN 1998
Hunac Ceel 1189
Hundred-Days Reforms 1898
Hundred Years War 1337, 1340, 1346, 1347, 1356, 1360, 1369, 1372, 1400, 1413, 1415, 1429, 1436, 1449, 1453
Hungary/Hungarians 1241, 1261, 1438, 1515, 1918, 1938, 1947
  Austria-Hungary see Austria-Hungary
  Christianity 997
  communism 1947
  Eastern block 1989
  Habsburg dynasty 1438, 1526
  Hungarian Rising 1956
  Mongols 1344
  national government 1848, 1849
  Ottoman conquest 1541
  self-administration 1711
HUNS 170 BCE, 91 BCE, 43 BCE, 140, 311, 316, 374, 383, 430, 441, 450, 451, 452
  Onogur 681
  White see Hepthalites
Hunt, Walter 1849
Hunt, William Holman 1852
Huntsman, Benjamin 1740
HURONS 1649
HURRIANS 1550 BCE
HUS, JAN 1413, 1415
HUSSEIN I, king of Jordan 1953, 1970
HUSSEIN IBN ALI 1916, 1924
Husseinid dynasty 1705
Hussites 1413, 1415, 1419, 1434
Hussite Wars 1419, 1420, 1430,

1434
Hutton, James 1795
Hutu 1959, 1996
HUXLEY, ALDOUS 1932
HUXLEY, THOMAS 1893
HUYGENS, CHRISTIAAN 1657, 1678
Hydaspes, battle of 326 BCE
HYDER ALI, sultan of Mysore 1761, 1781, 1782
hydraulics 60
hydroelectricity 1886
hydrogen, discovery 1766
hydrogen bomb 1952
hygrometer 1783
HYKSOS 1700 BCE, 1640 BCE
HYPATIA 415
hypodermic syringe 1850

I

Ibáñez, Vicente Blasco 1898
Ibn al-Haytham 1010
IBN BATTUTAH 1349
IBN KHALDUN 1332
Ibn Omar al-Marrakashi 1262
Ibn Rushd see Averröes
Ibn Sina see Avicenna
Ibrahim I, Ottoman sultan 1648
IBRAHIM PASHA 1816
IBSEN, HENRIK 1867
ice ages 15,000 BCE, 9500 BCE, 1840
Iceland 874, 1940, 1944, 1973
ice machine 1865
Iceni people 60
Iconoclasm 726, 843
Icons 843, 1399
Idaho 1890
IDRIS I, king of Libya 1951, 1969
Idris III, king of Kanem 1571
Idrisid dynasty 789
Ienari 1787, 1793
IEYASU, TOKUGAWA 1598
Ikhshidids 905
Ilinois 1818
Ilkhanid dynasty 1253, 1335
IMHOTEP 2650 BCE
Imjin River, battle of 1951
impressionism 1874
INCAS 1200, 1300, 1340, 1437, 1438, 1450, 1460, 1463, 1470, 1471, 1490, 1520, 1525, 1532, 1533
India
  Afghan invasion 1752, 1755, 1761
  Anglo-Sikh War 1845, 1846, 1849
  Assam 1229
  Bengal 1338
  British 1612, 1639, 1661, 1685, 1690, 1700, 1717, 1731, 1746, 1748, 1751–84, 1790, 1792, 1801–04, 1817, 1856, 1858, 1899, 1919, 1947
  Chaghati khanate 1299, 1306
  Chinese border dispute 1962
  Cholas 925, 985, 1022, 1026, 1279
  Delhi Sultanate see Delhi Sultanate
  Europeans 1487, 1498, 1501–10, 1750–58, 1778
  federal republic 1950
  Ghaznavids 1000
  Gujarat 1297, 1538
  Gupta empire 320, 360, 375, 395, 405, 450, 495, 535
  Hinduism 1200 BCE, 900 BCE, 600 BCE 747, 780, 1303, 1336, 1664, 1669, 1674, 1992
  Indian National Congress 1885, 1932, 1936
  Indian (Sepoy) Mutiny 1857, 1858
  Islamic conquest 1192
  Jainism 557 BCE
  Jaunpur 1394
  Kanva dynasty 73 BCE, 10 BCE
  Kashmir 1346
  Magadha 545 BCE, 73 BCE, 10 BCE
  Marathas 1674, 1742, 1758

Maratha Wars 1775, 1779–82, 1803, 1817
Mauryan 321 BCE, 303 BCE, 280 BCE, 256 BCE, 187 BCE, 73 BCE
Mongol invasions 1222, 1299, 1306
Mughal *see* Mughal empire
Muslim League 1906
Pallava 925
Pandya dynasty 1279, 1311
partition 1947
Persian invasion 1739
Punjab 1708
Rajputs 747, 1192, 1303
Rashtrakuta dynasty 753
salt march 1930
Sangama dynasty 1336
Satavahana dynasty 10 BCE
Sikhs 1469, 1675, 1708, 1792, 1802, 1826, 1831, 1984
Sri Lankan civil war 1987
Sunga dynasty 73 BCE
Tamerlane invades 1398
Telingana 1323
trade 50 BCE, 1501, 1612, 1717, 1731, 1773, 1813
Vijayanagar 1336, 1367
war with Pakistan 1965
Indiana 1816
Indonesia 1949, 1963, 1966
Indus period, Early 3500 BCE
industrial art 1763
Indus Valley civilization 2800 BCE, 2600 BCE, 2300 BCE, 1900 BCE
infrared light 1800
Ingavi, battle of 1841
INGRES, JEAN 1808
INNOCENT III, Pope 1209
inoculation 1721, 1798
Inquisition 1477, 1483, 1966
insecticide 1939, 1969
insulin 1921, 1982
intelligence test 1905
Inter-American Conference 1942
interferon, discovery 1957
Intermediate-range Nuclear Forces (INF) treaty 1988
internal combustion engine 1876, 1885
International, First 1864
International Monetary Fund (IMF) 1944
in-vitro fertilization 1978
Ionesco, Eugène 1960
Ionian Islands 1798, 1864
Iowa 1846
Iran
Iran-Iraq War 1980–88
oil industry 1951
Pahlavi dynasty 1925, 1941, 1979
revolution 1979
US embassy hostages 1979, 1981
see also Persia
Iraq 1920, 1927, 1981, 1996, 1998
Arab Federation 1958
Ba'athist coup 1968
Baghdad Pact 1955, 1959
Gulf War 1990–91
Iran-Iraq War 1980–88
republic 1958
Ireland
Act of Union 1801
battle of the Boyne 1690
British rule 1171, 1763, 1791, 1798, 1801
Easter Rising 1916
famine 1845
Home Rule Bill 1886, 1893
nationalism 1882, 1919
partition and civil war 1922
Sinn Féin 1907
United Irishmen 1791, 1798
Whiteboys revolt 1763
see also Eire; Irish Free State; Northern Ireland; Republic of Ireland
Irgun terrorists 1946
Irish Free State 1922, 1932, 1937
Irish Republican Army (IRA) 1974

Irish Republican Brotherhood (Fenians) 1858, 1866
Irkutsk 1652
iron 1600 BCE, 400, 1100 BCE, 800 BCE, 580 BCE, 500 BCE
blast furnace 1709
cast 550 BCE
wrought 1784
Iron Age 1200 BCE, *1000* BCE, 750 BCE
IROQUOIS CONFEDERACY 1649, 1726, 1780
irrigation 5000 BCE
Irving, John 1978
Isaacs, Alick 1957
ISABELLA I, queen of Castile 1492
ISABELLA II, queen of Spain 1833, 1834, 1843, 1868
Isherwood, Christopher 1939
Ishiguro, Kazuo 1986
ISIDORE, Bishop of Seville 590
Islam 570, 622, 630, 632, 705
Ismailis 1835
Koran 635
Wahhabi sect 1744, 1816
Isle, Claude l' 1792
Isly, battle of 1844
ISMAIL, shah of Persia 1501, 1502
Ismailis 1835
ISMAIL PASHA 1863, 1879
isotopes, discovery 1913
Israel 1100, 1948
Arab-Israeli conflict 1949, 1967, 1973, 1978, 1979, 1993, 1997
Gaza strip 1957
invasion of Beirut 1982
Sinai peninsula 1982
Six-Day War 1967
West Bank 1967
Issus, battle of 333 BCE
Istanbul 1453
Grand Bazaar 1455
Topkapi Sarayi *1453*
see also Constaninople
Italian Somaliland 1934
Italy 1947
Austrian domination 1815, 1831, 1847, 1848, 1859
axis alliance 1936
Balkan Wars 1912, 1913
Carbonari 1820
Charlemagne 774
city-states 1033, 1228, 1253
Etruscans 1100 BCE, 900 BCE, 600 BCE
Fascism 1922
France and Spain fight for control 1521, 1525, 1528
French invasions 1494, 1499, 1501, 1509, 1511, 1513, 1702
Garibaldi 1849, 1860, 1862, 1867
Guelphs and Ghibellines 1198, 1218, 1227, 1260, 1277, 1381
Holy League 1511
Holy Roman Empire 1154, 1167
humanism 1325, 1396, 1402, 1429, 1445, 1486
Lateran Treaties 1929
liberal unrest 1820, 1821
Lombard League 1167
Lombards 568, 663, 774
monarchy 1821
Napoleonic Wars 1796–98, 1805, 1806, *1813*
nationalism 1831, 1843, 1848, 1849
Normans 1040
Ostrogoths 493
pact of steel 1939
Papal States 757
Red Brigade 1978
Renaissance 1325, *1465*
republic 1946
Triple Alliance 1882
unification 1858–61, *1866*
uprisings of 1848
World War I 1918

World War 2 *1939–45*
Young Italy movement 1832
see also individual city-states and kingdoms
ITURBIDE, AGUSTÍN DE 1822
Ituzaingo, battle of 1827
Itzcoatl, Aztec king 1426
Ivan I, grand duke of Moscow 1325
IVAN III, grand duke of Moscow 1462
IVAN IV, tsar of Russia 1547, 1558, 1564
Ivory Coast 1842, 1889, 1958, 1960
Iwo Jima 1945

J

JACKSON, ANDREW 1815, 1828
JACKSON, THOMAS "STONEWALL" 1861
Jacobins 1790
Jacobites 1715, *1745*, 1746
Jacquard, Joseph 1801
Jaffa 1799
Jagiello, king of Poland 1386
JAINISM 557 BCE
Jakarta 1619
Jamaica 1656, 1839, 1962
Jamdat Nasr period 3100 BCE
JAMES I, king of England 1603
JAMES II, king of England 1688, 1690, 1702
James VI, king of Scotland *see* James I, king of England
JAMES, HENRY 1881
JAMES, JESSE 1882
JAMES, WILLIAM 1902
JAMESON, LEANDER STARR 1894, 1895
Jamestown 1607
Janissaries 1625, 1648, 1807, 1826
JANSKY, KARL 1932
Japan
administrative reforms 1787
annexation of Korea *1910*
anti-foreign movement 1860, 1863, 1864
Azuchi-Momoyama period 1568
Buddhism 550, 1200, 1262, 1282
civil wars 1336
constitution 1947
daimyo 1477
Edo period 1600
emperor 1333, 1336, 1867, 1889, 1928
Forty-seven *ronin* 1703
Fujiwara clan 857
government 604
Heian period 794, 1156
Hideoshi 1584, 1590, 1598
invasion of China 1937
Meiji Restoration 1867
Mongols attempt invasion 1274, 1281
Muromachi shōgunate 1392
No drama 1370
Onin War 1467, 1477
Russo-Japanese War 1904, 1905
Satsuma Rebellion 1877
Shimabara rebellion 1637
Shintoism 1814
shōgunate 1192
Taika reforms 645
Tokugawa dynasty 1598, 1600
trade 1543, 1570, 1609, 1624, 1643, 1854
Twenty-One Demands 1915
World War 1 1914–18
World War 2 1940–46
Yamato clan 250
Jarry, Alfred 1896
Jaruzelski, Wojciech 1981
Jask, battle of 1620
Jaunpur 1394
Java 1292, 1330, 1377, 1389, 1811, 1816
Dutch control 1619, 1826, 1831
Jayavarman II, king of Angkor 800
Jay's Treaty 1794
Jean de Boulogne 1580
JEFFERSON, THOMAS 1776, 1800

JEFFREYS, ALEC 1984
Jemappes, battle of 1792
Jene, battle of 1806
Jeng Cheng-gong (Koxinga) 1662
Jenkin's Ear, War of 1739
JENNER, EDWARD *1798*
JEROME 385
Jerusalem
Crusades 1099, 1100, 1118, 1149, 1187, 1191, 1197, 1212, 1219, 1228
Dome of the Rock (Qubbat al-Sakhrah) 685
Irgun terrorists 1946
Islamic capture 1244
Jewish settlements 1929
Jordan annexes east 1950
Knights of St John *1291*
sack 70
Six-Day War 1967
Temple destroyed 586 BCE
World War 1 1917
Jesuits 1534, 1759, 1764, 1767
Jesus Christ 4 BCE, 30
Jesus II, emperor of Ethiopia 1755
jet engine 1937, 1942, 1952
jewellery 7000 BCE, 3000 BCE, 2600 BCE, *80*
Jews
final solution 1942, 1997
Irgun terrorists 1946
Jewish Revolts 66, 70, 132
Maccabeaus 167 BCE
Nazi Germany 1935, 1938, 1942
Warsaw ghetto 1943
Zionist movement 1917, 1929
see also Israel
Jia Qing, emperor of China 1796
Jiddah 1517
Jiménez, Pérez 1958
Jing, Japanese empress 369
JOAN OF ARC *1429*, 1431
JOFFRE, JOSEPH 1914
Johannesburg 1886, 1900
Johanson, Donald 1974
JOHN, king of England 1199, 1215
JOHN I, king of Portugal 1415
JOHN VI, king of Portugal 1822, 1823
JOHNSON, ANDREW 1865
JOHNSON, LYNDON 1963, 1964
JOHNSON, SAMUEL 1755, 1791
JOHN IV, emperor of Ethiopia 1872, 1889
Joint European TORUS 1991
Joinville, Jean, Sire de 1309
Jomon culture 10,000 BCE
JONES, INIGO 1619
JONES, JOHN PAUL 1779
Jones, William 1786
Jonestown, mass suicide 1979
Jong, Erica 1974
JONSON, BEN 1605
Joplin, Scott 1902
Jordan 1950
Arab Federation 1958
civil war 1970
Jordanian Arab Legion 1948
Joseph I, king of Portugal 1750
JOSEPH II, Holy Roman emperor 1765, 1781
JOSPIN, LIONEL 1997
JOSQUIN DESPREZ 1504
JOUET, LOUIS 1673
Jouffray d'Abbans, Horace de 1783
JOULE, JAMES 1843
JOYCE, JAMES 1922, 1939
JUAN CARLOS, king of Spain 1969, 1975
JUAREZ, BENITO 1858
Judaea 37 BCE
Judaism *see* Jews
JUGURTHA, king of Numidia 106 BCE
JULIAN, Roman emperor 361, 363
JULIANA, queen of the Netherlands 1948
Julian calendar 46 BCE
Julius II, Pope 1512
July Revolution 1830
JUNG, CARL 1912

Jung Chang 1992
Junot, Andache 1807
junta 1787
Jupiter 1979, 1994
Jurchen 1127, 1211
JUSTINIAN, Byzantine emperor *527*, 534
JUTES 420
Jutland 1348
   battle of 1916
JUVENAL 110

K

Kabila, Laurent 1996
Kabul 1504, 1826
Kadesh, battle of 1275 BCE
KAFKA, FRANZ 1925
Kahlenberg, battle of 1683
Kaiser Wilhelmland 1914
Kajar dynasty 1794
KALIDASA 405
Kalmar, Treaty of 1397
Kalmus, Herbert 1922
Kalowitz, Peace of 1699
kamikaze winds 1281
Kanami Motokiyo 1370
Kandahar 1709, 1722
KANDINSKY, WASSILY 1940
Kanem 800, 1571
Kang-Xi, emperor of China 1662
Kang Youwei 1898
Kaniska, king 78
Kano 1903
Kansas 1856, 1861, 1863
   War for Bleeding 1854
KANT, IMMANUEL 1781, 1788
Kanva dynasty 73 BCE, 10 BCE
Kao, Charles 1966
Kaobang, battle of 1950
Kaplan, Viktor 1912
KARAGEORGE 1804
Karamanli, Yusef 1801
Karamanlid dynasty 1714, 1835
Kara Mustafa 1683
KARIM KHAN 1750
Karnal, battle of 1739
Kashgaria 1874
Kashmir 1346, 1819, 1846, 1949
Kasparov, Gary 1997
Kasr-i-Shirim, Treaty of 1639
Kasserine Pass 1943
KASSITES 1530 BCE, 1400 BCE, 1154 BCE
Katanga 1891, 1963
KAUNDA, KENNETH 1964
KAUNITZ, WENZEL VON 1753
Kautsky, Karl 1891
KAY, JOHN 1733
Kayambugu, king of Buganda 1763
KEATS, JOHN 1820
Kekulé, Friedrich 1858
Keller, Helen 1908
KELLOGG, FRANK 1928
Kellogg-Briand Pact 1928
KELLY, NED 1880
KELVIN, WILLIAM 1848
Kelvin scale 1848
Keneally, Thomas 1982
KENNEDY, JOHN F. 1960, 1961, 1963
KENNEDY, ROBERT 1968
Kentucky 1769, 1792
Kenya 1886, 1907, 1920, 1952, 1953, 1964
KENYATTA, JOMO 1953, 1964
KEPLER, JOHANNES 1619
KERENSKY, ALEXANDER 1917
KEROUAC, JACK 1957
KEYNES, JOHN 1936
Khan, Aliwal 1545
khanates 1259
Khanbalik 1267
Khartoum 1823, 1885
Khiva 1873
Khmer 1369
Khmer Republic 1970
Khmer Rouge 1975–79
KHOISAN 1779
KHOMEINI, RUHOLLAH 1963, 1979
KHOSRU I, Sassanian king 540
KHOSRU II, Sassanian king 591, 612

KHRUSHCHEV, NIKITA 1953, 1959, 1964
Khyber pass 1879
Kiakhta, Treaty of 1727
Kiel Canal 1895
KIERKEGAARD, SØREN 1844
Kiev 858, 882, 944, 1240, 1901, 1943
KIM IL SUNG 1949
kindergarten 1841
KING, MARTIN LUTHER 1960, 1963, 1968, 1983
King George's War 1743, 1748
King Philip's War 1675
King's Mountain, battle of 1780
King William's War 1689
KIPLING, RUDYARD 1894
Kircher, Athanasius 1650
KIRCHHOFF, GUSTAV 1857
Kirchner, Ernst 1905
Kirkuk, battle of 1733
KISSINGER, HENRY 1973
KITCHENER, HORATIO 1896
KLEE, PAUL 1918
KLERK, F.W. DE 1989
Klu Klux Klan 1865, 1915
Knights of St John *1291*, 1309, 1522
Knights Templar *1118*, 1307
knitting machine 1589
KNOX, JOHN 1547
Kōbe earthquake 1995
KOCH, ROBERT 1882
Kodiak Island 1784
KOHL, HELMUT 1982
Konarak 1250
KONGO 1483, 1490
König, Friedrich 1811
Königsberg 1457
Konya, battle of 1832
KOONS, JEFF 1990
Köprülü, Muhammad 1656
Koran 635
Korea 1419, 1443, 1871
   French 1865
   independence 1895
   Japanese 369, 1592, 1597, 1882, 1884, 1895, 1896, 1907
   Manchurians 1635
   Mongols 1231
   North 1949, 1950
   South 1949, 1950, 1965
   Yi (Choson) dynasty 1392
Korean War 1950, 1951, 1953
KOSCIUSZKO, THADEUS 1794
Kosovo 1998, 1999
   battle of 1389
KOSSUTH, LOUIS 1849
KOSYGIN, ALEKSEI 1964
Kowloon 1898
Koxinga *see* Jeng Cheng-gong
Krakatoa 1883
Krak des Chevaliers 1271
Kraków 1995
   anti-Polish rising 1846
   Swedish capture 1702
   university *1364*
   World War I 1914
Krebs, Hans 1940
Kristallnacht 1938
KROPOTKIN, PETER 1902
KRUGER, PAUL 1883
KUBLAI KHAN *1260*, 1267, 1294
Kuckuk Kainarji, Treaty of 1774
Kujula Kadphises 50 BCE
Kulturkampf 1871, 1880
Kumanovo, battle of 1912
Kumasi 1874
Kumbi 1076
Kundera, Milan 1979
Kunersdorf, battle of 1759
Kuniyoshi, Yasuo 1940
Kuomintang 1913, 1917, 1924–28, 1949
Kurds 1515, 1922, 1930, 1991, 1995, 1996
Kuril Islands 1875
Kurozumi Munetada 1814
Kush 1900 BCE, 920 BCE, 591 BCE, 550 BCE

KUSHAN EMPIRE 50 BCE, *50*, 78, 90, 235, 240
Kushite dynasty 727 BCE, 671 BCE
KUSHITES 25 BCE
Kut-el-Amra 1915
Kuwait 1899, 1990
Kyoto 794

L

Ladysmith, siege of 1899, 1900
Laennec, Rene 1819
LAFAYETTE, MARQUIS DE 1780, *1789*
La Fontaine, Jean de 1678
La Galada temple 2300 BCE
Lagash 2450 BCE, 2350 BCE, 2310 BCE
Lagos 1861, 1906
Lagrange, Joseph 1787
Lahore 1242, 1523, 1752
Laibach, Congress of 1821
Lake Champlain, battle of 1814
Lake Peipus, battle of 1242
Lake Regillus, battle of 499 BCE
Lake Trasimene, battle of 217 BCE
Lalibela 1117, 1200, *1270*
LAMARCK, JEAN BAPTISTE 1809
Lamartine, Alphonse 1820
La Mettrie, Julien 1747
LANCASTER DYNASTY 1399, 1455
Land, Edwin 1932
land reclamation 1340
Landsteiner, Karl 1900
LANGLAND, WILLIAM 1362
Laocoön 1506
Laos 1353, 1479, 1953, 1975
LAO TZU 531 BCE
LAPLACE, PIERRE 1812
La Rochelle 1628
   battle of 1372
Lartet, Édouard 1868
LA SALLE, ROBERT DE 1682
LAS CASAS, BARTOLOMÉ DE 1541
Lascaux cave paintings *15,000* BCE
laser 1960
Las Navas de Toloso, battle of 1212
Lateran Treaties 1929
Latin empire 1204, 1261
Latin language 241 BCE
Latvia 1918, 1934
   independence 1990
   Soviet Union 1940
Laue, Max von 1912
Lausanne, Treaties of 1912, 1923
La Venta 900 BCE
LAVOISIER, ANTOINE 1774, 1789
LAW, JOHN 1717, 1720
law codes
   Body of Liberties
     (Massachusetts) 1641
   Code Napoléon 1804
   Hammurabi 1780 BCE
   Justinian 534
   Ming China 1397
   patents 1474
   Theodosius II 438
   Urukagina 2350 BCE
Lawrence, D.H. 1913
LAWRENCE, ERNEST 1931
LAWRENCE, T.E. 1917
League of Armed Neutrality 1780
League of German Princes 1785
League of Nations *1919*, 1920, 1926, 1944
League of Three Emperors 1872
LEAKEY, MARY 1978
Leary, Timothy 1968
Lebanon 1842, 1945, 1958
   civil war 1975, 1982, 1987
   Druze 1925
   republic 1926
Lechfield, battle of 955
Leclanché, Georges 1866
LE CORBUSIER *1952*
LEE, ANN 1774
LEE, ROBERT E. 1862, 1865
Lee, William 1589
LEEUWENHOEK, ANTON VAN *1680*
Leger, Fernand 1951
legionnaire's disease 1976
Legislative Assembly 1791
Legnano, Giovanni di 1360
LEIBNIZ, GOTTFRIED VON 1673,

1684, 1714
Leipzig 1813
Leizhou Bandao 1898
Le Loi 1418, 1428
LEMAITRE, GEORGES 1927
Lend-Lease 1941
LENIN, VLADIMIR ILYICH 1903, 1917, 1921, 1924
Leningrad
   siege 1941, 1943
   see also Petrograd; St Petersburg
Lennon, John 1980
Le Nôtre, André 1662
lenses 1010
   achromatic 1757
   microscope *1680*
   spectacles 1300, 1766
   telescope 1608, 1672
Leo III, Byzantine emperor 726
LEO III, Pope 800
LEO X, Pope 1517
LEONARDO DA VINCI 1480, *1500*, 1503
León and Navarre 1037
Leonov, Alexei 1965
LEOPOLD I, king of Belgium 1831
LEOPOLD II, king of Belgium 1865, 1876, 1881, 1884, 1885
LEOPOLD III, king of Belgium 1951
Leopoldville 1881
Leovigild, Visigoth king 583
Lepanto, battle of 1571
LEPIDUS 43 BCE
Lesotho 1868, 1966
LESSEPS, FERDINAND DE 1859
LESSING, DORIS 1950
Lessing, Gotthold 1766
LEVERRIER, URBAIN 1841
Levi, Carlo 1945
LEVI, PRIMO 1947
Lévi-Strauss, Claude 1949
Lewinsky, Monica 1998
LEWIS, MERIWETHER 1804
Lewis, Sinclair 1920
Lexington, battle of 1775
Leyden, siege of 1574
Leyden jar 1745
Lhasa 1717, 1904
L'Hôpital, Guillaume de 1696
Liaoyang, battle of 1904
LIBBY, WILLARD 1946
Liberia 1822, 1847
Library of Congress 1800
Libreville 1849
Libya 1510, 1914, 1940, 1971, 1980, 1986
   independence 1951
   Italy 1900, 1911, 1913, 1922, 1935
   Qaddafi 1969
Lichtenstein, Roy 1963
LICINIUS 324
Liegnitz, battle of 1241
light
   aberration 1728
   diffraction 1618
   Doppler effect 1848
   and electricity 1864
   emission and absorption spectra 1853
   emission spectroscopy 1857
   infrared 1800
   polarization 1808
   speed of 1676
   transverse wave theory 1821
   ultraviolet 1801
   wave theory 1678
lighthouse 280 BCE
lighting
   electric 1878, 1879
   fluorescent 1935
   mercury vapour lamp 1892
   neon 1910
   street 1809
Lima 1535
LIMBOURG brothers 1410
Lin, Maya 1982
LINCOLN, ABRAHAM *1860*, 1862, 1864, 1865
LINDBERGH, CHARLES 1925
Linde, Carl von 1876

1720, 1943
Constitutions of Melfi 1231
French control 1266, 1282
Pedro of Aragón 1282
Spanish control 1734, 1738
Siddhartha Gautama *see* Buddha
Siegen, Ludwig von 1654
SIEMENS, WERNER VON 1856
Siena 1260
Sierra Leone 1787, 1821
SIÈYES, EMMANUEL JOSEPH 1789
SIGISMUND, Holy Roman emperor
   1396, 1420, 1433
Sikhism 1469, 1675, 1708
Sikhs 1469, 1675, 1708, 1792,
   1802, 1809, 1819, 1826, 1831,
   1834, 1984
   Anglo-Sikh War 1845, 1846,
   1849
Sikorsky, Igor 1939
Silesia 1742
Silesian War
   First 1740
   Second 1744
Silk 2800 BCE, 561
Silk Road 97, 297, 1280
Silla 57 BCE, 668
Silva, Joaquim de 1789
Simon, Neil 1965
Simpson, James 1847
Sinai Peninsula 1906, 1982
Sinatra, Frank 1956
Sinclair, Upton 1917
Sind 1843
Singapore 1819, 1826, 1963
   independence 1959, 1965
SINGER, ISAAC 1851
Sinn Féin 1907
Sino-French War 1884
SIOUX 1875, 1876, 1877
Sitka 1799
SITTING BULL 1876
Sitwell, Edith 1916
Sivaji 1674
Six-Day War 1967
Skandagupta, Gupta king 450
Skylab space station 1973
skyscraper 1883
slavery and the slave trade 1445,
   1501, 1517, 1568, 1619, 1621,
   1720, 1739, 1790, 1873, 1883,
   1890, 1924
   anti-slavery movement 1700,
   1787, 1856–59
   asiento 1702, 1713
   Brazil 1888
   British empire 1807, 1834
   Clay Compromise 1850
   Congo 1892
   Dutch West Indies 1862
   France and French colonies
   1794, 1815
   Haiti 1791, 1798
   League of Nations 1926
   Liberia 1822
   Libreville 1849
   Missouri compromise 1820,
   1854
   Paulistas 1708
   South Africa 1717
   Underground Railroad 1838
   United States 1793, 1800, 1808,
   1820, 1831, 1838, 1854,
   1856–59, 1862, 1865
   War for Bleeding Kansas 1854
   Zanzibar 1897
Slav peoples 540, 582, 860
Slivnitza, battle of 1885
Slovakia 1993
Slovenes 1918
Sluys, battle of 1340
smallpox 541, 1721, 1798, 1978
smelting 5500 BCE, 1540
Smetana, Antanas 1926
SMITH, ADAM 1776
SMITH, JOHN 1607
SMITH, JOSEPH 1830
Smith, Theobald 1893
Smithsonian Institute 1846
Smolensk, battle of 1812
SMUTS, JAN 1916

Snellius 1618
Soba 1504
Sobrero, Ascanio 1846
Socialism 1878, 1879, 1890, 1906
Society of Friends *see* Quakers
Society of Jesus *see* Jesuits
SOCRATES 399 BCE
soda ash, Solvay process 1861
SODDY, FREDERICK 1913
sodium, discovery 1806
Sofala 1506
Sogdiana 329 BCE
Sokoto 1804, 1903
Solferino, battle of 1859
Solidarity 1980, 1981, 1989
SOLOMON, King of Israel 962 BCE
Solomonid dynasty 1270
SOLON 594 BCE
SOLVAY, ERNEST 1861
SOLZHENITSYN, ALEXANDER 1962
Somalia 1862, 1889, 1960, 1992,
   1994
Somme, battles of the 1916, 1918
SOMOZA, ANASTASIO 1936, 1979,
   1980
SONDHEIM, STEPHEN 1991
SONG DYNASTY 860, 1127, 1258
SONGHAI EMPIRE 1464, 1468, 1493,
   1517, 1591
SONTAG, SUSAN 1978
SOPHOCLES *430* BCE
Sorel, Georges 1908
sorghum *4250* BCE
SOTO, HERNANDO DE 1541
sound recording 1890, 1898, 1958,
   1982
South Africa 1883, 1895, 1907,
   1919
   African National Congress
   1964, 1994
   Afrikaners (Boers) *see*
   Afrikaners
   Apartheid 1949, 1984
   black homelands 1975
   Boer War 1899–1902
   British 1795, 1802, 1806, 1812,
   1815, 1820, 1837, 1843,
   1846, 1868, 1871, 1877,
   1910
   dominion status 1910
   Dutch settlers 1652, 1709,
   1717, 1730, 1760, 1778,
   1779, 1781, 1802
   economic sanctions against 1985
   Great Trek 1835
   Huguenot refugees 1688
   Mfecane Wars 1822
   republic 1961
   Sharpeville massacre 1960
   slavery 1717
   Soweto massacre 1975
   Suurveld Wars 1779, 1781,
   1789, 1793
   World War I 1915
   Zulu 1819, 1838, 1879
South African Republic 1856
South America
   Early Horizon period 1200 BCE
   Initial period 1200 BCE
South East Asian Treaty
   Organization (SEATO) 1954
Southern Ch'i dynasty 460
Southern Song dynasty 1127, 1279
South Sea Company 1710, 1720
Soviet-Chinese alliance 1960
Soviets, Congress of 1917
Soviet Union *see* Union of Soviet
   Socialist Republics
Soweto massacre 1975
space exploration 1903, 1957–76,
   1979, *1981*, 1983, 1990
space shuttle *1981*, 1986, 1990
Spain
   American Revolutionary War
   1779
   attempted coup 1981
   battle of Lepanto 1571
   Black Death 1347
   Bourbon dynasty 1700, 1733,
   1743, 1761
   Carlist Wars 1834, 1839, 1872
   Castile and Aragón united 1479

Christian 1008, 1037, 1085,
   1086, 1212, 1235, 1492
Civil War 1936, 1937, 1939
constitution 1836
Espartero dictatorship 1840,
   1842, 1843
European Community 1986
France and Spain fight for
   control of Italy 1521, 1525,
   1527, 1528
French Revolutionary Wars
   1793
Glorious Revolution 1868, 1869
Habsburg dynasty 1515, 1580,
   1700
Hundred Years War 1372
Inquisition 1477, 1483
Islamic 711, 756, 850, 976, 986,
   1008, 1037, 1085, 1086,
   1150, 1212, 1232, 1235,
   1236, 1340, 1569
junta 1787
liberal constitution 1812
liberal revolutions 1820, 1854
monarchy 1969, 1975
Nijmegen, Treaty of 1678
peace treaty with Ottoman
   Turks 1581
Peninsular War 1807–14
Portuguese independence 1385
republic 1873, 1931, 1936
unification under Ferdinand and
   Isabella 1492
War of the Austrian Succession
   1740–48
war with Britain 1796
War of Jenkin's Ear 1739
War of the Polish Succession
   1733–38
War of the Spanish Succession
   1702, 1704, 1706, 1709,
   1713
Spanish-American War 1898
Spanish Armada 1588
Spanish Succession, War of the
   1702, 1704, 1706, 1709, 1713
Sparta 499 BCE, 730 BCE, 669 BCE,
   582
   Corinthian War 396 BCE-386
   BCE
   Peloponnesian Wars 461 BCE,
   431 BCE, 421 BCE, 404 BCE
   Persian alliance 411 BCE
   Thirty Year peace agreement
   445 BCE
SPARTACUS 73 BCE
Sparticists 1919
spectacles 1300
   bifocal 1766
spectroheliograph 1910
Spencer, Percy 1945
SPENGLER, OSWALD 1918
SPENSER, EDMUND 1596
Spice Islands 1512, 1521, 1605,
   1623
   see also Moluccas
spinning frame *1769*
Spinning Jenny 1764
spinning wheel 1280
SPINOZA, BARUCH 1677
Spock, Benjamin 1946
Spotswood, Alexander 1716
Spurs, battle of the 1302
Sputnik satellites 1957
Spyri, Johanna 1880
squash, cultivation 7000 BCE,
   2200 BCE
Sri Lanka 1972
   Tamil Tigers 1987
   see also Ceylon
Srivijaya 710
Srong-brtsan 625
STAËL, MADAME DE 1813
STALIN, JOSEPH 1917, 1924, 1925,
   1928, 1930, *1937*, 1953
Stalingrad, siege 1942, 1943
Stamp Act 1765, 1766
Stamp Act Congress 1765
standardisation 1830
"Star Wars" 1983
States-General 1789

steamboat 1783, 1807
steam engine 60, 1698, 1705, 1765,
   1774, 1782, 1785, 1790, 1802
   compound 1845
   locomotive 1814
steam hammer 1839
steamship 1818, 1833, 1858
steam turbine 1884
steel
   Bessemer process 1856
   casting 1740
   galvanized 1742
   open-hearth manufacture 1863
   steel, pact of 1939
Stein, Gertrude 1933
STEINBECK, JOHN 1939
Steinway, Heinrich 1853
Stendhal (Henry Beyle) 1830
STEPHEN I, king of Hungary 997
STEPHENSON, GEORGE 1814, 1825
Sterne, Laurence 1760
stethoscope 1819
Stevenson, Robert 1883
Stevin, Simon 1586
Stirling, Robert 1816
stirrup 375
stock exchanges
   Bourse 1309
   computerisation 1987
   London 1571
   New York 1792, 1929, 1987
STOCKHAUSEN, KARLHEINZ 1988
stocking-frame 1589
stoics 300 BCE
Stolbovo, Peace of 1617
Stone Age 8,500 BCE, 8500 BCE
Stonehenge 3100 BCE, 2100 BCE,
   1900 BCE
Stono River 1739
Stoppard, Tom 1967
Storkyro, battle of 1714
Stoss, Viet 1489
STOWE, HARRIET BEECHER 1852
STRABO 10
Strachey, Lytton 1918
Strada, Zanobi da 1357
STRADIVARI, ANTONIO 1690
Straits Convention 1841
Straits Settlement 1826
Strassburg, Gottfried von 1210
Strategic Arms Limitation Treaty
   (SALT) 1970
Strategic Arms Reduction Talks
   (START) 1991
Strategic Defence Initiative (SDI)
   1983
Strauss, David 1836
STRAUSS, JOHANN 1867
STRAUSS, RICHARD 1896
STRAVINSKY, IGOR 1913
STRINDBERG, AUGUST 1888
stroboscope 1836
STROESSNER, ALFREDO 1955, 1989
Strutt, Jedebiah 1758
Stuart, Gilbert 1796
STUART DYNASTY 1371, 1603, 1625
   Jacobite rebellions 1715,
   1745, 1746
Stubbs, George 1762
Stuensee, John 1770, 1772
Sturgeon, William 1836
STURLUSON, SNORRI 1222
Sturm und Drang movement 1766
STUYVESANT, PETER 1655
Suarez, Adolfo 1977
sub-machine gun 1920
submarine 1798, 1914, 1915, 1958
SUCRE, ANTONIO DE 1825
Sudan 1820, 1823, 1882, 1884,
   1885, 1887, 1898, 1899
   independence 1956
   left-wing coup 1969
SUETONIUS 105
SUEVI 409, 583
Suez Canal 1859, 1869, 1875, 1889,
   1915, 1951, 1956
Suffragettes 1903
sugar beet 1747
sugar cane 1493
SUHARTO, RADEN 1966
SUI DYNASTY 581, 589
Sui Yang Jian, Chinese emperor 581